MW00473566

The Official Publication
of
The National Bed & Breakfast Association

# The Bed & Breakfast Guide

## For The
## United States, Canada,
## & the Caribbean

Listings With Description
1,650
Bed & Breakfast Homes & Inns
Plus
100 Reservation Services With
Over 9,000 Additional Bed & Breakfast
Accommodations

Also Including
The Host Recommended
Restaurant Guide Section

By
Phyllis Featherston
& Barbara Ostler

**The National Bed & Breakfast Association, Inc.**
**P.O. Box 332, Norwalk, Connecticut 06852**

Copyright 1991 by Phyllis Featherston and Barbara F. Ostler
All rights reserved.

Library of Congress Cataloging in Publication Data

ISBN #0-9611298-4-0

Cover and Book Design: Peter Featherston

Front Cover Picture: *Seven Gables Inn, 555 Ocean View Blvd.,
Pacific Grove, Ca*

Back Cover Picture: *The Harbor Lights Inn, 58 Washington St.,
Marlbehead, MA*

Typography & Graphics: R.I.S. Publishing, Westport, CT

Printed in the United States
Published by the National Bed & Breakfast Association, Inc.
P.O. Box 332, Norwalk, CT 06852

Distributed by The Talman Co., N.Y., N.Y.

This book is dedicated to the memory of Charles M. Featherston II, who founded The National B&B Association., Inc. His sudden and untimely death on May 23, 1982 ended his work on the original guide, but his influence can still be seen as his wife, Phyllis and daughter, Barbara constantly work to produce a B&B Guide that lists only the finest and professional B&B accommodations.

# *Preface*

The National Bed & Breakfast Association's fifth publication of The *Bed & Breakfast Guide for the United States, Canada and the Caribbean,* celebrates 11 years of Bed & Breakfast service to the traveler. This guide lists more than 1,650 individual Bed & Breakfast homes and inns with more than 400 pictures. Each listing is a *true* Bed & Breakfast guaranteeing either a full or continental breakfast. Through the **Reservation Service** section the traveler will find an additional 9,000 Bed & Breakfast accommodations.

This edition introduces our **Host Recommended Restaurant Section.** We list restaurants throughout the country that the individual hosts have recommended to their B&B guests through the years. This is a welcome service to the traveler using our Guide. It puts dining information at the travelers' fingertips as they travel between B&Bs or just out for a Sunday ride.

Also in this edition we are for the first time indicating which B&Bs give a commission to travel agents. This is done by placing an asterisk next the the city that the B&B is located in. By doing this we are expanding the scope of travelers who will be using B&Bs this year. It will now be advantagious for travel agents to introduce their clients to the wonderful world of Bed & Breakfast homes and inns.

# CONTENTS

# Contents (continued)

# Introduction

The Bed and Breakfast Guide of the United States and Canada is the *first* guide to compile and list ONLY those privately-owned homes and small inns which provide a night's lodging and include in their rates a full or continental breakfast.

Traveling in a more formal way, using motels or hotels, etc., is expensive and often uneventful and dull. Your personal contacts most often are with a desk clerk or an elevator operator – in most cases, not very memorable and hardly to be compared with spending an evening with a Kansas farm family or in a fisherman's ocean-front home in Nova Scotia. Having used the B and B method of travel here and abroad, we speak from personal experience. We now count many of the B and B proprietors as friends, whom we would always be glad to revisit and whose warm hospitality we will always cherish.

Not all Bed and Breakfast homes and inns are the same. Some are big, some small; some are owned and operated by an experienced innkeeper, some by an energetic housewife whose family has grown and whose home has space now that it never had in the past. If you are looking for uniformity of accommodation, you will not find it here...but, this is the beauty of our Association! Bed and Breakfast homes and inns conform in certain important respects. They must be clean, provide either a full or continental breakfast, must adhere to the listed rates in the Guide – these rates will include all taxes and surcharges.

We want you to enjoy staying at B and B's as much as we do. We do not want you, our guests, to be disappointed in any way; therefore, we suggest to you the following:

1. Call or write to confirm that a room will be available.
2. Inspect the room before you take it. The proprietor will be agreeable.
3. Verify the room rate and the provision of breakfast.
4. If children are part of the group, verify their accommodations.

WE WISH YOU HAPPY TRAVELING WHILE STAYING AT THE BED AND BREAKFAST HOMES AND INNS IN THE UNITED STATES AND CANADA!!

Sincerely,

*Phyllis Featherston*

Phyllis Featherston, President

*Barbara F. Ostler*

Barbara F. Ostler, Vice President
National Bed & Breakfast Association

# Introduction

Le Guide des Pensions des États Unis et du Canada est le premier guide qui compile et enregistre seulement les maisons et les petites auberges qui fournissent le logement pour la nuit et qui comprennent dans leurs tarifs un petit déjeuner complet ou léger.

Le voyage cérémonieux, avec les motels et les hôtels, etc., coûte cher et c'est souvent monotone et ennuyeux. Vos rapports personnels sont le plus souvent avec un concierge ou un opérateur d'ascenseur – d'habitude pas très mémorable et on ne peut pas comparer ces expériences á une nuit avec une famille à une ferme dans le Kansas ou une maison d'un pêcheur au bord de la mer en Nouvelle Écosse. Nous sommes restés à ces pensions ici et à l'étranger, et nous parlons de nos expériences personnelles. Maintenant beaucoup des propriétaires des pensions sont nos amis à qui nous voulons refaire des visites et nous chérirons toujours leur hospitalité.

Toutes les pensions et les auberges ne sont les mêmes. Quelquesunes sont grandes, les autres sont petites; quelquefois il y a un hôtelier, quelquefois il y a une ménagère dont les enfants sont partis et les chambres sont libres. Si vous cherchez l'uniformité de logement, vous ne la trouverez pas ici...mais voilà la beauté de notre association! Les pensions et les auberges respectent certains règlements. Il faut être propre; fournir un petit déjeuner complet ou léger; rester fidèle aux tarifs dans le Guide – taxes et services comprises.

Nous voulons que vous aimiez le séjour en pension autant que nous: Nous ne voulons pas que vous, nos invités, soyez déçus; alor nous vous recommandons le suivant:

1. Téléphoner ou écrire pour confirmer qu'une chambre vous attend.
2. Examiner le chambre avant de la prendre; le propriètaire le veut bien.
3. Vérifier le tarif et le petit déjeuner.
4. S'il y a des enfants dans le groupe, vérifier leurs chambres.

NOUS VOUS SOUHAITONS LE BON VOYAGE PENDANT VOTRE SÉJOUR DANS LES PENSIONS ET LES AUBERGES AUX ÉTATS-UNIS ET AU CANADA!!

À beintôt

*Phyllis Featherston*

Phyllis Featherston, President

*Barbara F. Ostler*

Barbara F. Ostler, Vice President
National Bed & Breakfast Association

# Introduction

La Guía de Pensiones de los Estados Unidos y de Canadá es la *primera* guía que compila y cataloga solamente las casas particulares y las posadas pequeñas que proveen alojamiento e incluyen en sus precios un desayuno completo o continental.

El viajar de un modo más formal, usando moteles o hoteles, etcétera, es caro y muchas veces, exento de acontecimientos notables, y aburrido. Sus contactos personales muchas veces son con un dependiente del escritorio del hotel o con un operador del ascensor – en la mayoría de los casos, no muy memorables y casi no pueden ser comparados con pasando una noche con na familia de una finca en Kansas o en una casa de un pescador frente al océano en Nova Scotia. Como hemos usado pensiones cuando viajando aquí y en el extranjero, hablamos de una experiencia personal. Ahora contamos a muchos de los propietarios de las pensiones como amigos, a quienes siempre estarémos alegres de visitar otra vez, y cuya hospitalidad ardiente siempre la apreciamos.

No todas las pensiones son iguales. Unas son grandes, otras pequeñas; unas son propiedad de y manejados por un posadero experto, otras por una ama de casa enérgica cuya familia ha crecida y cuya casa ahora tiene el espacio que nunca lo tenía en el pasado. Si Uds., buscan la uniformidad de acomodaciones, no la encontrarán aquí. . . pero, iesta es la belleza de nuestra asociación! Las pensiones conforman en ciertos, respectos importantes. Deben estar limpias, proveer o un desayuno completo o un desayuno continental, deben adherirse a los precias que están en la Guía – estos precios incluirán todos los impuestas y sobrecargas.

Queremos que Uds. gozan se estancia en las pensiones tanto como nosotros. No queremos que Uds., nuestros huespedes, sean desilusionados de ninguna manera; por eso, les sugerimos lo siguiente:

1. Llamar o escribir para confirmar que habrá una habitación.
2. Inspeccionar la habitación antes de tomarla. El propietario asentirá.
3. Verificar el precio de la habitación la provisión de desayuno.
4. Si niños son parte del grupo, verificar sus acomodaciones.

¡Les deseamos un buen viaje mientras que se queden en las pensiones de los Estados Unidos y de Canadá!

Adiós

*Phyllis Featherston*

Phyllis Featherston, President

*Barbara F. Ostler*

Barbara F. Ostler, Vice President
National Bed & Breakfast Association

# Becoming A Bed & Breakfast Host
## (For Private Homes & Family-Run Inns)

 If you have an extra bedroom or more and can set aside a bath with a tub or shower for guests you will have all the overhead you need to establish a Bed & Breakfast.

If you like meeting people, you will like being a Bed & Breakfast host. For those of any age who are looking to add to their income without leaving their home, starting a Bed & Breakfast might be the answer.

The Requirements Are Few:

1. A friendly greeting to the traveler.
2. Allow the traveler to inspect the room in advance of engaging it.
3. The bedroom must be clean with clean sheets and blankets.  All bath facilities must be clean with hot water, tub and/or shower.
4. Breakfast must be included in the price of the room.   Either a continental (juice/fruit, toast/roll, coffee/tea) or a full breakfast. Breakfast is usually served between  8:00 - 9:00 a.m.  and generally does not go beyond 9:30 - 10:00 a.m.
5. What you charge for the night's lodging is strictly up to you. All B&Bs are different in location, facilities and amenities. However, the price that you charge must include all taxes.*  There can be no hidden charges.  A deposit in advance may be required with the balance paid at checkout.
6. Before making the final decision about going into the Bed & Breakfast business, you should give thought as to whether or not this will be a part-time or a full-time business.  Will the operation be a seasonal one?  Will your family cooperate if they are asked to share their home with a traveler. It can be fun and most rewarding, but to run a quality and professional B&B requires hard work.  Owning  and operating a B&B requires your undivided attention. Cooking, cleaning and maintaining an excellent functioning B&B and congenial atmosphere inwhich to entertain your guests is a full-time business.  However, thousands of hosts are doing it and are enjoying all the wonderful people who come through their front door.   Once you finalize these personal questions, then proceed to your local zoning board and investigate zoning requirements and regulations.  If there is a Bed & Breakfast establishment already in your city or town, get in touch with

them and ask for their help regarding what local ordinances might be pertinent to your B&B business, such as start-up expenses, type(s) of insurance and fire codes.

For more in-depth information about establishing your own Bed & Breakfast home or inn, we suggest you contact A.M. Best Company, Inc., Ambest Road, Oldwick, NJ, 08858  (201) 439-2200 for their Underwriting Guide.

* State and local taxes should be verified with your city or town regulations.

# BED & BREAKFAST
# HOMES & INNS
# IN THE UNITED STATES

# ALABAMA

## The Heart of Dixie

Capitol: Montgomery
Statehood: December 14, 1819; the 22nd state
State Motto: We Dare Defend Our Rights
State Song: "Alabama"
State Bird: Yellowhammer
State Flower: Camellia
State Tree: Southern Pine

At one time everything in this state relied upon King Cotton; however, with the coming of the destructive Boll Weevil in the early 1900s, the Alabama farmer had to turn to planting other crops, including the peanut, to survive. As a result, the peanut crop was so successful it revived the economy and today Alabama is often referred to as "The Peanut Capitol of the World."

Along Alabama's southern shores can be found beautiful beaches and resorts. Its chief seaport, Mobile, on the Gulf of Mexico, is an exciting and bustling seaport. Its harbor is filled with ships from all over the world. The lovely old homes there reflect the style and grace of the early Spanish and French settlers.

The largest and perhaps the wealthiest city in Alabama is Birmingham, often called The Pittsburgh of the South because of its great steel mills and heavy industry. This city, however, is also known for its pioneering work in health and medical research in open heart surgery.

Among some of the most famous citizens that came from Alabama are Helen Keller, George Carver, Hugo Black and Booker T. Washington.

# ALABAMA

## Anniston *

Johnson, C. Robert
1025 Fairmont, 36201
(205) 236-1791

**Amenities:** 1,2,4,9,10,14,15,
16,17,18
**Breakfast:** F.

**Dbl. Oc.:** $91.80 - $156.60
**Sgl. Oc.:** $91.80 - $156.60
**Third Person:** $10.00

**The Noble House, A B&B Inn**—This house is the home of Anniston's founding family. Built in 1887, the house has been restored with all period furnishings. Evening aperitif served at no charge. Located in historic district. Six rooms, three private baths and three public baths. Three-room suite available.

## Ashville *

Sparks, Shirley & Mark
Hwy. 231 at 9th & 5th St., 35953
(205) 594-4366

**Amenities:** 1,9,10,12,16,17
**Breakfast:** F.
**Dbl. Oc.:** $55.00 - $75.00
**Sgl. Oc.:** $45.00 - $65.00
**Third Person:** $10.00
**Child:** $10.00

**Roses And Lace Country Inn**—A beautifully restored 1890 Victorian home. Listed in the *National Register of Historic Places.* Many fine antiques. Close to horse racing, Boaz outlet shopping and the Huntsville Space and Rocket Center. Two miles from I-59 and 15 minutes from I-20.

## N.E. Arab *

Allen, Billy J.
100 1st Ave., 35016
(205) 586-7038

**Amenities:** 6,9,10,16
**Breakfast:** F.

**Dbl. Oc.:** $45.00
**Sgl. Oc.:** $40.00

**Stamps Inn Bed & Breakfast**—Located atop Brindlee Mtn. in beautiful Mountain Lake region. This 1936 inn, renovated in 1988, has antique furnishings, colonial colors and wallcoverings throughout. Convenient to natural recreational areas, high-tech space-related areas & a nationally ranked shopping outlet center.

| | | | | |
|---|---|---|---|---|
| 1. No Smoking | 5. Tennis Available | 9. Credit Cards Accepted | 13. Lunch Available | 17. Shared Bath |
| 2. No Pets | 6. Golf Available | 10. Personal Checks Accepted | 14. Public Transportation | 18. Afternoon Tea |
| 3. No Children | 7. Swiming Available | 11. Off Season Rates | 15. Reservations Necessary | ★ Commissions given |
| 4. Senior Citizen Rates | 8. Skiing Available | 12. Dinner Available | 16. Private Bath | to Travel Agents |

# ALASKA

## The Last Frontier

Capitol: Juneau
Statehood: January 3, 1959; the 49th state
State Motto: North to the Future
State Song: "Alaska's Flag"
State Bird: Willow Ptarmigan
State Flower: Forget-Me-Not
State Tree: Sitka Spruce

Alaska, the largest state in the United States, is a fast growing and bustling state. Purchased from Russia in 1867 by Secretary William Seward for $7,200,000, it was at that time thought to be a foolish act and was called Seward's Folly. Today, it has vast fishing and lumber industries and her new and huge pipeline brings her latest natural resource, oil, to her sister states in the Union.

Tourists find their way to Alaska by means of plane or automobile across the Alaskan Highway, or by ferryboat up from the southwest coast of Washington and Canada.

Alaska has thousands of wild and untamed wilderness acres. Fisherman and hunters hunt the salmon, tuna, brown bear and caribous. The highest mountain peaks of North America are in this state and are a constant challenge to mountain climbers.

## Anchorage *

Dunlap, Betty
10661 Elies Dr., 99516
(907) 346-1957

**Amenities:** 1,2,9,11,15,17
**Breakfast:** F.
**Dbl. Oc.:** $65.00
**Sgl. Oc.:** $55.00
**Third Person:** $45.00
**Child:** under 10 yrs. - $10.00

**Alaska Cozy Comfort's**—Betty's bed and breakfast is a warm and large home just minutes from the bus stop and shopping. Close to Chugach State Park. Enjoy the city lights or a view of Mt.McKinley. Transportation available from airport or train upon request.

---

## Anchorage *

Helfrich, Mary
2200 Banbury Dr., 99504
(907) 333-1425

**Amenities:** 1,2,14,15,16,17
**Breakfast:** F.

**Dbl. Oc.:** $65.00
**Sgl. Oc.:** $55.00

**Anchorage Bed And Breakfast**—A warm Alaskan home located by the mountains and adjacent to the green belt. Easy access to main thoroughfares, bus routes and shopping. Nearby skiing and skating. Bikes on request. Outdoor jacuzzi. Open year round.

---

## Anchorage

Helms, Jeannie & George
4520 MacAlister Dr., 99515
(907) 243-4443

**Amenities:** 1,2,3,9,10,14,17
**Breakfast:** C. (F. after 8 a.m.)

**Dbl. Oc.:** $55.00
**Sgl. Oc.:** $45.00
**Third Person:** $20.00

**Down Home Bed & Breakfast**—Country atmosphere with city amenities. Near airport, public transportation, 24-hour superstore and restaurants.Walk to trout lake or just sit on the back porch and enjoy the rock garden and berry patch. Continental breakfast before 8 a.m. and Sundays. Full breakfast after 8 a.m.

---

## Anchorage *

Kerr, Cathy
950 P. St., 99501
(907) 272-3553

**Amenities:** 1,2,9,10,14,15,16, 17
**Breakfast:** F.

**Dbl. Oc.:** $55.00 - $65.00
**Sgl. Oc.:** $55.00 - $65.00
**Third Person:** $10.00
**Child:** $10.00

**The Lilac House**—An exceptional bed and breakfast, paying careful attention to details to make your stay memorable. Nearby restaurants, shops, museums and Coastal Trail. Beautiful furnishings, soothing atmosphere and quiet neighborhood. Great place to relax and unwind from your Alaskan travels.

---

| | | | |
|---|---|---|---|
| 1. No Smoking | 5. Tennis Available | 9. Credit Cards Accepted | 13. Lunch Available | 17. Shared Bath |
| 2. No Pets | 6. Golf Available | 10. Personal Checks Accepted | 14. Public Transportation | 18. Afternoon Tea |
| 3. No Children | 7. Swiming Available | 11. Off Season Rates | 15. Reservations Necessary | ★ Commissions given |
| 4. Senior Citizen Rates | 8. Skiing Available | 12. Dinner Available | 16. Private Bath | to Travel Agents |

# ALASKA

## Anchorage

Lindbloom, Connie
4151 Lakeridge Circle, 99502
(907) 243-1606

**Amenities:** 1,2,14,17
**Breakfast:** C. and F.

**Dbl. Oc.:** $60.00
**Sgl. Oc.:** $50.00
**Third Person:** $10.00
**Child:** $10.00

**Connie's Bed & Breakfast**—Ten minutes from airport. Close to shopping malls and public transportation. Nearby are several stocked trout lakes. A warm and comfortable room with Alaskan hospitality to relax in while planning your next busy day.

---

## Anchorage *

Putman, Mary
2903 W. 29th, 99517-1702
(907) 248-4255

**Amenities:** 1,8,10,14,15,17
**Breakfast:** F.

**Dbl. Oc.:** $70.00
**Sgl. Oc.:** $40.00 - $50.00

**Putman's B&B**—Only six minutes to airport. Near bike trails and bus lines. Restaurants and shopping within a mile. Off-street parking. Well-traveled hosts. Freezer space available.

---

## Anchorage

Roberts, Peter
145 W. 6th Ave., 99501
(907) 279-5293

**Amenities:** 1,9,10,11,15,16, 17
**Breakfast:** C. and F.

**Dbl. Oc.:** $55.00
**Sgl. Oc.:** $45.00
**Third Person:** $40.00

**Sixth & Bed & Breakfast**—Prime downtown location. Complimentary bicycles. Low winter rates. Seven blocks from railroad station. One block from museum and Federal Building.

---

## Fairbanks *

Hegarty, Kelley
204 Front St., 99701
(907) 452-3343, Fax: (907) 451-8522

**Amenities:** 1,2,8,11,14,17
**Breakfast:** C.
**Dbl. Oc.:** $75.00
**Sgl. Oc.:** $60.00
**Third Person:** $15.00
**Child:** $15.00

**An Old Alaskan Country Inn On The River's Edge**—Fish from under towering birches on acres of lush, flower-filled gardens of this lovely restored historic newspaper publisher's downtown home. Charming rooms. Antiques. Alaskan art throughout. Old-fashioned Alaskan hospitality. Very special winter activities.

---

| | | | |
|---|---|---|---|
| 1. No Smoking | 5. Tennis Available | 9. Credit Cards Accepted | 13. Lunch Available | 17. Shared Bath |
| 2. No Pets | 6. Golf Available | 10. Personal Checks Accepted | 14. Public Transportation | 18. Afternoon Tea |
| 3. No Children | 7. Swiming Available | 11. Off Season Rates | 15. Reservations Necessary | ★ Commissions given |
| 4. Senior Citizen Rates | 8. Skiing Available | 12. Dinner Available | 16. Private Bath | to Travel Agents |

# ALASKA

## Fairbanks

Mease, Wendy & Steve
1001 Dolly Varden Lane, 99709
(907) 479-2532

**Amenities:** 1,8,10,14,15,16
**Breakfast:** F.

**Dbl. Oc.:** $50.00
**Sgl. Oc.:** $45.00
**Third Person:** $10.00
**Child:** under 5 yrs. -
no charge

**Chena River Bed & Breakfast**—An elegant Alaskan home nestled amidst 10 acres of spruce trees on the Chena River. Minutes from University of Alaska, Fairbanks campus, musuem, Pump House Restaurant and Riverboat Discovery. Full sourdough breakfast. One block from bus line. Transportation available.

## Fairbanks

Noll, Levina
604 2nd St., 99701
(907) 451-8106

**Amenities:** 2,10,15,16,17
**Breakfast:** C.

**Dbl. Oc.:** $52.00 - $62.00
**Sgl. Oc.:** $40.00
**Third Person:** $12.00
**Child:** $10.00

**Midnight Sun Traveler**—In a quiet location near most local attractions. We offer either a shared bath or a suite with queen bed and a private bath.

## Fairbanks *

Reem, Bonnie & Richard
231 Iditarod, 99701
(907) 452-3240

**Amenities:** 1,2,10,16,17
**Breakfast:** F.

**Dbl. Oc.:** $54.00 - $59.40
**Third Person:** $10.80

**Beaver Bend Bed & Breakfast**—Located on the scenic Chena River near downtown Fairbanks. Nearby restaurants and shops. We are in a quie neighborhood, have a large garden and serve a fine Alaskan sourdough breakfast.

## Fairbanks

Vanasse, Deb & Tim
310 Rambling Rd., 99712
(907) 457-2664

**Amenities:** 1,10,11,17
**Breakfast:** F.

**Dbl. Oc.:** $45.00
**Sgl. Oc.:** $30.00
**Third Person:** $10.00
**Child:** under 12 yrs. - $5.00

**Hillside Bed & Breakfast**—A split-level home on an acre of wooded hillside featuring in-room TV, private kitchenette and laundry facilities. Clean and spacious Alaskan decor. Experienced B&B hosts have lived several years in the Alaskan bush as well as in Fairbanks.

| | | | |
|---|---|---|---|
| 1. No Smoking | 5. Tennis Available | 9. Credit Cards Accepted | 13. Lunch Available | 17. Shared Bath |
| 2. No Pets | 6. Golf Available | 10. Personal Checks Accepted | 14. Public Transportation | 18. Afternoon Tea |
| 3. No Children | 7. Swiming Available | 11. Off Season Rates | 15. Reservations Necessary | ★ Commissions given |
| 4. Senior Citizen Rates | 8. Skiing Available | 12. Dinner Available | 16. Private Bath | to Travel Agents |

## Fairbanks *

Welton, Leicha & Paul
4312 Birch Lane, 99708
(907) 479-0751

**Amenities:** 1,8,9,10,11,15,16,17
**Breakfast:** F.
**Dbl. Oc.:** $48.00
**Sgl. Oc.:** $38.00
**Third Person:** $10.00
**Child:** under 12 yrs. - $5.00

**Alaska's 7 Gables Bed & Breakfast**—Centrally located on 1-1/2 acres in a spacious Tudor home with a floral solarium, garden, waterfall, cathedral ceilings and antique stained glass. Featuring gourmet food, jacuzzi, laundry, phones, cable TV, bicycles, skis and canoe. Rooms or apartments with new beds.

## Gustavus *

Burd, H. Sandy
Box 37, 99826
(907) 697-2241

**Amenities:** 2,10,17
**Breakfast:** C.

**Dbl. Oc.:** $60.00
**Sgl. Oc.:** $40.00
**Third Person:** $20.00

**Good River Bed & Breakfast**—Discover the beauty of Glacier Bay and Gustavus using our log house as a home base. Delicious breakfast with homemade breads and jams, comfy beds, two full bathrooms and library. Bicycles and fishing poles available to enjoy the unspoiled surroundings. Rustic cabin also available.

## Gustavus *

Unrein, Annie & Al
Tong Rd.
Box 5, 99826
(907) 697-2288

**Amenities:** 1,2,10,12,13,15,16,17,18
**Breakfast:** F.
**Dbl. Oc.:** $128.00
**Sgl. Oc.:** $71.00
**Third Person:** $41.00
**Child:** no charge - $26.00

**Glacier Bay Country Inn**—A photographer's paradise, professional's retreat and fisherman's dream. Peaceful storybook setting —away from the crowds. Fresh seafoods, garden produce, homemade boat tours, fishing, kayaking, hiking. Courtesy van, bikes. Air fare arranged.

| | | | | |
|---|---|---|---|---|
| 1. No Smoking | 5. Tennis Available | 9. Credit Cards Accepted | 13. Lunch Available | 17. Shared Bath |
| 2. No Pets | 6. Golf Available | 10. Personal Checks Accepted | 14. Public Transportation | 18. Afternoon Tea |
| 3. No Children | 7. Swiming Available | 11. Off Season Rates | 15. Reservations Necessary | ★ Commissions given |
| 4. Senior Citizen Rates | 8. Skiing Available | 12. Dinner Available | 16. Private Bath | to Travel Agents |

# ALASKA

## Homer *

Seekins, Gert & Floyd
Box 1264, 99603
(907) 235-8996

**Amenities:** 1,2,6,7,8,9,10,11,
15,16,17,18
**Breakfast:** F.

**Dbl. Oc.:** $50.00 - $70.00
**Sgl. Oc.:** $45.00
**Third Person:** $10.00
**Child:** under 12 yrs. -
no charge

**Homer Bed & Breakfast**—Fantastic view: mountains, glaciers, beautiful Kachemak Bay. Modern cabin guest houses with complete kitchen facilities. TV, private bathrooms, outdoor wood sauna. Birds, moose, wildflowers. Salmon and halibut charters. Referral agency for other B&B activities in the area.

## Juneau

Urquhart, Judy
9436 N. Douglas Hwy., 99801
(907) 463-5886

**Amenities:** 1,4,8,9,10,12,13,
14,16,17
**Breakfast:** C. and F.

**Dbl. Oc.:** $65.00
**Sgl. Oc.:** $65.00
**Third Person:** $10.00
**Child:** under 12 yrs. -
no charge

**Blueberry Lodge B&B**—A handcrafted log lodge only minutes away from Alaska's capitol. Five bedrooms, lodge room and library. Beautiful view of inland ocean waterway. Five miles away from ski area. The B&B is surrounded by lush rain forests and Alpine meadows. Shuttle. Brochure available.

## Seward *

Freeman, Charlotte L.
Eagle Lane
P.O. Box 1734, 99664-1734
(907) 224-3939

**Amenities:** 1,2,3,16,17,18
**Breakfast:** F.

**Dbl. Oc.:** $55.00 - $65.00
**Sgl. Oc.:** $45.00 - $55.00
**Third Person:** $10.00

**Swiss Chalet Bed & Breakfast**—An old-time Alaskan offers gracious hospitality and comfortable, smoke-free atmosphere. Located one block off Seward Highway by the road to Glacier exit. A five-minute walk to Le Barn Appetite Restaurant. Seasonal service May through September.

## Seward *

Reese, Annette & Frances
Box 1157
Mile 1.7 Nash Rd., 99664
(907) 224-3614

**Amenities:** 1,2,4,8,10,11,
16,17
**Breakfast:** C.

**Dbl. Oc.:** $56.10 - $71.40
**Sgl. Oc.:** $45.90 - $61.20
**Third Person:** $10.00

**The White House Bed & Breakfast**—A country home with five large guest rooms surrounded by forests and majestic mountains. Four miles to Seward Boat Harbor and 10 miles to Glacier exit. Cross-country skiing in winter. Guest rooms, TV room and fully equipped kitchen on second level.

| | | | | |
|---|---|---|---|---|
| 1. No Smoking | 5. Tennis Available | 9. Credit Cards Accepted | 13. Lunch Available | 17. Shared Bath |
| 2. No Pets | 6. Golf Available | 10. Personal Checks Accepted | 14. Public Transportation | 18. Afternoon Tea |
| 3. No Children | 7. Swiming Available | 11. Off Season Rates | 15. Reservations Necessary | ★ Commissions given |
| 4. Senior Citizen Rates | 8. Skiing Available | 12. Dinner Available | 16. Private Bath | to Travel Agents |

## Soldotna *

Hanson, Elaine & Jim
P.O. Box 1050, 99669
(907) 262-1789

**Amenities:** 1,6,8,10,11,13,14, 15,16,17,18
**Breakfast:** F.

**Dbl. Oc.:** $69.00 & up
**Sgl. Oc.:** $49.00
**Third Person:** $15.00
**Child:** no charge - $10.00

**Denise Lake Lodge Bed & Breakfast**—Three miles from town and Kenal River. Log cabin and smaller cabins on the lake. Cross-country skiing, ice fishing and guided fishing trips arranged.

## Valdez

Ayotte, Angie
333 Klutina St., 99686
(907) 835-4929

**Amenities:** 2,10,11,16,17
**Breakfast:** F.

**Dbl. Oc.:** $65.00
**Sgl. Oc.:** $65.00

**Colonial Inn Bed & Breakfast**—Large, clean and comfortable rooms with pleasant atmosphere and scenic view. A nutritious Southern-style homemade breakfast is served at your convenience. Located in town. A five-minute walk to gift shops, restaurants, museum and ferry terminal.

## Valdez *

Case, Cheryl
325 Jago
P.O. Box 1838, 99686
(907) 835-2624

**Amenities:** 1,2,3,7,8,9,10,11, 14,15,17
**Breakfast:** C.

**Dbl. Oc.:** $65.00
**Sgl. Oc.:** $65.00
**Third Person:** $10.00

**Alpine Mountain Inn Bed & Breakfast**—A two-story cedar home. Open year round. Guests enjoy \privacy of entire first floor. Two bedrooms, bath, living/dining area, cable TV and private entrance. Within walking distance to restaurants, harbor and stores. Owners of Lil Fox Charters.

## Valdez

Dennis, Betty
606 So. Waterfall
Box 1153, 99686
(907) 835-2717

**Amenities:** 1,2,4,5,7,8,10, 11,17
**Breakfast:** C. Plus

**Dbl. Oc.:** $63.60
**Sgl. Oc.:** $63.60
**Third Person:** $15.00

**Forget-Me-Not Bed And Breakfast**—Prince William Sound hospitality at its best. Relax in one of our luxurious guest rooms. Enjoy our complimentary breakfast from 6:30 a.m. to 9:00 a.m. Walk to the nearbycruise ships, ferry and downtown area.

| | | | | |
|---|---|---|---|---|
| 1. No Smoking | 5. Tennis Available | 9. Credit Cards Accepted | 13. Lunch Available | 17. Shared Bath |
| 2. No Pets | 6. Golf Available | 10. Personal Checks Accepted | 14. Public Transportation | 18. Afternoon Tea |
| 3. No Children | 7. Swiming Available | 11. Off Season Rates | 15. Reservations Necessary | ★ Commissions given |
| 4. Senior Citizen Rates | 8. Skiing Available | 12. Dinner Available | 16. Private Bath | to Travel Agents |

## Wasilla *

Carswell, Louise & Ross
2651 E. Palmer Hwy., 99687
(907) 376-5868

**Amenities:** 1,9,10,15,17
**Breakfast:** F.
**Dbl. Oc.:** $65.00
**Sgl. Oc.:** $50.00
**Child:** under 12 yrs. - no charge

**Country Lakes Bed And Breakfast**—Handy, yet scenic and peaceful. Guest rooms and back-yard deck overlooks a quiet waterway leading to nearby Lake Wasilla. Hosts are longtime Alaskans. We do spectacular seaplane, glacier and wildlife tours. Remote cabin stays also available.

| | | | | |
|---|---|---|---|---|
| 1. No Smoking | 5. Tennis Available | 9. Credit Cards Accepted | 13. Lunch Available | 17. Shared Bath |
| 2. No Pets | 6. Golf Available | 10. Personal Checks Accepted | 14. Public Transportation | 18. Afternoon Tea |
| 3. No Children | 7. Swiming Available | 11. Off Season Rates | 15. Reservations Necessary | ★ Commissions given |
| 4. Senior Citizen Rates | 8. Skiing Available | 12. Dinner Available | 16. Private Bath | to Travel Agents |

11

# ARIZONA

## The Grand Canyon State

Capitol: Phoenix
Statehood: February 14, 1912; the 48th state
State Motto: God Enriches
State Song: "Arizona"
State Bird: Cactus Wren
State Flower: Saguaro
State Tree: Paloverde

Arizona is a vacation land of wonder and beauty. It has one of the oldest communities in the country, going back to the 1100's. Inhabited then by the Hopi Indians, it still is a home for many American Indians today.

No other state has as many national monuments as this state. It not only boasts of the Grand Canyon, one of the natural wonders of the world, but also giant dams such as Coolidge, Glen Canyon, Hoover, Parker and Roosevelt.

Hundreds of visitors and vacationers come here every year. Many remain and make it their second home. Its warm and easy climate make it a haven for senior citizens.

## *Flagstaff*

Dierker, Dorothea
423 W. Cherry, 86001
(602) 774-3249

**Amenities:** 1,2,3,5,8,10,17
**Breakfast:** C. (F. after 8:00 a.m.)

**Dbl. Oc.:** $40.00
**Sgl. Oc.:** $30.00
**Third Person:** $10.00

**Dierker House — Bed And Breakfast**—A charming home in old historic Flagstaff. Antiques, privacy and comfort with many extras. Three upstairs guestrooms share a private entrance, sitting room and sunny guest kitchen. A delicious breakfast is served at 8 a.m. in the dining room. A convenient location.

## *Flagstaff*

Wanek, Ray
685 Lake Mary Rd., 86001
(602) 774-8959

**Amenities:** 1,2,3,8,9,10,15,16,17
**Breakfast:** C.
**Dbl. Oc.:** $64.80 - $100.00
**Sgl. Oc.:** $54.00

**Arizona Mountain Inn**—Our old English inn is nestled in the pines three miles south of Flagstaff. Antiques, crystal and lace decorate each room and suite. A delicious continental breakfast is served in our lovely dining room. Relax in a quiet forest atmosphere.

## *Phoenix*

Talbott, Pauline
4702 E. Edgemont, 85008
(602) 840-3254

**Amenities:** 1,2,10,14,15,16
**Breakfast:** C.

**Dbl. Oc.:** $35.00
**Sgl. Oc.:** $35.00

**Talbott's Stop-Over**—A private entrance, TV, fireplace and refrigerator. Approximately five miles from the airport. Two miles from Scottsdale, Arizona State University, Indian ruins, museums, shopping and theatres. Nearby 24-hour restaurants, zoo and botanical gardens.

## *Phoenix* *

Trapp, Darrell
P.O. Box 41624, 85080
(602) 582-3868

**Amenities:** 2,4,5,6,7,9,10,11,
12,13,15,16,18
**Breakfast:** F.
(C. — summer)

**Dbl. Oc.:** $61.00 - $150.00
**Sgl. Oc.:** $61.00 - $97.00
**Third Person:** $12.00-
$24.00
**Child:** on request

**Westways "Private" Resort-Inn B&B**—Convenient to I-17. Executive estate area. Contemporary Spanish design on designer-landscaped grounds. Deluxe queen-bedded rooms. Resplendently simple elegance. Guests rate us five stars. Casual Western comfort with class."Where guests preserve their privacy."

| | | | |
|---|---|---|---|
| 1. No Smoking | 5. Tennis Available | 9. Credit Cards Accepted | 13. Lunch Available | 17. Shared Bath |
| 2. No Pets | 6. Golf Available | 10. Personal Checks Accepted | 14. Public Transportation | 18. Afternoon Tea |
| 3. No Children | 7. Swiming Available | 11. Off Season Rates | 15. Reservations Necessary | ★ Commissions given |
| 4. Senior Citizen Rates | 8. Skiing Available | 12. Dinner Available | 16. Private Bath | to Travel Agents |

## *Sedona* *

Bruno, Fran & Dan
P.O. Box 10095, 86336
(602) 282-7640

**Amenities:** 1,2,3,5,6,7,10,11,15,16,18
**Breakfast:** F.
**Dbl. Oc.:** $71.00 - $120.00
**Sgl. Oc.:** $65.00 - $115.00
**Third Person:** $15.00
**Child:** $15.00

**Bed & Breakfast At Saddle Rock Ranch**—HISTORY * ROMANCE * ANTIQUES * EL-EGANCE * Centrally located on a Old West movie ranch. Panoramic red rock vistas. Guest rooms feature rock fireplaces, antiques and views. Three acres of grounds. Gardens, pool and spa. Scrumptious food and afternoon snacks. Warm and friendly hosts.

## *Sedona* *

Page, Lea
P.O. Box 552, 86336
(602) 282-2833

**Amenities:** 1,10,15,16,17,18
**Breakfast:** F.

**Dbl. Oc.:** &60.50 - $88.00
**Third Person:** $7.00
**Child:** $7.00

**Sipapu Lodge**—Traditional hospitality of the Old West. Commune with nature during peaceful moments on our deck. Buffet-style breakfasts have Southwest flavor. Relics of Indian culture and family memorabilia are found throughout our home. Sedona's red rocks are waiting for you!

## *Sedona* *

Stevenson, Doris & Dick
595 Jordan Rd., 86336
(602) 282-6462

**Amenities:** 1,2,9,15,16
**Breakfast:** F.

**Dbl. Oc.:** $70.00 - $85.00
**Third Person:** $8.00

**"A Touch Of Sedona"** — **Bed And Breakfast**—Eclectic elegance. Furnished with stained-glass lamps and antiques with a mix of contemporary. Old-fashioned breakfast with home-baked breads. Within walking distance of uptown.

## *Tucson* *

Bryant, Debbi & Charles
1640 N. Campbell, 85719
(602) 795-3840

**Amenities:** 1,2,3,9,10,11,12,
14,16,18
**Breakfast:** C.(weekdays)
F.(weekends)

**Dbl. Oc.:** $95.00 - $120.00
**Sgl. Oc.:** $95.00 - $120.00
**Third Person:** $10.00
**Child:** under 12 yrs. -
no charge

**La Posada Del Valle**—An elegant 1920's inn located in the heart of Tucson. Lush gardens and mature orange trees perfume the air. Patios for sunning. Five richly appointed guest rooms. Gourmet breakfast and afternoon tea. Within walking distance to the University of Arizona and University Hospital.

| | | | |
|---|---|---|---|
| 1. No Smoking | 5. Tennis Available | 9. Credit Cards Accepted | 13. Lunch Available | 17. Shared Bath |
| 2. No Pets | 6. Golf Available | 10. Personal Checks Accepted | 14. Public Transportation | 18. Afternoon Tea |
| 3. No Children | 7. Swiming Available | 11. Off Season Rates | 15. Reservations Necessary | ★ Commissions given |
| 4. Senior Citizen Rates | 8. Skiing Available | 12. Dinner Available | 16. Private Bath | to Travel Agents |

## Tucson *

Hymer-Thompson, Karen
11155 W. Calle Pima, 85743
(602) 578-3058

**Amenities:** 1,2,15,16
**Breakfast:** F.
**Dbl. Oc.:** $58.08 - $68.64
**Sgl. Oc.:** $58.08 - $68.64
**Third Person:** $10.56

**Casa Tierra, An Adobe Bed And Breakfast Inn**—A unique Mexican-style adobe inn with arches, colorful tiles and vaulted brick and rough viga ceilings. Situated on 10 acres of saguaro cacti. Three rooms with private patios. Courtyards. Quiet. Birds. Sunsets. 3-1/2 miles from Arizona's Sonora Natural Monument.

## Tucson *

Lininger, Schuyler
306 N. Alvernon, 85711
(800) 456-5634,
(602) 325-3366

**Amenities:** 4,5,6,7,9,10,11,12,
13,14,16
**Breakfast:** C.

**Dbl. Oc.:** $76.00
**Sgl. Oc.:** $89.00
**Third Person:** $10.00
**Child:** under 2 yrs. - $6.00

**The Lodge On The Desert**—A garden hotel with the atmosphere of a Mexican hacienda. Five minutes from two golf courses, tennis courts and a major shopping center. Three miles east of the University of Arizona. A heated pool, shuffleboard, Ping-Pong, croquet and a library are on the grounds.

| | | | | |
|---|---|---|---|---|
| 1. No Smoking | 5. Tennis Available | 9. Credit Cards Accepted | 13. Lunch Available | 17. Shared Bath |
| 2. No Pets | 6. Golf Available | 10. Personal Checks Accepted | 14. Public Transportation | 18. Afternoon Tea |
| 3. No Children | 7. Swiming Available | 11. Off Season Rates | 15. Reservations Necessary | ★ Commissions given |
| 4. Senior Citizen Rates | 8. Skiing Available | 12. Dinner Available | 16. Private Bath | to Travel Agents |

# ARKANSAS

## Land of Opportunity

Capitol:  Little Rock
Statehood:  January 15, 1836; the 25th state
State Motto:  The People Rule
State Song:  "Arkansas"
State Bird:  Mockingbird
State Flower:  Apple Blossom
State Tree:  Pine

Arkansas is a southern state with comfortable weather, warm enough to make the visitor feel unhurried and relaxed. There are beautiful rugged mountains and the Ozark Valley, where hot and cold springs invite tourists to come and soothe their aches and pains. The Buffalo National River flows across the northern boundary of Arkansas and through the Ozark Plateau. Here one can swim, canoe, fish and shoot the rapids. Here, too, the Ozark Folk Center at Mountain View has preserved the ingenuity of the country people of this state and their mountain music, crafts and folklore. Twenty-five million tourists each year come here to see and enjoy this center.

There are two large cities in Arkansas, Little Rock and Fort Smith. Perhaps one of the most unique towns in all of the U.S. is Texarkana, built just across from the state of Texas, yet on the border of both states. One half of the town is in Texas and the other in Arkansas.

Arkansas' national hero is Gen. Douglas MacArthur. He was born in Little Rock in 1880.

## *Brinkley*

| | | |
|---|---|---|
| Prince, Stanley | **Amenities:** 1,2,3,9,10,12,13, | **Dbl. Oc.:** $44.00 |
| 127 W. Cedar, 72021 | 15,16 | **Sgl. Oc.:** $38.00 |
| (501) 734-4955 | **Breakfast:** F. | |

**The Great Southern Hotel**—Grand times and true Southern hospitality await you at The Great Southern Hotel.  Restored in true Victorian elegance.  Rooms reflect a quaint and homey atmosphere reminiscent of bygone days.  Fine dining in the award-winning Victorian Tea Room.

## *Clarksville*

Moody, Pat
101 Railroad Ave., 72830
(501) 793-6851

**Amenities:** 1,2,3,9,13,16,18
**Breakfast:** C.
**Dbl. Oc.:** $58.30
**Sgl. Oc.:** $47.70
**Third Person:** $10.60

**The May House Inn**—Located in the heart of the Arkansas Ozarks.  A lovely Victorian home built in 1905.  Furnished with period antiques and features The Ozarks Ritz Tea Room.  A wonderful place for a Victorian adventure.

## *Eureka Springs*

| | | |
|---|---|---|
| Dragonwagon, Crescent | **Amenities:** 9,10,11,12,14,16 | **Dbl. Oc.:** $95.00 - $150.00 |
| 515 Spring St., 72632 | **Breakfast:** F. | **Sgl. Oc.:** $90.00 - $145.00 |
| (501) 253-7444 | | **Third Person:** $10.00 |
| | | **Child:** under 5 yrs. - no charge |

**Dairy Hollow House**—A warm and indulgent country inn/restaurant. Fireplace, flowers, hot tub and heavenly breakfast delivered daily to your door in a basket.  Fresh seasonal, regional cuisine featured in our flower-framed restaurant.  Lodging in our 1880's farmhouse or spacious main house.

## *Eureka Springs*

| | | |
|---|---|---|
| Gavron, Barbara | **Amenities:** 1,3,6,7,9,10,11,14, | **Dbl. Oc.:** $71.50 |
| 11 Singleton, 72632 | 15,16,17 | **Sgl. Oc.:** $66.00 |
| (501) 253-9111 | **Breakfast:** F. | **Third Person:** $10.00 |

**Singleton House**—An old-fashion Victorian with a touch of magic. Whimsically decorated. An eclectic collection of treasures and antiques.  Breakfast served on the balcony overlooking the fantasy garden and fish pond.  Walk to the historic district, shops and cafes.  Romantic cottage available.

| | | | |
|---|---|---|---|
| 1. No Smoking | 5. Tennis Available | 9. Credit Cards Accepted | 13. Lunch Available | 17. Shared Bath |
| 2. No Pets | 6. Golf Available | 10. Personal Checks Accepted | 14. Public Transportation | 18. Afternoon Tea |
| 3. No Children | 7. Swiming Available | 11. Off Season Rates | 15. Reservations Necessary | ★ Commissions given |
| 4. Senior Citizen Rates | 8. Skiing Available | 12. Dinner Available | 16. Private Bath | to Travel Agents |

## Eureka Springs

| | | |
|---|---|---|
| McDonald, Denise & Michael | **Amenities:** 1,2,3,4,9,10,11,14, | **Dbl. Oc.:** $82.50 - $93.50 |
| 263 Spring St., 72632 | 15,16 | **Sgl. Oc.:** $82.50 |
| (501) 253-7853 | **Breakfast:** F. | **Third Person:** $15.00 |

**Bridgeford Cottage**—Nestled in the heart of Eureka Springs' historic district is our 1884 Victorian cottage. Each room has a private entrance, antique furnishings and private bath. Fresh coffee in your suite, color TV, air conditioning and a mouth-watering breakfast.

## Eureka Springs *

| | | |
|---|---|---|
| Simantel, Iris & William | **Amenities:** 1,2,6,7,9,10,11,14, | **Dbl. Oc.:** $52.00 - $89.00 |
| 35 Kings Hwy., 72632 | 15,16 | **Sgl. Oc.:** $52.00 - $89.00 |
| (501) 253-8916 | **Breakfast:** F. | **Third Person:** $12.00 |

**Hearthstone Inn B&B And Cottages**—An award-winning turn-of-the-century Victorian inn in the historic district. Nine guest rooms with antique furnishings, private baths and entrances. Cable TV. King, queen and double beds. Two charming cottages next to the inn. Located on trolley route.

## Fordyce

Phillips, Col. & Mrs. James
412 W. 4th St., 71742
(501) 352-7202

**Amenities:** 1,2,5,6,7,9,10,15,16
**Breakfast:** F.
**Dbl. Oc.:** $59.00
**Third Person:** $10.00
**Child:** $5.00

**Wynne Phillips House**—A gracious colonial revival mansion listed in the *National Register of Historic Places.* Furnished with antiques, Oriental rugs and family heirlooms. This is a place to enjoy old-fashion pleasures such as rocking on the porch, singing by the piano or taking a stroll.

## Hot Springs *

| | | |
|---|---|---|
| Bartlett, Helen | **Amenities:** 1,2,4,9,10,16 | **Dbl. Oc.:** $59.40 - $70.20 |
| 303 Quapaw, 71901 | **Breakfast:** F. | **Sgl. Oc.:** $48.60 |
| (501) 623-3258 | | **Third Person:** $10.00 |
| | | **Child:** under 14 yrs. - $5.00 |

**Vintage Comfort Bed & Breakfast Inn**—A 1907 Queen Anne home where guests are pampered with Southern hospitality. Ideal for weddings and honeymoons. Hot Springs National Park, hiking trails and famed bath-house row.

| | | | | |
|---|---|---|---|---|
| 1. No Smoking | 5. Tennis Available | 9. Credit Cards Accepted | 13. Lunch Available | 17. Shared Bath |
| 2. No Pets | 6. Golf Available | 10. Personal Checks Accepted | 14. Public Transportation | 18. Afternoon Tea |
| 3. No Children | 7. Swiming Available | 11. Off Season Rates | 15. Reservations Necessary | ★ Commissions given |
| 4. Senior Citizen Rates | 8. Skiing Available | 12. Dinner Available | 16. Private Bath | to Travel Agents |

# ARKANSAS

## Kingston *

Sullivan, MaryJo
HCR 30, Box 198, 72742
(501) 665-2986

**Amenities:** 1,4,9,10,11,17
**Breakfast:** F.

**Dbl. Oc.:** $55.00
**Sgl. Oc.:** $30.00
**Third Person:** $15.00

**Fools Cove Ranch**—A rustic setting high in the Ozarks. Fine accommodations and great food. Family farm with beautiful views and natural trails. A short drive to Buffalo River, Eureka Springs area and Branson, Missouri. Or just rest and relax in comfort under large oaks. Corrals for horses.

## Mountain Home

Ritlinger, Robert
1501 Hwy. 201 No., 72653
(501) 425-7557

**Amenities:** 1,2,6,10,15,16
**Breakfast:** F.

**Dbl. Oc.:** $41.00 - $46.00
**Third Person:** $5.00

**Mountain Home Country Inn**—A charming colonial home built in 1905. Furnished with wicker and antiques. Located between Bull Shoals, Norfork Lakes and White River. Choose from four air-conditioned rooms with ceiling fans and cable TV. Relax on the porch, deck or under huge oak trees.

| | | | | |
|---|---|---|---|---|
| 1. No Smoking | 5. Tennis Available | 9. Credit Cards Accepted | 13. Lunch Available | 17. Shared Bath |
| 2. No Pets | 6. Golf Available | 10. Personal Checks Accepted | 14. Public Transportation | 18. Afternoon Tea |
| 3. No Children | 7. Swiming Available | 11. Off Season Rates | 15. Reservations Necessary | ★ Commissions given |
| 4. Senior Citizen Rates | 8. Skiing Available | 12. Dinner Available | 16. Private Bath | to Travel Agents |

# CALIFORNIA

## The Golden State

Capitol: Sacramento
Statehood: September 9, 1850; the 31st state
State Motto: Eureka (I Have Found It)
State Song: "I Love You, California"
State Bird: California Valley Quail
State Flower: Golden Poppy
State Tree: California Redwood

The gold rush of 1848 started millions of people moving to California. Today more people live in the state than any other state in the union.

Farmers here have created some of the largest and most productive farms in all of our country. Their fruits, vegetables and nuts are shipped all over the U.S. California has the distinction of having the highest farm income in the nation.

Visitors visit California by the thousands every year. The wonderful climate and diversified beauty of this state, from the majestic redwood forest of the north and the giant sequoias of the Sierra Nevadas to the beautiful beaches and deserts in the south, make it a favorite vacation land.

The movie industry, located around Los Angeles, has brought excitement and glamour here as well as entertainment for the entire country since the early 1900's.

One of the most famous events of the year is perhaps the Tournament of Roses Parade in Pasadena on New Year's Day.

Our 37th President, Richard M. Nixon, is a native Californian, born in Yorbe Linda.

# CALIFORNIA

## Anaheim *

Ramont, Lois
856 So. Walnut St., 92802
(714) 778-0150

**Amenities:** 1,2,3,4,9,10, 14,16
**Breakfast:** F.

**Dbl. Oc.:** $55.00 - $80.00
**Sgl. Oc.:** $37.00 - $75.00
**Third Person:** $5.00
**Child:** $5.00

**Anaheim Country Inn**—A large and beautiful Princess Anne farmhouse built in 1910 on an acre of lawn and gardens. One mile from Disneyland. Graced by beveled leaded-glass windows and charming turn-of-the-century furnishings. Hot tub and laundry room available.

## Angwin

Lambeth, Corlene & Harold
415 Cold Springs Rd., 94508
(707) 965-3538

**Amenities:** 1,2,3,5,7,9,10,11,15,16,18
**Breakfast:** C.
**Dbl. Oc.:** $91.80 - $189.00
**Third Person:** $21.60

**Forest Manor Bed & Breakfast Inn**—A majestic English Tudor on 20 secluded acres above NapaValley. Massive hand-carved beams, vaulted ceilings, fireplaces, decks and large pool/spa. Described as "one ofthe most romantic country inns", a peaceful wooded sanctuary and a small, exclusive resort."

## Arroyo Grande *

Glass, Gina & John
407 El Camino Real, 93420
(800) 767-0083, (805) 489-5926

**Amenities:** 1,2,3,6,7,9,10,11,14,15,16,18
**Breakfast:** F.
**Dbl. Oc.:** $100.70 - $143.10
**Sgl. Oc.:** $90.10 - $132.50
**Third Person:** $21.20
**Child:** $21.20 (off-season only)

**The Village Inn**—An 1884 Victorian featuring Laura Ashley prints, antiques and eyelet. Modern conveniences. On California's central coast. Two suites. Five mini-suites. Evening horsd'oeuvres. Near San Luis Obispo, Hearst Castle, beaches, wineries and mineral springs.

| | | | | |
|---|---|---|---|---|
| 1. No Smoking | 5. Tennis Available | 9. Credit Cards Accepted | 13. Lunch Available | 17. Shared Bath |
| 2. No Pets | 6. Golf Available | 10. Personal Checks Accepted | 14. Public Transportation | 18. Afternoon Tea |
| 3. No Children | 7. Swiming Available | 11. Off Season Rates | 15. Reservations Necessary | ★ Commissions given |
| 4. Senior Citizen Rates | 8. Skiing Available | 12. Dinner Available | 16. Private Bath | to Travel Agents |

# CALIFORNIA

## Auburn *

Verhaart, Alicia & Anthony
164 Cleveland Ave., 95603
(916) 885-1166

**Amenities:** 1,6,8,9,10,11, 16,18
**Breakfast:** F.

**Dbl. Oc.:** $75.00 - $160.00
**Sgl. Oc.:** $75.00 - $160.00
**Third Person:** $75.00 - $160.00
**Child:** no charge

**Power's Mansion Inn**—A completely redecorated 100-year-old mansion. Located in the heart of the "gold country." Fifteen luxurious rooms, all with private bathrooms, phones and air conditioning. Honeymoon suites with fireplaces. Skiing, horseback riding, fishing and antiquing.

## Avalon (Santa Catalina Island) *

Michalis, Hattie & Robert
344 Whittley Ave.
P.O. Box 1381, 90704
(213) 510-2547

**Amenities:** 2,3,4,5,6,7,10,11, 14,15,16,17
**Breakfast:** C.

**Dbl. Oc.:** $117.00-$135.00
**Sgl. Oc.:** $117.00 - $133.75

**Gull House**—"With a touch of class." Large 660-square-foot suites, separate entrances, fireplace, morning room, refrigerator, pool, spa and barbecue on patio. Within walking distance to all attractions. Send S.A.S.E. for brochure. Two-night minimum. Taxi passes to and from Avalon Ferry.

## Avalon (Santa Catalina Island)

Olsen, Jon
125 Clarissa Ave.
P.O. Box 1881, 90704
(213) 510-0356

**Amenities:** 1,2,3,4,5,6,7,9,10, 11,16,18
**Breakfast:** C. and F.

**Dbl. Oc.:** $140.00 - $267.50
**Sgl. Oc.:** $140.00 - $267.50
**Third Person:** $25.00

**The Garden House Inn**—An elegant couples haven. Private baths. Lovely garden patio. Steps to beach. Ocean-view terraces. Buffet breakfast. AAA rating. Catalina Island just 28 miles off shore from Los Angeles.

## Big Bear Lake *

Knight, Phyllis
869 S. Knickerbocker
P.O. Box 3661, 92315
(714) 866-8221

**Amenities:** 1,2,5,6,7,8,9,10,15,16,17,18
**Breakfast:** F.
**Dbl. Oc.:** $91.68 - $161.88
**Sgl. Oc.:** $80.88 - $91.68
**Third Person:** $21.60
**Child:** under 10 yrs. - $11.80

**Knickerbocker Mansion**—A historic 10-room log home and carriage house on two acres of rolling lawn surrounded by a national forest. Within walking distance to village and restaurants. A peaceful retreat with old-world charm.

| | | | | |
|---|---|---|---|---|
| 1. No Smoking | 5. Tennis Available | 9. Credit Cards Accepted | 13. Lunch Available | 17. Shared Bath |
| 2. No Pets | 6. Golf Available | 10. Personal Checks Accepted | 14. Public Transportation | 18. Afternoon Tea |
| 3. No Children | 7. Swiming Available | 11. Off Season Rates | 15. Reservations Necessary | ★ Commissions given |
| 4. Senior Citizen Rates | 8. Skiing Available | 12. Dinner Available | 16. Private Bath | to Travel Agents |

# CALIFORNIA

## Burlingame

Fernandez, Elnora & Joe
1021 Balboa Ave., 94010
(415) 344-5815

**Amenities:** 3,5,6,7,10,14, 15,16
**Breakfast:** C.

**Dbl. Oc.:** $50.00
**Sgl. Oc.:** $35.00
**Third Person:** $10.00
**Child:** under 5 yrs. - $5.00

**Burlingame Bed & Breakfast**—We are three miles south of the San Francisco Airport. Restaurants, shops and buses are a block away. The train is six blocks away. Private upstairs quarters. King-size bed. Private bath. Separate eating area. View of cree Native flora and fauna. Italian and Spanish spoken.

## Calistoga

Dwyer, Scarlet
3918 Silverado Trail, 94515
(707) 942-6669

**Amenities:** 2,5,6,7,10,16,18
**Breakfast:** C. Plus
**Dbl. Oc.:** $92.12 - $135.32
**Sgl. Oc.:** $75.76 - $118.96
**Third Person:** $20.00
**Child:** under 15 yrs. - no charge

**Scarlett's Country Inn**—A secluded farmhouse set in a quiet mood of green lawns and tall pines overlooking the vineyards. Three exquisitely appointed suites, one with fireplace and wet bar. Breakfast in room or by woodland swimming pool. Close to wineries and spas. Children welcome. Air conditioning.

## Calistoga

O'Gorman, Debbie
3225 Lake Co. Hwy., 94515
(707) 942-6334

**Amenities:** 7,8,10,16,17
**Breakfast:** C.
**Dbl. Oc.:** $60.00 - $97.86
**Sgl. Oc.:** $60.00 - $97.86
**Third Person:** $5.36
**Child:** under 5 yrs. - no charge

**Hillcrest B&B**—Family owned since 1860. This rambling country home offers antique-filled rooms with balconies and breathtaking views of the valley. Enjoy swimming, hiking and fishing on our lovely grounds.

| | | | | |
|---|---|---|---|---|
| 1. No Smoking | 5. Tennis Available | 9. Credit Cards Accepted | 13. Lunch Available | 17. Shared Bath |
| 2. No Pets | 6. Golf Available | 10. Personal Checks Accepted | 14. Public Transportation | 18. Afternoon Tea |
| 3. No Children | 7. Swiming Available | 11. Off Season Rates | 15. Reservations Necessary | ★ Commissions given |
| 4. Senior Citizen Rates | 8. Skiing Available | 12. Dinner Available | 16. Private Bath | to Travel Agents |

# CALIFORNIA

## Calistoga *

Osborn, Pamela & Jack
109 Wapoo Ave., 94515
(707) 942-4200

**Amenities:** 1,2,9,11,16
**Breakfast:** F.

**Dbl. Oc.:** $107.30 - $149.10
**Third Person:** $22.00

**Brannon Cottage Inn**—Built by Sam Brannan, a founding father of Sacramento and San Francisco. The inn has played host to artists and authors. Located in the heart of the wine country. It offers a private entry, lovely gardens, nearby spa, gourmet restaurants, hiking, riding, gliders and swimming.

## Calistoga

Swiers, Alma & Don
4455 N. Saint Helena Hwy., 94515
(707) 942-0316

**Amenities:** 1,2,3,5,6,7,9,10,
15,16
**Breakfast:** F.

**Dbl. Oc.:** $90.00 - $110.00
**Sgl. Oc.:** $75.00 - $95.00
**Third Person:** $20.00
**Child:** $20.00

**Quail Mountain Bed & Breakfast**—A secluded and luxurious retreat. Located on 26 heavily forested acres 300 feet above the Napa Valley, with a vineyard on the property. Guest rooms have king beds and private baths. A lovely breakfast awaits the guests.

## Calistoga

Wheatley, Meg & Tony
1805 Foothill Blvd., 94515
(707) 942-4535

**Amenities:** 1,2,3,10,11,15,17
**Breakfast:** F.

**Dbl. Oc.:** $104.50 - $115.50
**Sgl. Oc.:** $104.50 - $115.50

**"Culvers," A Country Inn**—A beautifully restored 1875 Victorian home. All rooms have an aura of days gone by. Furnished with antiques throughout. We offer a full country breakfast, afternoon sherry, pool, spa and sauna. Close to wineries and mud baths. Many good restaurants are close by.

## Cambria

Kilpatrick, Valarie
2476 Main St., 93428
(805) 927-3222

**Amenities:** 4,5,9,10,1
**Breakfast:** C.

**Dbl. Oc.:** $110.00 - $126.50
**Sgl. Oc.:** $110.00 - $126.50
**Third Person:** $15.00
**Child:** over 12 yrs. - $15.00

**Olalieberry Inn**— A registered and historic home built in 1873. Six guest rooms with private baths. Antique furnishings. Walk to village. Near Hearts Castle, beaches, winieries and a fine bicycling area.

## Cambria *

Larsen, Anna
2555 MacLeod Way, 93428
(805) 927-8619

**Amenities:** 2,4,7,9,10,15,16
**Breakfast:** F.

**Dbl. Oc.:** $69.06 - $116.88
**Third:** $15.94
**Child:** under 5 yrs. - $5.31

**Pickford House Bed & Breakfast**—Eight rooms, some with fireplaces. King or queen beds. TVs. All rooms with antiques. Beach, shops and restuarants. Wine and cake at 5 p.m. in our 1860 bar. Senior citizen rates available on weekdays. Children welcome.

| 1. No Smoking | 5. Tennis Available | 9. Credit Cards Accepted | 13. Lunch Available | 17. Shared Bath |
| 2. No Pets | 6. Golf Available | 10. Personal Checks Accepted | 14. Public Transportation | 18. Afternoon Tea |
| 3. No Children | 7. Swiming Available | 11. Off Season Rates | 15. Reservations Necessary | ★ Commissions given |
| 4. Senior Citizen Rates | 8. Skiing Available | 12. Dinner Available | 16. Private Bath | to Travel Agents |

## Carlsbad *

Hale, Celeste
320 Walnut Ave., 92008
(619) 434-5995

Amenities:4,5,6,7,9,10
11,14,15, 16
Breakfast: C.

Dbl.Oc.:$93.00 - $165.00
Sgl.Oc.:$82.00 - $154.00
Child: over 12 yrs.-
no charage

**Pelican Cove Inn**—Feather beds optional. Fireplaces. Private baths and entries. Jacuzzi tubs. 200 yards from beach. Beach chairs and towels. Picnic baskets available. Amtrak and Palomar Airport courtesy pickup. Gift certificates. sun deck. Veranda and gazebo. Exquisite!

## Carmel

Alberson,Bob
Monte Verde (between 5th & 6th)
P.O. Box 2619, 93921
(408) 624-7917
**Amenities:** 6,9,10,11,16,18
**Breakfast:** C.
**Dbl. Oc.:** $110.00 - $126.00
**Sgl.Oc.:** $110.00 - $126.00
**Third:** $22.00

**Happy Landing Inn**—Fantastic! Private and quiet. It's like walking into a Beatrix Potter movie set. The rooms are decorated with beautiful antiques and flowers. Breakfast is served in your room by Aiko, our Japanese maid. Seeing Aiko every morning is a great way to wake up.

## Carmel *

Jones, Honey
P.O. Box 2747, 93921
(408) 624-7738

Amenities: 3,9,10,11,15,16
Breakfast: C.

Dbl. Oc.: $86.90 - $148.50
Third Person: $22.00

**Vagabond's House**—Eleven unique rooms with fireplaces. Surrounded by a court yard dominated by large oak trees where camellias, rhododendrons, hanging plants, ferns and flowers abound. Near shops, restaurants and art galleries.

## Clio

Miller, Karen & Don
P.O. Box 136, 96106
(916) 836-2387

Amenities: 1,2,6,7,8,9,10,13,
16,17
Breakfast: F.

Dbl. Oc.: $74.37 - $148.75
Third Person: $15.93
Child: $15.93

**White Sulphur Springs B&B**—For a unique journey into the past, come and stay with us. An atmosphere of comfort with elegance. Relax by the warm mineral pool or walk among the pine trees. One hour from Reno or Lake Tahoe. Located on Highway 89, south of Graeagle.

| | | | | |
|---|---|---|---|---|
| 1. No Smoking | 5. Tennis Available | 9. Credit Cards Accepted | 13. Lunch Available | 17. Shared Bath |
| 2. No Pets | 6. Golf Available | 10. Personal Checks Accepted | 14. Public Transportation | 18. Afternoon Tea |
| 3. No Children | 7. Swiming Available | 11. Off Season Rates | 15. Reservations Necessary | ★ Commissions given |
| 4. Senior Citizen Rates | 8. Skiing Available | 12. Dinner Available | 16. Private Bath | to Travel Agents |

# CALIFORNIA

## Cloverdale

Sauder, Ina & Allen
29955 River Rd., 95425
(707) 894-5956

**Amenities:** 1,2,5,6,7,9,10,15, 16,17,18
**Breakfast:** F.

**Dbl. Oc.:** $91.63 - $118.63
**Sgl. Oc.:** $91.63 - $118.63
**Third Person:** $25.00
**Child:** under 12 yrs. - $15.00

**Ye Olde Shelford House**—A wine country Victorian. A crisp, clean, light and airy inn with family antiques, quilts, dolls and delicious breakfast. Wine-barrel gazebo for wine sipping. Antique car wine tours, $60.00 — or "surrey & sip," $55.00(includes lunch). An inn to relax in.

## Coronado *

Bogh, Elizabeth A.
1017 Park Pl., 92118
(619) 435-9318

**Amenities:** 2,5,6,7,9,10,11,14,15,16
**Breakfast:** C.
**Dbl. Oc.:** $85.60
**Sgl. Oc.:** $64.20
**Third Person:** $10.00

**Coronada Village Inn**—One block from beach, town, restaurants and shops. Ten minutes to San Diego attractions. European in style. Decorated with antiques. Some canopy beds. Jacuzzis. New baths. The romance of yesterday mingled with today's comforts.

## Davenport

McDougal, Marcia
31 Davenport Ave., 95017
(408) 425-1818

**Amenities:** 1,2,9,10,12,13,14, 15,16
**Breakfast:** F.

**Dbl. Oc.:** $55.00 - $105.00
**Sgl. Oc.:** $55.00 - $105.00
**Third Person:** $10.00
**Child:** under 10 yrs. - no charge

**New Davenport Bed & Breakfast**—Nine miles north of Santa, halfway between Monterey and San Francisco. Twelve ocean-view rooms. Ocean access. Whale watching January to May. Nearby state elephant seal tours beaches, hiking and favorite coastal restaurant.

## Del Mar *

Holmes, Doris
410 15th St., 92014
(619) 481-3764

**Amenities:** 1,2,3,9,10,11,15, 16,17,18
**Breakfast:** C.

**Dbl. Oc.:** $75.00 - $145.00

**Rock Haus Inn**—A romantic getaway to a quaint seaside village. Ten rooms, four with private baths and one with fireplace. Most have ocean view and down comforters. Stroll to beach, restaurants and Amtrak.

---

| | | | |
|---|---|---|---|
| 1. No Smoking | 5. Tennis Available | 9. Credit Cards Accepted | 13. Lunch Available | 17. Shared Bath |
| 2. No Pets | 6. Golf Available | 10. Personal Checks Accepted | 14. Public Transportation | 18. Afternoon Tea |
| 3. No Children | 7. Swiming Available | 11. Off Season Rates | 15. Reservations Necessary | ★ Commissions given |
| 4. Senior Citizen Rates | 8. Skiing Available | 12. Dinner Available | 16. Private Bath | to Travel Agents |

## Elk

Triebess, Hildrun-Uta
6300 S. Hwy. 1
P.O. Box 367, 95432
(707) 877-3321

**Amenities:** 1,2,3,10,11,15,16
**Breakfast:** F.

**Dbl. Oc.:** $105.49 - $137.89
**Sgl. Oc.:** $94.87 - $127.27

**Elk Cove Inn**—An 1883 Victorian with spectacular ocean views from cabins and main house. Fireplaces. Full gourmet breakfast. Ready access to expansive driftwood-strewn beach. Relaxed, romantic atmosphere in a rural village. Near Mendocino and Anderson Valley wineries. Nearby hiking and biking.

## Eureka

Carter, Christie & Mark
1033 Third St., 95501
(707) 445-1390

**Amenities:** 1,2,3,5,6,9,10,11, 12,14,15,16,17,18
**Breakfast:** F.

**Dbl. Oc.:** $79.00 - $280.00
**Sgl. Oc.:** $69.00 - $189.00
**Third Person:** $25.00

**Carter House Inn**—"1989 Best Inn in America" - *Uncle Ben's*; "Best breakfast in California" - *California Magazine;* "Delightful, remarkable" - *Bon Appetit*; "One of the most captivating inns of the entire state" - *National Motorist*; "The best of the best" - *California Living*. Need we say more?

## Eureka *

Vieyra, Lily & Doug
1406 'C' St. (at 14th), 95501
(707) 444-3144,
(707) 443-6512

**Amenities:** 1,2,9,10,11,14,16, 17,18
**Breakfast:** F.

**Dbl. Oc.:** $85.00 - $105.00
**Sgl. Oc.:** $80.00 - $100.00
**Child:** adult rate

**An Elegant Victorian Mansion**—Eureka's most elegant and famous B&B in an area dominated by many elegant Victorian homes. Listed in the *National Register of Historic Places*. Finnish sauna, Swedish massage, hot tub, croquet, bicycles, hors d'oeuvres and carriage rides.

## Fort Bragg *

Bailey, Colette & John
615 N. Main, 95437
(707) 964-0640

**Amenities:** 1,2,5,6,7,9,10,11,16,18
**Breakfast:** F.
**Dbl. Oc.:** $70.20 - $162.00
**Sgl. Oc.:** $59.40 - $97.20
**Third Person:** $21.60 - $27.00

**The Grey Whale Inn**—A premier inn on the Mendocino coast. Fourteen spacious rooms with private baths. Each room has a special amenity: ocean, garden or hill views, fireplace, deck, patio, wheelchair access or whirlpool tub. Walk to beach and Skunk Train.

| | | | | |
|---|---|---|---|---|
| 1. No Smoking | 5. Tennis Available | 9. Credit Cards Accepted | 13. Lunch Available | 17. Shared Bath |
| 2. No Pets | 6. Golf Available | 10. Personal Checks Accepted | 14. Public Transportation | 18. Afternoon Tea |
| 3. No Children | 7. Swiming Available | 11. Off Season Rates | 15. Reservations Necessary | ★ Commissions given |
| 4. Senior Citizen Rates | 8. Skiing Available | 12. Dinner Available | 16. Private Bath | to Travel Agents |

# CALIFORNIA

## Fort Bragg *

Gundersen, Marilyn & Gene
700 N. Main St., 95437
(707) 964-9529

**Amenities:** 1,2,5,6,7,9,10,11,16
**Breakfast:** F.
**Dbl. Oc.:** $59.40 - $97.20
**Sgl. Oc.:** $52.92 & up
**Third Person:** $15.00
**Child:** $15.00

**Pudding Creek Inn**—Two 1884 Victorians connected by an enclosed garden court. Ten rooms with private baths, some with fireplaces. Complimentary breakfast features homemade coffee breads served hot, fresh fruit and specialty dish. Shops, sights, beaches, train depot and dining within an easy walk!

## Fort Bragg *

Sorrells, Anne
561 Stewart St., 95437
(707) 964-5555

**Amenities:** 1,2,9,10,11,14,
15,16
**Breakfast:** F.

**Dbl. Oc.:** $75.60 - $124.20
**Third Person:** $10.00
**Child:** under 3 yrs. -
no charge

**Avalon House**—A 1905 Craftsman house. Quiet neighborhood. Three blocks from ocean and two blocks from Skunk Train. Six rooms with private baths, some with fireplaces, spas and ocean views. The Mendocino coast is famous for its scenic beauty and unspoiled environment. 150 miles north of San Francisco.

## Freestone

Hoffman, Rosemary & Rogers
520 Bohemian Hwy., 95472
(707) 874-2526

**Amenities:** 1,3,9,10,15,16
**Breakfast:** F.

**Dbl. Oc.:** $85.00 - $92.00
**Sgl. Oc.:** $85.00 - $92.00
**Third Person:** $15.00

**Green Apple Inn**—An 1860's farmhouse set in a meadow backed by redwoods. Located on five acres in the historic district of Freestone, between Bodega Bay and the Russian River. Nearby are excellent restaurants and small family wineries.

## Fremont *

Medeiros, Anne & Keith
43344 Mission Blvd., 94539
(415) 490-0520

**Amenities:** 1,2,9,10,14,15,16
**Breakfast:** C.

**Dbl. Oc.:** $69.55 - $80.25
**Sgl. Oc.:** $69.55 - $80.25
**Third Person:** $15.00

**Lord Bradley's Inn**—A Victorian nestled below Mission Peak, adjacent to Mission San Jose. Historic areas. Hikers and kite fliers paradise. Victorian decorated. Common room. Garden patio. Parking. Easy access to San Francisco by Bay Area Rapid Transit. Great for small weddings or retirement parties.

| | | | |
|---|---|---|---|
| 1. No Smoking | 5. Tennis Available | 9. Credit Cards Accepted | 13. Lunch Available | 17. Shared Bath |
| 2. No Pets | 6. Golf Available | 10. Personal Checks Accepted | 14. Public Transportation | 18. Afternoon Tea |
| 3. No Children | 7. Swiming Available | 11. Off Season Rates | 15. Reservations Necessary | ★ Commissions given |
| 4. Senior Citizen Rates | 8. Skiing Available | 12. Dinner Available | 16. Private Bath | to Travel Agents |

# CALIFORNIA

## Geyserville *

Campbell, Mary Jane & Jerry
1475 Canyon Rd., 95441
(707) 857-3476

**Amenities:** 1,2,5,7,9,10,15, 16
**Breakfast:** F.

**Dbl. Oc.:** $108.00 - $135.00
**Sgl. Oc.:** $97.20 - $124.20
**Third Person:** $25.00
**Child:** $25.00

**Campbell Ranch Inn**—Located in the heart of the Sonoma County wine country on a 35-acre hilltop. Spectacular views, beautiful gardens, tennis court, pool, spa and bikes. Large rooms, king beds and balconies. Full-menu breakfast and homemade dessert in the evening.

---

## Groveland *

Mosley, Peggy
18767 Main St.
P.O. Box 481, 95321
(209) 962-4000

**Amenities:** 2,5,6,7,8,9,11,12, 13,16,17
**Breakfast:** C.

**Dbl. Oc.:** $48.60 - $97.20
**Sgl. Oc.:** $48.60 - $97.20
**Third Person:** $10.80
**Child:** under 12 yrs. - no charge

**The Groveland Hotel, A Historic Inn**—A restored 1849 gold rush adobe, 25 miles from Yosemite Park. Much history nearby. Pure luxury with down comforters, up-scale linens, period decor and European antiques. Warm, friendly and fun. Free pickup from Pine Mt. Lake General Aviation Airport. Conference room.

---

## Gualala *

Flanagan, Nancy & Loren
34591 S. Hwy., 95445
(707) 884-4537

**Amenities:** 1,2,3,5,6,7,9,10,16
**Breakfast:** F.
**Dbl. Oc.:** $102.60 - $124.20
**Sgl. Oc.:** $102.60 - $124.20

34591 So. Highway 1    Gualala, California, 95445    (707) 884-4537

**North Coast Country Inn**—Rustic redwood buildings on a forested hillside overlooking the ocean. Four large guest rooms, all with fireplaces, antiques, private bathroom, deck, hot tub and view.

---

## Gualala

Linscheid, Leslie
38300 Shoreline Hwy. One, 95445
(707) 884-3256

**Amenities:** 1,2,3,5,6,9,10,11, 12,14,16,17,18
**Breakfast:** F.

**Dbl. Oc.:** $81.00 - $173.00
**Sgl. Oc.:** $81.00 - $173.00
**Third Person:** $15.00

**The Old Milano Hotel & Restaurant**—The Pacific Ocean plays an important role on this three-acre estate. Built in 1905 and listed in the *Register of Historic Places*. The seven guest rooms are antique-filled. The restaurant features gourmet dining with award-winning wines.

---

1. No Smoking
2. No Pets
3. No Children
4. Senior Citizen Rates
5. Tennis Available
6. Golf Available
7. Swiming Available
8. Skiing Available
9. Credit Cards Accepted
10. Personal Checks Accepted
11. Off Season Rates
12. Dinner Available
13. Lunch Available
14. Public Transportation
15. Reservations Necessary
16. Private Bath
17. Shared Bath
18. Afternoon Tea
★ Commissions given to Travel Agents

# CALIFORNIA

## Guerneville

Rechberger, Diane
12850 River Rd., 95446
(707) 887-1033

**Amenities:** 1,2,9,10,12,15, 16,17
**Breakfast:** F.

**Dbl. Oc.:** $70.20 - $124.20
**Third Person:** $15.00

**Ridenhour Ranch House Inn**—Near Korbel Winery. A 1906 far house on 2-1/4 acres. American and English decor throughout. A hearty breakfast of homemade goodies. 1- 1/4 hours from San Francisco, in the Russian River resort area. Children 10 years and overwelcome.

## Half Moon Bay *

Baldwin, Eve & Terry
615 Mill St., 94019
(415) 726-9794

**Amenities:** 1,2,3,5,6,7,9,10, 14,15,16,18
**Breakfast:** F.

**Dbl. Oc.:** $178.00 - $254.00
**Sgl. Oc.:** $178.00 - $254.00
**Third Person:** $20.00

**Mill Rose Inn**—"The ideal English country inn" — *New York Times*. Relax and be pampered in a romantic seaside retreat just minutes from San Francisco. English country garden, TV, phones, champagne breakfast, private spa and luxury suites. AAA and Mobil approved. Wood-burning fireplaces in rooms.

## Half Moon Bay *

Fogli, Michael
407 Mirada Rd., 94019
(415) 726-6002

**Amenities:** 1,2,5,6,9,10,13, 16,18
**Breakfast:** F.

**Dbl. Oc.:** $145.65 - $269.85
**Sgl. Oc.:** $145.65 - $269.85
**Third Person:** $21.45

**Cypress Inn On Miramar Beach**—Located on a five-mile stretch of sandy beach. Every room has a private deck, fireplace, private bath and great ocean views. Just 1/2 hour from San Francisco. Gourmet breakfasts, afternoon tea and snacks. In-house massage therapist available.

## Half Moon Bay *

Lowings, Anne
779 Main St., 94019
(415) 726-1616

**Amenities:** 1,5,6,7,9,10,14,15, 16,18
**Breakfast:** F.

**Dbl. Oc.:** $70.20 - $205.20
**Sgl. Oc.:** $64.80
**Third Person:** $15.00
**Child:** $15.00

**Old Thyme Inn**—Your hosts at Old Thyme Inn are the Lowings family. They have restored this 1890's house back to its position of elegance on Main Street. The rooms are all individually decorated with antiques, prints and wallpaper. There are fireplaces, whirlpool tubs and herbs.

## Half Moon Bay *

Lowings, Simon
324 Main St., 94019
(415) 726-9123,
(800) 77B-NB4U

**Amenities:** 1,2,5,6,9,10, 11,16
**Breakfast:** C.

**Dbl. Oc.:** $91.80 - $129.60
**Sgl. Oc.:** $86.40 - $124.20
**Third Person:** $10.00
**Child:** under 10 yrs. - no charge

**Zaballa House**—In the mid-1800's, Estanislao Zabella was the first city planner and owner of the general store, several stables and a bar. The house is located in a garden setting. Some rooms have fireplaces and some double-size whirlpool tubs with private bathrooms. A buffet breakfast is served.

| | | | |
|---|---|---|---|
| 1. No Smoking | 5. Tennis Available | 9. Credit Cards Accepted | 13. Lunch Available | 17. Shared Bath |
| 2. No Pets | 6. Golf Available | 10. Personal Checks Accepted | 14. Public Transportation | 18. Afternoon Tea |
| 3. No Children | 7. Swiming Available | 11. Off Season Rates | 15. Reservations Necessary | ★ Commissions given |
| 4. Senior Citizen Rates | 8. Skiing Available | 12. Dinner Available | 16. Private Bath | to Travel Agents |

## Healdsberg

| | | |
|---|---|---|
| Villeneuve, Gina | **Amenities:** 1,2,3,6,7,9,10,15, | **Dbl. Oc.:** $79.00 - $133.00 |
| 10630 Wohler Rd., 95448 | 16,17 | **Sgl. Oc.:** $79.00 - $133.00 |
| (707) 887-9573 | **Breakfast:** F. | **Third Person:** $20.00 |

**The Raford House**—This gracious 100-year-old Victorian farmhouse sits among the vineyards in a tranquil country setting. It offers seven comfortable guest rooms, two with fireplaces. The Raford House is a historic landmark. Gina and Vince Villeneuve are the innkeepers.

## Healdsburg *

| | | |
|---|---|---|
| Claus, Joanne | **Amenities:** 1,2,5,6,7,9,10,14, | **Dbl. Oc.:** $75.43 - $145.63 |
| 321 Haydon St., 95448 | 15,16,17,18 | **Sgl. Oc.:** $70.11 - $135.63 |
| (707) 433-5228 | **Breakfast:** F. | **Third Person:** $16.11 |
| | | **Child:** over 12 yrs. - $16.11 |

**Haydon House Bed & Breakfast Inn**—A beautifully furnished Queen Anne Victorian. Comfortable rooms, lavish breakfast and warm hospitality in a quiet and relaxing atmosphere within minutes of many award-winning wineries. Located in the heart of the Sonoma wine country. Within walking distance of historic plaza.

## Idyllwild

Dugan, Diana
26370 Hwy. 243
P.O. Box 1818, 92349
(714) 659-3202

**Amenities:** 1,2,8,9,10,15,16
**Breakfast:** F.
**Dbl. Oc.:** $90.00 - $150.00

**Strawberry Creek Inn**—A rambling home in the pines and oaks of the San Jacinto Mountains. A 15-minute walk along the highway or Strawberry Creek to the village with many quaint shops and fine restaurants. Nine rooms with private baths, some with fireplaces. A honeymoon cottage with whirlpool tub.

## Idyllwild

| | | |
|---|---|---|
| Jones, Barbara | **Amenities:** 1,2,3,7,10,15,16, | **Dbl. Oc.:** $60.50 - $82.50 |
| 26770 Hwy. 243 | 17 | **Sgl. Oc.:** $60.50 - $82.50 |
| P.O. Box 1115, 92349 | **Breakfast:** C. | |
| (714) 659-4087 | | |

**Wilkum Inn**—Warm hospitality and personal comfort combine with an ambience of yesteryear, enhanced by handmade quilts, antiques and collectibles. In a pine-forested mountain village with unique shops, excellent restaurants, fine and performing arts. Hike or just relax.

| | | | | |
|---|---|---|---|---|
| 1. No Smoking | 5. Tennis Available | 9. Credit Cards Accepted | 13. Lunch Available | 17. Shared Bath |
| 2. No Pets | 6. Golf Available | 10. Personal Checks Accepted | 14. Public Transportation | 18. Afternoon Tea |
| 3. No Children | 7. Swiming Available | 11. Off Season Rates | 15. Reservations Necessary | ★ Commissions given |
| 4. Senior Citizen Rates | 8. Skiing Available | 12. Dinner Available | 16. Private Bath | to Travel Agents |

# CALIFORNIA

## Inverness

Storch, Suzanne
75 Balboa Ave., 94937
(415) 663-9338

**Amenities:** 10,15,16
**Breakfast:** F.

**Dbl. Oc.:** $135.00
**Sgl. Oc.:** $124.20
**Third Person:** $15.00
**Child:** $15.00

**Rosemary Cottage**—Romantic seclusion in a French country cottage. Large deck overlooks view and garden. Spacious main room with view furnished with antiques. Wood-stove fireplace. Fullye quipped kitchen. Bedroom has queen bed and private bath. Families welcome.

## Ione *

Hubbs, Melisande
214 Shakeley Lane
P.O. Box 322, 95640
(209) 274-4468

**Amenities:** 1,2,6,10,15,
16,17,18
**Breakfast:** F.

**Dbl. Oc.:** $55.00 - $85.00
**Sgl. Oc.:** $50.00 - $80.00
**Third Person:** $15.00
**Child:** $15.00

**The Heirloom**—Located in gold country, midway between Tahoe and Yosemite. This colonial antebellum is down a country lane. Romantic English garden, balconies, fireplaces, antiques, grand piano, memorable breakfast, gracious hospitality, rich history, wineries and natural beauty.

## Jackson *

Beltz, Jeannine & Vic
11941 Narcissus Rd., 95642
(800) 933-4393, (209) 296-4300

**Amenities:** 2,3,9,10,15,16
**Breakfast:** F.

**Dbl. Oc.:** $84.80 - $116.60
**Sgl. Oc.:** $74.20 - $106.00

**The Wedgewood Inn**—A replica Victorian tucked away on a wooded acreage. Six lavishly furnished guest rooms. Wood-burning stoves, antiques, balcony, terraced English gardens, spectacular gazebo and sparkling mountains. Secluded, yet central to all tourist areas and excellent dining.

## Jamestown *

Willey, Stephen
Main St.
P.O. Box 502, 95327
(209) 984-3446

**Amenities:** 2,3,6,7,8,9,10,11,
12,13,14,15,16,17
**Breakfast:** C.

**Dbl. Oc.:** $70.20 - $81.00
**Sgl. Oc.:** $70.20 - $81.00
**Third Person:** $10.80

**Historic National Hotel — Bed & Breakfast**—An 11-room, 1859 fully restored gold rush hotel with an outstanding restaurant and the original saloon. Classic cuisine and gracious service are only part of what we offer.

---

| | | | |
|---|---|---|---|
| 1. No Smoking | 5. Tennis Available | 9. Credit Cards Accepted | 13. Lunch Available | 17. Shared Bath |
| 2. No Pets | 6. Golf Available | 10. Personal Checks Accepted | 14. Public Transportation | 18. Afternoon Tea |
| 3. No Children | 7. Swiming Available | 11. Off Season Rates | 15. Reservations Necessary | ★ Commissions given |
| 4. Senior Citizen Rates | 8. Skiing Available | 12. Dinner Available | 16. Private Bath | to Travel Agents |

## Jenner *

Murphy, Sheldon & Richard
10400 Coast Hwy. 1, 95459
(800) 732-2377, (707) 865-2377

**Amenities:** 4,6,7,9,10,11,12,13,14,15,16
**Breakfast:** C.
**Dbl. Oc.:** $60.00 - $150.00
**Sgl. Oc.:** $50.00 - $140.00
**Third Person:** $15.00
**Child:** under 3 yrs. - no charge

**Murphy Jenner Inn**—An exceptionally romantic setting where the wine country meets the sea. Lovingly decorated rooms, suites and cottages with water views and coastal charm. Some with fireplaces and hot tubs. All with private baths and separate entrances. Fine dining on premises.

## Klamath

Hamby, Donna & Paul
451 Requa Rd., 95548
(707) 482-8205

**Amenities:** 2,3,9,10,12, 15,16,18
**Breakfast:** F.

**Dbl. Oc.:** $60.00
**Sgl. Oc.:** $60.00
**Third Person:** $15.00

**Requa Inn**—A historic inn overlooking the Klamath River. Located in the heart of the Redwood National Park, one mile from the ocean. Near beaches and redwood trails. Open March to October. Full dinner menu — steaks and seafood.

## Laguna Beach *

Sparkuhl, Barbara
1289 So. Coast Hwy., 92651
(714) 497-2446

**Amenities:** 1,4,7,9,10,11,14, 15,16,18
**Breakfast:** C.

**Dbl. Oc.:** $90.00 - $160.00
**Sgl. Oc.:** $80.00 - $140.00
**Child:** under 12 yrs. - no charge

**Hotel Firenze**—A historic 1927 hotel in the European tradition, just steps to the beach. Features 24 ocean-view rooms and suites decorated with fine antiques. Enjoy the sun on the private roof deck with a 360-degree view. Relax in the den/library, garden courtyard or in the front of the fire.

## Laguna Beach *

Taylor, Dee
1322 Catalina St., 92651
(714) 494-8945

**Amenities:** 2,5,6,10,14,15,16
**Breakfast:** C.

**Dbl. Oc.:** $91.80 - $162.00
**Sgl. Oc.:** $91.80 - $162.00
**Third Person:** $20.00
**Child:** under 6 yrs. - $10.00

**The Carriage House**—A charming New Orleans-style inn two blocks from the blue Pacific. Secluded and flowered courtyard. Parking. Private living room, bedroom and bath. Some two-bedroom suites with kitchens. Antiques. Close to everything.

| | | | |
|---|---|---|---|
| 1. No Smoking | 5. Tennis Available | 9. Credit Cards Accepted | 13. Lunch Available | 17. Shared Bath |
| 2. No Pets | 6. Golf Available | 10. Personal Checks Accepted | 14. Public Transportation | 18. Afternoon Tea |
| 3. No Children | 7. Swiming Available | 11. Off Season Rates | 15. Reservations Necessary | ★ Commissions given |
| 4. Senior Citizen Rates | 8. Skiing Available | 12. Dinner Available | 16. Private Bath | to Travel Agents |

## Laguna Beach *

Wietz, Annette & Henk
741 So. Coast Hwy., 92651
(714) 494-3004

**Amenities:** 2,5,6,7,9,10,11, 14,15,18
**Breakfast:** C. Plus

**Dbl. Oc.:** $100.00 - $175.00
**Sgl. Oc.:** $95.00 - $170.00
**Third Person:** $20.00
**Child:** under 10 yrs. - $10.00

**Eiler's Inn**—Experience European hospitality. Warm, yet elegant, rooms. Downtown location. Walk to restaurants and art galleries. Wine served in a beautiful courtyard with fountain. Exceptional breakfast. Living room with fireplace. Library with color TV. Great to relax and get away.

## La Jolla *

Cash, Sherry
P.O. Box 91223, San Diego,
92169-0869
(619) 456-9634

**Amenities:** 1,2,3,5,6,7,11,14, 15,16,17
**Breakfast:** C. and F.

**Dbl. Oc.:** $75.00 - $110.00
**Sgl. Oc.:** $70.00 - $105.00

**Westbourne Windansea Bed And Breakfast**—Rated "the best" by experienced B&B guests. One block to ocean. Within walking distance to village. Near all of San Diego's attractions. Plush and comfortable guestrooms, gourmet breakfasts and finest linens and towels. No expense spared to spoil and pamper you.

## Lake Arrowhead

Wooley, Kathleen & John
28717 Hwy. 1
P.O. Box 362, Skyforest, 92385
(714) 336-1483

**Amenities:** 1,2,3,4,5,6,7,8,9,10, 11,12,13, 15,16,18
**Breakfast:** F.
**Dbl. Oc.:** $89.00 - $185.00
**Sgl. Oc.:** $89.00 - $185.00
**Third Person:** $30.00
**Child:** under 12 yrs. - $30.00

**Storybook Inn**—High in the San Bernardino Mountains at historic rim of the world. Surrounded by stately pine and oak trees, including one of the oldest oak trees in the area. This million-dollar estate has nine romantic guest rooms, as well as a "call-of-the-wild" rustic cabin.

## Lemon Cove *

Bonette, Kay & Pat
33038 Sierra Hwy., 93244
(209) 597-2555

**Amenities:** 1,2,6,8,9,10, 15,16,17
**Breakfast:** F.

**Dbl. Oc.:** $49.00 - $89.00
**Sgl. Oc.:** $49.00 - $89.00
**Third Person:** $10.00
**Child:** under 5 yrs. - no charge

**Lemon Cove Bed & Breakfast**—Nestled among acres of orange groves, Lemon Cove B&B is near Sequoia National Park. Romantically decorated rooms include antiques, quilts and claw-foot tubs. Bridal suite has whirlpool tub, fireplace and balcony. Plantation breakfast served in English-style dining room.

| | | | | |
|---|---|---|---|---|
| 1. No Smoking | 5. Tennis Available | 9. Credit Cards Accepted | 13. Lunch Available | 17. Shared Bath |
| 2. No Pets | 6. Golf Available | 10. Personal Checks Accepted | 14. Public Transportation | 18. Afternoon Tea |
| 3. No Children | 7. Swiming Available | 11. Off Season Rates | 15. Reservations Necessary | ★ Commissions given |
| 4. Senior Citizen Rates | 8. Skiing Available | 12. Dinner Available | 16. Private Bath | to Travel Agents |

## *Little River*

Molnar, Carole
7001 N. Highway One
P.O. Box 357, 95456
(707) 937-0697

**Amenities:** 1,2,3,4,9,10,11,14,
15,16
**Breakfast:** C. Plus

**Dbl. Oc.:** $85.00 - $100.00
**Sgl. Oc.:** $85.00 - $100.00
**Third Person:** $15.00
**Child:** $15.00

**Victorian Farmhouse**—Built in 1877, located two miles south of the historic village of Mendocino. All rooms have either king- or queen-size beds with private baths. Most have fireplaces. During your stay, we are delighted to serve breakfast to your room.

## *Long Beach*

Brasser, Laura & Reuben
435 Cedar Ave., 90802
(213) 436-0324

**Amenities:** 1,9,10,14,
15,16,18
**Breakfast:** F.

**Dbl. Oc.:** $88.00 - $99.00
**Third Person:** $15.00

**Lord Mayor's Inn**—Fine hospitality at the elegantly restored 1904 home of Long Beach's first mayor. Five spacious bedrooms, each with a private bath, carry out the turn-of-the-century ambience. Walk to the nearby Convention Center, shopping mall and World Trade Center.

## *Los Angeles* *

Burns, Murray
1442 Kellam Ave., 90026
(213) 250-1620

**Amenities:** 1,2,4,5,7,9,10,14,
16,17,18
**Breakfast:** F.

**Dbl. Oc.:** $65.00
**Sgl. Oc.:** $49.00
**Third Person:** $15.00
**Child:** under 10 yrs. -
no charge

**Eastlake Victorian Inn**—An 1887 Victorian home in a historic neighborhood. Contains Victorian furnishings, stained glass and landscaped gardens. Full breakfast served in dining room, porch or room. Fresh flowers and fruit in rooms. Smoking allowed on porch and grounds only. Near downtown.

## *Los Angeles*

Moultout, Suzanne
449 N. Detroit St., 90036
(213) 938-4794

**Amenities:** 1,2,3,10,14,15,17
**Breakfast:** C.

**Dbl. Oc.:** $50.00
**Sgl. Oc.:** $45.00
**Third Person:** $15.00

**Paris Cottage**—A Spanish-style house located on a quiet street. Close to West Hollywood, downtown (Amtrak), Beverly Hills and beaches. Your hostess offers an attractive guest room and a shady yard with fruit trees. Hollywood Hills, CBS Studios, restaurants, theatres and museums are close by.

---

| | | | | |
|---|---|---|---|---|
| 1. No Smoking | 5. Tennis Available | 9. Credit Cards Accepted | 13. Lunch Available | 17. Shared Bath |
| 2. No Pets | 6. Golf Available | 10. Personal Checks Accepted | 14. Public Transportation | 18. Afternoon Tea |
| 3. No Children | 7. Swiming Available | 11. Off Season Rates | 15. Reservations Necessary | ★ Commissions given |
| 4. Senior Citizen Rates | 8. Skiing Available | 12. Dinner Available | 16. Private Bath | to Travel Agents |

# CALIFORNIA

## Los Angeles *

Woon-Ha, Kim
545 S. Serrano Ave., 90020
(213) 389-8823

Amenities: 4,6,8,9,14,
15,16, 18
Breakfast: C.

Dbl. Oc.: $100.00 (average
price)
Third Person: $10.00

**Happy Inn/Bed & Breakfast**—A beautifully remodeled inn located in a residential area of Wilshire district. Shop at Rodeo Drive, do business on Wilshire Blvd. or enjoy artistic treats of Melrose. Homey atmosphere and live attractions of L.A. make for a pleasant and best place to stay. Shuttle service provided.

## Mariposa

Foster, Richard J.
3871 Hwy. 49 S., 95338
(209) 966-2832

Amenities: 1,7,10,17
Breakfast: F.

Dbl. Oc.: $45.00
Sgl. Oc.: $40.00
Third Person: $7.00
Child: under 2 yrs. -
no charge

**The Pelennor, Bed & Breakfast At Bootjack**—Created for the traveler seeking economical lodging. An hour to Yosemite, a bit further to skiing. Bagpipes and Scottish lore. Hot tub and lap pool. Six rooms. Honeymoon suite coming soon.

## Mariposa

Haag, Janice & Donald
5636 Whitlock Rd., 95338
(209) 966-5592

Amenities: 1,2,10,15,17
Breakfast: C.

Dbl. Oc.: $40.00
Sgl. Oc.: $35.00
Third Person: $10.00

**Winsor Farms Bed And Breakfast**—A peaceful hilltop retreat. This one-story country home is seven miles from Mariposa, three miles off Highway 140 and 45 minutes to Yosemite National Park. You can also explore the gold rush history unique to this area.

## Mendocino

Allen, Thomas
44860 Main St.
P.O. Box 626, 95460
(707) 937-0246

Amenities: 1,2,3,9,10,
15,16,18
Breakfast: F.

Dbl. Oc.: $59.00 - $130.00
Sgl. Oc.: $59.00 - $130.00
Third Person: $5.00

**Mendocino Village Inn**—Hummingbirds, Picassos, 1882 Victorian, French-roast coffee, fuchsias, fireplaces, Vivaldi, country breakfasts, Pacific surf, Bokharas, fresh blackberries, four-poster beds, migrating whales and Chardonnay.

| | | | |
|---|---|---|---|
| 1. No Smoking | 5. Tennis Available | 9. Credit Cards Accepted | 13. Lunch Available | 17. Shared Bath |
| 2. No Pets | 6. Golf Available | 10. Personal Checks Accepted | 14. Public Transportation | 18. Afternoon Tea |
| 3. No Children | 7. Swiming Available | 11. Off Season Rates | 15. Reservations Necessary | ★ Commissions given |
| 4. Senior Citizens Rates | 8. Skiing Available | 12. Dinner Available | 16. Private Bath | to Travel Agents |

# CALIFORNIA

## Mendocino *

Reding, Joe
45020 Albion St., 95460
(707) 937-0289

**Amenities:** 2,5,6,7,9,10,11,12, 15,16,17
**Breakfast:** C.

**Dbl. Oc.:** $45.00 - $135.00
**Sgl. Oc.:** $45.00 - $135.00
**Third Person:** $15.00
**Child:** $15.00

**MacCallum House Inn**—Located in the center of the village of Mendocino. Besides the main house, there are unique cottages on the grounds. There is an award-winning restaurant and bar on the premises.

## Mendocino

Zahavi, Jake
11201 Lansing St., 95460
(707) 937-0551

**Amenities:** 1,2,9,10,11,15,16
**Breakfast:** F.

**Dbl. Oc.:** $75.00 - $168.00
**Third Person:** $15.00

**Agate Cove Inn**—Situated on a bluff above the Pacific Ocean with a breath taking view. Cozy and romantic cottages with fireplaces, ocean views and private baths. Full country breakfast is served in this 1860's farmhouse with beautifully landscaped gardens.

## Montara *

Bechtell, William R.
1125 Tamarind St., 94037
(415) 728-3946

**Amenities:** 1,2,3,6,7,9,10,14, 15,16
**Breakfast:** F.

**Dbl. Oc.:** $70.00
**Sgl. Oc.:** $60.00
**Third Person:** $15.00

**Montara B&B**—Just 20 miles south of San Francisco on the scenic California coast! Semi-rural area with nearby hiking, beaches and horseback riding. Private entrance, private bath, fireplace, ocean view, phone and TV. Full breakfast served in a solarium overlooking the garden.

## Montara *

Hoche-Mong, Emily & Raymond
835 George St.
P.O. Box 937, 94037-0937
(415) 728-5451

**Amenities:** 1,2,4,9,10,16,17,18
**Breakfast:** F.
**Dbl. Oc.:** $80.00 - $90.00
**Sgl. Oc.:** $80.00 - $90.00
**Child:** under 16 yrs. - $10.00

**Goose & Turrets Bed & Breakfast**—One-half mile from beaches, 20 minutes from San Francisco Airport, 25 miles south of San Francisco. A historic home in a quiet garden, creature comforts and super breakfasts. Near tide pools, horses, restaurants and galleries. Half-Moon Bay Airport and harbor pick - up. French spoken.

| | | | | |
|---|---|---|---|---|
| 1. No Smoking | 5. Tennis Available | 9. Credit Cards Accepted | 13. Lunch Available | 17. Shared Bath |
| 2. No Pets | 6. Golf Available | 10. Personal Checks Accepted | 14. Public Transportation | 18. Afternoon Tea |
| 3. No Children | 7. Swiming Available | 11. Off Season Rates | 15. Reservations Necessary | ★ Commissions given |
| 4. Senior Citizen Rates | 8. Skiing Available | 12. Dinner Available | 16. Private Bath | to Travel Agents |

# CALIFORNIA

## Napa

Campbell, Pearl
720 Seminary St., 94559
(707) 257-0789

**Amenities:** 1,2,3,7,9,10,15,16, 17
**Breakfast:** C.

**Dbl. Oc.:** $88.00 - $120.00
**Sgl. Oc.:** $88.00 - $120.00

**Coombs Residence Inn**—Victorian splendor — a home with a personality of its own. Down comforters and pillows, terry robes, afternoon refreshments and lots of T.L.C.

## Napa

Logan, Rosemary & Bruce
1436 G. St., 94559

(707) 252-8144

**Amenities:** 1,2,3,5,9,10, 11,15,16
**Breakfast:** Full

**Dbl. Oc.:** $93.93 - $138.13
**Sgl. Oc.:** $49.73 - $93.93(weekdays)
**Third Person:** $16.58

**Arbor Guest House**—This 1906 colonial transition home and carriage house have been completely restored for the comfort of guests. Rooms are beautifully appointed with antiques and have private baths and queen-size beds; some with fireplaces; one with a spa tub. Close to wineries.

## Napa *

Maddox, Sybil
7400 St. Helena Hwy., 94558
(707) 946-2785

**Amenities:** 1,2,3,5,6,9,10,11,15,16,17
**Breakfast:** C.
**Dbl. Oc.:** $100.00 - $162.00
**Sgl. Oc.:** $75.00
**Third Person:** $30.00

**Sybron House**—A Victorian inn located on a hill in the middle of the Napa Valley with magnificent views of the surrounding vineyards and wineries. Nearby private tennis court, excellent restaurants. Ballooning, biking, hiking, golf and mud baths are available.

## Napa

Morales, Carol
1137 Warren St., 94559
(707) 257-1444

**Amenities:** 1,2,5,6,9,10,11,15,16,18
**Breakfast:** F.
**Dbl. Oc.:** $99.45 - $143.65
**Third Person:** $20.00
**Child:** over 12 yrs. - $20.00

**The Napa Inn**—A beautiful Queen Anne Victorian built in 1899. Located on a quiet tree-lined street in the historic town of Napa.The five guest rooms, parlor and dining room are furnished with the owner's personal collection of antiques.

| | | | | |
|---|---|---|---|---|
| 1. No Smoking | 5. Tennis Available | 9. Credit Cards Accepted | 13. Lunch Available | 17. Shared Bath |
| 2. No Pets | 6. Golf Available | 10. Personal Checks Accepted | 14. Public Transportation | 18. Afternoon Tea |
| 3. No Children | 7. Swiming Available | 11. Off Season Rates | 15. Reservations Necessary | ★ Commissions given |
| 4. Senior Citizen Rates | 8. Skiing Available | 12. Dinner Available | 16. Private Bath | to Travel Agents |

## *Napa* *

Page, Mary & Jeff
5444 St. Helena Hwy., 94558
(707) 255-5907

**Amenities:** 1,2,6,9,10,14,15,
        16,18
**Breakfast:** C.

**Dbl. Oc.:** $102.60 & up
**Sgl. Oc.:** $102.60 & up
**Third Person:** $10.00
**Child:** over 10 yrs. - $10.00

**The Trubody Ranch B&B**—Two beautiful rooms in a restored Victorian water tower beside our 1872 farmhouse, surrounded by 127 acres of our own vineyard land. Enjoy our flower gardens and vineyard walks.

## *Nevada City*

Jones, Louise
449 Broad St., 95959
(916) 265-4660

**Amenities:** 1,2,5,6,10,15,16
**Breakfast:** F.
**Dbl. Oc.:** $95.00 - $145.00
**Sgl. Oc.:** $95.00 - $145.00
**Third Person:** $20.00
**Child:** $20.00

**Gramdm,ere's Inn**—A warm French country atmosphere on beautiful grounds. Listed in the *National Register of Historic Places*. Located right above downtown Nevada City. Offers homemade gourmet breakfasts in a relaxed decor. Central air-conditioning.

## *Nevada City*

Weaver, Mary Louise & Conley
109 Prospect St., 95959
(916) 265-5135

**Amenities:** 1,2,3,5,6,7,8,9,10,14,15,
        16,17,18
**Breakfast:** F.
**Dbl. Oc.:** $76.60 - $118.80
**Sgl. Oc.:** $70.20 - $113.80
**Third Person:** $20.00

**The Red Castle Inn**—Since 1963, this four-story 1857 landmark inn has welcomed guests to the pleasure of its company. "Tops my list ofplaces to stay" — *Gourmet Magazine*. Overlooks the queen city of the gold country. Terraced gardens, sweeping verandas and bountiful buffet. Eight guest rooms.

| | | | | |
|---|---|---|---|---|
| 1. No Smoking | 5. Tennis Available | 9. Credit Cards Accepted | 13. Lunch Available | 17. Shared Bath |
| 2. No Pets | 6. Golf Available | 10. Personal Checks Accepted | 14. Public Transportation | 18. Afternoon Tea |
| 3. No Children | 7. Swiming Available | 11. Off Season Rates | 15. Reservations Necessary | ★ Commissions given |
| 4. Senior Citizen Rates | 8. Skiing Available | 12. Dinner Available | 16. Private Bath | to Travel Agents |

# CALIFORNIA

## Nevada City *

Wright, Mrs. Miriam
517 W. Broad St., 95959
(916) 265-2815

**Amenities:** 1,2,5,6,7,8,9,10,
14,16,18
**Breakfast:** F.

**Dbl. Oc.:** $70.00 - $90.00
**Sgl. Oc.:** $70.00 - $90.00

**Downey House B&B**—Circa 1869. Light and comfortable rooms with views and private baths. Lush garden with waterfall. Sunroom, porch and parlor. Generous buffet breakfast. Near fine shops, restaurants, galleries, museums and theatre.

## Newport Beach

Lvetto, Christine
2306 W. Ocean, 92660
(714) 673-7030

**Amenities:** 2,5,6,7,9,11,12,13,
14,15,16
**Breakfast:** C.

**Dbl. Oc.:** $163.50
**Sgl. Oc.:** $163.50

**The Portofino Beach Hotel**—The inn offers an oasis of elegance and privacy. Enjoy the European ambience created for your pleasure throughout our well-appointed rooms. Some rooms with sun decks, jacuzzis marble bathrooms and fine antiques. All rooms located by the sea.

## Nipton

Freeman, Gerald
72 Nipton Rd.
HC #1, Box 357, 92364 (mail)
(619) 856-2335

**Amenities:** 2,9,17
**Breakfast:** C.

**Dbl. Oc.:** $48.15
**Sgl. Oc.:** $48.15
**Third Person:** $10.00
**Child:** under 3 yrs. -
no charge

**Hotel Nipton**—Located in the east Mojave national scenic area. Originally built in 1904. Restored in 1986. Offers panoramic view of the New York Mountains. Jacuzzi for star gazing. Thirty miles from Lake Mojave. Parlor decorated with old photos and antiques.

## Ojai

Nelson, Mary
210 E. Matilija, 93023
(805) 646-0961

**Amenities:** 1,3,5,6,7,9,10
**Breakfast:** C.

**Dbl. Oc.:** $90.00
**Sgl. Oc.:** $80.00

**Ojai Manor Hotel**—Originally a little brick schoolhouse and now Ojai's oldest building. The hotel is centrally located in lovely park-like surroundings. Six guest rooms share three baths.

## Orland *

Glaesman, Mary & Kurt
Route 3, Box 3176, 95963
(916) 865-4093

**Amenities:** 1,2,10,15,16,17
**Breakfast:** F.

**Dbl. Oc.:** $45.00 - $75.00
**Sgl. Oc.:** $45.00 - 475.00
**Third Person:** $15.00

**The Inn At Shallow Creek Farm**—The inn is a gracious farmhouse offering spacious rooms with carefully chosen antiques, creating a blend of nostalgia and comfortable country living. Breakfast features old-fashioned baked goods and an assortment of local fresh fruits and juices.

| | | | |
|---|---|---|---|
| 1. No Smoking | 5. Tennis Available | 9. Credit Cards Accepted | 13. Lunch Available | 17. Shared Bath |
| 2. No Pets | 6. Golf Available | 10. Personal Checks Accepted | 14. Public Transportation | 18. Afternoon Tea |
| 3. No Children | 7. Swiming Available | 11. Off Season Rates | 15. Reservations Necessary | ★ Commissions given |
| 4. Senior Citizen Rates | 8. Skiing Available | 12. Dinner Available | 16. Private Bath | to Travel Agents |

## Pacific Grove

Browncroft, Dawn Yvette
557 Ocean View Blvd., 93950
(408) 373-7673
**Amenities:** 2,3,6,7,10,14,15
**Breakfast:** F.
**Dbl.Oc.:** $137.50 - $203.50
**Sgle.Oc.:** $115.50 - $203.50

**Roserox Country Inn By-The-Sea**— An intimate, historic Victorian set on the shores of the Pacific Ocean. All rooms have breathtaking ocean views. Wine/cheese by the fireplace in the parlor. Snuggle under down comforters and let the ocean lull you to sleep. Walk to the acquarium and Cannery Row.

## Pacific Grove *

Cherry Kent
225 Central Ave., 93950
(408) 649-8436
**Amenities:** 1,2,9,10,14,15,16,18
**Breakfast:** C.
**Dbl.Oc.:** $104.50 - $181.50
**Sgl.Oc.:** $104.50 - $181.50
**Third:** $16.50

**Gatehouse Inn Bed & Breakfast**—This light and airy seaside Victorian offers eight uniquely decorated rooms. Many have ocean views, fireplaces, decks and private patios. All rooms have private baths, down comforters and period antiques. Close to restaurants, shops and acquarium.

## Pacific Grove *

Claudel, Shelley
643 Lighthouse Ave., 939500
(408) 375-1287
**Amenities:** 1,2,4,5,6,7,9
10,11,15,17,18
**Breakfast:** F.
**Dbl.Oc.:** $85.00 - $130.00
**Sgl.Oc.:** $85.00 - $130.00

**Gosby House**—A romantic 1887 Queen Anne Victorian mansion. Each room is individually decorated with period antiques and fluffy comforters. Many rooms have fireplaces. Walk to the beach, shops and aquarium. Borrow bikes. Dine in local restauratns. Wonderful honeymoon packages.

| | | | | |
|---|---|---|---|---|
| 1. No Smoking | 5. Tennis Available | 9. Credit Cards Accepted | 13. Lunch Available | 17. Shared Bath |
| 2. No Pets | 6. Golf Available | 10. Personal Checks Accepted | 14. Public Transportation | 18. Afternoon Tea |
| 3. No Children | 7. Swiming Available | 11. Off Season Rates | 15. Reservations Necessary | ★ Commissions given |
| 4. Senior Citizen Rates | 8. Skiing Available | 12. Dinner Available | 16. Private Bath | to Travel Agents |

## Pacific Grove

Flatley, Susan
555 Ocean View Blvd., 93950
(408) 372-4341

**Amenities:** 1,2,5,6,7,9,10,14,15,16,18
**Breakfast:** C.
**Dbl. Oc.:** $95.00 - $175.00
**Sgl. Oc.:** $95.00 - $175.00

**Seven Gables Inn**—An 1886 Victorian mansion overlooking the Pacific Ocean. Furnished throughout with fine European and American antiques. All ocean-view rooms with private baths. Generous light breakfast and four o'clock tea served in an elegant parlor. Smoking in garden only.

## Palo Alto *

Hall, Susan & Maxwell
555 Lytton Ave., 94301
(415) 322-8555

**Amenities:** 1,2,3,9,10
**Breakfast:** C.

**Dbl. Oc.:** $99.00 - $148.50
**Sgl. Oc.:** $99.00 - $148.50

**The Victorian On Lytton**—Offers a combination of forgotten elegance with a touch of European grace. All 10 rooms have sitting parlors and private baths. Fine restaurants and shops are one block away.

## Portola

Haman, Lynne & Jon
256 Commercial St., 96122
(916) 832-0107

**Amenities:** 1,5,6,7,8,10,17
**Breakfast:** F.

**Dbl. Oc.:** $42.43 - $63.64
**Third Person:** $5.00

**Upper Feather Bed & Breakfast**—Small-town comfort and hospitality in casual country style. No TV or radio, but we have board games, puzzles and popcorn for relaxing. Walk to railroad museum, restaurants, wild and scenic river and national forestlands. Only one hour from Reno entertainment.

## Pt. Reyes Station

Bartlett, Julie
39 Cypress
Box 176, 94956
(415) 663-1709

**Amenities:** 1,2,3,10
**Breakfast:** F.

**Dbl. Oc.:** $90.00 - $95.00
**Sgl. Oc.:** $85.00 - $90.00

**Thirty-Nine Cypress**—Situated on a bluff with a spectacular view of Pt. Reyes National Seashore. Country gardens; all redwood. Antiques. Oriental rugs and art collection. Horseback riding by arrangement. Hot tub.

| | | | | |
|---|---|---|---|---|
| 1. No Smoking | 5. Tennis Available | 9. Credit Cards Accepted | 13. Lunch Available | 17. Shared Bath |
| 2. No Pets | 6. Golf Available | 10. Personal Checks Accepted | 14. Public Transportation | 18. Afternoon Tea |
| 3. No Children | 7. Swiming Available | 11. Off Season Rates | 15. Reservations Necessary | ★ Commissions given |
| 4. Senior Citizen Rates | 8. Skiing Available | 12. Dinner Available | 16. Private Bath | to Travel Agents |

## *Rancho Cucamonga* \*

Isley, Janice
9240 Archibald Ave., 91730
(714) 980-6450

**Amenities:** 1,2,5,6,7,8,9,10, 12,14,15,16,17,18
**Breakfast:** F.

**Dbl. Oc.:** $66.00 - $138.00
**Sgl. Oc.:** $66.00 - $138.00

**Christmas House Bed & Breakfast Inn**—A 1904 Victorian mansion with seven fireplaces, intricate woodwork, stained glass and fine antiques. Located 40 miles east of Los Angeles. Close to Ontario International Airport. Gracious turn-of-the-century surroundings and hospitality.

## *Rancho Palos Verdes* \*

Exley, Ruth & Earle
4273 Palos Verdes Dr. So., 90274
(213) 377-2113

**Amenities:** 2,4,6,7,10,12,13, 14,15,16,18
**Breakfast:** F.

**Dbl. Oc.:** $55.00
**Sgl. Oc.:** $45.00
**Third Person:** $10.00
**Child:** under 10 yrs. - no charge

**The Exley House By The Sea**—A cozy home in suburban Los Angeles. Friendly atmosphere; ocean front; private beach; many tourist attractions; restaurants; beautiful views; quiet. Smoking is restricted.

## *San Diego* \*

Emerick, Carol & Robert
3829 Albatross St., 92103
(619) 299-1564

**Amenities:** 1,2,5,6,7,9,10,14,15,16
**Breakfast:** C.
**Dbl. Oc.:** $45.00 - $80.00
**Sgl. Oc.:** $45.00 - $80.00
**Third Person:** $10.00
**Child:** $10.00

**The Cottage**—Located one mile from San Diego Zoo and three miles from Sea World is a quiet retreat in the heart of the city. Offers two accommodations, each with private bath and entrance. Freshly baked bread is served with fruit and a beverage.

| | | | |
|---|---|---|---|
| 1. No Smoking | 5. Tennis Available | 9. Credit Cards Accepted | 13. Lunch Available | 17. Shared Bath |
| 2. No Pets | 6. Golf Available | 10. Personal Checks Accepted | 14. Public Transportation | 18. Afternoon Tea |
| 3. No Children | 7. Swiming Available | 11. Off Season Rates | 15. Reservations Necessary | ★ Commissions given to Travel Agents |
| 4. Senior Citizen Rates | 8. Skiing Available | 12. Dinner Available | 16. Private Bath | |

# CALIFORNIA

## San Diego

Grady, Jerri
P.O. Box 7695, 92167
(619) 225-9765

**Amenities:** 7,10,14,15,16
**Breakfast:** F.
**Dbl. Oc.:** $66.00

**Surf Manor And Cottages**—Charming one- and two-bedroom apts. and quaint cottages furnished with antiques. Near Sea World. Refrigerator stocked for self-catered breakfast. Weekly rates only July-August. Lower off-peak rates available. Bed and breakfast accommodations offered only from Sept.-June.

## San Diego

Milbourne, Dorothy A.
2330 Albatross St., 92101
(619) 233-0638

**Amenities:** 1,10,14,15,16
**Breakfast:** C.

**Dbl. Oc.:** $60.00 - $75.00
**Sgl. Oc.:** $60.00 - $75.00
**Third Person:** $10.00
**Child:** under 9 yrs. - $5.00

**Harbor Hill Guest House**—A three-level, 90-year-old home. Each level has a private entry and kitchen. All have private bath, TV, harbor views and sun deck overlooking garden. Minutes to Balboa Park Zoo, Old Town Trolley, Mexico ferry, Coronado Island and San Diego harbor. Families welcome. Studio apartment.

## San Diego *

Thiess, Angela & Don
2470 Heritage Park Row, 92110
(619) 295-7088

**Amenities:** 1,2,3,4,5,6,7,9,12, 14,15,16,17
**Breakfast:** F.

**Dbl. Oc.:** $87.00 - $131.00
**Sgl. Oc.:** $82.00 - $125.00
**Third Person:** $22.00

**Heritage Park Bed & Breakfast Inn**—Situated on a seven-acre Victorian park in the heart of Old Town. A perfect romantic getaway. Social hour every evening. Nightly showing of black-&-white vintage films. Furnished with antiques of the Victorian era. Five-minute walk to heart of Old Town, San Diego.

| | | | | |
|---|---|---|---|---|
| 1. No Smoking | 5. Tennis Available | 9. Credit Cards Accepted | 13. Lunch Available | 17. Shared Bath |
| 2. No Pets | 6. Golf Available | 10. Personal Checks Accepted | 14. Public Transportation | 18. Afternoon Tea |
| 3. No Children | 7. Swiming Available | 11. Off Season Rates | 15. Reservations Necessary | ★ Commissions given |
| 4. Senior Citizen Rates | 8. Skiing Available | 12. Dinner Available | 16. Private Bath | to Travel Agents |

## San Francisco

Bard, Joan
330 Edgehill Way, 94127
(415) 564-9339

**Amenities:** 15,16
**Breakfast:** C.

**Dbl. Oc.:** $80.00
**Sgl. Oc.:** $80.00
**Third Person:** $10.00
**Child:** $10.00

**Casita Blanca**—A charming cottage high on a hill, not far from Golden GatePark. Twin beds, complete kitchen, fireplace and patio. A country setting, yet in the heart of San Francisco. Parkingavailable.

---

## San Francisco

Baires, Emma
225 Arguello Blvd., 94118
(415) 752-9482

Amenities: 1,2,5,6,7,10,14,
15,16,17
Breakfast: C.

Dbl.Oc.:$55.50 - $83.25
Sgl.Oc.:$55.50 - $83.25
Third Person:$12.00
Child: $12.00

**Casa Arguello**—Comfortable rooms in a cheerful elegant flat. Fifteen minutes from the center of town. Near Golden Gate Park, restaurants and shops. Within walking distance of public transporttation.

---

## San Francisco *

Karr, Rodney
1057 Steiner St., 94115
(800) 228-1647, (415) 776-5462,
 Fax:(415) 776-0505

**Amenities:** 1,2,5,6,7,9,10,
14,15,16,17,18
**Breakfast:** C.
**Dbl. Oc.:** $111.00 - $330.00
**Sgl. Oc.:** $111.00 - $330.00
**Third Person:** $25.00

**The Chateau Tivoli**—A landmark mansion that was the residence of the owners of San Francisco's world-famous Tivoli Opera. Guests experience a time-travel journey back to San Francisco's golden age of opulence with the 1890's furnishings from theVanderbilts, Gettys, etc.

---

1. No Smoking
2. No Pets
3. No Children
4. Senior Citizen Rates
5. Tennis Available
6. Golf Available
7. Swiming Available
8. Skiing Available
9. Credit Cards Accepted
10. Personal Checks Accepted
11. Off Season Rates
12. Dinner Available
13. Lunch Available
14. Public Transportation
15. Reservations Necessary
16. Private Bath
17. Shared Bath
18. Afternoon Tea
★ Commissions given
to Travel Agents

# CALIFORNIA

## San Francisco

Kavanaugh, Robert
4 Charlton Ct., 94123
(415) 921-9784

**Amenities:** 2,10,14,15,16,17
**Breakfast:** C.

**Dbl. Oc.:** $127.50

**The Bed & Breakfast Inn**—A 10-room, intimate and luxurious inn located on a mews street in a trendy shopping area. Warm, helpful staff and lovely furnishings. This is the original B&B inn in San Francisco.

## San Francisco

Kreibich, Susan
847 Fillmore St., 94117
(415) 931-3083

**Amenities:** 1,5,9,10,14,15,16,
17,18
**Breakfast:** F.

**Dbl. Oc.:** $75.00 - $85.00
**Sgl. Oc.:** $65.00 - $75.00
**Third Person:** $15.00
**Child:** $10.00

**No Name Victorian B&B**—Located in one of the most photographed areas of San Francisco, the historic district of Alamo Square. The No Name B&B sits close to all the sights that make our city famous. Three of the five guest rooms have fireplaces. Hot tub and wine for guests to enjoy.

## San Francisco *

Moffatt, Ruth
431 Hugo St., 94122
(415) 661-6210

**Amenities:** 5,6,7,9,10,14,
15,17
**Breakfast:** C.

**Dbl. Oc.:** up to $62.00
**Sgl. Oc.:** up to $55.00
**Third Person:** $7.00

**Moffatt House**—Catch a view of fog-veiled Mt. Sutro from our simple 1903 Edwardian home, located just one block from the major attractions in Golden Gate Park. Enjoy complete shopping and excellent public transit to downtown and ocean beach. Safe area. Exercise club discount.

## San Francisco

Pritikin, Robert
2220 Sacramento St., 94115
(415) 929-9444

**Amenities:** 9,10,12,14,15,16,18
**Breakfast:** F.
**Dbl. Oc.:** $99.00 - $210.00
**Sgl. Oc.:** $84.00 - $195.00
**Third Person:** $15.00

**The Mansions**—Rates include sumptuous breakfast, flowers in rooms, billiard/game room, superb dining, sculpture gardens and so much more. Celebrated guests include Barbra Streisand, Andre Sakhrov and Robin Williams. This small family-owned inn is indeed a magic palace.

| | | | | |
|---|---|---|---|---|
| 1. No Smoking | 5. Tennis Available | 9. Credit Cards Accepted | 13. Lunch Available | 17. Shared Bath |
| 2. No Pets | 6. Golf Available | 10. Personal Checks Accepted | 14. Public Transportation | 18. Afternoon Tea |
| 3. No Children | 7. Swiming Available | 11. Off Season Rates | 15. Reservations Necessary | ★ Commissions given |
| 4. Senior Citizen Rates | 8. Skiing Available | 12. Dinner Available | 16. Private Bath | to Travel Agents |

# CALIFORNIA

## San Francisco *

Wamsley, Helvi O.
1902 Filbert, 94123
(415) 567-1526

**Amenities:** 1,2,9,10,14,15,16
**Breakfast:** C. Plus

**Dbl. Oc.:** $72.15 - $127.65
**Third Person:** $22.20

**Art Center & Wamsley Bed & Breakfast**—For everything you want a home to be. An inn in the"Emerald City" by the Golden Gate and Fisherman's Wharf. Then home, a warm and cozy suite with a microwave kitchen,TV, a fireplace and a quiet rest. With the dawn, fresh baked goodies coffee and a day on the town.

---

## San Francisco *

Widburg, Monica & Ed
2007 15th Ave., 94116
(415) 564-1751

**Amenities:** 1,2,3,5,6,7,10,14,
15,16
**Breakfast:** F.

**Dbl. Oc.:** $65.00
**Sgl. Oc.:** $50.00

Located in a quiet residential area with a lovely ocean view. This charming house offers one room for bed & breakfast. Nearby there is ample parking and public transportation. Twenty minutes from the airport.

---

## San Francisco *

Yuan, George
600 Presidio Ave., 94115
(415) 931-1875

**Amenities:** 1,2,3,9,15,16,
**17,18**
Breakfast: C.

**Dbl. Oc.:** $69.93 - $119.88

**The Monte Cristo**—Part of San Francisco since 1875. Located two blocks from the elegantly restored Victorian shops, restaurants and antique stores on Sacramento Street. Each room is elegantly furnished with authentic period pieces. Convenient transportation.

---

| | | | |
|---|---|---|---|
| 1. No Smoking | 5. Tennis Available | 9. Credit Cards Accepted | 13. Lunch Available | 17. Shared Bath |
| 2. No Pets | 6. Golf Available | 10. Personal Checks Accepted | 14. Public Transportation | 18. Afternoon Tea |
| 3. No Children | 7. Swiming Available | 11. Off Season Rates | 15. Reservations Necessary | ★ Commissions given |
| 4. Senior Citizen Rates | 8. Skiing Available | 12. Dinner Available | 16. Private Bath | to Travel Agents |

## San Gregorio *

Raynor, Lorraine
5086 La Honda Rd.
Rt.#1, P.O. Box 54, 94074
(415) 747-0810

**Amenities:** 1,2,6,9,10,16,18
**Breakfast:** F.
**Dbl. Oc.:** $60.00 - $105.00
**Third Person:** $15.00
**Child:** under 2 yrs - $5.00(crib)

**Rancho San Gregorio**—Warm hospitality and home-grown products featured in our breakfast feast make this coastal country retreat a traveler's respite. Fifteen creekside acres, apple orchards, gazebo, gardens, patios and decks. Five miles north of San Francisco and Santa Cruz.

## San Luis Obispo *

Dinshaw, Ann & Michael
1473 Monterey St., 93401
(805) 549-0321

**Amenities:** 1,2,4,9,11,14,16,18
**Breakfast:** F.
**Dbl. Oc.:** $68.90
**Sgl. Oc.:** $63.60
**Third Person:** $10.00
**Child:** under 5 yrs. - $5.00

**Adobe Inn**—Enjoy the comfort and convenience of this cozy, Southwestern-style inn. Visit Hearst Castle, picnic at a vineyard or escape to the beach. Picnic baskets and afternoon tea available. Your hosts will help you discover the best of San Luis Obispo.

## San Rafael *

Cassidy, Linda & Dan
531 'C' St., 94901
(415) 454-3140

**Amenities:** 1,2,3,4,5,10,11,14, 15,16,18
**Breakfast:** C.

**Dbl. Oc.:** $65.00
**Sgl. Oc.:** $55.00
**Third Person:** $10.00

**Casa Soldavini**—Step back in time and enjoy the beauty that surrounds this1930's wine maker's home located in historic Mission San Rafael. Three rooms individually decorated, antiques, piano, patio and gardens. Shops, restaurants, beaches and redwoods minutes away.

| | | | | |
|---|---|---|---|---|
| 1. No Smoking | 5. Tennis Available | 9. Credit Cards Accepted | 13. Lunch Available | 17. Shared Bath |
| 2. No Pets | 6. Golf Available | 10. Personal Checks Accepted | 14. Public Transportation | 18. Afternoon Tea |
| 3. No Children | 7. Swiming Available | 11. Off Season Rates | 15. Reservations Necessary | ★ Commissions given |
| 4. Senior Citizen Rates | 8. Skiing Available | 12. Dinner Available | 16. Private Bath | to Travel Agents |

## Santa Barbara

Canfield, Caroline
P.O. Box 20065, 93102
(805) 966-6659

**Amenities:** 1,5,6,7,10,14,16
**Breakfast:** C. Plus

**Dbl. Oc.:** $50.00
**Sgl. Oc.:** $45.00
**Third Person:** $10.00
**Child:** $5.00

**Ocean View House**—A wonderful location in Santa Barabara in a quiet, private home within walking distance of the ocean. Two rooms, one with queen bed and a den with double-bed divan, TVs, interesting books and collections. Decorated in antique charm. Two-day minimum.

## Santa Barbara *

Davies, Linda Sue
121 E. Arrellaga, 93101
(805) 963-7067

**Amenities:** 1,2,3,5,6,7,9,10, 11,14,16,17,18
**Breakfast:** F.

**Dbl. Oc.:** $84.00 - $170.00
**Third Person:** $20.00

**Simpson House Inn**—Elegantly restored and decorated 1874 Victorian estate, secluded in an acre of English gardens. Fresh flowers, antiques, fine art, English lace, Oriental carpets, bicycles, croquet. Walk to restaurants, shops, museums and historic area. Enjoy local wines, delicious foods.

## Santa Barbara *

Eaton, Jenise Suding
1908 Bath St., 93101
(805) 687-2300

**Amenities:** 1,2,5,6,7,9,10,11,13,14, 16,17,18
**Breakfast:** F.
**Dbl. Oc.:** $73.80 - $125.00
**Sgl. Oc.:** $73.80 - $125.00
**Third Person:** $20.00
**Child:** $20.00

Blue Quail Inn
BED AND BREAKFAST

**Blue Quail Inn And Cottages**—Cottages and suites in a delightful, relaxing country setting. Scrumptious full breakfast and evening refreshments. Bikes available. Three blocks to Sansum Clinic/Cottage Hospital. Close to town and beaches. Picnic lunches available.

## Santa Barabara

MacDonald, Carol
1323 Dela Vine, 93101
(805) 963-2283

**Amenities:** 1,2,9,10,11,14,16, 17
**Breakfast:** F.

**Dbl. Oc.:** $99.00 - $214.50

**Tiffany Inn**—Carol and Larry have succeeded in creating an environment where guests can relax in a beautifully restored Victorian which boasts a magnificent collection of antiques. Most rooms have fireplaces and private baths. Nearby beaches, restaurants and shops.

| | | | | |
|---|---|---|---|---|
| 1. No Smoking | 5. Tennis Available | 9. Credit Cards Accepted | 13. Lunch Available | 17. Shared Bath |
| 2. No Pets | 6. Golf Available | 10. Personal Checks Accepted | 14. Public Transportation | 18. Afternoon Tea |
| 3. No Children | 7. Swiming Available | 11. Off Season Rates | 15. Reservations Necessary | ★ Commissions given |
| 4. Senior Citizen Rates | 8. Skiing Available | 12. Dinner Available | 16. Private Bath | to Travel Agents |

## *Santa Barbara*

| | | |
|---|---|---|
| McIsaac, Vida-marie | **Amenities:** 1,2,5,6,7,9,10,11, | **Dbl. Oc.:** $93.50 - $192.50 |
| 420 W. Montecito St., 93101 | 14,15,16,18 | **Sgl. Oc.:** $93.50 - $192.50 |
| (800) 594-4633, (805) 962-8447 | **Breakfast:** F. | **Third Person:** 10.00 |

**Harbour Carriage House**—Simply elegant accommodations in the French country manner; in-room spas; fireplaces; private baths; mountain views; located next door to two historic homes; two to three blocks from the beach.

## *Santa Barbara*

| | | |
|---|---|---|
| Miller, Marie | **Amenities:** 1,2,10,14,15, | **Dbl. Oc.:** $45.00 - $65.00 |
| 435 E. Pedregosa, 93103 | 16,17 | **Sgl. Oc.:** $45.00 |
| (805) 569-1914 | **Breakfast:** C. | **Third Person:** $10.00 |
| | | **Child:** under 5 yrs. - no charge |

**Old Mission Inn**—Built in 1895. Large rooms with fireplaces. Located within walking distance of the Old Mission, Museum of Natural History and downtown. Ten minutes from beaches and wharf.

## *Santa Barbara* *

| | | |
|---|---|---|
| Stevens, Valli & Larry | **Amenities:** 1,2,5,6,7,10,14,15, | **Dbl. Oc.:** $65.00 |
| 340 N. Sierra Vista, 93108 | 16,18 | **Sgl. Oc.:** $55.00 |
| (805) 969-1272 | **Breakfast:** F. | **Third Person:** $30.00 |
| | | **Child:** $10.00 |

**Valli's View**—This beautiful home has hillside gardens, sunny patios, shady deck and ever-changing mountain view. Guest room has color TV, private bath with tub and shower. Relax in living room with glass of wine around grand piano and fireplace. Fresh fruit and veggies from garden in season

## *Santa Clara*

| | | |
|---|---|---|
| Wigginton, Theresa | **Amenities:** 1,2,4,5,6,7,9,10, | **Dbl.Oc.:** $65.00 - $90.00 |
| 1390 Madison St., 95050 | 14,15,16,17,18 | **Sgl.Oc.:** $65.00 - $90.00 |
| (408) 249-5541 | **Breakfast:** F. | **Third Person:** $10.00 |
| | | **Child:** under 10 yrs. - $10.00 |

**Madison Street Inn**—Just 10 minutes from San Jose Airport is an elegant Victorian inn with exquisite grounds. Only one hour from San Francisco and 1 1/4 hours from Monterey. The inn makes an ideal base for visitors to California. Antique filled rooms. Great breakfasts include Eggs Benedict.

## *Santa Cruz*

| | | |
|---|---|---|
| Margo, Margaret & Sal | **Amenities:** 1,2,9,14,16 | **Dbl. Oc.:** $104.03 - $136.88 |
| 2-3665 E. Cliff, 95062 | **Breakfast:** C. | |
| (408) 475-4657 | | |

**Pleasure Point Inn Bed & Breakfast**—Overlooks beautiful Monterey Bay. Walk to beaches and shopping villages. Plan an evening cruise on the "Margaret Mary." Relax on a sunny deck with a good book or dine at one of the fine restaurants in the area. Three guest rooms with private bath. One of the best surfing areas.

| | | | | |
|---|---|---|---|---|
| 1. No Smoking | 5. Tennis Available | 9. Credit Cards Accepted | 13. Lunch Available | 17. Shared Bath |
| 2. No Pets | 6. Golf Available | 10. Personal Checks Accepted | 14. Public Transportation | 18. Afternoon Tea |
| 3. No Children | 7. Swiming Available | 11. Off Season Rates | 15. Reservations Necessary | ★ Commissions given |
| 4. Senior Citizen Rates | 8. Skiing Available | 12. Dinner Available | 16. Private Bath | to Travel Agents |

# CALIFORNIA

## Santa Cruz

Young, Tricia & Scott
P.O. Box 66593, 95066
(415) 321-5195

**Amenities:** 1,2,3,6,7,9,10,11, 15,16
**Breakfast:** F.

**Dbl. Oc.:** $110.00
**Sgl. Oc.:** $110.00
**Third Person:** $10.00

**Valley View**—Secluded "no-host" mountain retreat. Walls of glass overlook thousands of redwoods in the forest. Hot spa on private deck. Cable TV, stereo, piano, fireplace and full kitchen. Two-night minimum. Ten minutes to Santa Cruz. 20 minutes to Silicon Valley.

## Sausalito

MacDonald, Elizabeth
16 El Portal, 94965
(415) 237-2033

**Amenities:** 9,10,14,15,16,17
**Breakfast:** C.

**Dbl. Oc.:** $88.00 - $176.00
**Sgl. Oc.:** $88.00 - $176.00
**Third Person:** $88.00 - $176.00
**Child:** no charge

**Sausalito Hotel**—Fifteen-room bed and breakfast done in Victorian antiques. Nearby restaurants and shops. Easily accessible ferries to San Francisco. Breakfast and parking included in room rate. Reservations required up to seven weeks in advance of stay.

## Seal Beach *

Bettenhausen, Marjorie
212 5th St., 90740
(213) 493-2416

**Amenities:** 1,2,4,7,9,10,14,15,16
**Breakfast:** F.
**Dbl. Oc.:** $168.95
**Sgl. Oc.:** $106.82
**Third Person:** $10.90
**Child:** under 5 yrs. - $5.45

**The Seal Beach Inn & Gardens**—An internationally honored French-Mediterranean-style country inn, 300 yards from the beach. Next to Long Beach. Elegant suites/rooms with private baths. Lavish breakfast. Walk to village shops and restaurants. Short drive toDisneyland.

## Solvang

Clark, Les B.
1564 Copenhagen Dr., 93463
(805) 688-0559

**Amenities:** 2,4,9,10,12,13,16
**Breakfast:** C.

**Dbl. Oc.:** $85.00 - $190.00
**Sgl. Oc.:** $85.00 - $190.00
**ThirdPerson:** $12.00
(rollaway)

**Tivoli Inn**—Twenty-nine individually decorated and designed wood-burning fireplace suites. Complimentary basket of fruit and chilled bottle of local wine on your night of arrival. Complimentary continental breakfast served to your room every morning of your stay.

---

1. No Smoking
2. No Pets
3. No Children
4. Senior Citizen Rates
5. Tennis Available
6. Golf Available
7. Swiming Available
8. Skiing Available
9. Credit Cards Accepted
10. Personal Checks Accepted
11. Off Season Rates
12. Dinner Available
13. Lunch Available
14. Public Transportation
15. Reservations Necessary
16. Private Bath
17. Shared Bath
18. Afternoon Tea
★ Commissions given to Travel Agents

## Sonoma *

Lewis, Donna
316 E. Napa St., 95476
(707) 996-5339

**Amenities:** 2,3,7,9,10,15,16, 17
**Breakfast:** C.

**Dbl. Oc.:** $74.52 - $145.80
**Third Person:** $20.80

**Victorian Garden Inn**—A restored 1870 Greek Revival with four guest rooms, each uniquely decorated with the guest's total comfort in mind. Beautiful gardens and winding paths surround the pool. Private entrances, baths and concierge services provided. Slip back to another era and a secluded sanctum.

## Sonora

Hoover, Charlotte & Fred
15305 Bear Cub Dr., 95370
(209) 533-1441

**Amenities:** 2,3,5,6,8,9,10,15, 16
**Breakfast:** F.

**Dbl. Oc.:** $80.00
**Sgl. Oc.:** $60.00

**Serenity**—Listen to the wind through the pines as you relax on the veranda. Large rooms. Private baths. Queen or twin beds, lace-trimmed linens and handmade comforters. Close to Gold Rush towns, quaint shops and excellent dining. Near Yosemite and National Forest.

## St. Helena

Bartel, Jami
1200 Conn. Valley Rd., 94574
(707) 963-4001

**Amenities:** 2,4,5,6,7,8,9,10, 11,14,15,16,18
**Breakfast:** C.

**Dbl. Oc.:** $105.00 - $265.00
**Sgl. Oc.:** $105.00 - $265.00
**Third Person:** $25.00

**Bartel's Ranch & Country Inn**—Internationally acclaimed 60-acre estate setting in world-famous wine country. Romantic and secluded. 10,000 acres. Game room, library, bicycles and vineyard view. Three miles from St. Helena. Private and peaceful. Smoking is limited. Children by special arrangement.

## St. Helena

Cunningham, Erika
285 Fawn Park, 94574
(707) 963-2887

**Amenities:** 1,2,3,4,5,6,7,10,11,12,13, 15,16,18
**Breakfast:** C.
**Dbl. Oc.:** $65.00 - $175.00
**Sgl. Oc.:** $55.00 - $65.00
**Third Person:** $10.00
**Child:** $10.00

# Erika's Hillside

**Erika's Hillside**—Enjoy a peaceful and romantic retreat. Nestled on a quiet hillside overlooking the vineyards in the heart of the Napa Valley wine country. Hot tub, fireplace, private entrance and private bath. European hospitality.

| | | | | |
|---|---|---|---|---|
| 1. No Smoking | 5. Tennis Available | 9. Credit Cards Accepted | 13. Lunch Available | 17. Shared Bath |
| 2. No Pets | 6. Golf Available | 10. Personal Checks Accepted | 14. Public Transportation | 18. Afternoon Tea |
| 3. No Children | 7. Swiming Available | 11. Off Season Rates | 15. Reservations Necessary | ★ Commissions given |
| 4. Senior Citizen Rates | 8. Skiing Available | 12. Dinner Available | 16. Private Bath | to Travel Agents |

## St. Helena *

Gevarter, Annette
9550 St. Helena Rd., 94574
(707) 944-0880, 963-8743

**Amenities:** 1,2,6,7,9,10,11,12,13,15,16
**Breakfast:** F.
**Dbl. Oc.:** $85.00 - $145.00
**Third Person:** $15.00
**Child:** $15.00

**Hilltop House Bed & Breakfast**—A secluded mountain hideaway in a romantic setting on 135 acres of unspoiled wilderness. Hilltop House gives a hang-glider's view of the Mayacamus Mountains. Only 12 minutes from St. Helena and Route 29. Reduced rates Sunday-Thursday and off-season.

---

## Stanford *

Young, Tricia & Scott
P.O. Box 4528, 94309
(415) 321-5195,
Fax: (415) 325-5121

**Amenities:** 1,2,3,5,6,7,9,10, 14,16
**Breakfast:** F.

**Dbl. Oc.:** $99.00
**Sgl. Oc.:** $99.00
**Third Person:** $20.00

**Adella Villa**—Exclusive, secluded one-acre 1920's estate. Pool, gardens, bicycles and barbecue. Piano in music foyer. 4,000- square-foot residence with all amenities. Antiques. Quiet atmosphere. Two bedrooms. Whirlpool tub. Close to Silicon Valley, San Francisco and Stanford University.

---

## Sutter Creek *

Fox, Min & Pete
77 Main St.
P.O. Box 159, 95685
(209) 267-5882

**Amenities:** 1,2,3,4,5,6,7,9,10, 15,16
**Breakfast:** F.

**Dbl. Oc.:** $100.73 - $143.13
**Sgl. Oc.:** $95.43 - $132.53

**Foxes In Sutter Creek**—Six elegant rooms with private baths, air conditioning,wood-burning fireplaces and covered parking. Full gourmet breakfast cooked to order and served to each room on silver service. Newspapers. Gazebo. Is downtown, near fine restaurants and shops. Rated three stars by Mobil.

---

## Sutter Creek

Kaplan, Ann & Al
15 Bryson Dr., 95642
(209) 267-9155

**Amenities:** 1,2,8,9,15,16,18
**Breakfast:** F.

**Dbl. Oc.:** $75.00 - $125.00
**Third Person:** $25.00

**Gold Quartz Inn**—A Victorian hideaway in the heart of the motherlode. It blends the warmth and romance of a bed and breakfast with the comfort and luxury of an elegant hotel. Located halfway between the Bay area and Lake Tahoe. Twenty-four guest rooms.

| | | | | |
|---|---|---|---|---|
| 1. No Smoking | 5. Tennis Available | 9. Credit Cards Accepted | 13. Lunch Available | 17. Shared Bath |
| 2. No Pets | 6. Golf Available | 10. Personal Checks Accepted | 14. Public Transportation | 18. Afternoon Tea |
| 3. No Children | 7. Swiming Available | 11. Off Season Rates | 15. Reservations Necessary | ★ Commissions given |
| 4. Senior Citizen Rates | 8. Skiing Available | 12. Dinner Available | 16. Private Bath | to Travel Agents |

# CALIFORNIA

## Tahoe City *

Knauss, Cynthia & Bruce
236 Grove St., 95730
(916) 583-1001

**Amenities:** 2,5,6,8,9,10, 14,17
**Breakfast:** F.

**Dbl. Oc.:** $75.20 - $113.40
**Sgl. Oc.:** $75.20 - $113.40
**Third Person:** $15.00
**Child:** $15.00

**Mayfield House**—A romantic five-bedroom bed and breakfast located 1/2 block from Lake Tahoe. Skiing, biking, hiking, golf and tennis. A beautiful Tahoe house, stone fireplace and fresh flowers. Breakfast served in your room or in the quaint breakfast nook.

## Ukiah *

Ashoff, Gilbert
2605 Vichy Springs Rd., 95482
(707) 462-9515

**Amenities:** 1,2,5,6,7,9,10,12, 13,14,15,16
**Breakfast:** C. Plus

**Dbl. Oc.:** $95.00
**Sgl. Oc.:** $75.00
**Third Person:** $25.00
**Child:** $25.00

**Vichy Springs Resort & Inn**—One of California's oldest operating hot springs resorts. Opened in 1854, the original buildings have been completely renovated. Swedish massage, herbal facials and full bodywraps. A quiet, healing environment that leaves you refreshed, renewed and invigorated.

## Ventura *

Flender Baida, Gisela
411 Poli St., 93001
(805) 643-3600

**Amenities:** 1,2,3,9,10,15,16
**Breakfast:** F.
**Dbl. Oc.:** $115.50 - $170.50
**Sgl. Oc.:** $110.00 - $165.00
**Third Person:** $22.00
**Child:** over 13 yrs. - $22.00

**"La Mer"**—The most European getaway in southern California. Each guest room represents a specific European country, all with private entrances and baths, ocean view and full Bavarian breakfast. A historical landmark that was built in 1890.

## Westport

Grigg, Sally & Charles
40501 N. Hwy. One,
P.O. Box 121, 95488
(707) 964-6725

**Amenities:** 9,10,11,15,16,17
**Breakfast:** F.

**Dbl. Oc.:** $54.00 - $104.00
**Third Person:** $15.00

**Howard Creek Ranch**—An 1867 rural ocean-front ranch on 20 acres; magnificent views; beach; mountains; creeks; sauna; pool; hot tub; fireplace; antiques; flower garden; cabins; parlor with piano; near redwoods.

| | | | | |
|---|---|---|---|---|
| 1. No Smoking | 5. Tennis Available | 9. Credit Cards Accepted | 13. Lunch Available | 17. Shared Bath |
| 2. No Pets | 6. Golf Available | 10. Personal Checks Accepted | 14. Public Transportation | 18. Afternoon Tea |
| 3. No Children | 7. Swiming Available | 11. Off Season Rates | 15. Reservations Necessary | ★ Commissions given |
| 4. Senior Citizen Rates | 8. Skiing Available | 12. Dinner Available | 16. Private Bath | to Travel Agents |

## *Whittier*

| | | |
|---|---|---|
| Davis, Coleen | **Amenities:** 1,2,5,6,7,10,12,13, | **Dbl. Oc.:** $60.00 |
| 11715 S. Circle Dr., 90601 | 14,15,16,18 | **Sgl. Oc.:** $55.00 |
| (213) 699-8427 | **Breakfast:** F. | **Third Person:** $15.00 |
| | | **Child:** uner 5 yrs. - $10.00 |

**Coleen's California Casa**—Three rooms, one suite, private bath, parking, private entrance, complimentary beverage, lunch and dinner. Near Disneyland, Knott's Berry Farm, Universal Studios and Queen Mary. Beach view, quiet patio, deck and guest refrigerator. Fun!

## *Yuba City*

| | | |
|---|---|---|
| Jones, Robert | **Amenities:** 1,7,10,12,14,15,16, | **Dbl. Oc.:** $65.00 - $85.00 |
| 212 C. Street, 95991 | 17 | **Sgl. Oc.:** $55.00 - $75.00 |
| (916) 674-1942 | **Breakfast:** C. | **Third Person:** $10.00 |
| | | **Child:** under 5 yrs. - no charge |

**Harkey House Bed & Breakfast Inn**—Offers a distinctive combination of Victorian charm and modern comfort. Intimate, charming and romantic. Enjoy true Victorian charm in one of our four rooms. Residence includes marble fireplaces, spa, pool, library, garden, antiques, piano and hammock.

| | | | | |
|---|---|---|---|---|
| 1. No Smoking | 5. Tennis Available | 9. Credit Cards Accepted | 13. Lunch Available | 17. Shared Bath |
| 2. No Pets | 6. Golf Available | 10. Personal Checks Accepted | 14. Public Transportation | 18. Afternoon Tea |
| 3. No Children | 7. Swiming Available | 11. Off Season Rates | 15. Reservations Necessary | ★ Commissions given |
| 4. Senior Citizen Rates | 8. Skiing Available | 12. Dinner Available | 16. Private Bath | to Travel Agents |

# COLORADO

## *The Centennial State*

Capitol: Denver
Statehood: August 1, 1876; the 38th state
State Motto: Nothing Without Providence
State Song: "Where the Columbines Grow"
State Bird: Lark Bunting
State Flower: Rocky Mountain Columbine
State Tree: Blue Spruce

Colorado, with its majestic rocky mountains and its cool refreshing climate, is a state tourists love to visit. It has unusual natural beauty, historic mining towns and old Indian cliff dwellings. It also is the home for the U.S. Air Force Academy.

Skiing is the big winter attraction. At Vale, Aspen and other well known areas, millions of dollars a year are spent on this sport by vacationers.

Tourists can still ride the old-time locomotive between Durango and Silverton, and the Cliff Palaces of the Indians such as Mesa Verde are a constant source of pleasure for those who enjoy Indian history.

Buffalo Bill's grave lies atop Lookout Mountain near Denver.

## Aspen *

Dolle, Norma
124 E. Cooper St., 81611
(303) 925-8455, (303) 925-6971

**Amenities:** 2,6,7,8,9,10,11,14,15,16
**Breakfast:** C.
**Dbl. Oc.:** $92.79 - $164.01
**Sgl. Oc.:** $92.79 - $164.01
**Third Person:** $21.58
**Child:** under 10 yrs. - $10.79

The SNOW QUEEN BED & BREAKFAST

**Snow Queen Victorian Lodge**—A quaint family-run lodge built in the 1880's. Offers bed and breakfast. It has a variety of rooms, all with private baths, plus two kitchen units. Reasonably priced. Close to center of town, shops, restaurants and ski lifts. Hot tub, fireplace, TV and phones.

## Boulder

Family, Finn
Main St.,
SSR, Gold Hill,, 80302
(303) 443-6475

**Amenities:** 1,2,10,12,13,15, 15,17
**Breakfast:** C.

**Dbl. Oc.:** $41.60
**Sgl. Oc.:** $41.60
**Third Person:** $20.00
**Child:** under 12 yrs. - $10.00

*The Bluebird Lodge—Listed in the Register of Historic Places.* A tiny mountain town. Comfortably restored three story log building. Nine bedrooms and two baths are on the second floor. Sitting rooms, library, dining room and hot tub are on the first floor. Seasonal.

## Cedaredge *

Record, Gail & Ray
2169 Highway 65, 81413
(303) 856-6836

**Amenities:** 1,2,8,10,16
**Breakfast:** F.

**Dbl. Oc.:** $46.35 - $56.65
**Sgl. Oc.:** $36.05 - $46.35
**Third Person:** $10.30
**Child:** under 12 yrs. - $5.15

**Cedars' Edge Llamas Bed And Breakfast**—A unique cedar home in a quiet country setting. Beautiful rooms with private decks and fantastic views. Watch the llamas frolic in the pastures below. Country breakfast served in your room or on deck. Minutes from great skiing, fishing and hunting. Relax and unwind.

| | | | |
|---|---|---|---|
| 1. No Smoking | 5. Tennis Available | 9. Credit Cards Accepted | 13. Lunch Available | 17. Shared Bath |
| 2. No Pets | 6. Golf Available | 10. Personal Checks Accepted | 14. Public Transportation | 18. Afternoon Tea |
| 3. No Children | 7. Swiming Available | 11. Off Season Rates | 15. Reservations Necessary | ★ Commissions given |
| 4. Senior Citizen Rates | 8. Skiing Available | 12. Dinner Available | 16. Private Bath | to Travel Agents |

# COLORADO

## Colorado Springs *

Clark, Sallie & Welling
1102 W. Pikes Peak Ave., 80904
(719) 471-3980

**Amenities:** 1,2,3,5,6,7,8,9,10,14,16
**Breakfast:** F.
**Dbl. Oc.:** $65.00 - $95.00

**Holden House — 1902 Bed & Breakfast**—A 1902 storybook Victorian home filled with antiques and family heirlooms. Honeymoon suite. Mountain views. Near historic Old Colorado City. Central to all Pikes Peak area. Helpful hosts and friendly resident cat, "Mingtoy."

## Denver *

Hillestad, Ann & Chuck
2147 Tremont Pl., 80205
(303) 296-6666

**Amenities:** 1,2,3,5,9,10,14,16
**Breakfast:** C.
**Dbl. Oc.:** $82.00 - $132.00
**Sgl. Oc.:** $71.00 - $121.00
**Third Person:** $11.00

**Queen Anne Inn**—Colorado's most award-winning inn with numerous national "Best Of" honors by *Country Inns magazine*. Luxurious, elegant, romantic and historic. Quiet downtown location. All private baths, phones, air-conditioning, music, art, heirlooms, flowers and views.

## Denver *

Peiker, Diane
1572 Race St., 80206
(800) 92-MARNE, (303) 331-0621

**Amenities:** 1,2,3,4,9,10,14,16,18
**Breakfast:** F.
**Dbl. Oc.:** $84.00 - $164.00
**Sgl. Oc.:** $73.00 - $164.00

**Castle Marne Bed And Breakfast**—A luxurious urban inn. Minutes from the airport, convention center, business district, hospitals, shopping and fine dining. Each room in this Victorian mansion is a unique experience in pampered luxury. A local and national historic structure.

| | | | | |
|---|---|---|---|---|
| 1. No Smoking | 5. Tennis Available | 9. Credit Cards Accepted | 13. Lunch Available | 17. Shared Bath |
| 2. No Pets | 6. Golf Available | 10. Personal Checks Accepted | 14. Public Transportation | 18. Afternoon Tea |
| 3. No Children | 7. Swiming Available | 11. Off Season Rates | 15. Reservations Necessary | ★ Commissions given |
| 4. Senior Citizen Rates | 8. Skiing Available | 12. Dinner Available | 16. Private Bath | to Travel Agents |

# COLORADO

## Durango *

Craig, Mary Ann
P.O. Box 1047, 81302
(303) 247-2176

**Amenities:** 1,2,5,6,7,8,10,15, 16,17
**Breakfast:** F.

**Dbl. Oc.:** $58.91 - $69.62
**Sgl. Oc.:** $42.84 - $53.55
**Third Person:** 15.00
**Child:** under 5 yrs. - $5.00

**Scrubby Oaks B&B**—Located on 10 acres overlooking Animas Valley. Three miles from Durango and 1/2 hour from Purgatory Ski Resort. Antiques, artworks, good books, patio, gardens and fireplaces.

## Durango *

Jackson, Innkeeper
35060 U.S. Hwy. 550, 81301
(303) 259-4396

**Amenities:** 1,2,3,6,8,9,10,15, 16,18
**Breakfast:** F.

**Dbl. Oc.:** $60.00 - $80.00
**Sgl. Oc.:** $55.00 - $75.00
**Third Person:** $15.00

**Logwood**—A red cedar and log-structured home and B&B by design. Large windows allow the natural beauty of Upper Animas Valley to be with you indoors. River and stream in view of the large deck and covered porch. Natural setting, trees, birds and country charm. Twelve miles north of Durango.

## Eaton

White, Nadine
515 Cheyenne Ave., 80615
(303) 454-3890

**Amenities:** 1,2,4,5,6,10,12,13, 16,17,18
**Breakfast:** F.

**Dbl. Oc.:** $40.00 - $55.00
**Sgl. Oc.:** $35.00 - $45.00
**Third Person:** $5.00
**Child:** $5.00

**The Victorian Veranda Bed & Breakfast**—A home built in 1894. Guests enjoy a view of the Rocky Mountains from the wrap-around porch. Bicycles built for two. Beautifully landscaped yard. Baby grand player piano. Whirlpool in private bath. Black marble fireplace and balcony in one bedroom. All rooms have antiques.

## Estes Park

Cotten, Kathleen & Ron
P.O. Box 1208, 80517
(303) 586-5104

**Amenities:** 1,2,5,6,7,8,10,13, 15,16,17,18
**Breakfast:** F.

**Dbl. Oc.:** $53.00
**Sgl. Oc.:** $44.00
**Third Person:** $9.00
**Child:** under 1 yr. - no charge

**Cottonwood House**—Enjoy old-fashioned hospitality in this immaculate circa 1927 home. Minutes from the heart of Estes Park and Rocky Mountain National Park. Full country breakfast served on a sunny porch with flowers.

---

| | | | |
|---|---|---|---|
| 1. No Smoking | 5. Tennis Available | 9. Credit Cards Accepted | 13. Lunch Available | 17. Shared Bath |
| 2. No Pets | 6. Golf Available | 10. Personal Checks Accepted | 14. Public Transportation | 18. Afternoon Tea |
| 3. No Children | 7. Swiming Available | 11. Off Season Rates | 15. Reservations Necessary | ★ Commissions given |
| 4. Senior Citizen Rates | 8. Skiing Available | 12. Dinner Available | 16. Private Bath | to Travel Agents |

## Estes Park *

Mansfield, Sue & Gary
P.O. Box 1910, 80517
(303) 586-4666

**Amenities:** 1,2,6,8,10,12,15,16
**Breakfast:** F.
**Dbl. Oc.:** $60.00 - $125.00
**Sgl. Oc.:** $50.00 - $115.00
**Child:** over 12 yrs. - $15.00

**RiverSong**—A romantic eight-room country inn, at the end of a winding country lane on 30 wooded acres. Breathtaking views of snow-capped peaks of the Rocky Mountain National Park. Most rooms have fireplaces and spacious soaking tubs for two. Hiking trails. A peaceful getaway!

## Estes Park

Wanek, Pat & Jim
560 Ponderosa Dr.
P.O. Box 898, 80517
(303) 586-5851

**Amenities:** 1,2,5,6,7,8,10,12, 13,15,17
**Breakfast:** C.

**Dbl. Oc.:** $47.00 - $52.50
**Sgl. Oc.:** $39.50 - $43.00
**Third Person:** $7.00 - $9.00
**Child:** over 10 yrs. - adult rate

**Wanek's Lodge At Estes**—A modern mountain inn on a ponderosa pine-covered hillside. Just a few miles from Rocky Mountain National Park. Woodbeams, stone fireplaces, plants and beautiful scenery provide a comfortable and relaxed atmosphere. Resident cat.

## Ft. Collins *

Clark, Sheryl & John
202 E. Elizabeth, 80524
(303) 493-2337

**Amenities:** 1,2,5,6,7,9,10,14, 15,16,17,18
**Breakfast:** F.

**Dbl. Oc.:** $45.00 - $55.00
**Sgl. Oc.:** $39.00 - $49.00
**Third Person:** 10.00

**Elizabeth Street Guest House**—A beautifully restored 1905 brick home furnished with antiques. A unique three-story doll house is in the entry. Scenic hiking and fishing are nearby. Colorado StateUniversity is one block east. Rocky Mountain National Park is a wonderful day trip. ENJOY!

## Loveland *

Wiltgen, Marilyn L.
217 W. 4th St., 80537
(303) 669-0798

**Amenities:** 1,2,4,5,6,7,9,10, 15,16,18
**Breakfast:** F.

**Dbl. Oc.:** $69.00 - $98.00
**Sgl. Oc.:** $59.00 - $88.00

**The Lovelander Bed & Breakfast**—A beautifully restored Victorian. Enjoy a leisurely breakfast on the veranda, or rise early for a hike or drive in Rocky Mountain National Park with a picnic basket packed just for you. Welcome to the sweetheart city, community of the arts!

| | | | |
|---|---|---|---|
| 1. No Smoking | 5. Tennis Available | 9. Credit Cards Accepted | 13. Lunch Available | 17. Shared Bath |
| 2. No Pets | 6. Golf Available | 10. Personal Checks Accepted | 14. Public Transportation | 18. Afternoon Tea |
| 3. No Children | 7. Swiming Available | 11. Off Season Rates | 15. Reservations Necessary | ★ Commissions given |
| 4. Senior Citizen Rates | 8. Skiing Available | 12. Dinner Available | 16. Private Bath | to Travel Agents |

## *Manitou Springs*
Goldstein, Wendy
Ten Otoe Pl., 80829
(719) 685-9684

**Amenities:** 1,2,9,10,15,16,17
**Breakfast:** F.
**Dbl. Oc.:** $50.00 - $77.00
**Sgl. Oc.:** $50.00 - $77.00

**Two Sisters Inn**—A gracious B&B situated at the base of Pikes Peak. One block to shops, restaurants and mineral springs in the historic district. Built in 1919 as a boarding house, it's now a quiet five-bedroom B&B with a cozy honeymoon cottage.A gourmet breakfast served.

## *Pagosa Springs*
Northcutt, Virginia & Sandy
3366 Hwy. 84, 81147
(303) 264-5646

**Amenities:** 2,6,7,8,10,12,13,16,17
**Breakfast:** F.
**Dbl. Oc.:** $64.31 - $133.00
**Sgl. Oc.:** $43.60
**Third Person:** $10.00
**Child:** $5.00 (crib)

**Echo Manor Inn**—"The Castle" - A Dutch Tudor with towers, turrets and gables. Ten guest rooms, suite for 14 and a honeymoon suite. Skiing, snowmobiling, rafting, hunting, fishing, hiking, mountain biking, hot tub and conference rooms. All meals are included in rates if you book the whole house.

## *Red Cliff* *
Wasmer, Mary
101 Eagle St., 81649
(303) 827-5333

**Amenities:** 1,2,8,9,10,15,16, 17,18
**Breakfast:** C.

**Dbl. Oc.:** $80.00
**Sgl. Oc.:** $70.00
**Third Person:** $15.00
**Child:** under 12 yrs. - $10.00

**The Pilgrim's Inn**—A charming Victorian home located 15 miles from Vail. A place to meet and plan excursions, paint, write or meditate. Escape the city and relax on a sunny deck or in a hot tub. Montain biking, skiing, camping or hiking in theNational Forest that surrounds the inn.

| | | | |
|---|---|---|---|
| 1. No Smoking | 5. Tennis Available | 9. Credit Cards Accepted | 13. Lunch Available | 17. Shared Bath |
| 2. No Pets | 6. Golf Available | 10. Personal Checks Accepted | 14. Public Transportation | 18. Afternoon Tea |
| 3. No Children | 7. Swiming Available | 11. Off Season Rates | 15. Reservations Necessary | ★ Commissions given |
| 4. Senior Citizen Rates | 8. Skiing Available | 12. Dinner Available | 16. Private Bath | to Travel Agents |

## Redstone *

Johnson, Rose Marie & Ken
0058 Redstone Blvd., 81623
(303) 963-3463

Amenities: 1,4,5,6,7,8,9,10,12,15,16,17
Breakfast: C.
Dbl. Oc.: $78.59 - $168.86
Sgl. Oc.: $78.59
Third Person: $20.00
Child: under 12 yrs. - $5.00

### CLEVEHOLM MANOR

Clevholm Manor ("the Historic Redstone Castle")—Nestled high in the Colorado Rockies, you can relive the elegance, grace and history of the Manor House at Redstone with an enchanting overnight stay. One mile from town, where restaurants and shops are available.

## Vail *

Rude, Beverly
145 N. Main, Minturn, 8164
(800) 344-1750,
(303) 827-5761

Amenities: 1,2,4,5,6,7,8,9,10, 11,12,13,15,16
Breakfast: C.

Dbl. Oc.: $74.66 - $162.30
Sgl. Oc.: $63.84 - $151.49
Third Person: $16.23
Child: $16.23

The Eagle River Inn—Rated as one of Colorado's top 10 bed and breakfasts. Upon entering this delightful inn, one is immediately surrounded by Southwestern charm. The rooms are good size and are extremely comfortable. We are just seven miles from the Vail Ski Resort.

## Winter Park

Mulligan, Shirley & Fred
148 Fern Way
Box 397, 80482
(303) 887-2877

Amenities: 1,2,3,5,6,7,8,10, 12,15,17,18
Breakfast: F.

Dbl. Oc.: $45.00 - $70.00
Sgl. Oc.: $35.00 - $55.00
Third Person: $15.00
Child: over 10 yrs. - $10.00

Mulligan's Mountain Inn—An oasis of relaxation surrounded by year-round activities. Whether it be winter sports or summer fun in the Rockies —return to the inn and relax in the outdoor jacuzzi or play in the game room.

## Woodland Park

Stoddard, Tim
236 Pinecrest Rd.
P.O. Box 5760, 80866
(800) 728-8282

Amenities: 1,2,3,8,9,10, 16,17
Breakfast: F.

Dbl. Oc.: $78.15 - $119.83
Sgl. Oc.: $78.15 - $119.83
Third Person: $26.05

Pikes Peak Paradise Bed & Breakfast—Unexcelled view of Pikes Peak! Peaceful and romantic. Personal and friendly service. Large theatre pipe organ. Near hiking, cross-country skiing, fossil beds, Aspen viewing, historic mining town and many tourist attractions.

| | | | | |
|---|---|---|---|---|
| 1. No Smoking | 5. Tennis Available | 9. Credit Cards Accepted | 13. Lunch Available | 17. Shared Bath |
| 2. No Pets | 6. Golf Available | 10. Personal Checks Accepted | 14. Public Transportation | 18. Afternoon Tea |
| 3. No Children | 7. Swiming Available | 11. Off Season Rates | 15. Reservations Necessary | ★ Commissions given |
| 4. Senior Citizen Rates | 8. Skiing Available | 12. Dinner Available | 16. Private Bath | to Travel Agents |

# CONNECTICUT

## *The Constitution State*

Capitol: Hartford
Statehood: January 9, 1788; the 5th state
State Motto: He Who Transplanted Still Sustains
State Song: "Yankee Doodle"
State Bird: Robin
State Flower: Mountain Laurel
State Tree: White Oak

It was the early Indians that named this state after the long tidal river of Connecticut that flowed through the state into Long Island Sound.

This New England state is proud of its history and goes back to 1639 when as a colony it adopted The Fundamental Orders of Connecticut.

Yale University is the 3rd oldest institution for higher learning and was established in New Haven in 1701. In 1748, the first American Law School was established in Litchfield, Connecticut.

Connecticut is known as the gadget state and its Yankee Peddlers traveled all over selling the craftsmanship of its citizens in clocks, brasswear, buttons, firearms, pins and combs.

Today, visitors can stroll the cobbled streets of the restored Mystic Seaport and visit the old stores, sea captains' homes and museums. The whaling ships, The Joseph Conrad and The Charles Morgan are a visitor's delight. In Groton, Connecticut, the submarine capitol of today's naval world, the first nuclear submarine, the Nautilus, was built.

# CONNECTICUT

## Ashford *

Matthews, Marian
125 Ashford Center Rd., 06278
(203) 429-0031

**Amenities:** 1,7,8,10,11,17,18
**Breakfast:** F.

**Dbl. Oc.:** $55.00
**Sgl. Oc.:** $50.00
**Third Person:** negotiable
**Child:** under 5 yrs. -
no charge

**Henrietta House Bed & Breakfast**—A cozy, historic 1740 colonial with original wide-board floors and five fireplaces. Situated on three acres for hiking, riding and skiing. Furnished with antiques and old-world, hand-crafted items. Homemade breads, jams, jellies. Near U. Conn. and Eastern Connecticut University

## Bolton

Smith, Cinde & Jeff
25 Hebron Rd., 06043
(203) 643-8538

**Amenities:** 1,2,5,6,7,8,10,15,
16,17
**Breakfast:** F.

**Dbl. Oc.:** $60.00 - $70.00
**Sgl. Oc.:** $45.00 - $55.00
**Third Person:** $10.00

**Jared Cone House**—Located in the center of Bolton. Queen-size beds. Scenic views. Bicycles and canoes available. Nearby antiques and berry farms. Full breakfast featuring our own maple syrup. Children welcome. No smoking in guest rooms.

## Branford

Malone, Anita
106 Sunny Meadow Rd., 06405
(203) 481-5802

**Amenities:** 1,2,15,16
**Breakfast:** F.

**Dbl. Oc.:** $65.00
**Sgl. Oc.:** $45.00

**Sunny Meadow Bed & Breakfast**—Ten minutes from Yale in costal Branford. Excellent seafood restaurants, beaches and historic landmarks are nearby.This clean, comfortable colonial home provides a relaxing atmosphere in a quiet neighborhood.

## Chester *

Momparler, Michael
123 Main St.
Box 370, 06412
(203) 526-9770

**Amenities:** 1,2,4,9,10,11,15,
16,17
**Breakfast:** F.

**Dbl. Oc.:** $55.00 - $85.00
**Sgl. Oc.:** $45.00 - $75.00
**Third Person:** $10.00
**Child:** over 6 yrs. - $10.00

**Chester Village Bed And Breakfast**—Unique restoration provides a relaxing retreat in a storybook setting. Toss care to the winds as you stroll to the area's finest dining, antique and artisan shops. Nearby river and shoreline attractions. Quiet, casual ambience with wholesome food and warm, accommodating hosts.

| | | | | |
|---|---|---|---|---|
| 1. No Smoking | 5. Tennis Available | 9. Credit Cards Accepted | 13. Lunch Available | 17. Shared Bath |
| 2. No Pets | 6. Golf Available | 10. Personal Checks Accepted | 14. Public Transportation | 18. Afternoon Tea |
| 3. No Children | 7. Swiming Available | 11. Off Season Rates | 15. Reservations Necessary | ★ Commissions given |
| 4. Senior Citizen Rates | 8. Skiing Available | 12. Dinner Available | 16. Private Bath | to Travel Agents |

## Clinton

Adams, Helen
21 Commerce St., 06413
(203) 669-1646

**Amenities:** 1,2,3,4,9,10,11,14,16
**Breakfast:** F.
**Dbl. Oc.:** $81.00
**Sgl. Oc.:** $64.80

**Captain Dibbell House**—Our 1866 Victorian features a spacious parlor with fireplace. Bedrooms furnished with antiques, heirlooms and auction findings. Fresh flowers, fruit baskets, home-baked savories for breakfast and snacks. A gazebo overlooking the gardens and footbridge.

---

## Coventry *

Kelleher, Joy & Bill
41 N. River Rd., 06238
(203) 742-6359

**Amenities:** 1,2,5,6,7,9,10,15, 16
**Breakfast:** F.

**Dbl. Oc.:** $60.00
**Sgl. Oc.:** $55.00
**Third Person:** $10.00
**Child:** under 6 yrs. - $5.00

**Special Joys**—Featuring romantic Victorian or cozy colonial rooms with private baths, balcony and entrances. Close to Caprilands Herb Farm, antique shops and University of Connecticut. Antique dolls, toy and Steiff shop and museum on premises. 40 minutes from Old Sturbridge Village. A real treat!

---

## East Haddam

Swartz, Molly & Dan
7 Norwich Rd., 06423
(203) 873-1677

**Amenities:** 2,3,6,7,9,10,12,14, 16,18
**Breakfast:** F.

**Dbl. Oc.:** $81.00 - $108.00
**Sgl. Oc.:** $81.00 - $108.00
**Third Person:** $15.00

**Bishopsgate Inn**—Built in 1818, the inn offers six charming guest rooms, all with private bath. The inn is located in the beautiful and historic Connecticut River Valley and is one block from the Goodspeed Opera House, "Home of the American Musical."

---

| | | | | |
|---|---|---|---|---|
| 1. No Smoking | 5. Tennis Available | 9. Credit Cards Accepted | 13. Lunch Available | 17. Shared Bath |
| 2. No Pets | 6. Golf Available | 10. Personal Checks Accepted | 14. Public Transportation | 18. Afternoon Tea |
| 3. No Children | 7. Swiming Available | 11. Off Season Rates | 15. Reservations Necessary | ★ Commissions given |
| 4. Senior Citizen Rates | 8. Skiing Available | 12. Dinner Available | 16. Private Bath | to Travel Agents |

## Greenwich

Pearson, Doreen & Tog
76 Maple St., 06830
(203) 869-2110

**Amenities:** 1,2,5,6,7,9,15,16,17,18
**Breakfast:** C.
**Dbl. Oc.:** $75.60 - $118.80
**Sgl. Oc.:** $54.00 - $86.40
**Third Person:** $10.00
**Child:** over 8 yrs. - $10.00

**Stanton House Inn**—A 27-room B&B, located on 22+ park-like acres in downtown Greenwich, 30 miles from New York City. This restored mansion, designed by Stanford White, boasts the ambience of yesterday with 20th-century conveniences. Children over eight years old only. Sprinkler system throughout.

## Ivoryton

Senner, Sally & Eldon
46 Main St., 06442
(203) 767-0330

**Amenities:** 2,5,7,9,10,11,15,16
**Breakfast:** C. Plus
**Dbl. Oc.:** $108.00 - $172.00
**Sgl. Oc.:** $108.00 - $172.00
**Third Person:** $27.00
**Child:** $27.00

**The Copper Beech Inn**—A handsome home of the last century. A magnificent copperbeech tree, country gardens, fine art and antiques. Exceptional country French cuisine. Thirteen elegant guestrooms with private baths. Relaxing retreat in picturesque lower Connecticut valley.

## Ledyard *

Betz, Frankie & Tom
528 Col. Ledyard Hwy., 06339
(203) 536-2022

**Amenities:** 5,6,7,10,15,16,17,18
**Breakfast:** F.
**Dbl. Oc.:** $69.88 - $102.13
**Child:** $26.88

**Applewood Farm Inn**—An 1826 center-chimney-colonial listed in the *National Register of Historic Places*. A farm setting. Six rooms, four with working fireplaces. Five minutes from Mystic attractions, I-95 and fine dining. Open year round.

| | | | | |
|---|---|---|---|---|
| 1. No Smoking | 5. Tennis Available | 9. Credit Cards Accepted | 13. Lunch Available | 17. Shared Bath |
| 2. No Pets | 6. Golf Available | 10. Personal Checks Accepted | 14. Public Transportation | 18. Afternoon Tea |
| 3. No Children | 7. Swiming Available | 11. Off Season Rates | 15. Reservations Necessary | ★ Commissions given |
| 4. Senior Citizen Rates | 8. Skiing Available | 12. Dinner Available | 16. Private Bath | to Travel Agents |

# CONNECTICUT

## Litchfield *

Zivic, Ferdinand J.
Rt. 202 & Tollgate Rd., 06759
(203) 567-4545

**Amenities:** 9,10,12,13,15,16
**Breakfast:** F.

**Dbl. Oc.:** $110.00 - $240.00
**Third Person:** $15.00

**Tollgate Hill Inn**—A 1745 inn listed in *National Register of Historic Places*. Twenty rooms, all with private baths, air-conditioning, TV, phones and some with fireplaces. Five suites. MAP or EP plans. Award-winning restaurants. 100 miles (two hours) to New York City. Brochure available.

## Mystic

Adams, Maureen
382 Cow Hill Rd., 06355
(203) 572-9551

**Amenities:** 1,2,3,4,10,11,15, 16
**Breakfast:** C.

**Dbl. Oc.:** $65.00 & up
**Sgl. Oc.:** $65.00 & up

**"The Adams House"**—A quaint country setting, just 1-1/2 miles from downtown Mystic. This 1790 home has three fireplaces. Lush greenery on one acre. Fully air-conditioned. Antiques and period decor.

## Mystic

Comolli, Dorothy M.
36 Bruggeman Pl., 06355
(203) 536-8723

**Amenities:** 10,11,15,16
**Breakfast:** C.

**Dbl. Oc.:** $85.00
**Sgl. Oc.:** $75.00
**Third Person:** $25.00

**Comolli's House**—Ideal for vacationers or business person who desires a homey respite while traveling. Immaculate home on quiet hill overlooking the Mystic Seaport complex. Convenient to Olde Mystic Village, the Aquarium, sightseeing, sporting activities, restaurants and shops. Cozy rooms and TV.

## Mystic *

Lucas, Kay & Ted
180 Cow Hill Rd., 06355
(203) 536-3033

**Amenities:** 1,2,10,11,16, 17,18
**Breakfast:** F.

**Dbl. Oc.:** $65.00 - $110.00
**Third Person:** $15.00
**Child:** under 2 yrs. - no charge

**"Brigadoon"**—A touch of Scotland in the heart of Mystic. A restored Victorian farmhouse, 1-1/4 miles from downtown Mystic. Relaxed, friendly atmosphere on one acre of lovely landscaped grounds. Afternoon tea at check-in. Baileys or a brandy in the evening.

---

| | | | | |
|---|---|---|---|---|
| 1. No Smoking | 5. Tennis Available | 9. Credit Cards Accepted | 13. Lunch Available | 17. Shared Bath |
| 2. No Pets | 6. Golf Available | 10. Personal Checks Accepted | 14. Public Transportation | 18. Afternoon Tea |
| 3. No Children | 7. Swiming Available | 11. Off Season Rates | 15. Reservations Necessary | ★ Commissions given |
| 4. Senior Citizen Rates | 8. Skiing Available | 12. Dinner Available | 16. Private Bath | to Travel Agents |

# CONNECTICUT

## New Haven *

Schneider, Steven
1201 Chapel St., 06511
(203) 777-1201

Amenities: 2,9,10,11,15,
16,18
Breakfast: C.

Dbl. Oc.: $125.00 - $175.00
Sgl. Oc.: $100.00 - $150.00
Third Person: $15.00

**The Inn At Chapel West**—Located in downtown New Haven within walking distance to Yale University and fine dining, theatre and shoppng. Each of the 10 guest rooms in this restored 19th-century residence contains a private bath, telephone, TV and air-conditioning. Private and elegant!

## New London *

Beatty, Captain Morgan
265 Williams St.
P.O. Box 647, 06320
(800) 347-8818, (203) 447-2600

Amenities: 1,2,4,5,6,7,9,10,11,14,16,18
**Breakfast:** F.
**Dbl. Oc.:** $81.00 - $189.00
**Sgl. Oc.:** $75.60 - $183.60
**Third Person:** $16.20
**Child:** $16.20

**Queen Anne Inn**—Capture the essence of the historic Mystic-New London shoreline area. In soothing Victorian elegance, enjoy the ultimate in intimacy, romance and comfort. A memorable breakfast and afternoon tea await you. Private baths, air-conditioning and fireplaces. Call about activities.

## New Milford

Hammer, Rolf T.
5 Elm St., 06776
(203) 354-4080

Amenities: 5,6,7,8,9,10,
15,16
Breakfast: C.

Dbl. Oc.: $71.00 - $92.00
Sgl. Oc.: $63.00 - $79.00
Third Person: $11.00
Child: under 12 yrs. - $7.00

**The Homestead Inn**—An 1853 Victorian with eight guest rooms at the top of the Green in the village center. Stroll to restaurants, shops and movie theatre. All rooms have private baths. Open all year. Near year-round recreation. AAA approved. Small six-room motel on property. Hearty continental breakfast.

## Norfolk

Tsukroff, Judy
Route 44, 06058
(203) 542-5108

Amenities: 1,2,5,7,8,9,10,17
Breakfast: F.

Dbl. Oc.: $51.88
Sgl. Oc.: $46.44
Third Person: $13.50

**Weaver's House**—Simple hospitality in a village of forested hills, with four mapped hiking parks. Village woodland pond for swimming. Biking, boating, antiquing, fine dining in all price ranges in the area. Summer music. Cross-country skiing in town, downhill skiing within 30 minutes.

| | | | | |
|---|---|---|---|---|
| 1. No Smoking | 5. Tennis Available | 9. Credit Cards Accepted | 13. Lunch Available | 17. Shared Bath |
| 2. No Pets | 6. Golf Available | 10. Personal Checks Accepted | 14. Public Transportation | 18. Afternoon Tea |
| 3. No Children | 7. Swiming Available | 11. Off Season Rates | 15. Reservations Necessary | ★ Commissions given |
| 4. Senior Citizen Rates | 8. Skiing Available | 12. Dinner Available | 16. Private Bath | to Travel Agents |

## Norfolk *

Zuckerman, Kim
Route 44, 06058
(203) 542-5100

**Amenities:** 2,4,5,7,8,9,10,11,
12,13,16,17,18
**Breakfast:** C.

**Dbl. Oc.:** $80.00 - $150.00
**Sgl. Oc.:** $40.00 - $110.00
**Third Person:** $20.00

**Blackberry River Inn**—A 225-year-old colonial inn located in northwestern Connecticut in the foothills of the Berkshires. Nineteen rooms, some with fireplaces. Serves fine continental country cuisine. Enjoy our relaxed, rural setting.

## North Stonington *

Gray, Ann & Tom
32 Main St., 06359
(203) 535-1736

**Amenities:** 1,4,5,6,7,10,11,15,16,18
**Breakfast:** F.
**Dbl. Oc.:** $91.80 - $162.00
**Sgl. Oc.:** $81.00

**Antiques And Accommodations**—A restored Victorian situated in a charming village 2 1/2 miles off I-95. Minutes from Mystic Seaport and Watch Hill beaches. Rooms furnished with antiques and canopy beds. Elegant four-course candlelight breakfast. Extensive gardens.

## Norwalk *

Stahl, Diane & Charles
72 Dry Hill Rd., 06851
(203) 847-0283

**Amenities:** 1,2,4,5,6,7,10,14,
15,16
**Breakfast:** C. Plus

**Dbl. Oc.:** $65.00
**Sgl. Oc.:** $65.00
**Third Person:** $25.00
**Child:** over 12 yrs. - $25.00

**Stahl's Suite Nest**—Enjoy a cozy, quiet suite, bedroom, living room and private bath. Upstairs with private entrance. Country decor, color TV and air-conditioning. Near I-95, beaches, fine restaurants and train to New York. A business person or married couple's "home away from home." Helpful hosts.

## Old Lyme

Janse, Donald
11 Flat Rock Hill Rd., 06371
(203) 434-7269

**Amenities:** 2,5,6,7,9,10,16
**Breakfast:** F.

**Dbl. Oc.:** $75.00
**Sgl. Oc.:** $65.00
**Third Person:** $12.00
**Child:** $12.00

**Janse, Helen And Donald Bed And Breakfast**—A large room with sitting area, antiques, air-conditioning and private bath. Custom saltbox. Park-like yard. Three miles from I-95. Quiet road, vintage stone walls, century-old maples. Near fine dining, shops, theatre and recreational sites. In-room bouquets and snacks. Special!

| | | | | |
|---|---|---|---|---|
| 1. No Smoking | 5. Tennis Available | 9. Credit Cards Accepted | 13. Lunch Available | 17. Shared Bath |
| 2. No Pets | 6. Golf Available | 10. Personal Checks Accepted | 14. Public Transportation | 18. Afternoon Tea |
| 3. No Children | 7. Swiming Available | 11. Off Season Rates | 15. Reservations Necessary | ★ Commissions given |
| 4. Senior Citizen Rates | 8. Skiing Available | 12. Dinner Available | 16. Private Bath | to Travel Agents |

# CONNECTICUT

## Portland

Hinze, Elaine
7 Penny Corner Rd., 06480
(203) 342-1856

Amenities: 1,2,4,6,8,10, 15,16
Breakfast: F.

Dbl. Oc.: $80.00
Sgl. Oc.: $70.00
Third Person: $35.00

**The Croft**—An 1822 country home in central Connecticut. The guest suite is accessed by a private entrance and has a living room/dining area, kitchen and private bath. One or two bedrooms, according to your needs. Convenient to Wesleyan University. Herb garden. Nearby golf and skiing.

## Ridgefield *

Armato, Diane
91 N. Salem Rd., 06877
(203) 438-HOWE

Amenities: 5,6,7,8,9,10,14,15, 17,18
Breakfast: C.

Dbl. Oc.: $91.80
Sgl. Oc.: $81.00
Third Person: $10.00
Child: under 10 yrs. -
no charge

**Epenetus Howe House**—Colonial New England lives in our 1725 home. Located 1-1/2 hours from New York City, 45 minutes from Stamford and White Plains. Award-winning restaurants and museums are nearby. Whether you're traveling for business or pleasure, we can provide you with a relaxing atmosphere.

## Salisbury *

Alexander, Doris & Dick
Route 44 E., 06068
(203) 435-9539

Amenities: 1,2,5,6,7,8,9,10, 12,13,17,18
Breakfast: F.

Dbl. Oc.: $65.00 - $85.00
Third Person: $22.00

**Yesterday's Yankee**—A 1744 home furnished with antiques. Provides three guest rooms, warm hospitality and full breakfast featuring home baking. Lime Rock park, Music Mountain, Appalachian Trail, antique shops, boating, fishing, independent schools and fine restaurants are nearby.

## Sherman *

Johnson, Sallee
29 Route 37 E., 06784
(203) 354-4404

Amenities: 1,2,5,6,7,8,9,10, 16,18
Breakfast: F.

Dbl. Oc.: $64.80 - $91.80
Sgl. Oc.: $64.80 - $91.80
Third Person: $15.00

**Barnes Hill Farm B&B**—Circa 1835. Furnished with antiques. Situated on acres of fields and woods. Outside jacuzzi. Open all year. Cross-country skiing on property. Candlewood Lake one mile away for boating and ice fishing.

---

| | | | |
|---|---|---|---|
| 1. No Smoking | 5. Tennis Available | 9. Credit Cards Accepted | 13. Lunch Available | 17. Shared Bath |
| 2. No Pets | 6. Golf Available | 10. Personal Checks Accepted | 14. Public Transportation | 18. Afternoon Tea |
| 3. No Children | 7. Swiming Available | 11. Off Season Rates | 15. Reservations Necessary | ★ Commissions given |
| 4. Senior Citizen Rates | 8. Skiing Available | 12. Dinner Available | 16. Private Bath | to Travel Agents |

## Somersville *

Lumb, Phyllis & Ralph
63 Maple St., 06072
(203) 763-1473

**Amenities:** 1,2,3,10
**Breakfast:** C.
**Dbl. Oc.:** $55.00 - $60.00
**Sgl. Oc.:** $55.00 - $60.00
**Third Person:** $15.00

**The Old Mill Inn**—Just five miles east of I-91, Exit 47. A gracious 14-room home in the middle of Tobacco Valley. Has a beautiful dining room overlooking lawn surrounded by trees, shrubs and flowers. Sitting room, cable TV and fireplace.

## South Windsor

Krawski, Bill
130 Buckland Rd., 06074
(203) 644-8486

**Amenities:** 5,6,7,10,12,13, 15,17,18
**Breakfast:** F.

**Dbl. Oc.:** $75.00 - $100.00
**Sgl. Oc.:** $50.00 - $75.00

**Cumon Inn**—Eight rooms with six shared baths in 1970 saltbox colonial on 20 acres with 100-mile view from Mt. Tom to Connecticut Valley and shore. Featured in *House Beautiful*. Adjacent restaurant features home-grown cooked meals. Gazebo, hot tub, 20 minutes to Crystal Lake and trout/bass fishing.

## South Woodstock

Naumann, Richard
94 Plaine Hill Rd., 06267
(203) 928-0528

**Amenities:** 4,5,6,8,9,10,11,12,13,16,18
**Breakfast:** C.
**Dbl. Oc.:** $70.20 - $151.20
**Sgl. Oc.:** $59.40 - $145.80
**Third Person:** $12.00
**Child:** under 5 yrs. - no charge

The Inn at
WOODSTOCK
HILL

**The Inn At Woodstock Hill**—A restored country estate sits proudly on 14 acres of rolling farmland. 19 guest rooms with private bath, TV and phone. Decorated in floral chintz. Wood-burning fireplaces throughout. Four-star restaurant with outdoor dining terrace and cozy bar. Come and make memories!

| | | | | |
|---|---|---|---|---|
| 1. No Smoking | 5. Tennis Available | 9. Credit Cards Accepted | 13. Lunch Available | 17. Shared Bath |
| 2. No Pets | 6. Golf Available | 10. Personal Checks Accepted | 14. Public Transportation | 18. Afternoon Tea |
| 3. No Children | 7. Swiming Available | 11. Off Season Rates | 15. Reservations Necessary | * Commissions given |
| 4. Senior Citizen Rates | 8. Skiing Available | 12. Dinner Available | 16. Private Bath | to Travel Agents |

# CONNECTICUT

## Staffordville *

Judd, Laura J. & Dr. Kirby E.
Beffa Rd., 06076
(203) 684-2124, (203) 684-5404

**Amenities:** 1,2,7,8,10,17
**Breakfast:** F.

**Dbl. Oc.:** $43.20 - $48.60
**Sgl. Oc.:** $43.20 - $48.60
**Third Person:** $10.00
**Child:** under 12 yrs. - $5.00

**Winterbrook Farm**—A 1770 colonial. Antique furnishings. Working farm. Mid-way from New York City to Boston, 10 miles from Mass. Pike, I-84, Old Sturbridge Village and Brimfield Flea Market. Quiet 60 acres. Swimming, cross-country skiing, maple sugaring, fishing, berry picking, sheep and lambs.

## Storrs *

Kollet, Elaine
418 Gurleyville Rd., 06268
(203) 429-1400

**Amenities:** 2,4,7,8,10,15,16
**Breakfast:** F.

**Dbl. Oc.:** $59.40
**Sgl. Oc.:** $37.80
**Third Person:** $16.20
**Child:** $5.40

**Farmhouse On The Hill Above Gurleyville**—An elegant Cape Cod house. Air-conditioned bedrooms. Within walking distance to University of Connecticut campus. We offer all activities at the university plus our sheep farm, fishing, canoes, bikes, hot tub and exercise equipment. Nearby sports program or musicals available.

## Uncasville

Samolis, Sandra
1851 Norwich-New London Tpke., 06382
(203) 848-3649

**Amenities:** 1,2,4,5,6,7,9,10,
14,15,16,18
**Breakfast:** C.

**Dbl. Oc.:** $77.76
**Sgl. Oc.:** $64.80
**Third Person:** $10.80
**Child:** $10.80

**1851 Guest House**—Located just 20 minutes from Mystic, our guest house has four lovely, spacious rooms with private bath. Since our innkeeper is an artist, our decor is interesting and unique.

## Wethersfield *

Bottaro, Sophie & Frank
184 Main St., 06109
(203) 563-4236

**Amenities:** 1,2,5,6,9,10,14,15,16,17,
**Breakfast:** F.
**Dbl. Oc.:** $65.00 - $75.00
**Sgl. Oc.:** $65.00 - $75.00
**Third Person:** $10.00
**Child:** under 2 yrs. - no charge

**Chester Bulkley House Bed & Breakfast**—Nestled in the historic village of Old Wethersfield, this classic Greek Revival brick house has been lovingly restored by the innkeepers to provide a warm and gracious New England welcome to the vacationer, traveler or business person.

| | | | |
|---|---|---|---|
| 1. No Smoking | 5. Tennis Available | 9. Credit Cards Accepted | 13. Lunch Available | 17. Shared Bath |
| 2. No Pets | 6. Golf Available | 10. Personal Checks Accepted | 14. Public Transportation | 18. Afternoon Tea |
| 3. No Children | 7. Swiming Available | 11. Off Season Rates | 15. Reservations Necessary | ★ Commissions given |
| 4. Senior Citizen Rates | 8. Skiing Available | 12. Dinner Available | 16. Private Bath | to Travel Agents |

# DELAWARE

## The First State

Capitol: Dover
Statehood: December 7, 1787; the 1st state
State Motto: Liberty and Independence
State Song: "Our Delaware"
State Bird: Blue Hen Chicken
State Flower: Peach Blossom
State Tree: American Holly

Delaware is called the first state because it was the first to ratify the Constitution of the United States. It is the second smallest state; however, it has so much diversification in industry and economy that it is thought of as a big state. Factories boom in the north and beautiful farmlands grace the southern part of Delaware. Rivers, bays and oceans are all part of this state. If a pollster wants to get a reading on anything, he usually comes here first. In this state there is a cross section of Americans and American industry.

DuPont, the largest chemical company in the world, has its headquarters here and its research division.

Delaware also has its pleasure side, too. The beaches along the Atlantic coast around Rehoboth and Bethany are great favorites with the tourists.

# DELAWARE

## Bridgevile

Nichols, John
303 Market St., 19933
(302) 337-3134

**Amenities:** 1,5,6,7,9,10,11,12, 13,15,17,18
**Breakfast:** F.

**Dbl. Oc.:** $50.00 - $75.00
**Third Person:** no charge
**Child:** no charge

**Teddy Bear B&B**—On U.S. 404, 40 minutes from Chesapeake Bay and the Atlantic Coast. Resort area. Four square, 1920 home with three guest rooms sharing one bath. Gourmet cooks. Great hospitality and a down-home relaxed atmosphere.

## Dover

DeZwarte, Sherry & Carolyn
305 S. Governors Ave., 19901
(302) 678-1242

**Amenities:** 2,9,10,16
**Breakfast:** F.

**Dbl. Oc.:** $43.00 - $58.00
**Sgl. Oc.:** $35.00 - $50.00
**Third Person:** $8.00

**The Inn At Meeting House Square**—Located in Dover's historic district, this 1849 inn offers old-style hospitality, along with distinctive and quality accommodations. Four rooms, each with TV, phone and air-conditioning. Walk to historic sites, restaurants, business and government districts. AAA approved.

## New Castle

Burwell, Irma & Richard
206 Delaware St., 19720
(302) 328-7736

**Amenities:** 1,2,5,9,10,14,17
**Breakfast:** C.

**Dbl. Oc.:** $40.00
**Sgl. Oc.:** $40.00

**William Penn Guest House**—Historic New Castle. A charming, restored historic home, circa 1682, located across from the Courthouse on the Square. The house is decorated in antiques. Four cheerful guest rooms with shared baths. One room with twin beds has a private bath.

## New Castle *

Rosenthal, Dr. Melvin
The Strand at the Wharf, 19720
(302) 323-0999, (302) 322-8944

**Amenities:** 2,5,9,10,12, 13,14,16
**Breakfast:** F.

**Dbl. Oc.:** $65.00 - $85.00
**Sgl. Oc.:** $65.00 - $85.00
**Third Person:** $10.00
**Child:** under 6 yrs. - no charge

**Jefferson House Bed & Breakfast**—A charming 200-year-old river front hotel next to the park in the historic district. Complimentary wine at affiliated restaurants. Off 295 near Philadelphia. William Penn landed here.

---

| | | | | |
|---|---|---|---|---|
| 1. No Smoking | 5. Tennis Available | 9. Credit Cards Accepted | 13. Lunch Available | 17. Shared Bath |
| 2. No Pets | 6. Golf Available | 10. Personal Checks Accepted | 14. Public Transportation | 18. Afternoon Tea |
| 3. No Children | 7. Swiming Available | 11. Off Season Rates | 15. Reservations Necessary | ★ Commissions given |
| 4. Senior Citizen Rates | 8. Skiing Available | 12. Dinner Available | 16. Private Bath | to Travel Agents |

## *Wilmington* *

Brill, Dot & Art
213 W. Crest Rd., 19803
(302) 764-0789

**Amenities:** 1,2,3,5,6,7,9,10,15,16,18
**Breakfast:** F.
**Dbl. Oc.:** $65.00
**Sgl. Oc.:** $55.00
**Third Person:** $20.00

**A Small Wonder Bed And Breakfast**—Awards for B&B hospitality/landscaping. Traditional suburban home close to I-95 exit, DuPont Chateau country. Outdoor pool/spa, A/C, TV, VCR, phone. Two rooms. Menu choice. Double/twin/king beds. Visit Nemours, Winterthur, Longwood, Hagley and Wyeth Museums and Old New Castle.

| | | | | |
|---|---|---|---|---|
| 1. No Smoking | 5. Tennis Available | 9. Credit Cards Accepted | 13. Lunch Available | 17. Shared Bath |
| 2. No Pets | 6. Golf Available | 10. Personal Checks Accepted | 14. Public Transportation | 18. Afternoon Tea |
| 3. No Children | 7. Swiming Available | 11. Off Season Rates | 15. Reservations Necessary | ★ Commissions given |
| 4. Senior Citizen Rates | 8. Skiing Available | 12. Dinner Available | 16. Private Bath | to Travel Agents |

# DISTRICT OF COLUMBIA

## *Washington, D.C.*

Founded: Site chosen — 1791
         Became capitol — 1800

Washington, D.C. is the capitol of the United States. It lies between Maryland and Virginia and it is the only American city or town that is not a part of a state.

The District is mainly made up of government buildings and monuments. Millions of people are employed here for the government, but they live outside the District.

Visitors flock here year round, but especially in the springtime when the cherry blossoms along the Potomac River Basin are in bloom. They come because it is a beautiful city, but mainly to see their government in action.

Some of the most popular attractions are the Capitol Building, the House of Congress and Senate, The White House, Lincoln's and Jefferson's Memorial and the Washington Monument. There are also the Smithsonian buildings, Ford's Theatre, the J.F.K. Center for the Performing Arts and many, many other government buildings and museums to visit. Guided tours are available and through your Congressman or Senator, admission passes can be obtained to watch Congress and the Senate when they are in session.

# DISTRICT OF COLUMBIA

## Washington

Courville, William
101 Fifth St., NE, 20002
(202) 547-1050

**Amenities:** 1,2,3,4,9,10,11, 14,15,17
**Breakfast:** C.

**Dbl. Oc.:** $73.65 - $84.75
**Sgl. Oc.:** $51.45 - $62.55
**Third Person:** $15.00

**Capitol Hill Guest House**—A Victorian row house located just three blocks behind the U.S. Supreme Court and U.S. Capitol in Capitol Hill historic district. Walk to monuments, museums, Folger Theatre and Union Station. Convenient to metro. Home to members of Congress staff, artists, scholars and lobbyists.

## Washington *

Fenstemaker, Rick
1845 Mintwood Pl., NW, 20009
(202) 667-6369

**Amenities:** 2,4,9,10,11,15, 16,17,18
**Breakfast:** C.

**Dbl. Oc.:** $51.45 - $106.95
**Sgl. Oc.:** $45.50 - $95.85
**Third Person:** $10.00

**The Kalorama Guest House**—A charming European-style bed and breakfast located on a quiet, tree-lined street in downtown D.C. Victorian townhouses filled with period antiques. Walk to metro, zoo, shops and restaurants.

## Washington *

PIieczenik, Roberta
2700 Cathedral Ave., NW, 20008
(202) 328-0860

**Amenities:** 2,4,9,10,11,16, 17,18
**Breakfast:** C.

**Dbl. Oc.:** $51.45 - $106.95
**Sgl. Oc.:** $45.50 - $95.85
**Third Person:** $10.00

**The Kalorama Guest House At Woodley Park**—Relish the charm of our European-style bed and breakfast. Victorian townhouses offering downtown convenience and old-fashioned hospitality. Complimentary breakfast and evening aperitif. Walk to metro, buses, fine restaurants, shops and the National Zoo.

## Washington

Reeds, The
P.O. Box 12011, 20005
(202) 328-3510

**Amenities:** 1,2,9,11,14,15,16, 17
**Breakfast:** C.

**Dbl. Oc.:** $79.20 - $90.30
**Sgl. Oc.:** $68.10 - $$79.20
**Third Person:** $16.65
**Child:** $5.55

**The Reeds**—A restored Victorian home located in downtown D.C. Decorated with many antiques. Just 12 blocks north of the American History Museum. The house has gardens and a Victorian porch. Friendly and interesting hosts. Convenient to public transportation.

---

| | | | | |
|---|---|---|---|---|
| 1. No Smoking | 5. Tennis Available | 9. Credit Cards Accepted | 13. Lunch Available | 17. Shared Bath |
| 2. No Pets | 6. Golf Available | 10. Personal Checks Accepted | 14. Public Transportation | 18. Afternoon Tea |
| 3. No Children | 7. Swiming Available | 11. Off Season Rates | 15. Reservations Necessary | ★ Commissions given |
| 4. Senior Citizen Rates | 8. Skiing Available | 12. Dinner Available | 16. Private Bath | to Travel Agents |

# FLORIDA

## The Sunshine State

Capitol: Tallahassee
Statehood: March 3, 1845; the 27th state
State Motto: In God We Trust
State Song: "Swanee River"
State Flower: Orange Blossom
State Tree: Sabal Palm

Florida is one of the best known states for vacationing and retirement. Its sunny climate beckons thousands of tourists and retirees every year. Its beautiful beaches, orange and grapefruit groves, palm and coconut trees blend to make it a vacationers paradise.

Walt Disney built his Disney World here and Cape Canaveral boasts of Apollo II's lift-off on its way to man's first landing on the moon.

St. Augustine, founded by a Spanish explorer in 1565, is the oldest city in the United States.

Many of Florida's cities are located on canals or waterways, making pleasure boating a way of life. Florida is often referred to as the Venice of the U.S.

## *Amelia Island* *

Caples, David
82 So. Fletcher Ave.
P. O. Drawer 1210, 32034
(904) 277-4851

**Amenities:** 2,4,5,6,7,9,10,11,15,16
**Breakfast:** C. Plus
**Dbl. Oc.:** $85.00 - $105.00
**Sgl. Oc.:** $85.00
**Third Person:** $10.00

**Elizabeth Pointe Lodge**—Reminiscent of a turn-of-the-century ocean front lodging, on a Barrier Island. Bike to nearby historic seaport village. Hearty breakfast, newspaper and fresh flowers daily. Goodies available all day in open, old-fashioned kitchen. Twenty rooms and suites.

## *Amelia Island*

Grable, Gary
584 So. Fletcher Ave., 32034
(904) 261-5878, (800) 872-8531

**Amenities:** 2,4,5,6,7,9,10,12,13,15,16
**Breakfast:** C.
**Dbl. Oc.:** $81.00
**Sgl. Oc.:** $60.00
**Third Person:** $5.00
**Child:** $5.00

**The 1735 House**—Century-old charm on the beach on a small Barrier Island. Full suites with private bath, bedroom and living area. Spectacular beach view with access. Antiques, wicker and nautical furnishings. Freshly baked pastries and morning newspaper delivered to your private suite daily.

## *Amelia Island* *

Warner, Karen & Bob
20 & 22 So. Third St.
P.O. Box 688, 32034
(904) 261-3300

**Amenities:** 1,2,5,6,7,9,10,12,13,16
**Breakfast:** F.
**Dbl. Oc.:** $59.00 - $128.00
**Sgl. Oc.:** $59.00 - $128.00
**Child:** $10.00

**Florida House Inn**—Located on Amelia Island in the heart of the 50-block historic district. Built in 1857 as a tourist hotel, today's guests can enjoy the same large porches and rooms, some with fireplaces. All with antiques, quilts and handmade rugs.

| | | | | |
|---|---|---|---|---|
| 1. No Smoking | 5. Tennis Available | 9. Credit Cards Accepted | 13. Lunch Available | 17. Shared Bath |
| 2. No Pets | 6. Golf Available | 10. Personal Checks Accepted | 14. Public Transportation | 18. Afternoon Tea |
| 3. No Children | 7. Swiming Available | 11. Off Season Rates | 15. Reservations Necessary | ★ Commissions given |
| 4. Senior Citizen Rates | 8. Skiing Available | 12. Dinner Available | 16. Private Bath | to Travel Agents |

## *Big Pine Key*

Threlkeld, Kathleen & Jon
Long Beach Dr.
P.O. Box 378, 33043
(305) 872-2878

**Amenities:** 2,3,5,6,7,10,11,15, **Dbl. Oc.:** $83.25
16                **Sgl. Oc.:** $83.25
**Breakfast:** F.         **Third Person:** $15.00

**Bed & Breakfast On The Ocean — Casa Grande**—A Spanish-style hacienda located on the Atlantic Ocean. All rooms have private baths, air-conditioning and small refrigerators. Lush garden patio and hot tub overlook a private beach. Nearby island excursions, reef trips, Key Deer and local restaurants.

## *Bradenton Beach* *

Kern, Becky
1703 Gulf Dr., 34217
(813) 778-6858

**Amenities:** 1,2,3,6,7,9,10,11,14,15,16,18
**Breakfast:** C. Plus
**Dbl. Oc.:** $71.50 & up
**Sgl. Oc.:** $71.50 & up

**The Duncan House**—On beautiful Anna Maria Island, is a pre-1910 Victorian home elegantly decorated with antiques, four private rooms with baths and warm hospitality. Close to major attractions.

## *Brandon*

Bergan, Eileen
917 Sunlit Court, 33511
(813) 653-3807

**Amenities:** 3,4,10,11,12,13,15, **Dbl. Oc.:** $48.00 - $52.00
16,17,18           **Sgl. Oc.:** $40.00
**Breakfast:** C. and F.     **Third Person:** $35.00
                 **Child:** under 5 yrs. -
                 no charge

**Florida — Themarilee Bed & Breakfast**—A hospitably run private home close to beaches, Disney World, Sea World, Busch Gardens and all the attractions. Choice of king, double or twin beds. Enjoy the comfort of this luxurious home with your English host. Transportation provided to and from the airport.

## *Cedar Key*

Rogers, Maria
Main St.
P.O. Box 460, 32625
(904) 543-5111

**Amenities:** 1,2,5,6,7,9,10,12, **Dbl. Oc.:** $74.20 - $100.70
13,15,16,17,18       **Third Person:** $10.00
**Breakfast:** F.         **Child:** under 6 yrs. - $5.00

**Historic Island Hotel**—This 10-room tabby-walled, Jamaican-style landmark island hotel is internationally known for its authenticity, gourmet-natural foods restaurant and romantic qualities. A full gourmet breakfast is included. Dinner offers fresh seafood, vegetarian specialties and originality.

| | | | | |
|---|---|---|---|---|
| 1. No Smoking | 5. Tennis Available | 9. Credit Cards Accepted | 13. Lunch Available | 17. Shared Bath |
| 2. No Pets | 6. Golf Available | 10. Personal Checks Accepted | 14. Public Transportation | 18. Afternoon Tea |
| 3. No Children | 7. Swiming Available | 11. Off Season Rates | 15. Reservations Necessary | ★ Commissions given |
| 4. Senior Citizen Rates | 8. Skiing Available | 12. Dinner Available | 16. Private Bath | to Travel Agents |

## Clearwater

Grimm, Vivian
3234 Tern Way, 34622
(813) 573-5825

**Amenities:** 1,2,5,6,7,14, 15,16,17
**Breakfast:** F.

**Dbl. Oc.:** $45.00
**Sgl. Oc.:** $30.00
**Third Person:** $10.00
**Child:** under 6 yrs. - no charge

**Bed & Breakfast Of Tampa Bay**—Quiet, country-club setting. The paintings and artifacts give this home an Oriental flair. Conveniently located to the beaches on the Gulf of Mexico, historic St. Petersburg, Tarpon Springs, Disney World, Busch Gardens and Sarasota. Near Highway 275. Swimming pool and bike riding available.

## Coleman

Martin, Jean
So. 301 (Behind Shady Brook Park)
P.O. Box 551, 33521
(904) 748-7867

**Amenities:** 1,2,9,10,12,13,15, 16,18
**Breakfast:** F.

**Dbl. Oc.:** $65.72 - $92.22
**Sgl. Oc.:** $37.10 - $76.32
**Third Person:** $15.00

**The Son's Shady Brook Bed & Breakfast**—Overlooks a spring-fed creek. A relaxing retreat forelderly, handicapped, newlyweds and others. Four beautiful, comfy bedrooms and baths. Within 100 miles to major Florida attractions. Air-conditioning, heat, piano and more. See to appreciate.

## Daytona Beach

Fisher, Vinton
444-448 So. Beach St., 32114
(904) 252-INNS
**Amenities:** 1,2,5,6,7,9,10,11,12, 14,15,16,18
**Breakfast:** F.
**Dbl. Oc.:** $60.00 - $170.00

**Live Oak Inn**—Listed in the *Register of Historic Places*. Best of both river and beach. 16 rooms, most with whirlpool or soaking tubs. Porches with views of historic garden or marina. Fine dining, afternoon tea and coffee. Meeting rooms. Special services for business travelers. Off-street parking.

## Daytona Beach *

Morgan, Becky Sue
3711 So. Atlantic Ave., 32127
(904) 767-3119

**Amenities:** 1,2,4,5,6,7,9,10, 11,13,14,16
**Breakfast:** F.

**Dbl. Oc.:** $81.75
**Sgl. Oc.:** $70.85
**Third Person:** $10.00
**Child:** under 18 yrs. - no charge

**Captain's Quarters Inn**—Daytona's first bed and breakfast inn. All ocean-front suites. Private balcony overlooks the ocean. Heated pool. Family operated for 26 years. Old-fashioned coffee shop. Freshly baked bread each morning. Newspaper daily. Wine and cheese at check-in. Unique gift shop. Guest laundry.

| | | | | |
|---|---|---|---|---|
| 1. No Smoking | 5. Tennis Available | 9. Credit Cards Accepted | 13. Lunch Available | 17. Shared Bath |
| 2. No Pets | 6. Golf Available | 10. Personal Checks Accepted | 14. Public Transportation | 18. Afternoon Tea |
| 3. No Children | 7. Swiming Available | 11. Off Season Rates | 15. Reservations Necessary | ★ Commissions given |
| 4. Senior Citizen Rates | 8. Skiing Available | 12. Dinner Available | 16. Private Bath | to Travel Agents |

# FLORIDA

## Florida City *

Newton, Mildred
40 N.W. 5th Ave., 33034
(305) 247-4413

**Amenities:** 4,10,15,16,17
**Breakfast:** F.

**Dbl. Oc.:** $38.85 - $61.05
**Sgl. Oc.:** $33.30 - $44.40
**Third Person:** $10.00
**Child:** no charge

**Grandma Newton's Bed And Breakfast**—Visit Grandma and the relaxed, country atmosphere of her 1914 historic two-story renovated country home. Minutes from national parks, Florida Keys and Miami. Spacious rooms with air-conditioning insure a peaceful rest that whets your appetite for our huge country breakfast.

## Haines City *

Rooks, Diane
106 So. First St., 33844
(813) 421-2242

**Amenities:** 5,6,7,9,11,12,13,15,16,18
**Breakfast:** F.
**Dbl. Oc.:** $60.00
**Sgl. Oc.:** $60.00
**Third Person:** $10.00
**Child:** $10.00

**Van Rook Inn**—A beautifully restored 1920's home. Five bedrooms with private bath, each decorated in a distinctive style with antiques. Close to all central Florida attractions. Tennis, golf, fishing, shuffleboard and swimming are all available nearby.

## Holmes Beach

Davis, Frank H.
5626 Gulf Dr., 34217
(813) 778-5444

**Amenities:** 1,2,3,7,9,10,11,14,16
**Breakfast:** F.
**Dbl. Oc.:** $85.00 - $115.00

**Harrington House B&B**—Circa 1925, directly on the Gulf. The house features a living room with a 20-foot-high beamed ceiling and a fireplace. Some guest rooms have either four poster, wicker or brass beds. Five rooms have French doors and a deck overlooking the pool, Gulf and beautiful sunsets.

| | | | | |
|---|---|---|---|---|
| 1. No Smoking | 5. Tennis Available | 9. Credit Cards Accepted | 13. Lunch Available | 17. Shared Bath |
| 2. No Pets | 6. Golf Available | 10. Personal Checks Accepted | 14. Public Transportation | 18. Afternoon Tea |
| 3. No Children | 7. Swiming Available | 11. Off Season Rates | 15. Reservations Necessary | ★ Commissions given |
| 4. Senior Citizen Rates | 8. Skiing Available | 12. Dinner Available | 16. Private Bath | to Travel Agents |

## Indian Shores  *

Meeks, Greta
19418 Gulf Blvd., #407, 34635
(813) 596-5424

**Amenities:** 1,2,5,6,7,10,14,
15,16,17
**Breakfast:** F.

**Dbl. Oc.:** $50.00
**Sgl. Oc.:** $40.00
**Third Person:** $10.00
**Child:** under 2 yrs. - $5.00

**Meeks B&B On The Gulf Beaches**—Our luxurious beach condominium overlooks the pool and Gul fbeaches. Sumptuous breakfast served. Nearby shopping and restaurants. An easy drive to Busch Gardens and DisneyWorld.

## Jacksonville

Kelly, Virginia & Charles
1217 Boulevard St., 32206
(904) 354-6959

**Amenities:** 1,2,4,5,6,7,10,14,
15,16
**Breakfast:** C.

**Dbl. Oc.:** $77.35
**Sgl. Oc.:** $66.30
**Child:** under 18 yrs. -
no charge

**1217 On The Boulevard**—Enjoy warm, Southern hospitality in a classic 1904 home. Located in historic Springfield, central to river front shops, restaurants and festivals galore. Discover some of Florida's best-kept secrets! Relax in elegant comfort. Complimentary wine and refreshments.

## Key West *

Amsterdam, Albert J.
511 Caroline St., 33040
(305) 294-5349

**Amenities:** 5,6,7,9,10,11,15,16
**Breakfast:** C.
**Dbl. Oc.:** $166.50 - $222.00
**Sgl. Oc.:** $166.50 - $222.00
**Third Person:** $27.75
**Child:** under 6 yrs. - no charge

**Curry Mansion Inn**—Nestled alongside the original 1899 Curry Mansion, the inn offers 15 elegant and romantic rooms, each opening onto a sparkling pool and surrounded by lush foliage of the Curry estate. All rooms have private baths, phones, air-conditioning and cable television.

## Key West

Beres, Joe
525 Simonton St., 33040
(305) 294-6712

**Amenities:** 2,3,7,9,11,15,16
**Breakfast:** C.
**Dbl. Oc.:** $105.45 - $294.15
**Sgl. Oc.:** $105.45 - $294.15
**Third Person:** $15.00

**The Watson House**—Circa 1860. A small, award-winning inn with distinctive, fully equipped guest suites/apartments in historic preservation district. Spa, pool and gardens. Adults only. Brochure available.

| | | | | |
|---|---|---|---|---|
| 1. No Smoking | 5. Tennis Available | 9. Credit Cards Accepted | 13. Lunch Available | 17. Shared Bath |
| 2. No Pets | 6. Golf Available | 10. Personal Checks Accepted | 14. Public Transportation | 18. Afternoon Tea |
| 3. No Children | 7. Swiming Available | 11. Off Season Rates | 15. Reservations Necessary | ★ Commissions given |
| 4. Senior Citizen Rates | 8. Skiing Available | 12. Dinner Available | 16. Private Bath | to Travel Agents |

## Key West *

Carlson, Jody
415 William, 33040
(305) 296-7274

**Amenities:** 2,3,8,12,13,18
**Breakfast:** C.

**Dbl. Oc.:** $125.00
**Sgl. Oc.:** $85.00

**The Popular House**—A 100-year-old Victorian located in the heart of the historic preservation district. Fine restaurants, shops and beaches within walking distance. Sauna and spa. Classic Caribbean casual. A viable and affordable alternative.

## Key West

Geibelt, Fred
512 Simonton St., 33040
(305) 294-9227

**Amenities:** 2,3,7,9,11,15,16
**Breakfast:** C.
**Dbl. Oc.:** $61.05 - $194.25
**Third Person:** $16.65

**Heron House**—The most central location in historic district. Three blocks from beach. Spacious sun decks and tropical gardens offer quiet privacy.

## Lake Helen *

Clauser, Marge & Tom
201 E. Kicklighter Rd., 32744
(904) 228-0310

**Amenities:** 1,2,3,4,9,10,11,15, 16,18
**Breakfast:** F.

**Dbl. Oc.:** $90.00
**Sgl. Oc.:** $80.00
**Third Person:** $10.00

**Clauser's Bed & Breakfast**—An 1880's Victorian home in a tranquil country setting. The feeling of yesteryear with porch rockers, heirlooms, linens and lace. Set among giant trees. It is a peaceful retreat, yet only 20 miles to Daytona and 40 miles to Orlando. A warm welcome awaits you.

---

| | | | | |
|---|---|---|---|---|
| 1. No Smoking | 5. Tennis Available | 9. Credit Cards Accepted | 13. Lunch Available | 17. Shared Bath |
| 2. No Pets | 6. Golf Available | 10. Personal Checks Accepted | 14. Public Transportation | 18. Afternoon Tea |
| 3. No Children | 7. Swiming Available | 11. Off Season Rates | 15. Reservations Necessary | ★ Commissions given |
| 4. Senior Citizen Rates | 8. Skiing Available | 12. Dinner Available | 16. Private Bath | to Travel Agents |

## Lake Wales *

Hinshaw, Vita
P.O. Drawer AC, 33859
(813) 676-6011

**Amenities:** 5,6,7,9,10,11,12,13,15,16
**Breakfast:** C.
**Dbl. Oc.:** $92.00
**Sgl. Oc.:** $81.00
**Third Person:** $13.00

**Chalet Suzanne Country Inn & Restaurant**—An imaginative, first-class country inn with 30 lovely guest rooms accented with antiques. Private baths, phones, cable TV and amenities. Four-star restaurant with more fine dining awards than any in Florida. Breakfast, lunch and dinner served daily. Centrally located.

## Marathon

Hopp, Jean E.
5 Man-O-War Dr., 33050
(305) 743-4118

**Amenities:** 2,5,6,7,9,11, 15,16
**Breakfast:** F.

**Dbl. Oc.:** $66.60 - $138.75
**Sgl. Oc.:** $61.05
**Third Person:** $11.10

**Hopp—Inn Guest House**—Located in the heart of the Florida Keys. We are on the ocean. Charter fishing, scuba and snorkling. All guest rooms with ocean view or ocean front. Each room has a private bath and a private entrance. Tropical setting in a quiet area. Children in one- or two-bedroom villas only.

## Neptune Beach

Rowland, Janet
119 Oak St., 32233
(904) 246-2415

**Amenities:** 1,2,7,14,15,16
**Breakfast:** C.

**Dbl. Oc.:** $45.00
**Sgl. Oc.:** $40.00

**Oceanside B&B**—200 feet from ocean. Two blocks to A1A. 18 miles east of Jacksonville. Large, twin bedroom, two bathrooms, kitchen, separate entrance, patio and parking. Total privacy within a home filled with family heirlooms. Restaurants and shops are within walking distance.

## Orlando *

Allen, Esther
2411 Virginia Dr., 32803
(407) 896-9916

**Amenities:** 1,5,6,7,14,15,17
**Breakfast:** C.

**Dbl. Oc.:** $47.70
**Sgl. Oc.:** $37.10
**Third Person:** $10.60
**Child:** under 10 yrs. - $10.60

**Esther's B&B**—Located near Disney World and Epcot Center. Breakfast includes homemade muffins or coffeecake, cheese, fresh fruit and a beverage. Enjoy a glass of sherry poolside or in an artistic atmosphere of pianos and needlepoint of old masters.

| | | | | |
|---|---|---|---|---|
| 1. No Smoking | 5. Tennis Available | 9. Credit Cards Accepted | 13. Lunch Available | 17. Shared Bath |
| 2. No Pets | 6. Golf Available | 10. Personal Checks Accepted | 14. Public Transportation | 18. Afternoon Tea |
| 3. No Children | 7. Swiming Available | 11. Off Season Rates | 15. Reservations Necessary | ★ Commissions given |
| 4. Senior Citizen Rates | 8. Skiing Available | 12. Dinner Available | 16. Private Bath | to Travel Agents |

## Orlando *

Freudenburg, Victor
532 Pinar Dr., 32825
(407) 277-4903

**Amenities:** 1,2,10,15,16
**Breakfast:** F.

**Dbl. Oc.:** $49,50
**Sgl. Oc.:** $38.50
**Third Person:** $5.50
**Child:** under 3 yrs. -
no charge

**Rio Pinar House**—A spacious nine-room home on the Rio Pinar Golf Course, near the East-West Expressway, Goldenrod exit. Convenient to the airport, downtown, Disney World and other attractions. Your hosts can recommend many nearby fine restaurants.

## Orlando

Leddon, Lillian
816 N. Summerlin Ave., 32803
(407) 896-5477

**Amenities:** 1,2,3,10,15,16
**Breakfast:** F.
**Dbl. Oc.:** $60.50
**Sgl. Oc.:** $49.50
**Third Person:** $22.00

**The Brass Bed Room & Breakfast**—A beautifully restored 1924 Dutch colonial located near I-4 and downtown. Guest room is upstairs with queen-size bed and private bath. Adjoining TV room can sleep third person. Relax on sun deck or patio after spending the day at nearby attractions.

## Orlando

Meiner, Charles E.
211 No. Lucerne Circle, 32801
(407) 648-5188

**Amenities:** 2,9,10,15,16
**Breakfast:** C.

**Dbl. Oc.:** $85.00 - $150.00
**Sgl. Oc.:** $85.00 - $150.00
**Third Person:** $15.00

**Norment-Parry Inn**—Consists of three buildings of distinctive styles: a classic Victorian home, 12 art-deco units and three Edwardian suites. All guest rooms are decorated in period furnishings and overlook a tropical courtyard praised as"an oasis in the heart of Orlando."

## Ormond Beach *

Rainey, Margaret
393 John Anderson Dr., 32176
(904) 672-5557

**Amenities:** 2,3,4,5,6,7,10,11,
14,15,16
**Breakfast:** F.

**Dbl. Oc.:** $95.00
**Sgl. Oc.:** $75.00
**Third Person:** $20.00
**Child:** under 3 yrs. -
no charge

**Tea House Gardens**—An early 1900's home with period decor. Just three blocks from the ocean. Nearby restaurants, shopping, musuem and art gallery. A large, private suite for two or three persons includes efficiency kitchen. Air-conditioning, pool, color cable TV and private entrance in quiet area.

| | | | | |
|---|---|---|---|---|
| 1. No Smoking | 5. Tennis Available | 9. Credit Cards Accepted | 13. Lunch Available | 17. Shared Bath |
| 2. No Pets | 6. Golf Available | 10. Personal Checks Accepted | 14. Public Transportation | 18. Afternoon Tea |
| 3. No Children | 7. Swiming Available | 11. Off Season Rates | 15. Reservations Necessary | ★ Commissions given |
| 4. Senior Citizen Rates | 8. Skiing Available | 12. Dinner Available | 16. Private Bath | to Travel Agents |

## Palmetto *

Kriessler, Bette
1102 Riverside Dr., 34221
(813) 723-1236

**Amenities:** 2,3,9,10,11,16,18
**Breakfast:** F.

**Dbl. Oc.:** $71.50 - $110.00
**Sgl. Oc.:** $71.50 - $110.00
**Third Person:** $16.50

**Five Oaks Inn**—A majestic waterfront home within walking distance to restaurants, town, marina, shops and churches. Near beaches and cultural area. Period decor, circa 1911. Listed in the *Register of Historic Places.* Complimentary cocktail and relaxed atmosphere.

## Pensacola

Liechty, Jeanne & Neil
7830 Pine Forest Rd., 32526
(904) 944-4816

**Amenities:** 1,2,4,9,10,15,16
**Breakfast:** F.

**Dbl. Oc.:** $86.11
**Sgl. Oc.:** $75.21
**Third Person:** $10.90
**Child:** under 18 yrs. -
no charge

**Liechty's Homestead Inn**—The inn has five guest rooms with private baths, TV and phones. We are known for our delicious Mennonite-prepared food. Full six-course breakfast includes Amish waffles. We are located off I-10, Exit 2, 1/2 mile south on left side.

## St. Augustine *

Burkley-Kovacik, Karen
70 Cuna St., 32084
(904) 829-2467

**Amenities:** 1,4,5,7,9,10,11,12,
13,15,16,18
**Breakfast:** C.

**Dbl. Oc.:** $52.92 - $102.80
**Sgl. Oc.:** $52.92 - $102.80
**Third Person:** $10.00

**Carriage Way Bed & Breakfast**—A restored 1883 Victorian structure in the historic district. Includes breakfast, cordials, newspapers, bicycles and cookies. Picnic lunches and honeymoon breakfast in bed available. Romantic atmosphere with canopy, four-poster and brass beds.

## St. Augustine

Constant, Mark
38 Marine St., 32084
(904) 824-2116

**Amenities:** 1,2,3,5,6,7,9,10,15,16
**Breakfast:** C.
**Dbl. Oc.:** $59.40 - $135.00
**Sgl. Oc.:** $48.60 - $135.00
**Third Person:** $10.80

Since 1886

**The Kenwood Inn**—For over a century, this lovely old Victorian inn has received visitors. Located in the historic district, the inn is within easy walking distance to all attractions. Rooms range in size and are decorated differently from each other to create a home-away-from-home feeling.

| | | | | |
|---|---|---|---|---|
| 1. No Smoking | 5. Tennis Available | 9. Credit Cards Accepted | 13. Lunch Available | 17. Shared Bath |
| 2. No Pets | 6. Golf Available | 10. Personal Checks Accepted | 14. Public Transportation | 18. Afternoon Tea |
| 3. No Children | 7. Swiming Available | 11. Off Season Rates | 15. Reservations Necessary | ★ Commissions given |
| 4. Senior Citizen Rates | 8. Skiing Available | 12. Dinner Available | 16. Private Bath | to Travel Agents |

# FLORIDA

## St. Augustine *

Upchurch, Sandra
22 Avenida Menendez, 32084
(904 829-2915

**Amenities:** 2,5,6,7,9,10,
16,18
**Breakfast:** F.

**Dbl. Oc.:** $65.00 - $115.00
**Sgl. Oc.:** $65.00 - $115.00
**Third Person:** $10.00

**Casa De La Paz**—Overlooking Matanzas Bay, this elegant Mediterranean-style inn graces St. Augustine's historic district. Each room is distinctive in style with imported linens. Enjoy the veranda views and Spanish courtyard. Gourmet breakfast and complimentary champagne.

## St. Petersburg *

Powers, Antonia & Gordon
1719 Beach Dr., S.E., 33701
(813) 823-4955

**Amenities:** 1,2,3,5,6,7,9,10,14,16,18
**Breakfast:** C.
**Dbl. Oc.:** $71.50
**Sgl. Oc.:** $60.50

**Bayboro House B&B**—Be our guest. Sink your feet into the sand and stay awhile. The perfect place to relax. Walk out the front door to swimming, sunning, beachcombing or sit on the veranda swing and enjoy refreshing breezes from Tampa Bay. Antiques and beautiful old furnishings are yours to enjoy.

## Stuart *

Bell, Jean
501 Akron Ave., 34994
(407) 220-9148

**Amenities:** 1,2,3,7,9,10,11,
15,16,18
**Breakfast:** C.

**Dbl. Oc.:** $95.00
**Sgl. Oc.:** $75.00

**The Homeplace**—Guests indulge themselves in the early 20th-century charm and hospitality of this 1913 home. Three bedrooms with baths, comfortably appointed with antiques. Continental breakfast features home-baked "old Florida" recipes and freshly picked fruits from the back yard.

## Tarpon Springs

Carbaugh, Kathy
928 Bayshore Dr., 34689
(813) 934-2829

**Amenities:** 1,2,7,10,15,16
**Breakfast:** C.

**Dbl. Oc.:** $55.00
**Sgl. Oc.:** $55.00

**Kreamer Bayou Bed & Breakfast**—This lovely new waterfront home is located in the heart of Tarpon Springs on Kreamer Bayou. You can relax around the pool or out on the dock. If you enjoy water sports, arrangements can be made for snorkeling, scuba diving or fishing.

| | | | |
|---|---|---|---|
| 1. No Smoking | 5. Tennis Available | 9. Credit Cards Accepted | 13. Lunch Available | 17. Shared Bath |
| 2. No Pets | 6. Golf Available | 10. Personal Checks Accepted | 14. Public Transportation | 18. Afternoon Tea |
| 3. No Children | 7. Swiming Available | 11. Off Season Rates | 15. Reservations Necessary | ★ Commissions given |
| 4. Senior Citizen Rates | 8. Skiing Available | 12. Dinner Available | 16. Private Bath | to Travel Agents |

## *Tarpon Springs**

Morrick, Cher & Ron
32 W. Tarpon Ave., 34689
(813) 938-9333

**Amenities:** 1,2,3,5,6,7,10,14,
15,16,17
**Breakfast:** C. Plus

**Dbl. Oc.:** $55.00 - $82.50
**Sgl. Oc.:** $49.50 - $77.00
**Third Person:** $10.00

**Spring Bayou Inn**—An elegant in-town Victorian home with modern conveniences.Walk to quaint village shops, sponge docks and restaurants. Stroll around the bayou. Golf, beaches, fishing and tennis are available nearby. Continental breakfast served in formal dining area.

## *Venice*

McCormick, Susan & Chuck
519 S. Harbor Dr., 34285
(813) 484-1385

**Amenities:** 2,7,10,11,14,
15,16,17
**Breakfast:** C.

**Dbl. Oc.:** $49.00 - $87.00
**Sgl. Oc.:** $49.00 - $87.00
**Third Person:** $15.00

**The Banyan House**—A Mediterranean-style house built in 1926. Victorian living room, garden with swimming pool, hot tub, banyan tree and brick courtyard. Two bedrooms with shared baths; three efficiencies with private baths. Walking distance to beaches, shops and restaurants.

## *West Palm Beach*

Keimel, Dennis
419 Thirty Second St.,33407
(407) 848-4064

**Amenities:** 5,6,7,10,11,15,16
**Breakfast:** C.
**Dbl. Oc.:** $65.00
**Sgl. Oc.:** $65.00
**Child:** Inquire for rates

**West Palm Beach Bed And Breakfast**—An enchanting "Key West" style cottage, tropical pool area. Private baths. Centrally located in historic neighborhood one block from waterway. Minutes to beaches and Palm Beach. Bicycles and off-street parking. A relaxing place to kick off your sandals!

## *West Palm Beach**

Lesky, Bonnie
P.O. Box 1336, 33407
(407) 863-1508

**Amenities:** 1,2,4,5,7,10,11,13,
15,16,17,18
**Breakfast:** F.

**Dbl. Oc.:** $55.00 - $65.00
**Sgl. Oc.:** $45.00 - $55.00
**Third Person** - $15.00
**Child:** under 10 yrs. -
$10.00

**Royal Palm House**—Located in the heart of the historic district and two blocks from the intra-coastal waterway. Charming, warm and hospitable. Set amidst a lush tropical garden with many citrus trees. Sit by our pool and enjoy the sun and lovely breeze from the Atlantic.

| | | | | |
|---|---|---|---|---|
| 1. No Smoking | 5. Tennis Available | 9. Credit Cards Accepted | 13. Lunch Available | 17. Shared Bath |
| 2. No Pets | 6. Golf Available | 10. Personal Checks Accepted | 14. Public Transportation | 18. Afternoon Tea |
| 3. No Children | 7. Swiming Available | 11. Off Season Rates | 15. Reservations Necessary | ★ Commissions given |
| 4. Senior Citizen Rates | 8. Skiing Available | 12. Dinner Available | 16. Private Bath | to Travel Agents |

## *Zolfo Springs*

Matheny, Mary Jane
Route 1, Box 292, 33890
(813) 735-0266 (after 6 p.m.)

**Amenities:** 1,2,3,6,7,10, 15,16
**Breakfast:** C.

**Dbl. Oc.:** $53.50
**Sgl. Oc.:** $48.15

**Double M Ranch Bed & Breakfast**—A working cattle and citrus ranch in central Florida. Many nearby golf courses as well as fishing, canoeing and riding. Within two hours to Disney World, Cypress Gardens and Ft. Myers. 4,500 acres on which to enjoy the country! Ranch tour available.

| | | | |
|---|---|---|---|
| 1. No Smoking | 5. Tennis Available | 9. Credit Cards Accepted | 13. Lunch Available | 16. Private Bath |
| 2. No Pets | 6. Golf Available | 10. Personal Checks Accepted | 14. Public Transportation | 17. Shared Bath |
| 3. No Children | 7. Swiming Available | 11. Off Season Rates | 15. Reservations Necessary | 18. Afternoon Tea |

# GEORGIA

## The Empire State of the South

Capitol: Atlanta
Statehood: January 2, 1788; the 4th state
State Motto: Wisdom, Justice and Moderation
State Song: "Georgia On My Mind"
State Bird: Brown Thrasher
State Flower: Cherokee Rose
State Tree: Live Oak

The state of Georgia is known for its natural beauty and it has many vacation resorts attracting visitors from all over the world. The climate is mild most of the time, but in the summer it tends to get quite warm and humid.

It is the largest state east of the Mississippi and one of the leading growers of peaches. It is often called The Peach State.

The first Girl Scout troop in America was organized here by Juliette Low in 1912 and the first painless surgery was performed by Dr. Long in 1842, when he operated on a patient using ether as an anesthetic for the first time.

The capitol, Atlanta, represents the modern south. Almost two million people live here. It also was the home of Dr. Martin Luther King, and he is buried here today.

Jimmy Carter, our 39th president, was born here.

# GEORGIA

## Acworth

Pettys, Jan & Bill
4965 No. Main St.
P.O. Drawer F, 30101
(404) 974-9485

**Amenities:** 1,2,4,5,6,7,10,12,
13,15,17
**Breakfast:** C.

**Dbl. Oc.:** $57.20
**Sgl. Oc.:** $46.80
**Third Person:** $10.00

**Jesse Lemon Bed & Breakfast**—An 1880's Victorian townhouse. Five comfortable bedrooms furnished in period antiques. Only 29 miles from downtown Atlanta. Visit Atlanta, Kennesaw Mountain, Lake Acworth and Lake Allatoona, White Water, Six Flags and Stone Mountain.

## Americus

Davis, JoAnn & Tony
Mask Rd.
Route 6, Box 50, 31709
(912) 924-4992

**Amenities:** 2,3,6,9,10,12,15,
16,18
**Breakfast:** F.

**Dbl. Oc.:** $58.30
**Sgl. Oc.:** $46.64

**Merriwood Country Inn**—A beautiful cypress and log Southern homestead close to historic sites. Enjoy porches, pond, bikes, yard games and country critters. Cozy rooms with antiques and family pieces. Regional cuisine served in carriage house. English country conference room.

## Americus

Morris, Troy
425 Timberlane Dr., 31709
(912) 924-4884

**Amenities:** 1,2,3,6,9,15,16
**Breakfast:** F.

**Dbl. Oc.:** $57.75
**Sgl. Oc.:** $47.25
**Third Person:** $10.00

**The Morris Manor**—Visit a stately Georgian colonial home in a quiet, rural setting at the edge of Americus. Here you will enjoy a wholesome atmosphere and Southern hospitality, including a bed-time snack, full breakfast and other amenities. Fresh fruit available in season.

## Atlanta *

Amin, Mit
65 Sheridan Dr., NE, 30305
(800) 232-8520, (404) 233-8520,
(404) 233-8047

**Amenities:** 5,7,9,10,14,15,16
**Breakfast:** C.
**Dbl. Oc.:** $75.00 - $90.00
**Sgl. Oc.:** $65.00 - $75.00
**Third Person:** $5.00

**Beverly Hills Inn**—A charming city retreat in the heart of Buckhead. A European-style inn with antique furnishings and Oriental rugs. Play the piano in the parlor, read in the library or enjoy the vast choice of good restaurants within a short five-minute drive.

---

| | | | | |
|---|---|---|---|---|
| 1. No Smoking | 5. Tennis Available | 9. Credit Cards Accepted | 13. Lunch Available | 17. Shared Bath |
| 2. No Pets | 6. Golf Available | 10. Personal Checks Accepted | 14. Public Transportation | 18. Afternoon Tea |
| 3. No Children | 7. Swiming Available | 11. Off Season Rates | 15. Reservations Necessary | ★ Commissions given |
| 4. Senior Citizen Rates | 8. Skiing Available | 12. Dinner Available | 16. Private Bath | to Travel Agents |

# GEORGIA

## Atlanta *

Heartfield, Sandra
182 Elizabeth St., NE, 30307
(404) 523-8633

**Amenities:** 2,4,10,15,16
**Breakfast:** C.

**Dbl. Oc.:** $40.00
**Sgl. Oc.:** $30.00
**Third Person:** $10.00
**Child:** under 8 yrs.
no charge

**Heartfield Manor**—A stately 1903 English Tudor, minutes from downtown. Experience a lovely Victorian neighborhood with the convenience of rapid transit to all parts of the city and airport. Walking distance to theatres, restaurants, pubs and shops. Rooms and suites available.

## Atlanta

Jones, Joan & Doug
223 Ponce de Leon Ave., 30308
(404) 875-9449

**Amenities:** 4,9,10,14,16,18
**Breakfast:** F. and C.

**Dbl. Oc.:** $84.75
**Sgl. Oc.:** $73.45
**Third Person:** $5.00
**Child:** under 5 yrs. - $5.00

**Woodruff Bed & Breakfast Inn**—Southern charm and hospitality await you, including a full Southern breakfast with grits. A restored Victorian home decorated with antiques and located in Atlanta's prestigious mid-town neighborhood near the most awarded restaurants. Y'all come.

## Atlanta

Thomas, Timothy
253 15th St., NE, 30309
(800) 446-5416

**Amenities:** 2,9,10,14,15,16,18
**Breakfast:** C.
**Dbl. Oc.:** $92.34 - $222.35

**Ansley Inn**—Located in the heart of the mid-town Atlanta arts and business district. Situated in a beautifully restored Tudor mansion, Ansley Inn offers 12 luxuriously appointed rooms, all with jacuzzi tubs. 24-hour staff.

## Augusta *

Hoopes, Mrs. E.S.
2259 Cumming Rd., 30904
(404) 738-5122

**Amenities:** 2,10,14,15,16
**Breakfast:** C.

**Dbl. Oc.:** $55.00 - $85.00
**Third Person:** $5.00

**Augusta House**—Inn with 10 bedrooms. Walk to Augusta College. 2-1/2 miles to Medical College and downtown. A lovely, authentic English manor on three acres of English gardens. Furnished in antiques, wicker, period furniture and leaded glass chandeliers. Modernized.

| | | | | |
|---|---|---|---|---|
| 1. No Smoking | 5. Tennis Available | 9. Credit Cards Accepted | 13. Lunch Available | 17. Shared Bath |
| 2. No Pets | 6. Golf Available | 10. Personal Checks Accepted | 14. Public Transportation | 18. Afternoon Tea |
| 3. No Children | 7. Swiming Available | 11. Off Season Rates | 15. Reservations Necessary | ★ Commissions given |
| 4. Senior Citizen Rates | 8. Skiing Available | 12. Dinner Available | 16. Private Bath | to Travel Agents |

## Brunswick *

Rose, Rachel
1108 Richmond St., 31520
(912) 267-6369

Amenities: 1,2,10,12,13,15,16, 17,18
Breakfast: F.

Dbl. Oc.: $50.00 - $80.00
Sgl. Oc.: $47.50
Third Person: $22.50
Child: under 12 yrs. - $12.50

Rose Manor Guest House—A circa 1890, elegantly restored and gracefully furnished Victorian bungalow. Gateway to the Golden Isles at Hanover Square in historic Old Town. Nestled among old southern trees laden with yards of Spanish moss surrounded by beautiful gardens. Charming ambience.

## Calhoun

Mayer, Joan & Vincent
764 Union Grove Ch. Rd. S.E.,
Adairsville (mail), 30103
(404) 625-3649

Amenities: 1,3,4,15,17,18
Breakfast: C.

Dbl. Oc.: $35.00
Sgl. Oc.: $30.00
Child: 6-12 yrs. - no charge

Old Home Place—A charming country home, circa 1855. Large rooms accented with antiques. 50-ft. front porch with rockers shaded by magnolias. Breakfast served in cheerful blue-and-white kitchen. Homemade muffins and jams our specialty. Two miles from I-75, Exit 129. Nearby restaurants and shops.

## Commerce *

Tomberlin, Dot & Tom
103 Homer St., 30529
(404) 335-3823

Amenities: 1,2,4,5,6,7,9,10, 16,17
Breakfast: F.

Dbl. Oc.: $55.00
Sgl. Oc.: $47.00
Third Person: $10.00

The Pittman House—Located in NE Georgia on U.S. Highway 441, three miles offI-85 at Exit 54, about half-way between Atlanta and Greenville, South Carolina. Discount mall, golf and watersports are located nearby. Antiques. Shoppers delight. Furnished in turn-of-the-century decor.

## Dahlonega

Middleton, David
Route 7, Box 150, 30533
(404) 864-5257

Amenities: 2,3,9,10,16
Breakfast: F.

Dbl. Oc.: $71.50 - $137.50
Sgl. Oc.: $49.50 - $115.50
Third Person: $16.50

Mountain Top Lodge At Dahlonega—Enjoy antique-filled rooms in a beautiful mountain setting. Cathedral ceiling greatroom, spacious decks and heated outdoor spa. All rooms with private bath, some have fireplaces and whirlpool tubs. Full country breakfast with homemade biscuits.

| | | | |
|---|---|---|---|
| 1. No Smoking | 5. Tennis Available | 9. Credit Cards Accepted | 13. Lunch Available | 17. Shared Bath |
| 2. No Pets | 6. Golf Available | 10. Personal Checks Accepted | 14. Public Transportation | 18. Afternoon Tea |
| 3. No Children | 7. Swiming Available | 11. Off Season Rates | 15. Reservations Necessary | ★ Commissions given |
| 4. Senior Citizen Rates | 8. Skiing Available | 12. Dinner Available | 16. Private Bath | to Travel Agents |

## Hamilton *

Neuffer, Janice M.
P.O. Box 115
Hwy. 27, 31811
(404) 628-5659

**Amenities:** 1,2,5,6,7,10,11,12,13,16,17,18
**Breakfast:** F.
**Dbl. Oc.:** $58.30 - $72.08
**Sgl. Oc.:** $50.88 - $65.72
**Child:** no charge - $5.00

**Wedgwood Bed & Breakfast**—Six miles south of Calaway Gardens. Make this spacious home yours while visiting the area. Little White House at Warm Springs is nearby. The 1850 home's decor is Wedgwood blue with white stenciling. The home radiates the warmth and hospitality of your hostess.

## Macon

Schwartz, P.J.
575 College St., 31201
(912) 745-0258

**Amenities:** 2,4,9,10,15,16
**Breakfast:** C.

**Dbl. Oc.:** $65.00 - $95.00
**Sgl. Oc.:** $60.00
**Child:** $60.00

**Stone Conner House**—In the historic district. A circa 1873, Queen Anne style brick home with lovely terrace. Warm hospitality. Three guest rooms, one with jacuzzi bath and sitting room. Complimentary beverages on arrival.

## Madison

Rasch, Christian
250 No. Second St., 30650
(404) 342-4400

**Amenities:** 5,6,7,10,12,13,16, 17
**Breakfast:** F.

**Dbl. Oc.:** $60.00
**Sgl. Oc.:** $45.00

**The Brady Inn**—Charming Victorian cottages with period furniture located in the town that Sherman "refused to burn." One block from downtown square. Walking tour of antebellum homes available. Pleasant accommodations, local lore and Southern hospitality.

## Marietta

Rowe, Brigita
236 Church St., 30060
(404) 426-1881

**Amenities:** 9,10,14,15,16
**Breakfast:** C.

**Dbl. Oc.:** $71.50
**Sgl. Oc.:** $60.50
**Third Person:** $10.00

**The Stanely House**—An elegant Victorian inn built in 1895. Located in historic Marietta. Within walking distance to shops, restaurants and theatre and 20 minutes to downtown Atlanta.

| | | | | |
|---|---|---|---|---|
| 1. No Smoking | 5. Tennis Available | 9. Credit Cards Accepted | 13. Lunch Available | 17. Shared Bath |
| 2. No Pets | 6. Golf Available | 10. Personal Checks Accepted | 14. Public Transportation | 18. Afternoon Tea |
| 3. No Children | 7. Swiming Available | 11. Off Season Rates | 15. Reservations Necessary | ★ Commissions given |
| 4. Senior Citizen Rates | 8. Skiing Available | 12. Dinner Available | 16. Private Bath | to Travel Agents |

# GEORGIA

## Mountain City *

Smith, James H.
York House Rd.
P.O. Box 126, 30562
(404) 746-2068

**Amenities:** 1,2,4,8,9,10,11,16
**Breakfast:** C.
**Dbl. Oc.:** $59.95 - $81.75
**Sgl. Oc.:** $54.50 - $59.95
**Third Person:** $10.00
**Child:** under 6 yrs. - no charge

Historic Bed And Breakfast Inn

**The York House, Inc.**—A 1886 inn listed in the *National Register of Historic Places*. Nestled among the North Georgia mountains. Close to recreational activities. Completely renovated. Guestrooms decorated with period antiques. A two-story inn with porches on both levels surrounded by towering trees.

---

## Sautee

Schwartz, Hamilton
Hwy. 255 N.
Rt. 1, Box 1476, 30571
(404) 878-3355

**Amenities:** 2,9,10,11,12,16
**Breakfast:** C.

**Dbl. Oc.:** $70.00
**Sgl. Oc.:** $40.00
**Third Person:** $17.00
**Child:** under 17 yrs. - $11.00

**The Stovall House**—Relax in an attentively restored 1838 farmhouse on 26 acres in the mountains near Helen. Five guest rooms with private baths, period antiques, handmade curtains and stenciling. Award-winning restaurant. Dinner - $15.00. It's a country experience.

---

## Sautee

Wunderlich, Ginger & Van
Route #1,
Box 1086, 30571
(404) 878-2580

**Amenities:** 1,2,3,10,15, 16,17,18
**Breakfast:** C. Plus

**Dbl. Oc.:** $50.00 - $65.00
**Sgl. Oc.:** $45.00
**Third Person:** $15.00
**Child:** over 12 yrs. - $15.00

**Woodhaven Chalet**—Near Alpine Helen, Georgia. A secluded mountain setting with nearby hiking and horseback riding. Air-conditioned, piano, balcony, sherry and wine. One unit with cooking facilities, fireplace and TV. Artwork for sale. Smoking on covered porches. Wine available.

---

| | | | |
|---|---|---|---|
| 1. No Smoking | 5. Tennis Available | 9. Credit Cards Accepted | 13. Lunch Available | 17. Shared Bath |
| 2. No Pets | 6. Golf Available | 10. Personal Checks Accepted | 14. Public Transportation | 18. Afternoon Tea |
| 3. No Children | 7. Swiming Available | 11. Off Season Rates | 15. Reservations Necessary | ★ Commissions given |
| 4. Senior Citizen Rates | 8. Skiing Available | 12. Dinner Available | 16. Private Bath | to Travel Agents |

# GEORGIA

## Savannah*

Bannerman, Lois
209 W. Jones St., 31401
(912) 236-1774

**Amenities:** 4,5,6,7,10,16
**Breakfast:** C.

**Dbl. Oc.:** $100.90
**Sgl. Oc.:** $94.35
**Third Person:** $37.85 -
$82.25 (suite)

**Jesse Mount House**—Luxurious three-bedroom suites in an elegant 1854 home. High, four-poster, canopied beds. Rare antiques. Gilded harps. Garden-level suite has full kitchen and beautiful walled garden with fountains. Complimentary breakfast, fruit, sherry and candies in your suite.

## Savannah*

Barnett, Anne
106 W. Jones St., 31401
(912) 234-6928

**Amenities:** 3,5,6,7,10,15,16
**Breakfast:** C.

**Dbl. Oc.:** $65.00
**Sgl. Oc.:** $65.00
**Third Person:** $20.00

**Remshart-Brooks House**—Enjoy the hospitality of this historic home. Features a terrace garden suite with bedroom, living room, bath and kitchen. Home-baked delicacies enhance the continental breakfast. Private front and back entrances. Off-street parking available.

## Savannah*

McAlister, Robert
117 W. Gordon St., 31401
(912) 238-0518

**Amenities:** 9,10,14,16,17
**Breakfast:** F.

**Dbl. Oc.:** $43.00 - $87.00
**Sgl. Oc.:** $34.00 - $47.00
**Third Person:** $5.00 -
$10.00
**Child:** under 5 yrs. -
no charge

**Bed And Breakfast Inn**—An 1853 restored Federalist townhouse in historic district. Poster beds, rare porcelain, Oriental carpets, books, original art, antiques and traditional furnishings. A lovely walled garden. Quiet and convenient. Situated in a residential area.

## Savannah*

Smith, J.B.
203 W. Charlton St., 31401
(912) 232-8055, (800) 227-0650

**Amenities:** 2,9,10,11,16,17
**Breakfast:** C.

**Dbl. Oc.:** $53.76 - $98.56
**Third Person:** $14.64

**Pulaski Square Inn**—This fine townhouse, built in 1853, is located in Savannah's historic district. It is beautifully restored and features original pine flooring, marble mantels and crystal chandeliers. It is furnished with antiques and traditional furniture.

1. No Smoking
2. No Pets
3. No Children
4. Senior Citizen Rates
5. Tennis Available
6. Golf Available
7. Swiming Available
8. Skiing Available
9. Credit Cards Accepted
10. Personal Checks Accepted
11. Off Season Rates
12. Dinner Available
13. Lunch Available
14. Public Transportation
15. Reservations Necessary
16. Private Bath
17. Shared Bath
18. Afternoon Tea
★ Commissions given
to Travel Agents

# GEORGIA

## Savannah *

Steinhauser, Susan
14 W. Hull St., 31401
(912) 232-6622

**Amenities:** 2,4,5,6,7,9,10,11,15,16,18
**Breakfast:** C.
**Dbl. Oc.:** $126.00 - $224.00
**Sgl. Oc.:** $112.00 - $224.00
**Third Person:** $10.00
**Child:** under 12 yrs. - no charge

**Foley House Inn**—Circa 1896. Located in the heart of the historic district. Every room is an individual masterpiece. Antiques, Oriental rugs, fireplaces and many rooms with oversized jacuzzies. A delicate blend of traditional aristocracy and contemporary finesse. Evening cordial.

---

## Savannah *

Sullivan, Virginia & Hal
102 W. Hall St., 31401
(912) 233-6800

**Amenities:** 2,5,6,7,9,14,16
**Breakfast:** C.

**Dbl. Oc.:** $84.00 - $135.00
**Sgl. Oc.:** $67.00 - $84.00
**Third Person:** $17.00
**Child:** under 2 yrs. - no charge

**The Forsyth Park Inn**—An elegantly restored Victorian mansion in the historic district. Rooms feature wet bars, fireplaces and whirlpool tubs. Evening wine social hour.

---

## Senoia

Boal, Jan & Bobby
252 Seavy St.
Box 177, 30276-0177
(404) 599-3905

**Amenities:** 2,6,9,10,12,13,15,16
**Breakfast:** F.
**Dbl. Oc.:** $79.50 - $100.00
**Sgl. Oc.:** $68.90 - $90
**Third Person:** $15.90
**Child:** under 2 yrs. - no charge

**The Veranda**—30 miles south of Atlanta Airport. Listed in the *National Register of Historic Places*. Built in 1907, this rambling neo-classic structure hosted many illustrious guests, including William Jennings Bryant and Civil War veterans. Antique collections, 1930 player-organ, air-conditioning and gourmet meals.

---

| | | | | |
|---|---|---|---|---|
| 1. No Smoking | 5. Tennis Available | 9. Credit Cards Accepted | 13. Lunch Available | 17. Shared Bath |
| 2. No Pets | 6. Golf Available | 10. Personal Checks Accepted | 14. Public Transportation | 18. Afternoon Tea |
| 3. No Children | 7. Swiming Available | 11. Off Season Rates | 15. Reservations Necessary | ★ Commissions given |
| 4. Senior Citizen Rates | 8. Skiing Available | 12. Dinner Available | 16. Private Bath | to Travel Agents |

# GEORGIA

## St. Marys*

Geismar, Jackie & Don
209 Osborne, 31558
(912) 882-7490

**Amenities:** 1,2,3,10,15,16
**Breakfast:** C. Plus

**Dbl. Oc.:** $66.00
**Sgl. Oc.:** $66.00

**Goodbread House Bed & Breakfast**—A carefully restored Victorian, circa 1880, with high ceilings, seven fireplaces, wide pine floors, original wood trim and antiques throughout. A short walk to Cumberland Island Ferry. Wine and cheese served evenings in thelounge.

## Thomaston *

Franklin, Betty
403 W. Gordon St., 30286
(404) 647-5477

**Amenities:** 2,5,9,15,16
**Breakfast:** C. Plus

**Dbl. Oc.:** $46.20 - $60.90
**Sgl. Oc.:** $44.10
**Third Person:** $2.10
**Child:** $2.10

**Gordon Street Inn**—Built in 1898, this Victorian inn is two blocks from the town square. All rooms have private baths, cable TV, heat/air units and phones. Brochure available.

## Thomaston

Grace, Barbara
327 W. Main St., 30286
(404) 647-2482

**Amenities:** 1,9,10,15,16,17
**Breakfast:** F.

**Dbl. Oc.:** $63.00
**Sgl. Oc.:** $52.50
**Third Person:** $10.50

**The Whitfield Inn**—Located 1-1/2 blocks off U.S.-19. Southern hospitality at its finest. Victorian with a touch of country. Five guestrooms, three baths and a live-in grandma. Full breakfast and tour of beautiful heart of Georgia and nearby Flint River. Canoe rental and shuttle available.

## Thomasville *

Muggridge, Gladys
1304 o. Broad St., 31792
(912) 226-7294

**Amenities:** 3,5,6,10,14,
16,17,18
**Breakfast:** F.

**Dbl. Oc.:** $51.84
**Sgl. Oc.:** $49.68
**Third Person:** $10.80
**Child:** $10.80

**Deer Creek**—A dream home where deer roam. One mile from plantation tours. Spectacular view from all rooms. Twenty-foot deck for guests. Fifteen miles from dog track and Florida lottery. Adjacent golf course where Ike played. A cedar home on two acres. Charming decor.

---

| 1. No Smoking | 5. Tennis Available | 9. Credit Cards Accepted | 13. Lunch Available | 17. Shared Bath |
| 2. No Pets | 6. Golf Available | 10. Personal Checks Accepted | 14. Public Transportation | 18. Afternoon Tea |
| 3. No Children | 7. Swiming Available | 11. Off Season Rates | 15. Reservations Necessary | ★ Commissions given |
| 4. Senior Citizen Rates | 8. Skiing Available | 12. Dinner Available | 16. Private Bath | to Travel Agents |

# GEORGIA

## Thomasville *

Walker, Anne-Marie
Route 3, Box 1010, 31792
(912) 377-9644

**Amenities:** 5,7,10,12,15,16
**Breakfast:** F.

**Dbl. Oc.:** $157.50
**Sgl. Oc.:** $105.00
**Third Person:** $25.00
**Child:** under 12 yrs. -
no charge

**Susina Plantation**—An 1841 Greek Revival plantation home, built by the noted architect John Wind, is situated on 115 acres of lawns and woodlands. Five-course dinner with wine is included in the rates. For a most delightful evening, experience good food and good company at its best!

## Winterville *

Durham, Phyllis
130 Beaver Trail, 30683
(404) 742-7803

**Amenities:** 1,4,10,15,16
**Breakfast:** F.

**Dbl. Oc.:** $35.00
**Sgl. Oc.:** $25.00
**Third Person:** $15.00
**Child:** under 12 yrs. -
$10.00

**Durham's Bed And Breakfast**—Enjoy a comfortable room in a very quiet country setting far from any traffic. Guest may relax in the woods by a stream and be given a tour of our organic farm. Only seven miles from Athens and the University of Georgia.

| | | | | |
|---|---|---|---|---|
| 1. No Smoking | 5. Tennis Available | 9. Credit Cards Accepted | 13. Lunch Available | 17. Shared Bath |
| 2. No Pets | 6. Golf Available | 10. Personal Checks Accepted | 14. Public Transportation | 18. Afternoon Tea |
| 3. No Children | 7. Swiming Available | 11. Off Season Rates | 15. Reservations Necessary | ★ Commissions given |
| 4. Senior Citizen Rates | 8. Skiing Available | 12. Dinner Available | 16. Private Bath | to Travel Agents |

# HAWAII

## *The Aloha State*

Capitol: Honolulu
Statehood: August 21, 1959; the 50th state
State Motto: The Life of the Land is Perpetuated
in Righteousness
State Song: "Hawaii Ponoi"
State Bird: Nene (Hawaiian Goose)
State Flower: Hibiscus
State Tree: Kukui


Hawaii is the only state that is completely set apart from the rest of the United States in North America. It consists of 132 beautiful islands, some larger than others, about 2,400 miles west of the United States.

These islands were first discovered by Captain Cook in 1778 and called the Sandwich Islands after the Earl of Sandwich. Inhabited then by only natives, the first white settlers were missionaries that came here in 1820. The Chinese and Japanese arrived later as laborers and workers for the plantations, but gradually entered the political and economic world here and today we have a happy mixture of many different peoples living and working together.

Hawaii's mild and beautiful climate beckons tourists from all over the world. Beautiful beaches have made swimming and surfing a way of life here.

Tourism and the pineapple and sugar industries form the leading source of income for this state.

## Kailua (Oahu) *

Martz, Jeanette & Bob
395 Auwinala Rd., 96734
(808) 261-0316

**Amenities:** 2,5,6,7,14,15,16
**Breakfast:** F.

**Dbl. Oc.:** $65.00
**Sgl. Oc.:** $65.00
**Third Person:** $20.00

**Papaya Paradise**—Just 20 miles from Waikiki and 1-1/2 hours from all attractions. Walk to Kailua Beach. Quiet and private, with 20X40 pool, jacuzzi, tropical plants and flowers. Private entry, TV and air-conditioning in each room. Beach, mats, chairs and coolers furnished.

## Kailua (Ohau)

Epp, Doris
19 Kai Nani Pl., 96734
(800) 999-6026, (808) 254-5030

**Amenities:** 5,6,7,10,14,15,16
**Breakfast:** C.

**Dbl. Oc.:** $95.00

**Oceanfront/White Sand Beach B&B**—A beachfront, two-room suite that sleeps four. Private entry, bath, TV, refrigerator and microwave oven. Quiet and private. Ideal for family. Walk the three-mile-wide sandy beach. Only 1/2 hour from Waikiki. Nearby horseback riding, windsurfing, restaurants and shopping.

## Kapaa (Kauai) *

Barker, Gordon
P.O. Box 740, 96746
(808) 822-3073

**Amenities:** 9,10,15,16
**Breakfast:** C. Plus

**Dbl. Oc.:** $49,00 - $71.00
**Sgl. Oc.:** $38.00 - $60.00
**Third Person:** $11.00
**Child:** under 10 yrs. - $5.50

**Kay Barker's Bed And Breakfast**—Located in a quiet rural area. Overlooks miles of pasture. Ten minutes from golf, tennis, beaches, restaurants and more. A large home with extensive library, TV room and Lanai to enjoy. Your host, Gordon, knows of the special places.

## Kapaa (Kauai)*

Knott, Robert
4561 Kuamoo Rd., 46746
(808) 822-2560

**Amenities:** 1,2,5,6,7,8,9,15,
16
**Breakfast:** C.

**Dbl. Oc.:** $87.20 - $109.00
**Sgl. Oc.:** $76.30 - $98.10

**Fern Grotto Inn**—A plantation home in a tropical garden, amidst towering palms. Stroll to the beach on the banks of a placid river. Slumber in queen beds. Full, private baths. Tropical breakfast served on elegant English china.

| | | | |
|---|---|---|---|
| 1. No Smoking | 5. Tennis Available | 9. Credit Cards Accepted | 13. Lunch Available | 17. Shared Bath |
| 2. No Pets | 6. Golf Available | 10. Personal Checks Accepted | 14. Public Transportation | 18. Afternoon Tea |
| 3. No Children | 7. Swiming Available | 11. Off Season Rates | 15. Reservations Necessary | ★ Commissions given |
| 4. Senior Citizen Rates | 8. Skiing Available | 12. Dinner Available | 16. Private Bath | to Travel Agents |

## Kapaa (Kauai)*

Ross, Leonora & Norm
6402 Kaahele St., 96746
(808) 822-7201

**Amenities:** 1,2,3,15,16
**Breakfast:** C.

**Dbl. Oc.:** $82.00
**Sgl. Oc.:** $82.00

**The Orchid Hut**—A bright, cozy, modern three-room cottage with kitchenette. Located between Kauai's north and south shore recreation areas. Short drive to beach, shopping and dining. Spectacular view of Wailua River. Quiet and private. Three-day minimum. 10% off for seven or more days.

## Keaau*

Peyton, Stephen E.
HCR 9558, 96749-9318
(808) 966-4600

**Amenities:** 2,3,4,15,16,17
**Breakfast:** F.

**Dbl. Oc.:** $55.00
**Sgl. Oc.:** $50.00
**Third Person:** $10.00

**Paradise Place Bed & Breakfast**—Volcano, ocean and mountain views surround this quiet rural hideaway. Kitchenette and private entrances to guest rooms overlooking tropical gardens. Centrally located to Hilo, active lava flows and Volcanos National Park. Relax in the Aloha spirit.

## Kihei (Maui)

Svenson, Carol & Kenneth
541 Kupulau Dr., 96753
(808) 879-7984

**Amenities:** 1,10,15,16
**Breakfast:** F.

**Dbl. Oc.:** $65.00
**Sgl. Oc.:** $60.00

**Whaler's Way**—Surrounded by breathtaking mountain and ocean views. Cool afternoon breezes. Tropical flower gardens and fruit trees. Island-style rooms feature feeling of "home." Colorful sunset views. It is Paradise!

## Kilauea*

Guyer, Kirby
4041 Ka'iana
P.O. Box 422, 96754
(808) 826-1130

**Amenities:** 6,7,10,12,13,15,16,18
**Breakfast:** C.
**Dbl. Oc.:** $65.00
**Sgl. Oc.:** $65.00

**Hale Ho'o Maha**—"House of rest" nestled atop the cliffs above Hanalei on the north shore of Kauai. Close to beaches, golf and riding. Seven-foot round bed in charmingly decorated single-story home with windows all around. Full gourmet kitchen available.

| | | | |
|---|---|---|---|
| 1. No Smoking | 5. Tennis Available | 9. Credit Cards Accepted | 13. Lunch Available | 17. Shared Bath |
| 2. No Pets | 6. Golf Available | 10. Personal Checks Accepted | 14. Public Transportation | 18. Afternoon Tea |
| 3. No Children | 7. Swiming Available | 11. Off Season Rates | 15. Reservations Necessary | ★ Commissions given |
| 4. Senior Citizen Rates | 8. Skiing Available | 12. Dinner Available | 16. Private Bath | to Travel Agents |

## Koloa*

Warner, Evelyn
1792 Pee Rd., 96756
(800) 733-1632, (808) 742-6757

**Amenities:** 1,5,6,7,9,10,11, 15,16
**Breakfast:** C.

**Dbl. Oc.:** $70.00 - $95.00
**Third Person:** $11.00
**Child:** $5.50

**Poipu Plantation**—One of the most unusual and attractive accommodations on Kauai offering affordable Paradise. Nine one- and two-bedroom units in Poipu. A short walk to beaches and restaurants. The B&B inn offers cheerful rooms and spacious common area. TVs in all units.

## Koloa, Kauai *

Seymour, Edee
3459 Lawai Loa Lane
Box 930, Lawai, Kallai, 96765
(808) 332-9300

**Amenities:** 1,2,3,5,6,7, 10,15,16
**Breakfast:** C. Plus

**Dbl. Oc.:** $70.95 - $103.55
**Sgl. Oc.:** $59.00 - $95.00
**Third Person:** $10.00

**Victoria Place**—Spacious and sky-lit with jungle and ocean view. All bedrooms have private baths and open onto pool and garden. Near beaches, boutiques, golf and botanical garden. Barrier free. We pamper: flowers, chocolate, homemade muffins and "Aloha."

## Pahoa-Kalapana*

Koob, Richard
Ocean Rd. 137, 96778
(800) 367-8047 Ext. 669, (808) 965-7828

**Amenities:** 1,2,4,5,7,9,11,12,13,15, 16,17,18
**Breakfast:** C.
**Dbl. Oc.:** $66.00
**Sgl. Oc.:** $55.00
**Third Person:** $18.00
**Child:** no charge - $9.00

**Kalani Honua Seaside Educational Retreat**—A Hawaiian country getaway with fresh ocean breezes, comfy lodging, delicious cuisine, optional health and educational programs. Olympic pool, spa, tennis, horses. Nearby national and state parks and secluded beaches. Color brochure. ALOHA!

| | | | | |
|---|---|---|---|---|
| 1. No Smoking | 5. Tennis Available | 9. Credit Cards Accepted | 13. Lunch Available | 17. Shared Bath |
| 2. No Pets | 6. Golf Available | 10. Personal Checks Accepted | 14. Public Transportation | 18. Afternoon Tea |
| 3. No Children | 7. Swiming Available | 11. Off Season Rates | 15. Reservations Necessary | ★ Commissions given |
| 4. Senior Citizen Rates | 8. Skiing Available | 12. Dinner Available | 16. Private Bath | to Travel Agents |

## *Poipu Beach, Kauai* *

Cichon, Dottie
2720 Hoonani Rd., 96756
(800) 552-0095, (808) 742-1146

**Amenities:** 1,2,4,5,6,7,9,10,11,14,15,16,18
**Breakfast:** C.
**Dbl. Oc.:** $98.49 - $136.79
**Sgl. Oc.:** $93.02 - $131.32
**Third Person:** $16.41
**Child:** $16.41

**Poipu Bed & Breakfast Inn**—A romantic 1933 plantation house in sunny Poipu. All luxurious rooms have the charm of old Hawaii plus every modern amenity: new private baths (two with whirlpools),TVs, VCRs, white wicker, pine antiques and the spirit of"Aloha." Walk to beach, shops, restaurants, etc.

## *Volcano*

Jeyte, Lorna & Albert
P.O. Box 116, 96785
(808) 967-7366

**Amenities:** 2,6,9,10,12,15,16
**Breakfast:** F.
**Dbl. Oc.:** $82.00 - $110.00
**Sgl. Oc.:** $82.00 - $110.00
**Third Person:** $15.00
**Child:** under 2 yrs. - no charge

**Kilauea Lodge**—A country inn one mile from Volcano's National Park. Pristine forest setting. Private baths. Six rooms with fireplaces. Area noted for family hikes, golf and heli-tours. The inn has excellent full-service dining with continental cuisine. Fresh, big-island products.

## *Waimanalo* *

Leonard, Mrs. Bernie
41-585 Flamingo, 96795
(808) 259-7404

**Amenities:** 4,6,7,10,15,16
**Breakfast:** C.

**Dbl. Oc.:** $65.40
**Sgl. Oc.:** $59.95

**Orchid Row Bed & Breakfast**—A unique hideaway that surrounds you with "Aloha" and orchids. There is only the sounds of birds and tradewinds in the air. Your charming rooms include your private sitting and dining room, TV, kitchenette and full bath.

| | | | | |
|---|---|---|---|---|
| 1. No Smoking | 5. Tennis Available | 9. Credit Cards Accepted | 13. Lunch Available | 17. Shared Bath |
| 2. No Pets | 6. Golf Available | 10. Personal Checks Accepted | 14. Public Transportation | 18. Afternoon Tea |
| 3. No Children | 7. Swiming Available | 11. Off Season Rates | 15. Reservations Necessary | ★ Commissions given |
| 4. Senior Citizen Rates | 8. Skiing Available | 12. Dinner Available | 16. Private Bath | to Travel Agents |

# IDAHO

## The Gem State

Capitol:  Boise
Statehood:  July 3, 1890; the 43rd state
State Motto:  It Is Forever
State Song:  "Here We Have Idaho"
State Bird:  Mountain Bluebird
State Flower:  Syringa (Mock Orange)
State Tree:  Western White Pine

Idaho is located in the Rocky Mountains with exciting scenery and enormous resources. Its natural wonders, such as Hells Canyon and the Craters of the Moon National Monument, thrill visitors to this state every year.

Idaho is also a skier's paradise where ski areas and ski trails are considered among the best in the world.

This state is a leading producer of silver and phosphate. The Snake River and its many dams have made for rich farmlands. The Idaho potato is its No. 1 farm product. More potatoes are grown here than in any other state in the union.

# IDAHO

## Ashton

Jessen, Nieca & Jack
Idaho Hwy. #20
Box 11, 83420
(208) 652-3356

**Amenities:** 1,2,6,7,8,10
**Breakfast:** F.
**Dbl. Oc.:** $45.00
**Sgl. Oc.:** $35.00
**Third Person:** $10.50

**Jessen's Bed & Breakfast**—This B&B is 1-1/2 miles south of Ashton on Highway U.S. 20 with Yellowstone National Park to the north, Jackson Hole and The Great Tetons to the east. Our home is comfortable and hospitable.

## Cascade *

Haynes, Diana
H.C. 72, 83611
(208) 382-4336

**Amenities:** 2,8,10,11,12,13,15, 16,17
**Breakfast:** F.

**Dbl. Oc.:** $80.25
**Sgl. Oc.:** $80.25

**Wapiti Meadow Ranch**—A wilderness retreat in the heart of Idaho's Salmon River Mountains. Enjoy fishing, hiking, snowmobiling and cross-country skiing. Relax in the outdoor spa surrounded by home-like back-country comfort. Hearty gourmet dining with three meals a day is included in your rates.

## Shoup

Smith, Marsha & Aubrey
49 Salmon River Rd., 83469
(208) 394-2121

**Amenities:** 1,7,8,9,10,12,15, 16,17,18
**Breakfast:** F.

**Dbl. Oc.:** $37.45 - $57.78
**Sgl. Oc.:** $32.10 - $55.64
**Third Person:** $5.00
**Child:** under 12 yrs. - $3.50

**Smith House Bed & Breakfast**—Situated on the Salmon River, 50 miles from Salmon, Idaho. Beautiful split-level log home with five warm and distinctively different guest rooms. Hot tub, orchard and library. Nearby fishing, float trips, hunting and skiing. Sample homemade wines. Gift shop. Weekly rates.

## Sun Valley *

Van Doren, Virginia
P.O. Box 182, 83353
(208) 726-3611

**Amenities:** 1,4,5,6,8,9,10,11, 14,15,16,18
**Breakfast:** F.

**Dbl. Oc.:** $95.00 - $150.00
**Sgl. Oc.:** $85.00 - $140.00
**Third Person:** $20.00

**River Street Inn**—Each parlor suite has a view, queen- and king-size beds, Japanese-style soaking tub, walk-in shower, TV, phone and small refrigerator. Large breakfast features pastries. On a quiet street central to all area activities.

| | | | |
|---|---|---|---|
| 1. No Smoking | 5. Tennis Available | 9. Credit Cards Accepted | 13. Lunch Available | 17. Shared Bath |
| 2. No Pets | 6. Golf Available | 10. Personal Checks Accepted | 14. Public Transportation | 18. Afternoon Tea |
| 3. No Children | 7. Swiming Available | 11. Off Season Rates | 15. Reservations Necessary | ★ Commissions given |
| 4. Senior Citizen Rates | 8. Skiing Available | 12. Dinner Available | 16. Private Bath | to Travel Agents |

# ILLINOIS

## The Land of Lincoln

Capital: Springfield
Statehood: December 3, 1818; the 21st state
State Motto: State Sovereignty, National Union
State Song: "Illinois"
State Bird: Cardinal
State Flower: Native Violet
State Tree: White Oak

Illinois boasts of having more people than any other state in the midwest, and the second largest city in the United States, Chicago. Its deep and rich soil has made for large-scale farming and its mighty deposits of coal have brought great prosperity.

The steel frames necessary for the building of sky scrapers were invented here. It resulted in the erection of some of the tallest buildings in the world, including Chicago's own Sears Towers.

Chicago is the crossroads of the country. Trains and barges leave here with the products of the midwest farms and take them from one coast to another, either by rail or waterways.

Historically, Illinois first won national attention when Abraham Lincoln debated Stephen Douglas on the subject of slavery. Although not born in the state, Lincoln's burial place in Springfield is a national shrine. Ulysses S. Grant's home in Galena is maintained as it was when he lived there. Built in 1856, it has been a state memorial since 1932.

Although our 40th President, Ronald Wilson Reagan, spent most of his life in California he was also born in this state in Tampico on 2/6/11.

The first successful railroad sleeping car was invented by George Pullman at Bloomington, Illinois in 1859. It pioneered a new way of travel for Americans.

# ILLINOIS

## Champaign

Erickson, Joan
2204 Brett Dr., 61821
(217) 356-5828

**Amenities:** 2,3,10,14,15, 16,17
**Breakfast:** F.

**Dbl. Oc.:** $47.70
**Sgl. Oc.:** $42.40

**Grandma Joan's Homestay**—A comfortable, comtemporary two-story home with multi-level decks, jacuzzi, two fireplaces, screened-in porch and a collection of modern and folk art. Nearby walking/bicycle paths. Located 10 minutes from the University of Idaho. Grandma pampers you with cookies and milk at bedtime.

---

## Champaign *

Gold, Rita
R.R. 3, Box 69, 61821
(217) 586-4345

**Amenities:** 1,2,6,10,15,16,17
**Breakfast:** C.

**Dbl. Oc.:** $42.40
**Sgl. Oc.:** $37.10

**The Golds Bed & Breakfast**—A restored nine-room 1874 farmhouse just off I-74 between Mahomet and Champaign. Antique furnishings. Relaxed family atmosphere. Views of sunrises, sunsets and surrounding cornfields. Near University of Illinois, museum, golf and antiquing. Call for brochure.

---

## Chicago

Custer, Irene
5210 So. Kenwood Ave., 60615
(312) 363-4595

**Amenities:** 2,14,16,17
**Breakfast:** C.

**Dbl. Oc.:** $50.00 - $60.00
**Sgl. Oc.:** $45.00
**Third Person:** $5.00
**Child:** under 10 yrs. - no charge

**Hyde Park House**—A Victorian with veranda, porch swing and attached greenhouse. Near the University of Chicago, McCormick Place, Museum of Science & Industry. 20 minutes by bus to Lake Michigan. Walking distance to many ethnic and American restaurants, parks, gift shops and art galleries.

---

## Chicago *

Sandoval, Elia
2022 No. Sheffield, 60614
(312) 327-6546

**Amenities:** 2,10,14,15,16,17
**Breakfast:** C.

**Dbl. Oc.:** $60.00 - $75.00
**Sgl. Oc.:** $50.00

**Bed & Breakfast Lincoln Park/Sheffield**—Excellent public transportation. Many fine neighborhood restaurants and shops. A renovated Victorian building with self-catering apartments. Suites available. Walk to DePaul University, zoo and lake. Two-bedroom apartment — $120.00 and up.

---

| | | | | |
|---|---|---|---|---|
| 1. No Smoking | 5. Tennis Available | 9. Credit Cards Accepted | 13. Lunch Available | 17. Shared Bath |
| 2. No Pets | 6. Golf Available | 10. Personal Checks Accepted | 14. Public Transportation | 18. Afternoon Tea |
| 3. No Children | 7. Swiming Available | 11. Off Season Rates | 15. Reservations Necessary | ★ Commissions given |
| 4. Senior Citizen Rates | 8. Skiing Available | 12. Dinner Available | 16. Private Bath | to Travel Agents |

# ILLINOIS

## Du Quoin *

Morgan, Francie & Tom
104 S. Line St., 62832
(618) 542-6686

**Amenities:** 2,9,10,13,15,16,17, 18
**Breakfast:** F.

**Dbl. Oc.:** $53.00 - $79.50
**Sgl. Oc.:** $47.70
**Third Person:** $10.60
**Child:** under 12 yrs. -
no charge

**Francie's**—A turn-of-the-century children's home restored to a five-bedroom inn. Walking distance to beautiful State Fairgrounds Park, tennis courts and swimming pool. Tour and history given. Arts and crafts shop in house. Air-conditioning. 20 miles west of Interstate 57.

---

## Galena

Green, Alyce
1000 S. Bench St., 61036
(815) 777-0222

**Amenities:** 1,2,3,9,10,11,15, 16
**Breakfast:** C.

**Dbl. Oc.:** $75.21 - $107.91
**Sgl. Oc.:** $67.69 - $97.12

**Captain Gear Guest House**—One of Galena's outstanding mansions. Built in 1855. Situated on four secluded acres. Within walking distance(3/4 of a mile) to downtown shops. Hearty continental breakfast. Private baths (one with a double whirlpool).

---

## Galena

Jensen, Flo & Roger
606 So. Prospect St., 61036
(815) 777-3883

**Amenities:** 1,2,4,9,10,11,15, 17,18
**Breakfast:** C.

**Dbl. Oc.:** $60.00
**Sgl. Oc.:** $55.00
**Third Person:** $10.00
**Child:** under 12 yrs. - $5.00

**Avery Guest House**—Located within Galena's historic district. Close to antique shops, fine restaurants and historic buildings. Scenic view from our porch swing. Breakfast in sunny dining room with bay window. Golf, tennis, swimming, hiking and skiing. Mississippi River is nearby.

---

## Galena

Lozeau, Pamela
513 Bouthillier, 61036
(815) 777-0557

**Amenities:** 2,3,9,10,12,16
**Breakfast:** C.
**Dbl. Oc.:** $71.00 - $136.50

**Stillman's Country Inn**—An 1858 Victorian mansion adjacent to General Grant's home. Features fine dining and weekend nightclub. All guestrooms have private baths.

---

| | | | | |
|---|---|---|---|---|
| 1. No Smoking | 5. Tennis Available | 9. Credit Cards Accepted | 13. Lunch Available | 17. Shared Bath |
| 2. No Pets | 6. Golf Available | 10. Personal Checks Accepted | 14. Public Transportation | 18. Afternoon Tea |
| 3. No Children | 7. Swiming Available | 11. Off Season Rates | 15. Reservations Necessary | ★ Commissions given |
| 4. Senior Citizen Rates | 8. Skiing Available | 12. Dinner Available | 16. Private Bath | to Travel Agents |

## Galesburg

Johnson, Gwen & Lyle
624 No. Cherry St., 61401
(309) 342-4107

**Amenities:** 1,2,9,10,14,15,17
**Breakfast:** C.

**Dbl. Oc.:** $40.00
**Sgl. Oc.:** $35.00
**Third Person:** $15.00
**Child:** $15.00

**Seacord House Bed & Breakfast**—An 1890's landmark house. Victorian decor. Lace curtains. Family antiques. Fresh homemade muffins daily. Close to Knox College and Sandburg birthplace site. Your schedule accommodated — hospitality is a family tradition.

## Havana *

Stephens, Shirley
112 No. Schrader St., 62644
(309) 543-3295

**Amenities:** 2,10,17
**Breakfast:** C.

**Dbl. Oc.:** $58.10
**Sgl. Oc.:** $36.97

**The McNutt Guest House**—Just steps from the scenic Illinois River. Restaurants, grocery stores and shops are within walking distance. A gracious and beautifully furnished eight-room home. Reserve a bedroom or the entire guest house which sleeps eight. Entire guest house - $132.05

## Jacksonville *

McKinley, Rosalee
Morton at Church St., 62650
(217) 245-2588

**Amenities:** 1,2,3,6,10,16,18
**Breakfast:** C. Plus
**Dbl. Oc.:** $58.45 - $63.75
**Sgl. Oc.:** $53.45 - $58.75
**Third Person:** $10.00
**Child:** over 12 yrs. - $10.00

**The 258 Inn Bed & Breakfast**—An 1854 Victorian home where guests are pampered. Relax in the library with a good book, a jigsaw puzzle or the evening news. Browse through our shops of antiques, collectibles, quilts or our bed-and-bath shop. Homemade breads for breakfast. 30 miles west of Springfield, IL.

## Lanark

Aschenbrenner, Maggie
540 W. Carroll St., 61046
(815) 493-2307

**Amenities:** 1,2,3,6,8,9,10,16,17
**Breakfast:** F.
**Dbl. Oc.:** $53.12 - $69.69
**Sgl. Oc.:** $53.12 - $69.69

**Standish House**—A traditional English B&B. 120 miles west of Chicago. Relaxing, small-town atmosphere. Walking distance to business district. Myles Standish heritage carried throughout with 18th-century English antiques, canopy beds and decor. Central air-conditioning.

| | | | |
|---|---|---|---|
| 1. No Smoking | 5. Tennis Available | 9. Credit Cards Accepted | 13. Lunch Available | 17. Shared Bath |
| 2. No Pets | 6. Golf Available | 10. Personal Checks Accepted | 14. Public Transportation | 18. Afternoon Tea |
| 3. No Children | 7. Swiming Available | 11. Off Season Rates | 15. Reservations Necessary | ★ Commissions given |
| 4. Senior Citizen Rates | 8. Skiing Available | 12. Dinner Available | 16. Private Bath | to Travel Agents |

## Mossville

Ramseyer, Holly & Dean
1416 E. Mossville Rd., 61552
(309) 579-2300

**Amenities:** 1,2,3,9,10,15,16, 17,18
**Breakfast:** C.

**Dbl. Oc.:** $69.00 - $90.00
**Sgl. Oc.:** $52.00

**Old Church House Inn**—Nestled in central Illinois near the Rock Island bike trail, this 1869 colonial-style church welcomes you to the plush warmth of a Victorian era. Enjoy flower gardens, afternoon tea, queen featherbeds and pampering amenities in Peoria's finest B&B. Children over 12 years welcome.

## Naperville *

Harrison, Lynn
26 No. Eagle St., 60540
(708) 420-1117

**Amenities:** 1,2,3,5,6,7,8,9,10, 14,15,16,17,18
**Breakfast:** F.

**Dbl. Oc.:** $74.12 - $139.52
**Sgl. Oc.:** $52.32 - $117.72
**Third Person:** $10.90

**Harrison House Bed & Breakfast**—Circa 1911. 25 miles west of Chicago in historic Naperville. Walk to fantastic restaurants, shops and historic sites. Five antique-filled, air-conditioned guest rooms. One bath with jacuzzi. Homemade chocolate-chip cookies. Friendly atmosphere. Let us pamper you.

## Nauvoo

Ortman, William J.
324 White St., 62354
(217) 453-2249, (217) 544-1357

**Amenities:** 1,2,5,6,10,15,17
**Breakfast:** C.

**Dbl. Oc.:** $53.50
**Sgl. Oc.:** $48.50
**Third Person:** $5.00

**Ortman's Bed & Breakfast**—Mormon country. Listed in the *National Register of Historic Places*. Often visited by Mormon Joseph Smith. Beautiful views. The area is the site of many Huck Finn and Mormon movies. The wine cellar is connected to the house by a tunnel. Open spring, summer and fall; winter by appointment.

## Nauvoo *

Starr, Marjorie
Box 291, RR 1, 62354
(217) 453-2771

**Amenities:** 1,2,6,10,16,17
**Breakfast:** F.

**Dbl. Oc.:** $50.88 - $61.48
**Sgl. Oc.:** $47.20
**Third Person:** $7.50
**Child:** under 6 yrs. - $5.00

**Mississippi Memories**—Gracious lodging on the bank of the Mississippi. Elegantly served full breakfast. Quiet wooded area, wildlife, bald eagles, barges drifting by and geode hunting. Air-conditioning, piano and fireplaces. Two miles from restored historic Nauvoo, Illinois. Five guest rooms.

## Oak Park

Mungerson, Cynthia V.
301 No. Scoville Ave., 60302
(708) 386-8623

**Amenities:** 1,2,3,10,14,15,16, 18
**Breakfast:** F.

**Dbl. Oc.:** $53.00 - $68.90
**Sgl. Oc.:** $47.70 - $58.30
**Third Person:** $10.00

**Toad Hall**—A 1909 colonial. Five miles from Chicago Loop in the Frank Lloyd Wright historic district. Old-world atmosphere and service. Victorian antiques, Oriental rugs and Laura Ashley furnishings. Private baths, TV and air-conditioning. Walk to 25 Wright masterpieces.

| | | | |
|---|---|---|---|
| 1. No Smoking | 5. Tennis Available | 9. Credit Cards Accepted | 13. Lunch Available | 17. Shared Bath |
| 2. No Pets | 6. Golf Available | 10. Personal Checks Accepted | 14. Public Transportation | 18. Afternoon Tea |
| 3. No Children | 7. Swiming Available | 11. Off Season Rates | 15. Reservations Necessary | ★ Commissions given |
| 4. Senior Citizen Rates | 8. Skiing Available | 12. Dinner Available | 16. Private Bath | to Travel Agents |

# ILLINOIS

## Peoria

Giles, Ruth
1506 W. Alta Rd., 61615
(309) 243-5977

**Amenities:** 10,15,17
**Breakfast:** C.

**Dbl. Oc.:** $30.00
**Sgl. Oc.:** $25.00
**Child:** $5.00

**Ruth's Bed & Breakfast**—Private home. Guest rooms with shared bath. Family atmosphere. Children welcome. Five acres to roam. Twenty minutes or less from city attractions. Nearby family restaurants.

## Petersburg

Carmody, Pat & Mike
207 So. 12th St., 62675
(217) 632-2350

**Amenities:** 1,2,5,6,10,17
**Breakfast:** F.

**Dbl. Oc.:** $53.00
**Sgl. Oc.:** $40.00 - $42.40
**Third Person:** $10.60
**Child:** $10.60

**Carmody's Clare Inn**—Built in 1874 and lovingly restored. Antiques re-create the ambience of yesteryear. Petersburg is adjacent to New Salem, where Lincoln served as postmaster and wooed Ann Rutledge. Lincoln's home, law office and tomb are 20 milesaway in Springfield.

## Prairie du Rocher *

Kennedy, Jan
#2 Duclos & Main
P.O. Box 163, 62277
(618) 284-3463

**Amenities:** 1,2,4,9,12,13,15,16
**Breakfast:** F.
**Dbl. Oc.:** 58.00 - $68.88
**Sgl. Oc.:** $45.00
**Third Person:** $42.00
**Child:** under 10 yrs. - $10.00

**La Maison Du Rocher Country Inn**—Come and join us in a step back through history to a French Victorian era — when hospitality to guests was served with grace and flair. Dine in an elegant country atmosphere. Shop our unique handcrafted gift display with one-of-a-kind items.

## Sycamore

Petersen, Donna & Howard
Route 2, Box 154
Quigley Rd., 60178
(815) 895-5386

**Amenities:** 1,2,5,6,7,10,
15,16
**Breakfast:** F.

**Dbl. Oc.:** $37.10 - $58.30
**Sgl. Oc.:** $37.10 - $47.70
**Third Person:** $10.00
**Child:** under 10 yrs. - $5.00

**Country Charm Inn**—A three-story farmhouse on a tree-topped knoll. Sunken fireplace, loft library, large screen TV viewing area, breakfast in formal dining room or on cozy front porch. Roam the farm, pet the animals and meet Champ, the trickhorse. Howard and Donna offer warmth and friendliness.

| | | | |
|---|---|---|---|
| 1. No Smoking | 5. Tennis Available | 9. Credit Cards Accepted | 13. Lunch Available | 17. Shared Bath |
| 2. No Pets | 6. Golf Available | 10. Personal Checks Accepted | 14. Public Transportation | 18. Afternoon Tea |
| 3. No Children | 7. Swiming Available | 11. Off Season Rates | 15. Reservations Necessary | ★ Commissions given |
| 4. Senior Citizen Rates | 8. Skiing Available | 12. Dinner Available | 16. Private Bath | to Travel Agents |

## *Wheaton*

Shipanik, Judy
301 W. Roosevelt Rd., 60187
(708) 690-2600

**Amenities:** 2,4,5,6,8,9,10,14,15,16
**Breakfast:** F.
**Dbl. Oc.:** $109.89 - $177.60
**Sgl. Oc.:** $109.89 - $177.60
**Third Person:** $16.65

**Wheaton Inn**—Exquisitely appointed in the tradition of Williamsburg. Each of the guest rooms has a distinctive personality. Eleven rooms have gas fireplaces and every room has an adjoining bath, many with jacuzzi tubs, all with European towel warmers.

| | | | | |
|---|---|---|---|---|
| 1. No Smoking | 5. Tennis Available | 9. Credit Cards Accepted | 13. Lunch Available | 17. Shared Bath |
| 2. No Pets | 6. Golf Available | 10. Personal Checks Accepted | 14. Public Transportation | 18. Afternoon Tea |
| 3. No Children | 7. Swiming Available | 11. Off Season Rates | 15. Reservations Necessary | ★ Commissions given |
| 4. Senior Citizen Rates | 8. Skiing Available | 12. Dinner Available | 16. Private Bath | to Travel Agents |

# *INDIANA*

## *The Hoosier State*

Capital: Indianapolis
Statehood: December 11, 1816; the 9th state
State Motto: Crossroads of America
State Song: "On the Banks of the Wabash"
State Bird: Cardinal
State Flower: Peony
State Tree: Tulip Tree

Indiana is a great steel producing state. Gary is its major industrial city, close to Lake Michigan. It produces steel products for the automobile industry. Indiana has always had a penchant for cars and their capacity for speed. This goes back to the late 1800's and the beginning of the Indianapolis races. These races continue even today, bringing thousands of racing enthusiasts here every Memorial Day to once again experience the thrill of the powerful racing machine.

Yet, Indiana has another side. In the southern hills of this state are those who live on quiet farms independent of everyone, content to do what strikes their fancy, from beekeeping to arts and crafts. This is a state that is very much Americana.

The Indianian likes to celebrate holidays, loves parades and picnics. He is neighborly and invites tourists to come and enjoy his state with him.

The weather most of the year is warm and enjoyable. Winter months get their share of the snow and cold.

# INDIANA

## Angola *

Goranson, Betsey
RR 6, Box 273, 46703
(219) 665-2690

**Amenities:** 1,2,9,10,15,16,17
**Breakfast:** C.

**Dbl. Oc.:** $40.00 & up
**Sgl. Oc.:** $29.00 & up
**Third Person:** $5.00
**Child:** under 2 yrs. -
    no charge

**Sycamore Hill Bed And Breakfast**—Exit 48 of I-69, seven miles south of the junction of I-80I-90 and I-69. Two-story colonial pillared home. Tucked away amid rolling meadows with a shady back yard. Nearby canoeing, fishing, tobogganing and cross-country skiing. Six-minute drive to state park.

## Beverly Shores *

Arobine, Pearl
Lake Front Dr., 46301
(219) 879-9120

**Amenities:** 1,7,11,12
**Breakfast:** C.

**Dbl. Oc.:** $60.00
**Sgl. Oc.:** $60.00
**Third Person:** $40.00

**Stoney Point**—At the water's edge. Enjoy the beach in summer and the shore in winter. Nautical decor.

## Chesterton

Wilk, Timothy
350 Indian Boundary, 46304
(219) 926-5781

**Amenities:** 2,3,5,6,7,8,9,10,
    12,13,15,16,18
**Breakfast:** F.

**Dbl. Oc.:** $71.00 - $82.50
**Sgl. Oc.:** $66.00 - $77.00
**Third Person:** $11.00

**Gray Goose Inn**—Gracious hospitality in dunes country. A charming English country house among towering oaks on private lake. Some rooms with fireplace. Near I-94 and I-80. Trails, boats and bikes.

## Clinton *

Savage, Laura & Lou
424 Blackman St., 47842
(317) 832-2762

**Amenities:** 2,6,15
**Breakfast:** C.

**Dbl. Oc.:** $47.25
**Sgl. Oc.:** $47.25
**Child:** under 18 yrs. -
    $10.00

**Pentreath House**—Edwardian elegance and Hoosier hospitality join forces! Relax on the front porch or sit by the fieplace. Two of three rooms have private baths. Walk downtown to shops and restaurants downtown. Close to scenic Parke Co., Indiana State University, St. Mary's and much more.

---

| | | | |
|---|---|---|---|
| 1. No Smoking | 5. Tennis Available | 9. Credit Cards Accepted | 13. Lunch Available | 17. Shared Bath |
| 2. No Pets | 6. Golf Available | 10. Personal Checks Accepted | 14. Public Transportation | 18. Afternoon Tea |
| 3. No Children | 7. Swiming Available | 11. Off Season Rates | 15. Reservations Necessary | ★ Commissions given |
| 4. Senior Citizen Rates | 8. Skiing Available | 12. Dinner Available | 16. Private Bath | to Travel Agents |

## Corydon

Wiseman, Blain H.
P.O. Box 95
Capitol and Chestnut Sts.,, 47112
(812) 738-2020, (812) 738-7430

**Amenities:** 1,2,5,6,7,9,10,11, 16

**Breakfast:** F.

**Dbl. Oc.:** $66.00 - $102.00
**Sgl. Oc.:** $66.00 - $102.00
**Third Person:** $15.00

**Kintner House Inn**—Listed on *National Register of Historic Places*. Located in historic downtown Corydon. Unique shops, fine restaurants, antique malls and horse-drawn carriage rides. Excursion train, village blacksmith and art glass factory are within walking distance.

## Crawfordsville *

Hardwick, John
3729 Old S.R. 32 W., 47933
(317) 362-5864

**Amenities:** 1,2,3,9,10,15,16, 17

**Breakfast:** C.

**Dbl. Oc.:** $47.50
**Sgl. Oc.:** $45.00
**Third Person:** $2.50

**Yount's Mill Inn**—A traditional bed and breakfast. Historic home on 10 acres along Sugar Creek. Listed in the *National Register of Historic Places* and site of the Yount Woolen Mills. Many antiques, including the dress Grandma wore when she eloped. Convenient to Wabash and Donnelys.

## Huntington *

Gernand, Jean
326 So. Jefferson, 46750
(219) 356-4218, (219) 356-9215

**Amenities:** 1,2,10,12,13,16,17, 18

**Breakfast:** F.

**Dbl. Oc.:** $42.00
**Sgl. Oc.:** $36.75
**Third Person:** $5.25
**Child:** under 8 yrs. - $3.15

**Purviance House Bed & Breakfast**—An 1859 Italianate/Greek Revival listed in the *National Register of Historic Places*. Lovingly restored and decorated. Comfy beds, TV, books, complimentary snacks; beverages. Near nature trails, lakes, and golf. On SR 5 and U.S. 224, just off I-69 and US 24 near Ft. Wayne.

## Indianapolis *

Morris, Joan H.
7161 Edgewater Pl., 46240
(317) 257-2660

**Amenities:** 1,2,3,15,16,18
**Breakfast:** F.

**Dbl. Oc.:** $60.50 - $77.00
**Sgl. Oc.:** $55.00 - $71.50
**Third Person:** $20.00

**The Nuthatch Bed And Breakfast**—B&B home in a resort-like setting, minutes north of downtown Indianapolis. A 1920's French country cottage with arched windows and leaded glass doors. The Nuthatch overlooks scenic White River. Romantic hideaway. Exciting breakfasts. Rates change for 500 Mile Race and NCAA.

| | | | |
|---|---|---|---|
| 1. No Smoking | 5. Tennis Available | 9. Credit Cards Accepted | 13. Lunch Available | 17. Shared Bath |
| 2. No Pets | 6. Golf Available | 10. Personal Checks Accepted | 14. Public Transportation | 18. Afternoon Tea |
| 3. No Children | 7. Swiming Available | 11. Off Season Rates | 15. Reservations Necessary | ★ Commissions given |
| 4. Senior Citizen Rates | 8. Skiing Available | 12. Dinner Available | 16. Private Bath | to Travel Agents |

## Indianapolis

Whitten, Loretta
5214 E. 20th Pl., 46218
(317) 356-3149

**Amenities:** 1,2,3,10,14,15,16, 18
**Breakfast:** F.

**Dbl. Oc.:** $49.50
**Sgl. Oc.:** $44.00

**Friendliness With A Flair**—Public transportation every half hour. Thirty minutes from the heart of the city. Two modern and tastefully furnished rooms. Complete breakfast served in a glassed in area. Tranquil wooded surroundings. Table games available.

## Jasper *

Roach, Gail
RR 3, Box 168, 47546
(812) 695-4500

**Amenities:** 1,15,17
**Breakfast:** C.

**Dbl. Oc.:** $45.00
**Sgl. Oc.:** $40.00
**Third Person:** $10.00
**Child:** under 6 yrs. - $8.00

**The Artist's Studio Bed & Breakfast**—A spacious 1920's bungalow with oak floors and wood-work, period furniture and antiques. Home of watercolor artist Gail Roach. Close to antique shops, Archabbey, Patoka Lake, Holiday World and Lincoln Land. Local art on display. Enjoy the rolling hills of southern Indiana.

## Koontz Lake *

Davison, Jan & Les
7514 No. Hwy. 23, 46574
(219) 586-7090

**Amenities:** 2,5,6,7,8,10,11,15, 17,18
**Breakfast:** C.

**Dbl. Oc.:** $52.50
**Sgl. Oc.:** $42.00
**Third Person:** $10.50
**Child:** under 10 yrs. - $5.25

**Koontz House Bed & Breakfast**—Come and enjoy the beautiful home Sam Koontz built on the west edge of Koontz Lake circa 1880. Large bedrooms. Color TV. Air conditioning. Swimming. Enjoy the lake. 23 miles to South Bend. 12 miles to Potatoe Creek State Park. Walk to lakeside restaurant, marina and antique shops.

## La Grange

Billman, Gloria & Duane
212 W. Factory
P.O. Box #5, 46761
(219) 463-4227

**Amenities:** 1,2,3,5,6,9,10,15, 16,17
**Breakfast:** C.

**Dbl. Oc.:** $61.95 - $72.45
**Sgl. Oc.:** $40.95
**Third Person:** $26.25

**The 1886 Inn Bed & Breakfast**—Very unique, yet affordable. Only 10 minutes east of the Shipshewana Auction and Flea Market Factory. Home of the annual Steam and Gas Engine Show. Known as Indiana's Amish country. Tour the homestead and learn the authentic history and beliefs of the Amish and Mennonites.

| | | | |
|---|---|---|---|
| 1. No Smoking | 5. Tennis Available | 9. Credit Cards Accepted | 13. Lunch Available | 17. Shared Bath |
| 2. No Pets | 6. Golf Available | 10. Personal Checks Accepted | 14. Public Transportation | 18. Afternoon Tea |
| 3. No Children | 7. Swiming Available | 11. Off Season Rates | 15. Reservations Necessary | ★ Commissions given |
| 4. Senior Citizen Rates | 8. Skiing Available | 12. Dinner Available | 16. Private Bath | to Travel Agents |

## Ligonier

Blue, Doris & Ronald
508 So. Cavin St., 46767
(219) 894-3668

**Amenities:** 1,2,3,9,10,16,18
**Breakfast:** C.

**Dbl. Oc.:** $47.25 - $57.75
**Sgl. Oc.:** $42.00
**Third Person:** $20.00

**Solomon Mier Manor Bed And Breakfast**—This home is in the *National Register of Historic Places*. Located in the center of Amish country. A Queen Anne classic completely furnished with antiques of the era. Enjoy the history of Ligonier and browse the antique shop. Relax and step back into history with us!

## Middlebury

Eash, Diane & Carl
205 S. Main St., 46540
(219) 825-9666

**Amenities:** 1,2,6,9,10,16
**Breakfast:** C.
**Dbl. Oc.:** $63.00
**Sgl. Oc.:** $57.75
**Third Person:** $10.50
**Child:** $10.50

**Varns Guest House**—Circa 1898, this fourth-generation family home has been lovingly restored. Features five bedrooms with private baths. Located in the heart of Amish country. Enjoy many nearby fine restaurants and quaint shops. Relax on the porch swing as horse-drawn buggies clip along.

## Middlebury

Swarm, Treva & Herb
Box 1191, 46540
(219) 825-5023

**Amenities:** 1,2,6,8,9,10,
15,16,17
**Breakfast:** F.

**Dbl. Oc.:** $49.95 - $60.00
**Sgl. Oc.:** $39.95
**Third Person:** $15.00

**Bee Hive Bed & Breakfast**—Located in an Amish community. Easy access to Indiana Turnpike. Snuggle under handmade quilts in a country home and wake up to the smell of muffins baking. Come prepared to relax and enjoy a quiet evening with a glass of ice tea.

## Middlebury

Yoder, Evelyn
504 So. Main,
P.O. Box 1396, 46540
(219) 825-2378

**Amenities:** 1,2,7,9,10,11,
15,17
**Breakfast:** F.

**Dbl. Oc.:** $52.50
**Sgl. Oc.:** $42.00
**Third Person:** $15.75
**Child:** under 12 yrs. -
$10.50

**Yoder's Zimmer Mit Furstuck Haus**—The Yoders enjoy sharing their Amish-Mennonite heritage in their beautiful Crystal Valley home located in the heart of Indiana's Amish country near the Shipshewana Flea Market. Their home is filled with various collections and antiques.

| | | | |
|---|---|---|---|
| 1. No Smoking | 5. Tennis Available | 9. Credit Cards Accepted | 13. Lunch Available | 17. Shared Bath |
| 2. No Pets | 6. Golf Available | 10. Personal Checks Accepted | 14. Public Transportation | 18. Afternoon Tea |
| 3. No Children | 7. Swiming Available | 11. Off Season Rates | 15. Reservations Necessary | ★ Commissions given |
| 4. Senior Citizen Rates | 8. Skiing Available | 12. Dinner Available | 16. Private Bath | to Travel Agents |

# INDIANA

## Nashville

Suanne, Shirley
St. Rd. 135 N., R.R. 3
Box 62, 47448
(812) 988-4537

**Amenities:** 2,9,10,15,17
**Breakfast:** C.

**Dbl. Oc.:** $66.00 - $71.50
**Sgl. Oc.:** $55.00
**Third Person:** $11.00
**Child:** under 12 yrs. -
    no charge

**Plain and Fancy/Traveler's Accommodations And Country Store**—A turn -of-the-century log home on wooded acerage, within walking distance to Nashville and Brown County's renowned arts and craft center. Antique decor. Nearby country store, te nnis, golf, swimming and skiing. A quiet weekend retreat.

## Paoli *

Cornwell, Terry
210 No. Gospel, 47454
(812) 723-4677

**Amenities:** 5,6,7,8,9,10,11,
    15,16
**Breakfast:** F.

**Dbl. Oc.:** $63.00
**Sgl. Oc.:** $47.25

**Braxtan House Inn**—Thomas Braxtan, son of the original Quaker settlers, was a business man who built this 1839 Victorian home. Oak, cherry, chestnut and maple woodwork are featured. The inn is furnished in antiques and highlighted with stained glass windows.

## Peru

Henderson, Zoyla & Carm
54 No. Hood, 46970
(317) 472-7151

**Amenities:** 1,3,5,6,7,8,9,10,
    15,16
**Breakfast:** F.

**Dbl. Oc.:** $60.00 - $68.00
**Sgl. Oc.:** $55.00 - $60.00
**Third Person$10.00**

**Rosewood Mansion - A Bed & Breakfast Inn**—Only three blocks from the center of town, this 1862 mansion surrounds you in elegance with its grand staircase, oak paneled library and oval dining room. The large guest rooms are decorated in antiques. Nearby are many sport activities and attractions such as the Air Force Museum.

## Rockport

Ahnell, Emil
Third at Walnut, 47635
(812) 649-2664

**Amenities:** 10,12,13,15,16
**Breakfast:** C.

**Dbl.Oc.:** $35.00 - $50.00
**Sgl. Oc.:** $32.00 - $40.00
**Third Person:** $5.00
**Child:** under 12 yrs. -
    no charge

**The Rockport Inn**—Built in 1855 with hand-hewn logs, much of the original structure is still intact. The downstairs contains four dining rooms seating from eight to 40 people. On the second floor are six guest rooms, each with a private bath, cable TV and air conditioning

| | | | | |
|---|---|---|---|---|
| 1. No Smoking | 5. Tennis Available | 9. Credit Cards Accepted | 13. Lunch Available | 17. Shared Bath |
| 2. No Pets | 6. Golf Available | 10. Personal Checks Accepted | 14. Public Transportation | 18. Afternoon Tea |
| 3. No Children | 7. Swiming Available | 11. Off Season Rates | 15. Reservations Necessary | ★ Commissions given |
| 4. Senior Citizen Rates | 8. Skiing Available | 12. Dinner Available | 16. Private Bath | to Travel Agents |

# INDIANA

## Shipshewana

Miller, Ruth
R. 2, Box 592, 46565
(219) 768-4221

**Amenities:** 1,2,6,9,10,15,17
**Breakfast:** C.

**Dbl. Oc.:** $63.00
**Sgl. Oc.:** $31.50
**Child:** under 2 yrs. -
    no charge

**Greenmeadow Ranch**—Northern Indiana's most charming bed and breakfast farmstead. Two miles from the Amish-Mennonite Visitors Center, Shipshewana Auction; many shops and attractions. A great place to relax. Animal friends, posies, bluebirds, gazebo, dolls, wagon, teddies, buggies and antiques.

## Syracuse

Kennedy, Jean & Robert
R# 4, Box 208-A, 46567
(219) 457-4714

**Amenities:** 1,2,6,7,9,17
**Breakfast:** F.
**Dbl. Oc.:** $55.00 - $60.00
**Sgl. Oc.:** $46.75

**Anchor Inn Bed & Breakfast**—Centrally located between South Bend and Fort Wayne, in the heart of Indiana's lake country. Lake Wawasee, Amish area and antique shops are nearby. Five guest rooms. Open year round.

## Tippecanoe

Bessinger, Betty
4588 S.R. 110
(219) 223-3288

**Amenities:** 1,2,7,10,12,
          13,15,16
**Breakfast:** F.

**Dbl. Oc.:** $47.25
**Sgl. Oc.:** $42.00
**Third Person:** $7.50

**Bessinger's Hillfarm Wildlife Regufe Bed And Breakfast**—This cozy log home overlooks the water area with 39 islands,. It has 2 guest rooms with private baths, plus a hide-away bed in the loft. Picnic gazebo, hiking and canoeing available.

## Vevay

Hine, Leo
RR #3, P.O. Box 191, 47043
(812) 427-2900

**Amenities:** 4,10,15,17,18
**Breakfast:** C.

**Dbl. Oc.:** $47.50 - $68.25
**Sgl. Oc.:** $$7.50 - $68.25
**Third Person:** $10.00

**Captains Quarters B&B**—Enjoy a restful night in a stately home built by riverboat captain Thomas T. Wright in 1838. It overlooks the beautiful Ohio River. Wake up to coffee, tea or hot chocolate served with delicious breakfast breads and fruit. Visit the historic towns of Vevay and Madison.

| | | | |
|---|---|---|---|
| 1. No Smoking | 5. Tennis Available | 9. Credit Cards Accepted | 13. Lunch Available | 17. Shared Bath |
| 2. No Pets | 6. Golf Available | 10. Personal Checks Accepted | 14. Public Transportation | 18. Afternoon Tea |
| 3. No Children | 7. Swiming Available | 11. Off Season Rates | 15. Reservations Necessary | ★ Commissions given |
| 4. Senior Citizen Rates | 8. Skiing Available | 12. Dinner Available | 16. Private Bath | to Travel Agents |

## *Washington*

Graham, David B.
101 W. Maple St., 47501
(812) 254-5562

Amenities: 4,10,15,16
Breakfast: C.
Dbl.Oc.: $75.00
Sgl.Oc.: $40.00

**Mimi's House**—A unique home filled with the furnishings and memorablilia of the Graham family, noted glass, truck and automobile manufacturers. Experience the 1920's and 1930's. It is listed in the *National Register of Historic Places* because of its history and prarie-style architecture.

| | | | | |
|---|---|---|---|---|
| 1. No Smoking | 5. Tennis Available | 9. Credit Cards Accepted | 13. Lunch Available | 17. Shared Bath |
| 2. No Pets | 6. Golf Available | 10. Personal Checks Accepted | 14. Public Transportation | 18. Afternoon Tea |
| 3. No Children | 7. Swiming Available | 11. Off Season Rates | 15. Reservations Necessary | ★ Commissions given |
| 4. Senior Citizen Rates | 8. Skiing Available | 12. Dinner Available | 16. Private Bath | to Travel Agents |

# IOWA

## The Hawkeye State

Capitol: Des Moines
Statehood: December 28, 1846; the 29th state
State Motto: Our Liberties We Prize and
            Our Rights We Will Maintain
State Song: "The Song of Iowa"
State Bird: Eastern Goldfinch
State Flower: Wild Rose
State Tree: Oak

Iowa is one of the greatest farming states in the United States, sometimes called the "Corn State", or "The Land Where The Tall Corn Grows". Back in the mid-1800's, many young people heeded the advice of Horace Greeley to "Go west, young man, go west", and they did. It was the beginning of a great love affair between man and the soil. Some of the most productive corn farms are here, and some of the best-fed livestock.

Iowa has many lakes and streams that offer fine fishing and swimming, but the greatest excitement of the year is the annual Iowa State Fair. Farmers from all over Iowa gather together to show their personal farm prizes, from hogs to preserves, each one competing for the coveted Blue Ribbon.

Herbert Hoover, our 31st president, was born in West Branch, Iowa.

# IOWA

## Atlantic

Stensvad, Barbara & Bruce
1409 Chestnut St., 50022
(712) 243-5652

**Amenities:** 1,2,3,5,6,7,9,10,
12,16,17,18
**Breakfast:** F.

**Dbl. Oc.:** $57.20 - $78.00
**Sgl. Oc.:** $49.09 - $70.72

**Chestnut Charm Bed & Breakfast**—An enchanting 1898 Victorian mansion in serene surroundings. Five elegant guest rooms, most with private bath. Two sunrooms and fountained patio. Wake up to the aroma of gourmet coffee. Come, relax and be pampered in style!

## Cartha

Kash, Martha
620 West, 500
(515) 377-2586

**Amenities:** 1,4,10,16,18
**Breakfast:** F.

**Dbl. Oc.:** $36.74
**Sgl. Oc.:** $31.50
**Third Person:** $10.00
**Child:** under 5 yrs. - $5.00

**Martha's Vineyard B&B**—Gracious country living near Ames and Des Moines. Third-generation home restored with family treasures. Enjoy nature on a working farm. A full Iowan breakfast with home-grown and homemade foods. Like a visit to Grandmother's home.

## Des Moines

Walser, Elaine
5938 S.W. McKinley Ave., 5032
(515) 285-4135

**Amenities:** 4,5,6,7,10,15,17
**Breakfast:** C.

**Dbl. Oc.:** $46.80
**Sgl. Oc.:** $36.40
**Third Person:** $20.80
**Child:** under 12 yrs. - $5.00

**Brownswood Bed And Breakfast**—Escape to Brownswood to find an acreage with quiet country charm. Easy access to historic Valley Junction, living-history farms, fine restaurants and shops. Enjoy indoor trampoline. Ski and walk in Browns woods. Air and water purification systems.

## Dubuque *

Delaney, Michelle
1492 Locust St., 52001
(319) 557-1492

**Amenities:** 1,9,10,11,16
**Breakfast:** F.
**Dbl. Oc.:** $49.05 - $81.75
**Sgl. Oc.:** $43.60 - $76.30
**Third Person:** $10.90
**Child:** under 10 yrs. - $5.45

**The Richards House**—An 1883 stick-style mansion. Original interior features over 80 stained-glass windows, seven varieties of woodwork, embossed wallcoverings and period furnishings. Working fireplaces and queen-size beds in guest rooms. Mid-week discounts.

| | | | |
|---|---|---|---|
| 1. No Smoking | 5. Tennis Available | 9. Credit Cards Accepted | 13. Lunch Available | 17. Shared Bath |
| 2. No Pets | 6. Golf Available | 10. Personal Checks Accepted | 14. Public Transportation | 18. Afternoon Tea |
| 3. No Children | 7. Swiming Available | 11. Off Season Rates | 15. Reservations Necessary | ★ Commissions given |
| 4. Senior Citizen Rates | 8. Skiing Available | 12. Dinner Available | 16. Private Bath | to Travel Agents |

# IOWA

## Greenfield

Wilson, Wendy & Henry
RR 1, Box 132, 50849
(515) 743-2031

Amenities:1,7,10,15,16
Breakfast: F.

Dbl. Oc.: $78.00
Sgl. Oc.: $78.00
Third Person: $10.00

**The Wilson Home**—Two beautiful and spacious rooms open onto large, indoor pool and deck areas. Enjoy poolside breakfast year round. Hunters - call for information on pheasant hunting. Aunique Iowa bed and breakfast experience.

## Homestead

Janda, Sheila & Don
Main St., 52236
(319) 622-3937

**Amenities:** 1,5,6,7,8,9,10,11,16,18
**Breakfast:** C.
**Dbl. Oc.:** $39.18 - $65.35
**Sgl. Oc.:** $39.18 - $65.35
**Third Person:** $5.45
**Child:** under 6 yrs. - $2.18

**Die Heimat Country Inn**—for "The home place" is decorated in an old-world way with the Amana handmade walnut and cherry furniture, quilts and many heirlooms throughout. Legend has it that it was the original stagecoach stop for the colonies.

## Iowa City

Haverkamp, Dorothy & Clarence
619 No. Linn St., 52245
(319) 337-4363

**Amenities**1,2,10,14,17
**Breakfast:** F.

**Dbl. Oc.:** $32.45 - $43.10
**Sgl. Oc.:** $27.00 - $32.45
**Third Person:** $5.00
**Child:** $5.00

**Haverkamps' Linn Street Homestay**—A large and comfortable 1908 Edwardian-style home filled with antiques and collections. Front porch with swing. One mile south of I-80, Exit 244. Close to University of Iowa campus. Short drive to Amana Colonies, Kalona, West Branch and Cedar Rapids.

## Marengo *

Walker, Loy
I-80, Exit 216
R.R. 1, Box 82, 52301
(319) 642-7787

**Amenities:** 1,2,5,6,7,10,12,15,
16,17
**Breakfast:** F.

**Dbl. Oc.:** $49,05 - $55.40
**Sgl. Oc.:** $38.15 - $43.60
**Third Person:** $16.35
**Child:** under 12 yrs. -
$10.00

**Loy's Bed And Breakfast**—A beautiful farm home on a large grain and hog farm three miles off I-80. Farm tour, recreation room and hunting. Visit the Amana Colonies, settled by inspirationalists; Kalona, an Amish community; Iowa City and Cedar Rapids. Hospitality at its best!

---

| | | | |
|---|---|---|---|
| 1. No Smoking | 5. Tennis Available | 9. Credit Cards Accepted | 13. Lunch Available | 17. Shared Bath |
| 2. No Pets | 6. Golf Available | 10. Personal Checks Accepted | 14. Public Transportation | 18. Afternoon Tea |
| 3. No Children | 7. Swiming Available | 11. Off Season Rates | 15. Reservations Necessary | ★ Commissions given |
| 4. Senior Citizen Rates | 8. Skiing Available | 12. Dinner Available | 16. Private Bath | to Travel Agents |

# IOWA

## McGregor

| | | |
|---|---|---|
| Lange, Rita | **Amenities:** 1,2,5,6,7,8,9,10, | **Dbl. Oc.:** $55.00 |
| 112 Main St., 52157 | 14,15,16 | **Sgl. Oc.:** $55.00 |
| (319) 873-3501 | **Breakfast:** C. | **Third Person:** $10.00 |
| | | **Child:** under 5 yrs. - |
| | | no charge |

**Rivers Edge Bed And Breakfast**—Overlooks the Mississippi River. Enjoy McGregor's breathtaking scenery, charming shops and quaint restaurants within easy walking distance. Nearby boating, skiing and hiking. Comfortable and spacious home with charming antiques and memorabilia. Full kitchen.

## Middle Amana

| | | |
|---|---|---|
| Hahn, Lynn | **Amenities:** 2,6,9,10,16 | **Dbl. Oc.:** $41.42 |
| P.O. Box 124, 52307 | **Breakfast:** C. | **Sgl. Oc.:** $38.15 |
| (319) 622-3029 | | **Third Person:** $5.00 |
| | | **Child:** $2.00 |

**Dusk To Dawn Bed And Breakfast Inn**—A unique combination of the traditional Amana setting with a touch of modern living. Located in historic Middle Amana. Join us on our spacious deck. Greenhouse. Jacuzzi. Private accommodatons available for six to 16 guests.

## Middle Amana

| | | |
|---|---|---|
| Rettig, Ray | **Amenities:** 1,2,3,6,7,10, | **Dbl. Oc.:** $45.00 - $50.00 |
| P.O. Box 5, 52307 | 16,17 | **Sgl. Oc.:** $45.00 - $50.00 |
| (319) 622-3386 | **Breakfast:** C. | |

**The Rettig House**—An old communal Amana kitchen house. Tastefully decorated with family heirlooms and authentic Amana antiques. Courtyard, porches, lawn swing, patio and park-like lawn. Tranquil atmosphere and charming old-world ambience make us distinctly different.

## Missouri Valley *

| | | |
|---|---|---|
| Strub, Electa | **Amenities:** 1,2,6,7,8,9,10,12, | **Dbl. Oc.:** $56.00 |
| RR 3, Box 129, 51555 | 13,17,18 | **Sgl. Oc.:** $51.00 |
| (712) 642-2418 | **Breakfast:** F. | **Child:** under 2 yrs. - $10.00 |

**Apple Orchard Inn Bed And Breakfast**—Relax and renew in tranquil couuntry setting. Stroll through the 26-acre apple orchard and pioneer museum "next door." View scenic and unique Loess Hills and Boyer Valley from your window. Three rooms, three baths, jacuzzi and air-conditioning. Nearby antiquing.

| | | | | |
|---|---|---|---|---|
| 1. No Smoking | 5. Tennis Available | 9. Credit Cards Accepted | 13. Lunch Available | 17. Shared Bath |
| 2. No Pets | 6. Golf Available | 10. Personal Checks Accepted | 14. Public Transportation | 18. Afternoon Tea |
| 3. No Children | 7. Swiming Available | 11. Off Season Rates | 15. Reservations Necessary | ★ Commissions given |
| 4. Senior Citizen Rates | 8. Skiing Available | 12. Dinner Available | 16. Private Bath | to Travel Agents |

## Newton *

Owen, Kay
629 1st. Ave. E., 50208
(515) 792-6833

**Amenities:** 1,9,10,12,16
**Breakfast:** F.
**Dbl. Oc.:** $60.00 - $165.00
**Sgl. Oc.:** $60.00 - $165.00
**Third Person:** $20.80
**Child:** $20.80

**LaCorsette Maison Inn**—Bed and breakfast at its most gracious! Contemporary comforts blend with turn-of-the-century charm in a mission-style "le mansion." Charming French bed chambers and beckoning hearths. Listed in the *National Register of Historic Places*. Gourmet dining. Off I-80.

## Spencer *

Nichols, Mary
RR 1, Hwy. 71 So., 51301
(712) 332-7719, (712) 332-7719

**Amenities:** 1,5,6,7,8,9,10,13,15,16,18
**Breakfast:** F.
**Dbl. Oc.:** $50.00 - $60.00
**Sgl. Oc.:** $50.00 - $60.00
**Third Person:** $10.00

**Hannah Marie Country Inn**—A country Victorian, air-conditioned, with horse barn available. Close to Iowa's great lakes, Westbend Grotto, golf, antique shops and shopping. Seen in *Innsider*, *Midwest Living, Country Woman and Brides*. Serving lunches and afternoon teas to public. Open March to mid-December.

## Tipton *

Mitchell, Dolores
508 E. Fourth St., 52772
(319) 886-2633

**Amenities:** 5,6,7,8,10,12, 15,17
**Breakfast:** F.

**Dbl. Oc.:** $57.20
**Sgl. Oc.:** $46.80
**Third Person:** $10.00
**Child:** under 12 yrs. - $5.00

**Victorian House Of Tipton**—Step back into another era as you enter this 16-room Eastlake-style home built in 1883. Unusual architectural features and antiques. Centrally located in eastern Iowa near historic and natural attractions. Nine miles north ofI-80 at Exit 267 to Tipton.

---

| | | | | |
|---|---|---|---|---|
| 1. No Smoking | 5. Tennis Available | 9. Credit Cards Accepted | 13. Lunch Available | 17. Shared Bath |
| 2. No Pets | 6. Golf Available | 10. Personal Checks Accepted | 14. Public Transportation | 18. Afternoon Tea |
| 3. No Children | 7. Swiming Available | 11. Off Season Rates | 15. Reservations Necessary | ★ Commissions given |
| 4. Senior Citizen Rates | 8. Skiing Available | 12. Dinner Available | 16. Private Bath | to Travel Agents |

# KANSAS

## The Sunflower State

Capitol: Topeka
Statehood: January 29, 1861; the 34th state
State Motto: To The Stars Through Difficulties
State Song: "Home On The Range"
State Bird: Western Meadow Lark
State Flower: Sunflower
State Tree: Cottonwood

Kansas is known as The Wheat State and The Breadbasket of America. It leads all other states in the production of wheat. The farmer is cowboy and rancher who grows cattle and grain at the same time. The wheat at harvest time stands so tall that it makes the land look like a huge sea of gold. It is a beautiful sight to see. In Kansas, wheat harvesting is the biggest part of farming. Machines roll through the fields, cutting and producing bushels of grain every minute.

Kansas is also nicknamed Cowboy Capitol of the World, suggesting Kansas' background as a cattle country. One of its most famous cities is Dodge. Visitors can see ruts made by wagons on the Santa Fe Trail. They can visit Pony Express stations and frontier forts, which were built to protect settlers from the Indians. Kansas is proud of its history and tries to keep a bit of it for all to enjoy.

Dwight D. Eisenhower's boyhood home is preserved at Abilene.

## Beloit

Langdon, Lois & Frank
800 Meadowlark Lane, 67420
(913) 738-5869

**Amenities:** 1,3,10,15,16
**Breakfast:** F.

**Dbl. Oc.:** $30.00
**Sgl. Oc.:** $25.00

**Lois' Bed & Breakfast**—West edge of Beloit, corner of Eighth and Meadowlark Lane. Near Waconda Lake. Post rock country — many lovely, native-stone homes and buildings. Newer home in quiet area. Share family living area and at-home atmosphere.

## Columbus

Meriwether, Margaret
322 W. Pine, 66725
(316) 429-2812

**Amenities:** 1,2,5,6,7,9,10,
16,17
**Breakfast:** C.

**Dbl. Oc.:** $32.00 - $43.00
**Sgl. Oc.:** $27.00 - $38.00
**Third Person:** $5.00

**Meriwether House Bed And Breakfast**—Located in beautiful S.E. Kansas, just two hours from Kansas City, Tulsa and Springfield. A quiet cottage filled with antiques and goodies, all for sale. Interior decor shop located within. Excellent fishing area. Small-town "friendliness and peaceful comfort."

## Concordia

Warren-Gully, Carrie
508 W. 7th, 66901
(913) 243-2192

**Amenities:** 1,2,5,6,7,9,10,16,17,18
**Breakfast:** F.
**Dbl. Oc.:** $35.00 - $45.00
**Sgl. Oc.:** $31.50 - $40.50
**Third Person:** $5.00
**Child:** under 10 yrs. - no charge

**Crystle's Bed And Breakfast**—Hospitality and charm overflowing! A beautiful 1880 home with original antiques decorate unique and creative rooms. Enjoy a delicious breakfast and discover historic Concordia. No one can resist Crystle's, where relaxation is served by the arm load!

## Great Bend *

Nitzel, Doris & Dale
Route 5, Box 153, 67530
(316) 793-7527

**Amenities:** 1,5,10,15,17
**Breakfast:** F.

**Dbl. Oc.:** $31.58
**Sgl. Oc.:** $26.31
**Third Person:** $5.26

**Peaceful Acres Bed & Breakfast**—A sprawling farmhouse, working windmill, small livestock, chickens and guineas. Five miles from Great Bend and close to many historical sites. Kitchen available. Children welcome.

---

| | | | |
|---|---|---|---|
| 1. No Smoking | 5. Tennis Available | 9. Credit Cards Accepted | 13. Lunch Available | 17. Shared Bath |
| 2. No Pets | 6. Golf Available | 10. Personal Checks Accepted | 14. Public Transportation | 18. Afternoon Tea |
| 3. No Children | 7. Swiming Available | 11. Off Season Rates | 15. Reservations Necessary | ★ Commissions given |
| 4. Senior Citizen Rates | 8. Skiing Available | 12. Dinner Available | 16. Private Bath | to Travel Agents |

## *Holyrood*

Schepmann, Ron
Route 1, Box 47, 67450
(913) 252-3309

**Amenities:** 1,2,5,6,7,9,10,
16,17
**Breakfast:** F.

**Dbl. Oc.:** $31.28 - $57.35
**Sgl. Oc.:** $26.13 - $52.13
**Third Person:** $10.43
**Child:** under 12 yrs. - $5.22

**Hollyrood House**—Built in 1916, it is located just 1/2 mile off Highway 156 in the center of the breadbasket. Relaxing atmosphere with lily ponds. Steak-and-eggs breakfast. Antiques, craftshops, porcelain dolls, art studio, wildlife, birdwatching, fishing and hunting.

## *Lyons*

Brubaker, Janice & Hugh
400 E. Commercial, 67554
(316) 257-5248

**Amenities:** 1,6,7,12,13,15,17
**Breakfast:** F.

**Dbl. Oc.:** $35.00
**Sgl. Oc.:** $35.00
**Third Person:** $10.00
**Child:** $5.00

**Quivira House**—"Heart of Indian country," antique shopping,Coronado/Quivira historical museum, Kanopolis Reservoir and Comosphere Lindsborg's "Little Sweden." Visit Central Kansas and explore.

## *Newton*

Goering, Norma
307 W. Broadway, 67114
(316) 283-2045

**Amenities:** 1,2,9,10,15,16,17
**Breakfast:** F.

**Dbl. Oc.:** $40.00 - $45.00
**Sgl. Oc.:** $35.00 - $40.00
**Child:** under 12 yrs. -
$10.00

**The Hawk House Bed And Breakfast Inn**—Turn-of-the-century elegance and modern-day comfort. Rooms fully furnished with period antiques and appointments. Full access to common rooms as well as many amenities. In the heart of wheatland and close to city center and running/walking trail.

## *Peabody*

Jones, Marilyn & Gary
R.F.D. 2, Box 185, 66866
(316) 983-2815

**Amenities:** 1,5,10,15,16
**Breakfast:** C. Plus

**Dbl. Oc.:** $35.00
**Sgl. Oc.:** $30.00
**Third Person:** $15.00
**Child:** $15.00

**Jones Sheep Farm B&B**—A turn-of-the-century house to yourself at the end of the road surrounded by sheep pasture. No TV and no phone. Peace and quiet. Twin beds, crib and double bed. Completely furnished in style reminiscent of 1930's. Walking distance to historic town at edge of hill.

| | | | | |
|---|---|---|---|---|
| 1. No Smoking | 5. Tennis Available | 9. Credit Cards Accepted | 13. Lunch Available | 17. Shared Bath |
| 2. No Pets | 6. Golf Available | 10. Personal Checks Accepted | 14. Public Transportation | 18. Afternoon Tea |
| 3. No Children | 7. Swiming Available | 11. Off Season Rates | 15. Reservations Necessary | ★ Commissions given |
| 4. Senior Citizen Rates | 8. Skiing Available | 12. Dinner Available | 16. Private Bath | to Travel Agents |

## WaKeeney *

Hendricks, Mary & Dave
Route 1, Box 93, 67672
(913) 743-2644

**Amenities:** 2,6,10,15,16,18
**Breakfast:** F.

**Dbl. Oc.:** $45.00
**Sgl. Oc.:** $40.00
**Third Person:** $10.00

**Thistle Hill Bed & Breakfast**—Located halfway between Kansas City and Denver, 1-1/2 miles from I-70, Exit 120. Modern, two story country ranch home. Porches, fireplace and antiques. Enjoy prairie wildflowers, hunting, farm and ranch fun, beautiful sunsets and serenity of the Kansas prairie.

## Wakefield

Nuttall, Phyllis & Dick
201 Dogwood
P.O. Box 342, 67487
(913) 461-5732

**Amenities:** 5,6,7,10,11,12,17
**Breakfast:** F.

**Dbl. Oc.:** $35.00 - $45.00
**Sgl. Oc.:** $30.00 - $40.00
**Third Person:** $15.00
**Child:** under 10 yrs. - $10.00

**The Rock House Bed'n Breakfast**—Oak warmth. Built in 1914. Gift shop. Three blocks through park to Milford Lake. Across the street from public pool. Fenced patio. Near arboretum and antique shops. Share entire home and craft room. Brochure available.

## Wakefield

Thurlow, Pearl
206 6th,
Route 1, Box 297, 67487
(913) 461-5596

**Amenities:** 1,5,6,7,10,15, 16,17
**Breakfast:** F.

**Dbl. Oc.:** $30.00 - $45.00
**Sgl. Oc.:** $20.00 - $30.00
**Third Person:** $8.00

**Bed 'n' Breakfast — Still Country**—Wakefield, population of 800, on Milford Lake. Excellent getaway, outstanding museum, arboretum, nature trails, sandy beaches, unlisted corners-dolls, quilts and crafts. 80- acre farm with fruit trees. Antiques and Eisenhower Center. Prize-winning pancakes. "Come spend a spell."

## Wichita

Eaton, Roberta
3910 E. Kellogg, 67218
(316) 689-8101

**Amenities:** 2,9,10,15,16
**Breakfast:** C.
**Dbl. Oc.:** $72.31 - $127.94
**Sgl. Oc.:** $55.63 - $105.69
**Third Person:** $16.69
**Child:** $16.69

**Max Paul...An Inn**—Three English Tudor cottages that include 14 rooms furnished with European antiques, featherbeds and cable/HBO. Some suites have fireplace, decks and "tub for two." Exercise room and spa opens onto garden. Centrally located for business, shopping, parks and museums.

| | | | |
|---|---|---|---|
| 1. No Smoking | 5. Tennis Available | 9. Credit Cards Accepted | 13. Lunch Available | 17. Shared Bath |
| 2. No Pets | 6. Golf Available | 10. Personal Checks Accepted | 14. Public Transportation | 18. Afternoon Tea |
| 3. No Children | 7. Swiming Available | 11. Off Season Rates | 15. Reservations Necessary | ★ Commissions given |
| 4. Senior Citizen Rates | 8. Skiing Available | 12. Dinner Available | 16. Private Bath | to Travel Agents |

# KENTUCKY

## *The Blue Grass State*

Capitol: Frankfort
Statehood: January 1, 1792; the 15th state
State Motto: United We Stand, Divided We Fall
State Song: "My Old Kentucky Home"
State Bird: Cardinal
State Flower: Goldenrod
State Tree: Kentucky Coffee Tree


Kentucky is a beautiful and diverse state. Lexington, the hon
of thoroughbred horses and horse farms, provides hundreds
people with work. Churchill Downes is one of Kentucky's bi
gest tourist attractions. During the horse racing season, peop
come from all over the world just for the thrill of seeing the:
beautiful horses compete against each other. This is Old Ke:
tucky at its best!

Southwest Kentucky is an area of caves formed by hug
underground deposits of limestone. One of the caves ofte
visited by tourists is The Mammoth. It streaches out and rur
underground like a suburban city's subway.

The eastern part of Kentucky is Appalachia, named for th
Appalachian Mts. Here people exist differently. Their employ
ment depends almost entirely upon the mining of coal. This i
the most important commodity in this region, and it brings goo
times and bad.

Tobacco growing and bourbon whiskey are also big busines:

Kentucky has a steady influx of tourists because it is such
pretty and interesting state. It also claims to have mild and co
fortable weather most of the time.

## Bardstown *

McCoy, Fran
111 W. Stephen Foster Ave., 40004
(502) 348-5551

**Amenities:** 1,9,10 **Dbl. Oc.:** $70.30
17,18 **Sgl. Oc.:** $59.48
**Breakfast:** C. **Third Person:** $5.00

**JAILER'S INN**—Originally used as a jail from 1819 to 1874. Now completely remodeled and decorated with antiques and Oriental rugs. Lovely landscaped courtyard. Come and spend "time" in our wonderful old jail.

## Bowling Green

Hunter, Dr. Norman & Ronna Lee
659 E. 14th Ave., 42101
(502) 781-3861

**Amenitie** 1,2,3,5,6,7, **Dbl. Oc.:** $50.00
10,11,15,16,17,18 **Sgl. Oc.:** $40.00
**Breakfast:** F.

**Bowling Green Bed & Breakfast**—This grey-shingled home is a historic landmark centrally located near Western Kentucky University, restored town square and restaurants. Relax in lounge, front porch or picnic area. Hosts are a professor and nurse who enjoy travel, photography, antiques, reading and writing.

## Bowling Green *

Livingston, Dr. & Mrs. David
5310 Morgantown Rd., 42101
(502) 843-4846

**Amenities:** 2,4,5,6,7,10,11,12,13,15,
16,17,18
**Breakfast:** F.
**Dbl. Oc.:** $49.50
**Sgl. Oc.:** $39.50
**Third Person:** $10.00
**Child:** under 12 yrs. - $10.00

**Alpine Lodge**—Hansomely decorated with timely and traditional antiques suited to express all the comforts of home. There are 12 spacious rooms that can accommodate up to 19 guests. Visit the area sights of Western Kentucky University, Mammoth Cave, Shakertown, Opryland and museum.

## Carrollton

Gants, Judith
406 HIghland Ave., 41008
(502) 732-4210

**Amenities:** 2,4,5,6,7,8,9,10, **Dbl. Oc.:** $65.40
15,16 **Sgl. Oc.:** $49.05
**Breakfast:** F. **Third Person:** $10.90
**Child:** under 10 yrs. - $5.45

**P.T. Baker House**—Be a pampered guest at a beautifully restored and appointed century-old Victorian home in a charming historic district. Easy walk to antique and craft shops; two miles from statepark; mid-way between Cincinnati and Louisville. A unique experience — an ideal getaway.

| | | | |
|---|---|---|---|
| 1. No Smoking | 5. Tennis Available | 9. Credit Cards Accepted | 13. Lunch Available | 17. Shared Bath |
| 2. No Pets | 6. Golf Available | 10. Personal Checks Accepted | 14. Public Transportation | 18. Afternoon Tea |
| 3. No Children | 7. Swiming Available | 11. Off Season Rates | 15. Reservations Necessary | ★ Commissions given |
| 4. Senior Citizen Rates | 8. Skiing Available | 12. Dinner Available | 16. Private Bath | to Travel Agents |

## Covington

Moorman, Bernard
215 Garrard St., 41011
(606) 431-2118

**Amenities:** 4,9,10,14,15,16
**Breakfast:** F.

**Dbl. Oc.:** $66.96 - $105.84
**Sgl. Oc.:** $59.40 - $97.20
**Third Person:** $10.80
**Child:** under 12 yrs. -
no charge

**Amos Shinkle Townhouse Bed And Breakfast**—Neighborly, posh, quiet and comfortable. Located in the heart of Covington's Riverside historic district. A restful getaway. Set in an area of dooryard gardens and buildings that resemble England's Chelsea, overlooking the River Thames. A 15-minute walk to Cincinnati.

## Georgetown

McKnight, Mr. & Mrs. Clay
350 N. Broadway, 40324
(502) 863-3514

**Amenities:** 10,16
**Breakfast:** C.

**Dbl. Oc.:** $67.84
**Sgl. Oc.:** $57.24
**Third Person:** $15.00
**Child:** under 12 yrs. -
$10.00

**Log Cabin Bed & Breakfast**—Enjoy this Kentucky log cabin (circa 1809). Shake roof and chinked logs. Completely private. Two bedrooms, fireplace and fully equipped kitchen. Five miles to Kentucky Horse Park and 12 miles north of Lexington. Children welcome.

## Georgetown

Porter, Annette & Felice
201 So. Broadway, 40324
(502) 863-3163

**Amenities:** 2,9,10,15,16
**Breakfast:** F.

**Dbl. Oc.:** $65.00
**Sgl. Oc.:** $55.00
**Third Person:** $10.00
**Child:** under 16 yrs. -
no charge

**Breckinridge House Bed & Breakfast**—This home, circa 1820, belonged to John C. Breckinridge, who ran against Abraham Lincoln for the Presidency. There are two suites furnished in antiques that include bedroom/sitting room, kitchen and bath. We feature homemade breads, pecan rolls, bacon, eggs and fresh fruit.

## Glasgow *

Carter, Henry
4107 Scottsville Rd., 42141
(502) 678-1000

**Amenities:** 2,4,9,15,16
**Breakfast:** C.

**Dbl. Oc.:** $52.47 - $63.07
**Sgl. Oc.:** $52.47 - $63.07
**Third Person:** $5.30
**Child:** under 6 yrs. -
no charge

**Four Seasons Country Inn**—A luxurious inn built in 1989. All 17 rooms are furnished with antique reproductions and queen-size four-poster beds, as well as modern amenities. Near Mammoth Cave, Barren River State Park and fine restaurants. Situated on three acres. Two miles from town on Highway 31-E.

| | | | |
|---|---|---|---|
| 1. No Smoking | 5. Tennis Available | 9. Credit Cards Accepted | 13. Lunch Available | 17. Shared Bath |
| 2. No Pets | 6. Golf Available | 10. Personal Checks Accepted | 14. Public Transportation | 18. Afternoon Tea |
| 3. No Children | 7. Swiming Available | 11. Off Season Rates | 15. Reservations Necessary | ★ Commissions given |
| 4. Senior Citizen Rates | 8. Skiing Available | 12. Dinner Available | 16. Private Bath | to Travel Agents |

## Louisville *

Lesher, Marianne
1359 So. Third St., 40208
(502) 635-1574

**Amenities:** 2,5,9,10,14,15,16, 17
**Breakfast:** C.

**Dbl. Oc.:** $50.00 - $165.00
**Sgl. Oc.:** $40.00 - $155.00
**Third Person:** $10.00
**Child:** under 10 yrs. - no charge

**Old Louisville Inn**—Wake up to the aroma of home-baked breads, muffins and popovers when you stay in one of our 11 guest rooms orsuites. Centrally located between the airport and downtown. Consider us your "home-away-from-home." Call for reservations and a brochure.

## Louisville *

Roosa, Nan-Ellen & Stephen A.
1132 So. First St., 40203
(502) 581-1914

**Amenities:** 11,14,15,16,17
**Breakfast:** C.

**Dbl. Oc.:** $58.00
**Sgl. Oc.:** $53.00
**Third Person:** $10.00
**Child:** under 5 yrs. - $5.00

**The Victorian Secret Bed & Breakfast**—A three story, 14-room brick mansion in historic old Louisville. Recently restored, the 110-year-old structure provides a peaceful setting for enjoying antiques and period furnishings. Washer/dryer, sun decks, off-street parking and color cable TV.

## Middlesboro

Richards, Susan
208 Arthur Heights, 40965
(606) 248-4299

**Amenities:** 1,2,3,6,9,10, 15,16,17
**Breakfast:** F.

**Dbl. Oc.:** $49.13
**Sgl. Oc.:** $43.67
**Third Person:** $16.38

**The Ridgerunner**—Nestled in the Cumberland Mountains of S.E. Kentucky, between Pine Mountain State Park and the National Park of Cumberland Gap. A Victorian house emphasizing a view and the peace of yesteryear. View the spectacular spring and fall mountain foliage from our 60-foot front porch.

## Morehead

Lake, Betty & Allen
910 Willow Dr., 40351
(606) 784-5421

**Amenities:** 2,10,15,17
**Breakfast:** F.

**Dbl. Oc.:** $45.00
**Sgl. Oc.:** $40.00

**Appalachian House**—A large, one-family home where five children have grown up and left. Our house is part museum and part home. It contains many collections. Betty is a potter. Allen is a wood carver. Both were teachers. Only one mile from I-64,off the Morehead exit.

| | | | | |
|---|---|---|---|---|
| 1. No Smoking | 5. Tennis Available | 9. Credit Cards Accepted | 13. Lunch Available | 17. Shared Bath |
| 2. No Pets | 6. Golf Available | 10. Personal Checks Accepted | 14. Public Transportation | 18. Afternoon Tea |
| 3. No Children | 7. Swiming Available | 11. Off Season Rates | 15. Reservations Necessary | ★ Commissions given |
| 4. Senior Citizen Rates | 8. Skiing Available | 12. Dinner Available | 16. Private Bath | to Travel Agents |

## Owensboro

| | | |
|---|---|---|
| Ramey-Ford, Joan | **Amenities:** 4,5,7,9,10,11,12, | **Dbl. Oc.:** $60.00 |
| 5931 Hwy. #56, 42301 | 13,15,16,18 | **Sgl. Oc.:** $50.00 |
| (502) 771-5590 | **Breakfast:** F. | **Third Person:** $5.00 |
| | | **Child:** under 3 yrs. - |
| | | no charge |

**Friendly Farms**—A separate guest cottage with a wood-burning stove on a 100-acre farm. Indoor and outdoor tennis courts, Nautilus fitness equipment, outdoor pool, horses, one mile of hiking trails, fishing and sauna. Located three miles west of the city, amid orchards and ponds. Nearby restaurants.

## Paducah

| | | |
|---|---|---|
| Harris, Beverly & David | **Amenities:** 1,2,3,9,10,14,15, | **Dbl. Oc.:** $42.40 - $63.60 |
| 201 Broadway, 42001 | 17 | **Sgl. Oc.:** $42.40 |
| (502) 442-2698 | **Breakfast:** C. | **Third Person:** $5.00 |

**Paducah Harbor Plaza Bed & Breakfast**—This B&B highlights the corner of Broadway and Second Street's historic district. Rare antique auto museum, antique shops, restaurants and theatres. One block from American Quilter's headquarters and museum.

## Somerset

| | | |
|---|---|---|
| Epperson, Ann | **Amenities:** 2,9,17 | **Dbl. Oc.:** $27.25 |
| 411 S. Main St., 42501 | **Breakfast:** F. | **Sgl. Oc.:** $23.00 |
| (606) 678-4675 | | **Third Person:** $10.00 |
| | | **Child:** under 6 yrs. - $5.00 |

**Shadwick House**—Set in the foothills of the Cumberland Mountains. It has been known for its Southern hospitality for over 70 years. The house is decorated in antiques, quilts and Kentucky crafts. Nearby are Lake Cumberland and Cumberland Falls.

| | | | | |
|---|---|---|---|---|
| 1. No Smoking | 5. Tennis Available | 9. Credit Cards Accepted | 13. Lunch Available | 17. Shared Bath |
| 2. No Pets | 6. Golf Available | 10. Personal Checks Accepted | 14. Public Transportation | 18. Afternoon Tea |
| 3. No Children | 7. Swiming Available | 11. Off Season Rates | 15. Reservations Necessary | ★ Commissions given |
| 4. Senior Citizen Rates | 8. Skiing Available | 12. Dinner Available | 16. Private Bath | to Travel Agents |

# LOUISIANA

## The Pelican State

Capitol: Baton Rouge
Statehood: April 30, 1812; the 18th state
State Motto: Union, Justice and Confidence
State Song: "Song of Louisiana"
State Bird: Brown Pelican
State Flower: Magnolia
State Tree: Bald Cypress

In 1803, the state of Louisiana was part of the Louisiana Purchase from France. The $15,000,000 sale doubled the size of the United States.

French and Spanish speaking people came and settled in New Orleans. Their descendants are referred to as Creoles. Later settlers arrived from Nova Scotia. Henry Wadsworth Longfellow wrote of this journey in his poem, Evangeline. The Acadians settled in Lafayette City and retained most of their old customs. As a result of this mixture of nationalities and customs, Louisiana and especially the city of New Orleans, is a most colorful and interesting place to visit. Over 4,000,000 tourists come here each year.

The main attraction is the Mardi Gras in New Orleans and the French Quarter. The merrymaking of Carnival commences on Twelfth Night, approximately two weeks before the start of Lent, and it continues until Mardi Gras, the day before Lent starts.

Louisiana is located along the beautiful Gulf of Mexico, with the Mississippi River flowing along its eastern border and through the state to Baton Rouge and New Orleans.

## Monroe *

La France, Kay & Cliff
185 Cordell Lane, 71202
(318) 325-1550

**Amenities:** 4,9,10,12,15,16, 18
**Breakfast:** F.

**Dbl. Oc.:** $65.00 - $75.00
**Sgl. Oc.:** $55.00 - $65.00
**Third Person:** $10.00
**Child:** under 12 yrs. - $5.00

**Boscobel Cottage**—Built in 1820. Listed on the *National Register of Historic Places*. Lovely country setting on scenic Ovachita River. Antique charm with all creature comforts. Stay in Chapelor Garonniere and step back in time. Wonderful getaway!

## Napoleonville

Marshall, Millie & Keith
4250 Hwy. 308, 70390
(504) 369-7151

**Amenities:** 1,9,10,12,15,16
**Breakfast:** C. and F.
**Dbl. Oc.:** $89.00 - $159.00

**Madewood Plantation House**—A Greek Revival mansion and a national historic landmark 75 miles from New Orleans. Canopied beds, antiques, family style dinner by candlelight. Oaks, cane fields and family cemetery. Featured in *Vogue, L.A. Times, New York Times, Innsider* and *BBC.*

## New Iberia

Munson, Pratt
544 E. Main St., 70560
(318) 365-1000

**Amenities:** 1,2,10,16
**Breakfast:** C.

**Dbl. Oc.:** $45.00
**Sgl. Oc.:** $35.00
**Child:** under 12 yrs. - $5.00

**Old Perry House**—Located in the middle of the historic district of New Iberia. Raised cottage with two bedrooms each with a private bath. Furnished with family antiques. Within walking distance of Shadows on the Tecne. Civil War buffs welcomed.

## New Iberia *

Nereaux, Jr., Ernie
442 E. Main, 70560
(318) 364-5922

**Amenities:** 1,10,12,15,16
**Breakfast:** F.

**Dbl. Oc.:** $80.00
**Sgl. Oc.:** $60.00
**Third Person:** $45.00

**Masion Marceline**—Victorian townhouse in the historic district. Off US-90, 22 miles south of I-10. One guest suite with private jacuzzi, bath, parlor and library. Full breakfast served in the garden gazebo. Lunch and candlelight dinner available by advance request.

| | | | |
|---|---|---|---|
| 1. No Smoking | 5. Tennis Available | 9. Credit Cards Accepted | 13. Lunch Available | 17. Shared Bath |
| 2. No Pets | 6. Golf Available | 10. Personal Checks Accepted | 14. Public Transportation | 18. Afternoon Tea |
| 3. No Children | 7. Swiming Available | 11. Off Season Rates | 15. Reservations Necessary | ★ Commissions given |
| 4. Senior Citizen Rates | 8. Skiing Available | 12. Dinner Available | 16. Private Bath | to Travel Agents |

## New Orleans

| | | |
|---|---|---|
| Brown, Sarah Margaret | **Amenities:** 1,2,3,11,14,16,17 | **Dbl. Oc.:** $45.00 - $65.00 |
| 3660 Gentilly Blvd., 70122 | **Breakfast:** C. | **Sgl. Oc.:** $40.00 - $60.00 |
| (504) 947-3401 | | **Third Person:** $5.00 - $10.00 |

**New Orleans First B&B**—Safe convenient area of large 1930s' homes on tree lined boulevard. Off-street parking. On direct bus line to the French Quarter and downtown. Lovely bedroom with privatebath; two bedroom suite with bath; cozy garage apartment.

## New Orleans *

| | | |
|---|---|---|
| Chauppette, Carol | **Amenities:** 9,10,11,16 | **Dbl. Oc.:** $65.00 - $195.00 |
| 621 Esplanade, 70116 | **Breakfast:** C. | **Sgl. Oc.:** $55.00 - $185.00 |
| (504) 947-1161, (800) 367-5858 | | **Third Person:** $15.00 |
| | | **Child:** under 8 yrs. - no charge |

**Lamothe House**—Offers all the "old South" enchantment one could wish for. Lavish 19th-century antiques. Complimentary Creole "little breakfast" served in an opulent dining room setting. The inn is located on a wide, tree-shaded Esplanade street on the eastern boundary of the Quarter.

## New Orleans *

| | | |
|---|---|---|
| Fertitta, Alma | **Amenities:** 2,3,4,10,11,14,15, 16 | **Dbl. Oc.:** $97.75 |
| 3924 Evangeline St. | | **Sgl. Oc.:** $74.75 |
| Chalmette, LA , 70043 | **Breakfast:** C. | **Third Person:** $15.00 |
| (504) 271-0228 | | |

**La Maison Orleans**—Built in 1805 in the historic Faubourg Marigny area. It is within walking distance of the French Quarter and many restaurants. Each suite has a double bed, sitting area, fireplace, phone and TV. Parking is across the street.

## New Orleans

| | | |
|---|---|---|
| Jensen, Joni | **Amenities:** 2,10,14,17 | **Dbl. Oc.:** $60.00 |
| 1631 Seventh St., 70115 | **Breakfast:** C. | **Sgl. Oc.:** $50.00 |
| (504) 897-1895 | | **Third Person:** $10.00 |
| | | **Child:** under 15 yrs. - $5.00 |

**Jensen's Bed & Breakfast**—A 100 year old Queen Victorian beautifully decorated with antiques. Twelve- foot alcove ceilings and cypress doors. Located across the street from the garden district, an area known for its lovely homes. The trolley is one block away and is only a short ride to the French Quarter.

| | | | | |
|---|---|---|---|---|
| 1. No Smoking | 5. Tennis Available | 9. Credit Cards Accepted | 13. Lunch Available | 17. Shared Bath |
| 2. No Pets | 6. Golf Available | 10. Personal Checks Accepted | 14. Public Transportation | 18. Afternoon Tea |
| 3. No Children | 7. Swiming Available | 11. Off Season Rates | 15. Reservations Necessary | ★ Commissions given |
| 4. Senior Citizen Rates | 8. Skiing Available | 12. Dinner Available | 16. Private Bath | to Travel Agents |

# LOUISIANA

## New Orleans *

Prigmore, Maralee
2631 Prytania St., 70130
(504) 891-0457

**Amenities:** 9,10,11,14,15,16
**Breakfast:** C.

**Dbl. Oc.:** $65.00 - $175.00
**Sgl. Oc.:** $60.00 - $150.00
**Child:** under 2 yrs. -
no charge

**Sully Mansion**—Located in the heart of the garden district. Charming Queen Anne Victorian, circa 1890. Grand staircase, ten-foot doors, twelve- foot ceilings. Antiques are combined with today's furnishings. Ride the St. Charles street car to the main attractions.

## New Orleans

Spencer, David
915 Royal St., 70116
(504) 522-5558

**Amenities:** 2,9,14,15,16
**Breakfast:** C.

**Dbl. Oc.:** $94.85 & up
**Sgl. Oc.:** $83.75
**Third Person:** no charge
**Child:** no charge

**The Cornstalk Hotel**—A small elegant Victorian with fourteen rooms. *National Register* Hotel located in the New Orleans French Quarter. Near riverboats, antque shops etc. by day and Jazz Bourbon Street's world class restaurants by night. Parking available. 24 hour staff. Southern hospitality.

## New Roads *

Armstrong, Mary Ann
605 E. Main, 70760
(504) 638-6254

**Amenities:** 10
**Breakfast:** F.

**Dbl. Oc.:** $45.00
**Sgl. Oc.:** $40.00
**Third Person:** $5.00

**Pointe Coupee Bed & Breakfast**—Accommodations in three historic homes in downtown New Roads near False River and the Mississippi. Cajun food. Historic tours. A step back in time. Follow L.A. Hwy. 1 north of Baton Rouge.

## Port Vincent *

Schmieder, Fran
16520 Airport Rd., Prairieville, 70769
(504) 622-2850

**Amenities:** 1,2,4,7,9,10,12,15,
16
**Breakfast:** F.

**Dbl. Oc.:** $60.00 - $100.00
**Sgl. Oc.:** $60.00 - $100.00

**Tree House In The Park**—Cajun cabin in the swamp. Large bedroom with double jacuzzi tub, queen size waterbed, private hot tub on sun deck, heated pool and lower deck. Boat slip. Fishing dock. Double kayak float trip. Fireplace. Picture windows overlook three acres of trees and three ponds.

| | | | |
|---|---|---|---|
| 1. No Smoking | 5. Tennis Available | 9. Credit Cards Accepted | 13. Lunch Available | 17. Shared Bath |
| 2. No Pets | 6. Golf Available | 10. Personal Checks Accepted | 14. Public Transportation | 18. Afternoon Tea |
| 3. No Children | 7. Swiming Available | 11. Off Season Rates | 15. Reservations Necessary | ★ Commissions given |
| 4. Senior Citizen Rates | 8. Skiing Available | 12. Dinner Available | 16. Private Bath | to Travel Agents |

## *Shreveport*

Harris, James R.
2439 Fairfield Ave., 71104
(318) 424-2424

**Amenities:** 1,2,3,4,9,10,14,15,16
**Breakfast:** F.
**Dbl. Oc.:** $85.00 - $125.00

**Twenty Four Thirty Nine Fairfield, "A Bed And Breakfast"** — This fabulous home offers Victorian elegance and Southern charm. Decorated in English antiques, down bedding and Amish quilts. Private whirlpool baths. Balconies overlook landscaped gardens with gazebo, park bench, Victorian swing, fountain and lamp posts.

---

## *Shreveport*

Limscomb, Jane
2221 Fairfield Ave., 71104
(318) 222-0048

**Amenities:** 1,2,9,10,15,16
**Breakfast:** C.

**Dbl. Oc.:** $95.00 - $108.15
**Sgl. Oc.:** $65.00 - $77.25
**Third Person:** $10.00

**Fairfield Place**—Elegant 1890's inn located in the beautiful Highland historic restoration district. Spacious rooms decorated with European and American antiques including European feather beds. Enjoy the Victorian charm and quiet serene atmosphere.

---

## *St. Francisville*

Dittloff, Lyle
524 Royal St.
P.O. Box 1461, 70775
(504) 635-4791

**Amenities:** 2,6,10,12,16
**Breakfast:** C.

**Dbl. Oc.:** $71.50
**Sgl. Oc.:** $55.00
**Third Person:** $10.10
**Child:** under 2 yrs. -
no charge

**Barrow House**—Circa 1809. Located on historic Royal Street in a quiet neighborhood of antebellum homes. Rooms have period antiques. A cassette walking tour is included. Visit six area plantations or play golf. Gourmet candlelight dinner for guests.

---

| | | | | |
|---|---|---|---|---|
| 1. No Smoking | 5. Tennis Available | 9. Credit Cards Accepted | 13. Lunch Available | 17. Shared Bath |
| 2. No Pets | 6. Golf Available | 10. Personal Checks Accepted | 14. Public Transportation | 18. Afternoon Tea |
| 3. No Children | 7. Swiming Available | 11. Off Season Rates | 15. Reservations Necessary | ★ Commissions given |
| 4. Senior Citizen Rates | 8. Skiing Available | 12. Dinner Available | 16. Private Bath | to Travel Agents |

## St. Francisville *
Fillet, Florence & Dick
118 No. Commerce, 70775
(504) 635-6502, Fax: (504) 635-6421

**Amenities:** 2,6,12,13,16
**Breakfast:** C.
**Dbl. Oc.:** $53.90 - $64.90
**Sgl. Oc.:** $42.90 - $53.90
**Third Person:** $8.00
**Child:** under 6 yrs. - no charge

**The St. Francisville Inn**—Located in the heart of Louisiana plantation country. Nine guest rooms open onto a New Orleans style courtyard. This restored home, circa 1880, has a restaurant and a guest parlor with a spectacular ceiling medallion decorated with Mardi Gras masks.

| | | | | |
|---|---|---|---|---|
| 1. No Smoking | 5. Tennis Available | 9. Credit Cards Accepted | 13. Lunch Available | 17. Shared Bath |
| 2. No Pets | 6. Golf Available | 10. Personal Checks Accepted | 14. Public Transportation | 18. Afternoon Tea |
| 3. No Children | 7. Swiming Available | 11. Off Season Rates | 15. Reservations Necessary | ★ Commissions given |
| 4. Senior Citizen Rates | 8. Skiing Available | 12. Dinner Available | 16. Private Bath | to Travel Agents |

142

# MAINE

## The Pine Tree State

Capitol: Augusta
Statehood: March 15, 1820; the 23rd state
State Motto: I Direct or I Guide
State Song: "State of Maine Song"
State Bird: Chickadee
State Flower: White Pine Cone and Tassel
State Tree: White Pine

Of all the New England states, Maine is perhaps the largest and best known for its beautiful Atlantic coastline. Traveling along the rugged coast of Maine, a visitor can see and visit many lighthouses, fishing villages and beautiful sandy beaches.

For hundreds of years, the forest of Maine was the mainstay of its economy, and it remains that way today. However, with the modernization of machinery, the business of logging has become much safer. Paper and paper products are Maine's big business.

Maine is also known for growing potatoes. It supplies 8% of the nation's harvest.

Visitors to Maine can enjoy real clambakes. The lobsters and clams for these clambakes are found right in the Maine waters.

Maine's weather for the most part is cool. This kind of weather attracts vacationers in the summer and skiers in the winter. It has become a big vacation area.

## *Bar Harbor*

Bergman, Scott
Route 3, Box 1938, 04609
(800) 582-3681, (207) 288-5591

**Amenities:** 1,2,3,9,11,15,16,18
**Breakfast:** C.
**Dbl. Oc.:** $90.35 - $139.10
**Sgl. Oc.:** $90.35 - $139.10
**Third Person:** $20.00
**Child:** over 16 yrs. - $20.00

**Heathwood Inn**—A newly renovated Victorian farmhouse, minutes from Acadia National Park and downtown Bar Harbor. Rooms are elegantly decorated with antiques. Guest rooms contain TVs and luxurious private baths with dual steam showers. Honeymoon suite has a six-foot jacuzzi and king-size lace canopy bed.

## *Bar Harbor* *

Burns, Marian
69 Mt. Desert St., 04609
(207) 288-4263 (in Maine),
(800) 553-5109

**Amenities:** 2,6,7,9,10,11,15, 16,18
**Breakfast:** C. Plus (buffet)
**Dbl. Oc.:** $85.60 - $144.45
**Sgl. Oc.:** $85.60 - $144.45
**Third Person:** $10.00

**Mira Monte Inn**—A gracious 17-room Victorian, beautifully renovated with antiques, period furnishings and private baths. Some rooms with fireplaces and/or balconies. Common rooms. Quiet porches and terraces. Two-acre estate grounds. Open mid-May to late-October. Five-minute walk to waterfront.

## *Bar Harbor*

Chester, Dorothy & Mike
72 Mt. Desert St., 04609
(207) 288-4970

**Amenities:** 1,2,3,5,6,7,9,10, 11,14,15,16,18
**Breakfast:** F.
**Dbl. Oc.:** $96.30 - $112.35
**Sgl. Oc.:** $96.30 - $112.35

**Holbrook House**—An in-town 1876 Victorian summer home on the historic corridor. Within a five-minute walk to shops, restaurants and ocean. One mile to Acadia National Park. Ten bedrooms, all with private baths. Ample on-premises parking and bicycle storage.

## *Bar Harbor*

Noyes, Malcome
106 West St., 04609
(207) 288-3759
Amenities:1,2,5,6,7,8,9,10,11,15,16
**Breakfast:** C.
**Dbl. Oc.:** $79.00 - $149.00
**Sgl. Oc.:** $79.00 - $149.00
**Third Person:** $20.00
**Child:** $20.00

**Manor House Inn**—An 1887 Victorian mansion furnished in authentic Victorian style. Several guest rooms have fireplaces and many overlook one acre of lawns and gardens. All the beauty and activities of Acadia National Park are at your doorstep.Walk to shops and restaurants.

| | | | |
|---|---|---|---|
| 1. No Smoking | 5. Tennis Available | 9. Credit Cards Accepted | 13. Lunch Available | 17. Shared Bath |
| 2. No Pets | 6. Golf Available | 10. Personal Checks Accepted | 14. Public Transportation | 18. Afternoon Tea |
| 3. No Children | 7. Swiming Available | 11. Off Season Rates | 15. Reservations Necessary | ★ Commissions given |
| 4. Senior Citizen Rates | 8. Skiing Available | 12. Dinner Available | 16. Private Bath | to Travel Agents |

## Bar Harbor

O'Connell, Terence
39 Holland Ave., 04609
(207) 288-4563

**Amenities:** 1,2,5,6,7,8,9,10,11,16
**Breakfast:** C.
**Dbl. Oc.:** $75.00 - $150.00

**Castlemaine Inn**—Nestled on a quiet street in the village of Bar Harbor, only minutes from the magnificent Acadia National Park. The inn has 12 charming rooms, two lovely furnished apartments and a cozy two-room suite. All guest rooms have private baths, some with fireplaces, canopies and balconies.

## Bar Harbor

Schwartz, Susan
7 High St., 04609
(207) 288-4533

**Amenities:** 1,2,3,9,10,11,16, 17,18
**Breakfast:** F.

**Dbl. Oc.:** $69.55 - $101.65
**Sgl. Oc.:** $69.55 - $101.65
**Third Person:** $16.05

**Hearthside**—We invite you to join us for a relaxing stay in our newly redecorated 1907 home. Built as the private home for a doctor. Our guest rooms feature a blend of country and Victorian furnishings. Located in town on a quiet side street near shops, restaurants and the water.

## Bar Harbor

Suydam, Michele
12 Roberts Ave., 04609
(207) 288-2112

**Amenities:** 1,2,3,5,6,7,10,15, 16,17
**Breakfast:** C. Plus

**Dbl. Oc.:** $69.55 - $80.25

**Canterbury Cottage**—A Victorian cottage that has been tastefully restored to provide the comfort and modern conveniences of today. Located on a quiet street with a short walk to all shops, restaurants and harbor activities. A five-minute drive to Acadia National Park.

## Bath *

Lans ky, Gladys
60 Pearl St., 04530
(207) 443-1191

**Amenities:** 1,2,4,9,10,11,15, 17
**Breakfast:** C.

**Dbl. Oc.:** $48.15
**Sgl. Oc.:** $48.15

**Glad II**—A comfortable 1851 Victorian home. Nicholas, my four-legged concierge, and I look forward to welcoming you and making your stay with us memorable. Visit Reid State Park, Popham Beach and Maine Maritime Musuem. Shop in Freeport. Near Bowdoin College and Boothbay Harbor.

| | | | | |
|---|---|---|---|---|
| 1. No Smoking | 5. Tennis Available | 9. Credit Cards Accepted | 13. Lunch Available | 17. Shared Bath |
| 2. No Pets | 6. Golf Available | 10. Personal Checks Accepted | 14. Public Transportation | 18. Afternoon Tea |
| 3. No Children | 7. Swiming Available | 11. Off Season Rates | 15. Reservations Necessary | ★ Commissions given |
| 4. Senior Citizen Rates | 8. Skiing Available | 12. Dinner Available | 16. Private Bath | to Travel Agents |

# MAINE

## Bath *

Messler, Elizabeth & Vincent
45 Pearl St., 04530
(207) 443-6069

**Amenities:** 1,2,3,5,6,7,9,10,
11,16,17,18
**Breakfast:** F.

**Dbl. Oc.:** $64.20 - $80.25
**Third Person:** $15.00

**Packard House**—Relive the grand era of mid-19th century Bath, "City of Ships." An in-town, historic, classic Georgian home of ship builder Benjamin F. Packard. Period furnishings. Three guest rooms. Walk to restaurants and shops. Miles of beaches. Nearby museums, theatre and galleries.

## Bath *

Pollard, Sallie
No. Bath Rd.
RR 2, Box 85, 04530
(207) 443-4391

**Amenities:** 5,6,7,8,9,10,11,12,
16,17
**Breakfast:** F.

**Dbl. Oc.:** $55.00 - $70.00
**Sgl. Oc.:** $45.00
**Third Person:** $15.00

**Fairhaven Inn**—An old, established inn nestled into a hillside overlooking the Kennebec River. Beaches and cross-country ski trails. Mid-coast location. Year-round comfort. Country sights and sounds. Three miles from town.

## Bath *

Valdaski, Michele
1024 Washington St., 04530
(207) 443-5202

**Amenities:** 5,6,7,9,11,12,15,16,17
**Breakfast:** F.
**Dbl. Oc.:** $72.80 - $84.00
**Sgl. Oc.:** $67.80 - $79.00
**Third Person:** $25.00
**Child:** under 14 yrs. - $10.00

**1024 Washington**—An elegant and romantic atmosphere in historic district. Two beautiful beaches, wildlife sanctuary and Maine Maritime Museum. Fine restaurants, art galleries and a short drive to L.L.Bean! Come and enjoy our fresh flowers, fireplaces and music. Where memories are made.

---

| | | | |
|---|---|---|---|
| 1. No Smoking | 5. Tennis Available | 9. Credit Cards Accepted | 13. Lunch Available | 17. Shared Bath |
| 2. No Pets | 6. Golf Available | 10. Personal Checks Accepted | 14. Public Transportation | 18. Afternoon Tea |
| 3. No Children | 7. Swiming Available | 11. Off Season Rates | 15. Reservations Necessary | ★ Commissions given |
| 4. Senior Citizen Rates | 8. Skiing Available | 12. Dinner Available | 16. Private Bath | to Travel Agents |

# MAINE

## Belfast *

Heffentrager, Cathy & Carl
16 Pearl St., 04915
(207) 338-2304

**Amenities:** 1,2,5,6,7,8,10,11,15,16,18
**Breakfast:** F.
**Dbl. Oc.:** $53.50 - $80.25
**Sgl. Oc.:** $48.15 - $74.90
**Third Person:** $10.70

**The Jeweled Turret Inn**—An exquisite turreted, columned and gabled Queen Anne Victorian in a lovely historic village. Period decor. Antiques, lace and beautiful woodwork. Unique fireplaces, verandas and peaceful gardens. Walk to shops, restaurants and the harbor. Activities galore!

## Belfast *

Lightfoot, Phyllis & John
6 Northport Ave., 04915
(207) 338-4159

**Amenities:** 2,5,6,7,8,10,16,17,18
**Breakfast:** F.
**Dbl. Oc.:** $64.20 - $85.60
**Sgl. Oc.:** $53.50 - $74.90
**Third Person:** $10.00

**Frost House**—A Victorian home four blocks from water. Walk to town. Tandem bike, harbor cruises, croquet and badminton. Music at breakfast. Cookies and milk at night. Gardens and arbor. Routes 7/10 off Highway 1. One hour to Bar Harbor and 20 minutes to Camden. Stained glass and wood interior.

## Bethel *

Cheney, Dale & John
Rumford Rd., Route 2
HCR 61, Box 50, 04217
(207) 824-2002

**Amenities:** 1,2,6,7,8,9,10,11, 16,17
**Breakfast:** C.(summer) F.(winter)
**Dbl. Oc.:** $51.36 - $101.65
**Sgl. Oc.:** $40.66 - $80.25
**Third Person:** $25.00
**Child:** under 16 yrs. - $15.00

**Norseman Inn**—A 200-year-old Federal farmstead offering family-style hospitality. Quiet. Over five groomed acres. Five miles to downhill skiing. One mile to scenic Bethel. Fieldstone fireplaces in living and dining rooms. Newly renovated with the charm of a New England inn.

| | | | |
|---|---|---|---|
| 1. No Smoking | 5. Tennis Available | 9. Credit Cards Accepted | 13. Lunch Available | 17. Shared Bath |
| 2. No Pets | 6. Golf Available | 10. Personal Checks Accepted | 14. Public Transportation | 18. Afternoon Tea |
| 3. No Children | 7. Swiming Available | 11. Off Season Rates | 15. Reservations Necessary | ★ Commissions given |
| 4. Senior Citizen Rates | 8. Skiing Available | 12. Dinner Available | 16. Private Bath | to Travel Agents |

## Bingham

Gibson, Frances
Meadow St., 04920
(207) 672-4034

**Amenities:** 5,6,7,8,10,12,15, 17
**Breakfast:** F.

**Dbl. Oc.:** $50.00
**Sgl. Oc.:** $25.00
**Third Person:** $25.00

**Mrs. G.'s Bed & Breakfast**—An old Victorian home with four bedrooms. Within walking distance to shopping, church and white-water rafting on the Kennebec River. A quiet, warm and home-like atmosphere. A dormitory-style loft with 10 beds.

## Boothbay Harbor

Campbell, Diane
3 Eames Rd., 04538
(207) 633-2284

**Amenities:** 1,2,3,5,6,7,8,10, 11,15,16
**Breakfast:** C.

**Dbl. Oc.:** $70.00 - $90.00
**Third Person:** $15.00

**Anchor Watch Bed And Breakfast**—A warm welcome awaits you at our shorefront sea captain's house. Watch lobstermen hauling traps and lighthouses flashing. A short walk from our residential setting to dining, shops and boat trips. Homemade muffins. Efficiency available off-season.

## Boothbay Harbor

Thomas, George
71 Tonwsend Ave., 04538
(207) 633-4300

**Amenities:** 2,4,5,6,7,8,9,10,11,14,15,16
**Breakfast:** C.
**Dbl. Oc.:** $55.00 - $190.00
**Third Prson:** $25.00
**Child:** $10.00

**Harbour Towne Inn**—The finest B&B on the water's edge. Located on the waterfront. A short stroll to all activities. All private baths in this handsomely restored Victorian. All rooms are charming. A luxurious penthouse available. Scenic outside decks. Off-season senior citizen rates available.

## Boothbay, East

Morissette, Ellen
Murray Hill Rd., 04544
(207) 633-4551

**Amenities:** 1,2,6,7,9,10, 11,16
**Breakfast:** F.

**Dbl. Oc.:** $80.00 - $120.00
**Third Person:** $20.00

**Five Gables Inn**—A restored Victorian on Linekin Bay. All rooms have a water view and private bath. Some rooms have a fireplace. A gourmet breakfast is served. Very quiet and relaxing with a large veranda on which you can sit and view the bay.

| | | | | |
|---|---|---|---|---|
| 1. No Smoking | 5. Tennis Available | 9. Credit Cards Accepted | 13. Lunch Available | 17. Shared Bath |
| 2. No Pets | 6. Golf Available | 10. Personal Checks Accepted | 14. Public Transportation | 18. Afternoon Tea |
| 3. No Children | 7. Swiming Available | 11. Off Season Rates | 15. Reservations Necessary | ★ Commissions given |
| 4. Senior Citizen Rates | 8. Skiing Available | 12. Dinner Available | 16. Private Bath | to Travel Agents |

# MAINE

## Bridgton *

Starets, Jane & Dick
37 Highland Rd., 04009
(207) 647-3733

**Amenities:** 1,2,5,6,7,8,9,10,
15,16,17
**Breakfast:** F.

**Dbl. Oc.:** $72.76 - $117.70
**Sgl. Oc.:** $67.41 - $78.11
**Third Person:** $25.00
**Child:** under 12 yrs. -
$15.00

**Noble House**—A stately manor with private frontage on scenic Highland Lake. Canoe and foot pedal boat for guests' use. Sumptuous full breakfast. Family suites. Whirlpool baths. Nearby hiking, swimming, antiques, summer theatre and romantic restaurants. Cross-country and downhill skiing.

## Brunswick

Gventer, Rose
7 South St., 04011
(207) 729-6959

**Amenities:** 1,9,10,17
**Breakfast:** C.

**Dbl. Oc.:** $53.50
**Sgl. Oc.:** $42.80
**Third Person:** $10.70

**The Samuel Newman House**—An 1821 Federal-style house with seven guest rooms furnished in comfortable antiques. Adjacent to Bowdoin College and 10 minutes from L.L.Bean in Freeport. Delicious home-baked pastries and muffins. Open year round.

## Brunswick

Packard, Elizabeth & Peter
Bethel Point Rd. 2387, 04011
(207) 725-1115

**Amenities:** 1,2,7,10,11,15,17
**Breakfast:** F.
**Dbl. Oc.:** $70.00
**Sgl. Oc.:** $60.00
**Third Person:** $15.00

**Bethel Point Bed And Breakfast**—Peaceful oceanside comfort in 150-year-old home. Perfect view of ocean birds, seals and lobster boats. An opportunity for shoreline walks to explore the local coast. An easy drive to the area's specialties, such as Bowdoin College, Popham Beach, L.L.Bean and local restaurants.

## Camden

Davis, Mary & Jon
6 High St., 04843
(207) 236-9656

**Amenities** 1,2,3,5,6,7,8,9,10,
11,15,16,18
**Breakfast:** F.

**Dbl. Oc.:** $65.00 - $100.00
**Sgl. Oc.:** $60.00 - $90.00

**Windward House**—Enjoy the charm and comfort of our historic and beautifully restored Greek Revival home situated above picturesque Camden harbor. Guest rooms furnished with fine antiques and private baths. Enjoy our common rooms, gardens and gourmet breakfasts. Just steps to the harbor.

| | | | |
|---|---|---|---|
| 1. No Smoking | 5. Tennis Available | 9. Credit Cards Accepted | 13. Lunch Available | 17. Shared Bath |
| 2. No Pets | 6. Golf Available | 10. Personal Checks Accepted | 14. Public Transportation | 18. Afternoon Tea |
| 3. No Children | 7. Swiming Available | 11. Off Season Rates | 15. Reservations Necessary | ★ Commissions given |
| 4. Senior Citizen Rates | 8. Skiing Available | 12. Dinner Available | 16. Private Bath | to Travel Agents |

# MAINE

## Camden

Goodspeed, Don
60 Mountain St., 04843
(207) 236-8077

**Amenities:** 3,5,6,7,8,10,11,
16,17
**Breakfast:** C.

**Dbl. Oc.:** $63.00 - $80.00
**Sgl. Oc.:** $38.00 - $48.00
**Third Person:** $15.00
**Child:** $10.00

**Goodspeed Guest House**—An 1879 farmhouse with eight restored guest rooms. Antique clocks and furnishings throughout. Enjoy a continental breakfast on the sunny deck. A quiet location. Spacious grounds. Five blocks from the harbor.

## Camden *

Schmoll, Jody
67 Elm St. (U.S. Route 1), 04843
(207) 236-3196

**Amenities:** 1,5,6,7,8,9,10,11,12,13,
14,15,16,17,18
**Breakfast:** F.
**Dbl. Oc.:** $74.90 - $117.70
**Third Person:** $15.00
**Child:** $15.00

**Blue Harbor House, A Bed & Breakfast**—A classic New England Cape constructed prior to 1835. Completely restored and renovated. The inn provides every modern comfort while capturing that special essence of a bygone era. Walk to village, harbor and restaurants. Open year round.

## Camden *

Smith, Peter & Donny
22 High St., 04843
(207) 236-9636

**Amenities:** 1,2,3,5,6,7,8,9,10,11,
15.17,18
**Breakfast:** F.
**Dbl. Oc.:** $77.00
**Sgl. Oc.:** $66.35

**The Camden Main Stay Inn**—A comfortable bed, a hearty breakfast and a friendly innkeeper are found in this treasured old colonial home. Listed in the *National Register of Historic Places*. Located in Camden's historic district. The inn is a short five-minute walk from the harbor, shops and restaurants.

| | | | | |
|---|---|---|---|---|
| 1. No Smoking | 5. Tennis Available | 9. Credit Cards Accepted | 13. Lunch Available | 17. Shared Bath |
| 2. No Pets | 6. Golf Available | 10. Personal Checks Accepted | 14. Public Transportation | 18. Afternoon Tea |
| 3. No Children | 7. Swiming Available | 11. Off Season Rates | 15. Reservations Necessary | ★ Commissions given |
| 4. Senior Citizen Rates | 8. Skiing Available | 12. Dinner Available | 16. Private Bath | to Travel Agents |

# MAINE

## Capitol Island

Peckham, Kim
04538
(207) 633-2521

**Amenities:** 1,2,5,7,10,16,17
**Breakfast:** C.
**Dbl. Oc.:** $66.34 - $107.00
**Sgl. Oc.:** $48.15
**Third Person:** $10.00

**Albonegon Inn**—On a private island, four miles from Boothbay Harbor. It is perched on the rocks and offers outstanding views of nearby islands. It is a 19th-century, cottage-style building. Quiet and peaceful. Perfect for relaxing.

## Chamberlain

Hahler, M/M John J.
Route 32
Box 105, 04541
(207) 677-2386

**Amenities:** 2,3,6,7,10,16
**Breakfast:** C.

**Dbl. Oc.:** $58.00
**Sgl. Oc.:** $46.00
**Third Person:** $12.00

**Ocean Reefs On Long Cove**—Located on Long Cove. Four rooms. Two cabins. Watch waves break over the reef, lobstermen hauling traps and nature in its environment between tides. Choice of dining. Nature trails and sightseeing boat within two miles. Enjoy the coast from the rocks or the rockers.

## Chebeague Island

Bowden, Wendy & Kevin
Box 492, 04017
(207) 846-5155

**Amenities:** 1,4,5,6,7,9,10,11, 12,13,14,15,16,17, 18
**Breakfast:** C. and F.

**Dbl. Oc.:** $88.00 - $105.00
**Sgl. Oc.:** $77.00 - $97.00
**Third Person:** $15.00
**Child:** cribs - no charge

**Chebeague Island Inn**—An island getaway in a 20-room inn just a short boat trip from Portland. No phones or TV. Native island lobster and clams. Period 1926 antiques. Only inn and restaurant on the island. Full liquor license. Bikes. A 100 foot-long front porch with rockers. "The Crown Jewel of Casco Bay."

## Cherryfield

Conway, William
Park St.
P.O. Box 256, 04622
(207) 546-2780

**Amenities:** 1,2,5,6,7,10, 15,17
**Breakfast:** F.

**Dbl. Oc.:** $45.00
**Sgl. Oc.:** $40.00
**Third Person:** $10.00

**Ricker House**—A beautiful 1803 home in a quaint historic town on Narraguagus River. Centrally located for many activities in downeast coastal Maine. Rugged shorelines, lakes an drivers. Great seafood restaurants. Your hosts can help you get the most out of your visit.

| | | | | |
|---|---|---|---|---|
| 1. No Smoking | 5. Tennis Available | 9. Credit Cards Accepted | 13. Lunch Available | 17. Shared Bath |
| 2. No Pets | 6. Golf Available | 10. Personal Checks Accepted | 14. Public Transportation | 18. Afternoon Tea |
| 3. No Children | 7. Swiming Available | 11. Off Season Rates | 15. Reservations Necessary | ★ Commissions given |
| 4. Senior Citizen Rates | 8. Skiing Available | 12. Dinner Available | 16. Private Bath | to Travel Agents |

## Damariscotta

Hovance, Joseph R.
Route 129
HCR 64, Box 045F, 04543
(207) 563-5941

**Amenities:** 1,2,9,10,15,16,17
**Breakfast:** C.
**Dbl. Oc.:** $53.00 - $69.20
**Sgl. Oc.:** $48.15 - $63.85
**Third Person:** $10.70 - $15.70
**Child:** under 10 yrs. - $5.35

**Brannon-Bunker Inn**—An intimate and relaxing country B&B with river view. Mid-coast location. Seven rooms reflect the charm of yesterday with comforts of today. Private or shared baths. Selection of queen, double or twin beds. An antique shop in the inn! Nearby beach, lighthouse and fort shops.

## Eastport

McInnis, Ruth
Todd's Head, 04631
(207) 853-2328

**Amenities:** 1,10,16,17
**Breakfast:** C.

**Dbl. Oc.:** $40.00 - $75.00
**Sgl. Oc.:** $35.00
**Third Person:** $10.00
**Child:** under 8 yrs. -
no charge

**Todd House**—A center-chimney Cape, circa 1775, on Todd's Head. A unique good-morning staircase. A spectacular view of Passamaquoddy Bay. A library of local history items. Deck and barbecue facilities. Children and well-behaved pets welcome. Some rooms with private baths. Kitchenettes.

## Eliot

Raymond, Elaine
Route 101, 03903
(207) 439-0590

**Amenities:** 1,2,3,10,16,17,18
**Breakfast:** F.

**Dbl. Oc.:** $52.50 - $64.20
**Sgl. Oc.:** $37.00
**Third Person:** $20.00

**High Meadows B&B**—Open April-November. Ten guest rooms with queen, double or twin beds. A country setting. A colonial house built in 1736. Only 4-1/2 miles to shopping malls. 6-1/2 miles to historic New Hampshire.

## Freeport *

Bradley, Loretta & Alan
188 Main St., 04032
(207) 865-3289

**Amenities:** 1,2,6,7,9,11,
16,17
**Breakfast:** F.

**Dbl. Oc.:** $72.00
**Sgl. Oc.:** $55.00
**Child:** under 12 yrs. -
$10.00

**Captain Josiah Mitchell House**—One of the most historic houses in Maine. In town. Two blocks from L.L.Bean. A five-minute walk, passing centuries-old sea captains' homes, to all shops in town. Relax on our beautiful, peaceful veranda with antique wicker chairs and "remember-when" porch swing.

| | | | | |
|---|---|---|---|---|
| 1. No Smoking | 5. Tennis Available | 9. Credit Cards Accepted | 13. Lunch Available | 17. Shared Bath |
| 2. No Pets | 6. Golf Available | 10. Personal Checks Accepted | 14. Public Transportation | 18. Afternoon Tea |
| 3. No Children | 7. Swiming Available | 11. Off Season Rates | 15. Reservations Necessary | ★ Commissions given |
| 4. Senior Citizen Rates | 8. Skiing Available | 12. Dinner Available | 16. Private Bath | to Travel Agents |

# MAINE

## Freeport

| | | |
|---|---|---|
| Friedlander, Glyn & Jim | **Amenities:** 1,4,10,11,16, | **Dbl. Oc.:** $69.55 - $107.00 |
| Independence Dr., 04032 | 17,18 | **Third Person:** $15.00 |
| (207) 865-9295 | **Breakfast:** F. | **Child:** under 2 yrs. - $10.00 |

**The Isaac Randall House Bed And Breakfast**—An antique-furnished country inn within walking distance of downtown Freeport's exciting shopping (L.L.Bean). Air-conditioned bedrooms. Sumptuous breakfasts and evening snacks. Friendly ambience. Five wooded acres with pond.

## Freeport

| | | |
|---|---|---|
| Hassett, Edward | **Amenities:** 2,3,6,7,8,9,10,11, | **Dbl. Oc.:** $96.30 |
| 181 Main St., 04032 | 16 | **Sgl. Oc.:** $74.90 |
| (207) 865-1226 | **Breakfast:** F. | |

**181 Main Street Bed & Breakfast**—An 1840 Cape with country elegance, antiques and period appointments. Seven guest rooms, each with a private bath. In-town location. Walk to L.L.Bean and luxury outlets. Ample parking. Pool. Quiet location. AAA approved.

## Freeport *

| | | |
|---|---|---|
| Knudsen, Jr., Sigurd A. | **Amenities:** 1,2,6,7,8,9,10,11, | **Dbl. Oc.:** $102.00 - $124.00 |
| RR 3, Box 269C, 04032 | 16 | **Sgl. Oc.:** $87.00 - $109.00 |
| (207) 865-6566 | **Breakfast:** F. | **Third Person:** $15.00 |
| | | **Child:** $15.00 |

**The Bagley House**—Peace, tranquility and history abound in this magnificent 1772 country home. Antiques, handmade quilts and fireplaces. Six acres of fields, woods and flowers. A warm welcome awaits you. Just minutes from downtown Freeport's famous shopping.

## Freeport, South *

| | | |
|---|---|---|
| Ring, Gaila & Captain Thomas | **Amenities:** 1,2,3,7,8,10,11,13, | **Dbl. Oc.:** $69.55 - $133.75 |
| 25 Main St. | 16,17,18 | **Sgl. Oc.:** $58.85 - $107.00 |
| P.O. Box 146, 04078 | **Breakfast:** F. | **Third Person:** $16.05 |
| (207) 865-6112 | | **Child:** $16.05 |

**Atlantic Seal Bed And Breakfast**—Lovely harbor views year round. 1850 Cape. Cozy rooms, antiques, old-fashioned parlor with fireplace. Guest rooms feature sea breezes, fresh flowers, thick towels, homemade quilts and down comforters. Five minutes to L.L.Bean and outlet stores. Resident dog and cat.

## Harrison,

| | | |
|---|---|---|
| Cotton, Joyce & Paul | **Amenities:** 2,5,6,7,8,9,10,11, | **Dbl. Oc.:** $80.25 |
| Tolman Rd. | 16 | **Sgl. Oc.:** $58.85 |
| Box 551, 04040 | **Breakfast:** F. | **Third Person:** $15.00 |
| (207) 583-4445 | | **Child:** under 2 yrs. - no charge |

**Tolman House Inn**—A former carriage house art fully transformed into an inviting inn. Nine guest rooms with private baths and antique furnishings. The inn is situated on 100 acres with formal gardens. Cross-country skiing at our door. Take advantage of the nearby lakes.

| | | | | |
|---|---|---|---|---|
| 1. No Smoking | 5. Tennis Available | 9. Credit Cards Accepted | 13. Lunch Available | 17. Shared Bath |
| 2. No Pets | 6. Golf Available | 10. Personal Checks Accepted | 14. Public Transportation | 18. Afternoon Tea |
| 3. No Children | 7. Swiming Available | 11. Off Season Rates | 15. Reservations Necessary | ★ Commissions given |
| 4. Senior Citizen Rates | 8. Skiing Available | 12. Dinner Available | 16. Private Bath | to Travel Agents |

# MAINE

## Kennebunk

Ellenberger, Cathy
154 Port Rd., 04043
(207) 967-3824

**Amenities:** 2,4,5,6,7,9,10,11, 12,14,15,16,18
**Breakfast:** F.

**Dbl. Oc.:** $75.00
**Sgl. Oc.:** $60.00
**Third Person:** $50.00
**Child:** under 13 yrs. - $15.00

**Ellenberger's Guest House And Bed & Breakfast**—Located in the heart of the lower village. We offer a two-bedroom suite with a fireplaced living room. Enjoy a comfortable setting decorated with antiques. Walk to activities. One mile to the beach. Great breakfasts. Gallery I and antique shop on premises. Come and enjoy.

## Kennebunk

Foley, Maryellen & Tom
1917 Alewive Rd. (Route 35), 04043
(207) 985-2118

**Amenities:** 1,2,3,5,6,7,8,9,10, 16,17
**Breakfast:** C.

**Dbl. Oc.:** $69.55
**Sgl. Oc.:** $69.55

**The Alewife House**—A 1756 farmhouse with six acres of rolling hills. Furnished throughout with antiques. Quiet country atmosphere, yet close to the ocean. Antique shop. Guaranteed reservation with MasterCard or Visa. Four miles north of Exit 3 off the Maine Turnpike. Open year round.

## Kennebunk *

McAdams, Carolyn
57 Western Ave., 04043
(207) 967-4069

**Amenities:** 1,2,5,6,7,10,11,16, 17
**Breakfast:** F.

**Dbl. Oc.:** $64.20 - $80.25
**Sgl. Oc.:** $53.50 - $69.55
**Third Person:** $15.00

**Lake Brook B&B Guest House**—A turn-of-the-century farmhouse with comfortable rockers, great breakfasts, beautiful flower gardens and charming accommodations. Lake Brook is 1/2 mile from Dock Square and one mile from Kennebunk Beach. Come join us.

## Kennebunk

Yaeger, Murray
P.O. Box 1129, 04043
(207) 985-3770

**Amenities:** 2,9,10,11,15,16,18
**Breakfast:** F.
**Dbl. Oc.:** $90.00
**Sgl. Oc.:** $90.00
**Third Person:** $20.00

**Arundel Meadows Inn**—A 165-year-old farmhouse with seven guest rooms. Decorated with art and antiques. Three rooms with fireplaces. Two suites. Private bathrooms. Gourmet breakfasts. Five miles to Kennebunkport and beaches. Two miles north of Kennebunk on Route 1. Write for brochure/reservations.

---

| | | | | |
|---|---|---|---|---|
| 1. No Smoking | 5. Tennis Available | 9. Credit Cards Accepted | 13. Lunch Available | 17. Shared Bath |
| 2. No Pets | 6. Golf Available | 10. Personal Checks Accepted | 14. Public Transportation | 18. Afternoon Tea |
| 3. No Children | 7. Swiming Available | 11. Off Season Rates | 15. Reservations Necessary | ★ Commissions given |
| 4. Senior Citizen Rates | 8. Skiing Available | 12. Dinner Available | 16. Private Bath | to Travel Agents |

## *Kennebunkport* *

Copeland, Carol & Lindsay
Maine St.
P.O. Box 500-A, 04046
(207) 967-2117

**Amenities:** 5,6,7,9,10,11,15,16,18
**Breakfast:** C. or F.
**Dbl. Oc.:** $110.00 - $150.00
**Sgl. Oc.:** $110.00 - $150.00
**Third Person:** $15.00
**Child:** $8.00

**Maine Stay Inn And Cottages**—"Exceptional warmth and hospitality." An elegant B&B. Rooms, suites and charming garden cottages, some with fireplaces. Sumptuous breakfast and afternoon tea. Located in historic district. Walk to harbor, shops, galleries and restaurants. AAA and rated 3 diamond.

## *Kennebunkport*

Doane, Charles
Route 35
RR 3, Box 135, 04046
(207) 967-5766

**Amenities:** 1,2,9,10,11,16,18
**Breakfast:** F.
**Dbl. Oc.:** $89.25
**Sgl. Oc.:** $68.25
**Third Person:** $21.00
**Child:** under 10 yrs. - $10.50

**English Meadows Inn**—An 1860 Victorian farmhouse, operating as an inn for more than 80 years. Relax in the main house amid the works of nationally acclaimed local artists and antiques. For that special vacation, there is a large studio apartment and four-room cottage.

## *Kennebunkport*

Downs, Eva
South St., 04046
(207) 967-5151

**Amenities:** 1,5,6,7,8,9,10,11,15,16,18
**Breakfast:** F.
**Dbl. Oc.:** $89.06 - $176.55
**Third Person:** $21.40
**Child:** under 1 yr. - no charge

**The Inn On South Street**—Enjoy the comfortable elegance of this 19th-century Greek Revival home and the personal attention of the Downs family. Three spacious guest rooms and a luxurious suite, beautifully decorated with antiques. On a quiet street, yet close to restaurants, shops and the water.

| | | | | |
|---|---|---|---|---|
| 1. No Smoking | 5. Tennis Available | 9. Credit Cards Accepted | 13. Lunch Available | 17. Shared Bath |
| 2. No Pets | 6. Golf Available | 10. Personal Checks Accepted | 14. Public Transportation | 18. Afternoon Tea |
| 3. No Children | 7. Swiming Available | 11. Off Season Rates | 15. Reservations Necessary | ★ Commissions given |
| 4. Senior Citizen Rates | 8. Skiing Available | 12. Dinner Available | 16. Private Bath | to Travel Agents |

## *Kennebunkport* *

Kyle, Mary & William
South St.
P.O. Box 1333, 04046
(207) 967-2780

**Amenities:** 1,2,3,5,6,7,8,9,10,11,15,
16,17,18
**Breakfast:** F.
**Dbl. Oc.:** $69.55 - $96.30
**Sgl. Oc.:** $64.20 - $90.95
**Third Person:** $20.00

**Kylemere House 1818**—A beautifully appoined Federal seaport inn. Centrally located on a quiet street. Warm and inviting rooms, traditional hospitality and creative cuisine. Only a few minutes walk to the ocean, shops, restaurants and galleries. Seen in *Boston Globe* and *Glamour magazine*.

## *Kennebunkport* *

Ledda, Patricia
Locke St.
Box 646A, 04046
(207) 967-5632

**Amenities:** 2,3,4,6,9,10,11,15, **Dbl. Oc.:** $80.00 - $120.00
16,18 **Third Person:** $20.00
**Breakfast:** F.

**1802 House**—A charming bed and breakfast. A cozy atmosphere. Gourmt breakfast. Enjoy our warm hospitality and quiet setting. Overlooks the golf course and, of course, our President, when he is golfing. In the winter, enjoy our fireplaced rooms and in the summer, enjoy the cool ocean breezes.

## *Kennebunkport*

Reid, Elizabeth & Charles
Ocean Ave.
P.O. Box 2578, 04046
(207) 967-3315

**Amenities:** 5,6,7,10,11,16 **Dbl. Oc.:** $68.50 - $118.00
**Breakfast:** F. **Sgl. Oc.:** $52.00 - $77.00
**Third Person:** $16.00
**Child:** $10.00 - $12.00

**The Green Heron Inn**—A cozy, clean and comfortable inn located on scenic Ocean Avenue. Close to a small beach and within walking distance to Dock Square. The inn offers 10 guest rooms and one cottage, each with private bath, color TV and air-conditioning.

## *Kennebunkport*

Severance, Sandy & Mike
Gooch's Beach
P.O. Box 631, 04046-0631
(207) 967-4461

**Amenities:** 2,5,6,7,10,11,13, **Dbl. Oc.:** $99.00 - $176.00
13,16 **Sgl. Oc.:** $91.00 - $168.00
**Breakfast:** C. **Third Person:** $10.00

**The Seaside**—This 1756 inn has four guest rooms decorated with antiques. Open from late June until early September. Our 22-room inn has spacious rooms and overlooks our private and clean beach. Each room has two double beds, private patio or deck. Open year round.

| | | | |
|---|---|---|---|
| 1. No Smoking | 5. Tennis Available | 9. Credit Cards Accepted | 13. Lunch Available | 17. Shared Bath |
| 2. No Pets | 6. Golf Available | 10. Personal Checks Accepted | 14. Public Transportation | 18. Afternoon Tea |
| 3. No Children | 7. Swiming Available | 11. Off Season Rates | 15. Reservations Necessary | ★ Commissions given |
| 4. Senior Citizen Rates | 8. Skiing Available | 12. Dinner Available | 16. Private Bath | to Travel Agents |

## *Kennebunkport*

| | | |
|---|---|---|
| Shoby, Bernice & Frank | **Amenities:** 1,2,5,6,7,8,9,10, | **Dbl. Oc.:** $90.00 |
| Temple St. | 11,12,13,15,16 | **Sgl. Oc.:** $80.00 |
| P.O. Box 1123, 04046 | **Breakfast:** F. | **Third Person:** $20.00 |
| (207) 967-5773 | | |

**The Dock Square Inn**—A gracious Victorian B&B country inn. A former ship-builder's home located in the heart of historic Kennebunkport Village. Warm and congenial atmosphere. Full gourmet breakfast. Comfortable rooms, private baths and color cable TV.

## *Kennebunkport*

| | | |
|---|---|---|
| Sutter, Joan & David | **Amenities:** 1,2,3,5,6,7,8,9,10, | **Dbl. Oc.:** $101.65 - $181.90 |
| Pier Rd. | 11,12,13,16 | **Sgl. Oc.:** $101.65 - $181.90 |
| RR 2, Box 1180, 04046 | **Breakfast:** F. | **Third Person:** $26.75 |
| (207) 967-5564 | | |

**The Inn At Harbor Head**—A century-old, shingled waterfront cottage in the loveliest part of Kennebunkport—Cape Porpoise Harbor. Private baths. Wind chimes. Photographic breakfasts. Slow down, relax and unwind in the beautiful and uniquely furnished guest rooms. A smoke-free inn.

## *Kittery* *

| | | |
|---|---|---|
| Lamandia, Peter | **Amenities:** 1,9,10,11,16,17 | **Dbl. Oc.:** $58.85 - $90.95 |
| 29 Wentworth St., 03904 | **Breakfast:** F. | **Sgl. Oc.:** $53.50 - $85.60 |
| (207) 439-1489 | | **Third Person:** $10.70 |
| | | **Child:** $10.70 |

**Enchanted Nights Bed & Breakfast**—1880 Princess Anne Victorian. Ornate decor. Romantic French and English ambience. One mile to downtown Portsmouth, Kittery outlet malls, dining, dancing, scenic drives, historic homes and beaches. Central to Boston and Portland. Gourmet coffee, omelettes and pastries served.

## *Lincolnville Beach*

| | | |
|---|---|---|
| Curren, Lori | **Amenities:** 2,3,10,11,12, | **Dbl. Oc.:** $69.55 - $85.60 |
| The Other Rd. | 16,18 | **Sgl. Oc.:** $48.15 - $78.11 |
| P.O. Box 75, 04849 | **Breakfast:** F. | **Third Person:** $16.05 |
| (207) 236-3785 | | |

**Longville Inn**—A restored century-old Victorian "cottage" by the sea. Fireplaces, soft flannel sheets, fluffy towels, cozy comforters and pampering. Enjoy an afternoon shopping, sightseeing, walking the shore or just relaxing on the gazebo. Flower gardens in a country setting.

| | | | | |
|---|---|---|---|---|
| 1. No Smoking | 5. Tennis Available | 9. Credit Cards Accepted | 13. Lunch Available | 17. Shared Bath |
| 2. No Pets | 6. Golf Available | 10. Personal Checks Accepted | 14. Public Transportation | 18. Afternoon Tea |
| 3. No Children | 7. Swiming Available | 11. Off Season Rates | 15. Reservations Necessary | ★ Commissions given |
| 4. Senior Citizen Rates | 8. Skiing Available | 12. Dinner Available | 16. Private Bath | to Travel Agents |

## Little Deer Isle

Broadhead, Sophie
R.F.D. #1, Box 324, 04650
(207) 348-2540

**Amenities:** 2,5,6,7,10,15,16, 17,18
**Breakfast:** F.

**Dbl. Oc.:** $75.00 - $85.00
**Sgl. Oc.:** $60.00 - $70.00
**Third Person:** $18.00
**Child:** under 3 yrs. -
no charge

**Eggmoggin Inn**—A small, secluded coastal inn in a beautiful location and a view. On Eggemogin Beach, which is world-famous for sailing. The area is still unspoiled. Come and relax with us and enjoy life as it should be lived.

## Lubec

Childs, Lovetta
27 Summer St., 04652
(207) 733-2403

**Amenities:** 1,2,6,9,10,16,17, 18
**Breakfast:** F.

**Dbl. Oc.:** $58.85 - $80.25
**Sgl. Oc.:** $48.15 - $69.55
**Third Person:** $10.00
**Child:** $10.00

**Peacock House**—Built in 1860 by an English sea captain. This lovely old Victorian overlooks the Bay of Fundy. Seven bedrooms and five baths. Quiet ambience and unrivaled comfort. Nearby are Roosevelt's Campabello, Quoddy Head, golf and whalewatching.

## Lubec

Elg, E.M.
37 Washington, 04652
(207) 733-2487

**Amenities:** 1,2,3,6,10,15,16, 17
**Breakfast:** F.

**Dbl. Oc.:** $42.80 - $58.85
**Sgl. Oc.:** $42.80 - $58.85

**Breakers By The Bay**—Enjoy the breathtaking views of the sea from your own private deck. Rooms have handmade quilts and hand crocheted tablecloths. Located close to International Bridge which leads to Campobello and Roosevelt's house. Enjoy the beauty of Quoddy Head State Park.

## Mt. Desert

Worcester, Dorothy Lee
Riples Rd.
HCR 62, Box 189, 04660
(207) 244-5650

**Amenities:** 7,10,17
**Breakfast:** F.

**Dbl. Oc.:** $53.85 - $64.20
**Sgl. Oc.:** $53.85 - $64.20
**Third Person:** $10.35 -
$10.70
**Child:** $10.35 - $10.70

**Clover**—Clover is the only B&B on the lake on Bar Harbor's Mt.Desert Island, home of Acadia National Park. Located on Long Pond, the longest lake on any island in the world. 1 1/2 miles from the ocean, three miles from Acadia and 10 miles from Bar Harbor. Classy. Boats.

## Naples *

Hincks, Irene & Maynard
Lake House Rd.
P.O. Box 806, 04055
(207) 693-6226

**Amenities:** 2,5,6,7,8,9,10,11, 15,16
**Breakfast:** C.

**Dbl. Oc.:** $74.00 - $91.00
**Sgl. Oc.:** $66.60 - $81.90
**Third Person:** $10.00
**Child:** under 12 yrs. -
no charge

**Inn At Long Lake**—Unwind in this elegant 16-room inn. Located in the heart of the Sebago Lake area. You can enjoy four seasons of activities. Each tastefully decorated room has a private bath. Bask in the warm glow of a crackling fire in our 36-foot great room.

| | | | |
|---|---|---|---|
| 1. No Smoking | 5. Tennis Available | 9. Credit Cards Accepted | 13. Lunch Available | 17. Shared Bath |
| 2. No Pets | 6. Golf Available | 10. Personal Checks Accepted | 14. Public Transportation | 18. Afternoon Tea |
| 3. No Children | 7. Swiming Available | 11. Off Season Rates | 15. Reservations Necessary | ★ Commissions given |
| 4. Senior Citizen Rates | 8. Skiing Available | 12. Dinner Available | 16. Private Bath | to Travel Agents |

# MAINE

## Naples

Stetson, Arlene & David
Corner of Routes 302 & 114
RR1, Box 501, 04055
(207) 693-6365

**Amenities:** 4,5,6,7,8,9,10,11,
12,15,16,17,18
**Breakfast:** F.

**Dbl. Oc.:** $49.00 - $75.00
**Sgl. Oc.:** $39.00
**Third Person:** $10.00
**Child:** under 12 yrs. - $5.00

**The Augustus Bove House**—Your home away from home. A historic Hotel Naples restored for comfort and a relaxed atmosphere at affordable prices. Overlooks Long Lake. An easy walk to the water, shops, restaurants and recreation. Open all year. Off-season specials.

## New Harbor

Phinney Family, The
Northside Rd., Route 32, 04554
(207) 677-3727

**Amenities:** 1,2,6,7,9,10,11,12,
16
**Breakfast:** F.

**Dbl. Oc.:** $95.00 - $125.00
**Sgl. Oc.:** $70.00
**Third Person:** $16.00
**Child:** under 1 yr. -
no charge

**The Gosnold Arms**—On the historic Pemaquid peninsula. Attractive and comfortable rooms and cottages, most with water views. A glassed-in dining porch overlooking the harbor. Nearby lobster pounds, boat trips, historic sites, shops and beach. Congenial family atmosphere.

## Newcastle *

Forester, Martha & Jim
River Rd.
P.O. Box 17, 04553
(207) 563-8954

**Amenities:** 1,2,9,10,16,17
**Breakfast:** F.
**Dbl. Oc.:** $45.00 - $70.00
**Third Person:** $10.00

**Crown 'n' Anchor Inn**—A restored Greek Revival with a commanding view of the water. Fine period and Victorian furnishings throughout. Fireplaced parlor and large guest library. Full country gourmet breakfast by candlelight in the formal dining room. Near historic sites, shops and restaurants.

## Newcastle *

Markert, William
Glidden St., 04543
(207) 563-1309

**Amenities:** 1,2,5,6,7,8,9,10,
15,17
**Breakfast:** F.

**Dbl. Oc.:** $45.00 - $55.00
**Third Person:** $10.00

**The Markert House**—Four rooms with two shared baths in a 1900 Victorian on a hillside overlooking the Damariscotta River. Your host is an artist, photographer, gourmet cook and gardener. Reproduction Victorian veranda, antique furnishings and tasteful art.

---

| | | | | |
|---|---|---|---|---|
| 1. No Smoking | 5. Tennis Available | 9. Credit Cards Accepted | 13. Lunch Available | 17. Shared Bath |
| 2. No Pets | 6. Golf Available | 10. Personal Checks Accepted | 14. Public Transportation | 18. Afternoon Tea |
| 3. No Children | 7. Swiming Available | 11. Off Season Rates | 15. Reservations Necessary | ★ Commissions given |
| 4. Senior Citizen Rates | 8. Skiing Available | 12. Dinner Available | 16. Private Bath | to Travel Agents |

## Newcastle *

Sprague, Chris & Ted
04553
(207) 563-5685

**Amenities:** 1,2,3,6,7,8,9,10, 11,12,15
**Breakfast:** F.

**Dbl. Oc.:** $103.70 - $115.90
**Sgl. Oc.:** $91.50 - $105.70

**The Newcastle Inn**—A country inn of distinction on the picturesque Damariscotta River. Romantic, pampering ambience (some canopy beds) and truly memorable, epicurean cuisine. *Maine Sunday Telegram* gave us four stars — "so flawless it seems like a dream." AAA rated the inn - three diamonds.

## Ogunquit *

Hartwell, James
118 Shore Rd., 03907
(207) 646-7210

**Amenities:** 2,5,6,7,9,10,11,15, 16
**Breakfast:** C.

**Dbl. Oc.:** $95.00 - $175.00
**Sgl. Oc.:** priced accordingly

**Hartwell House**—This inn welcomes you in the tradition of fine European country inns, while offering authentic New England charm. Stroll the Marginal Way past picture-postcard seascapes and rock formations. Ogunquit Beach and Perkins Cove are both within a few steps.

## Ogunquit

Sachon, Eeta
30 Bourne Lane
P.O. Box 1940, 03907
(207) 646-3891

**Amenities:** 2,3,9,10,11,16,17
**Breakfast:** C.

**Dbl. Oc.:** $65.00 - $118.00
**Sgl. Oc.:** $65.00 - $118.00
**Third Person:** $10.00

**The Morning Dove Bed And Breakfast**—An 1860's farmhouse furnished with antiques and European accents. A quiet and convenient location near shops, beaches and restaurants! Spectacular gardens. Owner is an interior designer.

## Pemaquid *

De Kahn, Kristina
Route 130
HC 62, Box 178, 04558
(207) 677-2845

**Amenities:** 2,6,7,9,10,15, 16,17
**Breakfast:** F.

**Dbl. Oc.:** $60.00 - $70.00
**Sgl. Oc.:** $55.00 - $65.00
**Third Person:** $10.00

**Little River Inn**—Enjoy a relaxing coastal Maine vacation in one of Maine's most historic and scenic areas. Select a traditional room or one of our rustic gallery rooms. Delicious banquet breakfast. Minutes from the lighthouse, beach, archaeological digs, New Harbor, galleries and shops.

## Rumford

Tucker, Joan
E. Bethel Rd.
Box 12, 04279
(207) 364-4986

**Amenities:** 2,6,7,8,10,13,17
**Breakfast:** F.

**Dbl. Oc.:** $53.50
**Sgl. Oc.:** $32.10
**Third Person:** $10.70
**Child:** under two - no charge

**The Last Resort Bed & Breakfast**—A colonial Cape in Rumford Corner nestled in the foothills of western Maine. Country comfort, charm and good homecooking are our specialities. Skiing within minutes. Nearby are two state parks and golf courses. Fishing, hiking and hunting are by the back door. Children welcome.

| | | | | |
|---|---|---|---|---|
| 1. No Smoking | 5. Tennis Available | 9. Credit Cards Accepted | 13. Lunch Available | 17. Shared Bath |
| 2. No Pets | 6. Golf Available | 10. Personal Checks Accepted | 14. Public Transportation | 18. Afternoon Tea |
| 3. No Children | 7. Swiming Available | 11. Off Season Rates | 15. Reservations Necessary | ★ Commissions given |
| 4. Senior Citizen Rates | 8. Skiing Available | 12. Dinner Available | 16. Private Bath | to Travel Agents |

# MAINE

## Southwest Harbor *

Brower, Gardiner
Clark Point Rd., 04679
(207) 244-5335

**Amenities:** 1,2,5,6,7,8,10,11,16,17
**Breakfast:** F.
**Dbl. Oc.:** $58.85 - $123.05
**Third Person:** $21.04

**Lindenwood Inn**—A warm and friendly inn overlooking the harbor on the quiet side of Acadia National Park. Nearby sightseeing, hiking, boating, shops and restaurants. Relax in the parlor or play our harpsichord. Children over 12 years welcome. Open all year.

## Southwest Harbor

Cervelli, Nancy & Tom
100 Main St.
P.O. Box 1426, 04679
(207) 244-5302

**Amenities:** 1,2,3,9,10,11,16,18
**Breakfast:** F.
**Dbl. Oc.:** $80.25 - $155.15
**Sgl. Oc.:** $79.90 - $144.45
**Third Person:** $15.00

**The Kingsleigh Inn**—A romantic, restored country inn overlooking picturesque Southwest Harbor. We offer gracious hospitality in a warm and cozy setting. Located minutes from Acadia National Park. Within walking distance to restaurants and shops.

## Southwest Harbor

Gill, Ann
Clark Point Rd.
Box 1006, 04679
(207) 244-5180

**Amenities:** 1,2,3,5,6,7,10,11,
15,16,17,18
**Breakfast:** F.

**Dbl. Oc.:** $55.00 - $60.00
**Sgl. Oc.:** $55.00 - $60.00
**Third Person:** $20.00
**Child:** over 12 yrs. - $20.00

**The Island House**—Relax in a gracious seacoast home on the quiet side of Mount Desert Island. A charming and private loft apartment across the street from the harbor. A five-minute walk to village and restaurant. A five-minute drive to Acadia National Park. Open May through October.

## Southwest Harbor

Hoke, Elizabeth
Clark Point Rd., 04679
(207) 244-9828

**Amenities:** 1,2,6,7,8,9,10,11,
16,17,18
**Breakfast:** F.

**Dbl. Oc.:** $58.85 - $101.65
**Third Person:** $16.05

**The Lambs Ear Inn**—Please come and visit our stately old Maine house. Comfortable and serene. Overlooks the harbor, away from the hustle and bustle. Crisp, fresh linens. A sparkling harbor view and a breakfast to remember. Be a part of this special village surrounded by Acadia National Park.

| | | | | |
|---|---|---|---|---|
| 1. No Smoking | 5. Tennis Available | 9. Credit Cards Accepted | 13. Lunch Available | 17. Shared Bath |
| 2. No Pets | 6. Golf Available | 10. Personal Checks Accepted | 14. Public Transportation | 18. Afternoon Tea |
| 3. No Children | 7. Swiming Available | 11. Off Season Rates | 15. Reservations Necessary | ★ Commissions given |
| 4. Senior Citizen Rates | 8. Skiing Available | 12. Dinner Available | 16. Private Bath | to Travel Agents |

# MAINE

## Southwest Harbor

Strong, Prentice
Main St.
Box 68, 04679
(207) 244-7102

**Amenities:** 2,5,6,7,8,10,11,15, 17,18

**Breakfast:** F.

**Dbl. Oc.:** $58.35
**Sgl. Oc.:** $48.15

**Penury Hall**—Guests are honorary family, but don't have to wash the dishes. Share our two cats and interest in art, antiques, gardening and sailing. The sauna will relax you after hiking or skiing. Scrumptious varied breakfasts. We play backgammon for blood! Reservations advised.

## Spruce Head

Smith, Terry & Norman
Clark Island Rd., 04859
(207) 594-7644

**Amenities:** 7,9,10,11,12,15,16, 17

**Breakfast:** F.

**Dbl. Oc.:** $73.00
**Sgl. Oc.:** $50.00
**Third Person:** $15.00
**Child:** under 3 yrs. - $5.00

**Craignair Inn**—A charming seaside inn located 18 miles off Route 1. Antique-filled dining room and adjoining sitting room create a cozy atmosphere. Fine continental cuisine in our restaurant, serving dinner to guests and public, with a fabulous view of the sea. Natural setting.

## Stockton Springs *

Christie-Wilson, Katherine & David
RFD 1, Box 639, 04981
(207) 567-3726

**Amenities** 1,2,7,10,17
**Breakfast:** C.

**Dbl. Oc.:** $53.50
**Sgl. Oc.:** $42.80
**Third Person:** $16.00

**Whistlestop Bed & Breakfast**—Gracious and comfortable lodging in a secluded ocean front setting, just 1/2 mile from Route 1. Two guest rooms, double or twin beds and a hearty continental breakfast. Enjoy a warm welcome year round. Brochure available.

## Sunset *

Pavloff, Eleanor L.
Goose Cove Rd., 04683
(207) 348-2508

**Amenities:** 2,5,6,7,10,12, 13,15,16

**Breakfast:** C. (F. summer)

**Dbl. Oc.:** $95.00 - $212.00
**Sgl. Oc.:** $48.00 - $84.00
**Third Person:** $10.00 - $100.00
**Child:** sliding scale

**Goose Cove Lodge On Deer Isle**—Rustic cottages and rooms. Fireplaces. Sun decks overlooking the ocean. Main lodge serving breakfast and dinner in summer. Continental breakfast only in spring and fall. Nature walks, boat trips, massage and family-style evening entertainment. Natural beauty and peace.

## Swan's Island

Joyce, Jeanne
Main St., 04685
(207) 526-4116

**Amenities:** 10,15,17,18
**Breakfast:** F.

**Dbl. Oc.:** $48.15
**Sgl. Oc.:** $37.45
**Third Person:** $16.05
**Child:** under 5 yrs. - $5.35

**Jeannie's Place B&B**—A 45-minute ferry ride from Bass Harbor. Breakfast includes fresh-baked bread and muffins plus eggs and bacon. Enjoy picnics, beachcombing and peaceful walks through forests and along the seashore. Two guest rooms overlook the ocean.

| | | | | |
|---|---|---|---|---|
| 1. No Smoking | 5. Tennis Available | 9. Credit Cards Accepted | 13. Lunch Available | 17. Shared Bath |
| 2. No Pets | 6. Golf Available | 10. Personal Checks Accepted | 14. Public Transportation | 18. Afternoon Tea |
| 3. No Children | 7. Swiming Available | 11. Off Season Rates | 15. Reservations Necessary | ★ Commissions given |
| 4. Senior Citizen Rates | 8. Skiing Available | 12. Dinner Available | 16. Private Bath | to Travel Agents |

## *Topsham*

Nelson, Mary Kay & Dewey
36 Elm St., 04086
(207) 725-2562

**Amenities:** 1,10,15,16
**Breakfast:** F.

**Dbl. Oc.:** $60.00
**Sgl. Oc.:** $60.00
**Third Person:** $10.00
**Child:** under 6 yrs. -
no charge

**Middaugh Bed & Breakfast**—Located in the historic district. Listed in the *National Register of Historic Places*. This 150-year-old Federal Greek Revival home is 10 minutes from L.L.Bean and Freeport. Centrally located between Camden, Boothbay Harbor and Portland. Big rooms. Private baths.

## *W. Boothbay Harbor* *

Kelley, G. Frank
P.O. Box 505, 04575
(207) 633-2544, (800) 633-ROCK

**Amenities:** 5,6,7,9,10,11,12,16
**Breakfast:** F.
**Dbl. Oc.:** $58.85 - $117.70
**Sgl. Oc.:** $58.85 - $117.70

Operating in the Boothbay Harbor
Region Since 1898
May to October

**The Lawnmeer Inn**—Craggy cliffs. Retreat. Sea breezes. Beethoven. Indian Pudding. Old-time Maine. Coon cat. Lighthouse. Serenity. Puffins. Porches. Lobsters. Herb garden. Adirondack chairs. New friends welcome. Open May to Oct.

## *Waldboro*

Slagel, Don
Route 32 S., 04572
(207) 832-4552

**Amenities:** 2,5,7,8,9,10,11,
16,17
**Breakfast:** F.

**Dbl. Oc.:** $55.00 - $70.00
**Sgl. Oc.:** $45.00 - $60.00
**Third Person:** $10.00
**Child:** under 2 yrs. -
no charge

**Le Va Tout**—"Go for it" at this gracious 1830 B&B. Three minutes from Route 1 on 32 South. Gallery and gardens open to visitors. Superbly located for mid-coast Maine travel. Reservations encouraged throughout the year.

## *Weld* *

Strunk, Martha
7 High St., Farmington, ME 04938
Webb Lake, 04285
(207) 778-4306, (207) 585-2243

**Amenities:** 2,5,6,7,9,10,11,12,
13,15,16,17
**Breakfast:** C.

**Dbl. Oc.:** $50.00 - $65.00
**Sgl. Oc.:** $40.00
**Third Person:** $10.00
**Child:** $10.00

**Kawanhee Inn Lakeside Lodge**—Rated #1 for unique and hidden spots in the west Maine mountains. Ten-bedroom lodge. Fieldstone fireplaces. Cathedral pines overlooking pristine Lake Webb. Mt. Blue hiking. Sandy beach. Canoes. Moose and loon watching. Restaurant. Open May - October 15.

| | | | |
|---|---|---|---|
| 1. No Smoking | 5. Tennis Available | 9. Credit Cards Accepted | 13. Lunch Available | 17. Shared Bath |
| 2. No Pets | 6. Golf Available | 10. Personal Checks Accepted | 14. Public Transportation | 18. Afternoon Tea |
| 3. No Children | 7. Swiming Available | 11. Off Season Rates | 15. Reservations Necessary | ★ Commissions given |
| 4. Senior Citizen Rates | 8. Skiing Available | 12. Dinner Available | 16. Private Bath | to Travel Agents |

# MAINE

## York *

Rothermel, Hannah & Dan
162 Chases Pond Rd., 03909
(207) 363-7244

**Amenities:** 1,2,10,11,16
**Breakfast:** F.

**Dbl. Oc.:** $64.20
**Sgl. Oc.:** $53.50
**Third Person:** $15.00
**Child:** under 6 yrs. -
    no charge

**Hannah's Loft**—A very quiet setting. Ten minutes from beaches, restaurants and shopping. Historic, scenic downtowns of York, Portsmouth and Ogunquit. Private baths, deck and entrances. Skylights. Refrigerator and microwave. 5% of rate is donated to the Maine Children's Cancer Program.

---

## York

Simonds, Harriet & John
241 Cider Hill Rd.
Route 91, 03909
(207) 363-5233

**Amenities:** 5,6,7,10,16
**Breakfast:** C.

**Dbl. Oc.:** $53.50
**Sgl. Oc.:** $48.15
**Third Person:** $10.70
**Child:** $10.70

**"A Summer Place"**—Charming rooms in a 1790 house. Secluded country setting. River view. Ten minutes to miles of sandy beaches. Many excellent restaurants and discount malls within five miles. The inn is 2.7 miles off Route 1 on Route 91.

---

## York

Sullivan, Frances & Frank
78 Long Sands Rd., 03909
(207) 363-2532

**Amenities:** 1,2,5,6,7,8,10,11,
    15,16,18
**Breakfast:** F.

**Dbl. Oc.:** $64.20
**Sgl. Oc.:** $53.50
**Third Person:** $20.00
**Child:** no charge - $10.00

**The Wild Rose Of York, B&B**—Our handsome colonial inn was built in 1814. Relax on the huge porch or by the fireplace. Play the piano. Rooms are cozy with antique beds and quilts. Two have fireplaces. Walk to the historic village. Bike to the beaches that area one mile away. Our waffles are a favorite.

---

## York Beach

Billings, Evelyn & Gil
7 Cross St., 03910
(207) 363-6292 (summer),
(207) 568-0785 (winter)

**Amenities:** 1,2,10,16,17
**Breakfast:** C.

**Dbl. Oc.:** $54.00 - $64.00
**Sgl. Oc.:** $48.00 - $59.00
**Third Person:** $10.00
**Child:** under 12 yrs. - $5.00

**Red Shutters**—A cozy B&B for non-smokers. A quiet setting. Five-minute walk to beach, shops, dining and entertainment. "Your home while you're here." You'll awaken to the aroma of homemade muffins baking for your breakfast. Open June - August.

---

| | | | | |
|---|---|---|---|---|
| 1. No Smoking | 5. Tennis Available | 9. Credit Cards Accepted | 13. Lunch Available | 17. Shared Bath |
| 2. No Pets | 6. Golf Available | 10. Personal Checks Accepted | 14. Public Transportation | 18. Afternoon Tea |
| 3. No Children | 7. Swiming Available | 11. Off Season Rates | 15. Reservations Necessary | ★ Commissions given |
| 4. Senior Citizen Rates | 8. Skiing Available | 12. Dinner Available | 16. Private Bath | to Travel Agents |

# MAINE

## York Beach

Duffy, Danielle & Dan
8 S. Main St.,(Route 1A), 03910
(207) 363-8952

**Amenities:** 1,2,3,4,5,6,7,10, 11,15,17,18
**Breakfast:** C.

**Dbl. Oc.:** $63.00
**Sgl. Oc.:** $53.00
**Child:** under 12 yrs. - $10.00

**Homestead Inn B&B**—Built in 1905. Four large and quiet rooms with panoramic ocean view. Fireplaced living room. Sun deck. Breakfast served in barn-board dining room with ocean view. Walk to beach, lighthouse, shops and restaurants. Enjoy sunset serenity. Let us pamper you! Let the seashore happen.

## York Beach

Jennings, Virginia
44 Freeman St., 03910
(207) 363-4087, (207) 748-0916

**Amenities:** 4,9,10,11,15,17
**Breakfast:** C.

**Dbl. Oc.:** $57.00
**Sgl. Oc.:** $48.15
**Third Person:** $10.70
**Child:** $5.35

**The Candleshop Inn**—Like a visit to Grandma's house — if Grandma lived in a quaint New England seaside village. An easy stroll to beach and town and an easy drive to nightlife and malls. Definitely not an impersonal motel! Return to a simple way of life. Come and join a new family!

## York Harbor

Cook, Kathie & Wes
570 York St.
Box 445, 03911
(207) 363-7264

**Amenities:** 2,3,10,11,16,17,18
**Breakfast:** F.
**Dbl. Oc.:** $69.55
**Sgl. Oc.:** $58.85
**Third Person:** $10.00

**Bell Buoy Bed & Breakfast**—At the Bell Buoy, there are no strangers — only friends who have not met. Our Victorian home offers casual elegance in a quiet setting. You may walk to the nearby beaches, sit on the porch or curl up by the fireplace. Minutes from I-95 and outlet shopping.

## York Harbor *

Dominguez, Garry
Route 1 A, 03911
(207) 363-5119

**Amenities:** 2,4,5,6,7,9,10,11, 12,13,14,15,16,17
**Breakfast:** C.

**Dbl. Oc.:** $95.23
**Sgl. Oc.:** $84.53
**Third Person:** $15.00
**Child:** under 12 yrs. - no charge

**York Harbor Inn**—A 1637 historic country inn with ocean-view lodging and dining. Charming rooms feature fireplaces, antiques, poster beds, private baths, phone, air-conditioning, jacuzzi, boating, beach and mega-outlet mall shopping. AAA and Mobil rated.

| | | | | |
|---|---|---|---|---|
| 1. No Smoking | 5. Tennis Available | 9. Credit Cards Accepted | 13. Lunch Available | 17. Shared Bath |
| 2. No Pets | 6. Golf Available | 10. Personal Checks Accepted | 14. Public Transportation | 18. Afternoon Tea |
| 3. No Children | 7. Swiming Available | 11. Off Season Rates | 15. Reservations Necessary | ★ Commissions given |
| 4. Senior Citizen Rates | 8. Skiing Available | 12. Dinner Available | 16. Private Bath | to Travel Agents |

# MARYLAND

## *The Old Line State*

Capitol:  Annapolis
Statehood:  April 28, 1788, the 7th state
State Motto:  Manly Deeds, Womanly Words
State Song:  "Maryland, My Maryland"
State Bird:  Baltimore Oriole
State Flower:  Black-Eyed Susan
State Tree:  White Oak (Wye Oak)


Maryland was founded in 1634 by an Englishman named Calvert, who named it for Queen Henrietta Marie of England.

Francis Scott Keye wrote The Star Spangled Banner while watching the British bombard Fort McHenry during the War of 1812. He was inspired by the rockets and glare from the guns, and his inspiration became the National Anthem.

Today, Maryland is the bedroom for hundreds of government workers in Washington, D.C. The Baltimore harbor is one of the busiest on the eastern seaboard. Much of our imports from Europe come through here.

The Chesapeake Bay divides Maryland almost in half. In 1952, the world's first all-steel bridge over salt water was erected. Before this time, the people of each section of Maryland led entirely different lives, the country folk vs. the city folk.

Fishermen have wonderful fishing in the Chesapeake Bay. They are known all over the world for their oysters and clams.

The United States Naval Academy was established in Annapolis in 1845. It is a tourist attraction for hundreds of people every year.

## *Annapolis*

| | | |
|---|---|---|
| Clark, Mel | **Amenities:** 1,2,9,10,14, | **Dbl. Oc.:** $68.25 - $89.25 |
| 262 King George St., 21401 | 15,16,17 | **Sgl. Oc.:** $68.25 - $89.25 |
| (301) 268-3106 | **Breakfast:** C. | **Child:** no charge - |
| | (F. on weekends) | $10.00 |

**Casa Bahia**—An 1860's three-story house located in the Annapolis historic district. Furnished in a contemporary Southwestern style. During pleasant weather, breakfast is served outdoors on the patio, beside a pond filled with fish and aquatic plants.

---

## *Annapolis* *

| | | |
|---|---|---|
| Grovermann, Norma | **Amenities:** 1,2,3,6,9,10, | **Dbl. Oc.:** $78.75 |
| 232 Prince George St., 21401 | 14,15,17 | **Sgl. Oc.:** $63.00 |
| (301) 263-6418 | **Breakfast:** F. | |

**Prince George Inn Bed & Breakfast**—A delightful Victorian townhouse in the historic area. Furnished with antiques and art. Close to shops, restaurants, the U.S. Naval Academy, museums and city dock. Guests can enjoy a parlor, porches, courtyard and a gazebo. Lots of extra touches for guests' comforts.

---

## *Annapolis* *

| | | |
|---|---|---|
| Liedlich, Susan | **Amenities:** 1,2,9,10,14,17 | **Dbl. Oc.:** $63.00 - $78.75 |
| 149 Prince George St., 21401 | **Breakfast:** C. | **Sgl. Oc.:** $57.75 - $73.50 |
| (301) 268-6277 | | **Third Person:** $15.75 |
| | | **Child:** under 3 yrs. - |
| | | no charge |

**Ark & Dove Bed And Breakfast**—Located in the historic district. Visitors will find shops, restaurants, U.S. Naval Academy, St. John's College, cruise boats and Georgian mansions that are all within walking distance. Antiques adorn this B&B which spans three centuries. Bathrobes and toiletries provided.

---

## *Annapolis*

| | | |
|---|---|---|
| Ren, Lilith | **Amenities:** 1,2,3,10,14,15,16, | **Dbl. Oc.:** $68.25 - $105.00 |
| 161 Green St., 21401 | 17,18 | **Third Person:** $25.00 |
| (301) 268-9750 | **Breakfast:** C. | |

**Shaw's Fancy Bed & Breakfast**—Elegant suites with queen beds and private baths. Relax on our porch swing or in our hot tub. Great romantic getaway. Let us pamper you! Special packages on request. Within walking distance to dozens of restuarants, shops, historic homes and the U.S. Naval Academy.

---

| | | | | |
|---|---|---|---|---|
| 1. No Smoking | 5. Tennis Available | 9. Credit Cards Accepted | 13. Lunch Available | 17. Shared Bath |
| 2. No Pets | 6. Golf Available | 10. Personal Checks Accepted | 14. Public Transportation | 18. Afternoon Tea |
| 3. No Children | 7. Swiming Available | 11. Off Season Rates | 15. Reservations Necessary | ★ Commissions given |
| 4. Senior Citizen Rates | 8. Skiing Available | 12. Dinner Available | 16. Private Bath | to Travel Agents |

# MARYLAND

## Annapolis *

Schrift, Jeanne & Claude
110 Prince George St., 21401
(301) 268-5555

**Amenities:** 1,2,9,10,14,15, 16,17
**Breakfast:** C.

**Dbl. Oc.:** $75.48 - $133.20
**Sgl. Oc.:** $64.38 - $122.10
**Third Person:** $11.10
**Child:** under 1 yr. no charge

**Gibson's Lodgings**—Three houses in historic Annapolis — one 18th-century Georgian, one 19th-century stucco and a new house with aunique conference room — offer 21 guest rooms and suites, parlors and dining rooms. All are furnished in antiques. Parking. Walk to everything.

## Annapolis *

Wolfrey, Jo Anne & Don
One College Ave., 21401
(301) 263-6124

**Amenities:** 1,2,3,10,14,15,16
**Breakfast:** C.

**Dbl. Oc.:** $160.00
**Sgl. Oc.:** $160.00
**Third Person:** $18.00

**College House Suites**—Elegant historic-district. Homes with private suites for sophisticated travelers. Nestled between U.S. Naval Academy and St. John's College. Easy walk to historic buildings, city dock, restaurants, shops, galleries, theatre, live music and sailing. Two-night minimum.

## Annapolis *

Zuchelli, Robert
8 Martin St., 21401
(310) 626-1506

**Amenities:** 1,2,3,5,6,7,10,11, 14,15,16,17
**Breakfast:** C.

**Dbl. Oc.:** $75.00 - $120.00
**Sgl. Oc.:** $75.00 - $120.00

**William Page Inn**—Located in the center of the historic district, within minutes of city docks and Naval Academy. It is furnished in authentic antiques and provides off-street parking.

## Baltimore

Bragaw, Paul
1601 Bolton St., 21217
(301) 728-1179

**Amenities:** 1,2,9,10,14,15,16
**Breakfast:** C.

**Dbl. Oc.:** $90.00 - $140.00
**Sgl. Oc.:** $90.00 - $140.00
**Third Person:** $25.00

**Mr. Mole Bed & Breakfast**—On historic Bolton Hill. An 1840's row house on a tree-lined street. Period decor with many antiques. Music room has concert grand piano. Two-bedroom suites with sitting rooms. Walk to symphony, opera and metro. Close to Inner Harbor, without any downtown congestion.

---

| | | | |
|---|---|---|---|
| 1. No Smoking | 5. Tennis Available | 9. Credit Cards Accepted | 13. Lunch Available | 17. Shared Bath |
| 2. No Pets | 6. Golf Available | 10. Personal Checks Accepted | 14. Public Transportation | 18. Afternoon Tea |
| 3. No Children | 7. Swiming Available | 11. Off Season Rates | 15. Reservations Necessary | ★ Commissions given |
| 4. Senior Citizen Rates | 8. Skiing Available | 12. Dinner Available | 16. Private Bath | to Travel Agents |

# MARYLAND

## Baltimore *

Cooley, Linda
1125 N. Calvert St., 21202
(301) 752-7722

**Amenities:** 2,9,10,14,15,16
**Breakfast:** C.
**Dbl. Oc.:** $120.00
**Sgl. Oc.:** $100.00

**Society Hill Government House**—Eighteen spacious rooms elegantly decorated with antiques and artwork. Personalized service, charming atmosphere, complimentary parking, local telephone calls and inner-city van service. Wine offered in parlor.

---

## Baltimore *

Gondzor, Stanley
205 W. Madison St., 21201
(301) 728-6550

**Amenities:** 2,4,9,10,11,14,15, 16,18
**Breakfast:** C.

**Dbl. Oc.:** $72.80 - $106.40
**Sgl. Oc.:** $61.60 - $89.60
**Third Person:** $10.00
**Child:** under 12 yrs. - no charge

**The Shirley Madison Inn**—A Victorian mansion decorated with the elegance of a bygone era. A short walk to Inner Harbor and city's cultural corridor. Landscaped courtyard. Victorian and Edwardian antiques. Complimentary continental breakfast and evening sherry.

---

## Baltimore

Grater, Betsy
1428 Park Ave., 21217-4230
(301) 383-1274, Fax: (301) 728-8957

**Amenities:** 7,9,10,14,15,16,17
**Breakfast:** F.
**Dbl. Oc.:** $67.20 - $72.80
**Sgl. Oc.:** $56.00
**Third Person:** $16.80
**Child:** $16.80

**Betsy's B&B**—A petite estate in a downtown historic neighborhood. A four-story row house on a tree-lined street with a brass railing and white marble steps. Spacious rooms with 12-foot ceilings. Antiques and unique wall decorations. Hot tub. A center-hall stair to fourth-floor skylight.

---

| | | | |
|---|---|---|---|
| 1. No Smoking | 5. Tennis Available | 9. Credit Cards Accepted | 13. Lunch Available | 17. Shared Bath |
| 2. No Pets | 6. Golf Available | 10. Personal Checks Accepted | 14. Public Transportation | 18. Afternoon Tea |
| 3. No Children | 7. Swiming Available | 11. Off Season Rates | 15. Reservations Necessary | ★ Commissions given |
| 4. Senior Citizen Rates | 8. Skiing Available | 12. Dinner Available | 16. Private Bath | to Travel Agents |

# MARYLAND

## Baltimore

Jeschke, Charlotte & Curt
111 W. Mulberry St., 21201
(301) 576-0111

**Amenities:** 1,2,3,5,6,7,10,12,
13,14,15,17
**Breakfast:** F.

**Dbl. Oc.:** $65.00
**Sgl. Oc.:** $65.00

**Mulberry House**—A downtown B&B. Park your car and walk to most attractions and the best restaurants. Amenities 5, 6, 7,12 and 13 are available, but not on the premises. An 1830 townhouse with antiques. Intimate. Host on the premises. Brochure available on request.

---

## Baltimore

Paulus, Lucie
2406 Kentucky Ave., 21213
(301) 467-1688

**Amenities:** 1,2,4,5,6,10
**Breakfast:** F.

**Dbl. Oc.:** $60.00
**Sgl. Oc.:** $55.00

**The Paulus Gasthaus**—Located in a lovely residential area. Three miles from Inner Harbor and all downtown attractions. We offer quality accommodations and Gemutlichkeit. Hostess speaks fluent German and some French.

---

## Bel Air

Fox, Dorothy & Howard
Tudor Hall, 21014
(301) 838-0466

**Amenities:** 2,3,4,7,10,12,13,
15,16,17,18
**Breakfast:** C.

**Dbl. Oc.:** $50.00
**Sgl. Oc.:** $50.00

**Tudor Hall**—Home of the Maryland Booths. An 18th-century Gothic Revival cottage built as a country retreat by Junius Brutus Booth (1796-1852). The birthplace of Tom Edwin and John Wilkes Booth. Twenty minutes to downtown Harbor Place.

---

## Berlin *

Jacques, Stephen
2 N. Main St.
(301) 641-3589
**Amenities:** 2,5,6,9,10,11,12,13,15,16
**Breakfast:** C.
**Dbl.Oc.:** $60.00 - $108.00
**Sgl.Oc.:** $60.00 - $108.00

**Atlantic Hotel Inn & Restaurant**—Built in 1895, this restored Victorian is lcoated in the heart of Berlin's historic district. Antique shops, museums are within walking distance. Eight miles from Ocean City and Assateague National Seashore. Four star restaurant and piano lounge on premises.

---

| | | | | |
|---|---|---|---|---|
| 1. No Smoking | 5. Tennis Available | 9. Credit Cards Accepted | 13. Lunch Available | 17. Shared Bath |
| 2. No Pets | 6. Golf Available | 10. Personal Checks Accepted | 14. Public Transportation | 18. Afternoon Tea |
| 3. No Children | 7. Swiming Available | 11. Off Season Rates | 15. Reservations Necessary | ★ Commissions given |
| 4. Senior Citizen Rates | 8. Skiing Available | 12. Dinner Available | 16. Private Bath | to Travel Agents |

# MARYLAND

## Bridgetown *

McAuilfe, Marion
Route 312, 21620
(800) 345-4665, Ext. 609

**Amenities:** 4,9,10,12,13,
15,16
**Breakfast:** C. and F.

**Dbl. Oc.:** $116.00
**Third Person:** $21.00

**The Chesapeake Gun Club**—Gunning and lodging for the hunting enthusiast. Created for discriminating sportsmen and sportswomen accustomed to the very finest in service and accommodations. Ideal environment for a romantic interlude, family vacation or corporate retreat.

## Cambridge

Brannock, Shirley S.
215 Glenburn Ave., 21613
(301) 228-6938

**Amenities:** 2,9,10,16
**Breakfast:** C.

**Dbl. Oc.:** $80.00 - $90.00
**Sgl. Oc.:** $80.00 - $90.00
**Third Person:** $10.00
**Child:** $10.00

**Commodore's Cottage**—Two private cottage suites in a quiet garden setting near a river. Antiques, art, maritime museum, bicycling, birdwatching, touring and a blackwater wildlife refuge. Nearby seafood restaurants. Air-conditioning, TV, phone and kitchen. Continental breakfast served in cottage.

## Chesapeake City *

McAuilfe, Marion
P.O. Box 609, Chestertown, 21620
(800) 345-4665, Ext. 609

**Amenities:** 4,5,6,7,9,10,12,
13,15,16
**Breakfast:** C.

**Dbl. Oc.:** $68.00 - $100.00
**Third Person:** $21.00

**The Blue Max Inn**—A Georgian home built in 1844. Located in the heart of the city. Relax on three porches or meet other guests in two comfortable parlors. The inn took its name from Jack Hunter's The Blue Max, a book about the highest honor in the German Air Force. Families welcome.

## Chestertown

Brook, Mrs. Marge
R.3, Box 360, 21620
(301) 778-5540

**Amenities:** 1,2,4,5,6,7,10,
15,16,18
**Breakfast:** F.

**Dbl. Oc.:** $63.00 - $70.00
**Sgl. Oc.:** $63.00 - $65.00
**Third Person:** $10.00
**Child:** $10.00 (if not in crib)

**Radcliffe Cross**—A pre-Revolutionary (circa 1725) brick house with many original features. We invite you to enjoy a delightful night's lodging and breakfast amidst the colonial charm of yesteryear. Weekend rates available.

## Chestertown

Maisel, Mary Susan
231 High St., 21620
(301) 778-2300

**Amenities:** 2,5,6,7,10,15,
16,18
**Breakfasrt:** C.

**Dbl. Oc.:** $75.00 - $125.00
**Third Person:** $25.0
**Child:** under 3 yrs. -
no charge

**The White Swan Tavern**—The tavern was built in 1730 and is beautifully restored. Located in 18th-century Chestertown on Maryland's eastern shore. Each guest receives complimentary wine and fruit.

| | | | |
|---|---|---|---|
| 1. No Smoking | 5. Tennis Available | 9. Credit Cards Accepted | 13. Lunch Available | 17. Shared Bath |
| 2. No Pets | 6. Golf Available | 10. Personal Checks Accepted | 14. Public Transportation | 18. Afternoon Tea |
| 3. No Children | 7. Swiming Available | 11. Off Season Rates | 15. Reservations Necessary | ★ Commissions given |
| 4. Senior Citizen Rates | 8. Skiing Available | 12. Dinner Available | 16. Private Bath | to Travel Agents |

## Chestertown *

McAuilfe, Marion
114 Washington Ave., 21620
(800) 345-4665, Ext. 609

**Amenities:** 4,5,7,9,10,12,13
14,15,16
**Breakfast:** C.

**Dbl. Oc.:**$53.00 - $115.00
**Third Person:**$21.00

**Hill's Inn**—A Victorian inn built in 1877. Located in the heart of town. Restored to its original charm, the dining room and double parlor feature plaster moldings Walk to historic Washington College and shops. Families welcome.

## Chestertown *

McAuilfe, Marion
P.O. Box 609, 21620
(800) 345-4665, Ext. 609

**Amenities:** 4,5,6,7,9,10,12,13
15,16
**Breakfast:** C.

**Dbl. Oc.:**$90.00 - $174.00
**Third Person:**$21.00

**Great Oak Manor**—A historic, waterfront Georgian manor situated on Chesapeake Bay. Stroll through 12 acres of landscaped grounds or enjoy a private sandy beach for swimming and rafting. Families welcome. Facilities for weddings, receptions, family reunions and business meetings.

## Chestertown *

McAuilife, Marion
Rolph's Wharf Rd., 21620
(800) 345-4665, Ext. 609

**Amenities:** 4,7,9,10,12,13,
**15,16**
**Breakfast:** C

**Dbl. Oc.:** $90.00 - $121.00
**Third Person:** $21.00

**The Inn At Rolph's Wharf**—A Victorian inn built in 1830. Nestled on six acres, near a sweeping bend of the Chester River. The inn is completly restored and offers the use of a deep-water marina.

## Deale

Eicens, Margaret
5960 Vacation Lane, 20751
(301) 867-0998,
(301) 261-9580

**Amenities:** 1,5,10,16

**Breakfast:** C.

**Dbl. Oc.:** $63.00
**Sgl.Oc.:** $52.50 - $63.00
**Third Person:** $10.00
**Child:** under 10 yrs. -
no charge

**Makai Pierside B&B**—Situated in a rural setting on the waterfront near Washington D.C. All new. Large rooms with TV, refrigerator and coffee maker. Restaurants within walking distance or by water taxi. Fishing charters arranged. Boaters can dock boats on premises or next door at the marina.

## Easton *

McAuilfe, Marion
14 No. Auroa St., 21601
(800) 345-4665, Ext. 609

**Amenities:** 4,5,6,7,9,10,12,13,
14,15,16
**Breakfast:** C.

**Dbl. Oc.:** $65.00 - $81.00
**Third Person:** $22.00

**The McDaniel House**—A charming circa 1890 Victorian house. Located in the historic section of Easton. Relax on the wrap-around porch or in a more formal atmosphere of the living room. Within walking distance to other historic points of interest. Available for informal business meetings.

| | | | | |
|---|---|---|---|---|
| 1. No Smoking | 5. Tennis Available | 9. Credit Cards Accepted | 13. Lunch Available | 17. Shared Bath |
| 2. No Pets | 6. Golf Available | 10. Personal Checks Accepted | 14. Public Transportation | 18. Afternoon Tea |
| 3. No Children | 7. Swiming Available | 11. Off Season Rates | 15. Reservations Necessary | ★ Commissions given |
| 4. Senior Citizen Rates | 8. Skiing Available | 12. Dinner Available | 16. Private Bath | to Travel Agents |

## Ellicott City

Osantowski, Margo & John
4344 Columbia Rd., 21043
(301) 461-4636

**Amenities:** 1,2,3,9,10,15,16,17
**Breakfast:** C.
**Dbl. Oc.:** $73.50 - $94.50

**The Wayside Inn**—Minutes from the historic mill town of Ellicott City. Many specialty shops and the B&O Railroad Museum. For the business traveler, we are near Columbia, Maryland and convenient to Annapolis, Baltimore and Washington, DC. Gift certificates are available.

## Frederick

Compton, Beverly & Ray
7945 Worman's Mill Rd., 21701
(301) 694-0440

**Amenities:** 1,2,3,10
**Breakfast:** C.
**Dbl. Oc.:** $75.00 - $90.00
**Sgl. Oc.:** $65.00 - $80.00
**Third Person:** $15.00

**"Spring Bank" — A B&B Inn**—In *National Register of Historic Places*. The former home of a gentleman farmer/banker. Original 1880 details and period furnishings. Situated on 10 acres. Three miles north of Frederick's historic district. Nearby fine dining.

## Frederick *

Mullican, Shirley & Dwight
9549 Liberty Rd., 21701
(301) 898-7128

**Amenities:** 1,2,3,5,6,7,10,16  **Dbl. Oc.:** $75.00 - $85.00
**Breakfast:** C.

**Middle Plantation Inn**—A rustic bed and breakfast on 25 acres built of stone and logs. Drive through horse country to the village of Mt Pleasant. Located several miles east of Frederick. Furnished with antiques that have 19th-century ambience. Each room has a private bath, air-conditioning and TV.

## Gaithersburg *

Danilowicz, Suzanne & Joe
18908 Chimney Pl., 20879
(301) 977-7377

**Amenities:** 1,2,5,6,7,10,14,15,  **Dbl. Oc.:** $52.50
16,17  **Sgl. Oc.:** $42.00
**Breakfast:** F.  **Third Person:** $15.00
**Child:** under 10 yrs
no charge

**Gaithersburg Hospitality Bed & Breakfast**—Located in Montgomery Village. Nearby restaurants, shopping and recreation. This luxurious home is furnished with family pieces and has your comfort and pleasure in mind. It offers all amenities and is a 35-minute drive to Washington, D.C. via car or metro. Offers home cooking.

| | | | | |
|---|---|---|---|---|
| 1. No Smoking | 5. Tennis Available | 9. Credit Cards Accepted | 13. Lunch Available | 17. Shared Bath |
| 2. No Pets | 6. Golf Available | 10. Personal Checks Accepted | 14. Public Transportation | 18. Afternoon Tea |
| 3. No Children | 7. Swiming Available | 11. Off Season Rates | 15. Reservations Necessary | ★ Commissions given |
| 4. Senior Citizen Rates | 8. Skiing Available | 12. Dinner Available | 16. Private Bath | to Travel Agents |

## *Hagerstown*

Day, Shirley & Donald
Route 9, Box 330, 21740
(301) 797-4764

**Amenities:** 1,2,3,4,6,10,15,16,17,18
**Breakfast:** F.
**Dbl. Oc.:** $73.50
**Sgl. Oc.:** $63.00

**Beaver Creek House**—Comfort, relaxation and hospitality await you at this antique-filled Victorian home. Located in a beautiful country setting near I-70 and I-81. Nearby fine restaurants, recreation, historic sites and antiquing. Complimentary sherry. Mid-week rates.

## *Hagerstown*

Lehman, Irene
Downsville Pike
R.D. 3, Box 150, 21740
(301) 582-1735

**Amenities:** 1,5,6,7,10,12, 13,16,17
**Breakfast:** F.

**Dbl. Oc.:** $50.00 - $70.00
**Sgl. Oc.:** $50.00 - $70.00
**Third Person:** $9.00
**Child:** $3.00 - $5.00

**Lewrene Farm Bed & Breakfast**—A colonial home on a 125-acre farm for tourists, families, business people, small seminars and family gatherings. Large living room, fireplace, piano, antiques and six bedrooms with either poster or canopy beds. Near Antietam battlefield, Harpers Ferry and C&O Canal.

## *Havre de Grace*

Traub, Mark
301 So. Union Ave., 21078
(301) 939-5200

**Amenities:** 2,5,6,7,8,9,10,12,14,16,17
**Breakfast:** F.
**Dbl. Oc.:** $69.95 - $90.95
**Sgl. Oc.:** $69.95 - $90.95

**The Vandiver Inn**—Turn-of-the-century charm and Victorian hospitality await you at The Vandiver Inn, Havre de Grace's finest guest inn. One block from Chesapeake Bay and a short walk to fine restaurants and four marinas make The Vandiver Inn the traveler's choice.

## *New Market*

Rimel, Terry & Tom
9 W. Main St.
P.O. Box 299, 21774
(301) 865-5055

**Amenities:** 2,3,5,6,9,10,11,16, 17,18
**Breakfast:** F.

**Dbl. Oc.:** $63.00 - $105.00
**Sgl. Oc.:** $52.50 - $68.25

**National Pike Inn**—A Federal home in a quaint historic village with four air-conditioned and beautifully furnished guest rooms. Relax in our private courtyard surrounded by lavish azalea gardens or stroll through town, with over 30 antique shops, a general store and fine dining. No children under 10.

| | | | | |
|---|---|---|---|---|
| 1. No Smoking | 5. Tennis Available | 9. Credit Cards Accepted | 13. Lunch Available | 17. Shared Bath |
| 2. No Pets | 6. Golf Available | 10. Personal Checks Accepted | 14. Public Transportation | 18. Afternoon Tea |
| 3. No Children | 7. Swiming Available | 11. Off Season Rates | 15. Reservations Necessary | ⋆ Commissions given |
| 4. Senior Citizen Rates | 8. Skiing Available | 12. Dinner Available | 16. Private Bath | to Travel Agents |

## New Market

Rossig, Jane
17 Main St.
Box 237, 21774
(301) 865-3318

**Amenities:** 2,3,5,8,10,15,16
**Breakfast:** F.

**Dbl. Oc.:** $89.25
**Sgl. Oc.:** $78.75
**Third Person:** $10.00

**Strawberry Inn**—A professionally run B&B serving guests for the past 17 years. The restored 1837 Maryland farmhouse has five antique-furnished guest rooms. On the grounds is a restored log house with all the facilities for a small business meeting. Brochure. Children over seven only.

## North East *

Demond, Lucia & Nick
102 Mill Lane, 21901
(301) 287-3532

**Amenities:** 1,2,9,10,15,17
**Breakfast:** F.

**Dbl. Oc.:** $55.00 - $65.00
**Sgl. Oc.:** $50.00 - $60.00

**The Mill House**—On-site survey of Maryland Historic Trust. Circa 1710. Furnished with antiques. Three acres of grounds including mill ruins on a tidal creek. Two miles south of I-95, Exit 100. Less than one hour to points of interest in a tri-state area.

## Olney *

Polinger, Helen
16410 Batchellor's Forest Rd., 20832
(301) 774-7649

**Amenities:** 1,7,9,15,16,17
**Breakfast:** F.
**Dbl. Oc.:** $68.25 - $115.50
**Sgl. Oc.:** $68.25 - $115.50
**Third Person:** $31.50

**The Thoroughbred Bed And Breakfast**—A beautiful 175-acre estate. Many fine race horses were raised here. Full breakfast, hot tub, swimming pool, pooltable and piano. You may stay in the main house or quaint, renovated 1900 farmhouse. Twelve miles to Washington, D.C. and six miles to metro. Come and relax with us.

## Oxford

Clark, Eleanor & Jerry
110 N. Morris St.
P.O. Box 658, 21654
(301) 226-5496

**Amenities:** 2,3,5,6,7,10,
16,17
**Breakfast:** C. Plus

**Dbl. Oc.:** $81.00 - $91.80
**Sgl. Oc.:** $81.00 - $91.80
**Third Person:** $16.20

**1876 House**—Oxford's only B&B. Relax and enjoy the restful atmosphere in a restored 19th-century Victorian home. Queen Anne period furnishings, Oriental carpets, 10-foot ceilings and wide-planked floors. Breakfast is served in the formal dining room 8:00 - 9:30 a.m. Open Jan. 2 - Dec. 23.

| | | | |
|---|---|---|---|
| 1. No Smoking | 5. Tennis Available | 9. Credit Cards Accepted | 13. Lunch Available | 17. Shared Bath |
| 2. No Pets | 6. Golf Available | 10. Personal Checks Accepted | 14. Public Transportation | 18. Afternoon Tea |
| 3. No Children | 7. Swiming Available | 11. Off Season Rates | 15. Reservations Necessary | ★ Commissions given |
| 4. Senior Citizen Rates | 8. Skiing Available | 12. Dinner Available | 16. Private Bath | to Travel Agents |

# MARYLAND

## Rock Hall *

McAuilfe, Marion
Route 2, Box 204, 21661
(800) 345-4665, Ext. 609

**Amenities:** 4,7,9,10,12,
13,15,16
**Breakfast:** C.

**Dbl. Oc.:** $79.00 - $153.00
**Third Person:** $21.00

**Huntingfield Manor**—A gracious waterfront manor reminiscent of yesteryear on Maryland's historic eastern shore. Located on 200 acres, one mile south of Rock Hall on the west side of Eastern Neck Island Road. Rock Hall is one of the last refuges of Maryland's famous watermen. Many sights.

## Salisbury *

Wallace, Dru
804 Spring Hill Rd., 21801
(301) 742-4887

**Amenities:** 1,2,3,4,9,15,
16,17,
**Breakfast:** C.

**Dbl. Oc.:** $59.40 - $70.20
18   **Sgl. Oc.:** $54.00

**White Oak Inn**—A warm, hospitable lakeside colonial home set on five acres of lush trees. Enjoy the wildlife and beautiful sunsets. A historic town of fine restaurants, antique shops, zoo,college and nearby beaches. Cruise the Wicomico River on the Paddle Queen.

## Vienna

Altergott, Elise & Harvey
111 Water St.
P.O. Box 98, 21869
(301) 376-3347

**Amenities:** 2,5,9,10,17
**Breakfast:** F.

**Dbl. Oc.:** $63.00
**Sgl. Oc.:** $58.00

**The Tavern House**—An authentically restored colonial tavern on the Nanticoke River. Escape the 20th century and discover Eastern Shore hospitality. For those who enjoy looking at the river and marshes, watching an osprey in flight or a leisurely walk. Near Black Water Refuge.

---

| | | | |
|---|---|---|---|
| 1. No Smoking | 5. Tennis Available | 9. Credit Cards Accepted | 13. Lunch Available | 17. Shared Bath |
| 2. No Pets | 6. Golf Available | 10. Personal Checks Accepted | 14. Public Transportation | 18. Afternoon Tea |
| 3. No Children | 7. Swiming Available | 11. Off Season Rates | 15. Reservations Necessary | ★ Commissions given |
| 4. Senior Citizen Rates | 8. Skiing Available | 12. Dinner Available | 16. Private Bath | to Travel Agents |

# MASSACHUSETTS

## *The Bay State*

Capital: Boston
Statehood: February 6, 1788; the 6th state
State Motto: By The Sword We Seek Peace,
　　　　　　But Peace Only Under Liberty
State Song: "All Hail To Massachusetts"
State Bird: Chickadee
State Flower: Mayflower
State Tree: American Elm

Much of the history of our country began in this state. The Pilgrims landed in Plymouth in 1620 and the Boston Tea Party took place in Boston Harbor on Dec. 16, 1773. The historic ride of Paul Revere on April 19, 1775 is still reenacted each year, and the battlefields of Lexington and Concord remain a great tourist attraction.

Massachusetts, a champion of education, boasts of having the oldest college in our country. Harvard College was established in 1636 in Cambridge, and the first public library was started here when John Harvard gave his collection of books to the college. Today, in this state, there are over 75 fine colleges and higher institutions of learning.

The vacationer will find beautiful beaches from Newburyport on the north shore to Cape Cod on the south shore. The lovely Berkshire Hills in the western part of the state provide the stage for the Annual Berkshire Music Festival. Downtown Boston, and especially Quincy Market, is a haven of entertainment, gourmet restaurants and lovely shops. The Boston skyline, with its new buildings, reflect the Bostonian's initiative for progress set forth by their forefathers. Throughout the state, large industrial and technological companies are springing up because of the proximity to the educational facilities that are here.

The people of Massachusetts are very proud of their colonial heritage and often express it in their style of home and decor.

Presidents John Adams, John Quincy Adams, John F. Kennedy and George Herbert Walker Bush, our 41st President, were all born here.

# MASSACHUSETTS

## Attleboro *

Logie, Caroline & Jim
18 French Farm Rd., 02703
(508)226-6365

**Amenities:** 1,4,6,7,10,11,
14,16,17,18
**Breakfast:** F.

**Dbl. Oc.:** $55.00 - $70.00
**Sgl. Oc.:** $45.00 - $60.00
**Third Person:** $15.00
**Child:** under 6 yrs. -
no charge

**Emma C.'s Bed And Breakfast**—Enjoy the warmth and hospitality in this "country colonial" home. Guest rooms complete with antiques, quilts, fresh flowers, air-conditioning and TVs. Enjoy the sun deck in summer and wood stove in winter. Near train to Boston and Providence. Ten minutes to Wheaton College.

## Attleboro

Schaefer, Allana
203 No. Main St., 02703
(508) 222-6022

**Amenities:** 1,2,5,6,9,10,14,
16,17,18
**Breakfast:** F.

**Dbl. Oc.:** $55.00 - $72.00
**Sgl. Oc.:** $44.50 - $72.00
**Third Person:** $10.00

**The Col. Blackinton Inn**—Situated on the Bungay River, 1/2 mile to the Boston train and 1-1/2 miles to I-95. Sixteen guest rooms, two parlors, terrace and afternoon tea. Convenient to all attractions in S.E. New England. Business and pleasure travelers welcome. Available for small meetings and functions.

## Barnstable *

Bain, Fay & Donald
3660 Route 6A,
P.O. Box 856, 02630
(508) 362-8044

**Amenities:** 2,3,5,6,7,9,10,15,16
**Breakfast:** F.
**Dbl. Oc.:** $109.70 - $181.01
**Sgl. Oc.:** $109.70 - $181.01

**Ashley Manor**—A very special place. A secluded 1699 mansion in Cape Cod's historic area. Gracious, romantic and comfortable. Antiques and Oriental rugs. Beautifully appointed rooms and suites. All private baths. Fireplaces. New, private tennis court. Walk to beach and village.

## Barnstable *

Frazee, Robert
3026 Olde King's Hwy.
(Route 6A), 02630
(508) 362-8584

**Amenities:** 1,2,3,5,6,7,9,10,
11,15,16,17,18
**Breakfast:** C. Plus

**Dbl. Oc.:** $66.00 - $105.00
**Sgl. Oc.:** $50.00 - $83.00

**The Henry Crocker House**—Cheerful, spotless, historic 1805 former tavern is gracious and inviting. Canopy beds, fireplaced common rooms, porch, terrace and lovely grounds. Walk to beach, whale watching, dining and antiquing. Complimentary breakfast, afternoon tea and bikes.

| | | | | |
|---|---|---|---|---|
| 1. No Smoking | 5. Tennis Available | 9. Credit Cards Accepted | 13. Lunch Available | 17. Shared Bath |
| 2. No Pets | 6. Golf Available | 10. Personal Checks Accepted | 14. Public Transportation | 18. Afternoon Tea |
| 3. No Children | 7. Swiming Available | 11. Off Season Rates | 15. Reservations Necessary | ★ Commissions given |
| 4. Senior Citizen Rates | 8. Skiing Available | 12. Dinner Available | 16. Private Bath | to Travel Agents |

## Barnstable

Gedrin, Genny
61 Pine Lane, 02630
(508) 362-8559

**Amenities:** 1,2,3,5,6,7,10, 15,16
**Breakfast:** C.

**Dbl. Oc.:** $65.00 - $70.00
**Sgl. Oc.:** $60.00 - $65.00

**Goss House**—Located on the quiet north side of mid-Cape Cod. Three rooms with private baths. No children under 12. Open May 15 through October 31.

## Barnstable Village

Chester, Evelyn
Powder Hill Rd., 02630
(508) 362-9356

**Amenities:** 2,3,5,6,7,9,10, 12,16,18
**Breakfast:** F.

**Dbl. Oc.:** $152.90 - $185.90
**Sgl. Oc.:** $152.90 - $185.90

**Cobb's Cove**—A romantic, secluded, timbered colonial inn on a 1643 historic site. Centrally located on Cape Cod's quiet northside. Spacious rooms with lovely water views, whirlpool tubs and terrycloth robes. Superb breakfasts on flower-and bird-filled patio.

## Boston *

Butterworth, Susan
27 Brimmer St., 02108
(617) 523-7376

**Amenities:** 1,2,14,15,16
**Breakfast:** F.
**Dbl. Oc.:** $95.00 - $115.00
**Sgl. Oc.:** $95.00 - $115.00
**Third Person:** $20.00
**Child:** $20.00

**Beacon Hill Bed & Breakfast**—Three blocks from "Cheers" in historically preserved, elegant downtown neighborhood. Three spacious rooms with fireplaces in enormous Victorian row house overlooking the Charles River Esplanade. Easy walk to tourist highlights, subway and public garage.

## Boston *

Cote, Dennis F.
82 Chandler St., 02116
(617) 482-0408

**Amenities:** 1,2,3,10,14,15,16
**Breakfast:** C. and F.
**Dbl. Oc.:** $95.00
**Sgl. Oc.:** $90.00

**82 Chandler Street**—Located in historic downtown off famous Copley Square, near the Hynes Convention Center. Beautifully restored 1863 red-brick townhouse. Finely furnished bedrooms with private bath and kitchenettes. Family-style breakfast served in penthouse kitchen. Easy walk to all city sites.

| | | | | |
|---|---|---|---|---|
| 1. No Smoking | 5. Tennis Available | 9. Credit Cards Accepted | 13. Lunch Available | 17. Shared Bath |
| 2. No Pets | 6. Golf Available | 10. Personal Checks Accepted | 14. Public Transportation | 18. Afternoon Tea |
| 3. No Children | 7. Swiming Available | 11. Off Season Rates | 15. Reservations Necessary | ★ Commissions given |
| 4. Senior Citizen Rates | 8. Skiing Available | 12. Dinner Available | 16. Private Bath | to Travel Agents |

# MASSACHUSETTS

## Boston *

Hagopian, Family , The
261 Newbry St., 02116
(617) 437-7666

**Amenities:** 1,2,9,14,16
**Breakfast:** C. and F.
**Dbl. Oc.:** $70.00 - $130.00
**Sgl. Oc.:** $60.00 - $120.00

**Newbury Guest House**—A 19th-century townhouse with 15 renovated rooms. Common parlor and outdoor patio on fashionable Newbury Street. Private baths. Parking available. Minutes from public transportation. Walking distance to entire city of Boston.

## Boston *

Houghton, Mimi
106 Chestnut St., 02108
(617) 227-7866

**Amenities:** 10,11,14,15,16,17
**Breakfast:** F.

**Dbl. Oc.:** $85.00
**Sgl. Oc.:** $75.00
**Third Person:** $15.00

**Beacon Hill Accommodations**—Close to "Cheers," Freedom Trail, fine shops and restaurants. Filled with antiques, books and paintings. Roof deck and central air-conditioning. Ideal for business or pleasure. Hostess is a native Bostonian — full of ideas for your stay.

## Boston

Locke, Judy
533 Newbury St., 02215
(617) 266-2583, (617) 227-3111

**Amenities:** 2,9,10,14,15,17
**Breakfast:** C.
**Dbl. Oc.:** $60.00
**Sgl. Oc.:** $50.00
**Third Person:** $10.00

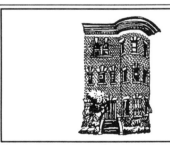

**The Newbury Inn**—A charming Victorian eight-room house located in the fashionable Back Bay area. Convenient to transportation and business center. Some rooms with ornate fireplaces.

## Boston *

Rosenbaum, Thomas
26 Chandler, 02116
(800) 842-3450, (617) 482-3450

**Amenities:** 2,9,11,14,15,16
**Breakfast:** C.

**Dbl. Oc.:** $92.15
**Sgl. Oc.:** $81.81
**Third Person:** $10.97
**Child:** under 12 yrs. -
no charge

**Chandler Inn**—A small hotel in the center of the city. The perfect option for the price-conscious traveler or tourist seeking a friendly spot. Located between Copley and Park Squares. We are within walking distance to most of Boston's historic sites.

| | | | | |
|---|---|---|---|---|
| 1. No Smoking | 5. Tennis Available | 9. Credit Cards Accepted | 13. Lunch Available | 17. Shared Bath |
| 2. No Pets | 6. Golf Available | 10. Personal Checks Accepted | 14. Public Transportation | 18. Afternoon Tea |
| 3. No Children | 7. Swiming Available | 11. Off Season Rates | 15. Reservations Necessary | ∗ Commissions given |
| 4. Senior Citizen Rates | 8. Skiing Available | 12. Dinner Available | 16. Private Bath | to Travel Agents |

## Boston *

| | | |
|---|---|---|
| Rugo, Vicki & Bob | **Amenities:** 2,4,10,14,15, | **Dbl. Oc.:** $55.00 - $80.00 |
| 47 Ocean St., 02124 | 16,17 | **Sgl. Oc.:** $45.00 - $70.00 |
| (617) 288-8867, (617) 282-5350 | **Breakfast:** C. | **Third Person:** $11.00 |
| | | **Child:** under 6 yrs. - |
| | | no charge |

**The Emma James House**—A spacious 1894 Victorian home with six guest rooms. Four miles south of downtown Boston and 15 minutes to I-93. Close to the Kennedy Library and Bayside Expo Center. Easy drive to Cape Cod. Parking. Children welcome. Brochure available.

## Boston *

| | | |
|---|---|---|
| Terwilliger, Christine & Bob | **Amenities:** 9,11,14,15,16,17 | **Dbl. Oc.:** $50.00 |
| Allston Station | **Breakfast:** C. | **Sgl. Oc.:** $35.00 |
| P.O. Box 364, 02134 | | **Third Person:** $10.00 |
| (617) 787-1860 | | **Child:** $10.00 |

**The Farrington Inn**—A small European-style bed and breakfast inn. Close to downtown Boston. Comfort, convenience and hospitality. An economical choice in one of the most expensive cities in the world. Located on the Green Line of the subway system.

## Boston

| | | |
|---|---|---|
| Walsh, Mary Lee | **Amenities:** 1,2,3,9,10, | **Dbl. Oc.:** $60.00 - $75.00 |
| Box 158, 02133 | 14,15,17 | **Sgl. Oc.:** $48.00 |
| (617) 479-6215 | **Breakfast:** C. (F. on weekends) | |

**Quincy Adams Bed And Breakfast**—An elegant Victorian home. Fireplaces, canopy bed and a jacuzzi. Downtown Boston and the Freedom Trail only 15 minutes away by subway or car. Located near restaurants, shops and the beach. Healthy and hearty breakfast served.

## Bourne *

| | | |
|---|---|---|
| Deasy, Terry & Paul | **Amenities:** 1,2,4,11,14, | **Dbl. Oc.:** $65.00 - $80.00 |
| 7 Coastal Way, 02532 | 15,16,17 | **Sgl. Oc.:** $55.00 - $70.00 |
| (508) 759-6564 | **Breakfast:** C. | **Third Person:** $15.00 |

**Cape Cod Canalside Bed & Breakfast**—A billion-dollar view of world-wide ships and fabulous yachts. Picnic table and hibachi. Separate guest area with six elegant rooms. Two-room suite with bath. Two additional bedrooms with bath. Fireplaced living room, cable TVs and refrigerator. Jog, canal walk and bike.

## Brewster *

| | | |
|---|---|---|
| DiCesare, Charles | **Amenities:** 2,3,5,6,9,11,14,15, | **Dbl. Oc.:** $75.00 - $125.00 |
| 1187 Old Kings Hwy., 02631 | 16,17 | **Sgl. Oc.:** $65.00 - $125.00 |
| (508) 896-2223 | **Breakfast:** F. | **Third Person:** $25.00 |
| | | **Child:** under 1 yr. - |
| | | no charge |

**Isaiah Clark House & Rose Cottage**—This sea captain's estate built in 1780 is a perfect setting for a colonial experience. Canopy beds and fireplaces. Five acres of land filled with lush plantings. The Swiss-trained innkeeper is famous for delicious breakfasts and the warmest hospitality on Cape Cod.

| | | | |
|---|---|---|---|
| 1. No Smoking | 5. Tennis Available | 9. Credit Cards Accepted | 13. Lunch Available | 17. Shared Bath |
| 2. No Pets | 6. Golf Available | 10. Personal Checks Accepted | 14. Public Transportation | 18. Afternoon Tea |
| 3. No Children | 7. Swiming Available | 11. Off Season Rates | 15. Reservations Necessary | ★ Commissions given |
| 4. Senior Citizen Rates | 8. Skiing Available | 12. Dinner Available | 16. Private Bath | to Travel Agents |

## *Brewster* *

Geisler, Marge & Jim
74 Locust Lane, 02631
(800) 526-3760, (508) 255-7045

**Amenities:** 1,2,3,5,6,7,8,10,15,
          16,17
**Breakfast:** F.
**Dbl. Oc.:** $65.00
**Sgl. Oc.:** $60.00

**Ocean Gold**—Located in peaceful setting next to Nickerson State Park. We offer a homey, friendly atmosphere, our own chickens for fresh eggs, homemade breads, jams and freshly ground coffee. Near top golf course that *Golf Digest* rates top 25.

## *Brewster* *

Rowan, Michele & Stephen
2553 Main St.
Box 1026, 02631
(508) 896-6114

**Amenities:** 2,5,6,7,9,10,11,12,
          13,15,16,17,18
**Breakfast:** F.

**Dbl. Oc.:** $44.00 - $100.00
**Sgl. Oc.:** $44.00 - $100.00
**Third Person:** $16.00
**Child:** under 3 yrs. -
          no charge

**Old Sea Pines Inn**—A romantic 1900's mansion, newly renovated and filled with antiques. Some rooms with fireplaces. 3-1/2 acres of privacy. Noted for charm, hospitality and cleanliness. Near lovely bayside beaches and bicycle trail. Air-conditioning. TV. Very personal service and attention.

## *Brookline* *

Lerman, Susan
P.O. Box 1142, 02146
(617) 566-2668

**Amenities:** 1,2,3,4,5,6,10,14,
          15,16,
**Breakfast:** F.

**Dbl. Oc.:** $86.00
**Sgl. Oc.:** $80.00

**The Carriage House**—A converted carriage house in one of Boston's most exclusive sections. Four miles to downtown. Queen or twin room with private bath, patio, den, full breakfast and parking. Well appointed and gracious 1925 red-brick home in estate area.

## *Chatham* *

DeHan, Margaret
359 Main St., 02633
(800) 332-4667,
(508) 945-9232

**Amenities:** 2,3,5,6,7,9,10,
          11,16
**Breakfast:** C.

**Dbl. Oc.:** $95.00 - $150.00
**Third Person:** $20.00

**Cranberry Inn At Chatham**—A landmark village inn, located in the lovely seaside village of Chatham on Cape Cod. Newly renovated with modern amenities, including private baths, TV, phone and air-conditioning. Four-poster beds and antiques. Resident innkeepers are old-house enthusiasts.

| | | | | |
|---|---|---|---|---|
| 1. No Smoking | 5. Tennis Available | 9. Credit Cards Accepted | 13. Lunch Available | 17. Shared Bath |
| 2. No Pets | 6. Golf Available | 10. Personal Checks Accepted | 14. Public Transportation | 18. Afternoon Tea |
| 3. No Children | 7. Swiming Available | 11. Off Season Rates | 15. Reservations Necessary | ★ Commissions given |
| 4. Senior Citizen Rates | 8. Skiing Available | 12. Dinner Available | 16. Private Bath | to Travel Agents |

# MASSACHUSETTS

## Chatham

Ferguson, Sharon & Thomas
22 Old Harbor Rd., 02633
(508) 945-4434

**Amenities:** 2,3,5,6,7,9,10,11,
14,15,16
**Breakfast:** F.

**Dbl. Oc.:** $104.22 - $142.61
**Sgl. Oc.:** $93.25 - $126.16

**The Old Harbor Inn**—Casual elegance beckons you to enchantment. English country comfort, queen or twin beds and full, private baths. Fireplaced gathering room. Buffet breakfast served in sunroom. Walk to everything. Pleasurable memory-making on the elbow of Cape Cod. AAA—rated three diamonds.

## Chatham

Piccola, Elsie
364 Old Harbor Rd., 02633
(800) 628-6972,
(508) 945-5859

**Amenities:** 1,2,3,5,6,7,9,10,
11,15,16,18
**Breakfast:** C.

**Dbl. Oc.:** $104.23 - $148.10

**Moses Nickerson House Inn**—Where memories begin. A quiet, romantic country inn built in 1839 for whaling captain Moses Nickerson. The seven guest rooms feature canopy beds, fireplaces, Oriental rugs and fine period antiques. Breakfast is served in the garden room.

## Chelmsford *

Pinette, Lorraine C.
4 Westview Ave.
P.O. Box 4141, 01824
(508) 256-0074

**Amenities:** 1,2,5,6,7,8,10,
15,17
**Breakfast:** C.

**Dbl. Oc.:** $50.00
**Sgl. Oc.:** $40.00
**Child:** under 10 yrs. -
$10.00

**Westview Landing**—A large contemporary on a tranquil pond. Boating, fishing and swimming in summer. During winter, relish the spa and rest by the fireplace. Thirty miles northwest of Boston. Near Routes 495, 93, 128 and 3.

## Cohasset

Watson, Tina
116 So. Main St., 02025
(617) 383-6205

**Amenities:** 10,14,17
**Breakfast:** C.

**Dbl. Oc.:** $50.00
**Sgl. Oc.:** $50.00
**Third Person:** $10.00

**Saltmarsh Farm**—This wonderful 1800 Victorian home, surrounded by an abundance of plantings and colorful gardens, offers a magnificent chance to experience the charm of a small seacoast village. The village and harbor are within walking distance, offering fine shops and restaurants.

## Concord *

Burch, Gregory
462 Lexington Rd., 01742
(508) 369-5610

**Amenities:** 2,10,11,16,18
**Breakfast:** C.

**Dbl. Oc.:** $110.00
**Sgl. Oc.:** $85.00
**Third Person:** $20.00
**Child:** $10.00

**Hawthorne Inn**—An 1870 colonial filled with antiques, quilts and modern and ancient artworks. Situated on land once owned by Emerson, Alcott and Hawthorne. Close to authors' homes, Walden Pond and the Old North Bridge. Site of first Revolutionary battle. Spiritually rejuvenating. Welcome.

| | | | |
|---|---|---|---|
| 1. No Smoking | 5. Tennis Available | 9. Credit Cards Accepted | 13. Lunch Available | 17. Shared Bath |
| 2. No Pets | 6. Golf Available | 10. Personal Checks Accepted | 14. Public Transportation | 18. Afternoon Tea |
| 3. No Children | 7. Swiming Available | 11. Off Season Rates | 15. Reservations Necessary | ★ Commissions given |
| 4. Senior Citizen Rates | 8. Skiing Available | 12. Dinner Available | 16. Private Bath | to Travel Agents |

# MASSACHUSETTS

## Concord *

Williams, Katie
1694 Main St., 01742
(508) 369-9119

**Amenities:** 1,2,5,6,7,8,9,10, 11,14,16,18
**Breakfast:** C. Plus

**Dbl. Oc.:** $75.00 - $85.00
**Sgl. Oc.:** $65.00 - $75.00
**Third Person:** $10.00

**The Colonel Roger Brown House**—A historic colonial house in restored mill complex, three miles from town center. Five rooms with country charm, air conditioning and private baths. Visit Concord's historic sights, Walden Pond and the Alcott House. Hearty buffet breakfast. Use of fitness club.

## Cotuit (Cape Cod)

Goldstein, Lynn & Jerry
451 Main St., 02635
(508) 428-5228

**Amenities:** 1,2,3,5,6,7,9,15, 16,17
**Breakfast:** C.

**Dbl. Oc.:** $54.85 - $71.30
**Sgl. Oc.:** $48.36 - $64.17
**Third Person:** $15.00

**Salty Dog Inn**—A restored Victorian home in a quaint seaside village near Hyannis, Falmouth, island boats, fine restaurants and theatre. Nearby warm-water beaches. Complimentary bikes. Private suite with canopy bed. Shared bath with king- or queen-size beds. "A bit of old Cape Cod."

## Cuttyhunk Island

Solod, Margo
1 Broadway, 02713
(508) 996-9292

**Amenities:** 2,7,9,10,11,12,13, 15,17
**Breakfast:** C.

**Dbl. Oc.:** $78.00
**Sgl. Oc.:** $78.00

**Allen House Inn**—Indulge yourself in simple, restful hospitality in a unique island setting. We offer cozy rooms, fine dining, surfcasting, beach walks, charter fishing and ocean swimming. A relaxed and unhurried atmosphere awaits you.

## Dartmouth, South

Brownell, Sally
322 Smith Neck Rd., 02748
(508) 992-0980

**Amenities:** 1,2,7,9,10,11,15, 16,18
**Breakfast:** F.

**Dbl. Oc.:** $75.00

**Salt Marsh Farm**—A 1775 Federal farmhouse on 90-acre nature preserve and organic farm. Laying hens. Tandem bike. Nearby beaches. Two very private rooms. Antiques, quilts, library and fireplaces. Home base for day trips to Boston, Cape Cod, the islands and Newport outlets. A quiet retreat.

## Dartmouth, South *

Scully, Meryl & Dan
631 Elm St.
Padanaram Village, 02748
(508) 996-4554

**Amenities:** 1,2,3,9,10,17,18
**Breakfast:** F.

**Dbl. Oc.:** $60.00
**Sgl. Oc.:** $50.00

**The Little Red House**—A charming gambrel colonial home overlooking a horse and cow pasture. Offers many country accents, antiques, a lovely living room with fireplace and a gazebo to enjoy in the backyard. It is close to the harbor, historic sites and major tourist areas.

| | | | | |
|---|---|---|---|---|
| 1. No Smoking | 5. Tennis Available | 9. Credit Cards Accepted | 13. Lunch Available | 17. Shared Bath |
| 2. No Pets | 6. Golf Available | 10. Personal Checks Accepted | 14. Public Transportation | 18. Afternoon Tea |
| 3. No Children | 7. Swiming Available | 11. Off Season Rates | 15. Reservations Necessary | ★ Commissions given |
| 4. Senior Citizen Rates | 8. Skiing Available | 12. Dinner Available | 16. Private Bath | to Travel Agents |

## Deerfield *

Whitney, Phyllis
330 No. Main St., 01373
(413) 665-3829

**Amenities:** 7,10,16,17
**Breakfast:** F.

**Dbl. Oc.:** $60.00 - $90.00
**Third Person:** $15.00

**Orchard Terrace Bed And Breakfast**—Located just four miles from historic Deerfield and central to five colleges. A lovely Georgian colonial situated on 11 acres. Nearby family ski areas. Only 10 miles to N.E. Morgan-horse show grounds. For those seeking something unique while in the Pioneer Valley.

## Dennis *

Brophy, Marie
152 Whig St., 02638
(800) 736-0160,
(508) 385-9928

**Amenities:** 1,2,9,10,11,15,16,
17,18
**Breakfast:** C. Plus

**Dbl. Oc.:** $55.00 - $99.00
**Sgl. Oc.:** $50.88
**Third Person:** $16.46

**Isaiah Hall B&B Inn**—Be enchanted by our country ambience and hospitality. A lovely 1857 farmhouse located in a quiet area within walking distance of beach, restaurants and shops. Private baths, decks, fireplace and queen beds available. Near bike trail, golf and tennis.

## Dennis *

Robinson, Diane
946 Main St., 02638
(508) 385-6317

**Amenities:** 2,3,5,6,7,9,10,11,
16,17,18
**Breakfast:** C. Plus

**Dbl. Oc.:** $55.00 - $110.00
**Sgl. Oc.:** $55.00 - $110.00
**Third Person:** $15.00

**The Four Chimneys Inn**—A relaxing, comfortable and charming Victorian home located in Dennis Village, the geographical center of Cape Cod. Nine bright rooms, spacious common areas, lovely gardens and grounds. Lake views. Walk to beach, playhouse, shops and museums.

## Dennisport *

Kelly, Gayle & Dan
152 Sea St.
P.O. Box 974, 02639
(508) 398-8470

**Amenities:** 1,2,5,6,7,9,10,11,17
**Breakfast:** F.
**Dbl. Oc.:** $55.00
**Sgl. Oc.:** $55.00
**Third Person:** $16.50

**The Rose Petal B&B**—An inviting 1872 home with attractive yard in a delightful seaside resort neighborhood. Full breakfast features pastries. Guest parlor with TV and piano. Walk to beach, shops and dining. Conveniently located in the heart of Cape Cod.

| | | | | |
|---|---|---|---|---|
| 1. No Smoking | 5. Tennis Available | 9. Credit Cards Accepted | 13. Lunch Available | 17. Shared Bath |
| 2. No Pets | 6. Golf Available | 10. Personal Checks Accepted | 14. Public Transportation | 18. Afternoon Tea |
| 3. No Children | 7. Swiming Available | 11. Off Season Rates | 15. Reservations Necessary | ★ Commissions given |
| 4. Senior Citizen Rates | 8. Skiing Available | 12. Dinner Available | 16. Private Bath | to Travel Agents |

## East Falmouth *

Peterson, Ann Marie
226 Trotting Park, 02536
(508) 540-2962

**Amenities:** 1,4,10,11,17
**Breakfast:** F.

**Dbl. Oc.:** $55.00
**Sgl. Oc.:** $50.00

**Bayberry Inn**—Come to Cape Cod! Lovely and inexpensive rooms. Set in the woods. Children and pets welcome. Old-fashion charm with modern comforts. One mile from shops and restaurants; two miles to beaches and island ferry. Open all year. Write for brochure.

## East Orleans *

Anderson, Donna
186 Beach Rd.
P.O. Box 756, 02643
(508) 255-1312

**Amenities:** 2,3,5,7,9,10,11,15,16,17
**Breakfast:** C.
**Dbl. Oc.:** $40.00 & up
**Third Person:** $20.00
**Child:** under 12 yrs. - $20.00

**Ship's Knees Inn**—A 160-year-old sea captain's home that offers an intimate setting with only a short walk to scenic Nauset Beach. Tennis and swimming on premises. Heated cottages available. Open all year.

## East Orleans *

Shand, Chris & LLoyd
202 Main St., Box 1016, 02643
(508) 255-8217

**Amenities:** 2,9,10,11,16
**Breakfast:** C.

**Dbl.Oc.:** $60.34 - $82.28
**Sgl.Oc.:** $54.85 - $76.79
**Third Person:** $10.00
**Child:** $5.00

**The Parsonage**—1770 cape home with five antique furnished rooms. Efficiency and cottage available. Close to Nauset Beach. Walk to restaurants. Great biking. Freshly baked breakfast served on the patio or to your room. Friendly and inviting.

## East Orleans *

Standish, Dorothy
163 Beach Rd., 02653
(508) 255-6654

**Amenities:** 2,4,5,6,7,9,10,11, 15,16,17
**Breakfast:** C. Plus

**Dbl. Oc.:** $35.00 - $85.00
**Sgl. Oc.:** $30.00 - $80.00
**Child:** under 6 yrs. - $15.00

**The Farmhouse" At Nauset Beach**—A quiet country inn. Walk to Nauset Beach and the Atlantic Ocean. Seashore setting. Open year round. Seasonal and off-season rates. Antiques. Some rooms have ocean views. Breakfast on a deck overlooking the ocean.

| | | | | |
|---|---|---|---|---|
| 1. No Smoking | 5. Tennis Available | 9. Credit Cards Accepted | 13. Lunch Available | 17. Shared Bath |
| 2. No Pets | 6. Golf Available | 10. Personal Checks Accepted | 14. Public Transportation | 18. Afternoon Tea |
| 3. No Children | 7. Swiming Available | 11. Off Season Rates | 15. Reservations Necessary | ★ Commissions given |
| 4. Senior Citizen Rates | 8. Skiing Available | 12. Dinner Available | 16. Private Bath | to Travel Agents |

## Eastham *

Aitchison, Nan
3085 County Rd., 02642
(508) 255-1886

**Amenities:** 1,2,3,4,5,6,7,9,10,11,
12,14,15,16,18
**Breakfast:** F.
**Dbl. Oc.:** $99.00

**The Over Look Inn, Cape Cod**—A gracious Victorian manor located on the beautiful outer Cape. Victorian billiard room, library, parlor, porches and garden. Close to ocean beach, bike trails, nature walks, whale watching, golf, windsurfing, antique and craftshops and fine restaurants. Scottish hospitality.

## Eastham, North *

Keith, Margaret
4885 State Hwy.(Route 6)
P.O. Box 238, 02651
(508) 255-6632

**Amenities:** 2,3,9,10,11,12,15, 16,17,18

**Breakfast:** F.

**Dbl. Oc.:** $76.00 - $116.00

**Penny House Inn**—An 18th-century sea captain's house opposite National Seashore. Beaches, bike and nature trails. Antiques, parlor, fireplaces, 12 rooms, country charm, beamed ceilings and wide-plank floors. On 1-1/2 acres of trees and lawn. Nearby fine dining.

## Edgartown *

Cortese, Jude
129 Main St., 02539
(508) 627-9655

**Amenities:** 2,5,6,7,9,10,11,14, 15,16,17

**Breakfast:** C.

**Dbl. Oc.:** $93.25 - $191.98
**Sgl. Oc.:** $93.25 - $191.98
**Third Person:** $16.40
**Child:** over 12 yrs. - $16.40

**Ashley Inn**—Nestled among spacious lawns, rose gardens and apple trees, the inn offers an attractive 1800's captain's home with country charm. Leisurely stroll to shops, beaches and fine foods. Eight bedrooms and two suites have been tastefully decorated with period antiques, brass and wicker. Join us.

## Edgartown *

Hall, Peggy
222 Upper Main St.
P.O. Box 1228, 02539
(508) 627-8137

**Amenities:** 2,3,5,6,7,9,10,11,15,
16,17,18
**Breakfast:** C.
**Dbl. Oc.:** $93.25 - $120.67
**Sgl. Oc.:** $82.28 - $120.67

**The Arbor**—This charming turn-of-the-century home is within a short stroll to the village shops, fine restaurants and bustling activity of Edgartown Harbor. The rooms are typically New England and filled with the fragrance of fresh flowers.

| | | | | |
|---|---|---|---|---|
| 1. No Smoking | 5. Tennis Available | 9. Credit Cards Accepted | 13. Lunch Available | 17. Shared Bath |
| 2. No Pets | 6. Golf Available | 10. Personal Checks Accepted | 14. Public Transportation | 18. Afternoon Tea |
| 3. No Children | 7. Swiming Available | 11. Off Season Rates | 15. Reservations Necessary | ★ Commissions given |
| 4. Senior Citizen Rates | 8. Skiing Available | 12. Dinner Available | 16. Private Bath | to Travel Agents |

# MASSACHUSETTS

## Edgartown

MacKenty, Maria & Jerry
40 Meeting House Way, 02539
(508) 627-8626

**Amenities:** 1,2,5,6,7,9,10, 11,15,17
**Breakfast:** F.

**Dbl. Oc.:** $77.00 - & up
**Sgl. Oc.:** $70.00 & up
**Third Person:** $15.00
**Child:** under 2 yrs. - no charge

**Meeting House Inn**—Warm hospitality awaits you at our 1750 colonial home located just two miles from the beach and town. Fine restaurants and shopping. Relax and enjoy our hot tub and experience the peace and quiet of our 58 acres.

## Edgartown

Maultz, Michael
35 Pease's Point Way
Box 2798, 02539
(508) 627-7289

**Amenities:** 2,9,10,11,15, 16,18
**Breakfast:** C.

**Dbl. Oc.:** $71.18 - $197.10
**Third Person:** $20.00

**Captain Dexter House Of Edgartown**—This charming 1840's inn is furnished with period antiques, canopy beds and working fireplaces. Located on a street of fine historic homes within three to four blocks of Edgartown's harbor, shops and restaurants. Complimentary continental breakfast and evening sherry.

## Edgartown

Nolan, Chloe D.
96 So. Summer St., 02539
(508) 627-4857

**Amenities:** 1,2,3,5,6,7,10,14, 15,16,17
**Breakfast:** C.

**Dbl. Oc.:** $100.00
**Sgl. Oc.:** $100.00
**Third Person:** $10.00

**Summer House**—A quaint, charming and recently renovated 150-year-old farmhouse. Large rooms with king beds. Short stroll to harbor and town. Beautiful garden. Spacious lawns and terraces. Best breads!

## Edgartown

Radford, Earle
56 No. Water St.
Box 1211, 02539
(508) 627-4794

**Amenities:** 2,5,6,7,10,11,14,15,16,17
**Breakfast:** C. and F.
**Dbl. Oc.:** $60.34 - $159.07
**Third Person:** $10.00
**Child:** $10.00

*Martha's Vineyard Island.*

**The Edgartown Inn**—A historic whale captain's home (1798) in the heart of town. All 12 bedrooms have tiled baths. More modest rates in captain's quarters and barn. Many antiques. Paneled dining room. Patio and garden. Daniel Webster and Nathaniel Hawthorne have stayed here.

---

| | | | |
|---|---|---|---|
| 1. No Smoking | 5. Tennis Available | 9. Credit Cards Accepted | 13. Lunch Available | 17. Shared Bath |
| 2. No Pets | 6. Golf Available | 10. Personal Checks Accepted | 14. Public Transportation | 18. Afternoon Tea |
| 3. No Children | 7. Swiming Available | 11. Off Season Rates | 15. Reservations Necessary | ★ Commissions given |
| 4. Senior Citizen Rates | 8. Skiing Available | 12. Dinner Available | 16. Private Bath | to Travel Agents |

## Edgartown

Smith, Linda
104 Main St.
P.O. Box 128, 02539
(508) 627-8633

**Amenities:** 2,4,5,6,7,9,10,11,14,16,18
**Breakfast:** C.
**Dbl. Oc.:** $105.00 - $205.00
**Sgl. Oc.:** $94.50 - $184.50
**Third Person:** $20.00
**Child:** $20.00

**Point Way Inn**—Enjoy our gardens, croquet and lemonade in the gazebo. In cooler months, afternoon tea is served before the fire in our library. All 14 rooms and suites have private baths, many with fireplaces and balconies. Complimentary courtesy car available.

## Fairhaven *

Reed, Kathleen
2 Oxford St., 02719
(508) 997-5512
**Amenities:** 2,5,6,7,9,10,15,16
**Breakfast:** C.
**Dbl. Oc.:** $47.00 - $74.00
**Sgl. Oc.:** $37.00 - $64.00
**Third Person:** $10.00

**Edgewater Bed And Breakfast**—A gracious waterfront home in the early whaling ship building area of historic Fairhaven. Spectacular water views. Close to historic areas, beaches and factory outlets. Five minutes from I-195. Five rooms (two with fireplaces and sitting rooms). Parking.

## Falmouth

Lloyd, Caroline & Jim
27 Main St., 02540
(508) 548-3786

**Amenities:** 1,2,3,5,6,7,10,11,14,
15,16,18
**Breakfast:** F.
**Dbl. Oc.:** $105.00 - $120.00
**Sgl. Oc.:** $85.00 - $105.00

**Mostly Hall Bed & Breakfast Inn**—This 1849 Southern plantation-styled house is located in the historic district by the village green. Near beaches and island ferries. Six large corner rooms with queen-size canopy beds and private baths. Gourmet breakfast. Bicycles. Garden gazebo and wrap-around veranda.

| | | | | |
|---|---|---|---|---|
| 1. No Smoking | 5. Tennis Available | 9. Credit Cards Accepted | 13. Lunch Available | 17. Shared Bath |
| 2. No Pets | 6. Golf Available | 10. Personal Checks Accepted | 14. Public Transportation | 18. Afternoon Tea |
| 3. No Children | 7. Swiming Available | 11. Off Season Rates | 15. Reservations Necessary | ★ Commissions given |
| 4. Senior Citizen Rates | 8. Skiing Available | 12. Dinner Available | 16. Private Bath | to Travel Agents |

## Falmouth

Long, Linda & Don
40 W. Main St., 02540
(508) 548-5621

**Amenities:** 1,2,3,5,6,7,10,11,14,16
**Breakfast:** F.
**Dbl. Oc.:** $70.00 - $110.00
**Sgl. Oc.:** $60.00 - $100.00
**Third Person:** $15.00 - $20.00

**Village Green Inn**—Elegant accommodations in a gracious old Victorian. Ideally located on historic village green. Delightful breakfasts feature delicious specialties. Walk or bike to fine shops, restaurants and beach. Relax amid 19th-century charm and warm hospitality.

## Falmouth

Sabo-Feller, Barbara
75 Locust St., 02540
(508) 540-1445

**Amenities:** 1,2,3,4,5,6,7,9,10,11,
14,15,16,18
**Breakfast:** F.
**Dbl. Oc.:** $88.00 - $98.00
**Sgl. Oc.:** $68.00 - $78.00
**Third Person:** $15.00
**Child:** over 12 yrs. - $15.00

**Captain Tom Lawrence House**—A beautiful 1861 whaling captain's residence in the historic district. Close to beach, bikeway, ferries and shops. Firm beds with canopies. Antiques, Steinway piano and fireplace. We grind our own flour from organic grain for delicious waffles, pancakes and breads. German spoken.

## Gayhead

LeBovit, Elise
Off State Rd., 02535
(508) 645-9018

**Amenities:** 7,9,10,11,14,
16,17
**Breakfast:** F.

**Dbl. Oc.:** $90.00 - $185.00
**Sgl. Oc.:** $75.00 - $170.00
**Third Person:** $15.00
**Child:** under 12 yrs. - $8.00

**Duck Inn**—The Martha's Vineyard's sunset. Ocean-view retreat with healthy gourmet breakfasts. A short walk to beach, cliffs, lighthouse, restaurants and shops. A 200-year-old farmhouse on 8-1/2 acres with fireplaces, decks, piano, hot tub and masseuse. Casual and eclectic antique setting.

## Gloucester *

Swinson, Ginny & Hal
83 Riverview, 01930
(508) 281-1826

**Amenities:** 2,3,5,7,10,11,
14,17
**Breakfast:** C.

**Dbl. Oc.:** $65.00 - $75.00
**Sgl. Oc.:** $60.00 - $70.00
**Third Person:** $10.00
**Child:** $10.00

**Riverview**—In historic Cape Ann on the Intercoastal Waterway. Enjoy boats and private beach from this renovated Victorian home. Nearby art colony, shopping, restaurants, great beaches and whale watching

| | | | | |
|---|---|---|---|---|
| 1. No Smoking | 5. Tennis Available | 9. Credit Cards Accepted | 13. Lunch Available | 17. Shared Bath |
| 2. No Pets | 6. Golf Available | 10. Personal Checks Accepted | 14. Public Transportation | 18. Afternoon Tea |
| 3. No Children | 7. Swiming Available | 11. Off Season Rates | 15. Reservations Necessary | ★ Commissions given |
| 4. Senior Citizen Rates | 8. Skiing Available | 12. Dinner Available | 16. Private Bath | to Travel Agents |

## Great Barrington *

Burdsall, Priscilla & Richard
RD 3, Box 125, 01230
(413) 528-4092

**Amenities:** 1,2,3,5,6,7,8,9,10,11,
15,16,17
**Breakfast:** F.
**Dbl. Oc.:** $70.00 & up

**Baldwin Hill Farm**—A hilltop farmhome with four bedrooms. Spectacular views. 450 acres for walks, hiking and biking. Maps and menus. Away from highway noise, but close to major routes. Easy access to summer, fall and winter attractions. Many excellent restaurants in the area. Wildlife.

## Great Barrington *

Harding, Jean & John          **Amenities:** 1,2,4,5,6,7,8,10,      **Dbl. Oc.:** $75.00 - $95.00
6 Berkshire Circle, 01230                15,16,17,18      **Sgl. Oc.:** $70.00 - $90.00
(203) 272-9461,          **Breakfast:** F.      **Child:** no charge
(413) 528-5995

**Ledgewood B&B**—A contemporary log home on two wooded acres. Close to several ski areas, lakes, state parks, Tanglewood, Jacob Pillow and other tourist attractions. Open only on weekends year round.

## Great Barrington

Littlejohn, Herb          **Amenities:** 2,3,5,6,7,8,10,11,      **Dbl. Oc.:** $63.42 - $84.56
1 Newsboy Monument Lane, 01230                17,18      **Sgl. Oc.:** $58.14 - $79.28
(413) 528-2882          **Breakfast:** F.

**Littlejohn Manor**—Savor Victorian charm dedicated to your comfort. Antiques enhance warmly furnished air-conditioned rooms. Near Tanglewood, Jacob Pillow, museums, fine dining and shops. Scenic views. Herb and flower gardens. Five miles to Butternut and Catamount skiing. Full English breakfast.

## Great Barrington

Miller, Lorraine & Daniel          **Amenities:** 1,2,3,10,11,15,17      **Dbl. Oc.:** $75.00
RD #4, Box 150, 01230          **Breakfast:** F.      **Sgl. Oc.:** $75.00
(413) 528-1028          **Third Person:** $15.00

**Hidden Acres — B&B In The Country**—Away from the noises of the main road, yet minutes to area attractions and ski slopes. Quiet and peaceful setting. Treated like friends instead of guests. Breakfast in a large, sunny kitchen — "all you can eat." Become a part of our family of friends.

| | | | | |
|---|---|---|---|---|
| 1. No Smoking | 5. Tennis Available | 9. Credit Cards Accepted | 13. Lunch Available | 17. Shared Bath |
| 2. No Pets | 6. Golf Available | 10. Personal Checks Accepted | 14. Public Transportation | 18. Afternoon Tea |
| 3. No Children | 7. Swiming Available | 11. Off Season Rates | 15. Reservations Necessary | ★ Commissions given |
| 4. Senior Citizen Rates | 8. Skiing Available | 12. Dinner Available | 16. Private Bath | to Travel Agents |

## Harvard *

Coolidge, Emilie & Frank
2 Brown Rd., 01451
(508) 456-3370

**Amenities:** 7,8,10,15,16,17
**Breakfast:** C.
**Dbl. Oc.:** $60.00
**Sgl. Oc.:** $50.00
**Third Person:** $10.00
**Child:** under 2 yrs. - no charge

**Deerhorn Farm B&B**—An unspoiled 300-year-old house in serene country setting with horses and beef cattle. Adjoins conservation land. Near fruitland museums. Close to Route 495, 25 minutes to historic Concord and one hour to Boston. Homemade bread and muffins.

## Harwich, West *

Connell, Eileen & Jack
77 Main St., 02671
(508) 432-9628

**Amenities:** 3,5,6,7,9,10,12,13, 14,15,16,18
**Breakfast:** F.

**Dbl. Oc.:** $90.00
**Third Person:** $25.00

**Cape Cod Sunny Pines B&B Inn**—Irish hospitality in a Victorian ambience reminiscent of a small Irish manor on the tip of the Cape. All suites. A/C, color TV, jacuzzi and pool. Central location on Cape Cod. Walk to water and bike trails. A day trip to the islands and whale watching. Complimentary evening social.

## Harwich, West *

Lockyer, Kathleen
186 Belmont Rd.
P.O. Box 444, 02671
(800) 321-3155, (508) 432-7766

**Amenities:** 5,6,7,9,10,11,14, 15,16
**Breakfast:** F.

**Dbl. Oc.:** $75.00 - $125.00
**Sgl. Oc.:** $65.00 - $100.00
**Third Person:** $15.00
**Child:** under 10 yrs. - $10.00

**The Lion's Head Inn**—A distinctive blend of the history of Cape Cod and amenities of a small resort. All guest suites have private baths, sitting areas and antique country decor. Full gourmet breakfast served poolside or fireside. Quiet wooded setting. Walk to beach, fine dining and shopping.

## Harwich, West *

Maguire, Lorraine
61 Share Rd., 02671
(508) 432-0493

**Amenities:** 2,3,5,6,7,9,10, 11,16
**Breakfast:** C.

**Dbl. Oc.:** $90.00
**Sgl. Oc.:** $75.00
**Third Person:** $10.00

**Seacrest Shores**—Ocean-front, beautifully appointed to enhance an ambience of warmth and hospitality. Private deck and entrance; perfect for honeymooners. Sail off our beach. color TV. Wonderful nearby shops. Lawn games. Quiet area. A wonderful place to relax and enjoy Cape Cod.

| 1. No Smoking | 5. Tennis Available | 9. Credit Cards Accepted | 13. Lunch Available | 17. Shared Bath |
| 2. No Pets | 6. Golf Available | 10. Personal Checks Accepted | 14. Public Transportation | 18. Afternoon Tea |
| 3. No Children | 7. Swiming Available | 11. Off Season Rates | 15. Reservations Necessary | ★ Commissions given |
| 4. Senior Citizen Rates | 8. Skiing Available | 12. Dinner Available | 16. Private Bath | to Travel Agents |

## *Harwichport* *

Ayer, Sara & Cal
74 Sisson Rd., 02646
(508) 432-9452

**Amenities:** 2,3,5,6,7,9,
10,15,16
**Breakfast:** C.

**Dbl. Oc.:** $65.00 - $70.00
**Sgl. Oc.:** $65.00 - $70.00

**The Coach House**—Quiet and comfortable elegance. King- and queen- size beds. Ideally located for bike trail to national seashore, whalewatching, fine beaches and day trips to the islands. Open May - October. Two-night minimum is requested. Brochure available.

## *Harwichport* *

Clayton, Mary Jane & Paul
255 Lower County Rd., 02646
(800) 272-4343, (508) 432-0337T

**Amenities:** 5,6,7,9,10,11,16,18
**Breakfast:** C.

**Dbl. Oc.:** $75.00 - $125.00
**Sgl. Oc.:** $75.00 - $125.00
**hird Person:** $12.50

**Bayberry Shores**—A walk-to-beach, brick-front Cape Cod home. Two large guest rooms and one suite. Private baths, TVs and refrigerators. Fireplaced common room and shady brick terrace. Also, one fireplaced efficiency suite. Children welcome and babysitting available.

## *Harwichport* *

Cunningham, Alyce & Wally
24 Pilgrim Rd., 02646
(800) 432-4345,
(508) 432-0810

**Amenities:** 2,5,6,7,8,9,10,14,
15,16
**Breakfast:** F.

**Dbl. Oc.:** $110.00 - $180.00
**Sgl. Oc.:** $110.00 - $180.00
**Third Person:** $20.00

**Dunscroft By-The-Sea**—A beautiful and private mile-long beach on Nantucket Sound. Romantic, quie and casual elegance. Designer linens, king/queen four poster beds with canopies. All private baths. Honeymoon cottage with fireplace. Walk to shops and restaurants. Efficiency suite also available.

## *Harwichport* *

Silverio, Janet
88 Bank St., 02646
(508) 432-3206

**Amenities:** 2,5,6,7,9,10,11,14,
15,18
**Breakfast:** C.
**Dbl. Oc.:** $82.28
**Third Person:** $12.00
**Child:** under 7 yrs. - no charge

**"The Inn On Bank Street"**—A Cape Cod bed and breakfast in the center of Harwichport. Five-minute walk to the ocean. Near bike trails, scenic harbors and gourmet restaurants. Six rooms have private baths and private entrances. A leisurely breakfast is served on the sun porch of this charming country inn.

| | | | | |
|---|---|---|---|---|
| 1. No Smoking | 5. Tennis Available | 9. Credit Cards Accepted | 13. Lunch Available | 17. Shared Bath |
| 2. No Pets | 6. Golf Available | 10. Personal Checks Accepted | 14. Public Transportation | 18. Afternoon Tea |
| 3. No Children | 7. Swiming Available | 11. Off Season Rates | 15. Reservations Necessary | ★ Commissions given |
| 4. Senior Citizen Rates | 8. Skiing Available | 12. Dinner Available | 16. Private Bath | to Travel Agents |

## Harwichport *

Van Gelder, Kathleen & David
85 Bank St., 02646
(800) 992-6550, (508) 432-0337

**Amenities:** 2,5,6,7,9,10,11,16
**Breakfast:** C.
**Dbl. Oc.:** $75.00 - $110.00
**Sgl. Oc.:** $75.00 - $110.00

**Captain's Quarters**—A 1850's Victorian with a classic wrap-around porch. Within walking distance to the beach. Five fine guestrooms (some with TVs and ceiling fans) have queen brass beds or twin beds. Perfect for honeymooners. Separate cottage on grounds. Walk to everything.

## Harwichport *

Van Gelder, Kathleen & David
326 Lower County Rd., 02646
(800) 272-4343, (508) 432-0337

**Amenities:** 2,5,6,7,9,10,11,16
**Breakfast:** C.
**Dbl. Oc.:** $75.00 - $125.00
**Sgl. Oc.:** $75.00 - $125.00
**Third Person:** $12.50

**Harbor Breeze**—Located across the road from picturesque Allen Harbor this country casual B&B offers nine rooms and family suites. All have private entrances and open on to the garden courtyard. Mini-fridges, TVs, pool and common room with microwave. Walk to beach, shops and dining.

## Hyannis *

Battle, Patricia
397 Sea St., 02601
(508) 771-7213

**Amenities:** 9,10,11,15,16
**Breakfast:** C.
**Dbl. Oc.:** $65.00 - $85.00
**Sgl. Oc.:** $45.00
**Third Person:** $10.00
**Child:** $10.00

**Sea Breeze Inn**—Our quaint, private location offers you a place to relax on our outdoor furniture, enjoy the sun and be cooled by the gentle sea breeze. All our rooms have private baths and some have water views. Three-minute walk to the beach. Convenient to the island ferries, shops and dining.

| | | | | |
|---|---|---|---|---|
| 1. No Smoking | 5. Tennis Available | 9. Credit Cards Accepted | 13. Lunch Available | 17. Shared Bath |
| 2. No Pets | 6. Golf Available | 10. Personal Checks Accepted | 14. Public Transportation | 18. Afternoon Tea |
| 3. No Children | 7. Swiming Available | 11. Off Season Rates | 15. Reservations Necessary | ★ Commissions given |
| 4. Senior Citizen Rates | 8. Skiing Available | 12. Dinner Available | 16. Private Bath | to Travel Agents |

## Hyannis

Boydston, Mary & Clark
162 Sea St., 02601
(508) 775-3595

**Amenities:** 1,2,3,6,7,9,10,11, 14,15,16
**Breakfast:** F.

**Dbl. Oc.:** $87.76
**Sgl. Oc.:** $87.76
**Third Person:** $20.00

**Elegance By-The-Sea Inn**—The Queen Anne home is within a short walk to beach, restaurants, golf and many activities. Enjoy a hearty breakfast with crystal, lace and classical music. Winter-theme weekends. Small, chic and select. A perfect base to explore the entire Cape.

## Hyannis

Siefkan, Barbara & John
Box 362, 02601
(800) 992-0096, (508) 775-5049

**Amenities:** 5,6,7
**Breakfast:** F.

**Dbl. Oc.:** $49.00
**Sgl. Oc.:** $49.00
**Third Person:** $15.00

**Cranberry Cove B&B**—A charming Cape Cod home situated on the edge of a cranberry bog. Within walking distance to island ferries, beaches and local restaurants. A true Cape Cod experience. Rustic and serene.

## Hyannis

Whitehead, J.B.
358 Sea St., 02601
(508) 775-8030

**Amenities:** 1,2,3,5,6,7,9,10, 16,17
**Breakfast:** F.

**Dbl. Oc.:** $60.34 - $93.25
**Sgl. Oc.:** $60.34 - $93.25
**Third Person:** $10.00

**The Inn On Sea Street**—A romantic, elegant Victorian inn just steps from the beach. Fireplace; large, quiet rooms; canopy beds; private baths; antiques; gourmet breakfast of homemade delights; fruit and cheese. Near island ferries and Kennedy compound. Warm and friendly atmosphere.

## Lanesboro *

Sullivan, Marianne & Dan
30 Old Cheshire Rd., 01237
(413) 442-0260,
(413) 443-0564

**Amenities:** 1,2,5,6,7,8,10, 15,17
**Breakfast:** F.

**Dbl. Oc.:** $75.00
**Sgl. Oc.:** $60.00
**Third Person:** $15.00
**Child:** under 3 yrs. - no charge

**The Tuckered Turkey**—Beautiful Berkshire location! Enjoy the cultural attractions in Lenox and Williamstown. Twenty minutes to the new Berkshire Mall. A restored 1800's farmhouse. Three guest rooms cater to special occasions. Three acres of views of the Berkshire Hills.

## Lenox *

Jacob, M/M Robert
15 Hawthorne St., 01240
(413) 637-3013

**Amenities:** 1,2,3,5,6,7,8,9, 10,11,16,18
**Breakfast:** F.

**Dbl. Oc.:** $60.00 - $145.00
**Third Person:** $20.00

**Brook Farm Inn**—There is poetry here. Shaded glen, pool, private bath and English tea. Near shops, Tanglewood and museums. Fall foliage. Fireplaces, large library and 650 volumes of poetry on tape. Twelve rooms. Children 15 and overwelcome.

| | | | | |
|---|---|---|---|---|
| 1. No Smoking | 5. Tennis Available | 9. Credit Cards Accepted | 13. Lunch Available | 17. Shared Bath |
| 2. No Pets | 6. Golf Available | 10. Personal Checks Accepted | 14. Public Transportation | 18. Afternoon Tea |
| 3. No Children | 7. Swiming Available | 11. Off Season Rates | 15. Reservations Necessary | ★ Commissions given |
| 4. Senior Citizen Rates | 8. Skiing Available | 12. Dinner Available | 16. Private Bath | to Travel Agents |

## Lenox *

Mears, Joan & Richard
5 Greenwood St., 01240
(413) 637-0975

**Amenities:** 2,5,6,7,8,9,10,11,
       15,16,18
**Breakfast:** F.
**Dbl. Oc.:** $80.00 - $190.00
**Sgl. Oc.:** $80.00 - $100.00
**Third Person:** $25.00
**Child:** $25.00

**Whistler's Inn**—Featured in *New York Magazine's* "Great Escapes." English Tudor mansion built in 1820 that captures the warmth and elegance of a bygone era. Eight acres of woodland and gardens. Antiques. Large library. Music room. Quiet. Central to town and Berkshires. Gracious accommodations.

## Lenox

Mekinda, Mario J.
141 Main St., 01240
(413) 637-0193

**Amenities:** 2,3,5,6,7,8,9,10,
      11,14,15,16
**Breakfast:** C.

**Dbl. Oc.:** $80.00 - $150.00
**Third Person:** $25.00

**Garden Gables Inn**—A 200-year-old inn. Located in the historic center of Lenox on five wooded acres dotted with gardens, maples and fruit trees. A 72-foot-long swimming pool. Reasonable rates with breakfast included. All 11 rooms have private baths. Open year round. Brochure available.

## Lenox

Miller, Rita
830 East St., 01240
(413) 442-2057

**Amenities:** 5,6,7,8,9,10,11,14,
      15,16,17,18
**Breakfast:** C. Plus

**Dbl. Oc.:** $45.00 - $145.00
**Sgl. Oc.:** $40.00 - $70.00
**Third Person:** $25.00
**Child:** $10.00

**East Country Berry Farm**—A historic colonial farmhouse. 20 acres. Mountain views. Tanglewood, theatre and dance festivals. Shakespeare & Co. Lush, colorful foliage. Fireplaced rooms. Canoe trip packages. Excellent restaurants, boutiques, museums and factory outlets.

## Lenox

Rolland, David
197 Main St., 01240
(413) 637-0562

**Amenities:** 2,5,6,7,8,10,11,15,16
**Breakfast:** C.
**Dbl. Oc.:** $80.00 - $315.00

**Cornell Inn**—In the heart of Lenox, convenient to all Berkshire attractions. Four-poster or brass beds, cozy fireplaces, landscaped gardens and a secluded sun deck. Nine bedrooms, each with a modern bath, antique furnishings and some with fireplaces to snuggle in front of on a nippy night.

| | | | | |
|---|---|---|---|---|
| 1. No Smoking | 5. Tennis Available | 9. Credit Cards Accepted | 13. Lunch Available | 17. Shared Bath |
| 2. No Pets | 6. Golf Available | 10. Personal Checks Accepted | 14. Public Transportation | 18. Afternoon Tea |
| 3. No Children | 7. Swiming Available | 11. Off Season Rates | 15. Reservations Necessary | ★ Commissions given |
| 4. Senior Citizen Rates | 8. Skiing Available | 12. Dinner Available | 16. Private Bath | to Travel Agents |

# MASSACHUSETTS

## Lenox *

Sherman, Betsy & Tom
19 Old Stockbridge Rd., 01240
(413) 637-9750

**Amenities:** 1,2,6,7,8,9,10,11, 16,18
**Breakfast:** F.

**Dbl. Oc.:** $65.00 - $155.00
**Sgl. Oc.:** $62.00 - $145.00
**Third Person:** $15.00

**Rookwood Inn**—Capture the spirit of a bygone era in our gracious Victorian inn. Period decor and English antiques. Peaceful and secluded, yet only a block from town center, shops and dining. A wonderful place to relax. Close to Tanglewood, galleries and skiing. Fifteen guest rooms.

---

## Lexington*

Halewood, Carol
2 Larchmont Lane, 02173
(617) 862-5404

**Amenities:** 1,2,3,5,6,7,10, 14,17
**Breakfast:** F.

**Dbl. Oc.:** $60.00
**Sgl. Oc.:** $50.00
**Third Person:** $15.00

**Halewood House**—A cozy Cape home within one mile of Lexington Center and I-95. Charming bedrooms with special touches, porch, patio and large, modern bath. Guest rooms separate from hostess' living area. Delightful breakfasts. No pets in house.

---

## Marblehead

Bacon, Margaret & Sandy
9 Gregory St., 01945
(617) 631-1890

**Amenities:** 1,2,5,7,9,10,11, 14,15,16
**Breakfast:** C.

**Dbl. Oc.:** $75.00
**Sgl. Oc.:** $65.00
**Child:** under 14 yrs. - $20.00

**Sea Street Bed And Breakfast**—A turn-of-the-century Victorian B&B ideally located in the historic waterfront district. Offers sparkling harbor views. Near fine restaurants, art galleries, antique shops and beaches. Easy access to Boston, Route 128, Salem and the North Shore.

---

## Marblehead

Blake, Susan
23 Gregory St., 01945
(617) 631-1032

**Amenities:** 1,2,3,5,7,10,14, 15,17
**Breakfast:** C.

**Dbl. Oc.:** $65.00
**Sgl. Oc.:** $55.00

**Harborside House**—A handsome 1830 colonial overlooking picturesque harbor. Two guest rooms with shared bath. Period dining room. Sunny breakfast porch. Fireplaced living room. Third-story deck. Near historic sites, antique shops and gourmet restaurants. Home-baked goods. Fat cat.

---

| | | | |
|---|---|---|---|
| 1. No Smoking | 5. Tennis Available | 9. Credit Cards Accepted | 13. Lunch Available | 17. Shared Bath |
| 2. No Pets | 6. Golf Available | 10. Personal Checks Accepted | 14. Public Transportation | 18. Afternoon Tea |
| 3. No Children | 7. Swiming Available | 11. Off Season Rates | 15. Reservations Necessary | ★ Commissions given |
| 4. Senior Citizen Rates | 8. Skiing Available | 12. Dinner Available | 16. Private Bath | to Travel Agents |

# MASSACHUSETTS

## Marblehead *

Conway, Peter
58 Washington St., 01945
(617) 631-2186

**Amenities:** 2,5,6,7,9,10,11,
          12,13,14,15,16
**Breakfast:** C.
**Dbl. Oc.:** $80.00 - $170.00
**Sgl. Oc.:** $80.00 - $170.00
**Third Person:** $15.00
**Child:** under 10 yrs. - no charge

**The Harbor Light Inn**—An elegant, restored 18th-century inn located just steps from great restaurants, shops, sailing and the historic waterfront. Air-conditioned rooms with private baths, four-poster canopy beds, jacuzzis and sun decks. Continental breakfast with homemade breads.

## Marblehead

Pabich, Diane & Richard
25 Spray Ave., 01945
(800) 446-2995,
(508) 741-0680

**Amenities:** 2,7,9,10,11,14,15,
          16,18
**Breakfast:** C.

**Dbl. Oc.:** $100.42 - $142.70
**Sgl. Oc.:** $100.42 - $142.70
**Third Person:** $10.57
**Child:** $10.57

**Spray Cliff On The Ocean**—A 1910 English Tudor summer home set high above the Atlantic. The inn provides a spacious and elegant atmosphere. The grounds include a brick terrace surrounded by lush flower gardens where eider ducks, cormorants and sea gulls abound. Spectacular views!

## Mashpee

Topalian, Sandra
15 Seconsett Point Rd.
P.O. Box 599W, 02536
(508) 548-3821 (summer), (508) 785-2250

**Amenities:** 1,2,7,10,15,17,18
**Breakfast:** F.
**Dbl. Oc.:** $95.00
**Sgl. Oc.:** $95.00
**Third Person:** $10.00
**Child:** under 18 yrs. - $10.00

**Mariners Cove Bed & Breakfast**—Saltwater-front contemporary. Private beach, panoramic ocean views, bubbling spa and private decks. South side of Cape Cod, between Falmouth and Hyannis. Near playhouse, antiques, shopping, water sports and ferry to islands. Spacious rooms. Elegant. Open June 20 - Labor Day.

---

| | | | |
|---|---|---|---|
| 1. No Smoking | 5. Tennis Available | 9. Credit Cards Accepted | 13. Lunch Available | 17. Shared Bath |
| 2. No Pets | 6. Golf Available | 10. Personal Checks Accepted | 14. Public Transportation | 18. Afternoon Tea |
| 3. No Children | 7. Swiming Available | 11. Off Season Rates | 15. Reservations Necessary | ★ Commissions given |
| 4. Senior Citizen Rates | 8. Skiing Available | 12. Dinner Available | 16. Private Bath | to Travel Agents |

## *Nantucket* *

Conway, Peter
26 No. Water St., 02554
(508) 228-0720

**Amenities:** 2,5,6,7,9,10,
11,16,17
**Breakfast:** C.

**Dbl. Oc.:** $70.00 - $140.00
**Sgl. Oc.:** $40.00 - $50.00
**Third Person:** $15.00
**Child:** under 5 yrs. -
no charge

**The Carlisle House Inn**—Built in 1765, this inn has maintained quality standards for over 100 years. This carefully restored inn is located just off the center of town. Hand-stenciled wallpapers, inlaid pine paneling, wide-board floors, rich Oriental carpets and working fireplaces.

## *Nantucket*

Gaw, Lee & Stuart
27 Fair St., 02554
(508) 228-6609

**Amenities:** 2,5,6,7,9,10,11,15,
16,17,18
**Breakfast:** C.

**Dbl. Oc.:** $75.00 - $150.00
**Third Person:** $20.00

**Great Harbor Inns**—Located in the historic district of Nantucket. Three beautiful old inns furnished with antiques, quilts and canopy beds. Most with private baths. Very romantic. Come and join us!

## *Nantucket* *

Hammer-Yankow, Robin
5 Ash St., 02554
(508) 228-1987

**Amenities:** 1,2,5,6,7,10,11,
15,16
**Breakfast:** C.

**Dbl. Oc.:** $90.00 - $130.00
**Third Person:** $20.00

**Cobblestone Inn**—Circa 1725. Five rooms. All private baths. Located on a quiet street in town. Just a few blocks from the ferry, shops, restaurants and museums. Enjoy our living room, sun porch or yard. Open year round.

## *Nantucket* *

Heron, Jean
10 Cliff Rd., 02554
(508) 228-0530

**Amenities:** 1,2,5,6,7,8,9,10,11,14,
15,16,17,18
**Breakfast:** C. Plus
**Dbl. Oc.:** $115.00 - $166.75
**Sgl. Oc.:** $92.00
**Third Person:** $35.00

**The Century House** —B&B Inn—Serving island travelers since the mid 1800's. In the residential section of the historic district. Short walk to beaches, restaurants, galleries, shops and museums. Antique appointments. Laura Ashley decor. Bountiful buffet breakfast and afternoon "happy hour." Friendly and warm.

| | | | | |
|---|---|---|---|---|
| 1. No Smoking | 5. Tennis Available | 9. Credit Cards Accepted | 13. Lunch Available | 17. Shared Bath |
| 2. No Pets | 6. Golf Available | 10. Personal Checks Accepted | 14. Public Transportation | 18. Afternoon Tea |
| 3. No Children | 7. Swiming Available | 11. Off Season Rates | 15. Reservations Necessary | ★ Commissions given |
| 4. Senior Citizen Rates | 8. Skiing Available | 12. Dinner Available | 16. Private Bath | to Travel Agents |

## *Nantucket*

Mannix, Bernadette
38 Orange St., 02554
(508) 228-1912

**Amenities:** 3,5,6,7,9,10,11,15,16,18
**Breakfast:** C.
**Dbl. Oc.:** $114.66 - $181.35

**The Four Chimneys**—Located in the heart of Nantucket Island's historic district. Four Chimneys is within a short walk from Main Street. Built in 1835, this beautiful sea captain's mansion has porches, fireplaces in five rooms, canopy beds and views of Nantucket Harbor and beyond.

## *Nantucket*

Parker, Mary & Matthew
7 Sea St., 02554
(508) 228-3577

**Amenities:** 1,2,5,6,7,9,10,11, 12,13,15,16
**Breakfast:** C.

**Dbl. Oc.:** $93.25 - & up
**Third Person:** $16.46

**Seven Sea Street Inn**—Enjoy our romantic country inn located in historic Nantucket. We will serve you an elegant continental breakfast each morning. In the evening, watch the sunset from our windows. Go for a walk or relax in our jacuzzi whirlpool. Your stay will be most enjoyable.

## *Northampton*

Lesko, Leona
230 No. Main St., 01060
(413) 584-8164

**Amenities:** 1,2,3,5,6,7,8,10,15,17
**Breakfast:** F.
**Dbl. Oc.:** $49.36
**Sgl. Oc.:** $43.88
**Third Person:** $15.00

**The Knoll**—A home of English Tudor design located in the five-college area of Northampton. Situated well off the road on a knoll overlooking 17 acres of farm and forest. In town, yet a country setting. Brochure available.

## *Oak Bluffs (Martha's Vineyard)*

Convery-Luce, Betsi
Seaview Ave.
Box 299BB, 02557
(508) 693-4187

**Amenities:** 2,3,7,9,10,11,14, 15,16,18
**Breakfast:** C.

**Dbl. Oc.:** $85.00 - $190.00

**The Oak House**—A historic Victorian government mansion, circa 1872, located on the beach. Ten elegant, theme rooms, each with private bath and most with balconies and ocean views. 25 percent discount off-season. Steps to ferry, beach, town and shuttle bus.

| | | | |
|---|---|---|---|
| 1. No Smoking | 5. Tennis Available | 9. Credit Cards Accepted | 13. Lunch Available | 17. Shared Bath |
| 2. No Pets | 6. Golf Available | 10. Personal Checks Accepted | 14. Public Transportation | 18. Afternoon Tea |
| 3. No Children | 7. Swiming Available | 11. Off Season Rates | 15. Reservations Necessary | ★ Commissions given |
| 4. Senior Citizen Rates | 8. Skiing Available | 12. Dinner Available | 16. Private Bath | to Travel Agents |

## Oak Bluffs (Martha's Vineyard) *

| | | |
|---|---|---|
| Katsomakis, Lisa | Amenities: 5,6,7,9,11,14, | Dbl. Oc.: $88.00 |
| 222 Circuit Ave., 02557 | 16,17 | Sgl. Oc.: $78.00 |
| (508) 693-7928 | Breakfast: C. | Third Person: $15.00 |
| | | Child: under 5 yrs. - no charge |

**Tivoli Inn**—Charming rooms and reasonable rates. Within walking distance to town, shops, restaurants, night life, beaches and ferries. Complimentary breakfast buffet. A great place with a clean and friendly atmosphere.

## Oak Bluffs, Martha's Vineyard

| | | |
|---|---|---|
| Zaiko, Pamela & Calvin | Amenities: 2,4,5,6,7,9,10,11, | Dbl. Oc.: $98.73 - $137.13 |
| 2 Pennacook Ave., 02557 | 13,14,15,16,18 | Sgl. Oc.: $88.73 - $127.13 |
| (508) 693-3955 | Breakfast: C. | Third Person: $15.00 |
| | | Child: no charge |

**The Beach House**—Located on the beautiful island of Martha's Vineyard. Directly across from a large beach. We offer queen-size brass beds, private baths and TV. Close to shops, restaurants, ferries, bike and moped rentals, tennis and golf, shuttle and tour busses.

## Peru

| | | |
|---|---|---|
| Halvorsen, Alice | Amenities: 6,8,10,15,16,17 | Dbl. Oc.: $40.00 - $45.00 |
| E. Windsor Rd., 01235 | Breakfast: F. | |
| (413) 655-8292 | | |

**Chalet d'Alicia**—This Swiss chalet-style home offers a private and casual atmosphere. Fresh, homemade breads and muffins round off a full country breakfast. Four resident cats and one dog make everyone welcome. Tanglewood, Jacob Pillow, Williamstown theatre and skiing are nearby.

## Petersham *

| | | |
|---|---|---|
| Day, Robert | Amenities: 2,6,8,9,10,16 | Dbl. Oc.: $84.56 |
| No. Main St., 01366 | Breakfast: C. | Sgl. Oc.: $63.42 |
| (508) 724-8885 | | Third Person: $15.86 |

**Winterwood At Petersham**—A 16-room Greek Revival mansion in the center of town. Five guest rooms, one is a two-room suite. All with private baths, most with fireplaces. Listed in the *National Register of Historic Places*. Located in the center of the state.

## Plymouth *

| | | |
|---|---|---|
| Smith, Janine & James | Amenities: 2,7,9,10,11,15, | Dbl. Oc.: $49.37 - $71.31 |
| 1 Morton Park Rd., 02360 | 16,17 | Sgl. Oc.: $43.88 - $60.34 |
| (508) 747-1730 | Breakfast: C. | Third Person: $5.05 |
| | | Child: $5.05 - $10.97 |

**Morton Park Place**—An 1860's N.E. colonial guest home furnished in Victorian and 20th-century pieces. Four guest bedrooms with private or semi-private baths. Two miles from Plymouth's historic district. One mile to Routes 3 and 44. Less than one hour to Boston, Cape Cod and Rhode Island.

| | | | | |
|---|---|---|---|---|
| 1. No Smoking | 5. Tennis Available | 9. Credit Cards Accepted | 13. Lunch Available | 17. Shared Bath |
| 2. No Pets | 6. Golf Available | 10. Personal Checks Accepted | 14. Public Transportation | 18. Afternoon Tea |
| 3. No Children | 7. Swiming Available | 11. Off Season Rates | 15. Reservations Necessary | ★ Commissions given |
| 4. Senior Citizen Rates | 8. Skiing Available | 12. Dinner Available | 16. Private Bath | to Travel Agents |

## Princeton

Morgan, Victoria E.
178 Westminster Rd., 01541
(508) 464-5600

**Amenities:** 1,7,8,9,10,12,15,
16,17,18
**Breakfast:** F.
**Dbl. Oc.:** $79.28
**Sgl. Oc.:** $71.35
**Third Person:** $10.57
**Child:** $10.57

**The Harrington Farm Country Inn And Restaurant**—Quiet and relaxing. Set on a hill surrounded by fields. Comfort, fine dining and hospitality is our trademark. Roam the gardens, read on the porch or cross-country ski from the back door. Open year round. Seven beautifully appointed guest

## Provincetown

Paoletti, Leonard
156 Bradford St., 02657
(508) 487-2543

**Amenities:** 2,3,9,11,15,16
**Breakfast:** C.

**Dbl. Oc.:**$84.24 - $87.42
**Sgl.Oc.:**$78.84 - $82.02
**Thrid Person:** $21.60

**Elephant Walk Inn**—A romantic country inn near Provincetown center. The spacious, elegantly furnished rooms all have private baths, color TVs, refrigerators and ceiling fans. Enjoy our large sun deck or lounge with your morning coffee. Free parking on the premises. Open April - October.

## Provincetown

Schoolman, David
22 Commercial ST., 02657
(508) 487-0706

**Amenities:** 2,5,6,7,10,11,14
**15,16,17**
**Breakfast:** C.

**Dbl. Oc.:**$70.00 - $162.00
**Sgl.Oc.:$70.00 - $162.00**
**Third Person:** $16.20
**Child:** under 1 yr. -
no charge

**Land's End Inn**—We overlook all of Cape Cod bay and offer Victorian comfort and quiet. Close to Provincetown and the National Seashore beaches. Guest rooms are homey and comfortable. Commonrooms offer quiet socializing or comtemplation. Beautiful views abound.

| | | | |
|---|---|---|---|
| 1. No Smoking | 5. Tennis Available | 9. Credit Cards Accepted | 13. Lunch Available | 17. Shared Bath |
| 2. No Pets | 6. Golf Available | 10. Personal Checks Accepted | 14. Public Transportation | 18. Afternoon Tea |
| 3. No Children | 7. Swiming Available | 11. Off Season Rates | 15. Reservations Necessary | ★ Commissions given |
| 4. Senior Citizen Rates | 8. Skiing Available | 12. Dinner Available | 16. Private Bath | to Travel Agents |

## Rockport

Kostka Gunter
65 Eden Rd., 01966
(508) 546-2823

**Amenities:** 2,4,5,6,7,9,10,11,15,16
**Breakfast:** C.
**Dbl. Oc.:** $86.00 - $97.00
**Sgl. Oc.:** $76.00 - $87.00
**Third Person:** $10.00

**Rocky Shores Inn and Cottages**—Enjoy the panoramic views of Thatcher Island and the open sea from this beautiful seaside inn. Rocky Shores is conveniently located between the picturesque harbor of Rockport and Gloucester and nearby beaches. A warm welcome awaits you for a great vacation.

## Rockport *

Petrino, Linda
156 Main St.,01966
(508) 546-9097

**Amenities:** 1,2,6,7,9,10,11
14,17
**Breakfast:** C.

**Dbl. Oc.:**$65.00
**Sgl.Oc.:**$50.00

**The Granite House Bed & Breakfast**—A charming home built of Rockport granite. Comfortable and tastefully decorated in the seacoast tradition. Within walking distance to art galleries, shops and fine restaurants. Our accommodations include dining area, living room and large sun deck.

## Salem

Kessler, Patricia
284 Lafayette St., 0197
(508) 744-4092

**Amenities:** 2,9,11,14,16,17
**Breakfast:** C.

**Dbl.Oc.:** $81.18 - $93.25
**Sgl. Oc.:** $81.18 - $93.25
**Third Person:** $9.00
**Child:** under 18 yrs. - $7.00

**Coach House Inn**—Return to the elegance of an earlier time. Built in 1879 by Captain E. Augustus Emmerton, a central figure in Salem's China trade. Guests enjoy cozy, comfortable rooms which retain the charm of this Victorian mansion. Private baths and off-street parking.

## Salem *

Pabich, Diane & Richard
7 Summer St., 01945
(800) 446-8924, (508) 741-0680

**Amenities:** 4,9,10,11,12,
13,14,16
**Breakfast:** C.

**Dbl. Oc.:** $87.76 - $109.70
**Sgl. Oc.:** $87.76 - $109.70
**Third Person:** $10.97
**Child:** $10.97

**The Salem Inn**—History-making hospitality. An 1834 sea captain's home featuring spacious, comfortably appointed guest rooms with a blend of period detail and antique furnishings. Some working fireplaces. Some-two room suites. Ideal for families. On Salem's Heritage Trail, near museums.

| | | | |
|---|---|---|---|
| 1. No Smoking | 5. Tennis Available | 9. Credit Cards Accepted | 13. Lunch Available | 17. Shared Bath |
| 2. No Pets | 6. Golf Available | 10. Personal Checks Accepted | 14. Public Transportation | 18. Afternoon Tea |
| 3. No Children | 7. Swiming Available | 11. Off Season Rates | 15. Reservations Necessary | ★ Commissions given |
| 4. Senior Citizen Rates | 8. Skiing Available | 12. Dinner Available | 16. Private Bath | to Travel Agents |

## Salem

Roberts, Ada May
16 Winter St., 01970
(508) 744-8304

**Amenities:** 1,2,3,9,11,14,16, 16,17
**Breakfast:** C.
**Dbl. Oc.:** $60.00 - $85.00

**Amelia Payson Guest House**—A fine example of Greek Revival architecture circa 1845. Elegantly restored. Guests enjoy charming accommodations. Located in the heart of historic Salem. A five-minute stroll to historic houses, museums, waterfront dining and train service.

## Sandwich *

Dickson, Elaine & Harry
152 Main St., 02563
(800) 388-2278

**Amenities:** 1,2,5,6,7,9,10,11, 16,17
**Breakfast:** F.
**Dbl. Oc.:** $55.00 - $82.00
**Third Person:** $10.00

**Captain Ezra Nye House**—Quiet, friendly hospitality in the heart of Sandwich, Cape Cod's oldest town. Nearby fine restaurants, museums, antique shops, beaches and the world-famous Heritage Plantation. Children six and over welcome. Voted one of Cape Cod's five best B&Bs in *WCOD's* best-of-the-Cape poll.

## Sandwich (Cape Cod) *

Lemieux, Reale J.
1-3 Bay Beach Lane
Box 151, 02563
(508) 888-8813

**Amenities:** 1,2,3,5,6,7,10,11, 15,16
**Breakfast:** C.
**Dbl. Oc.:** $100.00 - $150.00
**Third Person:** $25.00

**Bay Beach Bed & Breakfast**—Extraordinary ocean-front, overlooking beach and Cape Cod Bay. Honeymoon suite features whirlpool. Choose from three spacious and elegant guest suites, each with private bath, TV, phones, air conditioning and refrigerator. Visit nearby museums, historic sites and restaurants.

## Sandwich (Cape Cod) *

Merrell, Kay & David
158 Main St., 02563
(508) 888-4991

**Amenities:** 1,2,4,5,6,7,9,10, 11,14,16,17,18
**Breakfast:** F.
**Dbl. Oc.:** $60.33 - $82.27
**Sgl. Oc.:** $44.38 - $65.82
**Third Person:** $15.00

**The Summer House**—An elegant circa 1835 B&B featured in *Country Living Magazine*. Located in historic Sandwich Village. Antiques, hand-stitched quilts, large sunny rooms and English-style gardens. Walk to dining, shops and museums. Bountiful breakfast and afternoon tea elegantly served.

| | | | |
|---|---|---|---|
| 1. No Smoking | 5. Tennis Available | 9. Credit Cards Accepted | 13. Lunch Available | 17. Shared Bath |
| 2. No Pets | 6. Golf Available | 10. Personal Checks Accepted | 14. Public Transportation | 18. Afternoon Tea |
| 3. No Children | 7. Swiming Available | 11. Off Season Rates | 15. Reservations Necessary | ★ Commissions given |
| 4. Senior Citizen Rates | 8. Skiing Available | 12. Dinner Available | 16. Private Bath | to Travel Agents |

## Scituate *

Gilmour, Christine & Ian
18 Allen Pl., 02066
(617) 545-8221

**Amenities:** 1,2,3,9,10,11,15,16
         17,18
**Breakfast:** F.
**Dbl. Oc.:** $79.00 - $109.00
**Sgl. Oc.:** $79.00 - $109.00

**The Allen House**—An ocean view, Victorian elegance and the warm welome of English hosts in the heart of an unspoiled New England fishing town only one hour form Boston. Afternoon tea and quiet nights are preludes to a gourmet breakfast from your caterer-hosts who both cook.

## Sheffield

Maghery, Richard
Undermountain Rd.,
Route 41, 01257
(413) 229-2143

**Amenities:** 7,10,11,16
**Breakfast:** C.

**Dbl. Oc.:** $65.00 - $99.00
**Third Person:** $10.95

Ivanhoe Country House—Located in the Berkshire Hills. Nine rooms, all with private baths and two with kitchens. Swimming pool. 20 wooded acres. Near Tanglewood, antique shops, hiking trails, ski areas, golf and tennis. Excellent restaurants are nearby. Brochure available.

## Stockbridge *

Reynolds, Charles
Main St., South Lee, MA, 01260
(413) 243-1794

**Amenities:** 1,2,8,9,10,11,14,16
**Breakfast:** F.
**Dbl. Oc.:** $75.00 - $100.00
**Sgl. Oc.:** $75.00 - $95.00
**Third Person:** $15.00
**Child:** under 2 yrs. - $10.00

**Merrell Tavern Inn**—Stockbridge area. A historic, 18th-century stagecoach inn. Located in a small mountain village with two acres of grounds on a riverbank. Rooms with antiques, canopy beds and fireplaces. In National Register of Historic Places. Lower rates all weekdays, winter and spring.

## Sturbridge

Duquette, Agnes
72 Stallion Hill, 01566
(508) 347-3013

**Amenities:** 2,3,6,7,8,10,15,
         16,17
**Breakfast:** C.

**Dbl. Oc.:** $50.00
**Sgl. Oc.:** $60.00

**Bethlehem Inn**—Operated to help defray the cost of "Operation Bethlehem" in Sturbridge. Guests share the family living room and TV. Blueberry muffins, orange juice and coffee for breakfast. Wooded area by a babbling brook. Near Main Street, across from Old Sturbridge.

| | | | |
|---|---|---|---|
| 1. No Smoking | 5. Tennis Available | 9. Credit Cards Accepted | 13. Lunch Available | 17. Shared Bath |
| 2. No Pets | 6. Golf Available | 10. Personal Checks Accepted | 14. Public Transportation | 18. Afternoon Tea |
| 3. No Children | 7. Swiming Available | 11. Off Season Rates | 15. Reservations Necessary | ★ Commissions given |
| 4. Senior Citizen Rates | 8. Skiing Available | 12. Dinner Available | 16. Private Bath | to Travel Agents |

# MASSACHUSETTS

## Sudbury

MacDonald, Irene & Stuart
5 Checkerberry Circle, 01776
(508) 443-8660

**Amenities:** 1,2,5,6,10,15,17
**Breakfast:** F.

**Dbl. Oc.:** $60.00 - $65.00
**Sgl. Oc.:** $50.00 - $55.00
**Child:** $10.00 (crib)

**Checkerberry Corner Bed & Breakfast**—Located in the heart of historic Minutemen country. Minutes from Concord, Lexington, Wayside Inn and easy access to Boston. Quiet residential neighborhood. Fine restaurants are nearby. No smoking, please.

## Truro

Williams, Stephen
Route 6-A, Truro Center, 02666
(508) 349-3358

**Amenities:** 2,3,5,6,7,10,11,15,17
**Breakfast:** C.
**Dbl. Oc.:** $55.00
**Sgl. Oc.:** $50.00
**Third Person:** $10.00

**Parker House**—A warm, classic 1850 full Cape house with many antiques. Close to beaches and the charming narrow streets of Provincetown and Wellfleet. Open year round with a limited occupancy. Nearby restaurants.

---

## Tyringham *

Rizzo, Lilja & Joseph
Main Rd.,
Box 336, 01264
(413) 243-3008

**Amenities:** 1,2,5,6,7,8,10,11,
16,17,18
**Breakfast:** C.

**Dbl. Oc.:** $73.99 - $116.27
**Third Person:** $10.00
**Child:** under 2 yrs. -
no charge

**The Golden Goose**—A warm, friendly B&B inn nestled between Stockbridge, Lenox and Becket. Antiques, fireplaces and homemade breakfasts. Six guest rooms plus charming studio apartment. Beautiful year round. In the country, but close to Tanglewood, skiing and good restaurants.

---

## Vineyard Haven

Clarke, Mary & John
Box 1939, Owen Park, 02568
(508) 693-1646

**Amenities:** 5,6,7,9,10,11,14,15,16,17
**Breakfast:** C.
**Dbl. Oc.:** $99.00 - $160.00
**Third Person:** $15.00
**Child:** under 5 yrs. - $15.00

**Lothrop Merry House**—A charming 18th-century home overlooking the harbor. One block from the ferry. Beautiful views. Private beach. Seven rooms, some with fireplaces. Private baths. Sunfish, canoe and sailing charters available.

| | | | | |
|---|---|---|---|---|
| 1. No Smoking | 5. Tennis Available | 9. Credit Cards Accepted | 13. Lunch Available | 17. Shared Bath |
| 2. No Pets | 6. Golf Available | 10. Personal Checks Accepted | 14. Public Transportation | 18. Afternoon Tea |
| 3. No Children | 7. Swiming Available | 11. Off Season Rates | 15. Reservations Necessary | ★ Commissions given |
| 4. Senior Citizen Rates | 8. Skiing Available | 12. Dinner Available | 16. Private Bath | to Travel Agents |

## *Vineyard Haven*

Lengel, Alisa
100 Main St.
Box 2457, 02568
(508) 693-6564

Amenities: 2,9,10,11,15,
16,18
Breakfast: C.

Dbl. Oc.: $71.31 - $175.52
Third Person: $20.00

**Captain Dexter House Of Vineyard Haven**—The home of sea captain Rodolphas Dexter. Built in 1843. This country colonial inn is elegantly furnished with period antiques, original fireplaces and canopy beds. Enjoy a delicious, home baked continental breakfast. Walk to ferry, beach, shops and restaurants.

## *Vineyard Haven* *

Stavens, Darlene
4 Crocker Ave., 02568
(508) 693-1151

Amenities: 2,4,5,6,7,9,10,11,15,16
Breakfast: C.
Dbl. Oc.: $109.70 - $169.55
Third Person: $15.00
Child: under 12 yrs. - no charge

**The Crocker House Inn**—A charming Victorian inn with eight unique rooms and suites, all with private baths. Some feature private entrances with balconies and a fireplace. A home made continental breakfast is served in a lovely common area. Close to ferry, shops and restaurants

## *Ware* *

Skutnik, Margaret
14 Pleasant St., 01082
(413) 967-7847

Amenities: 1,4,5,6,7,10,11,15,16,17,18
Breakfast: F.
Dbl. Oc.: $47.00 - $65.00
Sgl. Oc.: $40.00 - $55.00
Third Person: $15.00
Child: under 4 yrs. - $10.00

**The 1880 Inn B&B**—Relax in yesterday's charm. Antiques, pumpkin hardwood floors, beamed ceilings and six fireplaces. Mid-point between historic Deerfield, Old Sturbridge, Boston and the Berkshires. One half hour to Amherst and New Hampshire. Quabbin Reservoir with fishing and hiking.

## *Wareham*

Murphy, Frances A.
257 High St., 02571
(508) 295-0684

Amenities: 1,2,5,6,7,8,9,10,
11,17,18
Breakfast: C.

Dbl. Oc.: $50.00
Sgl. Oc.: $50.00
Third Person: $10.00
Child: $10.00

**Mulberry Bed And Breakfast**—A circa 1840's home set on an acre of mulberry tree-shade dproperty in the historic area of Wareham. In this cozy, three-bedroom B&B, new friends enjoy a restful sleep, a hearty New England breakfast and hospitality. Close to Cape Cod.

| | | | |
|---|---|---|---|
| 1. No Smoking | 5. Tennis Available | 9. Credit Cards Accepted | 13. Lunch Available | 17. Shared Bath |
| 2. No Pets | 6. Golf Available | 10. Personal Checks Accepted | 14. Public Transportation | 18. Afternoon Tea |
| 3. No Children | 7. Swiming Available | 11. Off Season Rates | 15. Reservations Necessary | ★ Commissions given |
| 4. Senior Citizen Rates | 8. Skiing Available | 12. Dinner Available | 16. Private Bath | to Travel Agents |

## *Yarmouth, South*

Crowell, Mary & Walter
345 High Bank Rd., 02664
(508) 394-4182

**Amenities:** 2,10,11,15,16
**Breakfast:** C.

**Dbl. Oc.:** $80.00 - $100.00
**Third Person:** $15.00
**Child:** $15.00

**The Four Winds**—A 1712 sea captain's homestead in historic So. Yarmouth. Near beaches and bike trail. A carriage house sleeps six, with wood stove and kitchen. Available seasonally. Cottage sleeps three. Fireplace and kitchen. Suite with queen bed, sitting room, sleep sofa and wet bar.

## *Yarmouthport*

Perna, Malcolm
Route 6A, 277 Main St., 02675
(800) 999-3416, (508) 362-4348

**Amenities:** 1,4,5,6,7,,8,9,10,
11,12,13,15,14,16,
18
**Breakfast:** C.

**Dbl. Oc.:** $104.50
**Sgl. Oc.:** $84.50
**Third Person:** $20.00
**Child:** under 2 yrs. - $5.00

**The Colonial House Inn**—Offers old-world charm on the quiet side of Cape Cod, yet is minutes from shopping, beaches and night life. We provide you with "the best of all worlds." Indoor pool, TV, air conditioning and handicapped-accessible sun deck. All prices include dinner. Golfing year round.

## *Yarmouthport*

Tilly, Sven
101 Main St., 02675
(508) 362-4496

**Amenities:** 2,5,6,7,10,11,14,
16,17
**Breakfast:** C.

**Dbl. Oc.:** $66.00
**Sgl. Oc.:** $55.00
**Third Person:** $10.00
**Child:** $10.00

**Olde Captain's Inn**—On the Cape, a charmingly restored 160-year-old sea captain's home in the historic district. Walk to fine restaurants and craft shops. Large front and side porch for breakfast and relaxing. Third night free.

| | | | | |
|---|---|---|---|---|
| 1. No Smoking | 5. Tennis Available | 9. Credit Cards Accepted | 13. Lunch Available | 17. Shared Bath |
| 2. No Pets | 6. Golf Available | 10. Personal Checks Accepted | 14. Public Transportation | 18. Afternoon Tea |
| 3. No Children | 7. Swiming Available | 11. Off Season Rates | 15. Reservations Necessary | ★ Commissions given |
| 4. Senior Citizen Rates | 8. Skiing Available | 12. Dinner Available | 16. Private Bath | to Travel Agents |

# MICHIGAN

## *The Wolverine State*

Capitol: Lansing
Statehood: January 26, 1837; the 26th state
State Motto: If You Seek Pleasant Peninsula, Look About You
State Song: "Michigan, My Michigan"
State Bird: Robin
State Flower: Apple Blossom
State Tree: White Pine

Michigan is known for its long history of automobile manufacturing. Henry Ford built his first automobile here in 1896. The city of Detroit became the center of this industry and is called 'The Automobile Capitol of the World.'

To get automobiles to market, it was necessary to use the waterways that are readily available here. The Soo Canals at Sault Ste. Marie are the busiest ship canals in the western hemisphere. The railroads played a big part in this new industry, too. In 1855, the first railroad in Michigan was the Erie and Kalamazoo, linking Michigan with Ohio.

The people of Michigan like to enjoy life. They are known for their delight in having tourists visit and, in fact, tourism is very big here. The residents of Michigan use more of their lands for recreation than anything else.

# MICHIGAN

## Ann Arbor

Rosalik, Andre
2759 Canterbury Rd., 48104
(313) 971-8110

**Amenities:** 2,3,10,14,15,16,17
**Breakfast:** F.
**Dbl. Oc.:** $57.20
**Sgl. Oc.:** $46.80

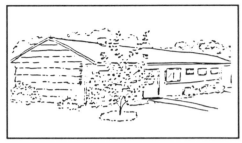

**The Urban Retreat**—A comfortable home on a quiet, tree-lined street. Minutes from downtown and the University of Michigan campus. Stroll in the adjacent 127-acre Country Farm Park. Pet the cats, watch the birds, smell the flowers and unwind. Two rooms available with antiques and period decor.

## Cadillac

Suhs, Hermann
214 No. Mitchell St., 49601
(616) 775-9563

**Amenities:** 2,5,6,7,8,9,10,11, 12,13,14,15,16
**Breakfast:** C.

**Dbl. Oc.:** $85.00
**Sgl. Oc.:** $70.00
**Third Person:** $10.00

**Hermann's European Inn**—Every convenience is yours in an old-world country setting atop a three-star European cafe and chefs deli. Hospitality unequaled. European flavor. Near lakes an skiing. Free parking, local phone calls, TVs and VCRs. Continental breakfast delivered to your door.

## Central Lake

Kooiman, Marilyn
2287 So. Main St.
P.O. Box 577, 49622
(616) 544-8122

**Amenities:** 1,2,3,5,6,7,10, 15,16
**Breakfast:** F.

**Dbl. Oc.:** $62.40
**Sgl. Oc.:** $52.00

**Bridgewalk Bed & Breakfast**—The footbridge is the first step to the special charm of Bridgewalk, leading you across a bubbling brook to the lawn and front porch shaded by old maple trees. Graciously appointed Victorian home. Many challenging golf courses, restaurants and nearby lakes.

## Coldwater

Schultz, Rebecca
215 E. Chicago St., 49036
(517) 279-8744

**Amenities:** 2,9,10,14,16
**Breakfast:** F.
**Dbl. Oc.:** $78.00 - $135.20
**Sgl. Oc.:** $78.00 - $135.20
**Third Person:** $20.00

**Chicago Pike Inn**—"Lodging in Victorian elegance." Six beautifully restored rooms surrounded by peace and tranquility. Located in a national historic district. We take pride in our "knack"of making your stay a memorable one.

| | | | | |
|---|---|---|---|---|
| 1. No Smoking | 5. Tennis Available | 9. Credit Cards Accepted | 13. Lunch Available | 17. Shared Bath |
| 2. No Pets | 6. Golf Available | 10. Personal Checks Accepted | 14. Public Transportation | 18. Afternoon Tea |
| 3. No Children | 7. Swiming Available | 11. Off Season Rates | 15. Reservations Necessary | ★ Commissions given |
| 4. Senior Citizen Rates | 8. Skiing Available | 12. Dinner Available | 16. Private Bath | to Travel Agents |

## Fennville

Witt, Shirley & David
626 W. Main St., 49408
(616) 561-6425

Amenities: 1,2,3,4,6,7,8,9,10,
          11,15,16,18
Breakfast: F.
Dbl. Oc.: $79.50
Sgl. Oc.: $69.90
Third Person: $15.00

**The Kingsley House**—An elegant Victorian built in 1886. Five guest rooms, private baths, beautiful decor, family antiques and an open oak stairway. Minutes from Saugatuck, Holland and Lake Michigan. Picnic area and bicycles available. Nearby playhouse theatre and excellent restaurants.

## Flint

Minore, Arletta
518 Avon St., 48503
(313) 232-6861

Amenities: 2,14,15,17
Breakfast: F.

Dbl. Oc.: $35.00
Sgl. Oc.: $30.00
Third Person: $10.00

**Avon House**—Enchanting Victorian home built in the 1880's. Filled with warm oak woodwork, window benches and antiques. Enjoy the turn-of-the-century Steinway grand in the parlor and a homemade breakfast in the formal dining room. Walking distance to downtown, cultural center, college and museums.

## Frankenmuth *

Kueffner, Margaret
176 Parker St., 48734
(517) 652-6839

Amenities: 4,5,6,7,10,15,
          16,17
Breakfast: F.

Dbl. Oc.: $50.00
Sgl. Oc.: $40.00
Third Person: $5.00
Child: under 5 yrs. -
        no charge

**The Kueffner Haus - Your Home Away**—A charming family home within easy walking distance to Frankenmuth's famous restaurants and major attractions. Upstairs two bedrooms include kitchenette and living room —ideal for extended stays. Corporate rates available.

## Glen Arbor *

Olson, Jenny & Bill
6680 Western Ave.
(M-109), 49636
(616) 334-4333

Amenities: 1,2,3,5,6,7,8,9,10,
          15,16,17
Breakfast: C.

Dbl. Oc.: $52.00 - $94.00
Sgl. Oc.: $52.00 - $94.00
Third Person: $12.00

**The Sylvan Inn**—A luxuriously renovated historic landmark inn with 14 charming rooms and suites. Spa/sauna. Carefully preserved historic charm in the heart of Sleeping Bear Dunes National Lakeshore. Easy access to fine dining, shopping, swimming, biking, downhill and cross-country skiing.

| 1. No Smoking | 5. Tennis Available | 9. Credit Cards Accepted | 13. Lunch Available | 17. Shared Bath |
| --- | --- | --- | --- | --- |
| 2. No Pets | 6. Golf Available | 10. Personal Checks Accepted | 14. Public Transportation | 18. Afternoon Tea |
| 3. No Children | 7. Swiming Available | 11. Off Season Rates | 15. Reservations Necessary | ★ Commissions given |
| 4. Senior Citizen Rates | 8. Skiing Available | 12. Dinner Available | 16. Private Bath | to Travel Agents |

## Grand Haven

Meyer, Susan
20009 Breton, Spring Lake, 49456
(616) 842-8409

**Amenities:** 2,7,8,9,10,11,14, 16,18
**Breakfast:** F.

**Dbl. Oc.:** $91.10
**Sgl. Oc.:** $91.10
**Third Person:** $26.50
**Child:** $26.50

**Seascape**—On a private Lake Michigan beach. Relaxing lakefront rooms. Enjoy the warm hospitality and cozy "country living" ambience of our nautical seashore home. Breakfast served in the gathering room with fieldstone fireplace or on deck. Both offer a panoramic view of Grand Haven Harbor.

## Grand Haven-Muskegon

Hewett, Virginia & John
60 W. Park St., Fruitport, 49415
(616) 865-6289

**Amenities:** 1,2,5,9,10,11,16
**Breakfast:** F.

**Dbl. Oc.:** $64.44 - $75.00
**Sgl. Oc.:** $64.44 - $75.00
**Child:** cot - no charge

**Village Park Bed & Breakfast**—Overlooking Spring Lake and Village Park with picnic area, tennis and boat launch. Relaxing common areas, decks, six charming guest rooms. Serving Grand Haven, Muskegon, Hoffmaster Park, Pleasure Island and race track. Wellness weekend packages available off-season. Historic setting.

## Grayling

Kellogg, Nancy & Duane
101 Maple St., 49738
(800) 762-8756, (517) 348-4921

**Amenities:** 1,4,6,7,8,9,10,11,14,15,16,17
**Breakfast:** F.
**Dbl. Oc.:** $52.00 - $67.60
**Third Person:** $10.00

**Borcher's Bed & Breakfast**—Full country breakfast and six plush guest rooms (two with private baths) in our country Victorian inn overlooking the AuSable River. Horseshoe pits, badminton, croquet, pool table, air-hockey and Ping-Pong. Packages for golf, fishing, cross-country and downhill skiing arranged.

| | | | | |
|---|---|---|---|---|
| 1. No Smoking | 5. Tennis Available | 9. Credit Cards Accepted | 13. Lunch Available | 17. Shared Bath |
| 2. No Pets | 6. Golf Available | 10. Personal Checks Accepted | 14. Public Transportation | 18. Afternoon Tea |
| 3. No Children | 7. Swiming Available | 11. Off Season Rates | 15. Reservations Necessary | ★ Commissions given |
| 4. Senior Citizen Rates | 8. Skiing Available | 12. Dinner Available | 16. Private Bath | to Travel Agents |

212

## *Holland*

Elenbaas, Robert
560 Central Ave., 49423
(616) 396-3664

**Amenities:** 1,5,6,7,8,9,10,11,16
**Breakfast:** F.
**Dbl. Oc.:** $55.00 - $85.00
**Third Person:** $10.00

**Dutch Colonial Inn**—A gracious Dutch colonial home built in 1930. Award-winning B&B features lovely family heirlooms, antiques, 1930 furnishings and elegant decor. Private baths with whirlpool tub. Hideaway suite. Close to Lake Michigan, Hope College and excellent shopping.

## *Holland*

McIntyre, Dr. & Mrs
13 E. 13th St., 49423
(616) 392-9886

**Amenities** 1,2,6,7,10,12,
14,16,17
**Breakfast:** C.

**Dbl. Oc.:** $53.00
**Sgl. Oc.:** $37.10
**Third Person:** $10.60

**McIntyre Bed And Breakfast**—A lovely, beautifully maintained home built in 1906. Antiques throughout. Sunny, air-conditioned rooms. Excellent beds. Off-street parking. Warm hospitality. Hearty continental breakfast. Near Hope College and downtown. No smoking or drinking.

## *Holland* *

Verwys, Bonnie
6 E. 24th St., 49423
(616) 396-1316

**Amenities:** 1,2,3,5,6,7,8,10,
15,16,17
**Breakfast:** F.

**Dbl. Oc.:** $60.00 - $80.00
**Sgl. Oc.:** $45.00 - $65.00

**The Parsonage 1908**—Rated superior by our guests in Michigan B&B Assoc.'s survey. A true European B&B in a quiet residential setting. Four guest rooms. Privacy and enjoyment. Five minutes to Lake Michigan, theatre and dining; 10 minutes to Saugatuck; three hours to Chicago, Dearborn and Traverse City.

## *Hudson*

Sutton, Barbara & Justin
18736 Quaker Rd., 49247
(517) 547-6302

**Amenities:** 1,2,4,5,6,7,9,10,15,17
**Breakfast:** F.
**Dbl. Oc.:** $57.20
**Sgl. Oc.:** $52.00
**Child:** under 7 yrs. - $7.50

**Sutton's Weed Farm Bed & Breakfast**—This seven-gable Victorian farmhouse, built in 1873, is like going back to Grandma's. Filled with family antiques. Located on 180 acres of woods, trails, wildlife, birds, etc. Ancient maple trees are still tapped for syrup to be enjoyed at the breakfast table. Nearby good restaurants.

| | | | |
|---|---|---|---|
| 1. No Smoking | 5. Tennis Available | 9. Credit Cards Accepted | 13. Lunch Available | 17. Shared Bath |
| 2. No Pets | 6. Golf Available | 10. Personal Checks Accepted | 14. Public Transportation | 18. Afternoon Tea |
| 3. No Children | 7. Swiming Available | 11. Off Season Rates | 15. Reservations Necessary | ★ Commissions given |
| 4. Senior Citizen Rates | 8. Skiing Available | 12. Dinner Available | 16. Private Bath | to Travel Agents |

## Lowell

Barber, Ardis
2534 Alden Nash NE, 49331
(616) 897-8142

**Amenities:** 6,8,9,10,15,17
**Breakfast:** F.

**Dbl. Oc.:** $39.50
**Sgl. Oc.:** $31.20
**Third Person:** $10.00
**Child:** under 2 yrs. - $10.00

**McGee Homestead B&B**—Come and join us in this 100-year-old country farmhouse with private entrance to three spacious guest rooms (two with shared bath) and a small kitchen. Come and relax by the fire or walk through acres of orchards. It's just like going to Grandma's!

## Mackinac Island *

Bacon, Jane & Mike
Box 285, 49757
(906) 847-6234

**Amenities:** 2,5,6,7,9,10,11,14,15,16
**Breakfast:** C.
**Dbl. Oc.:** $119.60 - $208.00
**Sgl. Oc.:** $119.60 - $208.00
**Third Person:** $20.80
**Child:** under 3 yrs. - $8.32

**Metivier Inn**—Located in the downtown historic district. A charming country home-like inn offers 19 rooms and two efficiency apartments. Cozy living room with wood-burning stove. Porches with wicker furniture. Unique Victorian summer resort. No automobiles.

## Marquette

Stabile, Linda & Frank
2403 U.S. 41 W., 49855
(906) 225-1393

**Amenities:** 1,2,7,9,10,15,16,17,18
**Breakfast:** C.
**Dbl. Oc.:** $107.00
**Sgl. Oc.:** $107.00

**Michigamme Lake Lodge**—A grand lodge situated on Lake Michigamme, 30 miles west of Marquette. A 1934 log construction with nine rooms and a gathering room with a 2-1/2 story stone fireplace. In *State Register of Michigan Historic Sites*. Swim, fish, hike, bike, canoe and relax.

## Northport

McCann, Barbara
Route 1, Box 169-F, 49670
(616) 386-5260

**Amenities:** 1,2,5,6,7,8,10,
11,16
**Breakfast:** F.

**Dbl. Oc.:** $75.00
**Sgl. Oc.:** $60.00
**Third Person:** $15.00
**Child:** under 10 yrs. - $8.00

**Mapletree Inn B&B**—This inn is flanked by a pond, spreading maple and birch trees and a relaxing deck. Guests enjoy serenity and generous space in our two-bedroom suite and rave about Barb's homemade muffins and fruit-filled breakfasts. Queen beds. Crib. TV. Deposit required.

| | | | | |
|---|---|---|---|---|
| 1. No Smoking | 5. Tennis Available | 9. Credit Cards Accepted | 13. Lunch Available | 17. Shared Bath |
| 2. No Pets | 6. Golf Available | 10. Personal Checks Accepted | 14. Public Transportation | 18. Afternoon Tea |
| 3. No Children | 7. Swiming Available | 11. Off Season Rates | 15. Reservations Necessary | ★ Commissions given |
| 4. Senior Citizen Rates | 8. Skiing Available | 12. Dinner Available | 16. Private Bath | to Travel Agents |

## Northville *

Lapine, Susan
501 W. Dunlap, 48167
(313) 349-3340

**Amenities:** 1,2,9,10,16
**Breakfast:** F.

**Dbl. Oc.:** $72.80 - $156.00
**Sgl. Oc.:** $72.80 - $156.00
**Third Person:** $10.00
**Child:** $10.00

**The Atchinson House Bed & Breakfast Inn**—A magnificent 1882 Victorian in the heart of historic district. Four blocks from quaint downtown. Authentically restored in period antiques. Quiet and relaxing. Enjoy nearby fine dining, shops, sports and tourist attractions. Lavish guest rooms with sumptuous breakfasts.

## Omena

Phillips, Mary Helen
13140 Isthmus Rd., 49674
(616) 386-7311

**Amenities:** 1,2,5,6,7,8,10,11,15,
          16,17,18
**Breakfast:** F.
**Dbl. Oc.:** $80.00
**Sgl. Oc.:** $65.00

**Omena Shores Bed & Breakfast**—Enjoy Lee Lanau County's quiet beauty. Our home is a lovingly restored 1858 barn with original hand-hewn beams. Rooms individually decorated with wicker and antiques. Orchards, vineyards, lakes and sweeping vistas abound. Superb dining. Open year round.

## Owosso *

Holmes, Carol A.
1251 No. Shiawassee, 48867
(517) 723-4890

**Amenities:** 2,5,6,9,10,15,16,
          17,18
**Breakfast:** C.

**Dbl. Oc.:** $60.00
**Sgl. Oc.:** $55.00
**Third Person:** $10.00
**Child:** under 12 yrs. -
          $10.00

**Mulberry House Bed & Breakfast**—Three lovely rooms await your visit where you will be greeted with warmth and hospitality. You may be awakened by the wonderful aroma of an elegant breakfast being prepared for you. Visit Curwood Castle, walk the Riverwalk and visit the area's attractions.

## Plymouth

Smith, Creon
827 W. Ann Arbor Trail, 48170
(313) 453-1620

**Amenities:** 9,10,12,13,14,15,
          16
**Breakfast:** F.

**Dbl. Oc.:** $76.44
**Sgl. Oc.:** $66.04
**Third Person:** $10.40
**Child:** under 12 yrs. -
          no charge

**The Mayflower Bed & Breakfast Hotel**—Features include a complimentary breakfast for guests, elegant but cozy surroundings and a reputation for good food and hospitality. Located in the heart of Plymouth, within walking distance of 150 charming shops.

| | | | |
|---|---|---|---|
| 1. No Smoking | 5. Tennis Available | 9. Credit Cards Accepted | 13. Lunch Available | 17. Shared Bath |
| 2. No Pets | 6. Golf Available | 10. Personal Checks Accepted | 14. Public Transportation | 18. Afternoon Tea |
| 3. No Children | 7. Swiming Available | 11. Off Season Rates | 15. Reservations Necessary | ★ Commissions given |
| 4. Senior Citizen Rates | 8. Skiing Available | 12. Dinner Available | 16. Private Bath | to Travel Agents |

## Port Huron

Secory, Lynne & Lew
1229 7th St., 48060
(313) 984-1437

**Amenities:** 2,9,10,12,13,14,15,16,17
**Breakfast:** C.
**Dbl. Oc.:** $46.80 - $62.40

**The Victorian Inn**—Features fine dining and guest rooms in authentically restored Victorian elegance. One hour north of metropolitan Detroit, this fine inn features classically creative cuisine and gracious service. Knowledgeable wine list. Pier Points Pub at lower level.

---

## Port Sanilac *

Denison, Shirley
111 So. Ridge (M-25), 48469
(313) 622-8800

**Amenities:** 1,2,4,5,6,7,9,10, 16
**Breakfast:** C.

**Dbl. Oc.:** $54.00
**Sgl. Oc.:** $54.00
**Third Person:** $15.60
**Child:** $15.60

**Raymond House Inn**—An 1872 antique-filled Victorian on Lake Huron. All private baths in seven rooms. Marina and boating, chartered fishing. Limited smoking. Children restricted. Ninety miles north of Detroit. Thirty miles north of Port Huron. Open April through October.

---

## Saginaw

Zuehlke, Danice
1631 Brockway, 48602
(517) 792-0746

**Amenities:** 1,2,5,6,8,9,10,15, 16,17,18
**Breakfast:** F.

**Dbl. Oc.:** $70.20 - $91.60
**Sgl. Oc.:** $70.20 - $91.60
**Third Person:** $10.00
**Child:** $10.00

**Brockway House Bed & Breakfast**—This Southern colonial mansion has been a historic treasure for generations. Now Zuehlkes invite you to share the enchantment and elegance of a classic B&B, where a warm hearth and personal family attention are part of the daily menu. Wonderful food.

---

## Saline *

Grossman, Shirley
9279 Macon Rd., 48176
(313) 429-9625

**Amenities:** 2,3,4,5,6,8,9,10, 15,16,17
**Breakfast:** F.

**Dbl. Oc.:** $52.00 - $68.00
**Sgl. Oc.:** $27.00 - $47.00
**Third Person:** $15.00
**Child:** over 10 yrs. - $15.00

**The Homestead Bed & Breakfast**—An 1851 brick farmhouse. Comfort, country and Victorian elegance. Walk, relax or cross-country ski. Fifteen minutes to Ann Arbor and Ypsilanti. Forty minutes to Detroit or Toledo. Children over 10 welcome.

---

| 1. No Smoking | 5. Tennis Available | 9. Credit Cards Accepted | 13. Lunch Available | 17. Shared Bath |
| 2. No Pets | 6. Golf Available | 10. Personal Checks Accepted | 14. Public Transportation | 18. Afternoon Tea |
| 3. No Children | 7. Swiming Available | 11. Off Season Rates | 15. Reservations Necessary | ★ Commissions given |
| 4. Senior Citizen Rates | 8. Skiing Available | 12. Dinner Available | 16. Private Bath | to Travel Agents |

## *Saugatuck*

Indurante, Dan
132 Mason St., 49453
(616) 857-8851

**Amenities:** 1,2,5,6,7,8,9,10, 11,16,17
**Breakfast:** C.

**Dbl. Oc.:** $58.00 - $79.00
**Sgl. Oc.:** $58.00 - $79.00
**Third Person:** $10.00
**Child:** under 6 yrs. - no charge

**The Red Dog Bed & Breakfast**—A comfortable place to stay in the heart of Saugatuck, steps away from restaurants, shopping and the boardwalk. Built in 1879. Six air-conditioned guest rooms, four with private baths. Open all year. Visit our ice cream parlor, a Saugatuck tradition for over 25 years.

## *Saugatuck* *

Simcik, Denise & Michael
900 E. Lake St.
P.O. Box 881, 49453
(616) 857-4346

**Amenities:** 1,2,3,5,6,7,8,9,10, 11,12,13,14,16
**Breakfast:** C.

**Dbl. Oc.:** $49.00 - $93.64
**Third Person:** $15.00

**Twin Gables Country Inn**—Overlooking the lake, this state historic inn is totally air-conditioned and features 14 guest rooms with private baths. Furnished with antiques and country. Summer guests can enjoy our side garden park with its outdoor pool. In winter, guests can use the indoor hot tub and cozy

## *Saugatuck* *

Tatsch, Cindi & Terry
633 Pleasant, 49453
(616) 857-2919

**Amenities:** 1,2,4,5,6,7,8,9,10, 11,14,17
**Breakfast:** C.

**Dbl. Oc.:** $79.50 - $100.70
**Sgl. Oc.:** $79.50 - $100.70
**Third Person:** $15.00

**Kemah Guest House**—A restored residential home located on a 2-1/2 acre lot. Three blocks from downtown Saugatuck. A short safe, walk to a variety of activities. Accommodates 10-12 people in five bedrooms. Common rooms include recreation room with pool table and Rathskeller Room.

## *Sawyer*

Lasco, Dale
5682 Sawyer Rd., 49125
(616) 426-4848

**Amenities:** 1,2,3,9,10,16,17
**Breakfast:** C.

**Dbl. Oc.:** $114.40
**Sgl. Oc.:** $114.40
**Third Person:** $26.00

**The Sawyer Country Inn**—Less than 1/2 mile from I-94 in southwest Michigan's harbor country. A beautiful and tranquil setting away from it all. The inn provides serene and comfortable antique-furnished accommodations for naturalists, sports enthusiasts or those who just want to rest.

| | | | |
|---|---|---|---|
| 1. No Smoking | 5. Tennis Available | 9. Credit Cards Accepted | 13. Lunch Available | 17. Shared Bath |
| 2. No Pets | 6. Golf Available | 10. Personal Checks Accepted | 14. Public Transportation | 18. Afternoon Tea |
| 3. No Children | 7. Swiming Available | 11. Off Season Rates | 15. Reservations Necessary | ★ Commissions given |
| 4. Senior Citizen Rates | 8. Skiing Available | 12. Dinner Available | 16. Private Bath | to Travel Agents |

## South Haven

Yelton, Joyce & Jay
140 No. Shore Dr., 49090
(616) 637-5220

**Amenities:** 1,2,5,6,7,8,9,10,15,16
**Breakfast:** F.
**Dbl. Oc.:** $74.20 - $132.50
**Sgl. Oc.:** $74.20 - $132.50

**Yelton Manor Bed & Breakfast**—Southern hospitality with Victorian elegance on scenic Lake Michigan. Eleven charming guest rooms with private baths. Central air conditioning. Nearby beaches, marinas, shops and restaurants. Ideal for business meetings and seminars. Open all year. Reservations preferred.

## St. Joseph

Swisher, Bill
1900 Lakeshore Dr., 49085
(616) 983-4881

**Amenities:** 2,5,6,7,8,9,10, 11,16
**Breakfast:** C.

**Dbl. Oc.:** $55.00 - $95.00
**Sgl. Oc.:** $55.00 - $95.00
**Third Person:** $10.00
**Child:** $10.00

**South Cliff Inn B&B**—Luxurious accommodations with a relaxed atmosphere. Many antique and custom-designed furnishings. Enjoy breathtaking sunsets over Lake Michigan from our new decks. Central A/C and heat for year-round comfort. Homemade breakfast in our lakeside sunroom.

## Suttons Bay *

Sutherland, Mary
613 St. Mary's Ave., 49682
(616) 271-4300

**Amenities:** 6,7,10,17
**Breakfast:** C.

**Dbl. Oc.:** $60.00
**Sgl. Oc.:** $50.00
**Third Person:** $10.00

**Open Windows Bed And Breakfast**—Built in 1885, this Victorian-era farmhouse, with fireplace, is within walking distance of unique shops and restaurants. It is beautifully furnished with family heirlooms and antiques complemented by flower gardens and a lovely front porch for viewing the bay.

## Traverse City *

Cump, Dorothy
2856 Hammond Rd. E., 49684
(616) 947-9806

**Amenities:** 1,2,6,7,8,9,10,11,17
**Breakfast:** F.
**Dbl. Oc.:** $62.40
**Sgl. Oc.:** $57.20
**Third Person:** $10.00

**Cherry Knoll Farm Bed & Breakfast**—Come! Enjoy the friendly atmosphere of this century-old Victorian farmhouse situated on 115 acres in the heart of Michigan's Riviera of the North. Near summer and winters ports. Spectacular fall colors and spring blossoms. Welcome!

| | | | |
|---|---|---|---|
| 1. No Smoking | 5. Tennis Available | 9. Credit Cards Accepted | 13. Lunch Available | 17. Shared Bath |
| 2. No Pets | 6. Golf Available | 10. Personal Checks Accepted | 14. Public Transportation | 18. Afternoon Tea |
| 3. No Children | 7. Swiming Available | 11. Off Season Rates | 15. Reservations Necessary | ★ Commissions given |
| 4. Senior Citizen Rates | 8. Skiing Available | 12. Dinner Available | 16. Private Bath | to Travel Agents |

# MINNESOTA

## The Gopher State

Capitol: St. Paul
Statehood: May 11, 1858; the 32nd state
State Motto: The Star of the North
State Song: "Hail! Minnesota"
State Bird: Common Loon
State Flower: Pink and White Lady's Slipper
State Tree: Norway Pine

Minnesota is the land of ten thousand lakes. Many of its cities and towns are named for lakes, falls or rapids. For every 20 acres of land, there is an acre of water. It is a popular playground for campers and canoers, with its many acres of wilderness along each lake site. Water skiing was developed here and the blue lakes attract swimmers, boaters and fishermen.

This state's million dairy cows make it a leading butter producing state. And with its flour mills it isn't hard to see how it got the name of "the bread and butter state."

The city of Duluth is its major port on Lake Superior. From here the grain and manufactured products of Minnesota are shipped to the Great Lakes cities and overseas.

The Mayo Clinic was established at Rochester in 1889 by Dr. William W. May and his two sons, William and Charles. It is one of the greatest medical research centers in the world.

## Fergus Falls

| | | |
|---|---|---|
| Nims, Judy | **Amenities:** 1,2,4,8,10,15,16, | **Dbl. Oc.:** $75.00 - $85.00 |
| R.R. 2, Box 187A, 56537 | 17,18 | **Sgl. Oc.:** $55.00 |
| (218) 739-2915 | **Breakfast:** F. | **Third Person:** $15.00 |

**Bakketopp Hus**—A wooded lake setting where one can relax by the fire, on the decks or in the spa. Natural wood patio windows and antique furnishings create an ambience of tranquility and solitude. Nearby ski trails, golf, antiques and restaurants. Visit - enjoy.

## Grand Marais *

| | | |
|---|---|---|
| Beattie, Mary & Scott | **Amenities:** 1,2,8,9,10,11,15, | **Dbl. Oc.:** $65.00 - $85.00 |
| Gunflint Trail | 16,17 | **Sgl. Oc.:** $60.00 - $80.00 |
| P.O. Box 181, 55604 | **Breakfast:** F. | **Third Person:** $13.00 |
| (218) 387-1276 or (800) 542-1226 | | |

**Pincushion Mountain Bed & Breakfast**—Three miles from Grand Marais. A contemporary home sits on forested ridgeline overlooking north shore of Lake Superior 1,000 feet below. Four guest rooms. Country decor. Great hiking, mountain biking, cross-country ski trails at door-step. Lodge-to-lodge hiking. Free brochure.

## Grand Marais

| | | |
|---|---|---|
| Kerber, Viola & Jack | **Amenities:** 1,2,3,9,10,15,17 | **Dbl. Oc.:** $69.00 - $74.00 |
| P.O. Box 963, 55604 | **Breakfast:** F. | **Sgl. Oc.:** $66.00 - $71.00 |
| (218) 387-1571 | | **Third Person:** $15.00 |

**The Superior Overlook B&B**—A contemporary home with private area for guests. Three guest rooms, two bathrooms, sauna and family room. Grand Marais is located on the north shore of Lake Superior, 40 miles from the Canadian border. All winter and summer activities are nearby. Open all year.

## Hendricks *

| | | |
|---|---|---|
| Larson, Joan & Lanford | **Amenities:** 1,2,9,10,15,16,17 | **Dbl. Oc.:** $35.00 - $45.00 |
| Route 1, Box 141, 56136 | **Breakfast:** F. | **Sgl. Oc.:** $30.00 - $35.00 |
| (507) 275-3740 | | **Third Person:** $10.00 |
| | | **Child:** under 17 yrs. no charge |

**Triple L Farm Bed & Breakfast**—A large, remodeled 1890 white frame house on a working family farm. Crops grown include corn and beans. Hogs are raised from farrow to finish. Guest rooms are furnished with some antiques. Homemade quilts on each bed. Country road hiking and biking.

| | | | | |
|---|---|---|---|---|
| 1. No Smoking | 5. Tennis Available | 9. Credit Cards Accepted | 13. Lunch Available | 17. Shared Bath |
| 2. No Pets | 6. Golf Available | 10. Personal Checks Accepted | 14. Public Transportation | 18. Afternoon Tea |
| 3. No Children | 7. Swiming Available | 11. Off Season Rates | 15. Reservations Necessary | ★ Commissions given |
| 4. Senior Citizen Rates | 8. Skiing Available | 12. Dinner Available | 16. Private Bath | to Travel Agents |

## Lutsen *

Lindgren, Shirley
Country Rd. 35, W191, 55612
(218) 663-7450

**Amenities:** 2,4,5,6,7,8,9,10,15,16,17
**Breakfast:** F.
**Dbl. Oc.:** $75.00 & up
**Sgl. Oc.:** $70.00 & up
**Third Person:** $15.00
**Child:** $15.00

**Lindgren's Bed And Breakfast**—A very gracious, very special 1920's log home on the north shore of Lake Superior. Picture yourself with the lake on one side and the warmth of a roaring fire in the magnificent stone fireplace on the other side. Sauna, color TVs and VCR. Jeep Safari available. Chartered fishing.

## Minneapolis

Moses, Bill
2321 Colfax Ave. So., 55405
(612) 377-5946

**Amenities:** 1,2,3,5,6,7,8,9,14, 15,17
**Breakfast:** C.
**Dbl. Oc.:** $75.00
**Sgl. Oc.:** $65.00

**Brasil House**—Near the lakes, theatres, museums, fine restaurants and all the finest shopping. It is also on the public transit system. This warm, hospitable and beautiful brick home welcomes gays and other minorities and is just south of downtown.

## Minneapolis *

Zosel, Nan
2304 Fremont Ave. So., 55405
(612) 377-5118

**Amenities:** 9,10,14,17
**Breakfast:** F.
**Dbl. Oc.:** $49.27
**Sgl. Oc.:** $43.80
**Third Person:** $5.47
**Child:** under 12 yrs. - $5.47

**Nan's Bed & Breakfast**—An 1895 Victorian family home. Antique furniture. A short walk to theatres, restaurants, shopping and scenic lakeside walking paths. Friendly, outgoing hosts always have time to give directions to where you want to go. One block from bus stop. Maps available.

## Morris

Berget, Karen
410 East 3rd St., 56267
(612) 589-4054

**Amenities:** 2,5,6,7,10,15,17
**Breakfast:** F.
**Dbl. Oc.:** $35.00 - $40.00
**Sgl. Oc.:** $30.00 - $35.00
**Third Person:** $2.00

**The American House**—A Victorian home decorated with antiques and country charm. Ride our tandem bike on scenic trails. Within walking distance to area restaurants and shops. Located one block from University of Minnesota - Morris campus.

| | | | |
|---|---|---|---|
| 1. No Smoking | 5. Tennis Available | 9. Credit Cards Accepted | 13. Lunch Available | 17. Shared Bath |
| 2. No Pets | 6. Golf Available | 10. Personal Checks Accepted | 14. Public Transportation | 18. Afternoon Tea |
| 3. No Children | 7. Swiming Available | 11. Off Season Rates | 15. Reservations Necessary | ★ Commissions given |
| 4. Senior Citizen Rates | 8. Skiing Available | 12. Dinner Available | 16. Private Bath | to Travel Agents |

# MINNESOTA

## North Branch

Olson, Gloria & Lowell
15140 400th St., 55056
(612) 583-3326

**Amenities:** 1,4,8,10,11,15,
16,17
**Breakfast:** F.

**Dbl. Oc.:** $80.00 - $100.00
**Sgl. Oc.:** $75.00
**Third Person:** $20.00

**Red Pine Log Bed & Breakfast**—Uniquely designed and handcrafted by Lowell in 1985 on 30 acres. All exposed logs. Awesome 25-foot ceiling, log staircase, balconies and skylights. Suite-size rooms with queen or king beds. 1 hour to Twin Cities. Two night minimum stay. Near cross-country skiing. Ceramics.

## Rochester

Martin, Mary
723 2nd St. So.W., 55902
(507) 289-5553

**Amenities:** 1,2,5,6,7,8,9,10,
14,15,16,18
**Breakfast:** F.

**Dbl. Oc.:** $75.90
**Sgl. Oc.:** $64.90

**Canterbury Inn Bed & Breakfast**—A Victorian landmark with all new private baths (tub and showers), central air conditioning, off-street parking. Walk to Mayo Clinic, gourmet dining, excellent antique shops. Fabulous full breakfasts (in bed if desired), afternoon tea-time, hors d'oeuvres, tea and wine.

## Spring Valley *

Chase, Jeannine & Bob
508 N. Huron Ave., 55975
(507) 346-2850

**Amenities:** 1,2,5,6,7,8,9,10,
15,16,18
**Breakfast:** F.

**Dbl. Oc.:** $63.60 - $79.50
**Sgl. Oc.:** $58.30 - $74.20
**Third Person:** $10.60
**Child:** under 5 yrs. -
no charge

**Chase's**—Second Empire 1879 mansion. In *National Register of Historic Places*. Farm-style breakfast. Near caves, hiking & biking trails, canoeing, trout fishing, birding, Amish area, state parks, Laura Ingalls Wilder sites and antique shops.

## St. Paul

Gustafson, Donna
984 Ashland, 55104
(612) 227-4288

**Amenities:** 1,2,5,6,7,10,14,15,16,17,18
**Breakfast:** C.
**Dbl. Oc.:** $58.30 - $95.40
**Sgl. Oc.:** $47.70 - $84.80
**Third Person:** $10.00
**Child:** $10.00

**Chatsworth B&B**—A spacious lace-curtained Victorian home in quiet and convenient neighborhood. Fifteen minutes from airport and downtown Minneapolis. Walk to shopping areas. Two whirlpool baths.

---

| | | | | |
|---|---|---|---|---|
| 1. No Smoking | 5. Tennis Available | 9. Credit Cards Accepted | 13. Lunch Available | 17. Shared Bath |
| 2. No Pets | 6. Golf Available | 10. Personal Checks Accepted | 14. Public Transportation | 18. Afternoon Tea |
| 3. No Children | 7. Swiming Available | 11. Off Season Rates | 15. Reservations Necessary | ★ Commissions given |
| 4. Senior Citizen Rates | 8. Skiing Available | 12. Dinner Available | 16. Private Bath | to Travel Agents |

# MISSISSIPPI

## *The Magnolia State*

Capital: Jackson
Statehood: December 10, 1817; the 20th state
State Motto: By Valor and Arms
State Song: "Go Mis-sis-sip-pi"
State Bird: Mockingbird
State Flower: Magnolia
State Tree: Magnolia

Once a land of quiet towns, Mississippi is fast becoming an urbanized state. Although the cotton growing industry is still an important industy here, more and more people are being employed in the lumber and manufacturing of wood product industries.

Because Mississippi has a warm climate with long summers and short winters, more tourists are vacationing here and finding it an enjoyable retreat. There are large, sunny beaches along the Gulf Coast and fine hotels. Costumed guides are available to show visitors through the handsome mansions and plantations. There is also excellent hunting and fishing, but most of all, genteel and wonderful southern hospitality.

## Long Beach *

Mertz, Dr. Karl C.
7416 Red Creek Rd., 39560
(800) 729-9670,
(601) 452-3080

**Amenities:** 1,2,4,5,6,7,8,10, 11,15,16,18
**Breakfast:** C.

**Dbl. Oc.:** $43.00 - $65.00
**Sgl. Oc.:** $32.00 - $54.00
**Third Person:** $11.00
**Child:** under 6 yrs. - no charge

**Red Creek Colonial Inn**—A three-story, circa 1899, raised French cottage situated on 11 acres of live oaks and magnolias. Located less than one mile south of I-10, Long Beach Exit 28 and five miles north of Beach Hwy. 90. A 64-foot front porch. Antiques and six fireplaces. Nearby swimming and golf.

## Lorman *

Hylander, Col. & Mrs. Walt
Route 552, 39096
(601) 437-4215

**Amenities:** 2,9,10,16
**Breakfast:** F.
**Dbl. Oc.:** $95.40
**Sgl. Oc.:** $63.60
**Third Person:** $26.50
**Child:** under 12 yrs. - $26.50

**Rosswood Plantation**—A stately 1857 mansion on a working 100-acre plantation. Offers luxury, privacy, exquisite antiques, Civil War history, hospitality and more. Ideal for honeymoons. In the *National Register of Historic Places*. AAA rated 3 diamonds. Near Natchez and Vicksburg.

## Natchez *

Byrne, Loveta
712 N. Union, 39120
(601) 442-1344

**Amenities:** 2,7,9,10,12,13,16
**Breakfast:** F.

**Dbl. Oc.:** $81.75 - $136.25
**Sgl. Oc.:** $70.85
**Third Person:** $21.80
**Child:** $21.80

**The Burn**—This three-story mansion was built in 1832 and is one of Natchez's most historic homes. It is noted for its semi-spiral stairway, unique gardens and exquisite collection of antiques. Owner occupied and operated by Tony and Loveta Byrne.

## Natchez *

Epperson, Durell
211 Clifton Ave., 39120
(601) 446-5730

**Amenities:** 2,10,15,16
**Breakfast:** F.

**Dbl. Oc.:** $75.00 - $110.00
**Third Person:** $20.00

**Riverside**—Overlooks the Mississippi River. Beautiful rooms with antiques. In the center of town. Private baths and Tester beds. Antebellum house built in 1858. Listed in the *National Register of Historic Places*. TVs in guest rooms. Tour of house included. Children over 12 welcome.

| | | | | |
|---|---|---|---|---|
| 1. No Smoking | 5. Tennis Available | 9. Credit Cards Accepted | 13. Lunch Available | 17. Shared Bath |
| 2. No Pets | 6. Golf Available | 10. Personal Checks Accepted | 14. Public Transportation | 18. Afternoon Tea |
| 3. No Children | 7. Swiming Available | 11. Off Season Rates | 15. Reservations Necessary | ★ Commissions given |
| 4. Senior Citizen Rates | 8. Skiing Available | 12. Dinner Available | 16. Private Bath | to Travel Agents |

# MISSISSIPPI

## Port Gibson *

Lum, M/M William D.
1207 Church St., 39150
(601) 437-4350, (601) 437-5300,
 (800) 729-0240

**Amenities:** 1,2,5,6,7,10,16
**Breakfast:** F.
**Dbl. Oc.:** $65.00 - $75.00
**Sgl. Oc.:** $60.00 - $65.00
**Third Person:** $15.00 - $20.00

**Oak Square**—An antebellum mansion in the town General U.S. Grant said was "too beautiful to burn." Heirloom antiques. Canopy beds. In *National Register of Historic Places*. Located on U.S. Highway 61, between Natchez and Vicksburg, one mile off Natchez Trace Parkway.

## Vicksburg *

Burns, May
1010 First East, 39180
(601) 636-4931, (800) 262-4822

**Amenities:** 7,9,10,11,16
**Breakfast:** F.

**Dbl. Oc.:** $80.25 - $123.05
**Sgl. Oc.:** $74.90 - $117.70
**Third Person:** $16.05

**Anchuca**—A beautiful 1830 Greek Revival mansion with magnificent period antiques and artifacts. Gas-burning chandeliers. Brick courtyards and landscaped gardens. Guest rooms in slave quarters. Guest cottage and one room in main house. AAA and rated four diamonds.

## Vicksburg *

Mackey, Estelle & Ted
2200 Oak St., 39180
(601) 636-1605, (800) 862-1300

**Amenities:** 1,2,7,9,10,11
**Breakfast:** F.
**Dbl. Oc.:** $65.00 - $105.00
**Sgl. Oc.:** $65.00 - $75.00

**Cedar Grove**—A magnificent mansion inn, circa 1840. The largest antebellum home in Vicksburg. Romantic gasoliers throughout the house. Eighteen guest rooms, all with private baths and beautifully furnished. Pool and spa. Situated on four acres.

## Vicksburg

Whitney, Bettye & Cliff
601 Klein, 39180
(800) 444-7421, (601) 636-7421

**Amenities:** 6,9,10,16
**Breakfast:** F.

**Dbl. Oc.:** $75.00 - $95.00
**Sgl. Oc.:** $65.00 - $85.00
**Third Person:** $20.00
**Child:** $15.00

**The Corners**—A four-diamond, AAA-approved mansion with the understated elegance of a comfortable home and the ambience of an old, luxurious Southern mansion. Parterre garden and 68-foot gallery across the front with a spectacular view of the Mississippi River. Evening beverage and tour of the home.

| | | | |
|---|---|---|---|
| 1. No Smoking | 5. Tennis Available | 9. Credit Cards Accepted | 13. Lunch Available | 17. Shared Bath |
| 2. No Pets | 6. Golf Available | 10. Personal Checks Accepted | 14. Public Transportation | 18. Afternoon Tea |
| 3. No Children | 7. Swiming Available | 11. Off Season Rates | 15. Reservations Necessary | ★ Commissions given |
| 4. Senior Citizen Rates | 8. Skiing Available | 12. Dinner Available | 16. Private Bath | to Travel Agents |

# MISSOURI

## Show Me State

Capitol:  Jefferson City
Statehood:  August 10, 1821; the 24th state
State Motto:  The Welfare Of The People Shall Be
                      The Supreme Law
State Song:  "The Missouri Waltz"
State Bird:  Bluebird
State Flower:  Hawthorne
State Tree:  Flowering Dogwood

Missouri is a state of yesterday's history and today's progress. Lewis and Clark started their trek to the Pacific Coast in 1804 from St. Louis, then called The Gateway to the West. The Pony Express originated in St. Joseph in 1860 and traveled across the west to Sacramento, California, bringing mail for the first time from one coast to another. The ice cream cone, hot dog and iced tea were all introduced and made popular at the 1904 St. Louis World's Fair. Jesse James was born here, as well as Samuel Clemens, who grew up to write about the adventures he and his friends had along the Mississippi River, and signed his name Mark Twain.

Today, the St. Louis Gateway Arch is the nation's tallest man-made monument and remains the symbol of St. Louis, The Gateway to the West. It is an important transportation city, with buying and selling of everything from cattle to antiques.

Tourism has become a very important part of Missouri's economy, and the climate during most of the year is pleasant enough to bring visitors here and, in some cases, very often to stay.

President Truman was born here and died here.

# MISSOURI

## Branson *

Coats, JoAnne & Bill
Indian Point Rd.
HCR 1, Box 1104, 65616
(417) 638-2978

**Amenities:** 1,2,7,9,10,11, 15,16
**Breakfast:** F.

**Dbl. Oc.:** $53.75 - $86.00
**Sgl. Oc.:** $48.50 - $75.00
**Third Person:** $7.00

**Josie's Bed & Breakfast**—A peaceful getaway. A rustic contemporary lakefront home. Gourmet food. Porch with panoramic view of Table Rock Lake. Cathedral ceilings and fireplace. Marina, famous Silver Dollar City and country music shows. Swimming and fishing in the vicinity. Also has a whirlpool.

## Branson *

Gaines, Jeanne
521 W. Atlantic
P.O. Box 1369, 65616
(417) 334-2280

**Amenities:** 1,2,5,6,7,10,15, 16,17
**Breakfast:** F.

**Dbl. Oc.:** $55.00
**Sgl. Oc.:** $55.00
**Third Person:** $20.00
**Child:** $10.00

**Gaines Land Bed And Breakfast**—A contemporary home within easy walking distance to downtown Branson. Exclusive use of large common room opening onto patio, hot tub and swimming pool. Breakfast served in formal dining room or on the deck overlooking the pool and patio. Refreshments served on arrival.

## Branson

Kelly, Opal
120 - 4th St., 65616
(417) 334-0959

**Amenities:** 2,3,4,5,6,10,16
**Breakfast:** F.
**Dbl. Oc.:** $50.00 - $65.00
**Third Person:** $10.00

**Branson House B&B Inn**—Beautiful 1920's home, hillside setting, air-conditioning, front porch overlooking downtown Branson and lake area. Walking distance to antique shops, restaurants and lake. A short drive to music shows and Silver Dollar City. Nearby fishing and boating area. Rooms furnished with antiques.

## Cape Girardeau *

Neumeyer, Teresa & Tom
25 So. Lorimier, 63701
(314) 335-0449

**Amenities:** 1,2,5,6,7,10,15, 16,18
**Breakfast:** F.

**Dbl. Oc.:** $50.00
**Sgl. Oc.:** $45.00
**Third Person:** $10.00
**Child:** under 12 yrs. - $5.00

**The Olive Branch Bed & Breakfast**—Three bedrooms with private baths. Home is a Craftsman bungalow with a veranda, fireplaces and plenty of rocking chairs. Resident cat. In residential area, close to restaurants, shops and Mississippi River. Year-round swimming and ice skating are nearby.

---

| | | | |
|---|---|---|---|
| 1. No Smoking | 5. Tennis Available | 9. Credit Cards Accepted | 13. Lunch Available | 17. Shared Bath |
| 2. No Pets | 6. Golf Available | 10. Personal Checks Accepted | 14. Public Transportation | 18. Afternoon Tea |
| 3. No Children | 7. Swiming Available | 11. Off Season Rates | 15. Reservations Necessary | ★ Commissions given |
| 4. Senior Citizen Rates | 8. Skiing Available | 12. Dinner Available | 16. Private Bath | to Travel Agents |

# MISSOURI

## Carthage

Brewer, Archie
R.R. 1, Box 203, 64836
(417) 358-6312

**Amenities:** 1,10,14,15,17
**Breakfast:** C.

**Dbl. Oc.:** $50.00
**Sgl. Oc.:** $40.00
**Third Person:** $20.00
**Child:** under 16 yrs. -
$10.00

**Brewers Maple Lane Farm B&B**—This 20-room Victorian home is in the *National Register of Historic Places*. Our farm is ideal for family vacations. 22-acres with a lake, picnic area, play ground and animals for petting. We specialize in church groups (retreats), offering a 20% discount if stay is more than one day.

## Carthage *

Henry, Nancy & Nolan
1106 Grand, 64836
(417) 358-0683

**Amenities:** 2,3,9,10,16,17
**Breakfast:** F.

**Dbl. Oc.:** $47.82

**The Leggett House**—A Victorian Carthage stone house on historic drive. Large rooms with period decor. Air conditioning. Elevator. Walking distance to historic square. Off-street parking. Near Precious Moments Chapel, Red Oak II and Powers Museum. Many well-preserved historic houses and churches.

## Carthage

Scoville, Ella Mae
1157 So. Main St., 64836
(417) 358-6145

**Amenities:** 1,2,10,16
**Breakfast:** F.

**Dbl. Oc.:** $42.62
**Sgl. Oc.:** $26.64

**Hill House**—A 20-room brick Victorian mansion built in 1887 with 10 fireplaces, stained glass, pocket doors and antique store on third floor. Historic Carthage has famous courthouse, Civil War battleground and Victorian houses open for tours and museum.

## Eminence

Peters, Lynett
HCR 1, Box 11, 65466
(314) 226-3233

**Amenities:** 2,7,10,11,15,16
**Breakfast:** C.
**Dbl. Oc.:** $51.25
**Sgl. Oc.:** $51.25
**Third Person:** $8.00
**Child:** under 2 yrs. - no charge

**River's Edge B&B Resort**—All rooms with private entrance and bath. Overlooks the river. From the deck, it's just steps down to our private beach for campfires, floating, swimming, fishing, hiking and lounging. Also has spas and Ping-Pong. Next to town. Perfect for a scenic and fun trip.

| | | | | |
|---|---|---|---|---|
| 1. No Smoking | 5. Tennis Available | 9. Credit Cards Accepted | 13. Lunch Available | 17. Shared Bath |
| 2. No Pets | 6. Golf Available | 10. Personal Checks Accepted | 14. Public Transportation | 18. Afternoon Tea |
| 3. No Children | 7. Swiming Available | 11. Off Season Rates | 15. Reservations Necessary | ★ Commissions given |
| 4. Senior Citizen Rates | 8. Skiing Available | 12. Dinner Available | 16. Private Bath | to Travel Agents |

# MISSOURI

## Eminence

Tastad, Wes
P.O. Box 276, 65466
(314) 226-3642

**Amenities:** 4,5,7,9,10,11,12,
13,15,16
**Breakfast:** F.

**Dbl. Oc.:** $50.00
**Sgl. Oc.:** $50.00
**Third Person:** $10.00
**Child:** under 12 yrs. -
no charge

**Eminence Canoes, Cottages & Campgrounds**—Enchanting and informal B&B cottages nestled on 30 acres await to welcome you to Ozark Mountain tranquility. Located in the heart of Missouri's largest national park. Canoe, swim, hike and unwind.

## Fulton *

Logan, Deb & Bob
310 W. 7th, 65251
(314) 642-9229

**Amenities:** 1,9,10,15,16,17
**Breakfast:** F.

**Dbl. Oc.:** $58.42
**Sgl. Oc.:** $47.80
**Third Person:** $10.65
**Child:** under 10 yrs. - $5.35

**Loganberry Inn**—Experience the charm of this turn-of-the-century Victorian. Five antique-filled guest rooms, three with private baths. Rock on porches or read by the fireside in our elegant parlor. Walk to shops and Churchill Memorial. Caring innkeepers is our trademark.

## Gravois Mills

Blochberger, Min
P 223 Rd.
RR 3, Box 338-D, 65037
(314) 372-2481

**Amenities:** 1,2,4,6,7,8,12,13,
16,17,18
**Breakfast:** C. and F.

**Dbl. Oc.:** $55.00
**Sgl. Oc.:** $27.50
**Third Person:** $5.00

**Lingerlong**—Arrive by boat or car. Enjoy fishing, water skiing or sunning on one of the multi-level decks. Or sit in front of a blazing fire and enjoy an afternoon tea or an evening snack provided by the hostess. Beautiful Soap Creek Cove on the Lake of the Ozarks.

## Hannibal *

Andreotti, Donalene & Mike
213 So. 5th St., 63401
(314) 221-0445

**Amenities:** 2,5,6,7,9,10,15,
16,18
**Breakfast:** F.

**Dbl. Oc.:** $55.00 - $85.00
**Sgl. Oc.:** $50.00 - $80.00
**Third Person:** $10.00

**Fifth Street Mansion B&B**—A historic 1858 mansion providing Victorian charm, contemporary comforts and gracious hospitality. All rooms have private baths, air-conditioning, antiques and period decor. Walk to Mark Twain's home, historic district shops and restaurants.

## Hannibal

Feinberg, Irv
R.R. #1, 63401
(314) 221-2789

**Amenities:** 1,2,3,5,6,7,9,10,
14,15,16,17,18
**Breakfast:** F.

**Dbl. Oc.:** $59.00 - $120.00
**Sgl. Oc.:** $59.00 - $120.00
**Third Person:** $10.50

**Garth Woodside Mansion**—A nationally noted 1871 Victorian country estate that once hosted Mark Twain. Beautifully restored with original furnishings and magnificent flying staircase. Pampered elegance and nightshirts for you to wear. Stroll to our pond filled with 39 fish.

| | | | |
|---|---|---|---|
| 1. No Smoking | 5. Tennis Available | 9. Credit Cards Accepted | 13. Lunch Available | 17. Shared Bath |
| 2. No Pets | 6. Golf Available | 10. Personal Checks Accepted | 14. Public Transportation | 18. Afternoon Tea |
| 3. No Children | 7. Swiming Available | 11. Off Season Rates | 15. Reservations Necessary | ★ Commissions given |
| 4. Senior Citizen Rates | 8. Skiing Available | 12. Dinner Available | 16. Private Bath | to Travel Agents |

# MISSOURI

## Hermann *

Birk, Gloria & Elmer
700 Goethe St., 65041
(800) 748-7883, (314) 486-2911

**Amenities:** 1,2,3,9,10,15,16,17
**Breakfast:** F.
**Dbl. Oc.:** $48.67 - $68.90
**Sgl. Oc.:** $48.67
**Third Person:** $13.43

**Birk's Gasthaus**—A 104-year-old Victorian mansion. Bed and breakfast everyday except first two weekends a month, when you can be a detective and solve a murder mystery. Write or call for information. Seven private baths and two shared baths.

## Independence *

Arthurs, Peggy & Tim
601 W. Maple, 64050
(816) 461-6814

**Amenities:** 2,4,7,9,10,11,14, 16,18
**Breakfast:** F.
**Dbl. Oc.:** $60.00
**Sgl. Oc.:** $55.00
**Third Person:** $5.00

**Arthurs Horse & Carriage House**—A beautifully restored 1885 home. Designer coordinated throughout. Guests have use of courting parlor and porches. Air conditioning and TV. Close to Truman's home, nine historic Independence sites. Sports complex, downtown Kansas City, Worlds of Fun and Country Club Plaza.

## Jackson *

Wischmann, Patricia
203 Bellevue, 63755
(314) 243-7427

**Amenities:** 1,2,5,6,7,10,12,13, 16,17,18
**Breakfast:** F.
**Dbl. Oc.:** $65.00
**Sgl. Oc.:** $55.00
**Third Person:** $15.00
**Child:** under 12 yrs. - $10.00

**Trisha's Bed & Breakfast**—A late Victorian near nostalgic Steam Train in a small town. Only two hours south of St. Louis on I-55. Elegant gourmet breakfast served by candlelight. Tastefully decorated with antiques and rich in local history. Experienced and congenial hostess. Finest hospitality.

---

| | | | | |
|---|---|---|---|---|
| 1. No Smoking | 5. Tennis Available | 9. Credit Cards Accepted | 13. Lunch Available | 17. Shared Bath |
| 2. No Pets | 6. Golf Available | 10. Personal Checks Accepted | 14. Public Transportation | 18. Afternoon Tea |
| 3. No Children | 7. Swiming Available | 11. Off Season Rates | 15. Reservations Necessary | ★ Commissions given |
| 4. Senior Citizen Rates | 8. Skiing Available | 12. Dinner Available | 16. Private Bath | to Travel Agents |

## *Jamesport*

Richardson, Rebecca J.
P.O. Box 227, 64648
(816) 684-6664

**Amenities:** 9,10,11,12,13,16
**Breakfast:** F.
**Dbl. Oc.:** $64.00
**Sgl. Oc.:** $64.00
**Third Person:** $13.00
**Child:** under 6 yrs. - no charge

**Richardson House Bed And Breakfast**—An antique-filled Victorian in Amish community. Perfect for family adventure or romantic retreat. You'll enjoy the whole house to yourself. Sleeps eight. Amish shops, antiques, fishing, biking, catered meals, babysitting, cable TV and air-conditioning.

---

## *Kansas City* *

Litchfield, Carolyn & Ed
217 E. 37th St., 64111
(816) 753-2667

**Amenities:** 2,5,9,10,15,16
**Breakfast:** F.

**Dbl. Oc.:** $64.00 - $117.00
**Sgl. Oc.:** $64.00 - $117.00
**Third Person:** $10.00
**Child:** under 1 yr. -
no charge

**Doanleigh Wallagh Inn**—Located between the Plaza and Crown Center, the inn offers 12 rooms in two architecturally interesting houses, both built in 1907. Each guest room has a private bath, cable TV with four movie channels, phone and air conditioning. Houses have a comfortable, elegant and romantic feeling.

---

## *Kansas City* *

Mills, Pat & Ian
3605 Gillham Rd., 64111
(816) 753-1269

**Amenities:** 1,2,5,9,10,14,15,
16,17,18
**Breakfast:** F.

**Dbl. Oc.:** $70.00 - $80.00
**Sgl. Oc.:** $70.00 - $80.00
**Third Person:** $10.00
**Child:** $10.00

**Milford House**—A beautifully restored 100-year-old home, conveniently situated one mile from the Plaza, Crown Center and historic Westport. Your hosts combine traditional English with Southern hospitality to provide a memorable and most enjoyable stay.

---

## *Parkville* *

Coons, Lola & Bill
Route 22, 64152
(816) 891-1018

**Amenities:** 2,5,6,7,8,10,
16,18
**Breakfast:** F.

**Dbl. Oc.:** $69.05
**Sgl. Oc.:** $58.42
**Third Person:** $15.93
**Child:** under 5 yrs. - $5.31

**Down-To-Earth Lifestlyes**—An 86-acre farm between Kansas City Airport and downtown Kansas City. Pond fishing, indoor pool, guest parking and entrance. Lounge with refrigerator, phones, TVs and radios. Great room with piano, fireplace, etc. Weekday special-order breakfast. Weekend brunch. Quiet country.

---

| | | | |
|---|---|---|---|
| 1. No Smoking | 5. Tennis Available | 9. Credit Cards Accepted | 13. Lunch Available | 17. Shared Bath |
| 2. No Pets | 6. Golf Available | 10. Personal Checks Accepted | 14. Public Transportation | 18. Afternoon Tea |
| 3. No Children | 7. Swiming Available | 11. Off Season Rates | 15. Reservations Necessary | ★ Commissions given |
| 4. Senior Citizen Rates | 8. Skiing Available | 12. Dinner Available | 16. Private Bath | to Travel Agents |

## Platte City *

Soper, Betty & Don
15880 Interurban Rd., 64079
(816) 431-5556

**Amenities:** 2,5,6,7,8,9, 10,15,16
**Breakfast:** C.

**Dbl. Oc.:** $61.91 - $93.38
**Sgl. Oc.:** $56.66
**Third Person:** $7.34

**Basswood Country Inn Resort**—An elegant country French inn with four suites and a 1935 two-bedroom lakeside cottage. Wooded. Stocked lakes. Pool. Five miles to Kansas City Airport. Close to two historic towns, antiques and two meeting facilities. Situated on 74 acres. Minutes from Kansas City.

## Springfield *

Ballard, Curt
1701 So. Fort, 65807
(417) 831-7242

**Amenities:** 1,2,9,10,13,14,16,18
**Breakfast:** F.
**Dbl. Oc.:** $55.00 - $130.00
**Sgl. Oc.:** $55.00 - $130.00
**Third Person:** $10.00
**Child:** $10.00

**The Mansion At Elfindale Bed & Breakfast Inn**—Enjoy one of the 13 tastefully appointed suites in this *Historic Register* turn-of-the-century mansion. Tea awaits you in the parlor. A full breakfast is served in the tea room. This christian B&B offers a tranquil experience in the heart of the Ozarks.

## Springfield

Brown, Karol & Nancy
900 E. Walnut, 65806
(417) 864-6346

**Amenities:** 1,5,7,9,10,11,13,15,16,18
**Breakfast:** F.
**Dbl. Oc.:** $75.00
**Sgl. Oc.:** $75.00
**Third Person:** $10.00

**Walnut Street Inn**—An 1894 Queen Anne Victorian showcase home located in the heart of the city within walking distance to fine restaurants, theatres and musuems. Enjoy charming rooms filled with antiques. Savor local wine and cheese and indulge in our sumptuous gourmet breakfast.

## St. Charles

York, Patricia
338 So. Main St., 63301
(314) 946-6

**Amenities:** 1,2,3,10,15,16
**Breakfast:** C.

**Dbl. Oc.:** $85.00
**Sgl. Oc.:** $85.00

**The St. Charles House**—An elegant, romantic and antique-furnished suite located in the heart of a 10-block historic district with over 100 shops and restaurants. Large back porch overlooks two parks and the Missouri River. Just 20 minutes to St.Louis. "For a truly special experience."

| | | | |
|---|---|---|---|
| 1. No Smoking | 5. Tennis Available | 9. Credit Cards Accepted | 13. Lunch Available | 17. Shared Bath |
| 2. No Pets | 6. Golf Available | 10. Personal Checks Accepted | 14. Public Transportation | 18. Afternoon Tea |
| 3. No Children | 7. Swiming Available | 11. Off Season Rates | 15. Reservations Necessary | ★ Commissions given |
| 4. Senior Citizen Rates | 8. Skiing Available | 12. Dinner Available | 16. Private Bath | to Travel Agents |

## St. Louis *

Milligan, Sarah & Jack
2156 Lafayette Ave., 63104
(314) 772-4429

**Amenities:** 1,2,10,14,16,17
**Breakfast:** F.

**Dbl. Oc.:** $45.00 - $65.00
**Sgl. Oc.:** $40.00 - $60.00
**Third Person:** $10.00
**Child:** under 16 yrs. - $7.00

**Lafayette House**—"In the center of things to do in St. Louis." An 1876 historically significant brick Queen Anne mansion overlooking Lafayette Park. Extensive library and collections. Third-floor suite with kitchen. Resident cats. Transportation pick-up arranged for a small fee.

## St. Louis *

Sundermeyer, Susan & Chuck
P.O. Box 8095, 63156
(314) 367-5870

**Amenities:** 1,2,6,9,10,14,
15,16
**Breakfast:** F.

**Dbl. Oc.:** $70.00 - $85.00
**Sgl. Oc.:** $70.00 - $85.00
**Third Person:** $15.00
**Child:** $15.00

**Coachlight Bed & Breakfast**—A turn-of-the-century brick home in the historic central west end. Within walking distance to unique shops, galleries, outdoor cafes and elegant mansions. Fine antiques, Laura Ashley fabrics, down comforters and generous, homemade breakfast.

## St. Louis *

Winter, Kendall
3522 Arsenal St., 63118
(314) 664-4399

**Amenities:** 1,2,5,6,7,9,10,14,
15,16,17,18
**Breakfast:** C. Plus

**Dbl. Oc.:** $54.30
**Sgl. Oc.:** $47.65
**Third Person:** $16.50

**The Winter House B&B**—A ten room Victorian home with turret built in 1897. Tower Grove Park, which adjoins the Missouri Botanical Gardens has lighted tennis courts and jogging trails and is within walking distance of our B&B. Tea and piano entertainment are included on weekends by reservation.

## Ste. Genevieve *

Beckerman, Rob
1021 Market St., 63670
(314) 883-5881

**Amenities:** 2,5,6,7,9,10,
16
**Breakfast:** F.

**Dbl. Oc.:** $50.70 - $61.40
**Sgl. Oc.:** $40.00 - $50.00
**Third Person:** $10.00
**Child:** under 6 yrs. - $5.00

**Steiger Haus**—Situated in historic Ste. Genevieve (established in 1735) near restored French colonial tour homes. Steiger Haus(1880) features private suites, an indoor swimming pool and special murder-mystery weekends.

## Stockton

Smith, Mary
809 South St., 65785
(417) 276-2345

**Amenities:** 1,2,3,10,15,17
**Breakfast:** F.

**Dbl. Oc.:** $40.00
**Sgl. Oc.:** $40.00

**Our Happy House Bed & Breakfast**—An early traditional home located two blocks from the square in the quaint town of Stockton. Five minutes from the clear waters of Stockton Lake. Large, shady yard for outdoor lounging. Outdoor gas grill available to guests.

| | | | |
|---|---|---|---|
| 1. No Smoking | 5. Tennis Available | 9. Credit Cards Accepted | 13. Lunch Available | 17. Shared Bath |
| 2. No Pets | 6. Golf Available | 10. Personal Checks Accepted | 14. Public Transportation | 18. Afternoon Tea |
| 3. No Children | 7. Swiming Available | 11. Off Season Rates | 15. Reservations Necessary | ★ Commissions given |
| 4. Senior Citizen Rates | 8. Skiing Available | 12. Dinner Available | 16. Private Bath | to Travel Agents |

## *Warrensburg* *

Wayne, Sandra & Bill
Route 3, Box 130, 64093
(816) 747-5728

**Amenities:** 1,2,9,10,11,12,13,
15,17,18
**Breakfast:** F.

**Dbl. Oc.:** $47.00
**Sgl. Oc.:** $42.00
**Third Person:** $11.00

**Cedarcroft Farm Bed & Breakfast**—Old-fashioned country hospitality. Country comfort pl full country breakfast in antique filled 1867 family farmhouse with tub/shower and central air/ heat. Explore 80 acres of secluded woods, meadows and streams. Hosts are Civil War re-enactors and retired United States Air Force.

## *Washington* *

Davis, Kathleen & Charles
3 Lafayette, 63090
(314) 239-2417

**Amenities:** 1,2,5,6,7,10,11,16
**Breakfast:** F.
**Dbl. Oc.:** $65.00 - $75.00
**Sgl. Oc.:** $50.00 - $60.00
**Third Person:** $10.00

**Washington House Bed And Breakfast**—A circa 1837 authentically restored inn on the Missouri River which features: river views, canopy beds, antique furnishings, complimentary wine and full breakfast. Only 50 minutes west of St. Louis.

## *Washington*

Jones, Karen
438 W. Front St., 63090
(314) 239-5025

**Amenities:** 2,5,6,7,9,10,
15,16,17
**Breakfast:** C.

**Dbl. Oc.:** $45.00 - $70.00
**Sgl. Oc.:** $35.00 - $55.00
**Third Person:** $10.00
**Child:** over 5 yrs. - $10.00

**Schwegmann House Bed And Breakfast**—One hour west of St. Louis. Visit historic sites, hike wilderness trails, discover unique shops, enjoy excellent cuisine, tarry along the wide Missouri's romantic valley...and stay in an historic home.

| | | | | |
|---|---|---|---|---|
| 1. No Smoking | 5. Tennis Available | 9. Credit Cards Accepted | 13. Lunch Available | 17. Shared Bath |
| 2. No Pets | 6. Golf Available | 10. Personal Checks Accepted | 14. Public Transportation | 18. Afternoon Tea |
| 3. No Children | 7. Swiming Available | 11. Off Season Rates | 15. Reservations Necessary | ★ Commissions given |
| 4. Senior Citizen Rates | 8. Skiing Available | 12. Dinner Available | 16. Private Bath | to Travel Agents |

# MONTANA

## The Treasure State

Capitol: Helena
Statehood: November 8, 1889; the 41st state
State Motto: Gold and Silver
State Song: "Montana"
State Bird: Western Meadow Lark
State Flower: Bitterroot
State Tree: Ponderosa Pine

This is Big Sky Country, the land of mountain goats and grizzly bears. Montana is the fourth largest state in the union. The mountains, the old gold camps and the vast lonely distances still make a visitor feel close to the American frontier.

The beautiful and exciting Glacier National Park is visited by hundreds of tourists every year. Sportsman from all over the world travel here to fish, hunt and enjoy the national forest, ranches and lodges.

Montana has its share of gold and silver mines as well as the largest deposit of copper in the world.

# *Bigford*

Doohan, Margot
675 Ferndale Dr., 59911
(406) 837-6851

**Amenities:** 1,4,5,6,7,8,9,10,
11,15,16,17
**Breakfast:** F.

**Dbl. Oc.:** $60.00 - $85.00
**Sgl. Oc.:** $50.00 - $75.00
**Third Person:** $15.00
**Child:** under 5 yrs. -
no charge

**O'Duachain Country Inn B&B**—Gracious tri-level log home on five acres near Flathead, Swan Lakes and Bigfork Mountain. Pristine grounds with exotic birds and wildlife. Antique decor, hot tub, spa and large decks enhance the wild and beautiful surroundings. Full breakfast is a gourmet delight. Luxurious and serene.

# *Bozeman*

Crowle, Patricia
9986 Happy Acres W., 59715
(406) 587-3651

**Amenities:** 1,2,8,9,10,15,16,
17,18
**Breakfast:** F.

**Dbl. Oc.:** $65.00
**Sgl. Oc.:** $45.00
**Third Person:** $10.00
**Child:** under 5 yrs. -
no charge

**Sun House Bed & Breakfast**—A quiet country retreat eight miles southwest of Bozeman, Montana. Near ski areas, fishing and Yellowstone National Park. This unique, passive-solar home features wildlife, sunsets, horse boarding and deluxe accommodations with jacuzzi.

# *Bozeman* *

Hillard, Doris & Larry
11521 Axtell County Rd., 59715
(406) 763-4696

**Amenities:** 1,2,3,6,7,8,10,12,
13,14,15,16,17
**Breakfast:** F.

**Dbl. Oc.:** $62.40
**Sgl. Oc.:** $36.40
**Child:** under 5 yrs. -
no charge

**Hillard's Bed & Breakfast And Guest House**—Located on 11 acres. Quiet and peaceful setting. Within walking distance to Gallatin River (blue-ribbon trout). Close to major airport. Ten miles to Bozeman and 25 miles to Big Sky and Bridger ski resorts. Various big-game hunting nearby. Babysitting available.

# *Great Falls* *

Matthews, Marge
1204 4 Ave. No., 59401
(406) 452-9001

**Amenities:** 4,5,6,7,8,10,12,13,
14,16,17,18
**Breakfast:** F.

**Dbl. Oc.:** $47.00
**Sgl. Oc.:** $42.00
**Third Person:** $10.00
**Child:** under 10 yrs. - $5.00

**The Chalet Bed & Breakfast Inn**—A stick Victorian chalet located across from the C.M. Russell Museum. Former governor's home. Guest rooms vary from quaint and cozy to spacious and elegant. Refreshments in the butler's pantry. Parlor fireplace. The grace and charm of a bygone era with modern comforts.

| | | | | |
|---|---|---|---|---|
| 1. No Smoking | 5. Tennis Available | 9. Credit Cards Accepted | 13. Lunch Available | 17. Shared Bath |
| 2. No Pets | 6. Golf Available | 10. Personal Checks Accepted | 14. Public Transportation | 18. Afternoon Tea |
| 3. No Children | 7. Swiming Available | 11. Off Season Rates | 15. Reservations Necessary | ★ Commissions given |
| 4. Senior Citizen Rates | 8. Skiing Available | 12. Dinner Available | 16. Private Bath | to Travel Agents |

# MONTANA

## Jordan *

Trumbo, Sylvia & John
Hill Creek Route
Box 325, 59337
(406) 557-2224

**Amenities:** 10,12,13,15,16,
17,18
**Breakfast:** F.

**Dbl. Oc.:** $50.00
**Sgl. Oc.:** $40.00
**Third Person:** $10.00

**Hill Creek Guest Ranch**—Rustic, yet modern cabins. Family-style meals on working ranch. Tours of fossil beds, C.M.R. Game Range and Fort Peck Lake. Abundant wildlife, photography and hiking.

## Livingston *

McCutcheon, Pam
405 W. Lewis, 59047
(406) 222-7699

**Amenities:** 5,6,7,8,9,10,11,
13,16,17
**Breakfast:** C. Plus

**Dbl. Oc.:** $57.20 - $67.60
**Sgl. Oc.:** $52.00 - $62.40
**Third Person:** $5.00
**Child:** under 12 yrs. -
no charge

**The Talcott House**—Elegant, but unpretentious. Located just three blocks from downtown Livingston. We cater to travelers, outdoor enthusiasts and families. Complete exercise facilities, dog kennels and large-screen TV. Mountain bike rentals and more.

## Loma *

Sorensen, Donald
HCR 67, Box 50, 59460
(800) 426-2926

**Amenities:** 1,2,3,9,10,17
**Breakfast:** F.

**Dbl. Oc.:** $85.00
**Sgl. Oc.:** $65.00
**Third Person:** $25.00

**Virgelle Mercantile**—Your ghost town getaway! Enjoy restored rooms above a 1912 general store in Virgelle, a ghost town along the wild and scenic Missouri River. Shop for antiques downstairs, canoe the river, follow the Lewis-Clark trail or just relax on the porch.

## Polson

Hunter, Mrs. Ruth
802 7th Ave. W., 59860
(406) 883-2460

**Amenities:** 1,2,5,6,7,10,
14,15,16
**Breakfast:** C.

**Dbl. Oc.:** $26.00
**Sgl. Oc.:** $15.60
**Third Person:** $5.20

**Ruth's Bed & Breakfast**—One block from the city limits on Flathead River, with a view of the mountains. There is a cottage away from the home with porta-potties. Shared bath and showers can be used in main home. One room in main home. Nearby res

| | | | |
|---|---|---|---|
| 1. No Smoking | 5. Tennis Available | 9. Credit Cards Accepted | 13. Lunch Available | 17. Shared Bath |
| 2. No Pets | 6. Golf Available | 10. Personal Checks Accepted | 14. Public Transportation | 18. Afternoon Tea |
| 3. No Children | 7. Swiming Available | 11. Off Season Rates | 15. Reservations Necessary | ★ Commissions given |
| 4. Senior Citizen Rates | 8. Skiing Available | 12. Dinner Available | 16. Private Bath | to Travel Agents |

## Red Lodge *
Boggio, Carolyn & Kerry
224 So. Platt Ave., 59068
(406) 446-3913

**Amenities:** 1,2,3,4,6,8,9,10,
16,17,18
**Breakfast:** C. Plus

**Dbl. Oc.:** $52.00 - $62.40
**Sgl. Oc.:** $46.80 - $52.00
**Third Person:** $10.40
**Child:** under 18 yrs. - $5.20

**Willows Inn**—Warm and inviting atmosphere. A lovely Victorian minutes from skiing, golf and magnificent mountain scenery. Charming and romantic rooms. Movies, books, games and afternoon refreshments. Delicious Finnish pastries. Large and airy sun deck. Two-bedroom family cottage available.

## Troy
Thompson, Mrs. Alex
15303 Bull Lake Rd., 59935
(406) 295-4228

**Amenities:** 7,8,10,17
**Breakfast:** F.

**Dbl. Oc.:** $46.60
**Sgl. Oc.:** $25.80
**Third Person:** $15.80

**Bull Lake Guest Ranch**—Located mid-way on Highway 56. Beautiful Bull Lake on the west and Cabinet Wilderness on the east. Scenic trail rides. Six modern, comfortable rooms with three shared baths. Primitive cabin sleeps six with use of showers. By day or week. Meals extra. Family-style meals.

| | | | |
|---|---|---|---|
| 1. No Smoking | 5. Tennis Available | 9. Credit Cards Accepted | 13. Lunch Available | 17. Shared Bath |
| 2. No Pets | 6. Golf Available | 10. Personal Checks Accepted | 14. Public Transportation | 18. Afternoon Tea |
| 3. No Children | 7. Swiming Available | 11. Off Season Rates | 15. Reservations Necessary | ★ Commissions given |
| 4. Senior Citizen Rates | 8. Skiing Available | 12. Dinner Available | 16. Private Bath | to Travel Agents |

# NEBRASKA

## The Cornhusker State

Capitol: Lincoln
Statehood: March 1, 1867; the 37th state
State Motto: 'Equality Before The Law'
State Song: "Beautiful Nebraska"
State Bird: Western Meadow Lark
State Flower: Goldenrod
State Tree: Cottonwood

The name Nebraska comes from the Oto Indian word, "Nebrathka" meaning flat water. Nebraska was a flat area of vast land with very cold winters and extremely hot summers when the first pioneers arrived. They came to farm and evidence of their hard labor can be seen where hundreds of trees first planted for shade, still stand today. "D" Street in Lincoln is famous for the many huge Oak trees that remain a symbol of these first settlers.

Every year, thousands of visitors drive the Nebraska Hwy that follows the Oregon and Morman trails. Ruts left by the pioneer's covered wagons can be seen along the roadside. In Gothesburg the Pony Express Station stands reminding us of where fresh supplies of horses were kept for the early mail carriers.

Today Omaha is the state's largest city and the center of trade and industry for eastern Nebraska and western Iowa. The capitol long ago moved from the open prairie is at Lincoln and is the second largest city of this state.

The leading crop is corn, but during WW II Nebraska farmers produced millions of tons of corn, oat, potatoes and wheat to meet the wartime shortage.

Nebraska is very proud of its well known sons & daughters: 38th President Gerald Ford, William Jennings Bryant, Willa Cather, Father Edward Flanagan, founder of Boys' Town, and Buffalo Bill Cody whose frontier ranch home still stands at Scout Rest near North Platte.

# NEBRASKA

## Crawford *

Anderson, Ruth N.
HCR 76, Box 39A, 69339
(308) 665-2364

**Amenities:** 6,7,8,9,10,11,12, 13,14,15,16,17
**Breakfast:** F.

**Dbl. Oc.:** $45.00 - $50.75
**Sgl. Oc.:** $39.50
**Third Person:** $10.00
**Child:** under 8 yrs. - no charge

**Butte Ranch**—Country cottage. Comfortable quarters. Solitude. You are cradled by Mother Nature. Welcome to my home!

---

## Grand Island *

Hank, Lois
1124 W. 3rd St., 68801
(308) 381-6851

**Amenities:** 1,9,10,15,17
**Breakfast:** F.

**Dbl. Oc.:** $50.00
**Sgl. Oc.:** $45.00
**Third Person:** $15.00
**Child:** under 10 yrs. - $5.00

**Kirschke House B&B**—A 1902 Victorian home, decorated in period furnishings and antiques. A wooden hot tub adds to the old-world charm in this lantern-lit brick wash house. Your hostess welcomes you to come and relax. Enjoy and experience yesterday today.

---

## Omaha

Jones, Donald
1617 S. 90th St., 68124
(402) 397-0721

**Amenities:** 6,10,15,16
**Breakfast:** C.

**Dbl. Oc.:** $25.00
**Sgl. Oc.:** $15.00
**Child:** under 3 yrs. - no charge

**Private Residence**—A large, comfortable home on one acre of land. Five minutes from I-80. Near large shopping centers and race tracks. Homemade cinnamon rolls for a delicious breakfast in the enclosed gazebo — weather permitting.

---

## Omaha *

Swoboda, Jeannie
140 N. 39th St., 68131
(402) 553-0951

**Amenities:** 5,6,9,10,14,16,17
**Breakfast:** C.

**Dbl. Oc.:** $62.32 - $73.47
**Sgl. Oc.:** $51.17 - $62.32
**Third Person:** $10.00
**Child:** $7.00

**The Offutt House**—"Chateauesque" mansion, built in 1894, is located in the historic "Gold Coast" area. Comfortable spacious rooms. Furnished with antiques and some with fireplaces. Located near downtown and the historic Old Market, which offers many beautiful shops and excellent restaurants.

---

| 1. No Smoking | 5. Tennis Available | 9. Credit Cards Accepted | 13. Lunch Available | 17. Shared Bath |
| 2. No Pets | 6. Golf Available | 10. Personal Checks Accepted | 14. Public Transportation | 18. Afternoon Tea |
| 3. No Children | 7. Swiming Available | 11. Off Season Rates | 15. Reservations Necessary | ★ Commissions given |
| 4. Senior Citizen Rates | 8. Skiing Available | 12. Dinner Available | 16. Private Bath | to Travel Agents |

## *Paxton*

Meyer, Gwen
Box 247, 69155
(308) 239-4265

**Amenities:** 1,2,3,9,10,16,17
**Breakfast:** F.
**Dbl. Oc.:** $45.00 & up
**Sgl. Oc.:** $33.00 & up
**Third Person:** $15.00
**Child:** under 12 yrs. - $10.00

**Gingerbread Inn—**We invite you to enjoy warm hospitality and relax in the atmosphere of a bygone era. Beautiful gazebo and private picnic grounds. Relax on porch swing. Awaken to the smell of a sumptuous, homemade breakfast. Gingerbread cookies are among the special touches.

| | | | | |
|---|---|---|---|---|
| 1. No Smoking | 5. Tennis Available | 9. Credit Cards Accepted | 13. Lunch Available | 17. Shared Bath |
| 2. No Pets | 6. Golf Available | 10. Personal Checks Accepted | 14. Public Transportation | 18. Afternoon Tea |
| 3. No Children | 7. Swiming Available | 11. Off Season Rates | 15. Reservations Necessary | ★ Commissions given |
| 4. Senior Citizen Rates | 8. Skiing Available | 12. Dinner Available | 16. Private Bath | to Travel Agents |

# NEVADA

## *The Silver State*

Capitol: Carson City
Statehood: October 31, 1864; the 36th state
State Motto: All for Our Country
State Song: "Home Means Nevada"
State Bird: Mountain Bluebird
State Flower: Sagebrush
State Tree: Single Leaf Pinon

In this state, rich deposits of silver ore were discovered in 1859. Virginia City became the site of one of the largest bonanzas of silver ore discovered by Henry Comstock. The massive strike brought hundreds of prospectors rushing to Nevada to 'strike it rich'. Some did, but many others did not. Along with mining came ranching, but in early 1869 when mining became less lucrative, gambling was legalized and the beginning of the state's largest and fastest growing industries began, tourism.

Over twenty million people visit this state each year. They enjoy the night life and gambling of Las Vegas, Reno, Lake Tahoe and Virginia City, as well as the summer and winter sports.

Hoover Dam is another tourist attraction. Man-made, and one of the highest concrete dams in the world, measuring 726 ft. from base to crest.

# NEVADA

## East Ely

Lindley, Jane & Norman
220 E. 11th St.
P.O. Box 151110, 89315-1110
(702) 289-8687

**Amenities:** 1,2,3,9,10,15,16
**Breakfast:** F.

**Dbl. Oc.:** $74.00
**Sgl. Oc.:** $62.00
**Third Person:** $7.00

**Steptoe Valley Inn**—Elegant, romantic five room Ely City historic building. 1/2 block from Nevada Northern Railway Museum. Private balconies and rose garden. Hosts operate small personalized scenic and historic back country tours and tours to the Great Basin National Park from June - Sept.

## Reno *

Walters, Caroline
136 Andrew Lane, 89511
(702) 849-0772

**Amenities:** 1,4,7,9,10,16,17
**Breakfast:** F.

**Dbl. Oc.:** $64.00
**Sgl. Oc.:** $54.00
**Third Person:** $10.00
**Child:** over 8 yrs. - $10.00

**Bed & Breakfast — South Reno**—The inn faces 10,000- foot Mt. Rose. Beamed ceiling and early-American decor. Casual. Ski, gamble, be entertained in posh hotels or cruise Lake Tahoe. Swimming pool, decks, poster queen beds, 10-room house, cable TV, separate sitting room and afternoon wine.

## Unionville

Jones, Mitzi & Lew
Star Route #79, 89418
(702) 538-7585

**Amenities:** 1,10,12,13,15,16,17
**Breakfast:** F.
**Dbl. Oc.:** $58.00
**Sgl. Oc.:** $48.00
**Child:** under 10 yrs. - $15.00

**Old Pioneer Garden B&B Guest Ranch**—Located in an 1860's mining town, one day drive from San Francisco or Salt Lake City. We have 120 acres, a trout stream and ghost town ruins. We raise our own fruits, vegetables, sheep, goats, geese and chickens. Guests delight in discovering this unique treasure.

| | | | |
|---|---|---|---|
| 1. No Smoking | 5. Tennis Available | 9. Credit Cards Accepted | 13. Lunch Available | 17. Shared Bath |
| 2. No Pets | 6. Golf Available | 10. Personal Checks Accepted | 14. Public Transportation | 18. Afternoon Tea |
| 3. No Children | 7. Swiming Available | 11. Off Season Rates | 15. Reservations Necessary | |
| 4. Senior Citizen Rates | 8. Skiing Available | 12. Dinner Available | 16. Private Bath | * Commissions given to Travel Agents |

# NEW HAMPSHIRE

## *The Granite State*

Capitol: Concord
Statehood: June 21, 1788; the 9th state
State Motto: Live Free or Die
State Song: "Old New Hampshire"
State Bird: Purple Finch
State Flower: Purple Lilac
State Tree: White Birch

The White Mountains make this New England state one of the most beautiful of all. Mt. Washington, the tallest mountain in this range, is one of the most popular attractions for visitors. It brings great excitement to the winter skier, and is a summer tourist delight. The mountain can be climbed either by foot, car or cog-railroad. In any case, it is not easy, and not everyone makes it to the top.

New Hampshire was settled in 1633 and the people worked the land and quarries. Factories sprung up, but in the late '30s and early '40s, they either moved south or closed completely. People had to look elsewhere for an income. Tourism became that other income. Today, tourism is a major source of income for this state.

The taxes are very low here and the people wish to keep them this way. Because of this, more and more people are moving here.

Daniel Webster and our 14th president, Franklin Pierce, were both born in New Hampshire.

## Andover, East *

Sherman, M/M Bradford
107 Maple St.
P.O. Box 107, 03231
(603) 735-6426

**Amenities:** 1,2,4,9,10,11,16,17
**Breakfast:** F.
**Dbl. Oc.:** $54.00 - $70.00
**Sgl. Oc.:** $43.00 - $54.00
**Third Person:** $16.00

**Patchwork Inn**—An 1805 village colonial on three acres. Cross-country and downhill skiing. Lake and mountain views. Walk to beach. Furnished with antiques, pewter and braided rugs. Three common rooms, all with fireplaces. Piano. Breakfast features family-made genuine honey and maple syrup.

## Antrim *

Brown, Jeremy
Miltimore Rd.
RR 2, Box 201, 03440
(603) 588-2407

**Amenities:** 1,7,8,10,17
**Breakfast:** F.

**Dbl. Oc.:** $53.50
**Sgl. Oc.:** $37.45
**Third Person:** $16.05

**Upland's Inn**—A handsome 1840 farmhouse on 32 beautiful rural acres. Nearby downhill and cross-country skiing, swimming and mountain climbing. Casual New England country ambience. Nine comfortable rooms and three sitting rooms. Groups welcome. Inn may be reserved.

## Ashland *

Paterman, Betsy
43 Highland St.
P.O. Box 819, 03217-0819
(603) 968-3775

**Amenities:** 2,5,6,7,8,9,10,11,16
**Breakfast:** F.
**Dbl. Oc.:** $81.00
**Sgl. Oc.:** $81.00
**Third Person:** $10.80

**Glynn House "Victorian" Inn**—A romantic escape in the heart of the White Mountains and lakes region of New Hampshire. "Golden Pond" area. Gracious four-bedroom Victorian filled with antiques and old-world hospitality. Jacuzzi bath and fireplace. Quaint New England town off I-93, Exit 24. Gourmet breakfast.

| | | | | |
|---|---|---|---|---|
| 1. No Smoking | 5. Tennis Available | 9. Credit Cards Accepted | 13. Lunch Available | 17. Shared Bath |
| 2. No Pets | 6. Golf Available | 10. Personal Checks Accepted | 14. Public Transportation | 18. Afternoon Tea |
| 3. No Children | 7. Swiming Available | 11. Off Season Rates | 15. Reservations Necessary | ★ Commissions given |
| 4. Senior Citizen Rates | 8. Skiing Available | 12. Dinner Available | 16. Private Bath | to Travel Agents |

# NEW HAMPSHIRE

## Bartlett *

Dindorf, Mark
Route 302, 03812-0327
(603) 374-2353

**Amenities:** 8,9,10,11,16,
17,18
**Breakfast:** F.

**Dbl. Oc.:** $69.00
**Sgl. Oc.:** $48.00 - $58.00
**Third Person:** $38.00 -
$45.00
**Child:** under 12 yrs. -
no charge

**The Country Inn At Bartlett**—A bed and breakfast inn for hikers, skiers and outdoor lovers in the White Mountains. Enjoy a hearty breakfast, relax by the fireside and unwind in the outdoor hot-tub. Choose a room in the main inn or one of the cozy cottage rooms. We welcome you to New Hampshire's White Mountains.

## Bethlehem

Barber, Mary Lou & Jerry
Main St., 03574
(603) 869-5869

**Amenities:** 1,2,3,6,9,10,11,15,16
**Breakfast:** F.
**Dbl. Oc.:** $65.00 - $80.00
**Sgl. Oc.:** $50.00 - $65.00
**Third Person:** $40.00

**Maplewood Inn Bed & Breakfast**—Located in the heart of the White Mountains near Franconia Notch State Park. Free golf available at Maplewood Country Club and Bethlehem Country Club. Choose one of our six bedrooms. From I-95, take Exit 40 for 3-1/2 miles east on Route 302.

## Bethlehem

Burns, Robert
Main St., 03574
(603) 869-3389

**Amenities:** 1,2,5,6,7,8,9,10,
11,16,18
**Breakfast:** F.
**Dbl. Oc.:** $70.00
**Sgl. Oc.:** $40.00
**Third Person:** $11.00

**The Mulburn Inn**—A sprawling summer estate built in 1913 as a family retreat known as the Ivie House on the Woolworth estate. We have seven spacious and elegant rooms, all with private baths. Minutes from Franconia Notch and Mt. Washington attractions. AAA rated.

---

| | | | |
|---|---|---|---|
| 1. No Smoking | 5. Tennis Available | 9. Credit Cards Accepted | 13. Lunch Available | 17. Shared Bath |
| 2. No Pets | 6. Golf Available | 10. Personal Checks Accepted | 14. Public Transportation | 18. Afternoon Tea |
| 3. No Children | 7. Swiming Available | 11. Off Season Rates | 15. Reservations Necessary | ★ Commissions given |
| 4. Senior Citizen Rates | 8. Skiing Available | 12. Dinner Available | 16. Private Bath | to Travel Agents |

## Bethlehem

Sims, Louise
trawberry Hill, 03574
(603) 869-2647

**Amenities:** 2,5,6,7,8,9,10,11,16,18
**Breakfast:** F.
**Dbl. Oc.:** $64.80 - $75.60
**Sgl. Oc.:** $54.00
**Third Person:** $16.20
**Child:** under 5 yrs. - no charge

**The Bells**—Quiet, in-town location. Walk to golf, tennis, antiques and fine dining. Luxurious suites. Romantic cupola. Private baths. Nearby skiing and all White Mountain attractions. Just off Main Street. (Route 302. Primary route between Maine and Vermont.) Open all year.

## Bradford *

Mazol, Connie & Tom
Main St., 03221
(603) 938-5309

**Amenities:** 5,6,7,8,9,10,12,15,16
**Breakfast:** F.
**Dbl. Oc.:** $74.50 - $85.40
**Sgl. Oc.:** $69.50 - $80.40
**Third Person:** $15.15
**Child:** $15.15

**The Bradford Inn**—An 1899 inn. A small hotel from inception. Today, the inn has 12 rooms and suites, cozy parlors and a restaurant with fireplaces. Lots of old-fashioned charm in the decor and hospitality. J. Albert's Restaurant serves excellent New England cuisine.

## Campton *

Preston, Susan & Nicholas
Mad River Rd., 03223
(603) 726-4283

**Amenities:** 1,2,4,5,6,7,8,10, 11,12,16
**Breakfast:** F.

**Dbl. Oc.:** $70.00
**Sgl. Oc.:** $35.00
**Third Person:** $20.00
**Child:** under 12 yrs. - $10.00

**The Mountain Fare Inn**—1845 farm style home. Fresh and welcoming. White Mountain village. Flowers, foliage, biking, hiking and skiing. Two hours north of Boston. Perfect stop between Vermont and Maine. Reunions, small groups (20). Guided hikes. Bring your family to New Hampshire!

## Centre Harbor *

Lauterbach, Barbara
Old Meredith Rd.
P.O. Box 1605, 03226
(603) 253-4334

**Amenities:** 1,3,7,8,10,15,17
**Breakfast:** F.

**Dbl. Oc.:** $59.40
**Sgl. Oc.:** $54.00
**Third Person:** $15.00

**Watch Hill**—Within walking distance to the beach and shops. Historic Watch Hill offers warm, Yankee hospitality. A 1772 house on two acres overlooking Lake Winnipesaukee. Enjoy a full gourmet breakfast in a tasteful setting of English and American antiques.

| | | | | |
|---|---|---|---|---|
| 1. No Smoking | 5. Tennis Available | 9. Credit Cards Accepted | 13. Lunch Available | 17. Shared Bath |
| 2. No Pets | 6. Golf Available | 10. Personal Checks Accepted | 14. Public Transportation | 18. Afternoon Tea |
| 3. No Children | 7. Swiming Available | 11. Off Season Rates | 15. Reservations Necessary | ★ Commissions given |
| 4. Senior Citizen Rates | 8. Skiing Available | 12. Dinner Available | 16. Private Bath | to Travel Agents |

## Claremont *

Albee, Debbie & Frank
25 Hillstead Rd., 03743-3399
(603) 543-0603

**Amenities:** 1,2,5,6,7,8,10,15,16,17
**Breakfast:** F.
**Dbl. Oc.:** $70.20 - $102.60
**Third Person:** $16.20

**Goddard Mansion B&B**—A delightful 18-room 1905 mansion. Elegant, yet "homey." Eight unique guest rooms. Natural breakfast. Smoke-free! Mountain view. Peaceful and quiet. Musical host. Puzzles and games available. Great antiquing country. Nearby fine dining. Short drive to historic points of interest.

## Conway *

Lein, Lynn & Bob
148 Washington St., 03818
(603) 447-3988

**Amenities:** 1,2,5,6,7,8,9,10,11,16,17,18
**Breakfast:** F.
**Dbl. Oc.:** $59.00 - $73.00
**Sgl. Oc.:** $38.00 - $49.00
**Third Person:** $15.00
**Child:** under 13 yrs. - $10.00

**Mountain Valley Manner B&B.**—A historic Victorian B&B located near the Kancamagus Highway, Mt. Cranmore, Attitash and Wildcat skiing. Just a mosey from two 19th-century kissing bridges and outlet shopping. Enjoy air-conditioned rooms, antiques, waterbed, pool and family-sized rooms.

## Effingham

Simmons, Clinton
Townhouse Rd.
Box 290, RR 1, 03814
(603) 539-6517

**Amenities:** 2,10
**Breakfast:** F.

**Dbl. Oc.:** $48.60
**Sgl. Oc.:** $43.20
**Third Person:** $10.00
**Child:** $10.00

**Buttermilk Farm**—Find serenity and natural beauty in the foothills of the White Mountains. A restored 1832 stagecoach stop with lovely guest rooms and a hearty country breakfast. Enjoy golf, fishing, antiquing, cross-country skiing and hiking. Bird watching is excellent.

## Fitzwilliam *

Terpstra, Kathleen & Michael
186 Depot Rd., 03447
(603)585-3344

**Amenities:** 1,2,5,6,8,10,13, 15,16,18
**Breakfast:** F.

**Dbl. Oc.:** $70.20
**Sgl. Oc.:** $64.80
**Third Person:** $10.00
**Child:** $10.00

**Hannah Davis House**—The aroma of homemade breads, freshly ground coffee brewing and a welcoming bowl of popcorn. An unhurried and hearty breakfast. That comfy feeling of country quilts, crisp antique linens and wood-burning fireplaces in a sunny and warmly restored 1820 Federal.

| | | |
|---|---|---|
| 1. No Smoking | 5. Tennis Available | 9. Credit Cards Accepted | 13. Lunch Available | 17. Shared Bath |
| 2. No Pets | 6. Golf Available | 10. Personal Checks Accepted | 14. Public Transportation | 18. Afternoon Tea |
| 3. No Children | 7. Swiming Available | 11. Off Season Rates | 15. Reservations Necessary | ★ Commissions given |
| 4. Senior Citizen Rates | 8. Skiing Available | 12. Dinner Available | 16. Private Bath | to Travel Agents |

## *Franconia* *

Kerivan, Kate
Easton Valley Rd.
P.O. Box 15, 03580
(603) 823-7775

**Amenities:** 1,2,3,8,9,10,11,15, 16,17,18
**Breakfast:** F.

**Dbl. Oc.:** $60.00 - $130.00
**Sgl. Oc.:** $50.00 - $75.00
**Third Person:** $20.00

**Bungay Jar Bed & Breakfast**—Set in Robert Frost's Easton Valley. Mountain views and private woodlands bounded by a river and national park. King-size suites, sauna, balconies, fireplace and country antiques throughout. Home built from an 18th-century barn. Hosts are avid hikers and skiers. Memorable!

## *Franconia*

Morris, Alec
Easton Rd., 03580
(603) 823-5542

**Amenities:** 5,6,7,8,9,10,11,12,13,16
**Breakfast:** F.
**Dbl. Oc.:** $90.95
**Sgl. Oc.:** $74.90
**Third Person:** $16.05
**Child:** under 4 yrs. - no charge

**Franconia Inn**—Set on 107 acres in a valley below Franconia Notch. The inn's 34 guest rooms are decorated simply, yet beautifully. Elegant American cuisine, beach, classical wines and black-tie service are all part of the inn's quiet, country sophistication. Families welcome!

## *Franconia*

Steele, Bill
Wells Rd.,
RR Box 33,, 03580
(603) 823-5501

**Amenities:** 2,4,5,6,8,9,11,12, 16,17
**Breakfast:** F.

**Dbl. Oc.:** $75.60
**Sgl. Oc.:** $59.40
**Third Person:** $10.80
**Child:** under 6 yrs. - no charge

**The Horse & Hound Inn**—Off Route 18, toward Cannon Mountain on a quiet country road, yet near all activities. Twelve-room traditional inn. Fine dining, lounge, patio and large yard for parties or receptions. Crib rental - $10.00.

## *Franconia*

Vail, Brenda, John & Shannon
Easton Valley Rd.
RFD 1, Box 75, 03580
(603) 823-7061

**Amenities:** 1,2,5,6,7,8,9,10,12,14,17
**Breakfast:** F.
**Dbl. Oc.:** $60.00
**Sgl. Oc.:** $40.00
**Third Person:** $27.00
**Child:** $27.00

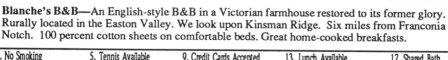

**Blanche's B&B**—An English-style B&B in a Victorian farmhouse restored to its former glory. Rurally located in the Easton Valley. We look upon Kinsman Ridge. Six miles from Franconia Notch. 100 percent cotton sheets on comfortable beds. Great home-cooked breakfasts.

| | | | | |
|---|---|---|---|---|
| 1. No Smoking | 5. Tennis Available | 9. Credit Cards Accepted | 13. Lunch Available | 17. Shared Bath |
| 2. No Pets | 6. Golf Available | 10. Personal Checks Accepted | 14. Public Transportation | 18. Afternoon Tea |
| 3. No Children | 7. Swiming Available | 11. Off Season Rates | 15. Reservations Necessary | ★ Commissions given |
| 4. Senior Citizen Rates | 8. Skiing Available | 12. Dinner Available | 16. Private Bath | to Travel Agents |

# NEW HAMPSHIRE

## Freedom

Daly, Marjorie & Bob
1 Maple St.
Box 478, 03836
(603) 539-4815

**Amenities:** 1,2,5,6,7,8,9, 10,17
**Breakfast:** F.

**Dbl. Oc.:** $64.80
**Sgl. Oc.:** $43.20
**Child:** under 12 yrs. - $10.00

**Freedom House Bed 'n' Breakfast**—Minutes off Routes 25 and 153. Offering genuine New England charm and hospitality, with a hearty country breakfast. No smoking in the house, please. Charmingly decorated with Victorian country.

## Greenfield *

Mangini, Vic
Box 400, 03047
(603) 547-6327

**Amenities:** 4,5,6,7,8,9,10,12, 13,15,16,17
**Breakfast:** F.

**Dbl. Oc.:** $49.00 - $65.00
**Sgl. Oc.:** $49.00 - $65.00
**Third Person:** $20.00
**Child:** $20.00

**Greenfield Inn**—Just 1-1/2 hours from Boston in the valley of Mt. Monadonck. Minutes to skiing and backpacking. Fine restaurants. Newly restored. Near state park. Honeymoon suites. Catered small weddings. Free brochure.

## Hampton *

Hornberger, Mary & John
252 Winnacunnet Rd., 03842
(603) 929-0443

**Amenities:** 2,5,6,7,8,9,10,11,16
**Breakfast:** F.
**Dbl. Oc.:** $70.00 - $100.00
**Sgl. Oc.:** $60.00
**Third Person:** $10.00
**Child:** $10.00

**The Inn At Elmwood Corners**—Memorable breakfasts and comfy country decor await you in this 1870 colonial inn. One mile to ocean and walking distance to village. Terry robes, cookies, games and TV in guest's sitting room. Near tax-free outlet shopping, orchards, summer theatre, etc.

## Hampton Beach

Windemiller, Debbie & Skip
365 Ocean Blvd., 03842
(603) 926-3542

**Amenities:** 1,2,5,6,7,9,11,14,16
**Breakfast:** C.
**Dbl. Oc.:** $95.00 - $120.00
**Third Person:** $26.00

**The Oceanside**—An elegantly appointed New England inn on the ocean front across from sandy beach. Ten tastefully decorated rooms with private baths, many with period antiques. Intimate breakfast cafe. Sun decks. Easy walk to activities and restaurants. Central A/C and heat.

| | | | | |
|---|---|---|---|---|
| 1. No Smoking | 5. Tennis Available | 9. Credit Cards Accepted | 13. Lunch Available | 17. Shared Bath |
| 2. No Pets | 6. Golf Available | 10. Personal Checks Accepted | 14. Public Transportation | 18. Afternoon Tea |
| 3. No Children | 7. Swiming Available | 11. Off Season Rates | 15. Reservations Necessary | ★ Commissions given |
| 4. Senior Citizen Rates | 8. Skiing Available | 12. Dinner Available | 16. Private Bath | to Travel Agents |

## Holderness *

Webb, William
Route 3, Box 680, 03245
(603) 968-7269

**Amenities:** 1,2,3,9,10,16,17
**Breakfast:** F.

**Dbl. Oc.:** $85.00 - $95.00
**Sgl. Oc.:** $55.00 - $65.00
**Third Person:** $25.00

**The Inn On Golden Pond**—An 1879 colonial home with nine bright and cheerful guest rooms. Surrounded by 50 wooded acres. Across the road is Squam Lake, the setting for the film "On Golden Pond." Open year round.

## Intervale

Davies, Eileen
Route 16, 03845
(603) 356-2224

**Amenities:** 2,9,10,11,16,17
**Breakfast:** C.

**Dbl. Oc.:** $51.84 - $99.36
**Sgl. Oc.:** $43.20
**Third Person:** $16.20
**Child:** $16.20

**Wildflowers Guest House**—Filled with Victorian antiques and located 1-1/2 miles from North Conway Village, our small B&B inn specializes in your comfort and convenience. We look forward to sharing our home with you here in the heart of the Mt. WashingtonValley.

## Jackson

Crocker, Robin
Route 16A, Box 359, 03846
(603) 383-6666

**Amenities:** 2,5,6,7,8,9,10,11,16,17
**Breakfast:** C. ( F. in winter)
**Dbl. Oc.:** $60.00 - $85.00
**Sgl. Oc.:** $50.00 - $75.00
**Third Person:** $20.00

**The Village House**—A 10-bedroom B&B that offers country living and warm hospitality. Swimming pool, tennis court, skiing, hiking, golfing, horseback riding, fine dining, shopping and Mt.Washington Valley attractions are at our doorstep.

## Jackson *

Levine Family, The
Route 16,
Pinkham Notch, 03846
(800) 537-9276, (603) 383-6822

**Amenities:** 4,5,6,7,8,9,10,11,12,13,
14,16,17,18
**Breakfast:** F. (C. in off-season)
**Dbl. Oc.:** $120.00
**Sgl. Oc.:** $85.00
**Third Person:** $25.00
**Child:** under 13 yrs. - no charge

**Dana Place Inn**—A century-old inn at base of Mt. Washington on 10 acres along Ellis River. Cozy rooms, fine dining, pub, indoorpool, jacuzzi, tennis, hiking, fishing and cross-country skiing on site. Alpine skiing, golf and attractions nearby. Special package plans available.

| 1. No Smoking | 5. Tennis Available | 9. Credit Cards Accepted | 13. Lunch Available | 17. Shared Bath |
|---|---|---|---|---|
| 2. No Pets | 6. Golf Available | 10. Personal Checks Accepted | 14. Public Transportation | 18. Afternoon Tea |
| 3. No Children | 7. Swiming Available | 11. Off Season Rates | 15. Reservations Necessary | ★ Commissions given |
| 4. Senior Citizen Rates | 8. Skiing Available | 12. Dinner Available | 16. Private Bath | to Travel Agents |

## Jaffrey

McNeill, Ellen & Frank
5 Ingalls Rd., 03452
(603) 532-7278

**Amenities:** 1,2,5,6,7,8,10,15, 16,17
**Breakfast:** F.

**Dbl. Oc.:** $75.00
**Sgl. Oc.:** $64.80
**Third Person:** $25.00

**Lilac Hill Acres Bed & Breakfast**—A historic 1840 home. Beautiful views. Surrounded by 50 acres of rolling meadows. Two hours from Boston. Nearby summer playhouses. Fireplace in guest sitting room.

## Jaffrey *

Miller, Barry
Route 124 E., 03452
(603) 532-6637

**Amenities:** 1,2,3,6,7,8,9, 10,16
**Breakfast:** F.

**Dbl. Oc.:** $81.00
**Sgl. Oc.:** $70.20
**Third Person:** $16.20

**The Benjamin Prescott Inn**—A beautifully restored 1853 Greek Revival home furnished with antiques. True hospitality, cleanliness and private baths. Overlooks a working dairy farm. Unwind and relax at a pace gone by. Near Cathedral of the Pines, Mt.Monadnock, historic sites and antique shops.

## Jefferson

Brown, Gregory W.
RFD 1, Box 68A, 03583
(603) 586-7998

**Amenities:** 1,2,4,5,6,7,8,9,10, 11,14,15,16,17,18
**Breakfast:** F.
**Dbl. Oc.:** $50.00 - $70.00
**Sgl. Oc.:** $45.00 - 465.00
**Third Person:** $10.00
**Child:** $6.00

**The Jefferson Inn**—Near Mt. Washington. 360-degree mountain views, wrap-around porch with rockers, acres of fields and a swimming pond. Near five golf courses. Superb hiking. Family suites. Nearby cross-country and downhill skiing. Skating rink, summer theatre and mountain bike trails.

## Jefferson

Fyon, Joanna
Route 115, 03583
(603) 586-4598

**Amenities:** 1,2,7,8,9,10,16,17
**Breakfast:** C.
**Dbl. Oc.:** $50.00 - $70.00
**Sgl. Oc.:** $39.00
**Third Person:** $10.00

**Stag Hollow Inn And Llama Keep**—Nestled in sunny meadows below Mt. Washington. Comfortable turn-of-the-century farmhouse. Antiques, down comforters and fireplace. Surrounded by 800,000 acres of national forest offering hiking, canoeing, bicycling and llama treks! A wildlife haven for naturalists.

| | | | | |
|---|---|---|---|---|
| 1. No Smoking | 5. Tennis Available | 9. Credit Cards Accepted | 13. Lunch Available | 17. Shared Bath |
| 2. No Pets | 6. Golf Available | 10. Personal Checks Accepted | 14. Public Transportation | 18. Afternoon Tea |
| 3. No Children | 7. Swiming Available | 11. Off Season Rates | 15. Reservations Necessary | ★ Commissions given |
| 4. Senior Citizen Rates | 8. Skiing Available | 12. Dinner Available | 16. Private Bath | to Travel Agents |

# NEW HAMPSHIRE

## Jefferson

Leslie, Janet
Davenport Rd., 03583
(603) 586-4320

**Amenities:** 1,2,9,10,11,15, 16,18
**Breakfast:** F.

**Dbl. Oc.:** $63.00
**Sgl. Oc.:** $53.00
**Third Person:** $22.00
**Child:** under 16 yrs. - no charge

**Davenport Inn**—An elegant 1809 colonial farmhouse offers a perfect place to relax. Very secluded. Mountain views. Enjoy reading by our fireplace or on our wrap-around porch. Local hiking, swimming, skiing, golf, etc. Delicious breakfasts and nightly dessert.

## Laconia *

Blazok, Maureen
1047 Union Ave., 03246
(603) 528-4185

**Amenities:** 1,5,6,7,8,9,10,11, 16,17
**Breakfast:** F.

**Dbl. Oc.:** $60.00 - $65.00
**Sgl. Oc.:** $50.00 - $55.00
**Third Person:** $12.00
**Child:** under 2 yrs. - no charge

**Tin Whistle Inn**—Share the charm, warmth and elegance of our post-Victorian home. Minutes away from boating, beaches and skiing. Enjoy the views from a large veranda overlooking Pagus Bay on Lake Winnipesaukee. No-need-for-lunch type breakfast. Centrally located in the lakes region.

## Laconia

Damato, Diane
R 1, Box 335, 03246
(603) 524-0087

**Amenities:** 1,5,6,7,10,15,16, 17,18
**Breakfast:** F.

**Dbl. Oc.:** $58.85 - $69.55
**Sgl. Oc.:** $53.50 - $64.20
**Third Person:** $16.05

**Ferry Point House**—Is a gracious country Victorian built in the 1800's as a summer retreat on Lake Winnisquam. Spend lazy moments on the 60 foot veranda or in our gazebo. Antique furnishings and decor speak of a by-gone era. Breakfast is a special treat! We are open from May — October.

## Lincoln

Deppe, Loretta & William
Pollard Rd.
P.O. Box 562, 03251
(603) 745-8517

**Amenities:** 1,2,5,6,7,8,9,10,11,17
**Breakfast:** F.
**Dbl. Oc.:** $59.40
**Sgl. Oc.:** $37.80
**Third Person:** $16.20
**Child:** $16.20

The Red Sleigh Inn
Bed & Breakfast

**The Red Sleigh**—Family-run inn with mountain views from each window, just off the scenic Kancamagus Highway. One mile to Loon Mountain ski area, Waterville and Cannon. Many summer attractions and superb fall foliage. Nearby shopping, dining and theatre. Barbecue facilites available.

| | | | | |
|---|---|---|---|---|
| 1. No Smoking | 5. Tennis Available | 9. Credit Cards Accepted | 13. Lunch Available | 17. Shared Bath |
| 2. No Pets | 6. Golf Available | 10. Personal Checks Accepted | 14. Public Transportation | 18. Afternoon Tea |
| 3. No Children | 7. Swiming Available | 11. Off Season Rates | 15. Reservations Necessary | ★ Commissions given |
| 4. Senior Citizen Rates | 8. Skiing Available | 12. Dinner Available | 16. Private Bath | to Travel Agents |

## Littleton *

Carver, Ann
247 W. Main St., 03561
(603) 444-2661

**Amenities:** 2,3,5,6,7,8,9,10, 12,15,16,17
**Breakfast:** F.

**Dbl. Oc.:** $40.00 - $90.00
**Sgl. Oc.:** $35.00 - $85.00

**Beal House Inn**—Built in 1833 as a farmhouse in Littleton. The house connected to the barn by a carriage house. Antique-filled guest rooms. Fireside breakfast. Fourteen rooms, 12 with private baths. From I-93, take Exit 42 to Routes 18 and 302.

## New Ipswich *

Bankuti, Ginny & Steve
Porter Hill Rd.
P.O. Box 208, 03071
(603) 878-3711

**Amenities:** 1,2,3,8,9,10,15,16,17,18
**Breakfast:** F.
**Dbl. Oc.:** $54.00 - $64.80
**Sgl. Oc.:** $46.20 - $48.60
**Third Person:** $43.20
**Child:** 8-18 yrs. - $16.20

**The Inn At New Ipswich**—A graceful 1790 home surrounded by stone walls and fruit trees. Six spacious guest rooms. Leisurely hearthside breakfasts. Only minutes to numerous antique shops, ski areas and hiking trails. Come and relax, read by the fire, rock on the porch and enjoy the quiet for awhile.

## New London

Rich, Margaret & Grant
125 Pleasant St., 03257
(603) 526-6271

**Amenities:** 1,2,3,5,6,7,8,9,10, 12,15,16
**Breakfast:** F.

**Dbl. Oc.:** $90.00 - $102.00
**Sgl. Oc.:** $60.00 - $65.00
**Third Person:** $30.00
**Child:** $30.00

**Pleasant Lake Inn**—Tucked away in a beautiful valley on five wooded acres with lakefront view. Eleven bedrooms recently renovated. Antiques, fireplace and quiet atmosphere. Guests may enjoy the views, walks and nature undisturbed by modern times.

## Newport

Tatem, Judi & Dick
HCR 63, Route 10, Box 3, 03773
(603) 863-3583,
(800) 367-2364

**Amenities:** 2,5,6,7,8,9,10,11, 12,13,
**Breakfast:** F.

**Dbl. Oc.:** $91.40 - $162.00
**Sgl. Oc.:** $75.60
**Third Person:** $21.60
**Child:** $5.00 (crib)

**The Inn At Coit Mountain**—Something more than a bed and breakfast. "Ohhh" is the best way to describe the library, with its oak paneling and granite fireplace. Sheer elegance! Breakfast is country-style or gourmet, as you wish.

| | | | |
|---|---|---|---|
| 1. No Smoking | 5. Tennis Available | 9. Credit Cards Accepted | 13. Lunch Available | 17. Shared Bath |
| 2. No Pets | 6. Golf Available | 10. Personal Checks Accepted | 14. Public Transportation | 18. Afternoon Tea |
| 3. No Children | 7. Swiming Available | 11. Off Season Rates | 15. Reservations Necessary | ★ Commissions given |
| 4. Senior Citizen Rates | 8. Skiing Available | 12. Dinner Available | 16. Private Bath | to Travel Agents |

## North Conway*

Begley, Ann & Hugh
P.O. Box 1817 FO,
Mt. Surprise Rd., 03860
(800) 882-9928
(603) 356-2625 (N.H. & Canada)

**Amenities:** 2,5,6,7,8,9,10,11
**Breakfast:** F.
**Dbl.Oc.:** $46.00 - $98.00
**Sgl.Oc.:** $38.00 - $75.00
**Third Person:** $17.00
**Child:** under 5 yrs. - no charge

**The Butonwood Inn**—A small country inn built in 1820. Tucked away on Mt. Surprise. Quiet and secluded yet only two miles to town and one mile to alpine skiing. Nine guest rooms with private and shared baths. TV rooms, fireplaced game room. Hiking and 60 K. groomed cross country trails from the door.

---

## North Conway *

Helfand, Judy & Dennis
Kearsarge Rd.
P.O. Box 1194, 03860
(603) 356-2044

**Amenities:** 2,5,6,7,8,9,10,11,12,16,17
**Breakfast:** F.
**Dbl. Oc.:** $60.00 - $110.00
**Sgl. Oc.:** $55.00 - $95.00
**Third Person:** $15.00 - $27.00
**Child:** under 12 yrs. - $10.00

**Cranmore Mt. Lodge**—A small country inn with resort facilities. We offer quiet rooms with shared baths. "Barn loft" offers new rooms with private baths, air-conditioning and color TV. Forty-bed dorm available for groups.

---

## North Conway*

Jackson, Claire
Kearsage Rd., 03860
(603) 356-9041

**Amenities:** 4,5,6,7,8,9,10,12, 15,16,18
**Breakfast:** F.

**Dbl. Oc.:** $98.00
**Sgl. Oc.:** $88.00
**Third Person:** $44.00
**Child:** under 12 yrs. - $22.00

**Peacock Inn**—Recapture romance in our intimate, classic country inn nestled in the heart of the scenic White Mountains, near the quaint village of North Conway. Mountain views, full country breakfast and private baths. Package plans available. Superior accommodations and service. ALA.

---

| | | | | |
|---|---|---|---|---|
| 1. No Smoking | 5. Tennis Available | 9. Credit Cards Accepted | 13. Lunch Available | 17. Shared Bath |
| 2. No Pets | 6. Golf Available | 10. Personal Checks Accepted | 14. Public Transportation | 18. Afternoon Tea |
| 3. No Children | 7. Swiming Available | 11. Off Season Rates | 15. Reservations Necessary | ★ Commissions given |
| 4. Senior Citizen Rates | 8. Skiing Available | 12. Dinner Available | 16. Private Bath | to Travel Agents |

## North Conway

Whitley, Farley
River Rd., 03860
(603) 356-6788

**Amenities:** 5,6,7,8,10,14,17
**Breakfast:** C.
**Dbl. Oc.:** 49.00 - $55.00
**Sgl. Oc.:** $40.00
**Third Person:** $10.00

**The Center Chimney — 1787**—A cozy, affordable B&B in a quiet woodsy setting. Just off Main St. Saco River swimming, canoeing and fishing. Five-minute walk to free cross-country skiing and ice skating, shops, restaurants and summer theatre. Package plans available.

## North Woodstock *

Yarnell, Rosanna & Michael
$97.20Routes 3 & 112, 03262
(603) 745-3890

**Amenities:** 2,7,8,9,10,11,12, 16,17,18
**Breakfast:** F.

**Dbl. Oc.:** $43.20 -
**Sgl. Oc.:** $37.80 - $91.80
**Third Person:** $16.20
**Child:** under 6 yrs. -
no charge

**Wilderness Inn**—The "quintessential country inn" in the midst of the WhiteMountains. Furnished with antiques. The inn has five bedrooms and suites with private baths and two bedrooms which share a bath. Complimentary gourmet breakfast. Dinner available by reservation. Fireside tea served.

## Northwood *

Briggs, Janet & Douglas
Jenness Pond Rd., 03261
(603) 942-8619

**Amenities:** 1,7,8,9,10,17
**Breakfast:** F.

**Dbl. Oc.:** $60.00
**Sgl. Oc.:** $49.00
**Third Person:** $10.00
**Child:** under 3 yrs. -
no charge

**Meadow Farm Bed And Breakfast**—A lovely country setting on 60 acres of horse pastures and woods. Authentic 1770 colonial with original features. Furnished in period antiques. Swim, canoe, loon watch on lake with private beach or bring your horse. Cross-country skiing. Great getaway!

## Northwood *

Cody, David
Jenness Pond Rd.
RFD 1, Box 3205, Pittsfield, 03263 (mail)
(603) 942-5596

**Amenities:** 1,7,8,10,17,18
**Breakfast:** F.

**Dbl. Oc.:** $65.00
**Sgl. Oc.:** $65.00
**Third Person:** $65.00

**Wild Goose Farm**—A restored antique, pre-Revolutionary farm. Period furnishings. Canopy beds. Fireplaces. Enjoy this quiet, sylvan setting, serenity and sherry. Beach and canoeing on secluded pond. Full breakfast with homemade bread, jams and jellies. French also spoken.

| | | | |
|---|---|---|---|
| 1. No Smoking | 5. Tennis Available | 9. Credit Cards Accepted | 13. Lunch Available | 17. Shared Bath |
| 2. No Pets | 6. Golf Available | 10. Personal Checks Accepted | 14. Public Transportation | 18. Afternoon Tea |
| 3. No Children | 7. Swiming Available | 11. Off Season Rates | 15. Reservations Necessary | ★ Commissions given |
| 4. Senior Citizen Rates | 8. Skiing Available | 12. Dinner Available | 16. Private Bath | to Travel Agents |

## Plymouth

Crenson, Carolyn & Bill
RR 4, Box 1955, 03264
(603) 536-4476

**Amenities:** 2,3,5,6,7,8,9,10,
16,18
**Breakfast:** F.

**Dbl. Oc.:** $70.00 - $85.00
**Sgl. Oc.:** $70.00 - $85.00
**Third Person:** $20.00

**Crab Apple Inn**—An 1835 brick colonial. Lovely guest rooms, fireplaces, gourmet breakfast, patio, spacious grounds with brook, gardens and wooded paths. Private baths and gracious amenities. At gateway to White Mountains. Near ski areas and lakes.

## Portsmouth

O'Donnell, Sarah Glover
314 Court St., 03801
(603) 436-7242

**Amenities:** 1,2,6,7,8,9,10,11,
14,16
**Breakfast:** F.

**Dbl. Oc.:** $65.00 - $92.00
**Sgl. Oc.:** $49.00 - $76.00
**Third Person:** $23.00
**Child:** over 12 yrs. - $23.00

**The Inn At Strawberry Banke**—A quiet, relaxing colonial inn with seven comfortable rooms with private baths. In the heart of historic Portsmouth. A few short blocks from a working port, quaint shops,waterfront parks, historic homes, harbor cruises, great restaurants and dockside eateries.

## Portsmouth *

Stone, Catherine
69 Richards Ave., 03801
(603) 433-2188

**Amenities:** 1,2,5,6,7,9,10,11,
16,17,18
**Breakfast:** F.

**Dbl. Oc.:** $70.20 - $81.00
**Sgl. Oc.:** $59.40 - $70.20
**Third Person:** $16.20
**Child:** under 5 yrs. - $10.80

**Leighton Inn**—An 1809 Federal mansion on a quiet residential street, furnished in museum-quality period antiques. Summer breakfast served on porch overlooking perennial gardens and raspberry patch. Six-minute walk to Market Square and Strawberry Banke. Parking.

## Randolph

Bean, Vivian & Tom
Route 2, 03570
(603) 466-5715

**Amenities:** 2,6,7,8,9,10,
16,18
**Breakfast:** C.

**Dbl. Oc.:** $48.00
**Sgl. Oc.:** $34.00
**Third Person:** $10.00

**Grand View Lodge**—Rooms with private bath, color TV and small refrigerator. Spectacular view. Warm. Hospitable. "Your home away from home." Walk the area, hike the mountains, ski or just relax. Nearby restaurants and shopping. On-premises yarn and craft shop with "wool yarn from our own sheep."

## Rindge

Linares, Carmen
03461
(603) 899-5167, 899-5166

**Amenities:** 1,2,3,5,6,7,8,10,
14,16,17
**Breakfast:** F.

**Dbl. Oc.:** $55.00 - $65.00
**Sgl. Oc.:** $45.00

**Grassy Pond House**—An 1831 homestead nestled among 150 forested acres overlooking water and gardens. Convenient to main roads, restaurants, antique shops, weekly auctions, summer theater and craft fairs. Hike Grand Monadnock.

| | | | | |
|---|---|---|---|---|
| 1. No Smoking | 5. Tennis Available | 9. Credit Cards Accepted | 13. Lunch Available | 17. Shared Bath |
| 2. No Pets | 6. Golf Available | 10. Personal Checks Accepted | 14. Public Transportation | 18. Afternoon Tea |
| 3. No Children | 7. Swiming Available | 11. Off Season Rates | 15. Reservations Necessary | ★ Commissions given |
| 4. Senior Citizen Rates | 8. Skiing Available | 12. Dinner Available | 16. Private Bath | to Travel Agents |

# NEW HAMPSHIRE

## Rye

Marineau, Janice & Norman
1413 Ocean Blvd.
Route 1A, 03870
(603) 431-1413

**Amenities:** 1,2,6,7,8,10,15, 16,17
**Breakfast:** F.

**Dbl. Oc.:** $75.60 - $81.00
**Sgl. Oc.:** $64.80 - $70.20
**Third Person:** $15.00

**Rock Ledge Manor Bed & Breakfast**—A gracious and traditional seaside manor home. Its excellent location offers an ocean view. Formal rooms. Ideally located to all New Hampshire and southern Maine seacoast activities. Sandy beach. Open year round.

## Snowvillage *

Cutrone, Trudy, Peter & Frank
03849
(603) 447-2818

**Amenities:** 2,3,4,5,6,7,8,9,10, 11,12,13,15,16
**Breakfast:** F.

**Dbl. Oc.:** $62.00
**Sgl. Oc.:** $92.00
**Third Person:** $43.00
**Child:** 7 - 12 yrs. - $31.00

**Snowvillage Inn**—A romantic Austrian estate with glorious mountain view that was a writer's home. Antiques, fireplaces, lovely gardens, gourmet candlelight dinners, cross-country skiing, hike from door and relax in sauna. Quiet, no-traffic setting and only five miles to Conway. Tax-free shops.

## Stark*

Spaulding, Nancy & Victor
Covered Bridge Rd.,
RFD #1, Box 389, 03582
(603) 636-2644
*Amenities: 7,8,10,16*
**Breakfast:** F.

**Dbl. Oc.:** $45.00
**Sgl. Oc.:** $30.00
**Child:** under 16 yrs. - $10.00

**Stark Village Inn**—New England farmhouse located next to a covered bridge and a church. Quiet area. Three rooms with private baths. Fireplace and antiques. River frontage. Relax on our wrap-around porch. Canoe, hike, fish, hunt, cross-country ski and snowmobile. Next to White Mountains Nat'l Park.

## Sugar Hill

Hern, Meri & Mike
Main St., 03585
(603) 823-5695

**Amenities:** 5,6,7,8,9,10,12,16, 17,18
**Breakfast:** F.

**Dbl. Oc.:** $54.00 - $91.80
**Sgl. Oc.:** $43.20 - $70.20
**Third Person:** $10.00
**Child:** under 2 yrs. -
no charge

**The Hilltop Inn**—An 1895 Victorian inn filled with antiques in the heart of the White Mountains of Franconia Notch. Peaceful and homey with beautiful sunset views and a large country breakfast. Children and pets welcome. English cotton flannel sheets and cozy inviting rooms. $5.00 charge for crib.

| | | | |
|---|---|---|---|
| 1. No Smoking | 5. Tennis Available | 9. Credit Cards Accepted | 13. Lunch Available | 17. Shared Bath |
| 2. No Pets | 6. Golf Available | 10. Personal Checks Accepted | 14. Public Transportation | 18. Afternoon Tea |
| 3. No Children | 7. Swiming Available | 11. Off Season Rates | 15. Reservations Necessary | ★ Commissions given |
| 4. Senior Citizen Rates | 8. Skiing Available | 12. Dinner Available | 16. Private Bath | to Travel Agents |

# NEW HAMPSHIRE

## Sugar Hill

Johnston, Barbara W.
RR 1, Box 94, 03585
(603) 823-5341

**Amenities:** 2,5,6,7,8,10, 11,16

**Breakfast:** C.

**Dbl. Oc.:** $71.00 - $125.00
**Sgl. Oc.:** $52.00 - $125.00
**Third Person:** $25.00
**Child:** $25.00

**Ledgeland**—In the heart of the White Mountains. Superb view and natural setting. Comfortable, quiet and relaxing. Inn open late June to late October. Cottages with wood-burning fireplaces and kitchens open year round. A winter wonderland for skiers.

## Sutton Mills

Forand, Margaret & Norman
Grist Mill Rd.
RR 1, Box 151, 03221
(603) 927-4765

**Amenities:** 1,2,5,6,7,8,10,12, 15,17,18

**Breakfast:** F.

**Dbl. Oc.:** $48.60
**Sgl. Oc.:** $37.80
**Third Person:** $10.80
**Child:** $10.80

**The Village House At Sutton Mills, NH**—A newly restored 1857 country Victorian, tastefully decorated with antiques and old quilts. Overlooks quaint New England village. Nearby shopping, antiques and restaurants. Stroll down lane to yesteryear and the general store. Snowmobile and cross-country skiing right on premises.

## Wakefield, East

Bettencourt, Ann & Anthony
Acton Ridge Rd.
Box 142, 03830
(603) 522-8824

**Amenities:** 1,2,6,7,8,9,11,15, 16,17

**Breakfast:** C.

**Dbl. Oc.:** $50.00 - $60.00
**Sgl. Oc.:** $43.00 - $53.00
**Third Person:** $10.00
**Child:** under 12 yrs. - $6.00

**Lake Ivanhoe Inn**—A charming 1800's colonial home opposite lake. Five nicely decorated rooms. Private and shared baths. Waterviews, private beach, fishing and swimming. 45 minutes to White Mountains, Maine and New Hampshire coasts. 20 minutes to Lake Winnipesaukee. Abuts wooded camping/RV area.

## Warner

Baese, Deb & Marlon
Main St.
RFD 1, Box 11, 03278
(603) 456-3494

**Amenities:** 1,5,6,8,10,17
**Breakfast:** F.
**Dbl. Oc.:** $43.20
**Sgl. Oc.:** $43.20
**Third Person:** $5.00

**Jacob's Ladder Bed & Breakfast**—Conveniently located between I-89, Exits 8 and 9 at the heart of a quaint New England village. Four ski areas within 20 miles with cross-country and snowmobile trails on site. Early 1800's home on four acres furnished with antiques. Nearby lakes, crafts, shopping and antiques.

| | | | | |
|---|---|---|---|---|
| 1. No Smoking | 5. Tennis Available | 9. Credit Cards Accepted | 13. Lunch Available | 17. Shared Bath |
| 2. No Pets | 6. Golf Available | 10. Personal Checks Accepted | 14. Public Transportation | 18. Afternoon Tea |
| 3. No Children | 7. Swiming Available | 11. Off Season Rates | 15. Reservations Necessary | ★ Commissions given |
| 4. Senior Citizen Rates | 8. Skiing Available | 12. Dinner Available | 16. Private Bath | to Travel Agents |

# NEW HAMPSHIRE

## Wentworth

Kauk, Marie
East Side & Buffalo Rd., 03282
(603) 764-5896

**Amenities:** 2,7,9,10,15,16, 17,18
**Breakfast:** C.

**Dbl. Oc.:** $54.00 - $81.00
**Sgl. Oc.:** $54.00
**Third Person:** $10.00
**Child:** $10.00

**Hilltop Acres**—A charming early-1800's home. Antique furniture. Large pine-paneled recreation room with cable TV. Spacious grounds. Housekeeping cottages. Near hiking, swimming, antique and craft shops, restaurants and White Mountain attractions. Open June-October.

## Wentworth

LaBrie, Diane
Route 25 & Atwell Hill Rd.
P.O. Box 147, 03282
(603) 764-9600

**Amenities:** 1,9,10,16,17
**Breakfast:** F.

**Dbl. Oc.:** $70.00 - $81.00
**Sgl. Oc.:** $70.00 - $81.00
**Third Person:** $10.00
**Child:** under 8 yrs. - $5.00

**Mountain Laurel Inn**—Step back into the 19th century when you visit this 1840 colonial. Your romantically appointed room with king-size bed is distinctive and comfortable. Your leisurely breakfast in our dinig room will energize you for your day's activities in New Hampshire.

## Whitefield *

Maxwell, Winslow
Parker Rd., 03598
(603) 837-9717
**Amenities:** 1,2,8,10,12,13,15, 16,17,18
**Breakfast:** F.
**Dbl. Oc.:** $60.00 - $80.00
**Sgl. Oc.:** $40.00
**Third Person:** $10.00
**Child:** under 12 yrs. -    no charge

**Maxwell Haus B&B**—Charming country setting on 32 acres. Six beautiful bedrooms with a Victorian decor. Private suite. Elegant sitting room with fireplace. Guest library. Fine country dining. Gourmet plan/MAP. Seasonal packages. Cross-country skiing, snowmobile and hiking on property.

| | | | |
|---|---|---|---|
| 1. No Smoking | 5. Tennis Available | 9. Credit Cards Accepted | 13. Lunch Available | 17. Shared Bath |
| 2. No Pets | 6. Golf Available | 10. Personal Checks Accepted | 14. Public Transportation | 18. Afternoon Tea |
| 3. No Children | 7. Swiming Available | 11. Off Season Rates | 15. Reservations Necessary | ★ Commissions given |
| 4. Senior Citizen Rates | 8. Skiing Available | 12. Dinner Available | 16. Private Bath | to Travel Agents |

# NEW JERSEY

## *The Garden State*

Capitol: Trenton
Statehood: December 18, 1787; the 3rd state
State Motto: Liberty and Prosperity
State Bird: Eastern Goldfinch
State Flower: Purple Violet
State Tree: Red Oak

New Jersey is a state of hundreds of thousands of people. Most of these people live in the northern industrial area around Newark. They are hard working and are involved in just about every kind of manufacturing there is in America. Sixty of the largest companies we have in the United States have plants in New Jersey.

The New Jersey Turnpike is the busiest turnpike in the country, bringing people in and out of this state on their way either north, south, east or west.

There are many historic places to visit in New Jersey, and also some very beautiful beaches along the Atlantic coast. Vacationers love this state. Atlantic City and the boardwalk has been a tremendous tourist attraction for years.

Organized baseball was first played in Hoboken, New Jersey in 1846, and Grover Cleveland was born in Cadwell in 1837.

## Avon-By-The-Sea

Curley, Kathleen & Jim
109 Sylvania Ave., 07717
(908) 988-6326

**Amenities:** 1,2,4,7,11
**Breakfast:** C.
**Dbl. Oc.:** $65.00 - $95.00
**Sgl. Oc.:** $55.00 - $85.00
**Third Person:** $20.00

**The Avon Manor**—A gracious turn-of-the-century home for your special getaway. Enjoy breakfast in our sunny dining room, ocean breezes on our full wrap-around porch and the serenity of this small seaside town. Seven air-conditioned bedrooms. One block to beach.

---

## Bay Head *

Conover, Beverly
646 Main Ave., 08742
(201) 892-4664

**Amenities:** 1,2,5,6,7,9,10,11,
14,15,16,18
**Breakfast:** C. and F.

**Dbl. Oc.:** $100.00 - $135.00
**Sgl. Oc.:** $90.00 - $125.00
**Third Person:** $30.00

**Conover's Bay Head Inn**—New Jersey shore's finest antique filled B&B. Special touches for a memorable stay. A short walk to the ocean, shops and restaurants. A view from every window! All private baths. Tea served in winter. Full breakfast served on Sunday and during quiet times.

---

## Belmar *

Kelley, Alan
102 7th Ave., 07719
(201) 681-8950

**Amenities:** 1,2,3,4,7,10,11,
14,16,17
**Breakfast:** C.
**Dbl. Oc.:** $60.00 - $80.00
**Sgl. Oc.:** $35.00 - $52.00
**Third Person:** $20.00
**Child:** $10.00

**"The Shillelagh Inn"**—The inn offers a spectacular view of the ocean from a porch that connects to your room. Convenient to major antique areas, Atlantic City and fine dining. We will also cater to your special functions, including wedding parties, family reunions and retreats.

---

| | | | | |
|---|---|---|---|---|
| 1. No Smoking | 5. Tennis Available | 9. Credit Cards Accepted | 13. Lunch Available | 17. Shared Bath |
| 2. No Pets | 6. Golf Available | 10. Personal Checks Accepted | 14. Public Transportation | 18. Afternoon Tea |
| 3. No Children | 7. Swiming Available | 11. Off Season Rates | 15. Reservations Necessary | ★ Commissions given |
| 4. Senior Citizen Rates | 8. Skiing Available | 12. Dinner Available | 16. Private Bath | to Travel Agents |

262

## Cape May

Burow, Greg
609 Hughes St., 08204
(609) 884-7293

**Amenities:** 1,2,5,6,7,9,10,11,16,18
**Breakfast:** F.
**Dbl. Oc.:** $133.75 - $155.15
**Sgl. Oc.:** $133.75 - $155.15
**Third Person:** $16.05

**The Wooden Rabbit**—Located on the prettiest street in Cape May, in the heart of the historic district, surrounded by Victorian cottages. Decor is country. All rooms have private baths, air conditioning and TV. Two blocks to shops and fine food. Children welcome.

## Cape May

Carroll, Sue & Tom
635 Columbia Ave., 08204
(609) 884-8690

**Amenities:** 1,2,3,7,10,11,15,16,18
**Breakfast:** F.
**Dbl. Oc.:** $117.70 - $149.80
**Sgl. Oc.:** $107.00 - $139.10
**Third Person:** $21.20

**Mainstay Inn & Cottage**—"The jewel of them all has got to be the Mainstay"—*Washington Post*. Twelve large, antique-filled rooms. This former gentlemen's gambling club offers history, romance and hospitality. Nearby shops, restaurants, historic attractions and beaches.

## Cape May *

Kulkowitz, Mark H.
19 Jackson St., 08204
(609) 884-9619

**Amenities:** 5,6,7,9,10,11,12,13,
14,16,17
**Breakfast:** F.
**Dbl. Oc.:** $67.41 - $96.30
**Sgl. Oc.:** $56.71 - $85.60
**Third Person:** $21.40
**Child:** under 5 yrs. - $13.91

**Carroll Villa Bed & Breakfast**—Our 109-year-old Victorian hotel is 1/2 block from a dip in the ocean and a Victorian mall. Modestly priced rooms include full breakfast. Roll out of bed and come downstairs to our nationally acclaimed restaurant for one of the best breakfasts of your life — or dinner!

| | | | |
|---|---|---|---|
| 1. No Smoking | 5. Tennis Available | 9. Credit Cards Accepted | 13. Lunch Available | 17. Shared Bath |
| 2. No Pets | 6. Golf Available | 10. Personal Checks Accepted | 14. Public Transportation | 18. Afternoon Tea |
| 3. No Children | 7. Swiming Available | 11. Off Season Rates | 15. Reservations Necessary | ★ Commissions given |
| 4. Senior Citizen Rates | 8. Skiing Available | 12. Dinner Available | 16. Private Bath | to Travel Agents |

## Cape May*

LeDuc, Annie
301 Howard St., 08204
(609) 884-8409

Amenities: 2,5,6,7,9,10,11,12,
    14,15,16,17
Breakfast: F.
Dbl. Oc.: $110.00 - $145.00
Sgl. Oc.: $60.00 - $70.00
Third Person: $27.00
Child: under 14 yrs. $4.00 - $16.00

Original Drawing by Lynne Cherry

Chalfonte Hotel—A basic 1876 Victorian summer hotel with verandas, rocking chairs and delicious Southern fare. Separate dining room for children under seven years. Dinner is included in daily rate. Entertainment includes cocktail lounge, concerts, theater and tours. Mid-week discount.

## Cape May

Miller, Sandy & Owen
24 Jackson St., 08204
(609) 884-3368

Amenities: 2,3,5,6,7,9,10,11,
    14,15,16,18
Breakfast: F.
Dbl. Oc.: $90.00 - $130.00
Sgl. Oc.: $80.00 - $120.00
Third Person: $25.00

Windward House—Elegant Edwardian inn 1/2 block from the ocean and mall. Eight antique filled rooms with queen beds, private baths and air conditioning. Three sun and shade porches. Cozy parlor fireplace. Vintage clothing and other collectibles on display. Free parking, beach tags and bicycles.

## Cape May

Rein, Cathy & Barry
1513 Beach Dr., 08204
(609) 884-2228

Amenities:1,2,3,5,6,7,9,10,
    11,15,16,18
Breakfast: F.
Dbl. Oc.: $100.70 - $143.10
Sgl. Oc.: $90.10 - $132.50
Third Person: $26.50

COLVMNS BY THE SEA

Colvlmns By The Sea—Ocean front mansion filled with the charm of a bygone era when a summer cottage had 20 rooms, 12 foot ceilings and hand carved woodwork. Today Victorian antiques are balanced by modern comfort and informality. Great for history buffs, birders or just to relax.

| | | | |
|---|---|---|---|
| 1. No Smoking | 5. Tennis Available | 9. Credit Cards Accepted | 13. Lunch Available | 17. Shared Bath |
| 2. No Pets | 6. Golf Available | 10. Personal Checks Accepted | 14. Public Transportation | 18. Afternoon Tea |
| 3. No Children | 7. Swiming Available | 11. Off Season Rates | 15. Reservations Necessary | ★ Commissions given |
| 4. Senior Citizen Rates | 8. Skiing Available | 12. Dinner Available | 16. Private Bath | to Travel Agents |

## Cape May

Schmidt, Lorraine
29 Ocean St., 08204
(609) 884-4428

**Amenities:** 1,3,5,7,9,11,14,15, **Dbl. Oc.:** $90.00 - $200.00
16,18         **Sgl. Oc.:** $80.00 - $190.00
**Breakfast:** F.

**The Humphrey Hughes House**—Located in the primary historic district. Five houses from the beach. Circa 1903. Stained glass windows mark each landing of the staircase, and intricately carved chestnut columns add to the atmosphere in this 30- room mansion. Beautifully decorated in Victorian style.

## Cape May

Smith, Frank
619 Hughes St., 08204
(609) 884-0613

**Amenities:** 1,2,3,11,16,18    **Dbl. Oc.:** $133.00
**Breakfast:** F.           **Sgl. Oc.:** $116.00
**Third Person:** $25.00

**White Dove Cottage**—1866 Victorian home situated on a gas lit street in the historic district. Rooms and suites offer private baths, European antiques and period wallpapers. Full breakfast is served at a grand banquet table. Close to beach, restaurants, tennis, fishing and antique shops.

## Cape May *

Wood, Jan & Buddy
808 Wash. St., 08204
(609) 884-7123
**Amenities:** 1,2,5,6,7,9,10,11,
14,15,16
**Breakfast:** C. Plus
**Dbl. Oc.:** $80.25 - $117.70
**Third Person:** $10.70

**Woodleigh House**—A country Victorian, built in 1866 features collections of glass and Royal Copenhagen throughout along with Victorian antiques. Porches sport rockers and wicker. Secluded brick courtyards and rear gardens available to our guests.

## Denville

Bergins, Annette & Alex
11 Sunset Trail, 07834
(201) 625-5129

**Amenities:** 1,2,5,7,10,14,    **Dbl. Oc.:** $50.00
15,16             **Sgl. Oc.:** $45.00
**Breakfast:** F          **Child:** $10.00

**Lakeside B&B**—One mile from I-80 between New York City and Pennsylvania. Private guest quarters with a stunning view of the bay. Double bed in guest room plus a family room with a color TV. Swimming, boating, fishing, ice skating on the lake.

| | | | |
|---|---|---|---|
| 1. No Smoking | 5. Tennis Available | 9. Credit Cards Accepted | 13. Lunch Available | 17. Shared Bath |
| 2. No Pets | 6. Golf Available | 10. Personal Checks Accepted | 14. Public Transportation | 18. Afternoon Tea |
| 3. No Children | 7. Swiming Available | 11. Off Season Rates | 15. Reservations Necessary | ★ Commissions given |
| 4. Senior Citizen Rates | 8. Skiing Available | 12. Dinner Available | 16. Private Bath | to Travel Agents |

## Flemington

Studer, Judith
96 Broad St., 08822
(908) 782-8234

Amenities: 1,2,5,6,7,9,10,11,
14,15,16,17,18
Breakfast: C.

Dbl. Oc.: $64.20 - $96.30
Sgl. Oc.: $59.20 - $91.30
Third Person: $15.00

**Jerica Will - A Bed & Breakfast Inn**—Welcome to this gracious Victorian country home in the historic town center. Spacious sunny guestrooms, livingroom with fireplace, wicker filled screened porch. Champagne hot air ballon flights. Winery tours. Wonderful escape weekends. Corporate travellers welcome!

## Flemington *

Venosa, Pam
162 Main St., 08822
(908) 788-0247

Amenities: 1,2,4,6,7,9,10,14,
16,17
Breakfast: C.

Dbl. Oc.: $59.00 - $91.00
Sgl. Oc.: $54.00 - $86.00
Third Person: $15.00

**The Cabbage Rose Inn**—Just one hour from New York City and Philadelphia. Romantic Victorian with five luxurious antique filled guestrooms. All are air conditioned and most have private baths. Steps from outlet shops, galleries and restaurants. Bucks County, PA and New Jersey wineries minutes away.

## Jobstown

Sudler, Lyd
R.D. #1, Box 420, 08041
(609) 723-5364

Amenities: 2,10,15
Breakfast: F.

Dbl. Oc.: $50.00 - $85.00
Sgl. Oc.: $50.00

**Belle Springs Farm**—Comtemporary farmhouse with family heirlooms, Steinway, fireplace and air-conditioning. Deer. Breakfast with a view. Five miles from exit 7 of the New Jersey Turnpike, midway between Washington, DC and New York. 1/2 hour to Philadelphia or Princeton, NJ.

## Manahawkin

Carney, Maureen
190 N. Main St., 08050
(609) 597-6350

Amenities: 2,6,7,11,15,
16,17,18
Breakfast: C. and F.

Dbl. Oc.: $53.50 - $70.00
Sgl. Oc.: $42.80 - $65.00

**The Goose N Berry Inn**—1800's historic home comfortably furnished with period antiques. Tree shaded porches overlook the wooded acreage. Nearby are ocean beaches, boating, canoeing, preserve, antiquing and crafts. Thirty minutes to Atlantic City. Exit 63 on the Garden State Parkway.

## Ocean City *

Barna, Lois & Frank
637 Wesley Ave., 08226
(609) 391-9366

Amenities: 1,2,3,5,6,7,9,11,
14,16,17
Breakfast: C.

Dbl. Oc.: $64.20 - $74.90
Third Person: $10.70

**BarnaGate Bed & Breakfast**—A seashore country Victorian 3 blocks from the ocean, shopping, and restaurants. Five homey guest rooms with private and semi-private baths. Relax on the porch or in the cozy living room. Open all year. Close to Atlantic City and antique shopping. Homemade breads and muffins.

| | | | |
|---|---|---|---|
| 1. No Smoking | 5. Tennis Available | 9. Credit Cards Accepted | 13. Lunch Available | 17. Shared Bath |
| 2. No Pets | 6. Golf Available | 10. Personal Checks Accepted | 14. Public Transportation | 18. Afternoon Tea |
| 3. No Children | 7. Swiming Available | 11. Off Season Rates | 15. Reservations Necessary | ★ Commissions given |
| 4. Senior Citizen Rates | 8. Skiing Available | 12. Dinner Available | 16. Private Bath | to Travel Agents |

## Ocean City

Hand, Donna
519 5th St., 08226
(609) 399-2829

**Amenities:** 1,2,3,9,11,15,16,17,18
**Breakfast:** F.
**Dbl. Oc.:** $65.00 - $70.00
**Sgl. Oc.:** $45.00 - $50.00
**Third Person:** $10.00
**Child:** over 10 yrs. - $10.00

**New Brighton Inn Bed & Breakfast**—Magnificently restored Victorian. All rooms furnished with antiques. Enjoy breakfast on our sun porch or in the privacy of your room. Close to beach, bay, boardwalk, restaurants and shops. Relax in our charming and romantic ambience.

## Ocean City

Hydock, Patricia
1020 Central Ave., 08226
(609) 398-1698

**Amenities:** 2,5,6,7,9,10,11,14, 15,16,17
**Breakfast:** F.

**Dbl. Oc.:** $80.25
**Sgl. Oc.:** $70.25
**Third Person:** $10.00
**Child:** under 6 yrs. - no charge

**The Enterprise B&B Inn**—Breakfast is the focus of your stay at the Enterprise and it is one of the reasons we were recently chosen as "one of the best inns" by *Atlantic City magazine*. The pink exterior with white gingerbread frosting combine to create "a heart and flower theme." A little country at the shore.

## Ocean City

Loeper, Marj & John
401 Wesley Ave., 08226
(609) 399-6071

**Amenities:** 1,2,5,6,7,9,10,11,14,16,18
**Breakfast:** F.
**Dbl. Oc.:** $80.25 - $139.10
**Sgl. Oc.:** $80.25 - $139.10
**Third Person:** $10.70

**Northwood Inn (Bed & Breakfast)**—An elegantly restored 1894 Victorian. Beautification Award nominee. Nine distinctively decorated guest rooms, fully stocked library and air conditioning. Walk to beach, boardwalk, shops and restaurants. Eight miles south of Atlantic City. Warm personal service. Open year round.

| | | | |
|---|---|---|---|
| 1. No Smoking | 5. Tennis Available | 9. Credit Cards Accepted | 13. Lunch Available | 17. Shared Bath |
| 2. No Pets | 6. Golf Available | 10. Personal Checks Accepted | 14. Public Transportation | 18. Afternoon Tea |
| 3. No Children | 7. Swiming Available | 11. Off Season Rates | 15. Reservations Necessary | ★ Commissions given |
| 4. Senior Citizen Rates | 8. Skiing Available | 12. Dinner Available | 16. Private Bath | to Travel Agents |

## Ocean City *

| | | |
|---|---|---|
| Nunan, Virginia | **Amenities:** 2,4,5,6,7,9,10,11, | **Dbl. Oc.:** $81.32 - $171.20 |
| 5447 Central Ave., 08226 | 13,14,15,16 | **Sgl. Oc.:** $73.19 - $154.08 |
| (609) 399-0477 | **Breakfast:** C.(winter) | **Third Person:** $12.00 |
| | F.(summer) | **Child:** $10.70 - $12.84 |

**Top O The Waves, Inc.**—Relax on your own beach front deck. Enjoy the outstanding ocean view in comfort, warm hospitality and high standards of innkeeping. Walk on the beach or ride bikes on the boardwalk. Go antiquing, shopping, fishing or sailing. Visit the wineries. Play tennis or golf. Come and enjoy.

## Ocean City *

| | | |
|---|---|---|
| Rice, Nancy & John | **Amenities:** 1,2,5,6,7,9,10,14, | **Dbl. Oc.:** $64.20 - $85.60 |
| 604 Atlantic Ave., 08226 | 16,17 | **Sgl. Oc.:** $64.20 - $85.60 |
| (609) 398-4115 | **Breakfast:** C. Plus | |

**Bayberry Bed & Breakfast**—Come stay in our beautifully decorated bed and breakfast located one block from the Ocean City beach and boardwalk. Included is continental breakfast which is enjoyed on the wrap-around porch or in our formal dining room. All rates are discounted 10% on weekdays.

## Ocean Grove *

| | | |
|---|---|---|
| Chernik, Doris | **Amenities:** 2,4,5,7,10,11,14, | **Dbl. Oc.:** $35,00 - $60.00 |
| 26 Webb Ave., 07756 | 16,17 | **Sgl. Oc.:** $30.00 - $45.00 |
| (201) 774-3084 (summer), | **Breakfast:** C. | **Child:** under 12 yrs. - $5.00 |
| (212) 751-9577 (winter) | | |

**Cordova**—Century-old B&B located in historic Ocean Grove. Beautiful Victorian with old world charm. One block from the beach. Recently featured in *New Jersey magazine* as one of the seven best places on the New Jersey shore. Kitchen, BBQ and picnic area for guests. You will feel like family.

## Ocean Grove

| | | |
|---|---|---|
| Rechlin, Catherine & Thomas | **Amenities:** 1,2,7,10,12,13,14, | **Dbl. Oc.:** $30.00 - $45.00 |
| 28 Main Ave. | 15,16,17 | **Sgl. Oc.:** $26.00 |
| P.O. Box 68, 07756 | **Breakfast:** C. and F. | **Third Person:** $5.00 |
| (201) 775-1905 | | |

**Sampler Inn**—Fine food and lodging since 1917. Just a block from the ocean. New Jersey's oldest cafeteria. All baking done in house. Discover America's largest assemblage of original and authentic Victorian architecture. Enjoy our private collection of antique samplers.

| | | | | |
|---|---|---|---|---|
| 1. No Smoking | 5. Tennis Available | 9. Credit Cards Accepted | 13. Lunch Available | 17. Shared Bath |
| 2. No Pets | 6. Golf Available | 10. Personal Checks Accepted | 14. Public Transportation | 18. Afternoon Tea |
| 3. No Children | 7. Swiming Available | 11. Off Season Rates | 15. Reservations Necessary | ★ Commissions given |
| 4. Senior Citizen Rates | 8. Skiing Available | 12. Dinner Available | 16. Private Bath | to Travel Agents |

## *Salem* *

Abbott, Edward
100 Tide-Mill Rd., 08079
(609) 935-2798

**Amenities:** 2,3,15,16,17,18
**Breakfast:** F.

**Dbl. Oc.:** $60.00
**Sgl. Oc.:** $55.00
**Third Person:** $15.00

**Tide-Mill Farm**—Outside historic Salem (1675). An 1845 Greek revival with seven guest rooms available. Located about 1 1/2 hours from Atlantic City and 15 minutes from the Memorial Bridge and the New Jersey Turnpike. 53 waterfront acres with fishing, crabbing, hunting and trails.

## *Spring Lake* *

Kirby, Carol J. & John R.
19 Tuttle Ave., 07762
(201) 449-9031

**Amenities:** 1,2,3,5,6,7,9,10,11,
14,15,16,18
**Breakfast:** C. Plus
**Dbl. Oc.:** $107.00
**Sgl. Oc.:** $96.00

**Sea Crest By The Sea**—Escape to the romantic refuge of a luxurious inn by the sea. We will pamper you with hospitality that is friendly yet unobtrusive. A lovingly restored 1885 Victorian inn for ladies and gentlemen on a seaside holiday.

## *Spring Lake*

Sarkar, Angele
1505 Ocean Ave., 07762
(201) 449-5327

**Amenities:** 1,2,5,6,7,9,10,11,
14,15,16,17,18
**Breakfast:** F.

**Dbl. Oc.:** $100.00 - $150.00
**Third Person:** $35.00
**Child:** under 12 yrs. -
$35.00

**The Grand Victorian**—Located directly on the ocean. Gracious hospitality defines the ambience. Individually decorated rooms each with its unique charm and appeal. Walk to stores, golf courses and tennis courts. Complimentary refreshments and hors d'oeuvres.

## *Stockton*

Warsaw, Louise
6 Woolverton Rd., 08559
(609) 397-0802

**Amenities:** 2,3,5,6,7,9,10,15,
16,17,18
**Breakfast:** F.

**Dbl. Oc.:** $70.00 - $120.00
**Sgl. Oc.:** $70.00 - $120.00
**Third Person:** $15.00

**Woolverton Inn**—An elegant stone colonial Victorian manor house on a ten acre estate admist formal gardens and stately trees. Twelve antique filled rooms with privacy. Play croquet, horseshoes or ride our bicycles along the Delaware River. Sit by the fire and relax.

## *Woodbine*

Thurlow, Annette M.
RD #3, Box 298, 08270
(609) 861-5847

**Amenities:** 2,7,9,10,12,15,16,
17
**Breakfast:** F.

**Dbl. Oc.:** $65.00 - $95.00
**Third Person:** $20.00
**Child:** over 12 yrs. - $20.00

**Henry Ludlam Inn**—Romantic lakeside country B&B circa 1740 featuring bedrooms with working fireplaces. Four course gourmet breakfast features our famous stuffed french toast and peach melba by the fire with candlelight. Picnic baskets available. Featured in many magazines. A place for all seasons.

| | | | |
|---|---|---|---|
| 1. No Smoking | 5. Tennis Available | 9. Credit Cards Accepted | 13. Lunch Available | 17. Shared Bath |
| 2. No Pets | 6. Golf Available | 10. Personal Checks Accepted | 14. Public Transportation | 18. Afternoon Tea |
| 3. No Children | 7. Swiming Available | 11. Off Season Rates | 15. Reservations Necessary | ★ Commissions given |
| 4. Senior Citizen Rates | 8. Skiing Available | 12. Dinner Available | 16. Private Bath | to Travel Agents |

# NEW MEXICO

## *The Land of Enchantment*

Capitol: Santa Fe
Statehood: January 6, 1912; the 47th state
State Motto: It Grows As It Goes
State Song: "O Fair New Mexico"
State Bird: Road Runner
State Flower: Yucca Flower
State Tree: Pinon or Nut Pine

New Mexico is a warm and scenic country. Its magnificent scenery attracts visitors from everywhere. The days are mild and sometimes quite warm, but the evenings are cool and delightful.

Lovers of history can visit Indian ruins, frontier forts and Spanish missions. They can see homes and shops still made from dried adobe bricks. Mexican food is still the most popular food here and fine jewelry is sold along the streets by vendors at bargain prices.

The Palace of Governors, the oldest government building in the United States, is here, as well as the most interesting Carlsbad Caverns.

## *Albuquerque* *

Cosgrove, Mary
327 Arizona S.E., 87108
(505) 256-9462

**Amenities:** 1,2,5,6,7,8,9,10,
11,14,15,16
**Breakfast:** C.
**Dbl. Oc.:** $75.00
**Sgl. Oc.:** $65.00
**Third Person:** $10.00

**The Sandcastle**—Large rooms. Comfortable common room. Private garage is $5.00 a night when available. Off-street parking available. Close to Sandia, Kirkland Air Force Base, fairgrounds, University of New Mexico and restaurants. Youngsters 12 and over welcome.

## *Carrizozo*

Desjardins, Harold
911 12th St.
P.O. Box 63, 88301
(505) 648-2149

**Amenities:** 1,2,3,6,7,8,9,
12,13,16,17
**Breakfast:** F.
**Dbl. Oc.:** $60.00
**Sgl. Oc.:** $60.00

**Old Adobe Inn**—This 1904 adobe home was formerly the Temple Hotel. It's complete with antiques, collectibles and warm hospitality. Close to Capitan, where Smokey the Bear National Monument can be found, and Lincoln, where Billy the Kid made his last escape. Great skiing areas.

## *Cedar Crest*

O'Neil, Elaine
P.O. Box 444, 87008
(505) 281-2467

**Amenities:** 1,2,8,10,16,17
**Breakfast:** F.
**Dbl. Oc.:** $61.00 - $83.00
**Sgl. Oc.:** $61.00 - $83.00
**Third Person:** $10.00
**Child:** $10.00

ELAINE'S
A BED AND BREAKFAST

**Elaine's, A Bed And Breakfast**—Charm, elegance and hospitality in a beautiful three-story log home nestled in the evergreen forests of Sandia peaks. Vacationers can enjoy all the attractions of Santa Fe and Albuquerque plus the historic sites, galleries and shops along the historic Turquoise Trail.

| | | | |
|---|---|---|---|
| 1. No Smoking | 5. Tennis Available | 9. Credit Cards Accepted | 13. Lunch Available | 17. Shared Bath |
| 2. No Pets | 6. Golf Available | 10. Personal Checks Accepted | 14. Public Transportation | 18. Afternoon Tea |
| 3. No Children | 7. Swiming Available | 11. Off Season Rates | 15. Reservations Necessary | ★ Commissions given |
| 4. Senior Citizen Rates | 8. Skiing Available | 12. Dinner Available | 16. Private Bath | to Travel Agents |

# NEW MEXICO

## Farmington

Ohlson, Diana
3151 W. Main, 87401
(505) 325-8219

**Amenities:** 1,2,3,9,15,16
**Breakfast:** C.

**Dbl. Oc.:** $68.74
**Sgl. Oc.:** $58.16
**Third Person:** $10.56

**Silver Rose Inn**—A newly built adobe in traditional New Mexican style, sitting on the cliff side of the San Jaun and La Plata Rivers. Located near Chaco Canyon, Aztec, Salmon Ruins, Mesa Verde, Canyon de Chelly and the Navajo, Ute, Hopi and Apache reservations. A Navajo rug gallery to enjoy.

## Las Cruces *

Lundeen, Linda & Jerry
618 S. Alameda Blvd., 88005
(505) 526-3355, (505) 526-3327

**Amenities:** 9,10,16
**Breakfast:** C.

**Dbl. Oc.:** $50.00 - $80.00
**Sgl. Oc.:** $45.00 - $75.00
**Third Person:** $10.00

**Lundeen, Inn Of The Arts**—Located in downtown Las Cruces. A Mexican territorial, adobe. A gracious hacienda adjoining the Linda Lundeen Gallery. All eight rooms named after American artists. Private baths.

## Lincoln

Jordan, Cleis & Jeremy
Hwy. 380 E.
P.O. Box 27, 88338
(505) 653-4676, Fax: (505) 653-4671

**Amenities:** 1,2,6,8,9,10, 12,16
**Breakfast:** C. and F.

**Dbl. Oc.:** $59.00 - $97.00
**Sgl. Oc.:** $48.00 - $86.00
**Third Person:** $11.00

**Casa De Patron**—Billy the Kid slept in this handsome, quiet adobe home. Hand-hewn vigas. Tree-lined courtyard. Warm hospitality, music and a bountiful breakfast await our guests. A tradition continued "con gusto." Idyllic frontier village on scenic route to Carlsbad Caverns.

## Placitas

Butler, Rhea & Robert
Star Route, Box 501, 87043
(505) 867-5586

**Amenities:** 1,6,8,10,15,16
**Breakfast:** C.
**Dbl. Oc.:** $68.50 - $99.75
**Sgl. Oc.:** $68.50 - $99.75
**Third Person:** $11.00
**Child:** under 12 yrs. - $6.00

**Kensington House**—A charming, unique New Mexican B&B located on a spectacular high mesa within minutes of Santa Fe, Albuquerque and several Indian Pueblos. Sandia and Jemez Mountain Ranges and the Southwestern charm are all part of the magic! A beautiful and peaceful stay.

---

| | | | |
|---|---|---|---|
| 1. No Smoking | 5. Tennis Available | 9. Credit Cards Accepted | 13. Lunch Available | 17. Shared Bath |
| 2. No Pets | 6. Golf Available | 10. Personal Checks Accepted | 14. Public Transportation | 18. Afternoon Tea |
| 3. No Children | 7. Swiming Available | 11. Off Season Rates | 15. Reservations Necessary | ★ Commissions given |
| 4. Senior Citizen Rates | 8. Skiing Available | 12. Dinner Available | 16. Private Bath | to Travel Agents |

## Santa Fe *

Ambrose, Trisha
652 Canyon Rd., 87501
(800) 279-0755, (505) 988-5888

**Amenities:** 1,2,9,10,11,16
**Breakfast:** C.
**Dbl. Oc.:** $85.00 - $145.00
**Sgl. Oc.:** $85.00 - $125.00
**Third Person:** $15.00
**Child:** under 12 yrs. - no charge

**Canyon Road Casitas**—A small, luxurious inn located on Santa Fe's historic Canyon Road. A restored adobe with the finest Southwestern decor and amenities. Accommodations in queen feather beds, private baths, quilts, guest robes and private garden. An award-winning inn.

## Santa Fe

Bennett, Gloria
436 Sunset St., 87501
(505) 983-3523

**Amenities:** 1,2,5,6,7,8,10, 15,16
**Breakfast:** C.

**Dbl. Oc.:** $77.00
**Sgl. Oc.:** $60.00

**Sunset House**—Four blocks to Plaza. Fireplace in winter and decks with views in summer. Quiet and artistic atmosphere. Grand piano for those who play. Casitas also available.

## Santa Fe *

Gosse, Jean
2407 Camino Capitan, 87505
(505) 471-4053

**Amenities:** 1,2,6,7,8,10, 15,16
**Breakfast:** C.

**Dbl. Oc.:** $40.00
**Sgl. Oc.:** $35.00

**Jean's Place**—A private home in a quiet residental area offering one room only for guests. We have one dog and one cat living with us. This home is also an alternative (crystal) healing center. We are about 10-15 minutes by car from downtown Santa Fe.

## Santa Fe *

Schneider, Mary Jo
529 E. Palace Ave., 87501
(505) 986-1431

**Amenities:** 1,2,9,10,11,15, 16,17,18
**Breakfast:** C.
**Dbl. Oc.:** $76.73 - $120.58
**Sgl. Oc.:**
**Third Person:** $15.00

**Alexander's Inn**—For a cozy stay in Santa Fe, nestle in a bed and breakfast featuring the best of American country charm. Built in 1903, the inn has been newly renovated to offer modern comfort along with the romance and charm of earlier and simpler times.

| | | | | |
|---|---|---|---|---|
| 1. No Smoking | 5. Tennis Available | 9. Credit Cards Accepted | 13. Lunch Available | 17. Shared Bath |
| 2. No Pets | 6. Golf Available | 10. Personal Checks Accepted | 14. Public Transportation | 18. Afternoon Tea |
| 3. No Children | 7. Swiming Available | 11. Off Season Rates | 15. Reservations Necessary | ★ Commissions given |
| 4. Senior Citizen Rates | 8. Skiing Available | 12. Dinner Available | 16. Private Bath | to Travel Agents |

## Santa Fe *

Walter, Martin
122 Grant Ave., 87501
(505) 983-6678

**Amenities:** 1,2,5,7,8,9,10,11,13,
14,15,16,17
**Breakfast:** F.
**Dbl. Oc.:** $50.00 - $125.00
**Sgl. Oc.:** $50.00 - $125.00
**Third Person:** $15.00
**Child:** $15.00

**Grant Corner Inn**—A delightful bed and breakfast hotel in a restored colonial home two blocks from Santa Fe's historic Plaza. Restaurant serving gourmet breakfast to the public.

## Silver City *

McCormick, Myra B.
P.O. Box 1163, 88062
(505) 538-2538

**Amenities:** 4,10,12,13,14,16
**Breakfast:** F.

**Dbl. Oc.:** $93.29 - $104.14
**Sgl. Oc.:** $53.15
**Third Person:** 32.00
**Child:** under 6 mo. -
no charge

**Bear Mountain Guest Ranch**—A two-story hacienda, three casitas, private baths, amid pinyon- and juniper-clad hills on 160 acres. 160 miles from El Paso and 200 miles north of Silver City. Nature oriented. Dinner-table talk, bicycling, binding and botanizing. Rates include three home-cooked meals.

## Taos *

Carp, Benjamin
132 Frontier Rd.
P.O. Box 584, 87571
(505) 758-4446

**Amenities:** 1,2,5,6,7,8,10,16
**Breakfast:** F.

**Dbl. Oc.:** $60.00 - $85.00
**Sgl. Oc.:** $55.00 - $80.00
**Third Person:** $25.00
**Child:** under 12 yrs. -
$15.00

**American Artists Gallery House**—A charming Southwestern hacienda filled with artwork. Fireplaces, hot tub and gardens. Magnificent view of mountains. Minutes from Plaza, galleries and Ski Valley. No smoking, please. Five guest rooms.

## Taos *

Cheek, Mildred & Don
P.O. Box 2326, 87571
(505) 776-2913

**Amenities:** 1,2,8,9,10,16
**Breakfast:** F.

**Dbl. Oc.:** $50.00 - $80.00
**Sgl. Oc.:** $50.00 - $80.00
**Child:** $20.00

**Stewart House Gallery & Inn**—A unique bed and breakfast inn and fine art gallery in a Taos landmark. Magnificent mountain views. Minutes from Ski Valley, historic Plaza and the Pueblo.

| | | | |
|---|---|---|---|
| 1. No Smoking | 5. Tennis Available | 9. Credit Cards Accepted | 13. Lunch Available | 17. Shared Bath |
| 2. No Pets | 6. Golf Available | 10. Personal Checks Accepted | 14. Public Transportation | 18. Afternoon Tea |
| 3. No Children | 7. Swiming Available | 11. Off Season Rates | 15. Reservations Necessary | ★ Commissions given |
| 4. Senior Citizen Rates | 8. Skiing Available | 12. Dinner Available | 16. Private Bath | to Travel Agents |

## Taos *

Deveaux, Yolanda
P.O. Box 2331, 87571
(800) 866-6548

**Amenities:** 1,2,3,5,8,9,10,11, 15,16
**Breakfast:** F.

**Dbl. Oc.:** $140.00
**Sgl. Oc.:** $95.00
**Third Person:** $25.00

**Taos Country Inn At Rancho Rio Pueblo**—An elegantly restored 19th-century hacienda on 22 acres. One mile from the Plaza, surrounded by Indian meadows, cottonwoods, apple trees, mesa and the Rio Pueblo. Spacious suites feature kiva fireplaces, hand-carved furniture, fine art and cozy down comforters.

---

## Taos *

Hockett, Mary
Hwy 150,
P.O. Box 453, El Prado, 87529
(505) 776-2422

**Amenities:** 1,2,5,6,7,8,9,10, 11,14,15,16,18
**Breakfast:** F.

**Dbl. Oc.:** $92.11 - $173.40
**Third Person:** $10.00

**Salsa Del Salto Bed And Breakfast Inn**—A world-class bed and breakfast inn. This sophisticated Southwestern home offers a pool, hot tub and private tennis court. Elegant rooms, private baths, king-size beds and gourmet breakfast. Located between Taos and the famous Taos Ski Valley.

---

## Taos

McManus, Bonnie
137 Bent St., 87571
(505) 758-9790

**Amenities:** 1,5,7,8,9,10,16
**Breakfast:** C.

**Dbl. Oc.:** $103.90
**Sgl. Oc.:** $92.96
**Third Person:** $15.00
**Child:** under 7 yrs. - no charge

**Casa Feliz**—A beautiful adobe house on charming Bent Street, 1/2 block from Plaza. Southwest-style rooms. Private baths. In *National Historic Registe of Historic Places*. Guided outdoor-adventure tours. Nearby skiing, hiking, rafting and swimming.

---

## Taos

Pelton, Randy
109 Mabel Dodge Lane
P.O. Box 177, 87571
(505) 758-0287

**Amenities:** 1,2,9,10,15, 16,17,18
**Breakfast:** F.

**Dbl. Oc.:** $54.68 - $120.31
**Sgl. Oc.:** $43.75 - $92.97
**Third Person:** $21.87
**Child:** under 3 yrs. - $10.98

**Hacienda Del Sol**—Chosen by *USA Weekend* as one of the 10 most romantic inns. A circa 1800 adobe in a country setting, yet in town. Fireplaces, views, hand-crafted furniture and original art. One room has a jacuzzi and one a steam room! Large outdoor hot tub. Generous breakfast.

---

| | | | |
|---|---|---|---|
| 1. No Smoking | 5. Tennis Available | 9. Credit Cards Accepted | 13. Lunch Available | 17. Shared Bath |
| 2. No Pets | 6. Golf Available | 10. Personal Checks Accepted | 14. Public Transportation | 18. Afternoon Tea |
| 3. No Children | 7. Swiming Available | 11. Off Season Rates | 15. Reservations Necessary | ★ Commissions given |
| 4. Senior Citizen Rates | 8. Skiing Available | 12. Dinner Available | 16. Private Bath | to Travel Agents |

# NEW MEXICO

## Taos *

Vernon, Susan
Box 5303
405 Cordoba Rd., 87571
(505) 758-4777

**Amenities:** 1,2,5,6,7,8,9,10,
16,18
**Breakfast:** F.

**Dbl. Oc.:** $106.94 - $139.68
**Sgl. Oc.:** $96.03 - $139.68
**Third Person:** $16.37
**Child:** $10.91 - $16.37

**Casa De Las Chimeneas**—Located in the heart of Taos. Offers luxurious, traditionally styled accommodations. Nearby art galleries, historic sites, skiing and fine dining. Hot tub and private garden with fountains. Complimentary wine and hors d'oeuvres. Children's rates are for under 12 years.

## Truchas

Curtiss, Frank
P.O. Box 338, 87578
(505) 689-2374

**Amenities:** 1,2,8,10,12,17
**Breakfast:** F.

**Dbl. Oc.:** $50.00
**Sgl. Oc.:** $40.00
**Third Person:** $25.00
**Child:** under 10 yrs. -
$10.00

**Rancho Arriba**—A European-style B&B. A small working farm located on a Spanish colonial land grant. We have a spectacular view, rural location and an informal atmosphere. Rooms are located in the adobe hacienda and breakfast is cooked on a wood-burning stove.

---

1. No Smoking
2. No Pets
3. No Children
4. Senior Citizen Rates
5. Tennis Available
6. Golf Available
7. Swiming Available
8. Skiing Available
9. Credit Cards Accepted
10. Personal Checks Accepted
11. Off Season Rates
12. Dinner Available
13. Lunch Available
14. Public Transportation
15. Reservations Necessary
16. Private Bath
17. Shared Bath
18. Afternoon Tea
★ Commissions given
to Travel Agents

# NEW YORK

## *The Empire State*

Capitol: Albany
Statehood: July 26, 1788; the 11th state
State Motto: Ever Upward
State Song: "I Love New York"
State Bird: Bluebird
State Flower: Rose
State Tree: Sugar Maple

New York is a mecca for tourists. It offers something for everyone. Commercially, it is the greatest manufacturing state in the United States, and it far out-ranks all other states in foreign trade and wholesale and retail trade.

Besides everything else, it is the nation's center for transportation, banking and finance.

It is a farming state, as well. Some of the finest fruits and vegetables are grown here.

Tourists can find just about any kind of recreation in this state, from the quiet and beauty of its mountains and streams, to the Big Apple, New York City, the largest city in the state. New York City offers skyscrapers, the United Nations Building, Statue of Liberty, New York Stock Exchange, and numerous choices of theatres and sports.

Four presidents have been born in this state, Martin Van Buren, Millard Fillmore, Theodore Roosevelt, and Franklin D. Roosevelt.

## Albany *

Tricarico, Janice
531 Western Ave., 12203
(518) 482-1574

**Amenities:** 1,2,3,10,14,17
**Breakfast:** C.
**Dbl. Oc.:** $64.00
**Sgl. Oc.:** $49.00
**Third Person:** $15.00

**Pine Haven Bed & Breakfast**—A century-old, gracious Victorian located one mile from downtown. Within walking distance to restaurants, theatre and shopping. Furnished in antiques, iron and brass beds for a Victorian ambience in the heart of Albany. A half hour to Saratoge and 45 minutes to the Adirondacks.

## Amagansett *

Fariel, Robert
30 Atlantic Ave., 11930
(516) 267-3692

**Amenities:** 1,2,3,5,6,7,10,11, 14,15,16,17
**Breakfast:** F. (C. in summer)

**Dbl. Oc.:** $92.00 - $117.00
**Sgl. Oc.:** $48.00

**Sea Breeze Inn**—A turn-of-the-century house and guest cottages. This small family-owned-and-operated country inn is just two blocks from the ocean. Open year round. Quiet, spacious grounds with gardens, gazebo and an old-fashioned porch. In business with same owners for 33 years.

## Amenia

Flaherty, James
Leedsville Rd.
Box 26, 12501
(914) 373-9681

**Amenities:** 2,3,5,6,7,8,9,10, 12,13,15,16
**Breakfast:** F. (C. - Sundays)

**Dbl. Oc.:** $575.00 - $790.00

**Troutbeck**—A dazzling English manor with four-star cuisine and year-round pools on 442 acres. *Country Inns of New York* said:"Troutbeck must be considered one of the finest inns in the world." Rates cover from 5 p.m. Friday to 2 p.m. Sunday per couple, six meals and all spirits.

## Auburn *

Fitzpatrick, Patricia
102 South St., 13021
(315) 255-0196

**Amenities:** 2,4,5,6,7,8,9,10, 11,13,14,15,16,17, 18
**Breakfast:** F.

**Dbl. Oc.:** $80.25 - $101.65
**Sgl. Oc.:** $58.85
**Third Person:** $7.00
**Child:** under 5 yrs. - no charge

**The Irish Rose, A Victorian Bed & Breakfast**—Get away and step back into the past. A lovely turn-of-the-century Victorian B&B. Swimming pool and skiing. Four fireplaces. Within walking distance to historic homes. Wine trails. Great in all seasons. Your hosts will serve a full gourmet breakfast.

---

1. No Smoking
2. No Pets
3. No Children
4. Senior Citizen Rates
5. Tennis Available
6. Golf Available
7. Swiming Available
8. Skiing Available
9. Credit Cards Accepted
10. Personal Checks Accepted
11. Off Season Rates
12. Dinner Available
13. Lunch Available
14. Public Transportation
15. Reservations Necessary
16. Private Bath
17. Shared Bath
18. Afternoon Tea
★ Commissions given to Travel Agents

## Averill Park

Tomlinson, Thelma
Route 3, Box 301, 12018
(518) 766-5035

**Amenities:** 1,2,3,6,7,8,10,15, 17,18
**Breakfast:** F.

**Dbl. Oc.:** $53.50
**Sgl. Oc.:** $42.80

**Ananas Hus Bed And Breakfast**—A hillside ranch home on 30 acres. Decorated in early American decor. Panoramic views of the Hudson River Valley in West Stephentown. Beauty and tranquility. Near Jiminy Peak and Brodie ski areas, theatres and other cultural activities.

## Bellport

Buck, Carol
21 Brown's Lane, 11713
(516) 286-9421

**Amenities:** 1,2,10,11,14,17
**Breakfast:** F.

**Dbl. Oc.:** $64.50 - $69.88
**Sgl. Oc.:** $43.00
**Third Person:** $16.13
**Child:** under 5 yrs. -
  no charge

**Shell Cottage**—Located in a quaint village on the south shore. A 110-year-old house with three antique-decorated bedrooms, spacious common room and outside porch. Walk to village, fine restaurants and summer theatre. Easy access to ocean beaches. Bikes and canoeing.

## Berlin *

Evans, Edith & Robert
Route 22, 12002
(518) 658-2334

**Amenities:** 4,5,6,7,8,9,10,12, 13,15,16
**Breakfast:** F.

**Dbl. Oc.:** $60.00 - $75.00
**Sgl. Oc.:** $50.00 - $60.00
**Third Person:** $10.00
**Child:** under 2 yrs. -
  no charge

**The Sedgwick Inn**—A historic 1791 inn located in scenic Taconic Valley. Beautifully furnished with antiques. Close to Williamstown Theatre, Tanglewood and other Berkshire attractions. Near downhill and cross-country skiing. Renowned restaurant. Small motel unit behind main house.

## Bolton Landing

Hayes, Cheryl & Richard
7161 Lakeshore Dr.
P.O. Box 537, 12814
(518) 644-5941

**Amenities:** 1,2,3,5,6,7,8,9,10, 12,15,16
**Breakfast:** C.

**Dbl. Oc.:** $85.60 - $101.65
**Sgl. Oc.:** $69.55 - $85.60
**Third Person:** $26.75

**Hayes' Bed & Breakfast Guest House**—A 1900's cottage. Full of charm. Enjoy a panoramic view of the mountains or walk across the street to the beach and relax in the sun. Shopping, antiques, dining and all resort entertainment are just minutes away. A vacationland you will not forget.

---

| | | | |
|---|---|---|---|
| 1. No Smoking | 5. Tennis Available | 9. Credit Cards Accepted | 13. Lunch Available | 17. Shared Bath |
| 2. No Pets | 6. Golf Available | 10. Personal Checks Accepted | 14. Public Transportation | 18. Afternoon Tea |
| 3. No Children | 7. Swiming Available | 11. Off Season Rates | 15. Reservations Necessary | ★ Commissions given |
| 4. Senior Citizen Rates | 8. Skiing Available | 12. Dinner Available | 16. Private Bath | to Travel Agents |

## Bolton Landing *

Richards, Charles
6883 Lakeshore Dr., 12814-0186
(518) 644-2492

**Amenities:** 2,5,6,7,8,10,11,16,17
**Breakfast:** F.
**Dbl. Oc.:** $48.00 - $58.00
**Sgl. Oc.:** $32.00
**Third Person:** $11.00

**Hilltop Cottage B&B**—A renovated caretaker cottage on Lake George in the eastern Adirondacks. Walk to beach, restaurants and marinas. Three rooms with shared baths. Guest cabin. Pets here. Smoking limited. Breakfast on screened porch. German spoken. Knowledgeable hosts. An at-home atmosphere.

## Branchport (New York Finger Lakes Area.)

Lewis, Linda & Robert
453 W. Lake Rd., 14418
(607) 868-4603

**Amenities:** 1,2,5,6,7,8,9,10,
          15,16,17
**Breakfast:** F.
**Dbl. Oc.:** $65.00 - $85.00
**Sgl. Oc.:** $65.00 - $85.00
**Third Person:** $20.00
**Child:** $20.00

**Gone With The Wind On Keuka Lake**—The name paints the picture. An 1887 stone Victorian on 14 acres overlooking our quiet lake cove with picnic gazebo. Capture total relaxation and peace of mind enjoying solarium hot tub, fireplaces, delectable breakfasts, cheerful rooms, private beach with dock and walking trails.

## Brockport

Klein, Anne & Ronn
3741 Lake Rd., 14420
(716) 637-0220

**Amenities:** 2,3,5,6,10,
          15,17,18
**Breakfast:** F.

**Dbl. Oc.:** $55.00
**Sgl. Oc.:** $50.00
**Third Person:** $13.00

**The Portico Bed & Breakfast**—Hospitality abounds in this stately 1850 Greek Revival landmark. Near colleges, museums, lake, shops, farm market and fine restaurants. Spacious rooms, three fireplaces, soft music, antiques and porches contribute to gracious living in casual comfort.

| | | | | |
|---|---|---|---|---|
| 1. No Smoking | 5. Tennis Available | 9. Credit Cards Accepted | 13. Lunch Available | 17. Shared Bath |
| 2. No Pets | 6. Golf Available | 10. Personal Checks Accepted | 14. Public Transportation | 18. Afternoon Tea |
| 3. No Children | 7. Swiming Available | 11. Off Season Rates | 15. Reservations Necessary | ★ Commissions given |
| 4. Senior Citizen Rates | 8. Skiing Available | 12. Dinner Available | 16. Private Bath | to Travel Agents |

## Brooklyn

Paolella, Liana
113 Prospect Park W., 11215
(718) 499-6115

**Amenities:** 1,2,5,9,10,14,15,
16,17
**Breakfast:** F.

**Dbl. Oc.:** $100.00 - $125.00
**Sgl. Oc.:** $90.00 - $125.00
**Third Person:** $35.00
**Child:** under 3 yrs. -
no charge

**Bed And Breakfast On The Park**—Just two miles from downtown Manhattan. A short walk from Brooklyn Museum and Botanical Garden. This 1892 Victorian mansion with views of New York City and Prospect Park has been converted to an urban B&B. Offers a European atmosphere and generous hospitality.

## Burdett *

Martin, Joan
Finger Lakes National Forest
Picnic Area Rd., 14818
(607) 546-8566

**Amenities:** 1,2,4,7,8,9,10,
15,17,18
**Breakfast:** F.

**Dbl. Oc.:** $59.95 - $81.75
**Third Person:** $10.00
**Child:** over 12 yrs. - $10.00

**Red House Country Inn**—Near Watkins Glen and Seneca Lake, in 13,000-acre national forest with 28 miles of hiking and cross-country ski trails. Nearby wineries. A beautiful 1840 farmstead with antiques throughout. Children 12 and over welcome. Dinner rate is $14.90 per person.

## Canandaigua

Freese, Elizabeth
4761 Route 364, Rushville, 1454
(716) 554-6973

**Amenities:** 1,2,7,8,9,10,
11,17
**Breakfast:** F.

**Dbl. Oc.:** $54.00
**Sgl. Oc.:** $37.00
**Third Person:** $15.00
**Child:** $10.00

**Lakeview Farm B&B**—A country home on 170 acres overlooking Canandaigua Lake. Two lakeview, antique-furnished bedrooms with shared baths and upstairs sitting room. Enjoy views from lounge dining area. Nearby pond and beautiful ravine. Public beach, restaurants, concert area and lake attractions. A/C.

## Canandaigua *

Sullivan, Julie & John
2920 Smith Rd., 14424
(716) 394-9232

**Amenities:** 1,2,5,6,7,8,9,10,11,
12,14,15,16,17,18
**Breakfast:** F.
**Dbl. Oc.:** $70.00 - $175.00
**Sgl. Oc.:** $60.00 - $150.00
**Third Person:** $20.00
**Child:** under 2 yrs. - no charge

**J.P. Morgan House**—An incomparable 1810 stone mansion on 46 acres. Quiet. Balconies, jacuzzi, common room with fireplace, six fireplaces, screened porch and patio. Fax. 13 miles from Bristol Mountain, horse-drawn sleigh and wagon rides. Recommended by *Bon Appetit* and *Great Weekend Getaways*.

| | | | |
|---|---|---|---|
| 1. No Smoking | 5. Tennis Available | 9. Credit Cards Accepted | 13. Lunch Available | 17. Shared Bath |
| 2. No Pets | 6. Golf Available | 10. Personal Checks Accepted | 14. Public Transportation | 18. Afternoon Tea |
| 3. No Children | 7. Swiming Available | 11. Off Season Rates | 15. Reservations Necessary | ★ Commissions given |
| 4. Senior Citizen Rates | 8. Skiing Available | 12. Dinner Available | 16. Private Bath | to Travel Agents |

## Cazenovia *

Barr, H. Grey
5 Albany St.
U.S. Route 20, 13035
(315) 655-3431

**Amenities:** 2,6,7,8,9,10,12,15,16
**Breakfast:** C.
**Dbl. Oc.:** $73.83 - $133.75
**Sgl. Oc.:** $63.13 - $101.65
**Third Person:** $5.00 - $15.00

**Brae Loch Inn**—A family-run Scottish inn with old-world charm. Located across from beautiful Cazenovia Lake. Fine dining and Scottish gift shop.

## Chappaqua

Crabtree, Dick & John
11 Kittle Rd., 10514
(914) 666-8044

**Amenities:** 9,10,12,13,16
**Breakfast:** C.

**Dbl. Oc.:** $81.55
**Sgl. Oc.:** $92.45
**Third Person:** $10.00

**Crabtree's Kittle House**—Built in 1790, Crabtree's Kittle House maintains a distinctive blend of country style and comfort. Not to be missed are the dinner specialties of the house including crisp roast duckling and the freshest seafood available.

## Cherry Plain *

Rubin, Helane & Bob
Mattison Hollow
P.O. Box 92, 12040
(518) 658-2946

**Amenities:** 1,2,5,6,7,8,10,12,
15,16,17,18
**Breakfast:** F.

**Dbl. Oc.:** $117.70
**Sgl. Oc.:** $117.70
**Third Person:** $48.15
**Child:** under 6 yrs. -
no charge

**Mattison Hollow**—On the state border of Massachusetts, Vermont and New York. Situated in the Berkshires. Furnished with antiques. A secluded 1790 country home. Minutes from Tanglewood, Williamstown, skiing, hiking, pond and trout brook. Dinner of all natural food is included in the rates.

## Chestertown*

Taylor, Sharon
Friends Lake Rd., 12817
(518) 494-4751

**Amenities:** 1,2,5,6,7,8,9,10,
12,15,16,17
**Breakfast:** F.

**Dbl. Oc.:** $73.00 - $105.00
**Sgl. Oc.:** $45.00 - $80.00

**Friends Lake Inn**—A fully restored 19th-century country inn overlooking Friends Lake. Public rooms include a living room with fireplace, wide veranda and a lake-view lounge. Our award-winning dining room with fireplace is known for its regional and imaginative cuisine.

| | | | | |
|---|---|---|---|---|
| 1. No Smoking | 5. Tennis Available | 9. Credit Cards Accepted | 13. Lunch Available | 17. Shared Bath |
| 2. No Pets | 6. Golf Available | 10. Personal Checks Accepted | 14. Public Transportation | 18. Afternoon Tea |
| 3. No Children | 7. Swiming Available | 11. Off Season Rates | 15. Reservations Necessary | ★ Commissions given |
| 4. Senior Citizen Rates | 8. Skiing Available | 12. Dinner Available | 16. Private Bath | to Travel Agents |

## *Cooperstown* *

Grimes, Joan & Jack
RD #2, Box 514, 13326
(607) 547-9700

**Amenities:** 1,2,5,6,7,8,10,11, 15,16
**Breakfast:** F.

**Dbl. Oc.:** $55.00 - $80.00
**Sgl. Oc.:** $41.25 - $60.00
**Third Person:** $15.00
**Child:** under 2 yrs. - no charge

**The Inn At Brook Willow**—This pastoral retreat is just a skip over a creek that winds its way to the inn. Guests are welcomed into a Victorian home and reborn barn furnished with fine antiques. Before going to the Hall of Fame in the morning, you will enjoy a bountiful meal.

## *Cooperstown* *

Wolff, Margaret & Jim
P.O. Box 1048, 13326-1048
(607) 547-2501

**Amenities:** 1,2,5,6,7,8,10, 11,15,16,17
**Breakfast:** F.
**Dbl. Oc.:** $60.00
**Sgl. Oc.:** $50.00
**Third Person:** $10.00
**Child:** under 5 yrs. - no charge

**Litco Farms Bed & Breakfast.**—Three miles from Cooperstown. Well suited to families and couples. Enjoy our 20x40-foot pool and 70 acres with nature trails. Warm hospitality and marvelous breakfasts will make your visit with us memorable. Shop at Heartworks, our on-site quilt shop.

## *Coram*

Wilson, Mrs. Richard
24 Harrison Ave., 11727
(516) 732-6703

**Amenities:** 1,2,4,5,6,7,10,11, 14,15,16,17,18
**Breakfast:** F.

**Dbl. Oc.:** $55.00 - $75.00
**Sgl. Oc.:** $38.00 - $65.00
**Third Person:** $15.00
**Child:** under 12 yrs. - $10.00

**Be-Our-Guest, Ltd. — A Bed & Breakfast Place**—A comfortable and local home near beaches, golf, shops, ferry and museums. Also a referral service on Long Island, giving our guests a wide selection of homes, prices, locations and amenities. Nearby Port Jefferson, The Hamptons, Stony Brook and great hospitality!

## *Corning*

DePumpo, Mary
188 DeLevan Ave., 14830
(607) 962-2347

**Amenities:** 1,6,7,10,12,13,14, 16,17,18
**Breakfast:** F.

**Dbl. Oc.:** $73.85 - $81.75
**Sgl. Oc.:** $54.50 - $70.85
**Third Person:** $10.90

**The DeLevan House**—A Southern colonial overlooking Corning. Shared and private bath accommodations. Very quiet, private surroundings, full breakfast and warm hospitality. Open all year.

| | | | | |
|---|---|---|---|---|
| 1. No Smoking | 5. Tennis Available | 9. Credit Cards Accepted | 13. Lunch Available | 17. Shared Bath |
| 2. No Pets | 6. Golf Available | 10. Personal Checks Accepted | 14. Public Transportation | 18. Afternoon Tea |
| 3. No Children | 7. Swiming Available | 11. Off Season Rates | 15. Reservations Necessary | ★ Commissions given |
| 4. Senior Citizen Rates | 8. Skiing Available | 12. Dinner Available | 16. Private Bath | to Travel Agents |

## Corning

Donahue, Kathy & Joe
69 E. First St., 14830
(607) 962-6355

**Amenities:** 2,8,10,16,17
**Breakfast:** F.
**Dbl. Oc.:** $60.00 - $80.00
**Sgl. Oc.:** $45.00 - $55.00
**Third Person:** $15.00

**"1865" White Birch Bed And Breakfast**—Imagine a friendly and warm atmosphere in an 1865 Victorian setting. Cozy rooms await our guests with both private and shared baths. Awake to the tantalizing aromas of a full breakfast. Walk to museums, historic Market Street and glass center. The White Birch has it all!

## Corning *

Peer, Winnie & Dick
134 E. First St., 14830
(607) 962-3253

**Amenities:** 9,10,16,17,18
**Breakfast:** F.

**Dbl. Oc.:** $75.00 - $115.00
**Sgl. Oc.:** $65.00 - $108.00
**Third Person:** $20.00
**Child:** under 6 yrs. -
no charge

**Rosewood Inn**—Step back into an elegant time. Enjoy antique-filled guest rooms with private baths. Some with fireplaces. Walk to nearby restored Market Street, Corning's noted glass center, musuems and fine dining. Close to wineries, Watkins Glen racing and most finger lakes.

## Croten-on-Hudson *

Notarius, Barbara
49 Van Wyck St., 10520
(914) 271-6737

**Amenities:** 1,7,9,10,14,15,16,17
**Breakfast:** F.
**Dbl. Oc.:** $60.00 - $140.00
**Sgl. Oc.:** $45.00 - $110.75
**Third Person:** $10.00
**Child:** $10.00

**Alexander Hamilton House**—Westchester's first B&B, circa 1889, is a stately Victorian home on a cliff above the Hudson. Many antiques, air conditioning, swimming pool and piano. Close to West Point, the Sleepy Hollow restorations and the corporate area around White Plains. Suite with fireplace.

| | | | |
|---|---|---|---|
| 1. No Smoking | 5. Tennis Available | 9. Credit Cards Accepted | 13. Lunch Available | 17. Shared Bath |
| 2. No Pets | 6. Golf Available | 10. Personal Checks Accepted | 14. Public Transportation | 18. Afternoon Tea |
| 3. No Children | 7. Swiming Available | 11. Off Season Rates | 15. Reservations Necessary | ★ Commissions given |
| 4. Senior Citizen Rates | 8. Skiing Available | 12. Dinner Available | 16. Private Bath | to Travel Agents |

## Davenport

Hodge, Bill
Main St., 13750
(607) 278-5068

**Amenities:** 5,6,7,8,9,10,12,16,17
**Breakfast:** C.
**Dbl. Oc.:** $38.08 - $58.24
**Sgl. Oc.:** $20.14 - $38.16
**Third Person:** $10.60
**Child:** under 11 yrs. - $5.30

**Davenport Inn**—A historic tavern built in 1819, close to Cooperstown and Oneonta. Our dining room features corn fritters! Private and shared baths available. Five rooms. Reservations, please! Full breakfast served on Sundays from May 25 -December 9.

---

## Dolgeville

Naizby, Adrianna
44 Stewart, 13329
(315) 429-3249

**Amenities:** 2,6,7,8,9,10, 16,17
**Breakfast:** F.

**Dbl. Oc.:** $48.15
**Sgl. Oc.:** $42.80
**Third Person:** $10.00

**Adrianna Bed And Breakfast**—Located off Thruway, Exit 29 A. Cozy residence in charming village, featuring eclectic blend of antique and contemporary furnishings. Convenient to Saratoga, Cooperstown, Utica, historic sights and diamond mines. Air conditioning.

---

## Downsville

Adams, Nancy & Harry
Main St.
Route 206, 13755
(607) 363-2757

**Amenities:** 1,2,4,6,7,12, 13,17,18
**Breakfast:** F.

**Dbl. Oc.:** $50.00
**Sgl. Oc.:** $35.00
**Third Person:** $15.00
**Child:** under 6 yrs. - $10.00

**Adams' Farm House Inn**—Come and enjoy our country hospitality. We will pamper you with our hearty breakfast, afternoon sweets and an evening drink. Friendly conversation and information about the local Catskill area. Lots of nearby fishing and antiquing. We have a beautiful farmhouse.

---

## Dryden

Brownell, Margaret
9 James St.
P.O. Box 119, 13053
(607) 844-8052

**Amenities:** 1,2,5,6,7,8,10, 15,17
**Breakfast:** C.

**Dbl. Oc.:** $55.00 & up
**Sgl. Oc.:** $49.50 & up
**Third Person:** $11.00 & up
**Child:** under 1 yr. - no charge

**Margaret Thacher's Spruce Haven B&B**—A log home surrounded by tall spruce trees, giving the feeling of being in the woods. Quiet street. Within 12 miles of Ithaca, Cortland, lakes, golf, skiing, colleges, museums and restaurants.

---

| | | | |
|---|---|---|---|
| 1. No Smoking | 5. Tennis Available | 9. Credit Cards Accepted | 13. Lunch Available | 17. Shared Bath |
| 2. No Pets | 6. Golf Available | 10. Personal Checks Accepted | 14. Public Transportation | 18. Afternoon Tea |
| 3. No Children | 7. Swiming Available | 11. Off Season Rates | 15. Reservations Necessary | ★ Commissions given |
| 4. Senior Citizen Rates | 8. Skiing Available | 12. Dinner Available | 16. Private Bath | to Travel Agents |

## Eagle Bay

Bennett, Bonnie & Douglas
Big Moose Lake, 13331
(315) 357-2042

**Amenities:** 2,5,6,7,8,9,11,12,
13,15,16,17
**Breakfast:** C.

**Dbl. Oc.:** $35.00 - $80.00
**Child:** $8.00 (cot)

**Big Moose Inn**—Located on Big Moose Lake. Our 23rd year. Cozy Adirondack rooms, lakeside dining, cocktail lounge, guest lounge with fireplace and neighboring marina. Enjoy outdoor activities or just relax. Complimentary hot cider and fruit.

## Fair Haven

Brown, Sara
Stafford St.
Box 378, 13064
(315) 947-5817

**Amenities:** 1,2,4,9,10,11,17
**Breakfast:** C.

**Dbl. Oc.:** $60.00
**Sgl. Oc.:** $37.45
**Child:** under 12 yrs. -
$10.00

**Brown's Village Inn**—A country home offering old-fashioned hospitality in a warm and friendly atmosphere. In a quiet area within walking distance to shops and restaurants. Two miles to beach and Renaissance Faire. Antique shop on property.

## Fair Haven *

Frost, Chris & Brad
West Bay Rd.
Box 241, 13064
(315) 947-5331

**Amenities:** 1,2,8,9,10,11,
16,17
**Breakfast:** F.

**Dbl. Oc.:** $70.00
**Sgl. Oc.:** $35.00
**Third Person:** $35.00
**Child:** under 10 yrs. -
$25.00

**Frost Haven Resort, Inc.**—Comfortable and homey rooms overlooking peaceful Little Sodus Bay. A hearty, full breakfast served 5-9 a.m. Spacious grounds. Just steps from waterfront and docking facilities. Spectacular Lake Ontario trout and salmon fishing. We invite you to visit us. Open year round.

## Fair Haven *

Sarber, A. Kathleen
P.O. Box 390, 13064
(315) 947-5282

**Amenities:** 1,2,3,9,10,17
**Breakfast:** F.

**Dbl. Oc.:** $48.15
**Sgl. Oc.:** $37.45

**Black Creek Farm**—Relax in our restored, circa 1888, Victorian farmhouse offering two cozy antique-filled rooms with shared bath. Located just minutes from boating and swimming on Lake Ontario and the Renaissance Faire. A full breakfast served 5-9 a.m. Antique shop on premises.

| | | | | |
|---|---|---|---|---|
| 1. No Smoking | 5. Tennis Available | 9. Credit Cards Accepted | 13. Lunch Available | 17. Shared Bath |
| 2. No Pets | 6. Golf Available | 10. Personal Checks Accepted | 14. Public Transportation | 18. Afternoon Tea |
| 3. No Children | 7. Swiming Available | 11. Off Season Rates | 15. Reservations Necessary | ★ Commissions given |
| 4. Senior Citizen Rates | 8. Skiing Available | 12. Dinner Available | 16. Private Bath | to Travel Agents |

## Fleischmanns *

Ruff, Peggy
Main St., 12430
(914) 254-4884

**Amenities:** 5,6,8,9,10,14,16,17
**Breakfast:** F.
**Dbl. Oc.:** $65.00 - $85.00
**Sgl. Oc.:** $55.00 - $60.00
**Child:** under 3 yrs. - $10.00

**Timberdoodle Inn**—A sportsman's village Victorian in Catskill Mountains. Relaxed and comfortable environment. English country theme. Bountiful breakfasts. Ski nearby Belleayre slopes. Hike forest preserve trails. Fish world-famous streams. Trout fishing instructions available by host.

---

## Fulton *

Rice, Joyce
R.D. #1, Box 176, 13069
(315) 593-3699

**Amenities:** 1,2,6,9,10,15,16
**Breakfast:** F.

**Dbl. Oc.:** $64.20 - $90.00
**Sgl. Oc.:** $53.50 - $69.75
**Third Person:** $16.00

**Battle Island Inn**—A pre-Civil War farm estate, restored and furnished with period antiques. Golf and cross-country skiing across the road. Rooms include TV, phone, private bath and desk. Full breakfast served in our elegant 1840's dining room. Sit on one of four porches or stroll through the gardens.

---

## Geneva *

Schickel, Jr., Norbert H.
1001 Lochland Rd., 14456
(800) 3GENEVA, (315) 789-7190

**Amenities:** 1,2,5,6,7,8,9,10,11,
            12,13,16
**Breakfast:** C.
**Dbl. Oc.:** $169.00 - $322.00
**Sgl. Oc.:** $159.00 - $312.00
**Third Person:** $52.00
**Child:** $17.00 - $29.00

**Geneva On The Lake**—An elegant, small resort in New York's finger lakes wine district. Enjoy luxurious suites overlooking Seneca Lake. Furnished terrace, formal gardens, pool and sailing. Candlelight dining with live musical entertainment on the weekends. AAA and rated four diamond.

---

| | | | |
|---|---|---|---|
| 1. No Smoking | 5. Tennis Available | 9. Credit Cards Accepted | 13. Lunch Available | 17. Shared Bath |
| 2. No Pets | 6. Golf Available | 10. Personal Checks Accepted | 14. Public Transportation | 18. Afternoon Tea |
| 3. No Children | 7. Swiming Available | 11. Off Season Rates | 15. Reservations Necessary | ★ Commissions given |
| 4. Senior Citizen Rates | 8. Skiing Available | 12. Dinner Available | 16. Private Bath | to Travel Agents |

## *Germantown*

Mastro, Marcia & Dan
RD #3, Box 287, 12526
(518) 537-6945

**Amenities:** 1,2,4,5,6,7,9,10,
15,16,17
**Breakfast:** F.

**Dbl. Oc.:** $64.20
**Sgl. Oc.:** $53.50

**Fox Run Bed & Breakfast**—A beautiful 1807 colonial located amidst the Hudson Valley's most popular historic sites. Guests enjoy country hospitality and a warm, relaxed atmosphere. Spacious air-conditioned rooms and many extras that say "welcome." Bicycles. Open May 1 - October 31.

## *Gowanda*

Lay, Phyllis
R.D. #1, Box 543, 14070
(716) 532-2168

**Amenities:** 5,6,7,8,10,17
**Breakfast:** F.

**Dbl. Oc.:** $40.00
**Sgl. Oc.:** $30.00
**Third Person:** $10.00
**Child:** under 12 yrs. - $5.00

**The Tepee**—Located on the Cattaraugus Indian Reservation. Light, bright rooms. Seneca artifacts. Tours of Indian Reservation and Amish country. Indian pow-wow and fall festival features Indian food and crafts. Hot-air balloon rides can be arranged.

## *Grafton* *

Risedorf, Elsie & Ken
Route 2
Box 331, 12082
(518) 279-9489

**Amenities:** 10,12,13,17
**Breakfast:** F.
**Dbl. Oc.:** $58.00
**Sgl. Oc.:** $43.00
**Third Person:** $12.00
**Child:** under 10 yrs. - $5.00

**Grafton Inn Bed & Breakfast**—This country farmhouse, built in 1794, has had a "checkered career." Twenty miles to Bennington, Vermont; Williamstown, Massachusetts; and Albany, New York. Concerts, museums, discount shopping, hiking, hunting and cross-country skiing. Closed December 15 - February 15.

| | | | |
|---|---|---|---|
| 1. No Smoking | 5. Tennis Available | 9. Credit Cards Accepted | 13. Lunch Available | 17. Shared Bath |
| 2. No Pets | 6. Golf Available | 10. Personal Checks Accepted | 14. Public Transportation | 18. Afternoon Tea |
| 3. No Children | 7. Swiming Available | 11. Off Season Rates | 15. Reservations Necessary | ★ Commissions given |
| 4. Senior Citizen Rates | 8. Skiing Available | 12. Dinner Available | 16. Private Bath | to Travel Agents |

## *Greenville* *

Dalton, Letitia & Eliot
South St.
R.D. #1, Box 2, 12083
(518) 966-5219

**Amenities:** 2,5,6,7,8,9,10,11,12,
13,14,15,16,17,18
**Breakfast:** F.
**Dbl. Oc.:** $80.25 - $117.70
**Sgl. Oc.:** $58.85 - $96.30
**Third Person:** $25.00
**Child:** under 10 years - $15.00

**Greenville Arms**—This is a true country inn that has provided hospitality to travelers for 35 years. A full country breakfast is served in the brick-hearthed dining rooms. On-premise restaurant features outstanding cuisine. Pool and croquet provide relaxation and old-fashionedness.

## *Groton* *

Salerno, Doris
210 Old Peroville Rd., 13073
(607) 898-5786

**Amenities:** 1,2,4,5,6,7,8,10,
11,15,16
**Breakfast:** F.
**Dbl. Oc.:** $66.00
**Sgl. Oc.:** $44.00
**Third Person:** 22.00
**Child:** under 5 years - $11.00

**Austin Manor Bed & Breakfast**—A restored Victorian with 14 spacious rooms on 185 acres of land. Fifteen minutes from Cayuga Lake, CornellUniversity, downtown Ithaca, Cortland, finger lakes, wineries, gorges, waterfalls, hiking, skiing, restaurants, theatres, museums, boating and craft shops.

## *Hamlin* *

Hollink, Shirley
1960 Redman Rd., 14464-9635
(716) 964-7528

**Amenities:** 1,3,10,17,18
**Breakfast:** F.

**Dbl. Oc.:** $61.05
**Sgl. Oc.:** $55.50
**Third Person:** $23.20

**Sandy Creek Manor House**—A quiet country setting surrounds this 1910 English Tudor on six wooded acres and sandy creek. Stained-glass windows, an antique player piano and a massive front porch takes you back in time. One-half hour to Rochester and 1-1/2 hours to Niagara Falls along the Seaway Trail.

| | | | | |
|---|---|---|---|---|
| 1. No Smoking | 5. Tennis Available | 9. Credit Cards Accepted | 13. Lunch Available | 17. Shared Bath |
| 2. No Pets | 6. Golf Available | 10. Personal Checks Accepted | 14. Public Transportation | 18. Afternoon Tea |
| 3. No Children | 7. Swiming Available | 11. Off Season Rates | 15. Reservations Necessary | ★ Commissions given |
| 4. Senior Citizen Rates | 8. Skiing Available | 12. Dinner Available | 16. Private Bath | to Travel Agents |

## *Hammondsport*

Bowman, Manita & Jack
61 Lake St.
P.O. Box 586, 14840
(607) 569-2516

**Amenities:** 1,2,3,10,16
**Breakfast:** C. Plus
**Dbl. Oc.:** $76.30
**Sgl. Oc.:** $65.40

**The Bowman House, A Bed And Breakfast**—Quiet comfort in picturesque Hammondsport Village. Enjoy the charm of this 1800's Queen Anne Victorian home in a comfortably elegant style. Sitting rooms, library and large second-floor bedrooms with private baths. Gracious hosts, privacy and personal touches.

## *Hammondsport*

Carl, Linda & Walter
17 Sheather St.
P.O. Box 366, 14840
(607) 569-2440, (607) 569-3629

**Amenities:** 1,2,3,5,7,9,15,16, 17,18
**Breakfast:** F.
**Dbl. Oc.:** $62.00
**Sgl. Oc.:** $51.00

**J.S. Hubbs Bed And Breakfast**—Come and relax in our family home. This historic Greek Revival (ink bottle) house was built in 1840 and has been in our family for almost 100 years. We offer a suite, single and double rooms with two private baths and three halfs. One-half block from Lake Keuka.

## *Hammondsport*

Laufersweiler, Ellen & Bucky
11 William St., 14840
(607) 569-3402, (607) 569-3483

**Amenities:** 1,2,3,5,6,7,8,10,15,16
**Breakfast:** F.
**Dbl. Oc.:** $60.50 - $82.50
**Sgl. Oc.:** $55.00 - $66.00
**Third Person:** $22.00

**The Blushing Rose B&B**—The Blushing Rose B&B extends an invitation to relax in a restored country home with the comfort of today. Four rooms with private baths. Copious breakfasts. Nearby historic village, wineries, museums and Corning. Quietly romantic ruffles and lace.

| | | | | |
|---|---|---|---|---|
| 1. No Smoking | 5. Tennis Available | 9. Credit Cards Accepted | 13. Lunch Available | 17. Shared Bath |
| 2. No Pets | 6. Golf Available | 10. Personal Checks Accepted | 14. Public Transportation | 18. Afternoon Tea |
| 3. No Children | 7. Swiming Available | 11. Off Season Rates | 15. Reservations Necessary | ★ Commissions given |
| 4. Senior Citizen Rates | 8. Skiing Available | 12. Dinner Available | 16. Private Bath | to Travel Agents |

## Hampton Bays*

Ute, Mrs.
Box 106, 11946
(516) 728-3560

**Amenities:** 2,3,5,6,7,10,11,15,16
**Breakfast:** F.
**Dbl. Oc.:** $75.00 - $100.00
**Sgl. Oc.:** $70.00 - $95.00
**Third Person:** $25.00 - $30.00

**House On The Water**—Eighty miles east of New York City, seven miles to Southampton and two miles to ocean beaches. Two-acre garden on bay. Terrace, lounges and kitchen privileges. Bicycles, windsurfer and pedal boat. Quiet location. Rooms with private bath, TV, water view and private entrance.

## Hancock

Toth, Adele & Jim
RD 1, Box 232B, Walton, 13856
(607) 865-7254

**Amenities:** 1,2,4,6,8,10,14,15, 16,17
**Breakfast:** C.

**Dbl. Oc.:** $41.60 - $57.20
**Sgl. Oc.:** $36.40
**Third Person:** $15.60
**Child:** under 2 years - free crib

**Sunrise Inn Bed & Breakfast**—A 19th-century farmhouse with two cozy guest rooms. Cabin, woodstove, gazebo and antique shop. Trout creek for guests to enjoy in a peaceful, country setting. Family pets in residence. 135 miles northsest of New York City. Fine local dining.

## Hempstead (on Garden City line) *

Duvall, Wendy
237 Cathedral Ave., 11550
(516) 292-9219

**Amenities:** 1,2,14,15,16
**Breakfast:** F.

**Dbl. Oc.:** $64.80 - $81.00
**Sgl. Oc.:** $64.80 - $81.00
**Third Person:** $15.00
**Child:** under 6 yrs. - $10.00

**Duvall B&B**—Gracious old Dutch colonial nestled in trees. Fine restaurant and shops within a walk. Period decor. Restored antiques. Selected for two house tours. Air conditioning and color TV. Relax with cheese and wine on arrival. Near airports, train to New York City and Long Island.

## Hobart *

Barber, Joyce
R.D. #1, Box 191, 13788
(607) 538-9338

**Amenities:** 1,2,9,10,16
**Breakfast:** F.

**Dbl. Oc.:** $60.00
**Sgl. Oc.:** $55.00
**Child:** $10.00

**Breezy Acres Farm Bed & Breakfast**—Our guests return again and again because of the friendly atmosphere and great breakfasts. Immaculate and beautifully decorated guest rooms. All private baths. Jacuzzi, fireplaces and gift shop. 300 wooded acres. Close to skiing, hunting and fishing. Country hospitality.

| | | | |
|---|---|---|---|
| 1. No Smoking | 5. Tennis Available | 9. Credit Cards Accepted | 13. Lunch Available | 17. Shared Bath |
| 2. No Pets | 6. Golf Available | 10. Personal Checks Accepted | 14. Public Transportation | 18. Afternoon Tea |
| 3. No Children | 7. Swiming Available | 11. Off Season Rates | 15. Reservations Necessary | ★ Commissions given to Travel Agents |
| 4. Senior Citizen Rates | 8. Skiing Available | 12. Dinner Available | 16. Private Bath | |

## Hoosick Falls

Bar-Zeev, Karin
Route 67, No. Bennington,12090
(518) 686-4880

**Amenities:** 1,9,10,15,16,17

**Breakfast:** F.

**Dbl. Oc.:** $50.00 - $65.00
**Sgl. Oc.:** $50.00 - $65.00
**Third Person:** $15,00
**Child:** under 6 yrs. -
no charge

**The Gypsy Lady B&B**—Just six miles from Bennington, Vermont or a 1/2 hour from Albany, New York. This renovated stagecoach inn is warm and welcoming. A hot tub and sauna adds to the cozy ambience. Rural, yet convenient to all recreational and cultural amenities make us the perfect weekend getaway.

## Ithaca

Grunberg, Wanda
P.O. Box 581, 14851
(800) 274-4771

**Amenities:** 9,10,11,15,16,
17,18

**Breakfast:** F.

**Dbl. Oc.:** $58.85 - $69.55
**Sgl. Oc.:** $48.00 - $58.85
**Third Person:** $15.00
**Child:** under 3 yrs. -
no charge

**Log Country Inn**—The rustic charm of a log house at the edge of a 7,000-acre state forest. Modern accommodations provided in the spirit of international hospitality. Three rooms. Homey atmosphere. Quiet and peaceful.

## Ithaca

Tomlinson, Jeanne
224 Bostwick Rd., 14850
(607) 272-8756

**Amenities:** 1,9,10,15,16,17
**Breakfast:** F.

**Dbl. Oc.:** $70.00 - $110.00
**Sgl. Oc.:** $70.00 - $110.00
**Third Person:** $20.00
**Child:** under 8 yrs. - $10.00

**Glendale Farm Bed & Breakfast**—Five guest rooms and one cottage. Shared and private baths. Located in a charming country setting. We are convenient to Cornell University, Ithaca College, Cayuga Wine Trail and two state parks.

## Jamesvile *

Mentz, Nancy & Alex
3740 Eager Rd., 13078
(315) 492-3517

**Amenities:** 1,2,4,8,10,12,13,
17

**Breakfast:** C.

**Dbl. Oc.:** $55.00
**Sgl. Oc.:** $40.00
**Third Person:** $5.00
**Child:** under 5 yrs. - $5.00

**High Meadows B&B**—Enjoy country hospitality. High in the hills twelve miles south of Syracuse, New York. A plant filled solarium, fireplace and a magnificent view. Whatever your pleasure. A homemade continental breakfast awaits you. We are here to serve you and make your stay a pleasant one.

| | | | |
|---|---|---|---|
| 1. No Smoking | 5. Tennis Available | 9. Credit Cards Accepted | 13. Lunch Available | 17. Shared Bath |
| 2. No Pets | 6. Golf Available | 10. Personal Checks Accepted | 14. Public Transportation | 18. Afternoon Tea |
| 3. No Children | 7. Swiming Available | 11. Off Season Rates | 15. Reservations Necessary | ★ Commissions given |
| 4. Senior Citizen Rates | 8. Skiing Available | 12. Dinner Available | 16. Private Bath | to Travel Agents |

# NEW YORK

## Keene *

Wilson, Joe-Pete
Alstead Hill Rd., 12942
(518) 576-2221, Fax: (518) 576-2071

**Amenities:** 2,5,6,7,8,9,10,12,
13,15,16,17,18
**Breakfast:** F.
**Dbl. Oc.:** $108.00 - $130.00
**Sgl. Oc.:** $54.00 - $78.18
**Third Person:** $22.50
**Child:** under 2 yrs. - $12.50

**The Bark Eater Inn**—Located on a spacious farm, minutes from the Olympic Village of Lake Placid. All summer and winter activities available. Originally a stagecoach stopover, the inn is a haven for those who seek simple, but gracious, accommodations and memorable dining.

## Lake Placid

Billerman, Gail & Bill
59 Sentinel Rd., 12946
(518) 523-3419

**Amenities:** 2,8,10,11
**Breakfast:** F.

**Dbl. Oc.:** $45.00 - $65.00
**Sgl. Oc.:** $30.00
**Third Person:** $10.00

**Blackberry Inn**—A large colonial situated one mile from the center of town, close to all recreational and sightseeing activities. Newly redecorated rooms and a home-baked breakfast await our guests.

## Lake Placid *

Blazer, Cathy & Teddy
3 Highland Pl.,12946
(518) 523-2377

**Amenities:** 2,5,6,7,8,9,10,11,
14,16
**Breakfast:** F.

**Dbl. Oc.:** $53.50 - $91.00
**Sgl. Oc.:** $48.00 - $80.00
**Third Person:** $13.00 -
$16.00
**Child:** under 10 yrs. - $9.00

**Highland House Inn**—This inn/cottage is centrally located in a quiet residential setting in the village. All facilities are tastefully decorated. All have private baths. The cottage has all the comforts of home, including a fireplace. Blueberry pancakes are a renowned specialty!

## Lake Placid

Hoffman, Carol
31 Sentinel Rd., 12946
(518) 523-9350

**Amenities:** 1,2,9,10,16,17
**Breakfast:** C.

**Dbl. Oc.:** $42.80
**Third Person:** $7.00

**Spruce Lodge B&B**—A family-run lodge, close to all area activities. Located within the limits of Lake Placid, in the heart of the beautiful Adirondack Mountains.

---

| | | | |
|---|---|---|---|
| 1. No Smoking | 5. Tennis Available | 9. Credit Cards Accepted | 13. Lunch Available | 17. Shared Bath |
| 2. No Pets | 6. Golf Available | 10. Personal Checks Accepted | 14. Public Transportation | 18. Afternoon Tea |
| 3. No Children | 7. Swiming Available | 11. Off Season Rates | 15. Reservations Necessary | ★ Commissions given |
| 4. Senior Citizen Rates | 8. Skiing Available | 12. Dinner Available | 16. Private Bath | to Travel Agents |

## Lake Placid

Johnson, Carol & Roy
15 Interlaken Ave., 12946
(518) 523-3180

**Amenities:** 1,3,4,5,6,7,8,9,10, 12,15,16,18
**Breakfast:** F.

**Dbl. Oc.:** $122.00 - $186.00
**Sgl. Oc.:** $97.60
**Third Person:** $40.00

**Interlaken Inn & Restaurant**—A Victorian inn in the heart of Lake Placid featuring a gourmet restaurant and 12 uniquely decorated rooms. The inn has tin ceilings, a cozy fireplace in the living room and lots of lace and charm. Nearby, you can enjoy golf, skiing or any pleasures of the area.

## LeRoy

Choquet, Warren
7856 Griswold Circle, 14482
(716) 768-2340

**Amenities:** 2,6,9,10,15,16
**Breakfast:** C.

**Dbl. Oc.:** $48.00 - $59.00
**Sgl. Oc.:** $38.00
**Third Person:** $11.00

**Edson House**—Many nearby places to explore: Letchworth State Park (theGrand Canyon of the East); Niagara Falls; Genesee Country Museum; Sonnenberg Gardens in Canandaigua; museums and activities in Rochester; horse racing in Batavia and Hamlin Beach State Park. Private baths.

## Mt. Tremper

Caselli, Lou
Cmr. of Route 212 & Wittenberg Rd.
P.O. Box 51, 12457
(914) 688-5329

**Amenities:** 1,2,3,5,7,8,9,10, 15,16,17
**Breakfast:** F.
**Dbl. Oc.:** $64.20 - $96.30

**Mt. Tremper Inn**—Victorian ambience plus museum antiques await you in this 1850, 23-room mansion. Large parlor with fireplace, game/reading room and classical music. Near Woodstock and all ski slopes. No children/pets. Romantic. Elegant. Seen in the *New York Times* and many other feature articles.

## Newfane

Hoy, Peg & Bill
2516 Lockport Olcott Rd., 14108
(716) 778-9843

**Amenities:** 1,10,15,17
**Breakfast:** C.

**Dbl. Oc.:** $40.00
**Sgl. Oc.:** $30.00
**Third Person:** $10.00 - $20.00
**Child:** no charge - $5.00

**Creekside Bed & Breakfast**—A large country home. Four large and sunny bedrooms. Two full, shared baths. Outside deck overlooks creek with duck sand geese. Homemade muffins and jams. Three miles to Olcott Harbor and great fishing. Niagara Falls and Fort Niagara Park only one-half hour away.

| | | | | |
|---|---|---|---|---|
| 1. No Smoking | 5. Tennis Available | 9. Credit Cards Accepted | 13. Lunch Available | 17. Shared Bath |
| 2. No Pets | 6. Golf Available | 10. Personal Checks Accepted | 14. Public Transportation | 18. Afternoon Tea |
| 3. No Children | 7. Swiming Available | 11. Off Season Rates | 15. Reservations Necessary | ★ Commissions given |
| 4. Senior Citizen Rates | 8. Skiing Available | 12. Dinner Available | 16. Private Bath | to Travel Agents |

## *Newfield* *

Carroll-Carney, Diane
1076 Elmira Rd. (Ithaca town line), 14867
(607) 273-7133

**Amenities:** 1,2,3,9,10,11,14,15,16
**Breakfast:** F.
**Dbl. Oc.:** $85.00
**Sgl. Oc.:** $75.00
**Third Person:** $25.00
**Child:** under 14 yrs. - $25.00

**Decker Pond Inn**—An elegant 1830 inn next to state park. On 10 acres with a pond for fishing and skating. Close to colleges and downtown Ithaca. Two-room suite with fireplace. Beautiful rooms furnished with antiques. Veranda overlooks pond.

## *Nichols* *

Hoffman, Barbara & Harry
E. River Rd.
Box 285, 13812
(607) 699-3222

**Amenities:** 1,2,3,6,10,15,16,18
**Breakfast:** F.
**Dbl. Oc.:** $43.60 - $49.05
**Sgl. Oc.:** $43.60 - $49.05

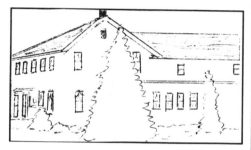

**Fawn's Grove Bed And Breakfast**—Country comfort and warm hospitality best describe Fawn's Grove. Bedrooms are beautifully furnished with queen-sized beds. Breakfast includes delicious homemade breads. Centrally located for trips to finger lakes, Corning Glass and Baseball Hall of Fame.

## *North Hudson*

Schoch, Patricia & Peter
Route 9, 12855
(518) 532-9255

**Amenities:** 2,5,6,7,8,10, 12,17
**Breakfast:** F.

**Dbl. Oc.:** $48.15 - $58.85
**Sgl. Oc.:** $37.45 - $48.15
**Third Person:** $16.05

**Pine Tree Inn B&B**—A turn-of-the-century classic Adirondack inn. Homemade breads with full breakfast. Near tourist attractions. Nearby cross-country and downhill skiing. Open all year. One-half mile north on Route 9 from Exit 29 on I-87.

| | | | |
|---|---|---|---|
| 1. No Smoking | 5. Tennis Available | 9. Credit Cards Accepted | 13. Lunch Available | 17. Shared Bath |
| 2. No Pets | 6. Golf Available | 10. Personal Checks Accepted | 14. Public Transportation | 18. Afternoon Tea |
| 3. No Children | 7. Swiming Available | 11. Off Season Rates | 15. Reservations Necessary | ★ Commissions given |
| 4. Senior Citizen Rates | 8. Skiing Available | 12. Dinner Available | 16. Private Bath | to Travel Agents |

## Parish

House, Frank
RD 2, County Route 38, 13131
(315) 625-7665

**Amenities:** 4,5,6,7,8,10, 11,17
**Breakfast:** C.

**Dbl. Oc.:** $42.80
**Sgl. Oc.:** $31.20
**Third Person:** $10.70
**Child:** under 13 yrs.
no charge

**Springbrook Farm Bed & Breakfast**—An apartment-like facility with four bedrooms. Each room has a double and a single bed. There is a fully equipped kitchen/lounge. A hot tub/spa is available. Beautiful country just 1-1/2 miles off Interstate 81 and 30 miles from Syracuse, Watertown and Oswego.

## Penn Yan *

White, Deborah
158 Main St., 14527
(315) 536-3101

**Amenities:** 1,2,5,6,7,8,9,10,15,16,18
**Breakfast:** F.
**Dbl. Oc.:** $69.55 - $80.25
**Sgl. Oc.:** $58.85 - $69.55
**Third Person:** $10.00
**Child:** $10.00

**The Fox Inn**—Located in Penn Yan, the center of the finger lakes wine district. An 1820 Greek Revival on manicured acre with gracious rose garden. Five bedrooms with private baths. Antiques and Orientals. Comfortable elegance in fine homeowned by the Fox family since 1888.

## Pittstown

Towne, Margaret
RD 2, Box 82, 12185
(518) 663-8369, (518) 686-7331

**Amenities:** 1,6,7,8,10,14,15, 16,17,18
**Breakfast:** F.

**Dbl. Oc.:** $35.00
**Sgl. Oc.:** $25.00
**Child:** no charge

**Maggie Towne's B&B**—Maggie Towne's B&B is just off Route 7. A lovely old colonial. Lawns and trees welcome playing children. Twenty miles to historic Bennington, Vermont. Thirty miles to Saratoga. No smoking, please. Enjoy a glass of wine on porch or by the fireplace. Free crib.

## Port Jefferson *

Burk, Kathleen
415 W. Broadway/Route 25A, 11777
(516) 474-1111

**Amenities:** 2,4,9,10,14,16,17,18
**Breakfast:** C.
**Dbl. Oc.:** $48.00 - $125.00
**Sgl. Oc.:** $48.00 - $125.00
**Third Person:** $10.00

**Compass Rose Bed & Breakfast**—An old home dating from the 1820's in a historic ship-building village known for its quaint shops and fine dining. It offers rooms and suites with a colonial atmosphere. Cable TV. Wine and cheese are served every evening in the rose parlor.

| | | | |
|---|---|---|---|
| 1. No Smoking | 5. Tennis Available | 9. Credit Cards Accepted | 13. Lunch Available | 17. Shared Bath |
| 2. No Pets | 6. Golf Available | 10. Personal Checks Accepted | 14. Public Transportation | 18. Afternoon Tea |
| 3. No Children | 7. Swiming Available | 11. Off Season Rates | 15. Reservations Necessary | ★ Commissions given |
| 4. Senior Citizen Rates | 8. Skiing Available | 12. Dinner Available | 16. Private Bath | to Travel Agents |

## Queensbury — Glens Falls

Crislip, Mr. & Mrs. Ned
Ridge Rd.
R.D. #1, Box 57, 12804
(518) 793-6869

Amenities: 1,5,7,8,9,10,11, 15,16
Breakfast: F.

Dbl. Oc.: $45.75
Child: $10.00

Crislip's Bed & Breakfast—Located in the Adirondack's resort area. It is a historic home featuring spacious and antique-filled rooms with private baths. Recreational and cultural sites nearby at Lake George and Saratoga. Off I-87. In winter, guests can ski on West Mountain.

## Randolph *

Hill, Bradley
252 Main St., 14772
(716) 358-9067

Amenities: 1,5,6,8,10,15,17
Breakfast: F.

Dbl. Oc.: $37.45
Sgl. Oc.: $32.10
Third Person: $10.70

The Colonial House—Located in the heart of western New York's Amish community. Comfortable guest rooms feature Amish furniture and quilts. Minutes from ski slopes, golf courses and Chautauqua Institute. Twelve miles east of Jamestown. Off Route 17 at Exit 16.

## Rhinebeck *

Kohler, Judy
31 Center St., 12572
(914) 876-8345

Amenities: 1,2,3,4,9,10, 16,18
Breakfast: F.

Dbl. Oc.: $147.25 - $218.89
Sgl. Oc.: $147.25 - $218.89
Third Person: $45.00

Village Victorian Inn—A romantic interlude awaits you. Gourmet breakfasts, antiques, canopy beds and private baths. Come and let us pamper you.

## Richfield Springs

Smith, Lona & George
72 E. Main St., 13439
(315) 858-2024

Amenities: 2,6,10,16,17
Breakfast: F.

Dbl. Oc.: $55.00 - $75.00
Sgl. Oc.: $40.00 - $65.00
Third Person: $15.00
Child: under 5 yrs. - $10.00

Summerwood—A gracious and spacious Victorian on three acres. Centrally located to Cooperstown, Glimmer glass Opera,antique shops, boating and fishing. Hosts offer company or privacy, a full gourmet breakfast, TV and complimentary beverage. Member of state, local and national associations.

## Richfield Springs

Watson, Karen & Bruce
23 Prospect St., 13439
(315) 858-1870

Amenities: 1,2,4,9,11,14,15, 16,17
Breakfast: F.

Dbl. Oc.: $65.00
Sgl. Oc.: $50.00
Third Person: $10.00
Child: $10.00

Country Spread Bed And Breakfast—Convenient to Cooperstown's museums and central Leatherstocking country. Families welcome! Enjoy warm and casual hospitality in our country-decorated home. Warm and delicious samplings from Karen's kitchen await you. Antiquing and all-season activities abound.

| | | | |
|---|---|---|---|
| 1. No Smoking | 5. Tennis Available | 9. Credit Cards Accepted | 13. Lunch Available | 17. Shared Bath |
| 2. No Pets | 6. Golf Available | 10. Personal Checks Accepted | 14. Public Transportation | 18. Afternoon Tea |
| 3. No Children | 7. Swiming Available | 11. Off Season Rates | 15. Reservations Necessary | ★ Commissions given |
| 4. Senior Citizen Rates | 8. Skiing Available | 12. Dinner Available | 16. Private Bath | to Travel Agents |

## *Rochester* *

Gallagher, Helen & Robert
1969 Highland Ave., 14618
(716) 442-4813

**Amenities:** 2,10,14,15,16,17
**Breakfast:** F.

**Dbl. Oc.:** $61.05 - $66.60
**Sgl. Oc.:** $55.50 - $61.05
**Third Person:** $30.00
**Child:** under 10 yrs. -
$10.00

**Highland Bed & Breakfast**—A gracious and traditional home located in a fine residential area of Rochester, two blocks off I-90 Expressway. Near museums and colleges. Hosts have been extending warm hospitality to guests since 1984. They offer information concerning area's cultural events. Member of *B&B of New York.*

## *Rochester*

Klein, Elinor
215 Dartmouth St., 14607
(716) 271-7872,
(716) 473-0778

**Amenities:** 1,2,3,10,14,15,
16,17,18
**Breakfast:** F.

**Dbl. Oc.:** $75.00
**Sgl. Oc.:** $65.00
**Third Person:** $30.00

**Dartmouth House**—Spacious 1905 Tudor in quiet and architecturally fascinating area. Walk to museums, antique shop s andrestaurants. Family antiques, Oriental rugs, beamed ceilings, fireplace and window seats. Great oak kitchen. Well-traveled hosts love pampering guests. Wonderful!

## *Rochester*

Whited, Cynthia
1883 Penfield Rd., Penfield, 14526 (mail)
(716) 385-3266

**Amenities:** 2,3,7,9,10,17
**Breakfast:** C.
**Dbl. Oc.:** $67.00 - $84.00
**Sgl. Oc.:** $50.00 - $70.00
**Third Person:** $15.00

**Strawberry Castle**—Step back to Victoriana in this classic Italianate mansion. Three acres of lawn, marshland and gardens with gracious pool provide a unique setting. Brass beds and lace await you. A diverse selection of fine nearby restaurants for your enjoyment. A special memory.

| | | | |
|---|---|---|---|
| 1. No Smoking | 5. Tennis Available | 9. Credit Cards Accepted | 13. Lunch Available | 17. Shared Bath |
| 2. No Pets | 6. Golf Available | 10. Personal Checks Accepted | 14. Public Transportation | 18. Afternoon Tea |
| 3. No Children | 7. Swiming Available | 11. Off Season Rates | 15. Reservations Necessary | ★ Commissions given |
| 4. Senior Citizen Rates | 8. Skiing Available | 12. Dinner Available | 16. Private Bath | to Travel Agents |

## Rye

Butler, Barbara & Kevin
130 Apawamis Ave., 10580
(914) 967-4670

Amenities: 2,5,7,9,10,11,13,
　　　　　　15,16,17,18
Breakfast: C.
Dbl. Oc.: $85.00 - $135.00
Third Person: $10.00
Child: under 3 yrs. - no charge

**Inn At Old Harbour**—A magnificent gingerbread Victorian overlooking Old Harbour. Listed in the *National Register of Historic Places*. Individually decorated guest rooms. All with period furnishings. Bountiful continental breakfast served in guest lounge or beautiful wrap-around porch.

## Saratoga Springs *

Benton, Kathleen
149 Union Ave., 12866
(518) 583-1173

Amenities: 1,2,3,4,5,6,7,8,
　　　　　　10,11,14,16
Breakfast: F.
Dbl. Oc.: $81.00
Third Person: $15.00
Child: $15.00

**Six Sisters Bed And Breakfast**—An 1880's Victorian charmer. Centrally located in historic city. Spacious rooms, private baths, large beds and a sumptuous breakfast. Stroll to museums, restaurants, downtown's unique and antique shops. Mineral bath/massage. Getaway package from November to April.

## Saratoga Springs *

Collins-Breslin, Andrea
200 Wall St., Schuylerville, 12871 (mail)
(518) 695-3693

Amenities: 1,2,3,5,6,7,8,9,10,
　　　　　　11,15,16,17,18
Breakfast: F.
Dbl. Oc.: $60.00 - $108.00
Sgl. Oc.: $60.00 - $108.00

**The Inn On Bacon Hill Bed & Breakfast**—Ten minutes from Saratoga Springs. Restored 16-room 1865 Victorian. Rural setting. Enjoy two parlors, baby grand piano, extensive library, marble fireplaces and many original architectural features unique to the inn. Sumptuous breakfast. Innkeeping courses offered.

| | | | | |
|---|---|---|---|---|
| 1. No Smoking | 5. Tennis Available | 9. Credit Cards Accepted | 13. Lunch Available | 17. Shared Bath |
| 2. No Pets | 6. Golf Available | 10. Personal Checks Accepted | 14. Public Transportation | 18. Afternoon Tea |
| 3. No Children | 7. Swiming Available | 11. Off Season Rates | 15. Reservations Necessary | ★ Commissions given |
| 4. Senior Citizen Rates | 8. Skiing Available | 12. Dinner Available | 16. Private Bath | to Travel Agents |

## Saratoga Springs *

Melvin, Stephanie & Bob
102 Lincoln Ave., 12866
(518) 587-7613

**Amenities:** 1,2,4,5,6,7,8,9,10,
11,14,16,17,18
**Breakfast:** C.
**Dbl. Oc.:** $59.40 - $97.20
**Sgl. Oc.:** $59.40 - $97.20

**The Westchester House**—A gracious 1885 Queen Anne Victorian inn. Seven guest rooms combine antique furnishings with up-to-date comforts. Enjoy our gardens, piano, extensive library and wrap-around porch. Near race tracks, museums, mineral spas, shops, restaurants, antiques and boating.

## Severance

Wildman, Helen
Sawmill Rd. & Route 74
P.O. Box 125, 12872
(518) 532-7734

**Amenities:** 1,4,5,6,7,10,
12,1315,17
**Breakfast:** F.

**Dbl. Oc.:** $50.00
**Sgl. Oc.:** $30.00
**Third Person:** $15.00
**Child:** under 10 yrs. -
$10.00

**The Bed House**—This charming Adirondack farmhouse has antique furnishings and guest parlor with fireplace. Tennis, beach and boating on 150 private acres on Paradox Lake. Hiking or sightseeing in nearby Pharoah Lake Wilderness and High Peaks region of Adirondack Park.

## Sharon Springs

Hargus, Rosita
Main St.
R.D. #1, 13459
(518) 284-2335

**Amenities:** 2,6,7,8,11,15,
17,18
**Breakfast:** F.

**Dbl. Oc.:** $65.00
**Sgl. Oc.:** $35.00
**Third Person:** $35.00
**Child:** under 12 yrs. -
$25.00

**Roses 'n' Lace Bed And Breakfast**—Between Howe Caverns and Cooperstown, at the junction of Routes 10 and 20. A charming Victorian home. Circa 1885. Restful weekend getaways, antiquing, sightseeing and more. Open weekends and holidays year round. Advance reservations required on weekdays.

| | | | |
|---|---|---|---|
| 1. No Smoking | 5. Tennis Available | 9. Credit Cards Accepted | 13. Lunch Available | 17. Shared Bath |
| 2. No Pets | 6. Golf Available | 10. Personal Checks Accepted | 14. Public Transportation | 18. Afternoon Tea |
| 3. No Children | 7. Swiming Available | 11. Off Season Rates | 15. Reservations Necessary | ★ Commissions given |
| 4. Senior Citizen Rates | 8. Skiing Available | 12. Dinner Available | 16. Private Bath | to Travel Agents |

## Southold *

Mooney-Getoff, Mary
1475 Waterview Dr., 11971
(516) 765-3356

**Amenities:** 1,4,5,6,7,15,17,18
**Breakfast:** F.
**Dbl. Oc.:** $70.00 - $75.00
**Sgl. Oc.:** $50.00 - $55.00
**Child:** under 6 yrs. - $10.00

**Goose Creek Guesthouse**—A spacious pre-Civil War farmhouse on the creek. Surrounded by six wooded acres. We are a resort area near the ferries to Montauk via Shelter Island and the ferry to New London.

## Spencer *

Brownell, Beatrice
178 No. Main St., 14883
(607) 589-5073

**Amenities:** 1,2,3,4,8,10, 11,15,17
**Breakfast:** F.

**Dbl. Oc.:** $45.00
**Sgl. Oc.:** $45.00
**Third Person:** $15.00

**A Slice Of Home**—Gracious hospitality and country atmosphere with a hearty breakfast on weekends and a continental on weekdays. Trout stream. Cross-country skiing. Located in the heart of the finger lakes, 20 minutes south of Ithaca via Route 34/96 and 30 minutes to Owego on Route 17.

## Stanfordville *

Kohler, Judy
Shelley Hill Rd., 12581
(914) 266-4239

**Amenities:** 1,2,3,9,10,16,18
**Breakfast:** F.

**Dbl. Oc.:** $252.56 - $335.75
**Sgl. Oc.:** $252.56 - $335.75
**Third Person:** $65.00

**Lacehouse Inn On Golden Pond**—A romantic interlude dedicated to just four couples. Jacuzzis for two, fireplaces, air conditioning, private decks and sumptuous breakfasts. A private lake for swimming, boating, fishing and savoring sunsets. A 22-acre estate, just 1-1/2 hours from New York City.

## Syracuse

Gero, Bernard
1402 James St., 13203
(315) 476-6541

**Amenities:** 1,2,3,5,6,8,10,14, 15,16,17,18
**Breakfast:** F.

**Dbl. Oc.:** $55.00
**Sgl. Oc.:** $50.00

**Benedict House**—The house was designed by Ward Wellington, the leading architect of the arts and craft movement at the turn of the century. Spacious rooms. Two to five miles from major highways, Syracuse University, LeMoyne College, malls, etc. Air-conditioned guest rooms with TVs.

| | | | | |
|---|---|---|---|---|
| 1. No Smoking | 5. Tennis Available | 9. Credit Cards Accepted | 13. Lunch Available | 17. Shared Bath |
| 2. No Pets | 6. Golf Available | 10. Personal Checks Accepted | 14. Public Transportation | 18. Afternoon Tea |
| 3. No Children | 7. Swiming Available | 11. Off Season Rates | 15. Reservations Necessary | ★ Commissions given |
| 4. Senior Citizen Rates | 8. Skiing Available | 12. Dinner Available | 16. Private Bath | to Travel Agents |

## Tannersville

Jozic, Stefania & Mirko
Route 23A, 12485
(518) 589-5560

**Amenities:** 4,5,6,7,8,9,11,12,
16,17
**Breakfast:** F.

**Dbl. Oc.:** $65.00 - $85.00
**Sgl. Oc.:** $45.00 - $70.00
**Third Person:** $15.00
**Child:** under 10 yrs. -
$15.00

**Washington Irving Lodge**—A classic country inn/B&B situated in the Catskill region/Hunter Mountain ski area. Charming rooms with private baths. Cocktail lounge. Period decor. Restored antiques. Spacious front porch. On eight acres.

## Warrensburg *

Carrington, Florence & Ken
2 Hudson St., 12885
(518) 623-2449

**Amenities:** 2,3,5,6,7,8,9,10,
11,12,13,16,17
**Breakfast:** F.
**Dbl. Oc.:** $95.00
**Sgl. Oc.:** $75.00
**Third Person:** $20.00

**The Merrill Magee House**—A historic house in the heart of an Adirondack village known for antiquing and year-round outdoor recreation. Luxurious rooms. Fine dining. Cozy pub. Secluded garden. Outdoor pool and jacuzzi.

## Waterloo

Anderson, Carol & Paul
1248 Routes 5 & 20, 13165
(315) 539-8325

**Amenities:** 1,2,5,6,7,8,9,10,
15,16,17
**Breakfast:** F.

**Dbl. Oc.:** $53.50
**Sgl. Oc.:** $48.15

**Front Porch Bed & Breakfast**—A charming Victorian home between Seneca and Cayuga Lakes. Near Rochester and Syracuse. Rolling hills are dotted with vineyards and wineries. Enjoy four seasons of recreation and scenic beauty. Three bedrooms and two baths. Ample breakfast served in hospitable surroundings.

## Watertown

Brown, Marsha
253 Clinton St., 13601
(315) 788-7324

**Amenities:** 1,2,3,5,6,7,8,9,10,
15,16,17,18
**Breakfast:** F.

**Dbl. Oc.:** $74.90 - $85.60
**Sgl. Oc.:** $58.85 - $69.55
**Third Person:** $15.00

**Starbuck House**—A 17-room Italianate mansion, circa 1864. Two blocks from downtown. A haven for corporate travelers and tourists on holiday. The warmth and hospitality of a B&B. Amenities of a small European hotel. Gourmet breakfast. One mile from Exit 45 off I-81.

| | | | | |
|---|---|---|---|---|
| 1. No Smoking | 5. Tennis Available | 9. Credit Cards Accepted | 13. Lunch Available | 17. Shared Bath |
| 2. No Pets | 6. Golf Available | 10. Personal Checks Accepted | 14. Public Transportation | 18. Afternoon Tea |
| 3. No Children | 7. Swiming Available | 11. Off Season Rates | 15. Reservations Necessary | ★ Commissions given |
| 4. Senior Citizen Rates | 8. Skiing Available | 12. Dinner Available | 16. Private Bath | to Travel Agents |

## *Watkins Glen*

Gerth, Heidi
P.O. Box 245, 14878
(607) 535-7909

**Amenities:** 1,2,7,8,9,10,11,
16,17
**Breakfast:** F.

**Dbl. Oc.:** $53.50
**Sgl. Oc.:** $42.80
**Third Person:** $15.00

**Vintage View Bed And Breakfast**—An 1865 farmhouse. Stroll through vineyards, visit our llamas, take a dip in the pool or relax and enjoy the views. Located within an easy drive to all Finger Lake attractions. We are open year round. Chartered fishing on Seneca Lake available. Grill and picnic area.

## *Westhampton Beach* *

Collins, Elsie
2 Seafield Lane, 11978
(516) 288-1559,
(800) 346-3290

**Amenities:** 1,2,3,5,7,10,11,
14,15,16
**Breakfast:** F.

**Dbl. Oc.:** $193.50 (suites
only)
**Third Person:** $50.00

**1880 Seafield House**—A hidden 100-year-old bed and breakfast country retreat. The perfect place for a romantic hideaway, a weekend of privacy or just a change of pace from city life. The Seafield estate includes a short brick walkway to the ocean beach and outstanding restaurants.

## *Wevertown*

Cole, Douglas
Route 28
P.O. Box A, 12886
(518) 251-2194, (800) 950-2194

**Amenities:** 5,6,8,9,10,11,
12,15,16
**Breakfast:** F.

**Dbl. Oc.:** $74.90
**Sgl. Oc.:** $42.80
**Child:** under 3 - no charge

**Mountainaire Adventures**—Located in Adirondack Park near Saratoga, Lake George and Gore Mountain ski area. Complimentary hot drink, sauna and hot tub. Beer and wine served. Ski, raft, canoe, fish and hike. Bike rentals, clinics and guided trips. Fun and relaxation for the whole family. Chalet rental.

## *Windham*

Seidel, Lorraine
Route 23, W., 496
(518) 734-4079

**Amenities:** 2,6,7,8,9,10,11,14,
15,16,17,18
**Breakfast:** F.

**Dbl. Oc.:** $74.90 - $85.60
**Sgl. Oc.:** $74.90 - $85.60
**Third Person:** $15.00
**Child:** $15.00

**Country Suite Bed & Breakfast**—Charming Victorian farmhouse. Turn-of-the-century elegance. Furnished with family heirlooms. Fireplace, full breakfast. Private or shared baths. Fine restaurants, antiquing and hiking. Two miles from "Ski Windham" in the Catskill Mountains. A note worthy luxury.

| | | | |
|---|---|---|---|
| 1. No Smoking | 5. Tennis Available | 9. Credit Cards Accepted | 13. Lunch Available | 17. Shared Bath |
| 2. No Pets | 6. Golf Available | 10. Personal Checks Accepted | 14. Public Transportation | 18. Afternoon Tea |
| 3. No Children | 7. Swiming Available | 11. Off Season Rates | 15. Reservations Necessary | ★ Commissions given |
| 4. Senior Citizen Rates | 8. Skiing Available | 12. Dinner Available | 16. Private Bath | to Travel Agents |

# NORTH CAROLINA

## The Tar Heel State

Capitol: Raleigh
Statehood: November 21, 1789; the 12th state
State Motto: To Be, Rather Than To Seem
State Song: "The Old North State"
State Bird: Cardinal
State Flower: Flowering Dogwood
State Tree: Pine

The brown gold of the ripe tobacco leaf has made North Carolina prosperous and the leading grower of tobacco in our country. Nothing is more exciting to the tobacco farmer than to take his product to town and listen to the auctioneer chanting his tobacco prices.

Another prosperous industry in the state is furniture. From the early settlers' own pine trees and pioneering style, came perfect pieces of furniture and the beginning of what became another prosperous industry for North Carolina.

Situated along the Atlantic seacoast, tourists can enjoy swimming as well as visiting the beautiful gardens, historical battlefields and gracious southern mansions.

The first airplane flight by the Wright Brothers took place at Kitty Hawk, and both presidents Andrew Johnson and James Polk were born in this state.

## Arden (South Asheville)

Bass, Jan
150 Royal Pines Dr., 28704
(704) 684-1847

**Amenities:** 4,7,8,9,10,11,12, 15,16,17,18
**Breakfast:** F.

**Dbl. Oc.:** $55.00 - $70.00
**Sgl. Oc.:** $50.00 - $65.00
**Third Person:** $5.00
**Child:** $5.00

**Blake House Inn**—This 1847 Gothic building was a Confederate hospital as well as a summer estate for Charlestonians. Five bedrooms, two with private baths, fireplaces and ambience. Dining available. Seven minutes from the Biltmore estate and Carl Sandburg's home. Rafting nearby.

## Asheville *

The Education Center, Inc.
87 Richmond Hill Dr., 28806
(919) 273-9409, (704) 252-7313,
 (800) 545-9238

**Amenities:** 1,2,6,8,9,10,12,13,15,16
**Breakfast:** F.
**Dbl. Oc.:** $86.40 - $189.00

**Richmond Hill Inn**—An elegant and historic inn overlooking the Blue Ridge Mountains. Twelve luxurious guest rooms. Private baths. Gracious service and amenities. Gourmet restaurant. Listed in the *National Register of Historic Places.*

## Asheville

Faber, Helen & Fred
100 Reynolds Heights, 28804
(704) 254-0496

**Amenities:** 2,5,6,7,8,10,16,17,18
**Breakfast:** C.
**Dbl. Oc.:** 54.00 - $91.80
**Sgl. Oc.:** $48.60 - $83.16
**Third Person:** $16.20

**The Old Reynold Mansion**—A bed and breakfast in a circa 1855 antebellum mansion. Beautifully restored with furnishings from a bygone era. A country setting amidst acres of trees and mountains. Wood-burning fireplaces. Verandas. Pool. Listed in the *National Register of Historic Places.*

| | | | |
|---|---|---|---|
| 1. No Smoking | 5. Tennis Available | 9. Credit Cards Accepted | 13. Lunch Available | 17. Shared Bath |
| 2. No Pets | 6. Golf Available | 10. Personal Checks Accepted | 14. Public Transportation | 18. Afternoon Tea |
| 3. No Children | 7. Swiming Available | 11. Off Season Rates | 15. Reservations Necessary | ★ Commissions given |
| 4. Senior Citizen Rates | 8. Skiing Available | 12. Dinner Available | 16. Private Bath | to Travel Agents |

# NORTH CAROLINA

## Asheville

Fain, Karen, Regina & Sam
177 Cumberland Ave., 28801
(704) 254-3608

**Amenities:** 2,3,5,6,9,10,
14,15,16
**Breakfast:** F.

**Dbl. Oc.:** $78.75
**Sgl. Oc.:** $68.25
**Third Person:** $21.00

**Carolina Bed & Breakfast**—A warm and comfortable turn-of-the-century home conveniently located in the historic Montford district. Five charming guest rooms with antiques and collectibles. Seven fireplaces, two porches and acres of beautiful gardens. Truly a home-away-from-home.

## Asheville *

Gaither, Nancy & Gary
230 Pearson Dr., 28801
(704) 253-5644

**Amenities:** 2,3,9,10,13,16
**Breakfast:** F.

**Dbl. Oc.:** $79.00
**Sgl. Oc.:** $74.00
**Third Person:** $10.00

**Cornerstone Inn**—A four-bedroom Dutch Tudor furnished with heirloom antiques. Surrounded by huge hemlocks. We are within walking distance of downtown and the Botanical Gardens. Full gourmet breakfasts. Full bath in each room. Evening sherry and cookies lovingly served.

## Asheville

LoPresti, Linda & Jim
62 Cumberland Circle, 28801
(704) 254-2244

**Amenities:** 1,2,4,5,9,10,
15,16,18
**Breakfast:** F.

**Dbl. Oc.:** $73.50 - $105.00
**Sgl. Oc.:** $63.00 - $78.75
**Third Person:** $15.75
**Child:** over 12 yrs. - $15.75

**Applewood Manor**—A fine old colonial manor located on two acres in Asheville's historic district. Antiques, collectibles, fine linens and lace help to re-create the ambience of the early 1900's. Come and romance yourselves.

## Asheville

McEwan, Barbara
674 Biltmore Ave., 28803
(704) 252-1389

**Amenities:** 1,2,3,9,10,11,14,
16,17,18
**Breakfast:** C.

**Dbl. Oc.:** $70.20 - $113.40
**Sgl. Oc.:** $63.72 - $106.92
**Third Person:** $16.20

**Cedar Crest Victorian Inn**—An 1890 Queen Anne mansion listed in the *National Register of Historic Places*. Lavish interior, carved oak paneling and authentic period decor with antique furnishings. Croquet, pitch and gardens. Located 1/4 mile from theBiltmore House and one mile from downtown.

## Asheville

Spradley, Karen & Andy
53 Saint Dunstans Rd., 28803
(704) 253-3525

**Amenities:** 1,2,9,10,13,15,16
**Breakfast:** F.

**Dbl. Oc.:** $78.75 - $94.50
**Sgl. Oc.:** $63.00
**Third Person:** $15.00

**Corner Oak Manor**—This lovely English Tudor home is surrounded by oak, maple and pine trees. It is decorated with antiques, weavings and many fine hand-crafted items. The gracious amenities include a full gourmet breakfast, outdoor jacuzzi, fireplace and baby grand piano.

| | | | | |
|---|---|---|---|---|
| 1. No Smoking | 5. Tennis Available | 9. Credit Cards Accepted | 13. Lunch Available | 17. Shared Bath |
| 2. No Pets | 6. Golf Available | 10. Personal Checks Accepted | 14. Public Transportation | 18. Afternoon Tea |
| 3. No Children | 7. Swiming Available | 11. Off Season Rates | 15. Reservations Necessary | ★ Commissions given |
| 4. Senior Citizen Rates | 8. Skiing Available | 12. Dinner Available | 16. Private Bath | to Travel Agents |

# NORTH CAROLINA

## Asheville

Turcot, Marge
119 Dodge St., 28803
(704) 274-1604

**Amenities:** 2,9,10,15,16,17
**Breakfast:** C.

**Dbl. Oc.:** $50.00 - $60.00
**Sgl. Oc.:** $45.00 - $55.00
**Third Person:** $5.00
**Child:** under 2 yrs. -
no charge

**Reed House**—A comfortable 1892 Queen Anne Victorian near the Biltmore estate. A working fireplace in every room. Breakfast on the porch. Relaxing rocking chairs everywhere. Children welcome. Listed in the *National Register of Historic Places*. The Reed House is a local historic property.

## Asheville (Weaverville) *

VanderElzen, Karen & John
26 Brown St., 28787
(704) 658-3899

**Amenities:** 1,2,5,6,7,8,9,10,
15,16
**Breakfast:** F.

**Dbl. Oc.:** $59.40
**Sgl. Oc.:** $48.60
**Third Person:** $10.80
**Child:** under 2 yrs. -
no charge

**Dry Ridge Inn**—A historic farmhouse 10 minutes north of Asheville. Large guest rooms with country antiques and handmade quilts. Gift shop features local arts and crafts. Friendly, small town atmosphere. Close to shopping, attractions and the Blue Ridge Parkway.

## Asheville *

Vogel, Lynn, Marion & Rick
100 & 116 Flint St., 28801
(704) 253-6723

**Amenities:** 1,2,3,9,10,14,16
**Breakfast:** F.
**Dbl. Oc.:** $81.00
**Sgl. Oc.:** $64.00
**Third Person:** $20.00

*Flint Street Inns.*

**Flint Street Inns**—Two lovely old family homes offering the best in bed and breakfast accommodations. Charming guest rooms, some with fireplaces and all with air-conditioning. The inns are within a comfortable walking distance to shops and restaurants. A full Southern-style breakfast is served.

## Asheville

Wyatt, Evelyn
230 Pearson Dr., 2880

(704) 253-5644

**Amenities:** 1,2,3,9,10,14,15
16,18

**Breakfast:** F.

**Dbl.Oc.:** $68.25
**Sgl.Oc.:** $57.75

**Third Person:** $10.50

**Cornerstone Inn**—Restored Dutch Tudor home in the heart of the historic district. Filled with American and European antiques. Minutes form all local attractions and downtown. Southern hospitality is a way of life for your hostess, Evelyn Wyatt.

| | | | |
|---|---|---|---|
| 1. No Smoking | 5. Tennis Available | 9. Credit Cards Accepted | 13. Lunch Available | 17. Shared Bath |
| 2. No Pets | 6. Golf Available | 10. Personal Checks Accepted | 14. Public Transportation | 18. Afternoon Tea |
| 3. No Children | 7. Swiming Available | 11. Off Season Rates | 15. Reservations Necessary | ★ Commissions given |
| 4. Senior Citizen Rates | 8. Skiing Available | 12. Dinner Available | 16. Private Bath | to Travel Agents |

## Asheville *

Willard, Linda & Ross
64 Linden Ave., 28801
(704) 254-9336

**Amenities:** 1,2,5,6,7,8,9,10, 11,16,18
**Breakfast:** F.

**Dbl. Oc.:** $70.20 - $81.00
**Sgl. Oc.:** $48.00 - $55.00
**Third Person:** $10.00

**Aberdeen Inn**—A hospitable, country-style bed and breakfast close to downtown and the Biltmore house. Wood-burning fireplaces in four of our nine bedrooms. Wicker rockers on the porch. Wine. Books. Cable TV. Great breakfasts. We will make your stay special. Welcome to our home.

## Beaufort

Kwaak, William
305 Front St., 28516
(919) 728-7036

**Amenities:** 1,2,4,5,6,7,9,10, 11,12,13,15,16
**Breakfast:** C. and F.

**Dbl. Oc.:** $81.00 - $135.00
**Sgl. Oc.:** $45.00
**Third Person:** $15.00
**Child:** under 10 yrs. - $10.00

**The Cedars Inn**—Vacation in this circa 1768 colonial inn located in the seaport town of Beaufort. Swim, fish or collect shells on the outer banks. Golf, tennis and boating are available. Finish your day with a fine gourmet dinner in our intimate inn.

## Beaufort *

Steepy, Kay & Philip
7345 Bramblewood Lane, 46254
(317) 297-8242
**Amenities** 1,2,3,4,6,7,9,10, 11,15,16
**Breakfast:** C. Plus
**Dbl. Oc.:** $82.00
**Sgl. Oc.:** $82.00
**Third Person:** $12.00

**Delmar Inn**—Located in the historic town of Beaufort, the inn, built in 1866, offers three antique furnished guest rooms. Stroll to the harbor, shops and musuem. A short drive to the beach, fort or the outer bank's ferry. The inn is on Beaufort's historic homes tour.

## Beech Mountain *

Archer, Bonny & Joe
Route 2, Box 56A, 28604
(704) 898-9004

**Amenities:** 2,6,7,8,9,11, 12,16
**Breakfast:** F.

**Dbl. Oc.:** $68.25 - $99.75
**Sgl. Oc.:** $68.25 - $99.75
**Third Person:** $8.40
**Child:** $8.40

**Archers Inn**—Perched on the side of Beech Mountain overlooking the surrounding mountains. Fireplaces in all the rooms. Fourteen guest rooms, 13 have a porch or deck and 11 have along-range view. Large TV. Post-and-beam construction. Carriage rides available.

| | | | | |
|---|---|---|---|---|
| 1. No Smoking | 5. Tennis Available | 9. Credit Cards Accepted | 13. Lunch Available | 17. Shared Bath |
| 2. No Pets | 6. Golf Available | 10. Personal Checks Accepted | 14. Public Transportation | 18. Afternoon Tea |
| 3. No Children | 7. Swiming Available | 11. Off Season Rates | 15. Reservations Necessary | ★ Commissions given |
| 4. Senior Citizen Rates | 8. Skiing Available | 12. Dinner Available | 16. Private Bath | to Travel Agents |

# NORTH CAROLINA

## Belhaven

Smith, Axson
600 E. Main St., 27810
(919) 943-2151,
(800) 346-2151 (in N. Carolina)

**Amenities:** 2,5,6,7,8,9,10,
11,12,14,15,16
**Breakfast:** C.
**Dbl. Oc.:** $42.00 - $78.75
**Sgl. Oc.:** $42.00 - $78.75
**Third Person:** $10.00

**River Forest Manor — Country Inn**—Built in 1897 and operated as a country inn since 1947. World-famous buffet smorgasbord with over 65 dishes each night. All rooms have a Victorian decor with modern facilities. Come and enjoy our fine food, pool and jacuzzi. Located on the waterfront.

## Black Mountain

Headley, Wilhelmina
North Fork Rd.
Route 1, Box 269, 28711
(704) 669-6762

**Amenities:** 1,2,5,6,7,10,16
**Breakfast:** F.

**Dbl. Oc.:** $40.00 - $55.00
**Sgl. Oc.:** $35.00 - $50.00
**Third Person:** $10.00
**Child:** under 10 yrs. - $5.00

**Bed And Breakfast Over Yonder**—Comfortable and secluded. Eighteen acres of mountain, wildflower gardens and rock terraces surround this house. Views of the highest peaks in the east. Nine miles from the Blue Ridge Parkway. Antique and craft shop, hiking trails, white-water rafting and gem hunting.

## Black Mountain

Miller, Barbara Dehaan
P.O. Box 965, 28711
(704) 669-8303

**Amenities:** 2,10,11,16
**Breakfast:** C.

**Dbl. Oc.:** $48.60 - $59.40
**Sgl. Oc.:** $43.20
**Third Person:** $10.00
**Child:** under 2 yrs. -
no charge

**The Blackberry Inn**—A red brick Colonial set on a secluded hilltop surrounded by oaks and evergreens. All private baths. Near antique and craft shops. Just 15 minutes from Asheville.

## Boone

Probinsky, Jean
209 Meadowview Dr., 28607
(704) 262-3670

**Amenities:** 2,5,6,7,8,10,14,
15,17
**Breakfast:** C.

**Dbl. Oc.:** $40.00
**Sgl. Oc.:** $35.00
**Third Person:** $10.00
**Child:** $10.00

**Grandma Jean's Bed & Breakfast**—Hook a trout, sit a spell, ride a horse, climb a mountain, hike a trail, ski a slope, play 18 holes or buy some folk art. Charming 60-year-old country home is in the heart of the Blue Ridge Mountains near Grandfather Mountain.

| | | | | |
|---|---|---|---|---|
| 1. No Smoking | 5. Tennis Available | 9. Credit Cards Accepted | 13. Lunch Available | 17. Shared Bath |
| 2. No Pets | 6. Golf Available | 10. Personal Checks Accepted | 14. Public Transportation | 18. Afternoon Tea |
| 3. No Children | 7. Swiming Available | 11. Off Season Rates | 15. Reservations Necessary | ★ Commissions given |
| 4. Senior Citizen Rates | 8. Skiing Available | 12. Dinner Available | 16. Private Bath | to Travel Agents |

## Brevard

Bourget, Eileen
410 E. Main St., 28712
(704) 884-2105

**Amenities:** 1,2,9,10,11,
12,15,16,17
**Breakfast:** F.
**Dbl. Oc.:** $55.00 - $65.00
**Sgl. Oc.:** $50.00 - $55.00
**Third Person:** $10.00

**The Inn At Brevard**—Listed in the *National Register of Historic Places*. This beautiful old home has been completely restored and offers a warm, European-style welcome to the Blue Ridge traveler. Open March through December 20.

## Brevard

Ong, Lyn
412 W. Probart St., 28712
(704) 884-9349

**Amenities:** 1,2,10,11,15,
16,17
**Breakfast:** F.

**Dbl. Oc.:** $50.76 - $60.48
**Sgl. Oc.:** $43.20 - $49.68
**Third Person:** $10.80

**The Red House**—Built in 1851, this B&B has been lovingly restored and furnished with family antiques. Come by and relax on our porch in the mountains.

## Bryson City *

Adams, Ruth
Fryemont Rd.
P.O. Box 816, 28713
(704) 488-3472

**Amenities:** 2,4,9,10,11,12,
15,16,17
**Breakfast:** F.

**Dbl. Oc.:** $80.00
**Sgl. Oc.:** $75.00
**Third Person:** $45.00
**Child:** under 12 yrs. -
$15.00

**Randolph House Inn**—Visit western North Carolina's most exclusive bed and breakfast inn. Only 10 miles from the Great Smoky Mountains National Parkway. Snuggled away in the Bryson City of yesteryear. This historic landmark, built in 1895, offers seven guest rooms and fine food.

## Chapel Hill

Kelly, Jane & Bob
NC 54 at Mebane Oaks Rd.
P.O. Box 267, 27514
(919) 563-5583

**Amenities:** 2,5,6,10,15,16,18
**Breakfast:** F.

**Dbl. Oc.:** $78.00 - $115.00
**Sgl. Oc.:** $68.00 - $90.00
**Third Person:** $15.00

**The Inn At Bingham School**—An award-winning, restored headmasters home. Listed in the *National Register of Historic Places*. Five rooms with private baths. Cottage with whirlpool bath. On 10 acres of rolling land. Only 15 minutes to Chapel Hill. Near Duke University. Full breakfast and p.m. refreshments.

| | | | | |
|---|---|---|---|---|
| 1. No Smoking | 5. Tennis Available | 9. Credit Cards Accepted | 13. Lunch Available | 17. Shared Bath |
| 2. No Pets | 6. Golf Available | 10. Personal Checks Accepted | 14. Public Transportation | 18. Afternoon Tea |
| 3. No Children | 7. Swiming Available | 11. Off Season Rates | 15. Reservations Necessary | ★ Commissions given |
| 4. Senior Citizen Rates | 8. Skiing Available | 12. Dinner Available | 16. Private Bath | to Travel Agents |

## *Charlotte*

Dearien, Peggy & Frank
5901 Sardis Rd., 28270
(704) 365-1936

**Amenities:** 1,2,3,9,10,15,16
**Breakfast:** F.

**Dbl. Oc.:** $86.58
**Sgl. Oc.:** $75.48
**Third Person:** $15.00

**The Homeplace**—Located in southeast Charlotte on 2-1/2 acres with garden gazebo and wrap-around porch. A 1902 restored Victorian with three rooms. Decorated in country charm. Warm and friendly atmosphere. Antiques and quilts.

## *Charlotte* *

Dyer, Janet & Rob
6221 Amos Smith Rd., 28214
(704) 399-6299

**Amenities:** 1,2,6,7,9,10,15,16
**Breakfast:** F.
**Dbl. Oc.:** $65.00 - $95.00
**Sgl. Oc.:** $65.00 - $95.00
**Third Person:** $5.00
**Child:** under 12 yrs. - no charge

**Still Waters**—A refurbished log house on two wooded acres. Porch, deck and a garden. 480- feet of lakefront on Lake Wylie with boat slips and ramp. Located just west of the airport,with good access to I-85, I-77 and the Billy Graham Parkway. Convenient to the Charlotte area attractions.

## *Charlotte* *

Kelley, Shirley K.
122 E. Morehead, 28204
(704) 376-3357

**Amenities:** 2,4,9,10,14,15,16
**Breakfast:** C.

**Dbl. Oc.:** $91.00
**Sgl. Oc.:** $79.00
**Third Person:** $12.00
**Child:** under 10 yrs. -
     no charge

**Morehead Inn**—A Southern estate endowed with quiet elegance. Spacious public areas with intimate fireplaces. Luxurious private rooms furnished with English and American antiques. Just minutes from uptown Charlotte in historic Dillworth.

## *Durham*

Ryan, Barbara
106 Mason Rd., 27712
(919) 477-8430

**Amenities:** 2,5,6,7,9,10,15,
     16,17,18
**Breakfast:** F.

**Dbl. Oc.:** $59.40 - $102.60
**Sgl. Oc.:** $54.00
**Third Person:** $10.80

**Arrowhead Inn**—A restored 1775 manor and carriage house on four rural acres. Four private baths and four shared baths. Hearty full breakfast, home baking and preserving. Close to Duke University, historic attractions, Museum Of Life And Science and antiquing. Seven miles to I-85.

| | | | |
|---|---|---|---|
| 1. No Smoking | 5. Tennis Available | 9. Credit Cards Accepted | 13. Lunch Available | 17. Shared Bath |
| 2. No Pets | 6. Golf Available | 10. Personal Checks Accepted | 14. Public Transportation | 18. Afternoon Tea |
| 3. No Children | 7. Swiming Available | 11. Off Season Rates | 15. Reservations Necessary | ★ Commissions given |
| 4. Senior Citizen Rates | 8. Skiing Available | 12. Dinner Available | 16. Private Bath | to Travel Agents |

## Edenton *

Edwards, Jane & Arch
300 No. Broad St., 27932
(919) 482-3641

**Amenities:** 2,5,6,7,10,16,18
**Breakfast:** C. (F. on Sundays)
**Dbl. Oc.:** $86.40
**Sgl. Oc.:** $54.00
**Third Person:** $15.00
**Child:** $15.00

**The Lords Proprietors' Inn**—"It is one of the friendliest and best-managed inns I have ever visited." - James T. Yenkel, *The Washington Post*. Twenty elegant, spacious rooms in Edenton's historic district. Winter weekends include tour of private historical homes and dinner.

## Edenton

Oliver, Fran & Rich
Route 4, Box 370, 27932
(919) 482-2282

**Amenities:** 2,9,16
**Breakfast:** F.

**Dbl. Oc.:** $60.00
**Sgl. Oc.:** $55.00
**Third Person:** $5.00

**Trestle House Inn**—Elegant lodge on 70 acres with a 20-acre lake. Private tiled bathrooms. Remote TV with HBO. Stone fireplaces, exercise room and game room.

## Franklin

Farrell, Jean & George
238 E. Hickory Knoll Rd., 28734
(704) 524-9666

**Amenities:** 1,2,6,8,9,10, 12,16
**Breakfast:** F.

**Dbl. Oc.:** $54.00 - $64.80
**Third Person:** $10.00

**Hickory Knoll Lodge**—Located high and secluded in the Great Smoky Mountains. Enjoy hiking in pristine woodlands, fishing for trout on premises or relaxing on our big front porch. King- and queen-sized beds with jacuzzi baths in over-sized rooms.

## Franklin

Oehser, Mary (Liz)
190 Georgia Rd., 28734
(704) 369-8985

**Amenities:** 2,5,6,10,16,17
**Breakfast:** F.

**Dbl. Oc.:** $54.00 - $64.80
**Sgl. Oc.:** $48.60
**Third Person:** $10.00

**Buttonwood Inn**—A small, mountain inn with a cozy-country feeling filled with antiques, quilts and collectibles. Enjoy a country to gourmet breakfast before gem mining, hiking, golfing, shopping or just relaxing on the deck. Your comfort and satisfaction is this inn's pleasure.

| | | | |
|---|---|---|---|
| 1. No Smoking | 5. Tennis Available | 9. Credit Cards Accepted | 13. Lunch Available | 17. Shared Bath |
| 2. No Pets | 6. Golf Available | 10. Personal Checks Accepted | 14. Public Transportation | 18. Afternoon Tea |
| 3. No Children | 7. Swiming Available | 11. Off Season Rates | 15. Reservations Necessary | ★ Commissions given |
| 4. Senior Citizen Rates | 8. Skiing Available | 12. Dinner Available | 16. Private Bath | to Travel Agents |

## Glenville

Carter, George
Big Ridge Rd., 28736
(704) 743-3094

**Amenities:** 1,2,3,5,6,7,10,15,
16,17
**Breakfast:** F.

**Dbl. Oc.:** $38.00
**Sgl. Oc.:** $22.00

**Mountain High**—Situated 4,200 feet up. Cool, quiet and beautiful mountain views. Resort area with lots to do. Horseback riding available. Excellent restaurants.

## Greensboro *

Green, JoAnne
205 No. Park Dr., 27401
(919) 274-6350

**Amenities:** 2,3,5,6,7,9,10,15,
16,17
**Breakfast:** C.

**Dbl. Oc.:** $59.40 - $81.00
**Sgl. Oc.:** $43.60 - $54.00
**Third Person:** $10.80

**Greenwood**—A 1905 home in the central historic district. Lovingly restored. Five guest rooms, guest kitchen, TV room and pool. Elegant decor with paintings and wood carvings from around the world. Park at our front door. Homemade breakfast features fresh squeezed orange juice.

## Henderson *

Cornell, Jean & Dick
Route 3, Box 610, 27536
(919) 438-2421

**Amenities:** 1,2,3,6,7,9,10,
15,16
**Breakfast:** F.

**Dbl. Oc.:** $90.75
**Sgl. Oc.:** $90.75

**La Grange Plantation Inn**—Nationally registered 18th-century plantation house on Kerr Lake. Near Virginia border. Award-winning restoration recognized by the *National Trust for Historic Preservation*. Five elegantly decorated and furnished rooms with private baths. Five miles from I-85.

## Hendersonville *

Carberry, Fred
755 No. Main St., 28792
(704)697-7778, (800)225-4700,
Fax: (704)697-8664

**Amenities:** 2,5,6,7,9,10,11,15,16
**Breakfast:** F.
**Dbl. Oc.:** $52.92 - $74.52
**Sgl. Oc.:** $45.36 - $52.92
**Third Person:** $10.80

**Claddagh Inn At Hendersonville**—Listed in the *National Register of Historic Places* and is AAA approved. All rooms feature a private bath, telephone and air-conditioning. Located two blocks from the downtown historic district. Enjoy the hospitality of a bygone era.

| | | | |
|---|---|---|---|
| 1. No Smoking | 5. Tennis Available | 9. Credit Cards Accepted | 13. Lunch Available | 17. Shared Bath |
| 2. No Pets | 6. Golf Available | 10. Personal Checks Accepted | 14. Public Transportation | 18. Afternoon Tea |
| 3. No Children | 7. Swiming Available | 11. Off Season Rates | 15. Reservations Necessary | ★ Commissions given |
| 4. Senior Citizen Rates | 8. Skiing Available | 12. Dinner Available | 16. Private Bath | to Travel Agents |

## *Hendersonville*

Sheiry, Diane & John
783 No. Main St., 28792
(800) 537-8195, (704) 693-9193

**Amenities:** 2,5,9,10,11,16
**Breakfast:** F.
**Dbl. Oc.:** $68.04 - $78.84
**Sgl. Oc.:** $62.64 - $73.44
**Third Person:** $10.80
**Child:** under 12 yrs. - no charge

**The Waverly Inn**—A recently restored 1898 Victorian listed with the *National Register of Historic Places*. Open all year. Fifteen rooms with private baths. Walk to excellent restaurants and shopping. Near the Biltmore Estate, Carl Sandburg's home, Blue Ridge Parkway and Flat Rock Playhouse.

## *Hertford*

Harnisch, Jenny
103 So. Church St., 27944
(919) 426-5809

**Amenities:** 1,2,9,10,14,15,16
**Breakfast:** F.
**Dbl. Oc.:** $47.25
**Sgl. Oc.:** $37.75
**Third Person:** $10.50
**Child:** under 10 yrs. - $5.25

**Gingerbread Inn**—Located on Bypass 17, 1-1/2 hours from North Carolina's outer bank beaches. Restored early-1900 home. Large rooms, king and queen beds, central air conditioning and free HBO TV. Famous gingerbread boy. Try our continental pastries at our bakery next door. Good fishing.

## *Highlands*

Alley, Donna & Chris
Hickory St.,
Route 1, Box 22B, 28741
(704) 526-2060

**Amenities:** 1,2,9,10,11,15, 16,18
**Breakfast:** F.

**Dbl. Oc.:** $70.00
**Sgl. Oc.:** $60.00
**Third Person:** $10.00
**Child:** $10.00

**Colonial Pines Inn**—A charming country inn on two acres. Large porch with views. Cozy parlor with fireplace and grand piano. Homemade breads are a specialty. Close to great shopping, dining and waterfalls. Separate guest house with fireplace and view. Open all year.

| | | | |
|---|---|---|---|
| 1. No Smoking | 5. Tennis Available | 9. Credit Cards Accepted | 13. Lunch Available | 17. Shared Bath |
| 2. No Pets | 6. Golf Available | 10. Personal Checks Accepted | 14. Public Transportation | 18. Afternoon Tea |
| 3. No Children | 7. Swiming Available | 11. Off Season Rates | 15. Reservations Necessary | ★ Commissions given |
| 4. Senior Citizen Rates | 8. Skiing Available | 12. Dinner Available | 16. Private Bath | to Travel Agents |

# NORTH CAROLINA

## Highlands

Hernandez, Jaunita
Route 2, Box 649N., 28741
(704) 526-4536

**Amenities:** 1,2,5,6,7,8,
10,15,16
**Breakfast:** F.

**Dbl. Oc.:** $68.00
**Third Person:** $10.0

**The Guest House**—A lovely contemporary home nestled in the tranquil mountains. Just moments from town. Close to all amenities: shopping, galleries, auctions, sports and fine dining. Enjoy the view while eating a delicious breakfast. A perfect place to relax and enjoy.

## Kenansville

Lennon, Iris
Hwy. 24 & 50, 28349
(919) 296-1831

**Amenities:** 2,6,9,10,12,
13,15,16
**Breakfast:** C.

**Dbl. Oc.:** $49.00
**Sgl. Oc.:** $42.00
**Third Person:** $12.00
**Child:** under 12 yrs. -
no charge

**Squire's Vintage Inn**—Located in the heart of Duplin County near historic Kenansville. Noted for its delicious cuisine and good taste. The rural setting adds to the privacy, intimacy and relaxation for an overall feeling of getting away from it all.

## Kill Devil Hills *

Combs, Phyllis
500 No. Virginia Dare Trail, 27948
(919) 441-6127

**Amenities:** 2,4,5,6,7,9,10,
11,15,16
**Breakfast:** C.

**Dbl. Oc.:** $80.00
**Sgl. Oc.:** $80.00
**Third Person:** $22.00

**Ye Olde Cherokee Inn**—Come and visit our big pink beach house, where you can dip your feet into the cool Atlantic Ocean only 600 feet away. Whether you want to sit in the sun or swim, fly or fish, sightsee or shop, study nature or history, this is the retreat for you.

## Lake Junaluska,

Cato, Wilma
One Atkins Loop, 28745
(704) 456-6486

**Amenities:** 1,2,5,6,7,10,12,
15,16,17
**Breakfast:** F.

**Dbl. Oc.:** $60.00
**Sgl. Oc.:** $40.00
**Third Person:** $15.00

**Providence Lodge**—Rustic with period furniture, good beds, claw-foot tubs and big porches. Delicious family style meals feature the best in country cooking. Nearby are the Blue Ridge Parkway, Great Smoky Mountains, Cherokee Indian Reservation and the Biltmore Estate.

| | | | |
|---|---|---|---|
| 1. No Smoking | 5. Tennis Available | 9. Credit Cards Accepted | 13. Lunch Available | 17. Shared Bath |
| 2. No Pets | 6. Golf Available | 10. Personal Checks Accepted | 14. Public Transportation | 18. Afternoon Tea |
| 3. No Children | 7. Swiming Available | 11. Off Season Rates | 15. Reservations Necessary | ★ Commissions given |
| 4. Senior Citizen Rates | 8. Skiing Available | 12. Dinner Available | 16. Private Bath | to Travel Agents |

## Lake Junaluska

Wright, Norma
21 No. Lakeshore Dr., 28745
(800) 733-6114

**Amenities:** 2,5,6,7,10,12,15,16,17
**Breakfast:** F.
**Dbl. Oc.:** $60.00
**Sgl. Oc.:** $40.00
**Third Person:** $15.00

**Sunset Inn**—Beautiful, rambling house with large porches. Views of lake and Smoky Mountains. A relaxing vacation or a restful stop between area attractions. Nearby are the CherokeeIndian Reservation, Maggie Valley, Biltmore Estate and Blue Ridge Parkway. Scrumptious homecooked meals.

## Lake Waccamaw

Garrell, Leroy M.
404 Lake Shore Dr.
P.O. Box 218, 28459
(919) 646-4744

**Amenities:** 6,7,10,15,17
**Breakfast:** F.

**Dbl. Oc.:** $52.50
**Sgl. Oc.:** $47.25
**Child:** Under 6 Yrs. - $5.25

**Bed And Breakfast By The Lake**—Spend a night with us on tranquil Lake Waccamaw. The quiet beauty and peaceful surroundings will long be remembered. Here you will awaken to the unmistakable smell of frying bacon and perking coffee. A full Southern breakfast tops off your stay.

## Manteo *

Miller, Bruce
Queen Elizabeth
P.O. Box 1822, 27954
(919) 473-1404, (800) 458-7069

**Amenities:** 1,2,4,6,7,9,11,12,
13,15,16
**Breakfast:** C.

**Dbl. Oc.:** $91.80 - $135.00
**Sgl. Oc.:** $91.80 - $135.00
**Third Person:** $10.00
**Child:** under 16 yrs. -
no charge

**The Tranquil House Inn**—28 room bed and breakfast inn on Shallowbag Bay offers lovely and unique accommodations. Wine, breakfast and bikes are complimentary. Within walking distance of shops, restaurants, movie theater and historic sites. Five- miles from the ocean.

## Mars Hill *

Wessel, Yvette
121 S. Main St., 28754
(704) 689-5722

**Amenities:** 2,5,6,7,8,9,
10,15,16
**Breakfast:** F.

**Dbl. Oc.:** $42.00 - $52.50
**Sgl. Oc.:** $42.00 - $52.50
**Third Person:** $10.00
**Child:** under 12 yrs. -
no charge

**Baird House**—85 year old brick charmer in garden setting. Furnished with fine antiques. Elegant yet homey. Tiny college town 18 miles north of Asheville.

| | | | |
|---|---|---|---|
| 1. No Smoking | 5. Tennis Available | 9. Credit Cards Accepted | 13. Lunch Available | 17. Shared Bath |
| 2. No Pets | 6. Golf Available | 10. Personal Checks Accepted | 14. Public Transportation | 18. Afternoon Tea |
| 3. No Children | 7. Swiming Available | 11. Off Season Rates | 15. Reservations Necessary | ★ Commissions given |
| 4. Senior Citizen Rates | 8. Skiing Available | 12. Dinner Available | 16. Private Bath | to Travel Agents |

# NORTH CAROLINA

## Mebane

Rice, Avis
Route 5, Box 137, 27302
(919) 563-1733

**Amenities:** 1,2,10,12,13, 15,16
**Breakfast:** F.

**Dbl. Oc.:** $50.00 - $60.00
**Sgl. Oc.:** $40.00 - $50.00

**The Ole Place**—A pre-Civil War cabin listed in the *National Register of Historic Places*. Queen-size beds, fireplace and jacuzzi. Relax on the porch, hike in the woods, or shop at the nearby outlet center. Near Duke and Chapel HillUniversities. Great for bird watchers.

## Mount Airy

Haxton, Ellen & Manford
2893 W. Pine St., 27030
(919) 789-5034

**Amenities:** 2,4,5,6,7,9,10,11, 12,13,15,16,17
**Breakfast:** C.

**Dbl. Oc.:** $52.50 - $89.25
**Sgl. Oc.:** $52.50 - $89.25
**Third Person:** $10.00
**Child:** $10.00

**Pine Ridge Inn**—1949 mansion, 2 miles east of I-79 and Hwy. 89. Private bedroom suites with private baths. Swimming pool. Large indoor hot tub. Excercise room. Transportation to and from the airport. Wine and cheese served.

## Murphy *

DeLong, Kate & Bob
500 Valley River Ave., 28906
(704) 837-9567

**Amenities:** 2,4,5,6,7,9,10, 11,15,16,18
**Breakfast:** F.
**Dbl. Oc.:** $70.20
**Sgl. Oc.:** $52.92
**Third Person:** $10.00
**Child:** no charge - $10.00

**Huntington Hall**—Patterned after an English B&B in a Victorian theme. Scrumptious full breakfast. Located 2 hours from Atlanta, Georgia, 3 hours from Greenville, South Carolina and 7 miles from the John C. Campbell Folk School. The area is perfect for rafting, canoeing, fishing and hiking.

## New Bern *

Cleveland, Lois
509 Pollack St., 28560
(919) 636-5553

**Amenities:** 1,2,9,10,16
**Breakfast:** F.

**Dbl. Oc.:** $81.00
**Sgl. Oc.:** $56.16
**Third Person:** $21.60
**Child:** under 6 yrs. -
no charge

**The Aerie**—One block from Tryon Palace. A Victorian inn located in New Bern's historic district. Rooms are individually decorated and furnished with antiques. A generous country breakfast is served each morning in our dining room.

| | | | | |
|---|---|---|---|---|
| 1. No Smoking | 5. Tennis Available | 9. Credit Cards Accepted | 13. Lunch Available | 17. Shared Bath |
| 2. No Pets | 6. Golf Available | 10. Personal Checks Accepted | 14. Public Transportation | 18. Afternoon Tea |
| 3. No Children | 7. Swiming Available | 11. Off Season Rates | 15. Reservations Necessary | ★ Commissions given |
| 4. Senior Citizen Rates | 8. Skiing Available | 12. Dinner Available | 16. Private Bath | to Travel Agents |

# NORTH CAROLINA

## New Bern *

Hansen, Diane
215 Pollock St., 28560
(919) 636-3810

**Amenities:** 2,5,6,9,10,16
**Breakfast:** F.

**Dbl. Oc.:** $75.60
**Sgl. Oc.:** $52.92
**Third Person:** $10.80
**Child:** $10.80

**Harmony House Inn**—Comfortable elegance in the historic district near Tryon Palace, restaurants and shops. Spacious Greek Revival inn, circa 1850, decorated with antiques, local reproductions and family history. Complimentary soft drinks and juices. Guest parlor. Porch with swings.

## Pinehurst

Ballard, Ann & Gene
Corner of Magnolia &
Chinquapin, 28374
(800) 526-5562, (919) 295-6900

**Amenities:** 1,5,6,7,9,10,
16,18
**Breakfast:** F.

**Dbl. Oc.:** $95.00
**Sgl. Oc.:** $59.00
**Third Person:** $20.00
**Child:** under 12 yrs. -
no charge

**The Magnolia Inn**—Built in 1896. Renovated and refurbished with Victorian furniture and accessories. Each of the 10 double rooms has a private bath with the original fixtures. Located in the village with shopping, dining and tours available. Access to Pinehurst Golf Courses.

## Salisbury

Webster, Gerry
220 S. Ellis St., 28144
(704) 633-6841

**Amenities:** 1,2,5,6,9,10,
14,16
**Breakfast:** C. Plus

**Dbl. Oc.:** $48.50 - $53.50
**Sgl. Oc.:** $43.50 - $48.50
**Third Person:** $11.00

**The 1868 Stewart-Marsh House**—Federal style home in the historic district. Screened porch with wicker furniture, cozy library, spacious guest rooms and antiques. Friendly, Southern hospitality. Historic sites, shopping and restaurants within walking distance. Tours of the historic district available.

## Sparta

Turbiville, Maybelline
E. Whitehead, 28675
(919) 372-8490

**Amenities:** 5,6,10,16
**Breakfast:** F.

**Dbl. Oc.:** $52.50
**Sgl. Oc.:** $36.75
**Third Person:** $10.00
**Child:** $10.00

**Turby-Villa**—Mimi & "Turby" Turbiville live in a large contemporary brick home 2 miles out in the country, near public golf courses and New River Canoeing. Set on 20 pastoral acres at the end of a long private drive. Each guest room has a private bath. Breakfast is served on a glassed-in porch.

## Spruce Pine

Ansley, Bill
101 Pine Ave., 28777
(704) 765-6993

**Amenities:** 1,2,4,6,7,8,9,10,
11,16
**Breakfast:** F.

**Dbl. Oc.:** $59.40 - $81.00
**Sgl. Oc.:** $48.60 - $70.20
**Third Person:** $10.80
**Child:** under 12 yrs. -
no charge

**Richmond Inn**—A half century old "country elegant" estate home nestled in the hills above town. Nearby are spectacular hiking trails, gem mining, skiing and crafts. Exit MM 331 off the Blue Ridge Parkway. We specialize in making our guests comfortable.

| | | | |
|---|---|---|---|
| 1. No Smoking | 5. Tennis Available | 9. Credit Cards Accepted | 13. Lunch Available | 17. Shared Bath |
| 2. No Pets | 6. Golf Available | 10. Personal Checks Accepted | 14. Public Transportation | 18. Afternoon Tea |
| 3. No Children | 7. Swiming Available | 11. Off Season Rates | 15. Reservations Necessary | ★ Commissions given |
| 4. Senior Citizen Rates | 8. Skiing Available | 12. Dinner Available | 16. Private Bath | to Travel Agents |

## Tryon *

Wainwright, Jennifer & Jeremy
200 Pine Crest Land, 28782
(800) 633-3001

**Amenities:** 2,5,6,7,9,10,12, 15,16
**Breakfast:** F.

**Dbl. Oc.:** $52.50 - $142.00
**Sgl. Oc.:** $42.00 - $130.00
**Third Person:** $28.00
**Child:** under 17 yrs. -
$17.50

**Pine Crest Inn**—Beautiful Blue Ridge country inn. 28 rooms, many with fireplaces. Cottages, cabins and the main inn on three peaceful acres. Close to gourmet restaurants, the Biltmore Estate, golf, tennis and magnificent scenery.

## Tryon

Weingartner, Anneliese & Ray
Howard Gap Rd.
P.O. Box 366, 28782
(704) 859-9114

**Amenities:** 2,7,9,10,12,15,16
**Breakfast:** F.

**Dbl. Oc.:** $58.80 - $78.75
**Sgl. Oc.:** $47.50 - $73.50
**Third Person:** $8.40
**Child:** $8.40

**Stone Hedge Inn**—Beautiful old estate on 28 acres at the base of the Blue Ridge Mountains. Some fireplaces, some kitchens. Restaurant guests enjoy continental cuisine while viewing a mountainside setting through picture windows. Rooms are decorated with antiques.

## Washington *

Hervey, Jeanne & Lawrence
400 E. Main St., 27889
(919) 946-7184

**Amenities:** 2,5,9,10,16
**Breakfast:** F.

**Dbl. Oc.:** $57.75 - $68.25
**Sgl. Oc.:** $47.25 - $57.75
**Third Person:** $10.50
**Child:** under 6 yrs. -
no charge

**Pamlico House**—Turn-of-the-century colonial revival home in the historic district. Large wrap-around porch, parlor, large formal dining room and elegant guest rooms. Air-conditioning and TV in each room. Telephone available. Located on historic Ablemarle tour route.

## Waynesville

Minick, Jeffrey
108 Pigeon St., 28786
(704) 456-7521

**Amenities:** 1,2,9,10,11,16
**Breakfast:** F.

**Dbl. Oc.:** $50.00
**Sgl. Oc.:** $40.00
**Third Person:** $10.00

**The Palmer House**—The inn was built before the turn-of-the-century and is located within one block of Main St. It is one of the last of Waynesville's once numerous tourist homes. Good food and friendly service. A home-away-from-home. Come and relax and enjoy the mountain view.

## Wilmington *

Ackiss, Catherine & Walker
No. 410 Orange St., 28401
(919) 251-0863,
(800) 476-0723

**Amenities:** 1,2,4,5,6,7,9,10, 14,15,16,18
**Breakfast:** F.

**Dbl. Oc.:** $65.00
**Sgl. Oc.:** $59.40
**Third Person:** $15.00

**Catherine's Inn on Orange**—Experience the warm, gracious hospitality of our restored 1875 home. Charming rooms furnished with antiques and reproductions. Located in historic downtown. Relax by our pool. After a tasty breakfast, enjoy nearby antique shops, galleries, museums and tours.

| | | | | |
|---|---|---|---|---|
| 1. No Smoking | 5. Tennis Available | 9. Credit Cards Accepted | 13. Lunch Available | 17. Shared Bath |
| 2. No Pets | 6. Golf Available | 10. Personal Checks Accepted | 14. Public Transportation | 18. Afternoon Tea |
| 3. No Children | 7. Swiming Available | 11. Off Season Rates | 15. Reservations Necessary | ★ Commissions given |
| 4. Senior Citizen Rates | 8. Skiing Available | 12. Dinner Available | 16. Private Bath | to Travel Agents |

## Wilmington

Anderson, Connie
520 Orange St., 28401
(919) 343-8128

**Amenities:** 1,10,14,16
**Breakfast:** F.

**Dbl. Oc.:** $65.00
**Sgl. Oc.:** $50.00
**Third Person:** $10.00
**Child:** under 2 yrs. -
no charge

**Anderson Guest House**—1851 Italianate townhouse overlooking private garden. Furnished with antiques and ceiling fans. Working fireplaces. Drinks upon arrival. A gourmet breakfast is served in the elegant dining room or on the porches. Walk to many sites and fine restaurants.

## Wilmington *

Benson, Kathleen
311 Cottage Lane, 28401
(919) 763-0511

**Amenities:** 1,2,6,10,16
**Breakfast:** C.

**Dbl. Oc.:** $69.70
**Sgl. Oc.:** $64.70
**Child:** under 12 yrs. -
no charge

**The Wine House**—Luxurious accommodations in the heart of the historic district. Enjoy the charm of the brick walled courtyard and the privacy of the separate guest house accommodations. Each room features a queen bed, fireplace, ceiling fan, wet bar, refrigerator and private bath.

## Wilmington,

Walsh, Kate
412 So. 3rd. St., 28401
(919) 762-8562

**Amenities:** 2,3,6,10,12,13,16
**Breakfast:** F.

**Dbl. Oc.:** $75.60
**Sgl. Oc.:** $90.20

**The Worth House - A Victorian Inn**—Elegant, private and luxurious this romantic Victorian inn is a dream come true! Guest rooms are furnished in antiques. Beds are dressed in fine linens. Private baths with thick white towels and imported soaps. An outstanding breakfast is served in bed or in the dining room.

## Winston-Salem *

Kirley, Shelley
612 Summit St., 27101
(919) 724-1074

**Amenities:** 2,3,10,11,14,
15,16,18
**Breakfast:** F.

**Dbl. Oc.:** $52.50 - $78.75
**Sgl. Oc.:** $52.50 - $73.50
**Third Person:** $10.00
**Child:** over 12 yrs. - $10.00

**Lady Anne's Victorian Bed & Breakfast**—Historic Victorian home circa 1890. Walking distance of downtown, fine restaurants and parks. Near historic Old Salem. Elegant antiques and Oriental rugs. Phones, cable TV, VCR, stereo and refrigerator. Evening dessert tray. Private entrance, porch and parlor for guests.

---

| | | | | |
|---|---|---|---|---|
| 1. No Smoking | 5. Tennis Available | 9. Credit Cards Accepted | 13. Lunch Available | 17. Shared Bath |
| 2. No Pets | 6. Golf Available | 10. Personal Checks Accepted | 14. Public Transportation | 18. Afternoon Tea |
| 3. No Children | 7. Swiming Available | 11. Off Season Rates | 15. Reservations Necessary | ★ Commissions given |
| 4. Senior Citizen Rates | 8. Skiing Available | 12. Dinner Available | 16. Private Bath | to Travel Agents |

# OHIO

## The Buckeye State

Capitol:  Columbus
Statehood:  March 1, 1803; the 17th state
State Motto:  With God, All Things Are Possible
State Song:  "Beautiful Ohio"
State Bird:  Cardinal
State Flower:  Scarlet Carnation
State Tree:  Buckeye

Ohio took its name from the Iroquois Indian word meaning something great. Ohio is great, and it has a mixture of great people with different living habits settled in pockets up and down this state. You can get the feeling you are in New England, West Virginia or Iowa, depending upon what section of the state you happen to be visiting.

Johnny Chapman, the original Johnny Appleseed, walked through Ohio sewing his apple seeds so that the frontier families might have fresh fruit. His orchards can still be found, but a modern Ohio has replaced his frontier land.

The state of Ohio is proud of her contribution to the space program. John Glenn, the first astronaut to orbit the world, and Neil Armstrong, the first astronaut to walk on the moon, both came from this state. Seven presidents were also born in Ohio: Grant, Hayes, Garfield, Harrison, McKinley, Taft and Harding.

## *Akron*

Pinnick, Jeanne & Harry
601 Copley Rd., 44320
(216) 535-1952

**Amenities:** 1,2,5,6,7,8,10,14,16,17
**Breakfast:** F.
**Dbl. Oc.:** $30.00
**Sgl. Oc.:** $24.00
**Third Person:** $6.00
**Child:** $6.00

**Portage House**—Two miles east of I-77. A three-story Tudor in the historic area of the ancient portage route between two river systems. Homemade breads and jams. Four doubles; one single. Smoking limited. Pets restricted.

## *Albany*

Hutchins, Sarah
9 Clinton St., 45710
(614) 698-6311

**Amenities:** 2,10,15,17,18
**Breakfast:** C.
**Dbl. Oc.:** $35.00 - $60.00
**Sgl. Oc.:** $20.00 - $30.00
**Third Person:** $5.00 - $15.00
**Child:** over 8 yrs - $5.00-$15.00

**The Albany House**—Experience today's comfort in yesterday's atmosphere. Historic house featuring antiques and collectibles in small village ten minutes from Athens and Ohio University. Super continental breakfast, afternoon and evening hors d'oeuvres.

## *Ashtabula*

Goode, Pat & Paul
1084 Walnut Blvd., 44004
(216) 964-8449

**Amenities:** 2,5,6,7,10,16,17
**Breakfast:** F.

**Dbl. Oc.:** $45.00 - $50.00
**Sgl. Oc.:** $35.00 - $40.00
**Third Person:** $15.00

**Michael Cahill B&B**—In Ashtabula Harbor, one of the oldest ports on Lake Erie. Large stick-style Victorian home built in 1887. Wap-around front porch, large parlors, convenience kitchen for guests. Short walk to restored historic shops, marine museum and Lake Erie.

## *Avon Lake*

Williams, Margaret
249 Vinewood, 44012
(216) 933-5089

**Amenities:** 1,2,3,4,7,10,]
15,16
**Breakfast:** F.

**Dbl. Oc.:** $40.00
**Sgl. Oc.:** $25.00

**Williams House**—Twenty miles west of Cleveland; four miles off I-90 on Ohio 83. One mile from Lake Erie public beach. Quiet residential area. Private bath.

| | | | |
|---|---|---|---|
| 1. No Smoking | 5. Tennis Available | 9. Credit Cards Accepted | 13. Lunch Available | 17. Shared Bath |
| 2. No Pets | 6. Golf Available | 10. Personal Checks Accepted | 14. Public Transportation | 18. Afternoon Tea |
| 3. No Children | 7. Swiming Available | 11. Off Season Rates | 15. Reservations Necessary | ★ Commissions given |
| 4. Senior Citizen Rates | 8. Skiing Available | 12. Dinner Available | 16. Private Bath | to Travel Agents |

## *Cincinnati*

Hackney, Gary
408 Boal St., 45210
(513) 421-4408

**Amenities:** 1,2,3,9,10,14,15, 16,17
**Breakfast:** F.

**Dbl. Oc.:** $65.00
**Sgl. Oc.:** $65.00
**Third Person:** $15.00

**Prospect Hill Bed And Breakfast**—This elegantly restored 1867 Italianate townhouse is nestled into a wooded hillside with spectacular views of downtown. Rooms offer woodburning fireplaces, bath robes, sofas and period antiques. Within walking distance to downtown Cincinnati.

## *Circleville*

Maxwell, Sue
610 So. Court St., 43113
(614) 477-3986

**Amenities:** 1,2,4,9,10,16,18
**Breakfast:** F.

**Dbl. Oc.:** $55.00 - $75.00
**Sgl. Oc.:** $50.00 - $70.00
**Third Person:** $10.00
**Child:** over 8 yrs. - $10.00

**Castle Inn**—Elegant 1900 mansion with many castle details such as towers, arches and a walled garden. Gourmet breakfast in museum-quality dining room. Located on a street of beautiful old homes. Walk to museums, restaurants and antique shops.

## *Columbus*

Lyle, Johna & James
825 Ebner St., 43206
(614) 443-9859

**Amenities:** 1,2,5,10,12,14,15,17
**Breakfast:** F.
**Dbl. Oc.:** $55.00
**Sgl. Oc.:** $45.00

**Lyle House, German Village Bed And Breakfast**—100-year-old home within walking distance of German village shops and restaurants. Furnished in antiques and 18th century reproductions. Piano, recorders, dulcimers and banjos for guests use. Air-conditioned rooms. One minute from downtown Columbus. Bikes available.

| | | | | |
|---|---|---|---|---|
| 1. No Smoking | 5. Tennis Available | 9. Credit Cards Accepted | 13. Lunch Available | 17. Shared Bath |
| 2. No Pets | 6. Golf Available | 10. Personal Checks Accepted | 14. Public Transportation | 18. Afternoon Tea |
| 3. No Children | 7. Swiming Available | 11. Off Season Rates | 15. Reservations Necessary | ★ Commissions given |
| 4. Senior Citizen Rates | 8. Skiing Available | 12. Dinner Available | 16. Private Bath | to Travel Agents |

# OHIO

## Danville

Acton, Joyce & Jim
29683 Walhonding Rd., 43014
(614) 599-6107

**Amenities:** 1,2,3,5,6,7,9,10,12,15,16
**Breakfast:** C. (F. on weekends)
**Dbl. Oc.:** $75.95 - $86.80
**Sgl. Oc.:** $54.25 - $86.80
**Third Person:** $27.13
**Child:** $16.28

**The White Oak Inn**—A true "country" inn located in an expansive private/public wooded area that ensures privacy. Antique furnishings. A large fireplaced common room. 50-foot front porch. Screen house. Three fireplaced rooms. Near Amish country, historic Ohio-Erie Canal village and antiquing.

---

## Delaware

Detrick, JoHelen
8870 Olentangy River Rd., 43015
(614) 885-5859

**Amenities:** 1,2,10,13,15, 16,17,18
**Breakfast:** F.

**Dbl. Oc.:** $52.00
**Sgl. Oc.:** $42.00
**Third Person:** $15.00
**Child:** over 5 yrs. - $15.00

**Olentangy River Valley B&B**—A brick and cedar home situated in the middle of 10 wooded acres. Just 15 minutes from Ohio Wesleyan University, Ohio State University and Otterbein College. We are completely isolated from the hustle and bustle. Rooms are spacious and comfortable.

---

## Dellroy

Etterman, Marie & James
4247 Roswell Road SW, 44620
(216) 735-2987

**Amenities:** 1,2,3,4,5,6,7,9, 10,16,17
**Breakfast:** C.

**Dbl. Oc.:** $46.00 - $60.00
**Sgl. Oc.:** $36.00 - $46.00
**Third Person:** $10.00
**Child:** over 10 yrs. - $10.00

**Pleasant Journey Inn**—An elegant 14-room restored post-Civil War mansion decorated in antiques. Centrally located near Atwood Lake. Rural setting 30 miles south of Canton and two hours from Cleveland and Pittsburgh. Owners are a retired Navy couple.

---

## East Fultonham

Graham, Dawn & Jim
7320 Old Town Rd., 43735
(614) 849-2728

**Amenities:** 2,5,6,7,10,12,13, 15,17
**Breakfast:** F.

**Dbl. Oc.:** $33.92
**Sgl. Oc.:** $28.62
**Third Person:** $10.60
**Child:** under 10 yrs. - $5.30

**Hill View Acres**—Located 10 miles southwest of Zanesville, off U.S. 22W Large, spacious home on 21 acres with pond. Enjoy the pool year-round spa or relax in family room by the fireplace. Country cooking a specialty. Area popular for antiquing, pottery and outdoor activities.

---

| | | | | |
|---|---|---|---|---|
| 1. No Smoking | 5. Tennis Available | 9. Credit Cards Accepted | 13. Lunch Available | 17. Shared Bath |
| 2. No Pets | 6. Golf Available | 10. Personal Checks Accepted | 14. Public Transportation | 18. Afternoon Tea |
| 3. No Children | 7. Swiming Available | 11. Off Season Rates | 15. Reservations Necessary | ★ Commissions given |
| 4. Senior Citizen Rates | 8. Skiing Available | 12. Dinner Available | 16. Private Bath | to Travel Agents |

## *Geneva-on-the-Lake*

Haffa, Grace & Earle
5162 Old Lake Rd., 44041
(216) 466-8013

**Amenities:** 1,5,6,7,15,17
**Breakfast:** C.

**Dbl. Oc.:** $39.00
**Sgl. Oc.:** $35.00

**Westlake House**—Renovated home with wash lavatories and ceiling fans in rooms. Double beds. Watch the sun rise and set on LakeErie. Two-minutes walk to the beach. Swing on the front porch or pitch horseshoes in the backyard.

## *Lexington*

Hiser, Ellen & Bill
8842 Denman Rd., 44904
(419) 884-2356

**Amenities:** 1,5,6,8,10,11,12,
15,16,17
**Breakfast:** F.

**Dbl. Oc.:** $65.00 - $85.00
**Sgl. Oc.:** $45.00 - $70.00
**Third Person:** $12.00
**Child:** under 5 yrs. -
no charge

**The White Fence Inn**—Located midway between Cleveland and Columbus off I-71. One-hundred-and-four year-old farmhouse on 73 acres with fishing pond. Six tastefully decorated guest rooms. Three fireplaces.Tempting breakfasts. Special anniversary package. Great country get away near Amish and Mohican State Park.

## *Louisville* *

Shurilla, Mary
1320 E. Main St., 44641
(216) 875-1021

**Amenities:** 1,2,6,10,17
**Breakfast:** F.

**Dbl. Oc.:** $50.00
**Sgl. Oc.:** $40.00
**Third Person:** $10.00
**Child:** under 6 yrs. - $5.00

**The Mainstay**—A century-old 12- room Victorian home with richly carved oak woodwork and antiques. Gracious hospitality. Minute from *Canton Pro Football Hall of Fame*. When you arrive enjoy complimentary fruit and cheese. 6:00 a.m. coffee served in your room.

## *Milan*

Susko, Sandra
304 S.R. 113 W.
P.O. Box 537, 44846
(419) 499-2435, (800) 843-2624

**Amenities:** 1,2,4,5,6,7,9,10,
11,12,13,14,15,17
**Breakfast:** F.

**Dbl. Oc.:** $60.00
**Sgl. Oc.:** $50.00
**Third Person:** $8.00
**Child:** under 6 yrs. -
no charge

**Coach House Inn Bed & Breakfast**—150- year-old clippership builder's home. 15 secluded acres overlooking historic Milan, birthplace of Thoma Edison, on the Huron River. Hardwood floors, fresh flowers,Victorian decor. Vacation packages. Cedar Point and LakeErie are minutes away. Canoes, woodland and bike trails.

| | | | |
|---|---|---|---|
| 1. No Smoking | 5. Tennis Available | 9. Credit Cards Accepted | 13. Lunch Available | 17. Shared Bath |
| 2. No Pets | 6. Golf Available | 10. Personal Checks Accepted | 14. Public Transportation | 18. Afternoon Tea |
| 3. No Children | 7. Swiming Available | 11. Off Season Rates | 15. Reservations Necessary | ★ Commissions given |
| 4. Senior Citizen Rates | 8. Skiing Available | 12. Dinner Available | 16. Private Bath | to Travel Agents |

# OHIO

## Millersburg

Kaufman, Alma J.
175 W. Adams St., 44654
(216) 674-0766

**Amenities:** 1,2,6,10,11,15,17
**Breakfast:** F.

**Dbl. Oc.:** $45.00 & up
**Sgl. Oc.:** $35.00 & up
**Child:** under 2 yrs. -
 no charge

**Adams St. Bed & Breakfast**—Small, comfortable B&B in remodeled century home in Amish country. Shared bath. Air conditioning. Browse in library. Walk to shops. Owner, formerly Amish, happy to share information. Resident cat welcomes guests. Good country cooking and homemade breads. No smoking.

## Nevada

Cover, Sherry & William
203 Hillcrest Street
P.O. Box 399, 44849
(614) 482-2869

**Amenities:** 1,5,6,7,9,10,16,
 17,18
**Breakfast:** F.

**Dbl. Oc.:** $55.00 - $70.00
**Sgl. Oc.:** $45.00
**Third Person:** $12.00
**Child:** under 5 yrs. -
 no charge

**Nevada Comfort B&B**—Victorian home situated in quaint historic town 1/2 mile east of Upper Sandusky and 1-1/2 miles south of U.S. 30. Choose from four beautifully decorated guest rooms. Families welcome. Nearby park, antique shops and a craft and gift shop.

## Old Washington

Wade, Ruth
Old National Rd.
Box 115, 43768
(614) 489-5970

**Amenities:** 7,10,17
**Breakfast:** C.

**Dbl. Oc.:** $38.00 - $40.00
**Sgl. Oc.:** $32.00
**Third Person:** $20.00
**Child:** under 10 yrs. -
 $10.00

**Zane Trace B&B**—Exit 85 off I-70. Brick Victorian built in 1859. Spacious, quiet rooms. Five miles from Salt Fork State Park, 20 miles east of Zane Grey Museum. Antique parlor, lovely staircase, high ceilings, exquisite woodwork, large porch, off-street parking. Small village seven miles east of Cambridge.

## Peninsula

Tolle, Jerry
1856 Main St., 44264
(216) 657-2900

**Amenities:** 2,3,5,6,7,8,10,
 11,15,17,18
**Breakfast:** F.
**Dbl. Oc.:** $45.00 - $50.00
**Sgl. Oc.:** $40.00 - $45.00
**Third Person:** $10.00 (cot)
**Child:** over 10 yrs. - $10.00

**Tolle House**—A cozy Victorian century home in peaceful, historic village. Antiques, shops and sidewalks. Private parlor for guests with TV and games. Porches with swings and rockers. Surrounded by a national park. Hike, bike, fish and explore. Working colonial farm. Train rides. Air conditioning.

| | | | |
|---|---|---|---|
| 1. No Smoking | 5. Tennis Available | 9. Credit Cards Accepted | 13. Lunch Available | 17. Shared Bath |
| 2. No Pets | 6. Golf Available | 10. Personal Checks Accepted | 14. Public Transportation | 18. Afternoon Tea |
| 3. No Children | 7. Swiming Available | 11. Off Season Rates | 15. Reservations Necessary | ★ Commissions given |
| 4. Senior Citizen Rates | 8. Skiing Available | 12. Dinner Available | 16. Private Bath | to Travel Agents |

## *Pickerington*

Maxwell, Sue
27 W. Columbus St., 43147
(614) 837-0932

**Amenities:** 1,2,3,4,5,9,10,
16,18
**Breakfast:** F.

**Dbl. Oc.:** $45.00 - $65.00
**Sgl. Oc.:** $40.00 - $60.00
**Third Person:** $5.00
**Child:** over 8 yrs. - $5.00

**Central House**—Formerly the Central Hotel, 1860-1938. Totally renovated. Looks like early photographs. Victorian antiques. On "old village" street with quaint shops. All rooms have top-quality mattresses. Park, tennis courts and playground behind the inn. Famous for giant cinnamon rolls!

## *Plain City*

Yoder, Claribel & Loyd
8144 Cemetery Pike, 43064
(614) 873-4489

**Amenities:** 1,2,4,10,17
**Breakfast:** F.
**Dbl. Oc.:** $55.00
**Sgl. Oc.:** $45.00
**Child:** under 10 yrs. - $5.00

**Yoders Spring Lake Bed & Breakfast**—Located 3/4 of a mile south of Plain City. 100-acre farm. Stocked five-acre fishing lake. Bicycling, jogging and walking paths. Amish restaurants and shops nearby. Thirty minutes from downtown Columbus, Ohio.

## *Poland*

Mely, Ginny & Steve
500 So. Main St., 44514
(216) 757-4116

**Amenities:** 2,5,6,7,9,10,16
**Breakfast:** C.

**Dbl. Oc.:** $50.00
**Sgl. Oc.:** $45.00
**Third Person:** $5.00
**Child:** $5.00

**The Inn At The Green**—A classically proportioned 1876 Victorian "Baltimore" townhouse located on the south end of the Poland Village Green. All bedrooms are light, airy and comfortably furnished with four poster beds and antiques. 1 1/2 miles from the restaurant and business section of Youngstown.

| | | | |
|---|---|---|---|
| 1. No Smoking | 5. Tennis Available | 9. Credit Cards Accepted | 13. Lunch Available | 17. Shared Bath |
| 2. No Pets | 6. Golf Available | 10. Personal Checks Accepted | 14. Public Transportation | 18. Afternoon Tea |
| 3. No Children | 7. Swiming Available | 11. Off Season Rates | 15. Reservations Necessary | ★ Commissions given |
| 4. Senior Citizen Rates | 8. Skiing Available | 12. Dinner Available | 16. Private Bath | to Travel Agents |

# OHIO

## Put-In-Bay

Barnhill, Barbara
910 State Route 257
P.O. Box 283, 43456
(419) 285-6181

**Amenities:** 1,2,3,7,10,15, 16,17
**Breakfast:** C. and F.

**Dbl. Oc.:** $60.00 - $75.00
**Sgl. Oc.:** $60.00 - $75.00

**The Vineyard B&B**—Situated on the east end of this charming island in LakeErie. Located on 20 acres which includes a six-acre vineyard and a private beach. One-hundred-and-thirty- year-old home full of family antiques. Three large bedrooms, one with private bath.

## Ripley

Kittle, Patricia & Glenn
201 No. Second St., 45167
(513) 392-4918

**Amenities:** 1,2,3,6,10,15,17,18
**Breakfast:** F.
**Dbl. Oc.:** $60.00
**Sgl. Oc.:** $60.00

**Baird House Bed And Breakfast Boutique**—If you enjoy casual country relaxing times away from the scurry of the city, then you will love it here near the Ohio River. Listed in the *National Register of Historic Places*. Circa 1825. Porches. Antique shops. A short drive to fine dining. Fifty miles east of Cincinnati.

## South Amherst

Isaac, Marjorie
111 White Birch Way, 44001
(216) 986-2090

**Amenities:** 1,2,5,6,7,8,10,12, 13,15,16,17,18
**Breakfast:** F.

**Dbl. Oc.:** $45.00
**Sgl. Oc.:** $40.00
**Third Person:** $10.00
(child)
**Child:** under 1 yr. -
no charge

**Birch Way Villa**—A large country manor with modern conveniences and comforts. Fresh spring water from an underground spring lake. Summer and fall guests will enjoy meals supplemented with fresh vegetables and fruit from a large garden and small orchid. Located on 19 acres of woods with a lake.

## Tiffin

Pinkston, Michael
2348 So. CR #19, 44883
(419) 447-4043

**Amenities:** 1,7,9,10,12,15, 16,17,18
**Breakfast:** C.

**Dbl. Oc.:** $85.00 - $110.00
**Sgl. Oc.:** $85.00 - $110.00

**Zelkova Inn**—Nestled in the woods, Zelkova Inn is a blend of grandeur and simplicity. Quiet except for the breeze blowing through the trees. Completely refurbished and filled with the finest furnishings and antiques. Centrally located between Cleveland, Columbus and Toledo, Ohio.

| | | | | |
|---|---|---|---|---|
| 1. No Smoking | 5. Tennis Available | 9. Credit Cards Accepted | 13. Lunch Available | 17. Shared Bath |
| 2. No Pets | 6. Golf Available | 10. Personal Checks Accepted | 14. Public Transportation | 18. Afternoon Tea |
| 3. No Children | 7. Swiming Available | 11. Off Season Rates | 15. Reservations Necessary | ★ Commissions given |
| 4. Senior Citizen Rates | 8. Skiing Available | 12. Dinner Available | 16. Private Bath | to Travel Agents |

# OHIO

## Tipp City

Nordquist, Thomas
1900 W. State
Route 571, 45371
(513) 667-2957

**Amenities:** 1,2,4,5,6,7,9,15,
16,17
**Breakfast:** F.

**Dbl. Oc.:** $68.90
**Sgl. Oc.:** $58.30
**Third Person:** $10.60
**Child:** under 12 yrs. -
no charge

**Willow Tree Inn**—A restored 1830 federal-styled manor house. Original outbuildings on site. Quiet and relaxing atmosphere. Decorated with antique furnishings. Four working fireplaces. Located 15 minutes north of Dayton. Close to airport. Take Exit 68 off I-75.

## Troy

Smith, F. June
434 So. Market St., 45373
(513) 335-1181

**Amenities:** 2,4,5,6,7,9,10,14,16
**Breakfast:** F.
**Dbl. Oc.:** $60.00
**Sgl. Oc.:** $40.00
**Third Person:** $10.00
**Child:** under 12 yrs. - $5.00

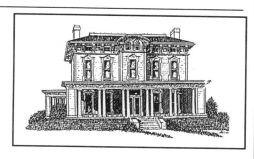

**H.W. Allen Villa Bed & Breakfast**—An 1874 Victorian mansion furnished with antiques. Rooms have private baths, air conditioning, TVs, phones and snackbars. Located north of Dayton near wineries, ATA trapshoot, International Air Show, hamvention, antiqueshops, Air Force Museum and Troy's Strawberry Festival.

## Westerville

Savage, Sally & Tom
93 College Ave., 43081
(800) 745-2678, (614) 882-2678

**Amenities:** 1,4,10,15,16,17
**Breakfast:** C.

**Dbl. Oc.:** $42.50 - $53.00
**Sgl. Oc.:** $37.00
**Third Person:** $10.00
**Child:** under 8 yrs. -
no charge

**Cornelia's Corner Bed & Breakfast**—Restored Victorian home (1850's) on Otterbein College campus. Walk to antique shops and eateries in uptown area. Our piano, porch, parlor and patio offer guests entertainment. Near gardens, parks, historic homes, Columbus Zoo, shopping malls and airport.

## Zanesfield

Failor, Joan
2875 Sandusky St., 43360
(513) 593-3746

**Amenities:** 2,3,5,7,8,10,
11,17
**Breakfast:** F.

**Dbl. Oc.:** $45.00
**Sgl. Oc.:** $35.00

**Myeerah's Inn Bed & Breakfast**—Located close to historic sites. Bikes may be borrowed by guests. Guest rooms are furnished with Ohio antiques, beautiful linens and fresh flowers. Hearty French country breakfasts such as egg strata, Swedish pancakes and fresh orange juice are served.

| | | | | |
|---|---|---|---|---|
| 1. No Smoking | 5. Tennis Available | 9. Credit Cards Accepted | 13. Lunch Available | 17. Shared Bath |
| 2. No Pets | 6. Golf Available | 10. Personal Checks Accepted | 14. Public Transportation | 18. Afternoon Tea |
| 3. No Children | 7. Swiming Available | 11. Off Season Rates | 15. Reservations Necessary | ★ Commissions given |
| 4. Senior Citizen Rates | 8. Skiing Available | 12. Dinner Available | 16. Private Bath | to Travel Agents |

# OKLAHOMA

## The Sooner State

Capitol: Oklahoma City
Statehood: November 16, 1907; the 46th state
State Motto: Labor Conquers All Things
State Song: "Oklahoma"
State Bird: Scissor-Tailed Flycatcher
State Flower: Mistletoe
State Tree: Redbud


Oklahoma was the last of the Indian territories in America. In 1893, the U.S. Government opened it up to the white man for settlement. The name Oklahoma was derived from two Indian words: "okla" for people, and "homa" for red. Some Indians have chosen to remain in the Ozark Hills and still speak Cherokee.

With the coming of irrigation, the land is now productive. However, for years the farmers had a difficult time. During the drought of the 1930's, this state suffered from the worst dry spell in years, and those who managed to stay alive pushed on with what little they had left to live in California. John Steinbeck wrote of them in his best seller, The Grapes of Wrath.

Natural gas and oil are the largest industries today in Oklahoma. It is one of the leading states in oil production.

Oklahoma's most famous personality was Will Rogers. He was a great American humorist and had much to say about many things. On this country, he is well remembered for saying, "There ought to be a law against anybody going to Europe until they have seen the things we have here."

## El Reno

Wiewel, Mrs. Ron
506 So. Evans Ave., 73036
(405) 262-9334

**Amenities:** 1,2,3,9,10,12, 13,15,16
**Breakfast:** F.

**Dbl. Oc.:** $43.00 - $69.00

**The Goff House Inn**—Step back into Oklahoma's past in a truly historic inn. Listed on the *National Register of Historic Places*. Three parlors and fireplaces. Walk to railroad museum, theatre and shops. El Reno is the crossroads of America. Route 66 and Highway 81. I-40 access exit 125. Come see us.

## Muskogee *

Lefler, Jean
501 No. 16th "Silk Stocking Ave.", 74401
(918) 683-0100

**Amenities:** 2,3,5,7,9,10,12,15, 16
**Breakfast:** F.

**Dbl. Oc.:** $66.50 - $105.00
**Sgl. Oc.:** $66.50 - $105.00
**Third Person:** $45.00

**Graham-Carroll House**—Just off I-40 near Tulsa. This majestic three-story home on "Silk Stocking Avenue" recalls the famous oil and Great Gatsby era. Famous for fine cuisine and sumptuous accommodations with suites, fireplaces, crystal chandeliers, marble floors, whirlpools and stained glass.

## Oklahoma City

Wright, Claudia
1841 NW 15th, 73106
(405) 521-0011

**Amenities:** 2,9,10,12,15,16
**Breakfast:** C.
**Dbl. Oc.:** $48.00 - $100.00
**Sgl. Oc.:** $43.00
**Third Person:** $20.00

**Grandison Inn**—Circa 1896. Brick and shingled three-story house surrounded by fruit trees, grapevine, lovely gardens and gazebo. Original stained glass and brass chandeliers. Country Victorian decor. Three fireplaces, parlor and third-floor suite. Close to downtown Interstates 35 and 40.

## Ramona

Agnew, Shauna & Jerry
Route 1, Box 1480, 74061
(918) 371-9868

**Amenities:** 1,2,7,9,10,12,13, 15,16,18
**Breakfast:** F.

**Dbl. Oc.:** $98.80 - $140.40
**Sgl. Oc.:** $98.80 - $140.40
**Third Person:** $20.00

**Jarrett Farm Country Inn**—Located twenty miles north of Tulsa on U.S. Highway 75. Lovely 230-acre horse farm. Two guest house suites with queen beds, living room and kitchen area. Elegant master suite in main house with king bed, sitting room and lavish bath. Dinner available for guests every night.

| | | | |
|---|---|---|---|
| 1. No Smoking | 5. Tennis Available | 9. Credit Cards Accepted | 13. Lunch Available | 17. Shared Bath |
| 2. No Pets | 6. Golf Available | 10. Personal Checks Accepted | 14. Public Transportation | 18. Afternoon Tea |
| 3. No Children | 7. Swiming Available | 11. Off Season Rates | 15. Reservations Necessary | ★ Commissions given |
| 4. Senior Citizen Rates | 8. Skiing Available | 12. Dinner Available | 16. Private Bath | to Travel Agents |

# OREGON

## *The Beaver State*

Capitol: Salem
Statehood: February 14, 1859; the 33rd state
State Motto: The Union
State Song: "Oregon, My Oregon"
State Bird: Western Meadow Lark
State Flower: Oregon Grape
State Tree: Douglas Fir

Oregon is noted for its mountains and coastal scenery. It is our most northwestern state, and forest covers almost half of it. It receives a tremendous amount of rain, which results in these forests and the beautiful green everywhere. Oregon leads the nation in lumber and in wood products. Much of this is exported, but most is used right here at home. The freezing and packing of home-grown fruits and the vast salmon, shrimp, crab and tuna industry are the main source of income for Oregon.

Vacationers love to visit this state. Millions come here every year to visit the beautiful parks and enjoy the excitement of camping in them. Mt. Hood is Oregon's majestic mountain, and a vacationer's paradise. It is perfect for the skier, hiker and climber.

# OREGON

## Ashland,

Reinhardt, Carmen & Joe
159 No. Main St., 97520
(503) 488-2901

**Amenities:** 1,2,5,6,7,8,9,10, 11,14,16,18
**Breakfast:** F.

**Dbl. Oc.:** $58.00 - $92.00
**Sgl. Oc.:** $53.00 - $89.00
**Third Person:** $25.00
**Child:** over 10 yrs. - $25.00

**Cowslip's Belle Bed & Breakfast**—Everyone asks for our recipes so here they are: cozy down comforters, chocolate truffles, teddy bears, antiques, Maxfield Parrish, peach pandowdy and scrumptious breakfasts. Located three blocks from theatres. Four rooms with queen or twin beds, private entrances and A/C.

## Ashland,

Treon, Donna
1819 Colestin Rd., 97520
(503) 482-0746

**Amenities:** 1,2,7,8,10,15,17
**Breakfast:** F.

**Dbl. Oc.:** $65.00
**Sgl. Oc.:** $60.00
**Third Person:** $15.00
**Child:** under 3 yrs. -
no charge

**Treon's Country Homestay Bed & Breakfast**—A peaceful B&B nestled in the tall pine forest south of Ashland. A pond for swimming and boating. Recreation room with pool table. Living room with fireplace. Guest kitchen. Barbecue area. Queen and twin beds. Families welcome! Hiking, biking and cross country skiing.

## Astoria,

Westling, Nola
3391 Irving Ave., 97103
(503) 325-8153

**Amenities:** 1,2,9,10,11,15,16
**Breakfast:** F.

**Dbl. Oc.:** $69.55 - $74.90
**Sgl. Oc.:** $64.20 - $69.55
**Third Person:** $10.00
**Child:** under 12 yrs. - $5.00

**Astoria Inn Bed & Breakfast**—Relax and be pampered in the comfort of our 1890 Victorian farmhouse. Lovely river and forest views. Quiet location. Two minutes from downtown. Music, movies and TV available. Visit the harp maker's workshop. Restored antiques blend beautifully with country French decor.

## Bend,

Bateman, Lorene
29 No.W. Greeley, 97701
(503) 382-4374

**Amenities:** 1,2,3,6,8,9,10,16
**Breakfast:** F.

**Dbl. Oc.:** $69.55 - $80.25
**Sgl. Oc.:** $58.85
**Third Person:** $15.00
**Child:** over 12 yrs. - $15.00

**Farewell Bend Bed & Breakfast**—Restored 70- year-old Dutch Colonial house. Four blocks from downtown shopping, restaurants and Drake Park on the Deschutes River. In winter ski Mount Bachelor. In summer golf and enjoy White River rafting. Complimentary wine or sherry. King beds, down comforters and terry robes.

| | | | |
|---|---|---|---|
| 1. No Smoking | 5. Tennis Available | 9. Credit Cards Accepted | 13. Lunch Available | 17. Shared Bath |
| 2. No Pets | 6. Golf Available | 10. Personal Checks Accepted | 14. Public Transportation | 18. Afternoon Tea |
| 3. No Children | 7. Swiming Available | 11. Off Season Rates | 15. Reservations Necessary | ★ Commissions given |
| 4. Senior Citizen Rates | 8. Skiing Available | 12. Dinner Available | 16. Private Bath | to Travel Agents |

## *Bend*

Kellum, Beryl
1054 N.W. Harmon Blvd., 97701
(503) 389-1680

**Amenities:** 2,3,5,6,7,8,10, 16,18
**Breakfast:** F.

**Dbl. Oc.:** $63.01 _ $84.41
**Sgl. Oc.:** $58.26 - $79.66
**Third Person:** $15.00

**Mirror Pond House**—A small inn at waters' edge where wild ducks and geese glide ashore. Near downtown. A quiet area. Big beds, private bath, sunny deck and guest canoe. Ski, fish, hike, golf, raft, shop or whatever. Evening wine and cheese rounds out a great day.

## *Brookings,*

Brugger, Sandra
21202 High Prarie Rd., 97415
(503) 469-2114 Ext. 4628,
(800) 327-2688

**Amenities:** 1,2,3,7,9,10,12,13, 15,16
**Breakfast:** F.

**Dbl. Oc.:** $75.00
**Sgl. Oc.:** $75.00
**Third Person:** $15.00
**Child:** under 10 yrs. - $15.00

**Chetco River Inn**—Relax in the peaceful seclusion of our private 35 acre forest, bordered on 3 sides by the river. Our inn is small and the number of guests is limited. Full country breakfast. Swimming, fishing, trails, horse shoes, archery await you! 30 minutes away from beaches.

## *Elmira*

McGillivray, Evelyn R.
88680 Evers Rd., 97437
(503) 935-3564

**Amenities:** 1,2,9,10,16
**Breakfast:** F.

**Dbl. Oc.:** $51.80 - $62.40
**Sgl. Oc.:** $41.80 - $52.40
**Third Person:** $25.90
**Child:** under 18 yrs. - $15.30

**McGillivray's Log Home Bed And Breakfast**—The best of yesterday with the comforts of today. King beds, private baths and air-conditioning. Breakfast usually prepared on the antique woodburning cook stove. Fourteen miles west of Eugene, OR on the way to the coast.

## *Eugene*

Brod, Barbara & Henri
988 Lawrence at Tenth, 7401
(503) 683-3160

**Amenities:** 9,10,12,14,15,16
**Breakfast:** C. Plus

**Dbl. Oc.:** $65.00 - $75.00
**Sgl. Oc.:** $55.00 - $65.00
**Third Person:** $10.00

**The Lyon And The Lambe**—An elegant home in a quiet neighborhood, only two blocks from the city center. Whirlpool bath, continental plus breakfast, complimentary aperitif and congenial hosts. Join us for an unexcelled visit in our bed and breakfast inn. Let us introduce you to the Emerald City.

| | | | |
|---|---|---|---|
| 1. No Smoking | 5. Tennis Available | 9. Credit Cards Accepted | 13. Lunch Available | 17. Shared Bath |
| 2. No Pets | 6. Golf Available | 10. Personal Checks Accepted | 14. Public Transportation | 18. Afternoon Tea |
| 3. No Children | 7. Swiming Available | 11. Off Season Rates | 15. Reservations Necessary | ★ Commissions given |
| 4. Senior Citizen Rates | 8. Skiing Available | 12. Dinner Available | 16. Private Bath | to Travel Agents |

## Eugene *

Getty, Jacki & Bob
640 Audel, 97404
(503) 688-6344 (voice or Todd)

**Amenities:** 1,2,5,6,7,9,10,14, 16,18
**Breakfast:** F.

**Dbl. Oc.:** $55.00
**Sgl. Oc.:** $50.00
**Third Person:** $15.00

**Getty's Emerald Garden Bed & Breakfast**—An architecturally interesting home in a country like setting. Large landscaped gardens with fruit, berries, and vegetables. Near most Eugene activities. Bikes and bike paths. Piano, TV/VCR and books. Park with pool. Sauna and hot tubs. You and your party are our only guests.

## Grants Pass

Althaus, Rosemary
762 NW 6th St., 97526
(503) 474-1374

**Amenities:** 1,2,5,6,10,17
**Breakfast:** F.
**Dbl. Oc.:** $65.00
**Sgl. Oc.:** $55.00
**Third Person:** $15.00

**Ahlf House Bed & Breakfast**—1902 Queen Anne Victorian. Architecturally interesting. The largest historic residence in Grants Pass. Furnished with fine antiques. This beautifully appointed home offers travelers pleasing accommodations. Located on the walking tour of national historic buildings of the town.

## Grants Pass

Hanson, Jacqueline
746 NW 6th St., 97526
(503) 479-4754

**Amenities:** 1,9,10,14,16
**Breakfast:** F.

**Dbl. Oc.:** $75.00
**Sgl. Oc.:** $65.00
**Third Person:** $20.00
**Child:** under 12 yrs. - no charge

**Wilson House Inn**—Historic landmark with elegant country charm located in the city. Four rooms with private baths. Each room is individually decorated in either early American, English, Victorian or French decor. Antiques throughout. Close to river, restaurants, theatre, shops and outdoor spa.

## Grants Pass *

Henry, Sheila & Victor
330 Humberd Lane, 97527
(503) 479-3650

**Amenities:** 1,2,6,7,8,9,10, 15,16
**Breakfast:** F.

**Dbl. Oc.:** $105.00
**Sgl. Oc.:** $105.00
**Third Person:** $20.00
**Child:** $20.00

**Country Paradise**—Romantic retreat nestled on five acres in a park setting. Elegant home. Private baths and entrances. King beds, swimming pool, wildlife, lawns, lily pond fountain and golf. Hearty breakfast served outdoors overlooking beautiful landscaping in the morning rays.

| | | | | |
|---|---|---|---|---|
| 1. No Smoking | 5. Tennis Available | 9. Credit Cards Accepted | 13. Lunch Available | 17. Shared Bath |
| 2. No Pets | 6. Golf Available | 10. Personal Checks Accepted | 14. Public Transportation | 18. Afternoon Tea |
| 3. No Children | 7. Swiming Available | 11. Off Season Rates | 15. Reservations Necessary | ★ Commissions given |
| 4. Senior Citizen Rates | 8. Skiing Available | 12. Dinner Available | 16. Private Bath | to Travel Agents |

## *Halfway* *

Olson, Mary Ellen
Rte. 1, Box 91, 97834
(503) 742-2990

**Amenities:** 1,2,4,8,9,11, 16,17
**Breakfast:** F.

**Dbl. Oc.:** $50.00 - $65.00
**Sgl. Oc.:** $35.00 - $45.00
**Third Person:** $25.00
**Child:** No charge - $12.50

**Birch Leaf Farm Bed & Breakfast**—Historic country house featuring sweeping views from the verandas. Pristine cross country snow fields. Raft or hike the Snake River, the Wallowas Mountains, or the National Recreation Area. Five bedrooms and a bunkhouse. Birding. Ponds and orchards on 42 acres. Horses available.

## *Hood River* *

Lee, Mac
1005 State St., 97031
(503) 386-1899

**Amenities:** 1,2,9,10,11,17
**Breakfast:** F.

**Dbl. Oc.:** $53.20 - $74.48
**Sgl. Oc.:** $47.88 - $69.16
**Third Person:** $10.00

**State Street Inn Bed & Breakfast**—Located in the heart of the scenic Columbia River Gorge. Dazzling view of Mount Adams and majestic Columbia. Close to skiing, wind surfing, hiking, restaurants and shopping. Casual elegance!

## *Jacksonville*

Groth, Patricia
240 E. Calif. st.
P.O. Box 13, 530
(503) 899-1942

**Amenities:** 1,2,9,10,11,12,13, 15,16
**Breakfast:** F.

**Dbl. Oc.:** $75.00
**Sgl. Oc.:** $65.00
**Third Person:** $10.00
**Child:** $10.00

**McCully House Inn**—Dining and lodging in historic Jacksonville. Three rooms with private baths. Full restaurant services. Lunch and dinner feature wonderful fresh meals, homemade breads and desserts. Walking distance to shopping, museums, Britt Music Festival.

## *Jacksonville*

Kraus, J.
175 E. California St., 97530
(503) 899-1900

**Amenities:** 9,10,12,13,16
**Breakfast:** F.

**Dbl. Oc.:** $75.00 - $175.00
**Sgl. Oc.:** $55.00 - $155.00
**Third Person:** $10.00
**Child:** $10.00

**Jacksonville Inn**—Built in 1861, this historic inn has eight air-conditioned rooms that are furnished with restored antiques. Luxurious honeymoon cottage. The award-winning restaurant is recommended by AAA and is open for lunch, dinner and sunday brunch. Over 700 wines.

## *Jacksonville*

Valletta, Patricia & John
455 No. Oregon
P.O. Box 1630, 97530
(503) 899-8938

**Amenities:** 1,2,6,7,8,9,10,11, 14,15,16
**Breakfast:** F.

**Dbl. Oc.:** $70.00 - $100.00
**Sgl. Oc.:** $70.00 - $100.00

**Judge TouVelle House**—An elegant historic home. Within walking distance to fine shops, restaurants, Britt Festival and nearby Shakespeare Festival. Enjoy the Pear Blossom Festival in the spring, the Britt Festival in summer and the Jazz Festival in the fall. Winter skiing and Victorian Christmas!

| | | | | |
|---|---|---|---|---|
| 1. No Smoking | 5. Tennis Available | 9. Credit Cards Accepted | 13. Lunch Available | 17. Shared Bath |
| 2. No Pets | 6. Golf Available | 10. Personal Checks Accepted | 14. Public Transportation | 18. Afternoon Tea |
| 3. No Children | 7. Swiming Available | 11. Off Season Rates | 15. Reservations Necessary | ★ Commissions given |
| 4. Senior Citizen Rates | 8. Skiing Available | 12. Dinner Available | 16. Private Bath | to Travel Agents |

## *Jacksonville* *

Winsley, Charlotte & George
540 E. California St.
P.O. Box 128, 97530 (mail)
(503) 899-1868

**Amenities:** 1,2,5,6,7,8,10,11, 14,15,16,17
**Breakfast:** F.

**Dbl. Oc.:** $70.00 - $90.00
**Sgl. Oc.:** $70.00 - $90.00
**Third Person:** $20.00

**Reames House, 1868**—Listed in the *National Register of Historic Places.* The perfect place to enjoy Jacksonville's music festivals, Ashland's Shakespeare, rafting, hiking, fishing and skiing.Victorian elegance, lace, twining roses and potpourri. Four guest rooms. Spacious garden setting.

## *Junction City*

Mode, Irma
94125 Love Lake Rd., 7448
(503) 998-1904

**Amenities:** 1,2,3,5,6,7,9,10, 15,16
**Breakfast:** F.

**Dbl. Oc.:** $63.60
**Sgl. Oc.:** $53.00

**Black Bart Bed & Breakfast**—A country bed and breakfast situated on 13 acres. Enjoy the quiet rural life for a day or more. Our home is over 100 years old and is filled with antqiues and collectibles. Our guest rooms capture the rustic heritage and country atmosphere. Borchure sent on request.

## *Lafayette*

Ross, Ronald
675 Hwy. 99 W., 97127
(503) 864-3740

**Amenities:** 1,2,10,16,18
**Breakfast:** C. and F.

**Dbl. Oc.:** $50.00
**Sgl. Oc.:** $50.00
**Third Person:** $10.00

**Kelty Estate Bed And Breakfast**—Built in 1872, this early colonial-style home is on the*National Register of Historic Places.* Located in the heart of the Oregon wine country, across the street from the Lafayette Antique Mall. Nearby are the Yamhill County Museum and wineries. One hour to the coast or mountains.

## *Lincoln City* *

Brey, Milton
3725 NW Keel, 97367
(503) 994-7123

**Amenities:** 1,2,5,6,7,9, 10,11,17
**Breakfast:** F.

**Dbl. Oc.:** $53.00 - $68.00
**Sgl. Oc.:** $53.00
**Third Person:** $15.00
**Child:** under 15 yrs. - $10.00

**Brey House Sea View Bed & Breakfast**—The ocean awaits you just across the street. This large Cape Cod house has all the makings of a great vacation. Resaurants and shopping within walking distance. Close to deep sea fishing and crabbing. Whale watching and storm watching from the Brey House.

| | | | | |
|---|---|---|---|---|
| 1. No Smoking | 5. Tennis Available | 9. Credit Cards Accepted | 13. Lunch Available | 17. Shared Bath |
| 2. No Pets | 6. Golf Available | 10. Personal Checks Accepted | 14. Public Transportation | 18. Afternoon Tea |
| 3. No Children | 7. Swiming Available | 11. Off Season Rates | 15. Reservations Necessary | ★ Commissions given |
| 4. Senior Citizen Rates | 8. Skiing Available | 12. Dinner Available | 16. Private Bath | to Travel Agents |

## *Portland*

Hall, Ms. Lori
125 S.W. Hooker St., 97201
(503) 222-4435

**Amenities:** 1,2,3,5,6,7,9,10,
      14,15,16,17
**Breakfast:** C. Plus
**Dbl. Oc.:** $80.00 - $110.00
**Sgl. Oc.:** $65.00 - $95.00
**Third Person:** $20.00 - $35.00

**General Hooker's B&B**—A casual, elegant Victorian in a quiet historic, downtown neighborhood. Preferred by business travelers for its superb location, amenities and creature comforts. Original art. View from the roof deck. Spa. TV. Air-conditioning. Knowledgeable hosts.

## *Portland*

Hartman, Katie & Christopher
2937 NE 20th Ave., 97212
(503) 281-2182

**Amenities:** 2,6,9,10,15,16,17
**Breakfast:** F.

**Dbl. Oc.:** $54.50 - $76.30
**Sgl. Oc.:** $49.05 - $76.30
**Third Person:** $10.90

**Heartmans Hearth A Bed & Breakfast**—Our 1911 arts-n-crafts home is just ten minutes from downtown and the airport. Antiques and contemporary art combine to create a relaxed atmosphere. Near convention center and Lloyd Center. Three blocks to the bus line. Art deco suite, jacuzzi and sauna available. Resident cat.

## *Portland*

Laughlin, Milli
5758 NE Emerson, 97218-2406
(503) 282-7892

**Amenities:** 1,2,5,6,7,8,10
      14,17
**Breakfast:** F.

**Dbl. Oc.:** $40.00 - $45.00
**Sgl. Oc.:** $35.00 - $40.00

**Hostess House**—Warmth and hospitality in a contemporary setting. Breakfast is served in the dining room overlooking the deep terraced yard. Large deck for sitting, reading or writing. A quiet residence adjacent to public transportation. Near main highway, arterials and airport.

## *Portland*

Sauter, Mary
4314 No. Mississippi Ave., 97217
(503) 284-5893

**Amenities:** 1,2,9,10,11,12,14,
      16,17,18
**Breakfast:** F.

**Dbl. Oc.:** $47.25 - $112.65
**Sgl. Oc.:** $31.70 - $108.10
**Child:** under 5 yrs. - $15.00

**John Palmer House**—45 minutes from Columbia Gorge, Mt. Hood and the wine country. One hour to the Pacific Ocean. Our beautiful Victorian can be your home-away-from-home. Award-winning decor. Gourmet chef. Your hosts delight in providing the extraordinary free color brochure.

| | | | | |
|---|---|---|---|---|
| 1. No Smoking | 5. Tennis Available | 9. Credit Cards Accepted | 13. Lunch Available | 17. Shared Bath |
| 2. No Pets | 6. Golf Available | 10. Personal Checks Accepted | 14. Public Transportation | 18. Afternoon Tea |
| 3. No Children | 7. Swiming Available | 11. Off Season Rates | 15. Reservations Necessary | ★ Commissions given |
| 4. Senior Citizen Rates | 8. Skiing Available | 12. Dinner Available | 16. Private Bath | to Travel Agents |

## Portland

Tebo, Marcelle & John
5733 SW Dickinson St., 7219
(503) 246-1839

**Amenities:** 1,2,10,14,17,18
**Breakfast:** F.

**Dbl. Oc.:** $54.50 - $49.05
**Sgl. Oc.:** $43.60 - $49.05

**Cape Cod B&B**—Located 10 minutes south of town off I-5 in a quiet area. Two rooms with queen and twin beds. Traditional and antique furniture. Outdoor spa in ivy-hedge enclosed garden. Near antique shops, wineries and Morman Temple. One hour to beach, Mt. Hood. and Columbia River Gorge.

## Seal Rock

Tarter, Barbara
6576 NW Pacific Coast Hwy 101, 97376
(503) 563-2259

**Amenities:** 1,2,3,9,10,15,16, 18
**Breakfast:** F.

**Dbl. Oc.:** $61.95 - $78.75
**Third Person:** $15.00
**Child:** no charge - $15.00

**Blackberry Inn**—12 miles south of Newport. 1940's Cape Cod. A short walk from the beach. Jacuzzi under the stars. Good food. Comfortable beds. Friendly outside pets. Acres of trails. Sitting area with fireplace. Near many tourist attractions.

## St. Helens *

Hopkins, Evelyn & Neal
105 South First, 97051
(503) 397-4676

**Amenities:** 1,2,4,6,10,15, 16,17
**Breakfast:** F.

**Dbl. Oc.:** $60.00
**Sgl. Oc.:** $40.00
**Third Person:** $10.00
**Child:** under 3 yrs. - no charge

**Hopkins House Bed & Breakfast**—Restored Dutch Colonial in waterfront national historic district. Close to Columbia River shops, musuem, restaurants, theatre and parks. Three guest rooms. Enjoy the fireplace, parlor, player piano and antiques.

## Tillamook

Still, Joy
3025 Gienger Rd., 97141
(503) 842-2265

**Amenities:** 1,2,3,10,12,16,17
**Breakfast:** F.

**Dbl. Oc.:** $45.00 - $60.00
**Sgl. Oc.:** $45.00 - $60.00
**Third Person:** $5.00

**Blue Haven Inn**—Built in 1916. Decorated with antiques. Situated in a quiet country setting. Individually decorated rooms. Full breakfast of your choice. Books, games, music and TV in the library. Antique shop on premises.

## Yachat *

Morgan, Baerbel & Sam
5985 Yachats River Rd., 97498
(503) 547-3813

**Amenities:** 1,2,9,16
**Breakfast:** F.

**Dbl. Oc.:** $65.00 - $95.00
**Sgl. Oc.:** $65.00 - $95.00
**Third Person:** $12.00

**Serenity Bed and Breakfast**—Located between Newport and Florence near Pacific Beauty. Gentle place to relax after countryside, forest and tidepool exploration. Minutes from Cade Perpetua, Sea Lion Cave, Heceta Lighthouse and covered bridge. Some rooms with private two-person jaccuzzi.

| | | | |
|---|---|---|---|
| 1. No Smoking | 5. Tennis Available | 9. Credit Cards Accepted | 13. Lunch Available | 17. Shared Bath |
| 2. No Pets | 6. Golf Available | 10. Personal Checks Accepted | 14. Public Transportation | 18. Afternoon Tea |
| 3. No Children | 7. Swiming Available | 11. Off Season Rates | 15. Reservations Necessary | |
| 4. Senior Citizen Rates | 8. Skiing Available | 12. Dinner Available | 16. Private Bath | ★ Commissions given to Travel Agents |

# PENNSYLVANIA

## *The Keystone State*

Capitol: Harrisburg
Statehood: December 12, 1787; the 2nd state
State Motto: Virtue, Liberty and Independence
State Bird: Ruffed Grouse
State Flower: Mountain Laurel
State Tree: Hemlock

Pennsylvania is enjoyed by tourists because it offers such a variety of things to see and do. It is the land where liberty began, the land of chocolate candy, steel mills, and the beginning of Little Leauge baseball.

One of the major attractions for tourists is the Liberty Bell in Philadelphia. This bell is a reminder to all Americans that here is where our Constitution was adopted and signed, giving all of us the right to private enterprise and initiative, and the right to live and worshop as we wish.

The steel mills in Pittsburgh, the beautiful Amish farms in Reading and Lancaster, the lively homes and cooking of the Pennsylvania Dutch throughout the heart of this state, is representative of what our forefathers visualized.

Pennsylvania offers scenic beauty and many historical attractions, from Valley Forge to the Gettysburg battlefields.

One of the oldest universities in our country is Pennsylvania University.

James Buchanan, our 15th president, was born here in 1791.

## *Adamstown* *

Berman, Thomas
62 W. Main St., 19501
(215) 484-0800, (800) 594-4808

**Amenities:** 1,2,3,4,7,9,10,11,
16,17,18
**Breakfast:** C.
**Dbl. Oc.:** $53.06 - $100.70
**Third Person:** $20.00

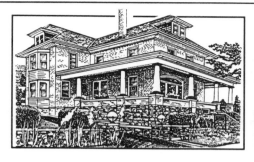

**Adamstown Inn**—Experience the simple elegance of a Victorian B&B with leaded glass doors, chestnut woodwork and Oriental rugs. It is located in a small town brimming with antique shops and minutes from outlet shopping. Master bedroom features a two-person jacuzzi. Highly acclaimed.

## *Airville*

Hearne, Ray
Muddy Creek Forks, 17302
(717) 927-6906

**Amenities:** 1,2,7,10,15,16,
17,18
**Breakfast:** F.

**Dbl. Oc.:** $63.60 - $90.10
**Sgl. Oc.:** $53.00 - $79.50
**Third Person:** $20.00
**Child:** under 15 years -
$15.00

**Spring House**—An 18th century historic stone B&B in a scenic river valley. Featherbeds to roses. Wood fires. Regional cooking. Restful rural solitude. Hiking, fishing,wineries and horseback riding. Near restaurants, musuems, Gettysburg, Lancaster and the Amish countryside.

## *Bird-In-Hand* *

Davis, Sally & Ed
2658 Old Philadelphia Pike
P.O. Box 270, 17505
(717) 393-4233

**Amenities:** 2,4,5,6,9,10,11,14,16
**Breakfast:** C.
**Dbl. Oc.:** $65.72
**Sgl. Oc.:** $65.72
**Third Person:** $10.60

**Greystone Manor Bed & Breakfast**—Located in the center of the Amish on two grassy acres. Rooms are in a French Victorian mansion and carriage house.Quilt and craft shop on premises. Farmers markets, outlets, Strasburg Railroad and other attractions are nearby.

| | | | | |
|---|---|---|---|---|
| 1. No Smoking | 5. Tennis Available | 9. Credit Cards Accepted | 13. Lunch Available | 17. Shared Bath |
| 2. No Pets | 6. Golf Available | 10. Personal Checks Accepted | 14. Public Transportation | 18. Afternoon Tea |
| 3. No Children | 7. Swiming Available | 11. Off Season Rates | 15. Reservations Necessary | ★ Commissions given |
| 4. Senior Citizen Rates | 8. Skiing Available | 12. Dinner Available | 16. Private Bath | to Travel Agents |

## *Boalsburg*

Allison, Arlene
126 E. Main St., 16827
(814) 466-6290

**Amenities:** 1,5,6,8,9,10,14,
15,16,17
**Breakfast:** F.

**Dbl. Oc.:** $68.50
**Sgl. Oc.:** $68.50
**Third Person:** $68.50
**Child:** under 12 yrs. -
$31.50

**Springfield House**—A restored Victorian home located in historic Boalsburg village, just five miles from Penn State University. Within walking distance to specialty shops, restaurants and museums.

## *Brackney* *

Frierman, Deborah & Howard
Tripp Lake Rd.
RD 1, Box 68, 18812
(717) 663-2645

**Amenities:** 1,2,6,7,8,9,10,12,
15,16
**Breakfast:** F.

**Dbl. Oc.:** $60.00
**Sgl. Oc.:** $50.00
**Third Person:** $15.00
**Child:** $15.00

**Indian Mountain Inn**—Country inn nestled in the mountains of NE PA. Eight rooms with queen-size beds. Whirlpool spa, liquor, dinner. Murder mystery weekends, fall foliage tours and more! 510 acres for hiking, hunting. Close to Alpine ski resorts. Woodstoves, game room, craft shop. $207/couple/weekend.

## *Brookville*

Swigart, Joan
Bluebird Hollow
R.D. #4, Box 217, 15825
(814) 856-2858

**Amenities:** 10,16,17,18
**Breakfast:** F.

**Dbl. Oc.:** $42.00 - $60.00
**Sgl. Oc.:** $37.00 - 55.00
**Third Person:** $10.00
**Child:** no charge - $10.00

**Bluebird Hollow Bed & Breakfast**—Let us pamper you in our 1894 restored farmhouse. Four miles south of Exit 13 (I-80), near Cook Forest, and 75 miles NE of Pittsburgh. Nestled on 17 acres. You'll bask in country hospitality and treated as extended family! Watch bluebirds from breakfast bay. Weekly rates available.

## *Canadensis*

Min, Dosoon G.
Route 447
P.O. Box 247, 18325
(717) 595-7262, (800) 842-0497

**Amenities:** 5,6,7,8,9,10,
11,12,16
**Breakfast:** F.

**Dbl. Oc.:** $63.60 - $84.80
**Sgl. Oc.:** $47.70 - $63.60
**Third Person:** $47.70 -
$63.60
**Child:** under 10 yrs. -
no charge

**Laurel Grove Inn & Resort**—In the heart of the Pocono vacation land. Easy access to shops and churches. Many local attractions. A gracious 100-year-old inn on 30 beautiful acres. One-room cottages. Motel units. Delicious meals. Dining room open to public. Recreation room. Reasonable rates. Reservations preferred.

| | | | |
|---|---|---|---|
| 1. No Smoking | 5. Tennis Available | 9. Credit Cards Accepted | 13. Lunch Available | 17. Shared Bath |
| 2. No Pets | 6. Golf Available | 10. Personal Checks Accepted | 14. Public Transportation | 18. Afternoon Tea |
| 3. No Children | 7. Swiming Available | 11. Off Season Rates | 15. Reservations Necessary | ★ Commissions given |
| 4. Senior Citizen Rates | 8. Skiing Available | 12. Dinner Available | 16. Private Bath | to Travel Agents |

## *Canadensis*

Pickett, Esther & William
Rt. 447 & Seese Hill Rd., 18325-007
(717) 595-7115

**Amenities:** 2,3,5,6,7,8,10,15,
16,17
**Breakfast:** C. Plus

**Dbl. Oc.:** $37.10 - $53.00
**Third Person:** $15.00

**Dreamy Acres**—Located in the heart of the Pocono Mountain vacationland on three acres of land with a stream flowing into a small pond. The lodge is 500 feet back from the highway giving it a pleasing quiet atmosphere. Bed and breakfast from May 1 through October 31.

## *Canadensis*

Robinson, Barb & Dick
RD 1, Box 630, 18325
(717) 595-3152

**Amenities:** 1,4,5,6,7,8,10,
11,15,16,17
**Breakfast:** F.
**Dbl. Oc.:** $45.00
**Sgl. Oc.:** $30.00
**Third Person:** $12.50

"Nearbrook"

**Nearbrook**—This 1930's charming home is surrounded by roses, rock gardens, woods and a stream. A hearty breakfast is served on the porch. Pocono hiking trails and points of interest are mapped out. A contagious informality encourages guests to use the piano, games, wooden trains and sleds.

## *Carlisle*

Fitting, Jeanne
McClures Gap Rd.
RD 3, Box 480, 17013
(717) 249-1455

**Amenities:** 1,2,3,6,10,12,
13,16
**Breakfast:** F.

**Dbl. Oc.:** $45.00
**Sgl. Oc.:** $40.00

**Alwayspring Farm**—A 45-acre farm in a rural setting. Ten minutes to Carlisle, Dickinson College and U.S. War College. Easy day trips to Gettysburg, Washington, D.C., Harrisburg and Hershey Park. Ten minutes to I-81; 20 minutes to Pennsylvania Turnpike.

## *Carlisle*

Line, Joan & Robert
2070 Ritner Hwy., 17013
(717) 243-1281

**Amenities:** 1,2,6,10,15,16,17
**Breakfast:** F.

**Dbl. Oc.:** $48.00 - $158.00
**Sgl. Oc.:** $35.00
**Third Person:** $12.00
**Child:** $12.00

**Line Limousin Farmhouse B&B**—Relax and unwind in an 1864 brick and stone farmhouse on 100 acres. Two miles to Exit 12 off I-81. French Limousine beef cattle are raised. Enjoy use of golf driving range, antiques, including player piano. Two rooms, private baths and king/twin extra-long beds.

| | | | |
|---|---|---|---|
| 1. No Smoking | 5. Tennis Available | 9. Credit Cards Accepted | 13. Lunch Available | 17. Shared Bath |
| 2. No Pets | 6. Golf Available | 10. Personal Checks Accepted | 14. Public Transportation | 18. Afternoon Tea |
| 3. No Children | 7. Swiming Available | 11. Off Season Rates | 15. Reservations Necessary | ★ Commissions given |
| 4. Senior Citizen Rates | 8. Skiing Available | 12. Dinner Available | 16. Private Bath | to Travel Agents |

## Christiana

Metzler, Minnie & Robert
107 Noble Rd., 17509
(215) 593-5535

**Amenities:** 1,2,6,10,15,17
**Breakfast:** F.

**Dbl. Oc.:** $38.00
**Sgl. Oc.:** $29.00
**Third Person:** $15.00
**Child:** $5.30 - $9.54

**Winding Glen Farm Guest Home**—A dairy farm situated in a beautiful valley. Guests stay in the 250-year-old farmhouse with 16-inch walls. Watch the cows being milked, go fishing in the creek or take a walk to the covered bridge. See our slide show. Handmade quilts for sale.

## Cooksburg *

Williams, E.F. Skip
Cook Forest - River Rd., 16217
(800) 648-6743

**Amenities:** 2,3,4,7,9,11,12, 13,15,16
**Breakfast:** C.

**Dbl. Oc.:** $60.00 - $106.00

**Clarion River Lodge**—A small, romantic country inn on the gentle Clarion River adjacent to Cook Forest Park. Fine dining and spirits. Only 20 rooms. Air conditioning, TV and queen or king beds. Great hiking, canoeing, biking, X-C skiing. Open year round.

## Cresco

Swingle, Kay
RD 2, Box 1051, 18326
(717) 676-4225

**Amenities:** 2,5,6,7,8,10,17
**Breakfast:** C.

**Dbl. Oc.:** $30.00
**Sgl. Oc.:** $25.00
**Third Person:** $10.00
**Child:** $10.00

**LaAnna Guest House**—A Victorian home on 25 acres. Furnished with antiques of the Empire and Victorian periods. Spacious rooms, quiet village, lovely walks, waterfalls, mountain views and privacy.

## Dallas

Rowland, Jeanette & Clifford
Route 1, Box 349, 18612-9604
(717) 639-3245

**Amenities:** 1,7,8,10,17,18
**Breakfast:** F.

**Dbl. Oc.:** $63.60
**Sgl. Oc.:** $63.60
**Third Person:** no charge
**Child:** no charge

**Ponda Rowland Bed & Breakfast**—A farm home furnished in colonial antiques. Fabulous antique collections. Fireplace. Scenic 130-acre farm and 30-acre wildlife area. Swimming, canoeing, fishing, hiking, ice skating, tobogganing and cross-country skiing on premises. Montage/Elk Mountain ski areas are nearby.

## Elizabethville *

Facinelli, Beth & Jim
30 W. Main St., 17023
(717) 362-3476,
 Fax: (717) 362-4571

**Amenities:** 1,2,6,7,9,10, 15,16
**Breakfast:** C.

**Dbl. Oc.:** $63.60
**Sgl. Oc.:** $58.30
**Third Person:** $5.30

**The Inn At Elizabethville**—A comfortable 12-room house furnished in arts and crafts/Mission Oaks style. Located on Route 209 in south central Pennsylvania. Five rooms with private baths. Fax, phone and copy service on site. Conference room seating for 16 available for seminars, meetings and small dinners.

| | | | |
|---|---|---|---|
| 1. No Smoking | 5. Tennis Available | 9. Credit Cards Accepted | 13. Lunch Available | 17. Shared Bath |
| 2. No Pets | 6. Golf Available | 10. Personal Checks Accepted | 14. Public Transportation | 18. Afternoon Tea |
| 3. No Children | 7. Swiming Available | 11. Off Season Rates | 15. Reservations Necessary | ★ Commissions given |
| 4. Senior Citizen Rates | 8. Skiing Available | 12. Dinner Available | 16. Private Bath | to Travel Agents |

## Emlenton

Burns, Cynthia
109 River Ave., 16373
(412) 867-2261

**Amenities:** 1,2,6,9,10,17
**Breakfast:** C.

**Dbl. Oc.:** $42.40
**Sgl. Oc.:** $42.40
**Third Person:** $10.60

**The Barnard House Bed & Breakfast**—A cozy retreat nestled along the banks of the Allegheny River. The many porches and all five bedrooms offer scenic views of the peaceful river. Antique shops, golfing (on the nation's oldest golf course) — all within five minutes.

## Ephrata

Donecker, H. William
318-324 No. State St., 17522
(717) 733-8696

**Amenities:** 2,5,6,7,9,10,12,
13,14,15,16
**Breakfast:** C. Plus
**Dbl. Oc.:** $62.54 -$137.80
**Sgl. Oc.:** $58.30 -$132.50
**Third Person:** $10.60
**Child:** $8.48

**The Guesthouse And 1777 House At Doneckers**—Country elegance, suites, jacuzzis and fireplaces. Complimentary breakfast. Gourmet restaurant. Exceptional fashion stores. Artists and art galleries. Historic Lancaster County.

## Ephrata

Lawson, Judith
287 Duke St., 17522
(717) 733-0263

**Amenities:** 4,7,9,10,11,12,13,
15,16,17
**Breakfast:** F.

**Dbl. Oc.:** $53.00 - $79.50
**Sgl. Oc.:** $53.00 - $79.50
**Third Person:** $10.00
**Child:** under 12 yrs. -
$10.00

**Gerhart House Bed And Breakfast**—Built when quality and aesthetics were considered. Parlor trimmed in native chestnut woodwork. Beds have handmade Mennonite quilts and freshly ironed linens. In the heart of Amish country. Near antique markets, Ephrata Cloister and fine restaurants. Full breakfast.

## Erwinna *

Strouse, Ronald
River Rd., 18920
(215) 294-9100

**Amenities:** 2,3,9,10,12,15,
16,18
**Breakfast:** C. Plus

**Dbl. Oc.:** $74.20 - $132.50
**Sgl. Oc.:** $47.70 - $68.90

**Evermay-on-the-Delaware**—Located in rural Bucks County on 25 acres of gardens and meadows. The country hotel, in the *National Register of Historic Places*, offers lodging, including breakfast and afternoon tea. An elegant dinner is served Friday, Saturday, Sunday and holidays.

| | | | |
|---|---|---|---|
| 1. No Smoking | 5. Tennis Available | 9. Credit Cards Accepted | 13. Lunch Available | 17. Shared Bath |
| 2. No Pets | 6. Golf Available | 10. Personal Checks Accepted | 14. Public Transportation | 18. Afternoon Tea |
| 3. No Children | 7. Swiming Available | 11. Off Season Rates | 15. Reservations Necessary | ★ Commissions given |
| 4. Senior Citizen Rates | 8. Skiing Available | 12. Dinner Available | 16. Private Bath | to Travel Agents |

## Gap *

Krackow, Eugenie
6051 Old Philadelphia Pike
(Route 340), 17527
(717) 442-3139

**Amenities:** 1,2,3,4,9,10,14,
15,16,17,18
**Breakfast:** F.
**Dbl. Oc.:** $58.00
**Sgl. Oc.:** $58.00

**Fassitt Mansion Bed And Breakfast**—In Pennsylvania Dutch country. This restored 1845 stone mansion offers beautifully decorated guest rooms in an area surrounded by Amish farms. Antiques and quilts can be found throughout the mansion. Four fireplaces add warmth and coziness to this special, romantic setting.

## Gettysburg *

Agard, Mimi
44 York St., 17325
(717) 337-3423

**Amenities:** 1,2,5,6,7,8,9,10,
11,15,16,17
**Breakfast:** F.
**Dbl. Oc.:** $70.00 - $85.00
**Sgl. Oc.:** $65.00
**Third Person:** $10.00

**The Brafferton Inn**—The first house built in Gettysburg's historic district. 1786 charm and hospitality. History surrounds you in this house and community — bullet holes in the guest room mantle, for example. Innkeepers delight in making your stay memorable. Easy access to sights and restaurants.

## Greenville

Ochs, Diane & Tom
32 Eagle St., 16125
(412) 588-4169

**Amenities:** 2,10,15,16,17
**Breakfast:** C.

**Dbl. Oc.:** $42.40 - $53.00
**Sgl. Oc.:** $37.10 - $47.70
**Third Person:** $10.60

**Phillips House 1890**—A 100-year-old restored Victorian home in western Pennsylvania, midway between Erie and Pittsburgh. Near I-80 and I-79. Greenville is the home of Theil College. The surrounding Lakeland area offers many outdoor activities. Antiques, quilts and comfort.

---

| | | | | |
|---|---|---|---|---|
| 1. No Smoking | 5. Tennis Available | 9. Credit Cards Accepted | 13. Lunch Available | 17. Shared Bath |
| 2. No Pets | 6. Golf Available | 10. Personal Checks Accepted | 14. Public Transportation | 18. Afternoon Tea |
| 3. No Children | 7. Swiming Available | 11. Off Season Rates | 15. Reservations Necessary | ★ Commissions given |
| 4. Senior Citizen Rates | 8. Skiing Available | 12. Dinner Available | 16. Private Bath | to Travel Agents |

# PENNSYLVANIA

## Hanover *

Hormel, Monna
315 Broadway, 17331
(717) 632-3013

**Amenities:** 2,3,5,6,7,8,9,
            10,16,18
**Breakfast:** F.
**Dbl. Oc.:** $74.20 - $100.70
**Sgl. Oc.:** $67.84 - $94.34

**Beechmont Inn**—Thirteen miles from Gettysburg. An elegant 1834 Federal period inn with seven rooms, antiques, private baths, gourmet breakfast, fireplace and air conditioning. Nearby antiquing, wineries and a large state park with a lake.

## Hawley *

Lazan, Judith & Sheldon
528 Academy St., 18428
(717) 226-3430

**Amenities:** 5,6,7,9
**Breakfast:** F.

**Dbl. Oc.:** $75.00
**Sgl. Oc.:** $45.00
**Third Person:** $25.00

**Academy Street B&B**—A historic Italianate Victorian B&B with seven large air-conditioned rooms. Elegant lodging. Gourmet breakfast. Northeast Poconos. All lake recreational activities are nearby. Four bedrooms with private baths. Three bedrooms with shared bath.

## Hershey

Long, Phyllis
50 Northeast Dr., 17033
(717) 533-2603

**Amenities:** 1,2,6,7,9,10,11,
            15,16,17
**Breakfast:** F.

**Dbl. Oc.:** $47.70
**Sgl. Oc.:** $47.70
**Third Person:** $5.30
**Child:** under 2 yrs. -
        no charge

**Pinehurst Inn B&B**—A country setting within walking distance of Hershey attractions. Twelve guest rooms, large dining room and living room with fireplace. Wonderful for family reunions or small seminars. Less than an hour's drive to Gettysburg and the Pennsylvania Dutch county of Lancaster.

## Holicong

Auslander, James
5358 Route 202
P.O. Box 202, 18928
(215) 794-5373

**Amenities:** 1,2,3,5,6,7,8,9,10,
            11,15,16,18
**Breakfast:** F.

**Dbl. Oc.:** $79.50 - $132.50
**Sgl. Oc.:** $79.50 - $132.50
**Third Person:** $20.00

**Ash Mill Farm**—1790 manor house. 11 sheep-filled acres. Meals and tea to strains of Mozart, Brahms and Vivaldi. Five rooms with antiques. Suite available. Minutes to New Hope and Peddlers Village. Featured in *Gourmet* and *Family Circle magazines*. Fireplaces, veranda and flowered patio. Nearby super shops.

---

| | | | | |
|---|---|---|---|---|
| 1. No Smoking | 5. Tennis Available | 9. Credit Cards Accepted | 13. Lunch Available | 17. Shared Bath |
| 2. No Pets | 6. Golf Available | 10. Personal Checks Accepted | 14. Public Transportation | 18. Afternoon Tea |
| 3. No Children | 7. Swiming Available | 11. Off Season Rates | 15. Reservations Necessary | ★ Commissions given |
| 4. Senior Citizen Rates | 8. Skiing Available | 12. Dinner Available | 16. Private Bath | to Travel Agents |

## *Intercourse*

Schoen, Robin & Sterling
313 Osceola Mill Rd., 17529
(717) 768-3758

**Amenities:** 1,2,3,10,17
**Breakfast:** F.

**Dbl. Oc.:** $89.50

**Osceola Mill House**—Located in scenic Lancaster County surrounded by old-order Amish farms in a quaint historic setting. The 1766 inn is decorated with period antiques and reproductions. We have been told that breakfast alone is worth the trip.

## *Kennett Square* *

Hicks, Anne
201 E. Street Rd., 19348
(215) 444-3903

**Amenities:** 2,5,6,7,8,10,
12,15,16,17,18
**Breakfast:** F.
**Dbl. Oc.:** $79.50
**Sgl. Oc.:** $47.70
**Third Person:** $10.00
**Child:** $10.00

**Meadow Spring Farm**—An 1836 farmhouse filled with family antiques, collection of dolls, cows and Santa Clauses. Situated in the Brandywine Valley, home of the Wyeths, Longwood Gardens and Winterthur. Full country breakfast served in the solarium or dining room.

## *Lahaska*

Eck, Claire M.
Rt. 202, Box 500, 18931
(215) 794-0440

**Amenities:** 1,2,3,4,8,9,10,11,
14,15,16,18
**Breakfast:** C.

**Dbl. Oc.:** $85.00 - $100.00
**Sgl. Oc.:** $85.00 - $100.00
**Third Person:** $20.00
**Child:** over 12 yrs. - $20.00

**Lahaska Hotel "A Fine Country Inn"**—Bed and breakfast lodging in beautiful Bucks County. Comfortable and clean rooms. Air-conditioning. Victorian country decor. Restaurant on premises serving lunch and dinner.

## *Lampeter*

Mason, Richard
837 Village Rd., 17537
(717) 464-0707

**Amenities:** 1,2,6,7,9,10,11,12,
14,16,17,18
**Breakfast:** F.

**Dbl. Oc.:** $47.70
**Sgl. Oc.:** $42.40
**Third Person:** $15.90
**Child:** under 12 yrs. -
$10.60

**The Walkabout Inn**—A 1925 Mennonite home in Amish countryside. Porches and English gardens. Tour pickup at inn. Information on antique/quilt auctions. Amish dinners. Guest rooms feature stenciling, antiques and quilts. Five-course Aussie breakfast. Honeymoon and anniversary specials.

| | | | | |
|---|---|---|---|---|
| 1. No Smoking | 5. Tennis Available | 9. Credit Cards Accepted | 13. Lunch Available | 17. Shared Bath |
| 2. No Pets | 6. Golf Available | 10. Personal Checks Accepted | 14. Public Transportation | 18. Afternoon Tea |
| 3. No Children | 7. Swiming Available | 11. Off Season Rates | 15. Reservations Necessary | ★ Commissions given |
| 4. Senior Citizen Rates | 8. Skiing Available | 12. Dinner Available | 16. Private Bath | to Travel Agents |

## Lancaster

Flatley, Sue & Jack
1105 E. King, 17602
(717) 293-1723

**Amenities:** 1,2,9,14,16,17
**Breakfast:** F.

**Dbl. Oc.:** $58.30 - $68.90

**O'Flaherty's Dingeldein House**—Come and make our home your home. Enjoy genuine warmth and hospitality in the homey atmosphere of the Dingeldein House. Our Dutch colonial home is traditionally appointed for your comfort for a restful stay in beautiful Lancaster County. Our breakfast will make your day.

## Lancaster *

Giersch, Carol & Bill
1400 E. King St., 17602
(717) 396-8928

**Amenities:** 1,2,11,14,17,18
**Breakfast:** F.

**Dbl. Oc.:** $48.00 - $59.00
**Sgl. Oc.:** $37.00
**Third Person:** $11.00
**Child:** under 17 yrs. - $5.50

**New Life Homestead Bed & Breakfast**—A stately 1912 brick home in center of Amish and historic area. The feeling of visiting your auntie, spoiling guests with flowers, fruit and candy. Air conditioning. Hearty breakfasts and evening treats. Tours arranged. Videos on Amish. Rest in the gardens. Mennonite family.

## Lancaster

Graybill, Dorothy
900 W. Main St., 17522
(717) 733-6094

**Amenities:** 1,5,6,7,9,10,12,15,18
**Breakfast:** F.
**Dbl. Oc.:** $65.00 - $115.00
**Sgl. Oc.:** $55.00 - $105.00
**Third Person:** $35.00
**Child:** under 12 yrs. - $20.00

**Historic Smithton Country Inn**—A smiling, welcoming inn. Every room has a fireplace, a four-poster or canopy bed, leather-upholstered furniture, books, reading lamps and optional featherbeds. Antiques, handmade things, chamber music, candles and quilts contribute to make a very romantic setting.

| | | | | |
|---|---|---|---|---|
| 1. No Smoking | 5. Tennis Available | 9. Credit Cards Accepted | 13. Lunch Available | 17. Shared Bath |
| 2. No Pets | 6. Golf Available | 10. Personal Checks Accepted | 14. Public Transportation | 18. Afternoon Tea |
| 3. No Children | 7. Swiming Available | 11. Off Season Rates | 15. Reservations Necessary | |
| 4. Senior Citizen Rates | 8. Skiing Available | 12. Dinner Available | 16. Private Bath | * Commissions given to Travel Agents |

## Lancaster *

Hartung, Brant
2014 Old Philadelphia Pike, 17602
(717) 299-5305

**Amenities:** 2,5,6,7,8,10,15,17
**Breakfast:** C.
**Dbl. Oc.:** $58.30 - $79.50
**Sgl. Oc.:** $58.30 - $79.50
**Third Person:** $10.00
**Child:** under 2 yrs. - no charge

**Witmer's Tavern — Historic 1725 Inn**—A historic 1725 inn, Lancaster's only authentic pre-Revolutionary inn still lodging travelers. Fireplaces. Fresh flowers in rooms. Romantic. Pandora's antique and quilt shop. In *National Register of Historic Places*. In Pennsylvania Dutch heartland. $15 charge if fireplace used.

---

## Lancaster

| | | |
|---|---|---|
| Mitrani, Jacqueline & Stephen | **Amenities:** 1,2,3,5,6,7,15, | **Dbl. Oc.:** $58.00 |
| 2129 Main St.,Churchtown 17555 | 16,17 | **Sgl. Oc.:** $48.00 |
| (215) 445-6713 | **Breakfast:** C. (weekdays) | **Third Person: $10.60** |
| | F. (weekends) | |

**The Foreman House Bed & Breakfast**—Located in Amish country in Lancaster County, surrounded by beautiful farmlands. Quilts and antiques in area to purchase. An elegant old home in a quaint village. Furnished with heirlooms and local art. Many repeat guests. Gregarious hosts.

---

## Lancaster *

Owens, Karen & Jim
1049 E. King St., 17603
(717) 397-1017

**Amenities:** 1,2,3,5,6,7,9,10,
14,15,16,18
**Breakfast:** F.
**Dbl. Oc.:** $80.00 - $115.00
**Sgl. Oc.:** $80.00 - $115.00
**Third Person:** $30.00

**The King's Cottage**—Escape to an elegant, award-winning *National Register* in near Amish farms. King/queen beds, private baths, full breakfast, afternoon tea, air conditioning and fireplaces. Antiques, crafts, quilt shopping and historic sites. Amish dinner available. AAA, Mobil listed — excellent.

---

| | | | | |
|---|---|---|---|---|
| 1. No Smoking | 5. Tennis Available | 9. Credit Cards Accepted | 13. Lunch Available | 17. Shared Bath |
| 2. No Pets | 6. Golf Available | 10. Personal Checks Accepted | 14. Public Transportation | 18. Afternoon Tea |
| 3. No Children | 7. Swiming Available | 11. Off Season Rates | 15. Reservations Necessary | ★ Commissions given |
| 4. Senior Citizen Rates | 8. Skiing Available | 12. Dinner Available | 16. Private Bath | to Travel Agents |

## *Lancaster*

Smith, Stuart
Route 23, Churchtown, (location)
2100 Main St., Narvon, 17555 (mail)
(215) 445-7794

**Amenities:** 2,5,6,7,8,9,10,12,15,16,17
**Breakfast:** F.
**Dbl. Oc.:** $49.00 - $95.00
**Sgl. Oc.:** $49.00 - $95.00
**Third Person:** $20.00
**Child:** over 12 yrs. - $20.00

**Churchtown Inn B&B**—Circa 1735. In the heart of Pennsylvania Dutch country. A historic stone mansion. Dinner with an Amish family arranged. Musical innkeeper. Special event weekends(murder mysteries, concerts, Victorian Ball, etc.) Five minutes to tourist attractions, antique markets and outlets.

## *Lancaster*

Thomas, Jean
2336 Hollinger Rd., 17602-4728
(717) 464-3050

**Amenities:** 1,2,5,6,7,10,11,
12,13,14,15,16,17
**Breakfast:** F.
**Dbl. Oc.:** $58.30
**Sgl. Oc.:** $37.10
**Third Person:** $15.90
**Child:** 6 - 13 yrs. - $10.60

**Hollinger House B&B**—Built by a tanner in 1870. Hosted by a Mennonite family. It's grand, but homey. Close to Amish country, good restaurants, farmers markets, outlets, historic attractions and much more. Tours arranged. Deposit requested. Children welcome (no charge for those under six).

## *Lancaster* *

Zook, Mary K.
1687 Lincoln Hwy. E., 17602
(717) 392-9412

**Amenities:** 10,11,14,15,16
**Breakfast:** C. Plus
**Dbl. Oc.:** $38.00 - $65.00
**Sgl. Oc.:** $36.00 - $60.00
**Third Person:** $12.00
**Child:** under 6 mo. - no charge

**Lincoln Haus Inn B&B, 1687**— Lincoln Hwy. Amish hostess. Unique oak stairs and floor. All private baths. New honeymoon—anniversary suite. Two-three day minimum. Centrally located. Picnic facilities and swings. If you stay a week, one day is free. Air conditioning. No alcoholic beverages.

| | | | | |
|---|---|---|---|---|
| 1. No Smoking | 5. Tennis Available | 9. Credit Cards Accepted | 13. Lunch Available | 17. Shared Bath |
| 2. No Pets | 6. Golf Available | 10. Personal Checks Accepted | 14. Public Transportation | 18. Afternoon Tea |
| 3. No Children | 7. Swiming Available | 11. Off Season Rates | 15. Reservations Necessary | ★ Commissions given |
| 4. Senior Citizen Rates | 8. Skiing Available | 12. Dinner Available | 16. Private Bath | to Travel Agents |

## Leola

Parmer, Jean W.
111 Turtle Hill Rd., 17540
(717) 656-6163

**Amenities:** 1,2,5,6,7,10,15,17, 18
**Breakfast:** F.

**Dbl. Oc.:** $45.00
**Sgl. Oc.:** $30.00
**Third Person:** $10.00
**Child:** under 3 yrs. - $5.00

**Turtle Hill Bed & Breakfast**—Very scenic, one mile off Routes 222 and 272. Overlooks Conestoga River near an old mill — photographer's paradise. Rural area. Neighboring Amish farms.

## Lewisburg

Boldurian, Natalie & Tony
Route 192W
RD 2, Box 573A, 17837
(717) 523-7197

**Amenities:** 1,2,9,10,16
**Breakfast:** C.
**Dbl. Oc.:** $65.00 - $95.00
**Sgl. Oc.:** $65.00 - $95.00
**Third Person:** $10.00

**The Inn On Fiddler's Tract**—A historic 1810 luxurious limestone home situated on 33 acres. Contains five suites, private library and a formal dining room featuring private-party dining. A jacuzzi, sauna and hiking trails are just a few things available to make your stay with us special.

## Lumberville

Nessler, Harry
River Rd., 18933
(215) 297-5661

**Amenities:** 1,2,10
**Breakfast:** F.

**Dbl. Oc.:** $65.00 & up

**1740 House**—Situated in the most charming section of Bucks County, this B&B inn offers guests 24 early-American rooms, each with private bath and either terrace or balcony overlooking the Delaware River.

## Mansfield

Crossen, Sylvia S. & Stuart
131 S. Main, 16933
(717) 662-7008

**Amenities:** 1,2,3,4,5,6,7,8,9, 10,12,13,15,16,17
**Breakfast:** F.

**Dbl. Oc.:** $44.52 - $63.60
**Sgl. Oc.:** $40.28 - $63.60
**Third Person:** $12.00
**Child:** under 3 yrs. - $3.00

**Crossroads Bed & Breakfast**—A 1926 Georgian style B&B with four large bedrooms. Situated in a small college community in the scenic mountain region of northern Pennsylvania. Nearby museums, hiking, boating and sightseeing. Lounge, game/card room available. Whirlpool tub, TV and air conditioning.

| | | | |
|---|---|---|---|
| 1. No Smoking | 5. Tennis Available | 9. Credit Cards Accepted | 13. Lunch Available | 17. Shared Bath |
| 2. No Pets | 6. Golf Available | 10. Personal Checks Accepted | 14. Public Transportation | 18. Afternoon Tea |
| 3. No Children | 7. Swiming Available | 11. Off Season Rates | 15. Reservations Necessary | ★ Commissions given |
| 4. Senior Citizen Rates | 8. Skiing Available | 12. Dinner Available | 16. Private Bath | to Travel Agents |

## Marietta

Vogt, Kathy & Keith
1225 Colebook Rd., 17547
(717) 653-4810

Amenities: 1,2,9,10,15,17
Breakfast: F.

Dbl. Oc.: $47.70
Sgl. Oc.: $31.80
Child: $10.60

**Vogt Farm Bed And Breakfast**—Our cheerfully decorated guest rooms are located in our 1865 brick farmhouse. Some amenities that we offer are: a family room with a TV and fireplace, air conditioning, terry robes and quiet porches for your pleasure. Central location for Lancaster, York and Hershey.

## Mercer

Stranahan, Ann & James
117 E. Market St., 16137
(412) 662-4516

Amenities: 1,2,5,6,7,15,16
Breakfast: F.

Dbl. Oc.: $63.60
Sgl. Oc.: $53.00
Third Person: $10.60

**Stranahan House Bed & Breakfast**—A 150-year-old colonial Empire-style home furnished with antiques. Historic area. Amish country. Five minutes from I-79 and I-80. Located in center of town just a few steps from county courthouse. Lunch and dinner are available nearby.

## Mertztown

Dimick, Dr. & Mrs. Dean
RD #2, Box 26, 19539
(215) 682-6197

Amenities: 1,2,5,8,9,10,15,16, 17,18
Breakfast: F.

Dbl. Oc.: $63.60 - $68.90
Sgl. Oc.: $53.00 - $58.30
Third Person: $31.80

**Longswamp Bed & Breakfast**—Over 200-year-old country home set in lush Berks County farmland. Minutes from Allentown. Near Amish. Innovative breakfasts prepared by owner. Excellent nearby restaurants. Five cultivated acres; 40 acres of woods. Superb music and books. A library for guests.

## Milford

Schneider, Stewart
RD 2, Box 9285, 18337
(717) 296-6322

Amenities: 1,2,7,8,9,10,11, 16,17
Breakfast: F.

Dbl. Oc.: $60.00 - $85.00
Sgl. Oc.: $60.00 - $85.00

**Black Walnut B&B Inn**—A tudor-style stone house with historic marble fireplace, 12 charming bedrooms with antique and brass beds. A 160-acre quiet and peaceful estate. Conveniently located near horseback riding, antiquing, golfing, skiing, rafting and canoeing on the Delaware River.

## Montoursville

Mesaris, Harold
RD 1, Box 11A, 17754
(717) 433-4340

Amenities: 5,6,7,8,10
Breakfast: C.

Dbl. Oc.: $53.00
Sgl. Oc.: $53.00
Third Person: $10.00

**The Carriage House At Stonegate**—Provides 1,400 square feet of privacy for guests on two floors with two bedrooms. Located in the middle of an all-season recreation area, minutes north of I-80. Situated off I-80 on an 1800's-era farm.

| | | | | |
|---|---|---|---|---|
| 1. No Smoking | 5. Tennis Available | 9. Credit Cards Accepted | 13. Lunch Available | 17. Shared Bath |
| 2. No Pets | 6. Golf Available | 10. Personal Checks Accepted | 14. Public Transportation | 18. Afternoon Tea |
| 3. No Children | 7. Swiming Available | 11. Off Season Rates | 15. Reservations Necessary | ★ Commissions given |
| 4. Senior Citizen Rates | 8. Skiing Available | 12. Dinner Available | 16. Private Bath | to Travel Agents |

## *Montrose*

Rose, Candace & Frederick
26 S. Main St., 18801
(717) 278-1124

**Amenities:** 5,6,8,9,10,12,13,
15,16,17
**Breakfast:** F.

**Dbl. Oc.:** $35.00 - $60.00
**Sgl. Oc.:** $35.00 - $60.00
**Third Person:** $10.00 -
$15.00
**Child:** under 10 yrs. - $5.00

**The Montrose House**—Open year round. Chef owned and operated. Within walking distance of shops and stately homes. Set in the Endless Mountains, the inn is a favorite with sports enthusiasts and vacationers. Fine dining and cozy rooms in an earlyAmerican setting.

---

## *Mount Joy*

Miller, Yvonne
1382 Pinkerton Rd., 17552
(717) 653-4028

**Amenities:** 5,6,9,10,15,16,
17,18
**Breakfast:** F.

**Dbl. Oc.:** $53.00
**Sgl. Oc.:** $31.80
**Third Person:** $10.60
**Child:** under 13 yrs.- $5.30

**Green Acres Farm**—Green Acres is the place to go. Between Lancaster Amish country and Hershey. A twelve-room farmhouse. Sleeps 26. One-hundred-and-sixty acre grain farm. Pony and cart, kittens, sheep and goat. Trampoline. Swings. Peaceful. Many options for activity. Antique shop. Dried flowers for sale.

---

## *Mount Joy*

Swarr, Gladys
305 Longenecker Rd., 17552
(717) 653-4655

**Amenities:** 1,2,5,6,9,10,
15,16
**Breakfast:** C. Plus

**Dbl. Oc.:** $58.30 - $63.60
**Sgl. Oc.:** $47.70 - $58.30
**Third Person:** $12.72
**Child:** $7.00

**Cedar Hill Farm**—A 1817 stone farmhouse overlooking peaceful stream. Charming air-conditioned bedrooms. All private baths. Honeymoon suite with private balcony. Near Amish country and Hershey. Host born on this working farm. Nearby renowned restaurants. Genuine farmers market on Tuesdays.

---

## *Mt. Pocono* *

Marsh, Tracy
Grange Rd.
HCR #1, Box 9A, 18344
(717) 839-9234
$10.60

**Amenities:** 1,2,4,6,7,8,9,10,
11,12,13,16,17,18
**Breakfast:** F.

**Dbl. Oc.:** $69.90 - $95.40
**Sgl. Oc.:** $58.30 - $84.80
**Third Person:** $21.20
**Child:** under 10 yrs. -

**Country Road Bed And Breakfast**—Situated on four secluded acres of woods and rolling hills. Five rooms freshly linened and detailed with comfortable and cozy quilts. Features brass and canopy beds. Minutes from skiing, horseback riding and family entertainment.

---

| | | | | |
|---|---|---|---|---|
| 1. No Smoking | 5. Tennis Available | 9. Credit Cards Accepted | 13. Lunch Available | 17. Shared Bath |
| 2. No Pets | 6. Golf Available | 10. Personal Checks Accepted | 14. Public Transportation | 18. Afternoon Tea |
| 3. No Children | 7. Swiming Available | 11. Off Season Rates | 15. Reservations Necessary | ★ Commissions given |
| 4. Senior Citizen Rates | 8. Skiing Available | 12. Dinner Available | 16. Private Bath | to Travel Agents |

# PENNSYLVANIA

## Muncy *

Smith, Marie Louise & David
307 S. Main St., 17756
(717) 546-8949

**Amenities:** 1,2,3,5,6,7,8,9,10,15,16,17
**Breakfast:** F.
**Dbl. Oc.:** $58.30
**Sgl. Oc.:** $37.10
**Third Person:** $10.60

**The Bodine House**—Enjoy soft candlelight, warm fireplaces and antiques in a restored townhouse built in 1805. Located in the Muncy national historic district. Three blocks from shops and restaurants. The local attractions include hiking, skiing, biking and antiquing.

## New Bloomfield *

Ulsh, Carol & David
41 W. Main St., 17068
(717) 582-2914

**Amenities:** 1,2,3,5,6,7,8,10, 15,16,17
**Breakfast:** F.
**Dbl. Oc.:** $53.00
**Sgl. Oc.:** $42.40
**Third Person:** $26.50

**The Tressler House Bed & Breakfast**—Relax in this spacious Federal-period home tastefully decorated with antiques. Small-town location. Nearby rural attractions and historic points. Close to Harrisburg, Hershey and Carlisle for added interests.

## New Hope

Cassidy, Robert
Routes 202 and 263
Peddler's Village,
Lahaska, 18931
(215) 794-4004

**Amenities:** 1,2,5,6,9,10,12,13, 16,18
**Breakfast:** C.
**Dbl. Oc.:** $116.60
**Sgl. Oc.:** $116.60
**Third Person:** $15.90
**Child:** under 1 yr. - no charge

**The Golden Plough Inn**—Each of the 45 elegant guest rooms reflect the charm of 18th-century American country style. Jacuzzis, balconies, fireplaces are amenities. All have private baths, dressing areas, refrigerators, air conditioning and TV. Next to Peddler's Village, six restaurants and 70 shops.

## New Hope *

Glassman, Carl
111 W. Bridge St., 18938
(215) 862-2570

**Amenities:** 1,2,3,5,6,7,8,10,14,16,17,18
**Breakfast:** C.
**Dbl. Oc.:** $68.90 - $169.60
**Sgl. Oc.:** $63.60 - $159.00
**Third Person:** $22.00
**Child:** $22.00 (if crib provided)

**Wedgwood Inn Of New Hope**—Voted 1989 "Inn of the Year" by *Inn Guidebook* readers. This Victorian painted lady sits on two acres and is steps from the village center. Innkeepers Nadine and Carl Glassman speak French, Dutch, Spanish and Hebrew. AAA and Mobil rated. Five fireplaces, A/C and turn-down service.

| | | | |
|---|---|---|---|
| 1. No Smoking | 5. Tennis Available | 9. Credit Cards Accepted | 13. Lunch Available | 17. Shared Bath |
| 2. No Pets | 6. Golf Available | 10. Personal Checks Accepted | 14. Public Transportation | 18. Afternoon Tea |
| 3. No Children | 7. Swiming Available | 11. Off Season Rates | 15. Reservations Necessary | ★ Commissions given |
| 4. Senior Citizen Rates | 8. Skiing Available | 12. Dinner Available | 16. Private Bath | to Travel Agents |

## North Wales *

Kratz, Steve
1005 Horsham Rd., 19454
(215) 362-7500

**Amenities:** 2,6,9,10,12,15,16
**Breakfast:** F.
**Dbl. Oc.:** $87.00 - $140.00
**Sgl. Oc.:** $80.00 - $130.00
**Third Person:** $15.00

**Joseph Ambler Inn**—Twenty-eight room colonial inn on 13 acres. Antiques and reproductions. Private baths. Excellent restaurant with cocktails in 1820 stone barn. Nearby golf and tennis. Museums, historic sites and antique shopping.

## Orrtanna

Martin, Mary
96 Hickory Bridge Rd., 17353
(717) 642-5261

**Amenities:** 1,2,6,8,9,10,12,15, 12,15,16
**Breakfast:** F.

**Dbl. Oc.:** $$69.00 - $79.00
**Sgl. Oc.:** $50.00 - $60.00

**Hickory Bridge Farm**—Only eight miles west of Gettysburg. Unique country dining and bed and breakfast. Farm-style dinners served in a Pennsylvania barn. Country cottages in a quiet wooded setting by a stream. Full breakfast served at restored 1750 farmhouse. Owned and operated for 15 years.

## Oxford *

Hershey, Arlene & Ephraim
15250 Limestone Rd., 19363
(215) 932-9257

**Amenities:** 1,7,8,10,16
**Breakfast:** C. and F.

**Dbl. Oc.:** $40.00
**Sgl. Oc.:** $25.00
**Third Person:** $10.00
**Child:** under 6 yrs. - $5.00

**Log House B&B**—A log country home in Chester County. Quiet. Away from traffic noise. Wooded area. Picnicing, hiking and bicycling. Special attractions. One-half hour from Amish country. Open all year. Weekly rates available.

## Paradise

Rohrer, Marion
505 Paradise Lane, 17562
(717) 687-7479

**Amenities:** 1,2,6,10,11,16,17
**Breakfast:** C.
**Dbl. Oc.:** $45.00 - $60.00
**Sgl. Oc.:** $40.00 - $55.00
**Third Person:** $10.00
**Child:** under 5 yrs. - $4.00

**Maple Lane Guest House**—Situated on a 200-acre farm in the heart of Amish country. Four guest rooms with antiques, quilts, needlework, stenciling, canopy and poster beds. Forty-mile view. Good food and attractions here in Lancaster County Dutch country.

| | | | | |
|---|---|---|---|---|
| 1. No Smoking | 5. Tennis Available | 9. Credit Cards Accepted | 13. Lunch Available | 17. Shared Bath |
| 2. No Pets | 6. Golf Available | 10. Personal Checks Accepted | 14. Public Transportation | 18. Afternoon Tea |
| 3. No Children | 7. Swiming Available | 11. Off Season Rates | 15. Reservations Necessary | ★ Commissions given |
| 4. Senior Citizen Rates | 8. Skiing Available | 12. Dinner Available | 16. Private Bath | to Travel Agents |

# PENNSYLVANIA

## Philadelphia *

Angelore, Laura
235 Chestnut St., 19106
(800) 624-2988

**Amenities:** 1,2,4,9,11,14,15, 16,18
**Breakfast:** C.

**Dbl. Oc.:** $105.45 - $144.30
**Sgl. Oc.:** $99.90 - $132.20
**Third Person:** $5.55
**Child:** under 18 yrs. - $5.55

**The Independence Park Inn**—Philadelphia's great little hotel located in the heart of America's most historic square mile adjoining Independence National Park, Liberty Bell and Penns Landing. Thirty-six designer-decorated rooms. Listed in the *National Register of Historic Places.*

## Quakertown,

Laumont, M.
Box 243, Old Bethlehem, 18951
(215) 536-4651

**Amenities:** 1,3,5,6,7,8,9, 10,12,15,16
**Breakfast:** C.

**Dbl. Oc.:** $90.00 - $132.00

**Sign Of The Sorrel Horse**—Built in 1749. Near Lake Nockamixon. Five antique filled rooms. Finest gourmet restaurant on premises. Near New Hope. Three star rated, AAA. French and German spoken.

## Reading

Staron, Norma & Ray
118 So. 5th St., 19602
(215) 374-6608

**Amenities:** 2,7,9,10,11,14, 15,16,17
**Breakfast:** F.

**Dbl. Oc.:** $64.00 - $75.00
**Sgl. Oc.:** $53.00 - $64.00
**Third Person:** $10.00

**Hunter House**—A restored, historic 1846 revival townhouse and a secluded 1905 annex on nearby "Mansion Row.". Relaxing, lovely and comfortable. TV and air conditioning. Close to famous outlet, antique shops, restaurants, historic sites and Amish country. A unique and sheltered urban experience.

## Ridgway

Shoemaker, Lois
Montmorenci Rd.
Box 17, 15853
(814) 776-2539

**Amenities:** 1,2,10,15,16,17,18
**Breakfast:** C. or F.
**Dbl. Oc.:** $40.00
**Sgl. Oc.:** $40.00
**Third Person:** $10.00
**Child:** under 6 yrs. - $10.00

**Faircroft Bed & Breakfast**—Two miles from Route 219. A warm, comfortable and quiet homestead on 75 acres of farmland. Next door to Allegheny National Forest. Area famous for scenery, outdoor recreation, good food, relaxation and fresh air. Antique decor. Young, middle-aged professional owners.

| | | | | |
|---|---|---|---|---|
| 1. No Smoking | 5. Tennis Available | 9. Credit Cards Accepted | 13. Lunch Available | 17. Shared Bath |
| 2. No Pets | 6. Golf Available | 10. Personal Checks Accepted | 14. Public Transportation | 18. Afternoon Tea |
| 3. No Children | 7. Swiming Available | 11. Off Season Rates | 15. Reservations Necessary | ★ Commissions given |
| 4. Senior Citizen Rates | 8. Skiing Available | 12. Dinner Available | 16. Private Bath | to Travel Agents |

## Ronks

Simpson, David
2574 Lincoln Hwy. E.
(Route 30 East), 17572
(717) 299-6005

**Amenities:** 1,2,9,10,15,17
**Breakfast:** F.

**Dbl. Oc.:** $55.00 - $65.00
**Sgl. Oc.:** $55.00 - $65.00
**Third Person:** $12.00

**Candlelite Inn Bed & Breakfast**—Surrounded by Amish farmlands. This 1920's brick farmhouse offers four clean, quiet rooms, sitting room with TV, central air/heat, phone and country breakfast. It is close to all attractions. There is also an antiques and collectibles shop on the premises.

## Scottdale *

Horsch, Ruth A. & James E.
Route 1, Box 634, 15683-9567
(412) 887-5404

**Amenities:** 1,5,6,7,8,10,15,
17,18
**Breakfast:** C.

**Dbl. Oc.:** $40.00 - $48.00
**Sgl. Oc.:** $36.00 - $40.00
**Third Person:** $15.00
**Child:** under 12 yrs. - $5.00

**Pine Wood Acres**—Situated in the Laurel Highlands of western Pennsylvania,10 miles from I-70 and I-76 exits at New Stanton. A country home with four acres of woods, gardens and herbs. Near Frank Lloyd Wright's Fallingwater and other attractions. Child in room between 13-18 years — $10.00 charge.

## Shawnee On Delaware

Cox, James
River Rd.
Box 265, 18356
(717) 421-2139

**Amenities:** 2,6,7,8,10,17,
**Breakfast:** F.

**Dbl. Oc.:** $63.60
**Sgl. Oc.:** $47.70
**Third Person:** $21.20
**Child:** under 13 yrs. - $15.90

**Eagle Rock Lodge In The Poconos**—Awake to a hearty breakfast served on a wicker-furnished porch overlooking the Delaware. This old country inn is nestled on 10-1/2 acres and include seven guest rooms and lots of lounging space. Close to all activities, sports, theatre and fine dining. Borders Water Gap National Park.

## Slippery Rock

McKnight, Sandra
152 Applewood Lane, 16057
(412) 794-1844

**Amenities:** 1,2,4,5,6,7,8,9,10,
13,16,18
**Breakfast:** F.

**Dbl. Oc.:** $79.00 - $115.00
**Sgl. Oc.:** $55.00 - $81.00
**Third Person:** $15.00
**Child:** under 18 yrs. - $10.00

**Applebutter Inn**—A restored 1844 farmhouse with 11 guest rooms. Features antiques, canopy beds and fireplaces. Original woodwork and floors. Gracious rural tranquility. Just 50 minutes north of Pittsburgh.

| | | | |
|---|---|---|---|
| 1. No Smoking | 5. Tennis Available | 9. Credit Cards Accepted | 13. Lunch Available | 17. Shared Bath |
| 2. No Pets | 6. Golf Available | 10. Personal Checks Accepted | 14. Public Transportation | 18. Afternoon Tea |
| 3. No Children | 7. Swiming Available | 11. Off Season Rates | 15. Reservations Necessary | ★ Commissions given |
| 4. Senior Citizen Rates | 8. Skiing Available | 12. Dinner Available | 16. Private Bath | to Travel Agents |

## *Somerset*

Jones, Janet
RD 6, Box 250, 15501
(814) 443-4978

**Amenities:** 5,6,7,8,9,10,11,16,17,18
**Breakfast:** F.
**Dbl. Oc.:** $85.00
**Sgl. Oc.:** $80.00
**Third Person:** $15.00
**Child:** under 12 yrs.- no charge

**Glades Pike Inn**—Since 1842, this inn has welcomed visitors to the scenic Laurel Mountains. A first-class bed and breakfast. Features five bedrooms with wood-burning fireplace, pine floors and high ceilings. Close to Seven Springs, Hidden Valley and Georgian Place outlet shops.

## *Starlight* *

McMahon, Judy & Jack
Box 27, 18461
(717) 798-2519

**Amenities:** 2,5,6,7,8,9,10,11,
12,13,14,15,16,17
**Breakfast:** F.

**Dbl. Oc.:** $79.50 - $106.00
**Sgl. Oc.:** $54.06 - $68.90
**Third Person:** $30.74
**Child:** 7-12 yrs. - $30.74

**The Inn At Starlight Lake**—Since 1909, this classic country inn has offered a lovely lake with year-round activities, from swimming to skiing. Twenty-six charming rooms and outstanding cuisine, all within a congenial, informal setting. Winding roads and quaint river towns complete the scene.

## *Starrucca*

Nethercott, Virginia & Roland
Main St., 18462
(717) 727-2211

**Amenities:** 2,5,6,8,9,10,
16,17
**Breakfast:** C.

**Dbl. Oc.:** $42.40 - $68.90
**Child:** $10.00

**Nethercott Inn**—An 1893 Victorian home located in a quiet village in the Endless Mountains. Nearby hunting, cross-country skiing and downhill skiing. Period decor. Furnished with antiques. Smoking limited.

## *Strasburg*

Joy, Debby
958 Eisenberger Rd., 17579
(717) 687-8585

**Amenities:** 1,2,10,11,16,18
**Breakfast:** F.

**Dbl. Oc.:** $31.80 - $53.00
**Sgl. Oc.:** $31.80 - $53.00
**Third Person:** $10.00
**Child:** no charge - $5.00

**The Decoy B&B**—Spectacular view. Quiet rural location in Amish farm country. Former Amish home. Four rooms, all with private baths. Air conditioned in summer. Near local attractions. Bicycle tours by advanced reservations. Two cats in residence. Open year round. Reservations appreciated.

| | | | |
|---|---|---|---|
| 1. No Smoking | 5. Tennis Available | 9. Credit Cards Accepted | 13. Lunch Available | 17. Shared Bath |
| 2. No Pets | 6. Golf Available | 10. Personal Checks Accepted | 14. Public Transportation | 18. Afternoon Tea |
| 3. No Children | 7. Swiming Available | 11. Off Season Rates | 15. Reservations Necessary | ★ Commissions given |
| 4. Senior Citizen Rates | 8. Skiing Available | 12. Dinner Available | 16. Private Bath | to Travel Agents |

# PENNSYLVANIA

## *Thompson*

Stark, Douglas
Main St., Route 171
RD 2, Box 36, 18465
(717) 727-2625

**Amenities:** 6,7,8,9,10,12,13, 16,17
**Breakfast:** F.

**Dbl. Oc.:** $35.00
**Sgl. Oc.:** $20.00
**Third Person:** $15.00
**Child:** under 5 yrs. - no charge

**Jefferson Inn**—Warm country atmosphere. Built in 1871 with a full-menu restaurant. Enjoy one of the most reasonable inns in northeast Pennsylvania. Rolling hills, lots of snow trails, skiing, hunting or just taking it easy.

## *Titusville* *

Rogalski, Charmaine
430 E. Main St., 16354
(814) 827-1592

**Amenities:** 6,10,16,17
**Breakfast:** C.
**Dbl. Oc.:** $58.30
**Sgl. Oc.:** $47.70
**Third Person:** $5.00
**Child:** under 16 yrs. - no charge

**McMullen House Bed And Breakfast**—Situated in the picturesque Oil Creek Valley. Minutes away from Drake Well Park, the world's first oil well. Also, the Oil Creek and Titusville Railroad can take you for a ride"through the valley that changed the world."

## *Valley Forge* *

Williams, Carolyn J.
Box 562, 19481
(215) 783-7838

**Amenities:** 1,4,5,6,7,8,9,10, 15,16,18
**Breakfast:** F.

**Dbl. Oc.:** $53.00 - $68.90
**Sgl. Oc.:** $31.80 - $47.70
**Third Person:** $10.60
**Child:** under 12 yrs. - $10.60

**Valley Forge Mountain B&B**—Near Philadelphia, Brandywine Valley, Lancaster County. Two wooded acres, guest parlor/fireplace, central air conditioning. Fine dining, theatre and shopping. California king suite, double sleigh bed, private bath. Your hosts are musician, equestrian, needlepointer, gourmands. Long terms.

| | | | | |
|---|---|---|---|---|
| 1. No Smoking | 5. Tennis Available | 9. Credit Cards Accepted | 13. Lunch Available | 17. Shared Bath |
| 2. No Pets | 6. Golf Available | 10. Personal Checks Accepted | 14. Public Transportation | 18. Afternoon Tea |
| 3. No Children | 7. Swiming Available | 11. Off Season Rates | 15. Reservations Necessary | ★ Commissions given |
| 4. Senior Citizen Rates | 8. Skiing Available | 12. Dinner Available | 16. Private Bath | to Travel Agents |

## Wellsboro *

Kaltenbach, Lee
Stony Fork Rd. (Kelsey Ave.)
R.D. #6, Box 106A, 16901
(717) 724-4954

**Amenities:** 1,2,5,6,7,8,9,10,
        11,12,13,15,16,17,18
**Breakfast:** F.
**Dbl. Oc.:** $53.00 - $99.50
**Sgl. Oc.:** $37.50
**Third Person:** $26.50
**Child:** $10.00

**Kaltenbach's Bed And Breakfast**—A spacious and attractive home on 72 acres. Two miles from Wellsboro. Turn left on Stony Fork Road. A warm, hospitable, small, family-run inn with 10 large rooms and fireplace. Golf package.

## West Chester *

Rupp, Winifred
409 S. Church St., 19382
(215) 692-4896

**Amenities:** 1,2,7,10,15,17
**Breakfast:** F.

**Dbl. Oc.:** $68.90
**Sgl. Oc.:** $63.60
**Third Person:** $15.90
**Child:** $5.30

**The Crooked Windsor**—A charming Victorian home. Centrally located in historic West Chester. Within a short driving distance to Longwood Gardens, Brandywine, museums, Wintertur, Valley Forge and other points of interest. Completely furnished with fine antiques. Pool and garden.

## Willow Street

Hershey, Debbie
2835 Willow St. Pike, 17584
(717) 464-5881

**Amenities:** 1,2,5,6,9,10,13,14,15,16,17
**Breakfast:** F.
**Dbl. Oc.:** $68.90
**Sgl. Oc.:** $47.70
**Third Person:** $15.00

**The Apple Bin Inn**—An 1860's structure featuring warm colonial charm with country decor. Relax, enjoy many amenities, full breakfast, patios, poster beds, color cable TV and air conditioning. Picnic lunches available. Bicycle beautiful Lancaster County countryside. Storage and maps available.

| | | | |
|---|---|---|---|
| 1. No Smoking | 5. Tennis Available | 9. Credit Cards Accepted | 13. Lunch Available | 17. Shared Bath |
| 2. No Pets | 6. Golf Available | 10. Personal Checks Accepted | 14. Public Transportation | 18. Afternoon Tea |
| 3. No Children | 7. Swiming Available | 11. Off Season Rates | 15. Reservations Necessary | ★ Commissions given |
| 4. Senior Citizen Rates | 8. Skiing Available | 12. Dinner Available | 16. Private Bath | to Travel Agents |

## *Wrightstown*

Butkus, Ellen & Richard
677 Durham Rd.
Route 413, 18940
(215) 598-3100

**Amenities:** 2,9,10,15,16,18
**Breakfast:** F.

**Dbl. Oc.:** $116.60
**Child:** under 12 yrs. -
$24.38

**Hollileif Bed & Breakfast Establishment**—Escape to country elegance. Minutes from New Hope, shopping and history. Experience 18th-century warmth in an antique-furnished farmhouse on 5-1/2 rolling acres. Romantic ambience, gourmet breakfasts, central A/C and fireplace. Midweek and extended-stay rates available.

## *York*

LaRowe, Lojan
Kreutz Creek Rd.
R.D. 24, Box 1042, 17406
(717) 757-5384

**Amenities:** 1,2,3,4,7,8,10,15,
16,18
**Breakfast:** C. and F.

**Dbl. Oc.:** $75.00
**Sgl. Oc.:** $65.00
**Third Person:** $10.00

**Cottage At Twin Brook Farm**—A two-hundred-year-old colonial farm nestled between three wooded ridges. Provides 55 acres of picturesque privacy. Brooks, ponds, woods, trails, fields and pastures. Member of *National Trust For Historic Preservation*. York, Lancaster and Gettysburg are nearby.

| | | | |
|---|---|---|---|
| 1. No Smoking | 5. Tennis Available | 9. Credit Cards Accepted | 13. Lunch Available | 17. Shared Bath |
| 2. No Pets | 6. Golf Available | 10. Personal Checks Accepted | 14. Public Transportation | 18. Afternoon Tea |
| 3. No Children | 7. Swiming Available | 11. Off Season Rates | 15. Reservations Necessary | ★ Commissions given |
| 4. Senior Citizen Rates | 8. Skiing Available | 12. Dinner Available | 16. Private Bath | to Travel Agents |

# RHODE ISLAND

## *Little Rhody*

Capitol: Providence
Statehood: May 29, 1790; the 13th state
State Motto: Hope
State Song: "Rhode Island"
State Bird: Rhode Island Red
State Flower: Violet
State Tree: Red Maple

Rhode Island is the smallest of the fifty states. Only 1,214 sq. miles, it lies on beautiful Narragansett Bay, just a little way out on the Atlantic Ocean.

It is quite a resort state. Thousands of visitors come here every year. The beaches afford plenty of swimming and boating.

In Newport, the tourist can take the Cliff Walk by the most beautiful mansions in the world, or see the America's Cup Sailboat Race off the coast of Newport.

Jewelry and silver seem to be the prime source of income for this state, along with tourism. The people of Rhode Island are very proud of their state, and love to have others come to see it. They make wonderful hosts.

## *Block Island*

Abrams, Joan
1 Spring St., 02807
(401) 466-2421, (401) 274-0262

**Amenities:** 9,10,11,12,16,18
**Breakfast:** F.
**Dbl. Oc.:** $80.00 - $300.00
**Third Person:** $25.00

**The 1661 Inn**—A restored inn overlooking the ocean. Most rooms with private bath, telephone, deck and ocean view. Some with jacuzzis. Dining room and deck with canopy overlooks the Atlantic. A three-minute walk to quaint harbor village and shops. Nearby beaches.

## *Block Island*

Abrams, Joan
1 Spring St., 02807
(401) 466-2421, (401) 274-0262

**Amenities:** 9,10,11,12,16,18
**Breakfast:** F.
**Dbl. Oc.:** $80.00 - $300.00
**Third Person:** $25.00

**Hotel Manisses**—Gracious Victorian rooms with private bath, telephone and some with jacuzzis. An elegant dining room and garden terrace serving Tapas and dinner. Open 3:00-12:00 p.m. Dinner reservations recommended. Outdoor deck with canopy. Nearby shops and beaches.

## *Block Island*

Connolly, Violette M. & Joseph   **Amenities:** 5,7,9,10,11,   **Dbl. Oc.:** $53.50 - $128.40
Spring St., 02807                               12,15,16,17    **Sgl. Oc.:** $37.45 - $80.25
(401) 466-2653                   **Breakfast:** F.

**The White House**—A gracious island mansion. Presidential autograph collection on display. French Provincial antiques throughout. Spectacular ocean views from the rooms. Limo service to the ferry and airport. Close to beaches and restaurants.

## *Block Island*

McQueeney, Claire & Stephen   **Amenities:** 2,3,4,5,7,9,10,11,   **Dbl. Oc.:** $80.00 - $125.00
High St., 02807                               14,15,16,17,18    **Sgl. Oc.:** $80.00 - $125.00
(401) 466-2494                   **Breakfast:** C.

**The Sheffield House**—An 1888 Victorian home in the historic district. Five minutes to the beach, shops and restaurants. Quiet, individually decorated rooms on a beautiful island. Country kitchen. Friendly and knowledgeable host. Lovely gardens.

| | | | |
|---|---|---|---|
| 1. No Smoking | 5. Tennis Available | 9. Credit Cards Accepted | 13. Lunch Available | 17. Shared Bath |
| 2. No Pets | 6. Golf Available | 10. Personal Checks Accepted | 14. Public Transportation | 18. Afternoon Tea |
| 3. No Children | 7. Swiming Available | 11. Off Season Rates | 15. Reservations Necessary | ★ Commissions given |
| 4. Senior Citizen Rates | 8. Skiing Available | 12. Dinner Available | 16. Private Bath | to Travel Agents |

## Block Island

Rose, Judith
Roslyn Rd., 02807
(401) 466-2021

**Amenities:** 2,5,7,9,11,15, 16,17
**Breakfast:** C.

**Dbl. Oc.:** $100.00 - $164.00
**Sgl. Oc.:** $100.00 - $164.00
**Third Person:** $30.00

**Rose Farm Inn**—Sea and country setting. Walking distance to beaches, town and ferries. Antique furnishings. King/queen beds, some with canopies and ocean view. Light buffet breakfast served on stone porch. Ferries from Galilee, Providence, Newport and New London, CT. Children over 12 welcome.

## Bristol *

Anderson, Wendy
956 Hope St.
P.O. Box 5, 02809
(401) 254-0230

**Amenities:** 1,4,5,6,7,10,12,13, 14,15,17,18
**Breakfast:** F.

**Dbl. Oc.:** $70.00 - $80.00
**Sgl. Oc.:** $55.00
**Third Person:** $12.00
**Child:** (under 10 years) Free

**The Joseph Reynolds House**—A 17th-century country mansion. National historic landmark. Located in lovely New England town on Narragansett Bay. Close to excellent bike path and state park. Easy access to Boston, Newport and Providence. Ideal for touring Southeast and Northeast.

## Jamestown

Lacaille, Lori
14 Union St., 02835
(401) 423-2641

**Amenities:** 4,5,6,7,9,10, 11,17
**Breakfast:** C.

**Dbl. Oc.:** $75.00
**Sgl. Oc.:** $50.00
**Third Person:** $10.00

**The Calico Cat Guest House**—A Victorian home 200 feet from Jamestown Harbour. Ten minutes away from beautiful Newport, with its many shops and restaurants, fishing, sailing, swimming and mansion tours.

## Middletown *

Lindsey, Anne
6 James St., 02840
(401) 846-9386

**Amenities:** 1,2,5,6,7,9,10,11, 14,15,16,17
**Breakfast:** C. + cereal

**Dbl. Oc.:** $66.60
**Sgl. Oc.:** $55.50

**Lindsey's Guest House**—Off-street parking. Deck and large yard. Nearby bird sanctuary and wildlife refuge. Newport's Cliff Walk, famous mansions, Tennis Hall of Fame, Ocean Drive and Yachting Museum. Walk to beaches and restaurants. Lower rates on weekdays.

## Narragansett

Snee, Mildred
191 Ocean Rd., 02882
(401) 783-9494

**Amenities:** 2,3,5,6,7,10, 17,18
**Breakfast:** F.

**Dbl. Oc.:** $53.00
**Sgl. Oc.:** $42.40
**Third Person:** $13.60

**The House Of Snee**—A turn-of-the-century Dutch colonial with a cozy porch facing the open Atlantic Ocean. Mystic Seaport and Newport are nearby. Within easy walking distance of beach, movies, restaurants and shops.

| | | | | |
|---|---|---|---|---|
| 1. No Smoking | 5. Tennis Available | 9. Credit Cards Accepted | 13. Lunch Available | 17. Shared Bath |
| 2. No Pets | 6. Golf Available | 10. Personal Checks Accepted | 14. Public Transportation | 18. Afternoon Tea |
| 3. No Children | 7. Swiming Available | 11. Off Season Rates | 15. Reservations Necessary | ★ Commissions given |
| 4. Senior Citizen Rates | 8. Skiing Available | 12. Dinner Available | 16. Private Bath | to Travel Agents |

# RHODE ISLAND

## Newport

Bayuk, Pam & Bruce
123 Spring St., 02840
(800) 525-8373

**Amenities:** 1,2,3,9,11,15,16,17
**Breakfast:** C.
**Dbl. Oc.:** $84.00 - $140.00
**Sgl. Oc.:** $84.00 - $140.00
**Third Person:** $15.00

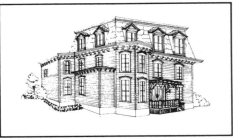

**The Pilgrim House Inn**—Lovely restored Victorian inn located in the heart of the historic district. Shops and restaurants within easy walking distance. Mansions close by. Homemade continental breakfast served on rooftop deck overlooking scenic Newport Harbor. A/C. Parking. Children over 12 welcome. Come see

---

## Newport

Brandeis, Paul
29 Pelham St., 02840
(401) 846-3324

**Amenities:** 1,5,6,7,9,10,11,15, 16,17
**Breakfast:** F.

**Dbl. Oc.:** $$65.00 - $95.00
**Third Person:** $15.00

**Inn Of Jonathan Bowen**—An elegant inn on a gas-lit historic hill. Located in the heart of activity. One-half block to the harbor. Renovated in 1987. Eclectic antique decor. Luxurious rooms. Safe, off-street parking. Walk everywhere. Famed mansions. Gourmet breakfast. Getaway plans.

---

## Newport *

Burke, Helen
Halidon Ave., 02840
(401) 847-8318

**Amenities:** 2,7,9,10,11, 15,16,17
**Breakfast:** C.

**Dbl. Oc.:** $85.00
**Sgl. Oc.:** $75.00
**Third Person:** $15.00

**Halidon Hill Guest House**—Modern and spacious rooms with ample on-site parking. A 10-minute walk to Hammersmith Farm and the beach. Convenient to shopping areas, local restaurants and mansions. Call for reservations.

---

## Newport

Droual, Margot
96 Pelham St., 02840
(401) 847-4400

**Amenities:** 2,9,10,11,15,16
**Breakfast:** C. and F.

**Dbl. Oc.:** $55.50 - $127.65
**Third Person:** $7.50
**Child:** under 12 yrs. -
no charge

**La Forge Cottage**—Classic Victorian makes this B&B one of the most pleasant inns around. On historic hill close to beaches and downtown. Private bath, TV, phone, A/C and refrigerator. Breakfast served to you in your room prepared by our own French chef. German and French spoken. Reservations.

---

| | | | | |
|---|---|---|---|---|
| 1. No Smoking | 5. Tennis Available | 9. Credit Cards Accepted | 13. Lunch Available | 17. Shared Bath |
| 2. No Pets | 6. Golf Available | 10. Personal Checks Accepted | 14. Public Transportation | 18. Afternoon Tea |
| 3. No Children | 7. Swiming Available | 11. Off Season Rates | 15. Reservations Necessary | ★ Commissions given |
| 4. Senior Citizen Rates | 8. Skiing Available | 12. Dinner Available | 16. Private Bath | to Travel Agents |

## Newport

Gallon, June & Audrey
32 Cranston Ave., 02840
401) 847-7094

**Amenities:** 1,2,5,6,7,10,11,14, 15,17

**Breakfast:** F.

**Dbl. Oc.:** $90.00
**Sgl. Oc.:** $84.00
**Third Person:** $36.60
**Child:** under 6 yrs. - no charge

**Clover Hill Guest House**—A gracious Victorian home built circa 1891. Within walking distance to the wharf area with its shops, restaurants and harbor. Minutes away is Bellevue Avenue and the famous mansions, Cliff Walk, 10-mile Ocean Drive and the beaches.

## Newport

Latimore, Parvine
353 Spring St., 02840
(401) 847-4767

**Amenities:** 2,3,4,9,10,11,12, 14,15,16

**Breakfast:** C. Plus

**Dbl. Oc.:** $75.00 & up
**Sgl. Oc.:** $75.00 & up
**Third Person:** $20.00
**Child:** over 12 yrs. - $20.00

**Spring Street Inn**—A charming Victorian home two blocks from the harbor. Walk to all Newport highlights. All rooms with private baths. Harbor-view suite with balcony for two-four people. Generous home-baked breakfast. On-site parking. Open all year round. VISA/MasterCard accepted.

## Newport *

Mailey, Susan
22 Channing St., 02840
(401) 846-6113

**Amenities:** 1,4,9,10,11, 14,15,17

**Breakfast:** C.

**Dbl. Oc.:** $75.00
**Sgl. Oc.:** $65.00
**Third Person:** $15.00
**Child:** no charge

**The Turn Of The Century Inn**—A Victorian cottage, centrally located to beaches and downtown Newport. The atmosphere is informal. The interior is decorated with antiques and whimsical collections.

## Newport

McCabe, Peg
16 Clarke St., 02840
(401) 846-5676

**Amenities:** 2,5,6,7,9,10,11,14, 15,17

**Breakfast:** C.

**Dbl. Oc.:** $61.60 - $89.60
**Sgl. Oc.:** $56.00

**Queen Anne Inn**—A restored Victorian townhouse with period furniture. Located in the historic district. Two blocks from harbor cruises, restaurants, etc. Parking. Fourteen rooms with seven shared baths. Minimum two-night stay weekends and three-night stay during holidays. Open April-October.

| | | | |
|---|---|---|---|
| 1. No Smoking | 5. Tennis Available | 9. Credit Cards Accepted | 13. Lunch Available | 17. Shared Bath |
| 2. No Pets | 6. Golf Available | 10. Personal Checks Accepted | 14. Public Transportation | 18. Afternoon Tea |
| 3. No Children | 7. Swiming Available | 11. Off Season Rates | 15. Reservations Necessary | ★ Commissions given |
| 4. Senior Citizen Rates | 8. Skiing Available | 12. Dinner Available | 16. Private Bath | to Travel Agents |

# RHODE ISLAND

## Newport

Moy, MariAnn & Ed
12 Clay St., 02840
(401) 849-6865

**Amenities:** 1,2,4,9,10,11,14,15,16
**Breakfast:** F.
**Dbl. Oc.:** $85.00 - $150.00
**Third Person:** $15.00

**Ivy Lodge**—Step back in time and stay in one of Newport's famous cottages in the heart of the mansion area. Only three blocks from the Cliff Walk. Gracious and romantic. Each room is individually decorated and hand-stenciled. Relax and unwind on our wicker-filled porch.

---

## Newport

Post, Dorothy
406 Bellevue Ave., 02840
(401) 847-0302

**Amenities:** 2,7,10,11,14, 15,16
**Breakfast:** C.

**Dbl. Oc.:** $105.00
**Sgl. Oc.:** $85.00
**Third Person:** $20.00
**Child:** $15.00

**"Wayside"**—A large, attractive and hospitable Georgian brick house with flower beds. Swimming pool. Bicycle storage. Games and books. A place to relax or to enjoy golf, tennis and sailing. A short walk to mansions and harbor-front activities. Newport is great fun all year!

---

## Newport *

Rogers, Rita & Sam
39 Clarke St., 02840
(401) 847-0640

**Amenities:** 2,3,5,6,7,9,10, 11,14,16,17
**Breakfast:** C.
**Dbl. Oc.:** $77.70 - $99.90
**Sgl. Oc.:** $77.70 - $99.90

**The Melville House**—Seven rooms furnished in colonial style in the heart of the historic district. One block from Brick Market and the wharfs. Stay at a colonial inn built circa 1750. In the *National Register of Historic Places*. Off-street parking. Complimentary sherry. Homemade breakfast.

---

## Newport *

Weintraub, Amy
23 Brinley St., 02840
(401) 849-7645

**Amenities:** 2,3,5,6,7,9,10,11, 14,15,16,17
**Breakfast:** C.

**Dbl. Oc.:** $95.20 - $140.00
**Sgl. Oc.:** $84.00 - $123.20
**Third Person:** $15.00

**Brinley Victorian Inn**—Romantic Victorian decor. Features satin and lace window treatments, period wallpapers, trompe l'eoi and faux finishes with 19th-century antiques. Friendly and relaxed atmosphere. Service provided by innkeepers who love their work. Park and walk to historic sites and beach.

---

| | | | |
|---|---|---|---|
| 1. No Smoking | 5. Tennis Available | 9. Credit Cards Accepted | 13. Lunch Available | 17. Shared Bath |
| 2. No Pets | 6. Golf Available | 10. Personal Checks Accepted | 14. Public Transportation | 18. Afternoon Tea |
| 3. No Children | 7. Swiming Available | 11. Off Season Rates | 15. Reservations Necessary | ★ Commissions given |
| 4. Senior Citizen Rates | 8. Skiing Available | 12. Dinner Available | 16. Private Bath | to Travel Agents |

## *Newport/Middletown* *

Canning, Polly
349 Valley Rd.
Route 214, 02840
(401) 847-2160

**Amenities:** 1,2,5,6,7,10,11,
15,16,17
**Breakfast:** C.

**Dbl. Oc.:** $82.25
**Sgl. Oc.:** $64.20

**Polly's Place**—A quiet retreat two minutes from Newport Harbor and beaches. Lovely large, clean rooms with homey atmosphere and delicious home-baked goodies. Polly also has a three-room apartment available by the week or longer. She is a native and a realtor. Helpful information offered.

## *Providence* *

Parker, Yvonne
46 Forest St., 02902
(401) 421-7194

**Amenities:** 1,2,9,14,15,17
**Breakfast:** C.
**Dbl. Oc.:** $63.60
**Sgl. Oc.:** $47.70
**Third Person:** $15.00

**Lansing House Bed & Breakfast**—Convenient to Brown University, Rhode Island School of Design and downtown Boston. Built in 1905. Listed in a city-wide survey of historic resources. The hostess is a former newspaper and TV journalist who now writes fiction. She has lived in Paris, Japan and many areas of the U.S.

## *Westerly* *

Madison, Ellen L.
330 Woody Hill Rd., 02891
(401) 332-0452

**Amenities:** 1,2,10,11,16,17
**Breakfast:** F.

**Dbl. Oc.:** $66.60
**Sgl. Oc.:** $49.95
**Third Person:** $10.00
**Child:** $10.00

**Woody Hill Guest House**—Retreat from your busy routine and entrench yourself in the peace and quiet of this antique-filled country home. Two miles form superb ocean beaches. Swing on the porch swing or explore the gardens.

## *Wyoming*

Stetson, Billie & Bill
161 New London Tpke., 02898
(401) 539-7233
**Amenities:** 5,6,7,10,17
**Breakfast:** C.
**Dbl. Oc.:** $53.00
**Sgl. Oc.:** $53.00
**Third Person:** $26.50
**Child:** under 10 yrs. - $10.00

**The Way Stop**—Circa 1757. Enjoy antiques, eclectic "stuff" and fireplaces in the cool evenings. The patio overlooks 50 acres of fields and woods. Also has a pond for swimming, fishing, canoeing or paddle boating. Beaches, Newport, Mystic and Providence are a short trip away.

| | | | | |
|---|---|---|---|---|
| 1. No Smoking | 5. Tennis Available | 9. Credit Cards Accepted | 13. Lunch Available | 17. Shared Bath |
| 2. No Pets | 6. Golf Available | 10. Personal Checks Accepted | 14. Public Transportation | 18. Afternoon Tea |
| 3. No Children | 7. Swiming Available | 11. Off Season Rates | 15. Reservations Necessary | ★ Commissions given |
| 4. Senior Citizen Rates | 8. Skiing Available | 12. Dinner Available | 16. Private Bath | to Travel Agents |

# SOUTH CAROLINA

## *The Palmetto State*

Capitol: Columbia
Statehood: May 23, 1788; the 8th state
State Motto: Prepared in Mind and Resources,
        While I Breathe, I Hope
State Song: "Carolina"
State Bird: Carolina Wren
State Flower: Carolina Jessamine
State Tree: Palmetto

South Carolina is a great state to visit, and for those who live there, it is a great place to call home. It stretches from the beautiful Appalachian foothills to the spacious and popular Atlantic Coast beaches.

It is home for more than three million energetic and resourceful people. These people share a common bond, whether they live in the larger municipalities of the Palmetto State or in its growing small towns and rural communities. That common bond is a commitment to preserving a quality of life which is their heritage and building upon it by encouraging businesses and industries to grow and prosper here.

South Carolina is a most gracious state and invites visitors to come and enjoy its beautiful beaches and flower gardens, and fish and hunt in its well-stocked fields and streams.

# SOUTH CAROLINA

## Anderson

Ryter, Myrna
1109 S. Main St., 29621
(803) 225-1109

**Amenities:** 2,5,6,7,9,10,12,14, **Dbl. Oc.:** $65.00
15,16            **Sgl. Oc.:** $52.00
**Breakfast:** C.         **Third Person:** $10.00

**Evergreen Inn**—A luxuriously restored mansion listed in *Register of Historic Places*. Specialty suites for a romantic getaway. Within walking distance to downtown antique shops and 20 minutes to Lake Hartwell. Next door to an award-winning, Swiss-owned restaurant in an elegant mansion.

## Beaufort

Harrison, Stephen R.
1009 Craven St., 29902
(803) 524-9030

**Amenities:** 1,2,3,5,6,7,9,10, **Dbl. Oc.:** $74.90 - $112.35
13,15,16       **Sgl. Oc.:** $64.20
**Breakfast:** F.       **Third Person:** $16.05

**The Rhett House Inn**—Nestled in historic Beaufort, this is an authentic B&B inn that beautifully re-creates the feeling of the "old" South. All guest rooms have been created for your comfort and convenience. All guest rooms have private baths and some have fireplaces.

## Beaufort

Mitchell, JoAnne
500 Washington St., 29902
(803) 522-8552

**Amenities:** 1,2,3,5,6,7,9,10, **Dbl. Oc.:** $69.55 - $101.65
15,16       **Sgl. Oc.:** $55.85 - $90.95
**Breakfast:** C.       **Third Person:** $10.00

**Trescot Inn**—A cheerful and inviting plantation house, moved to historic "Point" in 1976. Fully restored with central A/C. Begin and end your days on verandas, being serenaded by a variety of birds. Stroll or bike along streets lined with moss-draped oaks. Nearby shopping, beach and restaurants.

## Beaufort *

Roe, Eugene
601 Bay St., 29902
(803) 524-7720

**Amenities:** 5,6,7,9,10,14,15,16
**Breakfast:** F.
**Dbl. Oc.:** $70.00 - $80.00
**Sgl. Oc.:** $65.00 - $75.00
**Third Person:** $15.00
**Child:** $15.00

**Bay Street Inn**—A historic Greek Revival antebellum home on the water. Site of the movie "Prince of Tides" starring Streisand and Nolte. Museum-quality furnishings. Library, music room, 14 fireplaces. Gardens. Old South at its best. Near Hilton Head, Charleston and Savannah. See them all.

| | | | | |
|---|---|---|---|---|
| 1. No Smoking | 5. Tennis Available | 9. Credit Cards Accepted | 13. Lunch Available | 17. Shared Bath |
| 2. No Pets | 6. Golf Available | 10. Personal Checks Accepted | 14. Public Transportation | 18. Afternoon Tea |
| 3. No Children | 7. Swiming Available | 11. Off Season Rates | 15. Reservations Necessary | ★ Commissions given |
| 4. Senior Citizen Rates | 8. Skiing Available | 12. Dinner Available | 16. Private Bath | to Travel Agents |

# SOUTH CAROLINA

## Beech Island *

Zieger, Maggie & Ralph
1325 Williston Rd.
P.O. Box 117, 29841
(803) 827-0248

**Amenities:** 2,3,4,5,6,9,10,16
**Breakfast:** C.

**Dbl. Oc.:** $53.50
**Sgl. Oc.:** $48.15

**The Cedars Inn**—Gracious accommodations in an 1820's country manor house situated on 12 park-like acres. Six miles form Augusta, Georgia. Nearby attractions include: Redcliffe Plantation, Augusta Riverwalk Park, Aiken's Thoroughbred Horse Farm and polo games.

---

## Bluffton

Tuttle, Dana
Bridge St., 29910
(803) 757-2139

**Amenities:** 1,2,5,6,7,9,10,15,
16
**Breakfast:** F.

**Dbl. Oc.:** $65.00 - $85.00
**Sgl. Oc.:** $60.00 - $80.00
**Third Person:** $20.00

**The Fripp House Inn**—A historic landmark (circa 1835) in a quiet village on the May River. Private gardens with pool and fountains. A spacious home, family atmosphere and hearty food. Five minutes from Hilton Head Island.

---

## Charleston

Chapman, Ben
30 King St., 29401
(803) 577-2633

**Amenities:** 5,6,7,10,15,16
**Breakfast:** C.
**Dbl. Oc.:** $55.00 - $90.00
**Third Person:** $20.00

**Hayne House Bed And Breakfast**—One of the city's oldest B&B's (circa 1755) in the heart of the historic district. One block from Battery. Within walking distance to restaurants, shopping and Waterfront Park. Furnished in antiques. Piano, sitting room, lots of good books and porch with rockers. Bikes available.

---

## Charleston *

Fox, Laura
198 King St., 29401
(803) 723-7000

**Amenities:** 1,2,4,5,6,7,9,
11,16
**Breakfast:** C. and F.

**Dbl. Oc.:** $139.10
**Sgl. Oc.:** $123.05
**Third Person:** $10.70
**Child:** under 12 yrs. -
no charge

**Kings Courtyard Inn**—Located in the heart of antique and historic districts. An 1853 restored inn. Rates include continental breakfast, newspaper and evening turn-down with brandy and chocolate. Sherry upon arrival. *Historic Hotels of America*, AAA -four diamond approval.

---

| | | | | |
|---|---|---|---|---|
| 1. No Smoking | 5. Tennis Available | 9. Credit Cards Accepted | 13. Lunch Available | 17. Shared Bath |
| 2. No Pets | 6. Golf Available | 10. Personal Checks Accepted | 14. Public Transportation | 18. Afternoon Tea |
| 3. No Children | 7. Swiming Available | 11. Off Season Rates | 15. Reservations Necessary | ★ Commissions given |
| 4. Senior Citizen Rates | 8. Skiing Available | 12. Dinner Available | 16. Private Bath | to Travel Agents |

## Charleston *

Hancock, Aubrey
138 Wentworth St., 29401
(803) 577-709

**Amenities:** 1,2,3,9,10,11,16
**Breakfast:** F.

**Dbl. Oc.:** $85.00 - $150.00
**Sgl. Oc.:** $85.00 - $100.00

**Villa De La Fontaine Bed And Breakfast**—A classic revival porticoed mansion built in 1838. Restored and furnished with museum-quality furniture. Located in the heart of the historic area. Operated by a retired interior designer. Formal gardens.

## Charleston

Smith, B.J.
114 Rutledge Ave., 29401
(803) 722-7551

**Amenities:** 1,9,10,11,14, 16,17,18
**Breakfast:** C.

**Dbl. Oc.:** $50.00 - $85.00
**Sgl. Oc.:** $40.00 - $75.00
**Third Person:** $5.00 - $10.00
**Child:** under 12 yrs. - no charge

**Rutledge Victorian Guest House**—A century-old house in Charleston's historic district. Quaint yet elegant, with 12-foot ceilings, fireplaces and antiques. Decorative old porch, parking, air-conditioning and TV. A 10- to 20-minute walk to most sights. Student rates available.

## Charleston

Spell, Karen M.
2 Meeting St., 29401
(803) 723-7322

**Amenities:** 1,2,3,5,6,7,10,14, 15,16
**Breakfast:** C.

**Dbl. Oc.:** $85.00 - $135.00
**Third Person:** $20.00

**Two Meeting Street Inn**—Located in the historic district. Charleston's most renowned and elegant inn where guests enjoy the entire inn. No children under eight years. Located across from Battery Park on waterfront.

## Charleston

Spell, David
40 Rutledge Ave., 29401
(803) 722-0973

**Amenities:** 1,2,3,5,6,7, 10,14,15,16
**Breakfast:** C.
**Dbl. Oc.:** $95.00
**Sgl. Oc.:** $95.00
**Third Person:** $15.00

**Belvedere Guest House**—Offers hospitable accommodations in a gracious mansion overlooking Colonial Lake. Located in the historic district of downtown Charleston at the corner of Rutledge Avenue and Queen Street.

| | | | | |
|---|---|---|---|---|
| 1. No Smoking | 5. Tennis Available | 9. Credit Cards Accepted | 13. Lunch Available | 17. Shared Bath |
| 2. No Pets | 6. Golf Available | 10. Personal Checks Accepted | 14. Public Transportation | 18. Afternoon Tea |
| 3. No Children | 7. Swiming Available | 11. Off Season Rates | 15. Reservations Necessary | ★ Commissions given to Travel Agents |
| 4. Senior Citizen Rates | 8. Skiing Available | 12. Dinner Available | 16. Private Bath | |

# *SOUTH CAROLINA*

## *Charleston*

| | | |
|---|---|---|
| Weed, Diane Deardurff | **Amenities:** 1,2,5,6,7,10,11,14, | **Dbl. Oc.:** $75.00 - $80.00 |
| 105 Tradd St., 29401-2422 | 15,16,18 | **Sgl. Oc.:** $75.00 - $80.00 |
| (803) 577-0682 | **Breakfast:** C. | **Third Person:** $25.00 |
| | | **Child:** $25.00 |

**Country Victorian Bed And Breakfast**—Private entrances, antique iron and brass beds, old quilts and antique oak and wicker furniture. Located in the historic area within walking distance of everything. Relaxon piazza of this historic home and watch carriages pass by. Enjoy bicycles, free parking and many extras.

## *Charleston*

| | | |
|---|---|---|
| Widman, Richard | **Amenities:** 1,2,4,5,6,7,9,11, | **Dbl. Oc.:** $117.70 - $235.40 |
| 116 Broad St., 29401 | 16,18 | **Sgl. Oc.:** $96.30 - $235.40 |
| (803) 723-7999 | **Breakfast:** C. | **Third Person:** $16.05 |
| | | **Child:** under 12 yrs. - no charge |

**John Rutledge House Inn**—Located in the historic district. Built in 1763 by John Rutledge, a signer of the U.S. Constitution. Nightly turn-down, continental breakfast and newspaper delivered to your room. Wine served in the ballroom. AAA - four diamond and *Historical Homes of America* approved.

## *Columbia*

| | | |
|---|---|---|
| Vance, Dan | **Amenities:** 1,2,4,6,9,11, | **Dbl. Oc.:** $94.16 |
| 2003 Greene St., 29205 | 14,15,16 | **Sgl. Oc.:** $83.46 |
| (803) 765-0440, | **Breakfast:** C. | **Third Person:** $10.70 |
| (800) 622-3382 | | **Child:** under 12 yrs. - no charge |

**Claussen's Inn**—A historic restored inn. Adjacent to the University of South Carolina campus. Convenient to shopping, dining and downtown. Rates include continental breakfast, turn-down service with chocolates and brandy. Complimentary wine and sherry. AAA - four diamond award.

## *Georgetown*

| | | |
|---|---|---|
| Shaw, Mary | **Amenities:** 4,5,6,16 | **Dbl. Oc.:** $45.00 |
| 8 Cypress Court, 29440 | **Breakfast:** F. | **Sgl. Oc.:** $45.00 |
| (803) 546-9663 | | **Third Person:** $10.00 |
| | | **Child:** $10.00 |

**The Shaw House**—Lovely view overlooking Willowbank Marsh. Rocking chairs on the porch. Bird watching. Large guest room with private bath. Within walking distance of downtown. Fresh fruit. Wonderful restaurants. Turn-down service at night. We delight in our guests feeling at home.

---

| | | | | |
|---|---|---|---|---|
| 1. No Smoking | 5. Tennis Available | 9. Credit Cards Accepted | 13. Lunch Available | 17. Shared Bath |
| 2. No Pets | 6. Golf Available | 10. Personal Checks Accepted | 14. Public Transportation | 18. Afternoon Te |
| 3. No Children | 7. Swiming Available | 11. Off Season Rates | 15. Reservations Necessary | ★ Commissions give |
| 4. Senior Citizen Rates | 8. Skiing Available | 12. Dinner Available | 16. Private Bath | to Travel Agents |

## Johnston

Derrick, M/M Scott
602 Lee St.
P.O. Box 486, 29832
(803) 275-4552

**Amenities:** 2,6,10,15,16
**Breakfast:** C.

**Dbl. Oc.:** $50.00
**Sgl. Oc.:** $40.00
**Third Person:** no charge
**Child:** no charge

**The Cox House Inn**—A circa 1910 Victorian home. Located on Highway #121 in the middle of Johnston. Four suites, kitchen, living room and cable TV. Breakfast: cereal, juice and coffee left in kitchen of each suite. Persimmon Hill Golf Club is five minutes away. Antique and reproduction decorations.

## Leesville

Wright, Annabelle & Jack
244 W. Church St., 29070
(803) 532-2763

**Amenities:** 2,4,6,7,9,10,16
**Breakfast:** C.

**Dbl. Oc.:** $48.15
**Sgl. Oc.:** $42.80
**Third Person:** $5.00
**Child:** under 12 yrs. -
no charge

**Able House Inn**—A chateau estate 10 miles from I-20 on Route 1, 30 minutes from Columbia. Surrounded by pecan, pine and pink dogwood trees. Five charming guest rooms, imported antiques, air-conditioning, TV and stereo. Fresh popcorn and soda in the evenings. Closely supervised children welcome.

## Myrtle Beach

Ficarra, Ellen & Cos
407-71 Ave. N., 29577
(803) 449-5268

**Amenities:** 2,5,6,7,9,11,
14,15,16
**Breakfast:** C. Plus

**Dbl. Oc.:** $64.20 - $87.74
**Third Person:** $10.70
**Child:** under 12 yrs. - $6.42

**Serendipity, An Inn**—An award-winning, mission-style inn. 300 yards to ocean beach. Heated pool and jacuzzi. Secluded patio. Air conditioning, color TV and refrigerators. Shuffleboard and Ping-Pong. Dozens of golf courses. Nearby tennis. Convenient to all restaurants, amusements and shops.

## Pickens *

Schell, Sherry & George
4913 Scenic Hwy. 11, 29671
(803) 878-0078

**Amenities:** 1,2,4,6,7,9,10,13,
15,16,18
**Breakfast:** F.

**Dbl. Oc.:** $70.00
**Sgl. Oc.:** $70.00
**Third Person:** $10.00

**The Schell Haus**—This Victorian home sits on 11 wooded acres across from Table Rock State Park. Relax in the parlor, beautifully appointed guest rooms or by the pool. Hiking, waterfalls, antiquing and spectacular mountain views await you at the Schell Haus. No children under 12 years of age.

| | | | |
|---|---|---|---|
| 1. No Smoking | 5. Tennis Available | 9. Credit Cards Accepted | 13. Lunch Available | 17. Shared Bath |
| 2. No Pets | 6. Golf Available | 10. Personal Checks Accepted | 14. Public Transportation | 18. Afternoon Tea |
| 3. No Children | 7. Swiming Available | 11. Off Season Rates | 15. Reservations Necessary | ★ Commissions given |
| 4. Senior Citizen Rates | 8. Skiing Available | 12. Dinner Available | 16. Private Bath | to Travel Agents |

# SOUTH CAROLINA

## Ridgeland

Urbanek, Joe
Route 2, Box 3, 29936
(803) 726-5141

**Amenities:** 1,3,4,5,9,10,
16,17
**Breakfast:** C. Plus

**Dbl. Oc.:** $58.80
**Sgl. Oc.:** $48.10

**Lakewood Plantation**—A newly renovated 10-acre plantation. A lake with excellent fishing. 1800 period furnishings. Marble fireplace in the living room. Central heat/air. Beautiful spiral staircase. 1/2 hour to Hilton Head, Beaufort, NC and Savannah, GA. Heated kennel. Excellent nearby dining.

## Spartanburg

Finnegan, Joseph
279 St. George St., 32084
(904) 824-6068

**Amenities:** 1,2,7,9,10,15,16
**Breakfast:** C.
**Dbl. Oc.:** $60.00 - $125.00
**Third Person:** $8.00

**St. Francis Inn**—Built in 1791 and located in the historic district. We offer the charm of yesterday and the comfort of today. Complimentary bicycles, admission to the oldest house, fireplaces, color cable TV, private parking and a variety of accommodations are here for you to enjoy.

## Sumter

Carnes, Merilyn & Bob
6 Park Ave., 29150
(803) 773-2903

**Amenities:** 2,5,6,9,10,11,
16,17
**Breakfast:** C.

**Dbl. Oc.:** $55.00
**Sgl. Oc.:** $40.00
**Third Person:** no charge
**Child:** no charge

**Sumter Bed & Breakfast**—An 1896 home facing a quiet park. A sitting porch welcomes you to a private entrance and a bygone era. Inside, a Victorian staircase takes you to four charming guest rooms. Common rooms, phone, HBO, library, antiques, fresh orange juice and home-baked pastries.

---

| | | | | |
|---|---|---|---|---|
| 1. No Smoking | 5. Tennis Available | 9. Credit Cards Accepted | 13. Lunch Available | 17. Shared Bath |
| 2. No Pets | 6. Golf Available | 10. Personal Checks Accepted | 14. Public Transportation | 18. Afternoon Tea |
| 3. No Children | 7. Swiming Available | 11. Off Season Rates | 15. Reservations Necessary | ★ Commissions given |
| 4. Senior Citizen Rates | 8. Skiing Available | 12. Dinner Available | 16. Private Bath | to Travel Agents |

# SOUTH DAKOTA

## *The Sunshine State*

Capitol: Pierre
Statehood: November 2, 1889; the 40th state
State Motto: Under God The People Rule
State Song: "Hail, South Dakota"
State Bird: Ring-Necked Pheasant
State Flower: American Pasqueflower
State Tree: Black Hills Spruce

South Dakota is a land of rare beauty and unusual landscapes. It has fertile crop-growing land, canyons, the strange Badlands and the enchanting Black Hills.

The wild west look is still here. Buffaloes can be seen roaming Custer's State Park in herds.

South Dakota is visited by hundreds of tourists every year. Probably one of the most popular attractions is Mt. Rushmore. Here in 1928, Gutzon Borglum began a memorial to freedom and to the spirit of the American people. It took him and his small group of men 14 years to complete this task, but when he finished, the sculptured and carved faces of four of our greatest presidents, George Washington, Abraham Lincoln, Thomas Jefferson and Theodore Roosevelt, were enshrined here forever.

# SOUTH DAKOTA

## Canova

Skoglund, Delores & Alden
Route 1, Box 45, 57321
(605) 247-3445

**Amenities:** 7,10,12,13,17
**Breakfast:** F.

**Dbl. Oc.:** $60.00
**Sgl. Oc.:** $30.00
**Third Person:** $15.00 -
$20.00
**Child:** under 5 yrs. -
no charge

**Skoglund Farm**—Enjoy overnight on the prairie. Ride horses. See cattle, fowl and peacocks. Relax. Special attractions. Evening meal included in rates. Piano. The coffee pot is on. Feel at home.

## Chamberlain *

Cable, Alta & Frank
HC 69, Box 82A, 57325
(605) 734-6084

**Amenities:** 10,15,16,17
**Breakfast:** F.

**Dbl. Oc.:** $45.00
**Sgl. Oc.:** $35.00
**Child:** $10.00

**Riverview Ridge**—Country peace and quiet with a beautiful view of the Missouri River. A modern home with king or queen beds. Two miles north of downtown Chamberlain on Highway 50.

## Custer

Seaman, Carole & Mill
35 Centennial Dr., 57730
(605) 673-3333

**Amenities:** 1,2,6,7,8,10,
11,17,18
**Breakfast:** F.

**Dbl. Oc.:** $43.00 - $48.00
**Sgl. Oc.:** $37.50
**Child:** under 1 yr. -
no charge

**Custer Mansion Bed And Breakfast**—An 1891 historic Victorian Gothic on one acre. Charmingly restored. Offers Western hospitality and home-cooking in a unique setting of the beautiful Black Hills. Nearby biking, hiking, trout fishing and hunting. Near Custer State Park, Mount Rushmore and restaurants.

## Deadwood

Rowland, Joseph
22 Van Buren, 57732
(605) 578-3877

**Amenities:** 1,2,3,4,5,6,7,8,9,
10,12,13,14,16,18
**Breakfast:** F.

**Dbl. Oc.:** $69.55 - $90.95
**Sgl. Oc.:** $62.01 - $81.09

**The Adam's House**—An 1892 Victorian mansion. Elegant, romantic and embracing. A sanctuary in which to relax, romance, dream and experience a bygone era. A time to be pampered by our attentive staff.

## Hill City

Nash, Evelyn
HC 87, Box 75B, 57745
(605) 574-2316

**Amenities:** 2,15
**Breakfast:** C.

**Dbl. Oc.:** $35.00
**Sgl. Oc.:** $25.00

**Peaceful Valley Bed And Breakfast**—Located in the heart of the Black Hills. Centrally located to Mount Rushmore, Custer State Park, Custer City, Hill City's 1880 train, Black Hills Playhouse, Deadwood/Lead, Hot Springs, Spearfish and The Passion Play. Quiet, country living with lots of hiking trails.

| | | | | |
|---|---|---|---|---|
| 1. No Smoking | 5. Tennis Available | 9. Credit Cards Accepted | 13. Lunch Available | 17. Shared Bath |
| 2. No Pets | 6. Golf Available | 10. Personal Checks Accepted | 14. Public Transportation | 18. Afternoon Tea |
| 3. No Children | 7. Swiming Available | 11. Off Season Rates | 15. Reservations Necessary | ★ Commissions given |
| 4. Senior Citizen Rates | 8. Skiing Available | 12. Dinner Available | 16. Private Bath | to Travel Agents |

## Lead

LeMar, Mr. & Mrs. Jim
HC 37, Box 1220, 57754
(605) 584-3510

**Amenities:** 2,6,8,9
**Breakfast:** F.

**Dbl. Oc.:** $59.00 & up

**Cheyenne Crossing B&B**—A B&B in a true country store located in one of America's prettiest canyons. Year-round outdoor recreation center. Close to Mount Rushmore, Devils Tower, historic Deadwood and much more.

## Owanka

Reeves, Judy & Wes
R.R., Exit 90, 57767
(605) 798-5405

**Amenities:** 1,11,12,13,15, 16,18
**Breakfast:** C.

**Dbl. Oc.:** $40.00
**Sgl. Oc.:** $30.00
**Third Person:** $10.00
**Child:** under 8 yrs. -
no charge

**Country Bed And Breakfast**—Just 30 miles from Black Hills, home of Mount Rushmore, and 30 miles from The Badlands. Located in a quiet area and a great place to relax. Small family farm on 40 acres with access to kitchen. Horseback riding available. See the trail that covered wagons crossed to Deadwood.

## Philip

Thorson, Phillis & Leonard
HCR 02, Box 100, 57567
(605) 859-2120

**Amenities:** 1,10,15,17
**Breakfast:** F.

**Dbl. Oc.:** $40.00
**Sgl. Oc.:** $25.00
**Child:** under 12 yrs. -$5.00

**Thorson's Homestead**—Old-fashioned Western hospitality. A family-owned farm and ranch. A convenient stop on your way to the Badlands and Black Hills. Nearby is a small Lutheran church. Handicrafts are a hobby. Enjoy dancing, sports and visiting. Quiet and cozy. Twelve miles north of Highway 14 between Philip and Wall.

## Rapid City

Kuhnhauser, Audry
RR 8, Box 2400, 57702
(605) 342-7788

**Amenities:** 1,2,3,10,15,16
**Breakfast:** F.

**Dbl. Oc.:** $67.60
**Sgl. Oc.:** $62.40
**Third Person:** $15.00

**Audrie's Cranbury Corner Bed & Breakfast**—The ultimate in charm and old-world hospitality. Our spacious rooms are furnished in comfortable European antiques. Each room features a private entrance, private bath, fireplace, patio and private hot tub. Secluded Black Hills setting only seven miles west of Rapid City.

## Spearfish

Christensen, Patricia
432 Hillsview, 57783
(605) 642-2859

**Amenities:** 1,2,3,9,10,11,15, 16,17
**Breakfast:** F.

**Dbl. Oc.:** $52.00 - $62.40
**Sgl. Oc.:** $39.50
**Third Person:** $10.00

**Christensen's Country Home**—Enjoy relaxing and comfortable lodging in this beautifully decorated four-bedroom inn. One mile from B.H. Passion Play and within driving distance to all major B.H. attractions and historic Deadwood. Enjoy the 1840 billiards table and the special breakfasts. No children under 10 years of age.

| | | | |
|---|---|---|---|
| 1. No Smoking | 5. Tennis Available | 9. Credit Cards Accepted | 13. Lunch Available | 17. Shared Bath |
| 2. No Pets | 6. Golf Available | 10. Personal Checks Accepted | 14. Public Transportation | 18. Afternoon Tea |
| 3. No Children | 7. Swiming Available | 11. Off Season Rates | 15. Reservations Necessary | ★ Commissions given |
| 4. Senior Citizen Rates | 8. Skiing Available | 12. Dinner Available | 16. Private Bath | to Travel Agents |

# TENNESSEE

## *The Volunteer State*

Capitol: Nashville
Statehood: June 1, 1796; the 16th state
State Motto: Agriculture and Commerce
State Song: "Rocky Top Tennessee"
State Bird: Mockingbird
State Flower: Iris
State Tree: Tulip Poplar


Tennessee is a state of varied industries. In the east there are the coal mines; in the middle of the state, the farmers raise cattle and tobacco; and in the west there are large cotton plantations. But regardless, there is one thing everyone here enjoys, and that is Country Music, as played at the Grand Ole Opry in Nashville.

There is a lot of Civil War history here and beautiful scenic drives. However, the majority of visitors that come to Tennessee come first to see the Grand Ole Opry.

Three presidents were born and lived here: Andrew Jackson, James Polk and Andrew Johnson.

## *Chattanooga*

Alford, Rhoda & Robert
2501 Lookout Mountain Pkwy.,
37419
(615) 821-7625

**Amenities:** 1,2,10,15,17,18
**Breakfast:** C. Plus

**Dbl. Oc.:** $48.15 - $58.85
**Sgl. Oc.:** $37.45
**Third Person:** $10.00

**Alford House B. & B.**—A traditional-style home with Victorian decor. Relax in our gazebo as you view the mountain range or take a stroll up Lookout Mountain. Minutes from local attractions, shopping and fine dining. Wake-up coffee served. Check-in and check-out time is flexible.

## *Cleveland*

Brown, Beverlee
215 20th St., N.E., 37311
(615) 476-8029,
(615) 479-5311

**Amenities:** 1,2,4,5,6,7,9,11,
14,15,16,17,18
**Breakfast:** F.

**Dbl. Oc.:** $70.00
**Sgl. Oc.:** $60.00
**Third Person:** $10.00
**Child:** under 14 yrs. - $5.00

**Brown Manor**—A deluxe manor with special attention to personal service. In the heart of a quaint town on I-75. Chattanooga is 30 miles away. White-water rafting is 16 miles away. Glidder-Port is 20 miles away. National Forest - 10 miles away. Walking tours and biking. Privacy and pampering.

## *Cleveland* *

Chadwick, Winnie A.
2766 Michigan Ave. Rd., NE
Route 9, Box 107, 37312
(615) 339-2407

**Amenities:** 2,4,5,6,7,9,10,11,
12,15,16,17
**Breakfast:** F.

**Dbl. Oc.:** $37.00 - $42.00
**Sgl. Oc.:** $30.00
**Third Person:** $30.00
**Child:** under 5 yrs. -
no charge

**Chadwick House**—A charming family home set on three acres of woodland. Just five miles from I-75 and four miles from Cleveland. Irish host is world traveled. Nearby white-water rafting, Cherokee National Forest, Ruby Falls, The Lost Sea and good restaurants. A great place to relax and unwind.

## *Dandridge*

Franklin, Lucy & Hood
Route 5, Box 380, 37725
(615) 397-3470

**Amenities:** 2,5,6,7,8,10,
15,16,18
**Breakfast:** F.

**Dbl. Oc.:** $70.04
**Sgl. Oc.:** $53.87
**Third Person:** $10.77
**Child:** under 15 yrs. -
no charge

**Mill Dale Farm**—A hospitable working farmhouse one mile off I-40. Breakfast prepared with home-cured hams, breads, jams and jellies. Built and owned since 1843. The antique-filled antebellum home is centrally located for visits to mountains, lakes, arts, Gatlinburg and Pigeon Forge.

| | | | | |
|---|---|---|---|---|
| 1. No Smoking | 5. Tennis Available | 9. Credit Cards Accepted | 13. Lunch Available | 17. Shared Bath |
| 2. No Pets | 6. Golf Available | 10. Personal Checks Accepted | 14. Public Transportation | 18. Afternoon Tea |
| 3. No Children | 7. Swiming Available | 11. Off Season Rates | 15. Reservations Necessary | ★ Commissions given |
| 4. Senior Citizen Rates | 8. Skiing Available | 12. Dinner Available | 16. Private Bath | to Travel Agents |

## Dandridge

Price, Mary
Sugarfork Rd.
Route 1. Box 19, 37725
(615) 397-7327

**Amenities:** 6,9,10,16,17
**Breakfast:** C. and F.

**Dbl. Oc.:** $70.00
**Sgl. Oc.:** $48.00
**Third Person:** $27.50
**Child:** under 12 yrs. -
no charge

**Sugarfork Lodge Bed & Breakfast**—Situated in a tranquil setting on Douglas Lake. Three guest rooms with a fireplace in the common area. The Great Smoky Mountains, Dollywood, two colleges and two golf courses are close by. The lake is used year round for fishing and water sports.

---

## Gatlinburg

Burns, Connie & John
Route 3, Box 393, 37738
(615) 436-4668

**Amenities:** 1,2,3,10,12,
14,15,16
**Breakfast:** F.

**Dbl. Oc.:** $65.00 - $114.00
**Sgl. Oc.:** $58.00 - $98.00
**Third Person:** $17.00
**Child:** $17.00

**Buckhorn Inn**—A truly unique country inn offering peaceful seclusion with the feeling and tradition of early Gatlinburg. Establishedin 1938. Buckhorn Inn was built on a hillside facing the magnificent views of the Smokies and includes 40 acres ofwoodlands, meadows and quiet walkways.

---

## Gatlinburg

Butcher, Gloria
Route 2, Box 750, 37738
(615) 436-9457

**Amenities:** 1,2,5,6,7,8,9,10,
11,15,16,17,18
**Breakfast:** F.

**Dbl. Oc.:** $73.00
**Sgl. Oc.:** $68.00

**Butcher House Bed & Breakfast**—The only B&B on Ski Mountain. 2,800-foot elevation above Gatlinburg. Unparalleled view of the Great Smoky Mountains. Ambience, elegance, unique gourmet dining, guest kitchen, stone fireplaces, pristine beauty, horse-backriding, hiking, outlet malls, Dollywood and live theatre.

---

## Gatlinburg *

Mellor, Lee
Route 1, Box 273, 37738
(615) 436-5432

**Amenities:** 1,2,3,9,10,11,
15,16,18
**Breakfast:** F.
**Dbl. Oc.:** $66.80 & up
**Third Person:** $20.00

**The Colonel's Lady**—Re-creates the elegance and charm of an English country inn. Secluded in its own lush mountaintop grounds, yet it's still convenient to local attractions. Panoramic views of the Great Smoky Mountains, big and shaded verandas, 1,000-volume library and outdoor hot tub.

---

| | | | |
|---|---|---|---|
| 1. No Smoking | 5. Tennis Available | 9. Credit Cards Accepted | 13. Lunch Available | 17. Shared Bath |
| 2. No Pets | 6. Golf Available | 10. Personal Checks Accepted | 14. Public Transportation | 18. Afternoon Tea |
| 3. No Children | 7. Swiming Available | 11. Off Season Rates | 15. Reservations Necessary | ★ Commissions given |
| 4. Senior Citizen Rates | 8. Skiing Available | 12. Dinner Available | 16. Private Bath | to Travel Agents |

## Jonesborough

Robertson, Reva Jo
212 E. Main St., 37659
(615) 753-3039

**Amenities:** 1,2,10,16
**Breakfast:** F.

**Dbl. Oc.:** $60.00
**Sgl. Oc.:** $55.00
**Third Person:** $12.00
**Child:** $12.00

**Robertson House**—Conveniently located within the historic district of Tennessee's oldest town. Take a walking tour or explore the many craft and antique shops. Relax in comfortable surroundings and enjoy Southern hospitality at its best.

## Kodak *

Hickman, Hilda
734 Pollard Rd., 37764
(615) 933-3512

**Amenities:** 1,2,3,6,9,10,
15,16,18
**Breakfast:** F.

**Dbl. Oc.:** $55.00 - $75.00
**Sgl. Oc.:** $55.00 - $75.00
**Third Person:** $10.00

**Grandma's House**—Situated on a country lane in Dumpling Valley, two miles from I-40 at Exit 407. Hosts are both native east Tennesseans. Three guest rooms with private baths. Farm-style house has a fireplace in the dining room, a large porch, country quilts and antiques.

## Lynchburg

Rothfeldt, Harriet & Jim
Wiseman Rd.
Route 6, Box 126,
Shelbyville, 37160
(615) 759-4639

**Amenities:** 2,9,10,15,16,
17,18
**Breakfast:** C.

**Dbl. Oc.:** $41.04
**Sgl. Oc.:** $34.56
**Third Person:** $5.00
**Child:** under 5 yrs. -
no charge

**County Line Bed & Breakfast**—A two-story house, circa 1908, situated on a horse farm. Located 4-1/2 miles from Lynchburg and 45 minutes from the space center at Huntsville. Close to Jack Daniel Distillery, Miss Mary Bobo's Boarding House and many arts and crafts shops. Homemade breads. Warm hospitality.

## Memphis

Long, Samantha
217 N. Waldran, 38105
(901) 527-7174

**Amenities:** 2,4,9,10,14,15,16
**Breakfast:** C.

**Dbl. Oc.:** $50.00 - $70.00
**Sgl. Oc.:** $50.00 - $70.00
**Third Person:** $10.00
**Child:** under 2 yrs. -
no charge

**Lowenstein-Long House**—The house was built at the turn of the century and was restored in 1984. It is centrally located and convenient to many attractions. The house has beautiful mahogany woodwork and impressive plaster moldings. A great example of Victorian architecture.

## Murfreesboro

Deaton, Barbara & Robert
435 E. Main St., 37130
(615) 893-6030

**Amenities:** 2,10,11,15,16,17
**Breakfast:** C.

**Dbl. Oc.:** $45.00
**Sgl. Oc.:** $35.00
**Third Person:** $5.00
**Child:** under 12 yrs. - $2.50

**Clardy's Guest House**—A Victorian home in the historic district, furnished with antiques. House features 8'x8' stained glass, ornate woodwork and fireplaces. Just two miles from I-24 and 30 miles southeast of Nashville. Good antique shopping, touring and dining area.

| | | | |
|---|---|---|---|
| 1. No Smoking | 5. Tennis Available | 9. Credit Cards Accepted | 13. Lunch Available | 17. Shared Bath |
| 2. No Pets | 6. Golf Available | 10. Personal Checks Accepted | 14. Public Transportation | 18. Afternoon Tea |
| 3. No Children | 7. Swiming Available | 11. Off Season Rates | 15. Reservations Necessary | ★ Commissions given |
| 4. Senior Citizen Rates | 8. Skiing Available | 12. Dinner Available | 16. Private Bath | to Travel Agents |

# *TENNESSEE*

## *Pigeon Forge*

Hilton, Norma & Jack
1101 Valley Heights Dr., 37863
(615) 428-9765

**Amenities:** 2,4,5,6,7,8,9,10, 11,12,13,14,16,18
**Breakfast:** F.

**Dbl. Oc.:** $75.90 - $108.90
**Sgl. Oc.:** $64.00
**Third Person:** $10.00
**Child:** under 6 yrs. - $5.00

**Hilton's Bluff Bed & Breakfast Inn**—Elegant country living. Near Smoky Mountain National Park, Dollywood, outlet shopping, craft community, golf, fishing, hiking, skiing, horseback riding, historic tours and fine dining. Enjoy den with fireplace, gameroom, decks with rockers and outdoor hot tub.

## *Pigeon Forge*

Trombley, Yvonne
915 Colonial Dr., 37863
(615) 428-0370

**Amenities:** 1,2,9,10,11,14,15, 16,17
**Breakfast:** F.

**Dbl. Oc.:** $64.90 - $121.00
**Sgl. Oc.:** $53.90 - $110.00
**Third Person:** $10.00
**Child:** no charge

**Day Dreams Country Inn**—Enjoy a down-home country atmosphere. Our log home, situated on three acres, offers beautiful trees, gardens and a stream to sit and relax by. Within walking distance, you'll find outlet malls, Dollywood, the rest of Pigeon Forge and the Great Smoky Mountains.

## *Rugby*

Jones, Bill
Hwy. 52, P.O. Box 5252, 37733
(615) 628-5252

**Amenities:** 1,2,6,7,9,10,12,13, 15,16,17
**Breakfast:** F.

**Dbl. Oc.:** $97.00 & up
**Sgl. Oc.:** $78.00 & up

**Grey Gables Bed 'n' Breakfast**—Cumberland Plateau - An 1880 historic English colony. Grey Gables blends Victorian English and Tennessee country. Enjoy an evening meal, a country breakfast, white-wicker or country rockers, croquet, horseshoes and canoe rental. Shuttle access to golf, swiming, hiking and cycling.

## *Rugby*

Stagg, Barbara
Hwy. 52, 37733
(615) 628-2430

**Amenities:** 1,2,3,7,9,10,12,13, 15,16,17
**Breakfast:** F.

**Dbl. Oc.:** $55.00 - $65.00
**Sgl. Oc.:** $45.00 - $55.00
**Child:** 6-12 yrs. - $8.00

**Newbury House At Historic Rugby**—Pioneer cottages built in 1880. Restored and furnished with antiques. Listed in the *Register of Historic Places*. In a tranquil village near national and state parks. Historic building tours, craft commissary and Victorian bookshop. Century-old walking trails to adjacent river.

| | | | | |
|---|---|---|---|---|
| 1. No Smoking | 5. Tennis Available | 9. Credit Cards Accepted | 13. Lunch Available | 17. Shared Bath |
| 2. No Pets | 6. Golf Available | 10. Personal Checks Accepted | 14. Public Transportation | 18. Afternoon Tea |
| 3. No Children | 7. Swiming Available | 11. Off Season Rates | 15. Reservations Necessary | ★ Commissions given |
| 4. Senior Citizen Rates | 8. Skiing Available | 12. Dinner Available | 16. Private Bath | to Travel Agents |

# TENNESSEE

## Sevierville

Fleissner, Sue & Chuck
Route 6, Box 197, 37862
(615) 453-3997

**Amenities:** 2,3,7,10,15,16,17
**Breakfast:** F.

**Dbl. Oc.:** $70.04
**Sgl. Oc.:** $59.26

**Cove Country Inn**—A beautiful log home nestled in the mountains. Furnished in antiques and country primitives. Conveniently located near Pigeon Forge, Gatlinburg and Dollywood.

## Sevierville *

Miller, Fern
2803 Old Country Way, 37862
(615) 428-4858

**Amenities:** 1,2,3,4,5,6,7,8,9, 10,11,15,16,17,18
**Breakfast:** F.

**Dbl. Oc.:** $65.00 - $97.00
**Sgl. Oc.:** $54.00 - $87.00

**Milk & Honey Country Hideaway**—Close to Gatlinburg, Pigeon Forge, outlet malls and Great Smoky Mountain National Park. Large front porch, rockers, cozy rooms and hearty breakfasts. Warm hospitality in a quiet country setting.

## Tullahoma

Stricklin, Ethel
2303 Ovoca Rd., 37388
(615) 455-9496

**Amenities:** 4,6,7,9,10,15, 16,17
**Breakfast:** F.

**Dbl. Oc.:** $40.00 - $50.00
**Third Person:** $10.00

**Jennys Bed And Breakfast**—A suite with sitting room and twin beds with private bath and shower. Two bedrooms with double beds and shared bath with tub. Situated 3-1/2 miles from downtown Tullahoma. Quiet and restful location. Private entrance and screened patio room. Country quiet and city convenient.

| | | | | |
|---|---|---|---|---|
| 1. No Smoking | 5. Tennis Available | 9. Credit Cards Accepted | 13. Lunch Available | 17. Shared Bath |
| 2. No Pets | 6. Golf Available | 10. Personal Checks Accepted | 14. Public Transportation | 18. Afternoon Tea |
| 3. No Children | 7. Swiming Available | 11. Off Season Rates | 15. Reservations Necessary | ★ Commissions given |
| 4. Senior Citizen Rates | 8. Skiing Available | 12. Dinner Available | 16. Private Bath | to Travel Agents |

# TEXAS

## *The Lone Star State*

Capitol: Austin
Statehood: December 29, 1845; the 28th state
State Motto: Friendship
State Song: "Texas, Our Texas"
State Bird: Mockingbird
State Flower: Bluebonnet
State Tree: Pecan

Texas is second in size to Alaska. It is so big that when it entered the union, Congress gave it the right to divide into five states, but it preferred to remain one and BIG. It is called the Lone Star State because of the one lone star on its flag.

Many colorful people from history have come from Texas, including Davy Crockett, Jim Bowie and one of our more modern-day heros, President Lyndon B. Johnson.

Texas has many millionaires because of the great oil strikes there over the years. There is also much cattle, and great cattle farms. The King Ranch is perhaps the largest cattle-raising ranch in the world.

The cities of Houston, Dallas, San Antonio and Fort Worth are exciting places for the tourist to visit.

# TEXAS

## Austin

Jackson, Kay
12000 W. 22 1/2 St., 78705
(800) 747-9231

**Amenities:** 1,2,3,4,9,10,12,13,
14,15,16,17
**Breakfast:** F.

**Dbl. Oc.:** $54.00 - $69.00
**Sgl. Oc.:** $49.00 - $64.00
**Third Person:** $10.00

**The Wild Flower Inn**—A lovely 50 year old home located on a tree lined street. The inn is seven blocks west of the University of Texas campus and just a few minutes from the state capitol complex. Convenient to the LBJ Presidential Library. Close to hiking and biking trails and tennis courts.

## Austin *

Southard, Rejina & Jerry
908 Blanco, 78703
(512) 474-4731

**Amenities:** 1,3,9,10,14,15,16
**Breakfast:** C.
**Dbl. Oc.:** $55.37 - $100.57
**Sgl. Oc.:** $44.07 - $89.27
**Third Person:** $10.00

**Southard House**—A lovely 1890's home located off West 6th Street. Claw-foot tubs, antiques and porch sitting. Quiet, eclectic and relaxing. Walk to star-rated restaurants and unique shops. Charming bedrooms with phones. Freshly baked bread and seasonal fruit. Complimentary wine. Downtown area.

## Austin

Thurmond, Mrs. Peninnah
10817 Ranch Rd. 2222, 78730-1102
(512) 338-1817

**Amenities:** 5,6,7,9,10,15,16

**Breakfast:** F.

**Dbl. Oc.:** $65.00
**Sgl. Oc.:** $65.00
**Third Person:** $65.00
**Child:** $15.00

**Peaceful Hill Bed & Breakfast**—Located on a ranch high up in the beautiful rolling hills west of Austin. Native-stone country home overlooking the city skyline. Only 15 minutes to Lake Travis. Home-cooked reakfast served on the porch, dining room or by the fire.

## Dallas

Offerman, Amanda
4311 W. Lawther Dr., 75214
(214) 824-0673

**Amenities:** 1,3,5,6,7,9,12,13,
14,15,16,17
**Breakfast:** F.

**Dbl. Oc.:** $67.80 - $84.75
**Sgl. Oc.:** $61.10 - $84.75
**Child:** under 15 yrs. -
$13.10

**Lawther Place**—A beautiful historic estate on White Rock Lake. Fantastic view. Bicycling, jogging, sailing, tennis, billiards and weights. Just 10 minutes from downtown shopping, fine restaurants, sports events, etc. Relaxing, quiet and very romantic. Children in guest houses only.

| | | | | |
|---|---|---|---|---|
| 1. No Smoking | 5. Tennis Available | 9. Credit Cards Accepted | 13. Lunch Available | 17. Shared Bath |
| 2. No Pets | 6. Golf Available | 10. Personal Checks Accepted | 14. Public Transportation | 18. Afternoon Tea |
| 3. No Children | 7. Swiming Available | 11. Off Season Rates | 15. Reservations Necessary | ★ Commissions given |
| 4. Senior Citizen Rates | 8. Skiing Available | 12. Dinner Available | 16. Private Bath | to Travel Agents |

## Fort Worth

Hancock, Susan & Mark
109-1/2 West Exchange, 76106
(817) 626-1522

**Amenities:** 1,2,9,10,14,15,16,17,18
**Breakfast:** F.
**Dbl. Oc.:** $67.80 - $129.95
**Sgl. Oc.:** $67.80
**Third Person:** rollaway - $11.30

**Miss Molly's Hotel Bed & Breakfast**—Discover the living history of the cowboys and cattle along the red-brick streets of this 10-block historic district. In the middle of it all is Miss Molly's Hotel, once a primand proper hotel and later a popular bordello. Each of eight guest rooms furnished in Old West.

---

## Fredericksburg

Kothe, Naomi & Kermit
HC 10, Box 53A, 78624
(512) 669-2471

**Amenities:** 2,3,9,10,15,16,17
**Breakfast:** F.

**Dbl. Oc.:** $68.90
**Sgl. Oc.:** $68.90
**Third Person:** $21.20
**Child:** $21.20

**J Bar K Ranch Bed & Breakfast**—A large historic, German rock home with antique furnishings on a Texas hill country ranch. Just 15 minutes from Fredericksburg with its German heritage and architecture. Excellent restaurants and quaint shops. Real Texas hospitality. Children over seven years of age welcome.

---

## Galveston

Clark, Robert
2217 Broadway, 77550
(409) 765-8148, (800) 762-2632

**Amenities:** 1,2,3,4,6,7,9,10, 12,15,16
**Breakfast:** F.

**Dbl. Oc.:** $90.40 - $113.00
**Sgl. Oc.:** $90.40 - $113.00
**Third Person:** $11.30
**Child:** $11.30

**The White Horse Inn**—An elegant Victorian mansion built in 1884. Two rooms in main house. Four rooms in carriage house. Fourteen-foot ceilings, fireplaces and balconies. Antique and reproduction furniture. Close to historic district. Beautiful garden. Near museums and Strand district.

---

| | | | |
|---|---|---|---|
| 1. No Smoking | 5. Tennis Available | 9. Credit Cards Accepted | 13. Lunch Available | 17. Shared Bath |
| 2. No Pets | 6. Golf Available | 10. Personal Checks Accepted | 14. Public Transportation | 18. Afternoon Tea |
| 3. No Children | 7. Swiming Available | 11. Off Season Rates | 15. Reservations Necessary | ★ Commissions given |
| 4. Senior Citizen Rates | 8. Skiing Available | 12. Dinner Available | 16. Private Bath | to Travel Agents |

## *Galveston*

Hanemann, Helen R.
1805 Broadway, 77550
(409) 763-0194

**Amenities:** 10,15,17,18
**Breakfast:** F.
**Dbl. Oc.:** $129.95 - $152.25
**Sgl. Oc.:** $129.95 - $152.25
**Third Person:** $56.50
**Child:** under 6 yrs.- no charge

**The Guilded Thistle**—Enter into a wonderland of fanciful ambience, down-home elegance, superb service and bountiful amenities. Enjoy the memorable experience of choosing "one of the best guest residences Texas has to offer." - Texas Monthly Press.

## *Galveston* *

Mafrige, Nancy & Don
511 - 17th St., 77550
(409) 762-3235

**Amenities:** 2,3,4,9,10,14,15, 16,17
**Breakfast:** C.

**Dbl. Oc.:** $101.70 - $141.25
**Sgl. Oc.:** $101.70
**Third Person:** $22.60
**Child:** $22.6

**The Victorian Inn**—An 1899 Italianate villa home of a prominent cement contractor who built the first county seawall and the Galveston Water Works. Carved oak fireplaces, maple floors and stairwells. Spacious guest rooms, each with its own balcony. Smoking on porches. Children over 12 welcome.

## *Garland* *

Cushion, Nancy & Gene
417 Glen Canyon Dr., 75040
(214) 530-0819,
(214) 298-8586 (reservations)

**Amenities:** 1,2,3,9,15,16
**Breakfast:** F.

**Dbl. Oc.:** $52.85
**Sgl. Oc.:** $41.13
**Third Person:** $11.75

**Catnap Creek B&B**—These gracious hosts offer a peaceful wooded-creek setting. Hot tub, shaded patio overlooking the creek, vegetarian breakfasts and bicycles. The spacious guest room has a private entry, private bath and queen-size bed. Two cats are in residence.

| | | | |
|---|---|---|---|
| 1. No Smoking | 5. Tennis Available | 9. Credit Cards Accepted | 13. Lunch Available | 17. Shared Bath |
| 2. No Pets | 6. Golf Available | 10. Personal Checks Accepted | 14. Public Transportation | 18. Afternoon Tea |
| 3. No Children | 7. Swiming Available | 11. Off Season Rates | 15. Reservations Necessary | ★ Commissions given |
| 4. Senior Citizen Rates | 8. Skiing Available | 12. Dinner Available | 16. Private Bath | to Travel Agents |

## *Houston*

Swanson, Marguerite
921 Heights Blvd., 77008
(713) 868-4654

**Amenities:** 1,2,9,10,12,14,
15,16
**Breakfast:** F.

**Dbl. Oc.:** $55.00 - $60.00
**Sgl. Oc.:** $40.00 - $45.00

**Durham House**—A faithfully restored bed & breakfast on the *National Register of Historic Places*. Antique furnishings, player piano, gazebo and porch swing. Just 10 minutes from downtown. Weddings and murder mystery dinner parties. Elegant Victorian. Open all year.

## *Hunt*

Dickinson, Karl
P.O. Box 158, 78024
(512) 238-4681

**Amenities:** 1,2,4,5,6,9,10,11,
15,16
**Breakfast:** F.

**Dbl. Oc.:** $79.50 - $111.30
**Sgl. Oc.:** $79.50
**Third Person:** $15.00
**Child:** under 5 yrs. -
no charge

**River Bend B&B**—Come stay with us on the banks of the beautiful Guadalupe River under the cypress trees. Minutes from art galleries and antiquing. The B&B is built of native stone and has an antique decor. 55 acres. One half mile of river front.

## *Hunt*

Price, June F. & Donald A.
Rt. 1, Box 174-A, 78024
(512) 238-4531

**Amenities:** 1,2,3,10,12,
13,15,16
**Breakfast:** C. and F.

**Dbl. Oc.:** $55.00 - $65.00
**Sgl. Oc.:** $55.00
**Third Person:** $10.00

**Joy Spring Ranch B&B**—Beautiful hill country log cabin. Sleeps four. Complete kitchen. Near Kerrville, 87 miles northwest of San Antonio. 2,066 altitude on Guadalupe River. Many summer camps. Birding and hiking. Wildlife includes exotic deer and wild turkeys. 100 acre ranch. Private and secluded.

## *Marble Falls*

Scarborough, Joanne & Roger
1908 Redwood Dr.,
Granite Shoals, 78654
(512) 598-6448

**Amenities:** 1,2,6,7,10,16
**Breakfast:** F.

**Dbl. Oc.:** $58.30
**Sgl. Oc.:** $52.00
**Third Person:** $10.60
**Child:** under 12 yrs. -
no charge

**La Casita**—Nestled 50 feet behind the main house this private cottage is rustic and Texan on the outside yet throughly modern inside. Native Texan hosts can suggest wineries, parks, and river cruises, however, relaxing in a country setting is the main attraction.

| | | | | |
|---|---|---|---|---|
| 1. No Smoking | 5. Tennis Available | 9. Credit Cards Accepted | 13. Lunch Available | 17. Shared Bath |
| 2. No Pets | 6. Golf Available | 10. Personal Checks Accepted | 14. Public Transportation | 18. Afternoon Tea |
| 3. No Children | 7. Swiming Available | 11. Off Season Rates | 15. Reservations Necessary | ★ Commissions given |
| 4. Senior Citizen Rates | 8. Skiing Available | 12. Dinner Available | 16. Private Bath | to Travel Agents |

## *Mineola*

| | | |
|---|---|---|
| Sellers, Ron | **Amenities:** 1,2,4,5,6,9,10,12, | **Dbl. Oc.:** $82.50 |
| 411 E. Kilpatrick, 75773 | 13,16,17 | **Sgl. Oc.:** $72.50 |
| (214) 569-6560 | **Breakfast:** F. | **Third Person:** $10.00 |
| | | **Child: under 2 yrs. -** |
| | | no charge |

**Sellers' Corner**—1910 Greek Revival mansion with four guest rooms. Five minutes from town, shopping, theatre etc. Southern hospitality with country charm and elegance. Antique furnishings. Great for relaxation. Walking and biking areas. Thirty minutes from the famous Canton Trade Day.

## *Salado*

| | | |
|---|---|---|
| Sands, Cathy | **Amenities:** 1,2,5,6,7,9,10,15, | **Dbl. Oc.:** $69.20 - $90.50 |
| #1 Roseway | 16,17 | **Sgl. Oc.:** $69.20 - $90.50 |
| P.O. Box 500, 76571 | **Breakfast:** F. | **Third Person:** no charge |
| (817) 947-5999 | | **Child:** no charge |

**The Rose Mansion**—Located off of I-35 halfway between San Antonio and Dallas. Beautiful Victorian house built in 1873. Beautiful giant oak trees surround the inn. Located in a historic town with many unique shops and restaurants. Five rooms with fireplaces. Come enjoy the quiet.

## *San Antonio*

| | | |
|---|---|---|
| Cross, Alma & Steven | **Amenities:** 2,5,6,7,9,13,14,15, | **Dbl. Oc.:** $40.68 - $62.15 |
| 621 Pierce St., 78208 | 16,17 | **Sgl. Oc.:** $32.77 - $54.24 |
| (512) 223-9426 | **Breakfast:** C. and F. | **Third Person:** $9.00 |
| | | **Child:** no charge - $5.00 |

**Bullis House Inn**—Lovely historic Texas mansion minutes from downtown. Large columns, chandeliers, fireplaces and veranda. Eight rooms. Free parking. Located off I-35 next to historic Fort Sam Houston. Meeting facilities. Special weekday and honeymoon packages available. A Texas landmark.

## *San Antonio*

Daubert, Grace & Bob
300 West French Pl., 78212
(512) 733-1998

**Amenities:** 1,2,3,5,6,7,
10,14,15,16
**Breakfast:** C.
**Dbl. Oc.:** $75.00
**Sgl. Oc.:** $75.00

**Falling Pines B&B**—Historic restoration near the Alamo, river walking and downtown businesses. Three- story mansion constructed of brick and limestone. Entry level has paneling, oak floors and Oriental rugs. Second level has designer guest rooms. Third level is a unique suite. On a park like acre.

| | | | | |
|---|---|---|---|---|
| 1. No Smoking | 5. Tennis Available | 9. Credit Cards Accepted | 13. Lunch Available | 17. Shared Bath |
| 2. No Pets | 6. Golf Available | 10. Personal Checks Accepted | 14. Public Transportation | 18. Afternoon Tea |
| 3. No Children | 7. Swiming Available | 11. Off Season Rates | 15. Reservations Necessary | ★ Commissions given |
| 4. Senior Citizen Rates | 8. Skiing Available | 12. Dinner Available | 16. Private Bath | to Travel Agents |

# TEXAS

## San Antonio

Trevino, Maria
921 Matagorda, 78210
(512) 271-3040

**Amenities:** 1,2,9,10,11,14,15,
16,17
**Breakfast:** C.

**Dbl. Oc.:** $50.85 - $79.10
**Sgl. Oc.:** $50.85 - $79.10
**Third Person:** $10.00
**Child:** under 12 yrs. -
no charge

**Naegelin Bed & Breakfast**—1910 historical landmark colonial home in downtown area. Rich woodwork throughout the home. Four spacious bedrooms carefully furnished with antiques. Six blocks from the Alamo, Riverwalk and other downtown attractions.

---

## Tyler

Powell, Rebecca & Bert
415 South Vine, 75702
(214) 592-2221

**Amenities:** 1,2,5,6,7,9,10,
15,16
**Breakfast:** F.

**Dbl. Oc.:** $73.20
**Sgl. Oc.:** $61.90
**Third Person:** $11.30

**Rosevine Inn, Bed & Breakfast**—Located in the historic "brick street area" of Tyler. Near many shops. Enjoy our courtyard and outdoor hot tub. Refreshments are served on arrival and a delectible breakfast in the morning. The innkeepers enjoy visiting with their guests and acting as tour guides.

---

## Uvalde *

Durr, Carolyn & Ben
1149 Pearsall Rd.
P.O. Box 1829, 78802
(512) 278-8550

**Amenities:** 1,2,3,10,12,15,
16,18
**Breakfast:** C. and F.

**Dbl. Oc.:** $59.13
**Sgl. Oc.:** $59.13
**Child:** under one yr. -
$15.00

**Casa De Leona**—Spanish hacienda on the ruins of the Fort Inge historic site bordering the Leona River. A quiet retreat for small busniess meetings or art seminars. Wilderness trails for hiking and bird watching. Quiet hideaway for honeymooners and special occasions. Open year round.

---

| | | | | |
|---|---|---|---|---|
| 1. No Smoking | 5. Tennis Available | 9. Credit Cards Accepted | 13. Lunch Available | 17. Shared Bath |
| 2. No Pets | 6. Golf Available | 10. Personal Checks Accepted | 14. Public Transportation | 18. Afternoon Tea |
| 3. No Children | 7. Swiming Available | 11. Off Season Rates | 15. Reservations Necessary | ★ Commissions given |
| 4. Senior Citizen Rates | 8. Skiing Available | 12. Dinner Available | 16. Private Bath | to Travel Agents |

# UTAH

## The Beehive State

Capitol: Salt Lake City
Statehood: January 4, 1896; the 45th state
State Motto: Industry
State Song: "Utah, We Love Thee"
State Bird: Sea Gull
State Flower: Sego Lily
State Tree: Blue Spruce

Utah was settled in 1847 by the Mormon pioneers, led by Bringham Young. They were industrious people, and came to the west to live where they could express their religious beliefs as they wanted. Today most of the people of Utah live along the Wasatch Mountain area. Salt Lake City is a modern city with wide streets and tree-lined sidewalks. It has an open and very clean look. Tourists are attracted here from all over the country to hear the magnificent Mormon Chapel Singers and to see the Mormon church buildings.

Oil and copper have been the main occupation of the people of Utah for many years, but tourism has become a major source of income in the past 10 years. There are several National Parks here, including Bryce Canyon and Zion National Park.

## Kanab

Bantlin, Jeanne & Frank
106 W. 100 No., 84741
(801) 644-5079

**Amenities:** 1,2,3,6,9,10,16
**Breakfast:** C.

**Dbl. Oc.:** $64.40
**Sgl. Oc.:** $59.95

**Nine Gables Inn**—A 100-year-old historic home furnished with family antiques. Located close to Bryce and Zion National Parks, the Grand Canyon, Lake Powell and Pipe Spring National Monument. Also known as the Zane Grey House. There is one cat in residence.

---

## Kanab

Barden, Aprile & Ronald
30 N. 200 W., 84741
(801) 644-5952

**Amenities:** 1,2,3,6,9,11,16
**Breakfast:** F.

**Dbl. Oc.:** $42.00
**Sgl. Oc.:** $42.00

**Miss Sophie's Bed & Breakfast**—A restored 1800's home with an in-town location. Guestrooms have antiques and private baths. Kanab, hub to parks, is called "Little Hollywood" for its movie past. Nice weather. Open May to October.

---

## Moab *

Stucki, Marge & Richard
185 N. 300 E., 84532
(801) 259-2974

**Amenities:** 1,2,9,10,16,17
**Breakfast:** F.

**Dbl. Oc.:** $44.00 - $57.20
**Sgl. Oc.:** $38.50
**Third Person:** $8.80
**Child:** under 3 yrs. -
no charge

**Sunflower Hill Bed & Breakfast Inn**—Warm hospitality in a delightfully appointed country inn. Antiques, fireplace, guest dining room and charming bedrooms. Memorable breakfast buffet with great home baking. Queen and double beds. Flowered patios and gardens. Quiet. Off highway, near town center.

---

## Nephi

Gliske, Dorothy & Robert
110 So. Main St., 84648
(801) 623-2047

**Amenities:** 1,2,9,10,12,13,16
**Breakfast:** F.

**Dbl. Oc.:** $55.00
**Sgl. Oc.:** $50.00
**Third Person:** $10.60
**Child:** $10.60

**Whitmore Mansion**—This mansion combines Victorian elegance with warm and personal service, reflecting the charm of bygone days. Private baths and a hearty breakfast helps to ensure a pleasant stay.

---

## Park City

Daniels, Hugh
615 Woodside Ave., 84060-2639
(801) 645-8068, (800) 648-8068

**Amenities:** 1,2,5,6,7,8,9,10,
11,16
**Breakfast:** F.

**Dbl. Oc.:** $44.10 - $187.43
**Sgl. Oc.:** $44.10 - $181.92
**Third Person:** $16.54 -
$22.05
**Child:** under 13 yrs. - $5.52

**The Old Miners' Lodge - A Bed & Breakfast Inn**—Originally built in 1893 in the national historic district of Park City known for its magnificent skiing and golf. Ten guest rooms, including three suites. Thirty miles east of Salt Lake City. No smoking. Outdoor hot tub and many amenities.

---

| | | | | |
|---|---|---|---|---|
| 1. No Smoking | 5. Tennis Available | 9. Credit Cards Accepted | 13. Lunch Available | 17. Shared Bath |
| 2. No Pets | 6. Golf Available | 10. Personal Checks Accepted | 14. Public Transportation | 18. Afternoon Tea |
| 3. No Children | 7. Swiming Available | 11. Off Season Rates | 15. Reservations Necessary | ★ Commissions give |
| 4. Senior Citizen Rates | 8. Skiing Available | 12. Dinner Available | 16. Private Bath | to Travel Agents |

## Salt Lake City

Lind, Karl
6151 So. 900 E., 84121
(801) 268-8762

**Amenities:** 1,2,8,9,10,11,16
**Breakfast:** C.

**Dbl. Oc.:** $50.00 - $80.00
**Sgl. Oc.:** $50.00
**Third Person:** $10.00

**The Spruces Bed And Breakfast**—The Spruces is set amid tall spruces and a small quarter-horse breeding and training farm. It has four suites furnished with folk art and Southwestern touches. All have phone, TV and private baths. Two have kitchens. Ski slopes are within a one-half hour drive.

## St. George

Curtis, Donna
217 No. 100 W., 84770
(801) 628-3737

**Amenities:** 1,2,5,6,7,9,10,16
**Breakfast:** F.

**Dbl. Oc.:** $38.15 - $76.30
**Sgl. Oc.:** $27.25 - $76.30
**Third Person:** $10.00
**Child:** $10.00

**Seven Wives Inn**—Two side-by-side pioneer homes, one built in 1873 and the other built in 1883. Both are in the St. George historic district and are featured in the city's walking tour. Both are furnished in antiques and include original hand-grained massive woodwork. Swimming pool.

## Toquerville

Boyns, Debbie & Phil
650 Springs Dr.
P.O. Box 276, 84774
(801) 635-9964

**Amenities:** 3,5,6,7,8,10,
15,16
**Breakfast:** F.

**Dbl. Oc.:** $50.00
**Sgl. Oc.:** $40.00
**Third Person:** $10.00

**"Your Inn Toquerville"**—A secluded and spacious solar home on a 10-acre orchard with a spectacular mountain view. Homemade peach brandy by the fire or upstairs patio. King-size beds and sitting area. Coffee at your door. Gourmet breakfast. Only 17 miles to Zion National Park. Nearby trout fishing.

| | | | |
|---|---|---|---|
| 1. No Smoking | 5. Tennis Available | 9. Credit Cards Accepted | 13. Lunch Available | 17. Shared Bath |
| 2. No Pets | 6. Golf Available | 10. Personal Checks Accepted | 14. Public Transportation | 18. Afternoon Tea |
| 3. No Children | 7. Swiming Available | 11. Off Season Rates | 15. Reservations Necessary | ★ Commissions given |
| 4. Senior Citizen Rates | 8. Skiing Available | 12. Dinner Available | 16. Private Bath | to Travel Agents |

# VERMONT

## *The Green Mountain State*

Capitol: Montpelier
Statehood: March 4, 1791; the 14th state
State Motto: Vermont, Freedom and Unity
State Song: "Hail Vermont"
State Bird: Hermit Thrush
State Flower: Red Clover
State Tree: Sugar Maple


Vermont is called The Green Mountain State because of its beautiful and overwhelming green mountains. It is a state that receives much snow, and their longest season is winter. However, the other seasons, although shorter in length, are just as beautiful because of the colorful foliage and magnificent scenery.

Vermont is the only New England state that does not have a coastline, but its lovely lakes and recreational facilities more than make up for the lack of a seashore. Swimming and boating in the summer and the best of skiing in the winter makes Vermont a tourist paradise.

The tapping of their own maple trees brings the Vermonters the sugar to make maple sugar products for which they are so well known.

Presidents Chester A. Arthur and Calvin Coolidge were both born here.

## Alburg

Schallert, Dottie & Patrick
Blue Rock Rd.
Route 2, Box 149B, 05440
(802) 796-3736

**Amenities:** 1,2,3,6,7,8,10,15, 16,18
**Breakfast:** F.

**Dbl. Oc.:** $53.50 - $69.55
**Sgl. Oc.:** $53.50 - $69.55
**Third Person:** $10.00
**Child:** over 10 yrs. - $10.00

**Thomas Mott Bed & Breakfast**—An 1838 farmhouse on Lake Champlain. Four rooms with private baths. St. #78 to Thomas Mott B&B sign. South to lakeshore. One hour to Jay, Burlington and Montreal. 1-1/2 hours to Stow/Smugglers, etc. Canoes, horseshoes and fishing.

## Arlington *

Hardy, Joanne & George
RR #2, Box 2015, 05250
(802) 375-2269, (800) 882-2545

**Amenities:** 1,2,4,5,6,7,8,9, 10,12,16,17
**Breakfast:** F.
**Dbl. Oc.:** $70.00 - $100.00
**Sgl. Oc.:** $48.00 - $59.00
**Third Person:** $24.00
**Child:** 6 - 12 yrs. - $18.00

**Hill Farm Inn**—One of Vermont's original farm vacation inns. Located in two renovated farmhouses built in 1790 and 1830. Quiet, comfortable and relaxed atmosphere. Delicious country cooking, home grown vegetables and homemade jam to take home. Splendid mountain views.

## Arlington

Kenny, Mathilda
Sandgate Rd.
Box 2480, 05250
(802) 375-2272

**Amenities:** 3,7,10,12,13, 15,16,17,18
**Breakfast:** F.

**Dbl. Oc.:** $50.00 - $60.00
**Sgl. Oc.:** $25.00 - $30.00
**Third Person:** $20.00
**Child:** under 12 yrs. - $15.00

**The Evergreen Inn**—An old-fashioned country inn nestled in the Green River Valley off the beaten path. Casual and relaxed atmosphere. Beautiful scenery. Family owned and operated for 52 years. Home cooking and baking.

## Alburg

Masterson, Woody
Battenkill Rd., 05250
(8020 375-6372

**Amenities:** 1,2,7,8,9,10,11, 15,16,17,18
**Breakfast:** F.

**Dbl. Oc.:** $65.00
**Sgl. Oc.:** $40.00
**Third Person:** $20.00
**Child:** under 10 yrs. - $10.00

**Shenandoah Farm**—Experience New England in this lovingly restored 1820 colonial overlooking the Battenkill River. Wonderful Americana year round. Full "farm- fresh"breakfast is served daily.

| | | | |
|---|---|---|---|
| 1. No Smoking | 5. Tennis Available | 9. Credit Cards Accepted | 13. Lunch Available | 17. Shared Bath |
| 2. No Pets | 6. Golf Available | 10. Personal Checks Accepted | 14. Public Transportation | 18. Afternoon Tea |
| 3. No Children | 7. Swiming Available | 11. Off Season Rates | 15. Reservations Necessary | ★ Commissions given |
| 4. Senior Citizen Rates | 8. Skiing Available | 12. Dinner Available | 16. Private Bath | to Travel Agents |

# VERMONT

## Arlington

Wall, Peggy
Historic Route 7A
RR 2, Box 2440, 05250
(802) 362-4213

**Amenities:** 2,5,6,7,8,9,10, 16,17
**Breakfast:** F.

**Dbl. Oc.:** $70.00 - $115.00
**Sgl. Oc.:** $65.00 - $110.00

**The Inn At Sunderland**—A restored Victorian farmhouse nestled at the foot of Mt.Equinox, just south of Manchester. Comfortable rooms, antiques, fireplaces and porches with lovely mountain views.

---

## Barnet *

Pierce, Doris & George
Box 35, 05821
(802) 633-4100

**Amenities:** 6,7,8,10,16,17
**Breakfast:** C.

**Dbl. Oc.:** $53.50
**Sgl. Oc.:** $42.80

**The Old Homestead**—A real Vermont bed and breakfast inn located in picturesqueBarnet Village in Vermont's northeast kingdom. We provide a quiet and friendly atmosphere from which our guests may enjoy many attractions in rural northeastern Vermont.

---

## Bellows Falls *

Champagne, Helene
RD 1, Box 328, 05101
(802) 463-9008

**Amenities:** 1,2,4,8,9,10, 11,15
**Breakfast:** F.

**Dbl. Oc.:** $64.20
**Sgl. Oc.:** $48.15
**Third Person:** $21.40
**Child:** under 12 yrs. - $10.00

**Blue Haven Guest House**—An expanded 1830 schoolhouse that boasts a large farmhouse kitchen and cozy pine den that features a stone fireplace. Period rooms in a peaceful and pleasant Christian home. Less than two miles from town. Local historic train ride. Horse-and-buggy rides in season. Nearby biking and skiing.

---

## Belmont

Gorman, Mary
Box 62, 05730
(802) 259-2903

**Amenities:** 1,2,9,10,11,15,16
**Breakfast:** C. Plus
**Dbl. Oc.:** $68.00
**Sgl. Oc.:** $47.00
**Third Person:** $10.00
**Child:** $10.00

**The Leslie Place**—A peaceful setting on 100 acres near Weston. This lovingly restored 1840 farmhouse is close to ski areas, restaurants, theatre and shops. The relaxed, spacious interior and picturesque setting create a welcome retreat year round. Brochure available.

---

| | | | | |
|---|---|---|---|---|
| 1. No Smoking | 5. Tennis Available | 9. Credit Cards Accepted | 13. Lunch Available | 17. Shared Bath |
| 2. No Pets | 6. Golf Available | 10. Personal Checks Accepted | 14. Public Transportation | 18. Afternoon Tea |
| 3. No Children | 7. Swiming Available | 11. Off Season Rates | 15. Reservations Necessary | ★ Commissions given |
| 4. Senior Citizen Rates | 8. Skiing Available | 12. Dinner Available | 16. Private Bath | to Travel Agents |

# VERMONT

## Bethel *

Wolf, Lyle
RD 2, Box 60, 05032
(802) 234-9474

**Amenities:** 6,7,8,9,10,15, 16,17
**Breakfast:** C.

**Dbl. Oc.:** $50.00 - $95.00
**Sgl. Oc.:** $35.00 - $80.00
**Third Person:** $15.00
**Child:** $15.00

**Greenhurst Inn**—In the *National Register of Historic Places*. A Victorian mansion on the White River in the center of Vermont, with the elegance of another age. On Route 107, three miles west of I-89 in a quiet and rural setting. Mid way between Boston and Montreal.

## Brattleboro

Pusey, Patricia & William
RR 4, Box 668, 05301
(802) 464-3253

**Amenities:** 1,2,16,18
**Breakfast:** C. Plus

**Dbl. Oc.:** $65.00 - $85.00
**Sgl. Oc.:** $55.00 - $65.00
**Third Person:** $25.00

**Shearer Hill Farm**—A quiet and pristine farm setting. Family owned and operated. Open year round. Close to swimming, skiing, hiking and shopping. Well-groomed cross-country skiing trails on the premises. Maple syrup made at the farm in the spring. Bill and Patti Pusey, innkeepers.

## Brookfield *

Simpson, Pat & Peter
P.O. Box 494, 05036
(802) 276-3412

**Amenities:** 1,2,6,7,8,10,12, 15,16,17
**Breakfast:** F.
**Dbl. Oc.:** $83.00 - $116.00
**Sgl. Oc.:** $60.00 - $87.00
**Third Person:** $20.00 - $25.00

**Green Trails Country Inn**—By the famous floating bridge. A cozy and informal country inn — "like going home to grandma's." Decorated with quilts and antiques. Featured on the "Today" show. "The epitome of a country inn."

## Burlington

TeTreault, Arlene
251 Staniford Rd., 05401
(802) 862-2781

**Amenities:** 1,2,3,10,14,17
**Breakfast:** C.

**Dbl. Oc.:** $40.00
**Sgl. Oc.:** $35.00

**North Shore**—A lovely, traditional Burlington home three miles from downtown. Ideally located on a beautiful bike path for biking, walking and cross-country skiing. Fantastic view of Lake Champlain. One-half mile to public beaches. Shopping at Ethan Allen Shopping Center.

---

| | | | |
|---|---|---|---|
| 1. No Smoking | 5. Tennis Available | 9. Credit Cards Accepted | 13. Lunch Available | 17. Shared Bath |
| 2. No Pets | 6. Golf Available | 10. Personal Checks Accepted | 14. Public Transportation | 18. Afternoon Tea |
| 3. No Children | 7. Swiming Available | 11. Off Season Rates | 15. Reservations Necessary | ★ Commissions given |
| 4. Senior Citizen Rates | 8. Skiing Available | 12. Dinner Available | 16. Private Bath | to Travel Agents |

## *Cabot* *

Lloyd, Judy & Dan
P.O. Box 187, 05647
(802) 563-2819

**Amenities:** 1,2,10,11,
  12,16,17
**Breakfast:** F.
**Dbl. Oc.:** $55.00
**Sgl. Oc.:** $35.00

**Creamery Inn Bed And Breakfast**—A Federal-style home in a rural setting near Cabot Creamery. Guest rooms feature 1830's original stenciling that has been restored. Relax in sitting room, around fireplace or on porch. Snowmobile trails, country roads and picturesque surroundings. Delicious breakfasts.

## *Chelsea*

Papa, Mary Lee & James
Main St. (Route 110), 05038
(802) 685-3031

**Amenities:** 1,2,3,5,6,8,9,
  10,11,12
**Breakfast:** F.
**Dbl. Oc.:** $74.90 - $91.16
**Sgl. Oc.:** $74.90 - $91.16
**Third Person:** $15.00

**Shire Inn**—Chelsea is Vermont's quintessential small village and we're Vermont's finest small village inn. An 1832 brick Federal home. Gourmet dining. Four rooms with working fireplaces. All rooms have private baths. Scenery abounds.

## *Chester* *

Bowman, Barbara & Jean
P.O. Box 646, 05143
(802) 875-2674

**Amenities:** 6,7,8,9,10,11,
  15,16
**Breakfast:** F.

**Dbl. Oc.:** $32.10 - $107.00
**Sgl. Oc.:** $48.15 - $80.25
**Third Person:** $16.05 (cot)
**Child:** $16.05 (cot)

**Henry Farm Inn**—A 1700's farmhouse located on 50 acres of rolling hills and meadows. Seven spacious guest rooms, all with private baths and recently renovated. Comfy sitting rooms and a sunny dining room make you feel at home. Come and join us for a day or more.

---

| | | | |
|---|---|---|---|
| 1. No Smoking | 5. Tennis Available | 9. Credit Cards Accepted | 13. Lunch Available | 17. Shared Bath |
| 2. No Pets | 6. Golf Available | 10. Personal Checks Accepted | 14. Public Transportation | 18. Afternoon Tea |
| 3. No Children | 7. Swiming Available | 11. Off Season Rates | 15. Reservations Necessary | ★ Commissions given |
| 4. Senior Citizen Rates | 8. Skiing Available | 12. Dinner Available | 16. Private Bath | to Travel Agents |

# VERMONT

## Chester *

Strohmeyer, Janet & Don
Route 11 W., 05143
(802) 875-2525

**Amenities:** 2,4,5,6,7,8,9,10,
11,12,13,15,16
**Breakfast:** F.

**Dbl. Oc.:** $75.00
**Sgl. Oc.:** $50.00
**Third Person:** $12.00
**Child:** under 8 yrs. - $6.00

**The Stone Hearth Inn**—A lovely and informal country inn built in 1810. Ten restored guest rooms, all with private baths. Library and living room, pub and large recreation room. Near major ski areas and quaint villages. Perfect for families. Dinner $15.00 - $20.00 (advanced notice).

## Chester

Thomas, Georgette
Main St., #32, 05143
(802) 875-2412

**Amenities:** 1,5,6,7,8,9,10,16
**Breakfast:** F.

**Dbl. Oc.:** $75.00 - $95.00
**Sgl. Oc.:** $55.00 - $65.00
**Third Person:** $20.00
**Child:** under 14 yrs. - $10.00

**The Hugging Bear Inn & Shoppe**—A lovely Victorian, circa 1850. Six rooms with a teddy bear in every bed. Three family rooms, toys, TV and VCR. Nearby ski, tennis and golf areas. Children of all ages welcome. A magical place to stay. Two friendly cats in residence.

## Chester

Wright, Irene & Normon
Main St.
P.O. Box 708, 05143
(802) 875-2205

**Amenities:** 2,5,6,7,8,10,16
**Breakfast:** F.

**Dbl. Oc.:** $50.00 - $75.00
**Sgl. Oc.:** $40.00 - $60.00
**Third Person:** $10.00 - $15.00

**"Chester House"**—A village B&B of extraordinary charm and hospitality. Located across from the village green. The home was built in 1780 and is in the *National Register of Historic Places.* Easy access to skiing, cycling, antiquing, golfing or just enjoying the beauty of Vermont.

## Craftsbury

Schmitt, Penny
Main St., 05827
(800) 521-2233, (802) 586-9619

**Amenities:** 5,6,7,8,9,10,12,15,16
**Breakfast:** F.
**Dbl. Oc.:** $160.00 - $220.00
**Sgl. Oc.:** $110.00 - $120.00
**Child:** $45.00 - $60.00

**The Inn On The Common**—Beautifully decorated, superb cuisine and award-winning wine cellar. Video and book library. Gardens and spectacular views of the Green Mountains. Swimming pool, clay tennis court and English croquet. Nearby sports center with hiking trails, bike rentals and lake swimming.

| | | | |
|---|---|---|---|
| 1. No Smoking | 5. Tennis Available | 9. Credit Cards Accepted | 13. Lunch Available | 17. Shared Bath |
| 2. No Pets | 6. Golf Available | 10. Personal Checks Accepted | 14. Public Transportation | 18. Afternoon Tea |
| 3. No Children | 7. Swiming Available | 11. Off Season Rates | 15. Reservations Necessary | ★ Commissions given |
| 4. Senior Citizen Rates | 8. Skiing Available | 12. Dinner Available | 16. Private Bath | to Travel Agents |

## Cuttingsville

Smith, Donna & William
Lincoln Hill
Box 120, 05738
(802) 492-3367

**Amenities:** 2,6,7,8,10,15,16, 17,18
**Breakfast:** F.

**Dbl. Oc.:** $45.00
**Sgl. Oc.:** $25.00
**Third Person:** $10.00
**Child:** under 6 yrs. - $5.00

**Maple Crest Farm**—Located in the heart of the Green Mountains in the Rutland area. An 1808 farmhouse lovingly preserved for five generations. 27 rooms with beautiful views. Downhill and cross-country skiing and hiking. Central location to historic sites. Two-day minimum.

## Danby *

Dansereau, Lois & Paul
So. Main St.
RR 1, Box 66F, 05739
(802) 293-5567

**Amenities:** 2,6,7,8,9,10,12,15,16,17
**Breakfast:** F.
**Dbl. Oc.:** $92.02
**Sgl. Oc.:** $75.97
**Third Person:** $16.00
**Child:** under 10 yrs. - no charge

**Silas Griffith Inn**—Built in 1891 by Vermont's first millionaire. 17 antique-filled guest rooms. Spectacular mountain views. Near the Appalachian Trail, hiking, biking, antiquing, skiing and pool. Village location. Comfortable and homey. Large living room and library with fireplace.

## Danby

Edson, Anharad & Chip
Main St.
P.O. Box 221, 05739
(802) 293-5099

**Amenities:** 2,7,8,9,10,16, 17,18
**Breakfast:** F.

**Dbl. Oc.:** $53.00 - $69.00
**Sgl. Oc.:** $37.00 - $53.00
**Third Person:** $10.00
**Child:** under 2 yrs. - $5.00

**The Quails Nest Bed & Breakfast**—Nestled among the Green Mountains in a quiet Vermont village. Quiet and old-fashioned country fun in a circa 1835 antique-filled inn. Nearby skiing, hiking, swimming, fishing, country auctions, horseback riding, bicycling, canoeing and shopping.

## Derbyline

Moreau, Phyllis & Tom
46 Main St., 05830
(802) 873-3604

**Amenities:** 1,2,9,10,16,18
**Breakfast:** F.

**Dbl. Oc.:** $53.50 - $64.20
**Sgl. Oc.:** $42.80 - $53.50
**Third Person:** $10.00
**Child:** $10.00

**Derby Village Inn**—Located at the Canadian border in a quaint country village. Our elegant Victorian home is furnished with restored antiques. Join us for a relaxing stay and visit our town's international library and opera house.

| | | | |
|---|---|---|---|
| 1. No Smoking | 5. Tennis Available | 9. Credit Cards Accepted | 13. Lunch Available | 17. Shared Bath |
| 2. No Pets | 6. Golf Available | 10. Personal Checks Accepted | 14. Public Transportation | 18. Afternoon Tea |
| 3. No Children | 7. Swiming Available | 11. Off Season Rates | 15. Reservations Necessary | ★ Commissions given |
| 4. Senior Citizen Rates | 8. Skiing Available | 12. Dinner Available | 16. Private Bath | to Travel Agents |

# VERMONT

## East Burke *

Lewin, Beverly
RR 1, Box 81, 05832
(802) 467-3472

**Amenities:** 2,6,7,8,10,16,17
**Breakfast:** C.

**Dbl. Oc.:** $47.08 - $49.22
**Sgl. Oc.:** $38.52
**Third Person:** $20.00
**Child:** under 16 yrs. -
$10.00

**Burke Green Guest House**—A comfortable guest house in Vermont's unspoiled northeast kingdom. A spacious, remodeled farmhouse (circa 1840) on 30 country acres overlooking Burke Mountain. Near beautiful Willoughby Lake. Families welcome. Cat in residence.

## Essex Junction

Blake, Eva & Edward
36 Old Stage Rd., 05452
(802) 878-2589

**Amenities:** 1,2,6,10,15,16,17
**Breakfast:** F.

**Dbl. Oc.:** $50.00 - $60.00
**Sgl. Oc.:** $45.0 - $55.00
**Third Person:** $10.00

**Country Comfort B&B**—Country charm within easy reach of city sights. Offers a choice of room decor - country or Victorian. Jenny Lind room. Twin beds available. Grazing sheep and clucking hens complete the tranquil theme.

## Fairlee *

Wright, Sharon & Scott
S. Main St., 05045
(802) 333-4326, (800) 666-1946

**Amenities:** 1,2,4,5,6,7,8,9,10,
16,17
**Breakfast:** C.

**Dbl. Oc.:** $44.94 - $57.78
**Sgl. Oc.:** $40.66 - $53.50
**Third Person:** $6.00
**Child:** $6.00

**Silver Maple Lodge & Cottages**—A historic B&B country inn located in a scenic four-season resort area. Nearby canoeing, fishing, golf, hiking, tennis and hot-air balloon flights. Convenient to cross-country and downhill skiing. Dartmouth College is 12 miles away. Restaurant located next door.

## Hyde Park *

Wheelwright, Bidi & George
Box 146, 05655
(802) 888-5894

**Amenities:** 1,2,3,5,6,7,8,9,10,
12,13,15,16,17,18
**Breakfast:** F.

**Dbl. Oc.:** $83.46
**Sgl. Oc.:** $53.50

**Hyde Park House**—An elegant 1830 village house beautifully restored with sauna and jacuzzi. An English garden, fine library and antiques. A sportsman's paradise. Close to Stowe, Smugglers Notch and Jay Peak. Relax your body, ease your mind and soothe your soul.

## Jay

Angliss, Jane & Bob
Route 242, 05859
(802) 988-2643,
(800) 2227-7452 (outside Vermont)

**Amenities:** 2,7,8,9,12,15,16
**Breakfast:** C. (F. winter)

**Dbl. Oc.:** $80.25
**Sgl. Oc.:** $53.50
**Third Person:** $25.40

**Jay Village Inn**—A charming country inn located three miles from Jay Peak ski area. Fifteen guest rooms. A popular restaurant with great food and moderate prices. Pub, game room, sauna and TV. Enjoy the unspoiled, natural beauty of the "real Vermont." Specials during ski season.

| | | | |
|---|---|---|---|
| 1. No Smoking | 5. Tennis Available | 9. Credit Cards Accepted | 13. Lunch Available | 17. Shared Bath |
| 2. No Pets | 6. Golf Available | 10. Personal Checks Accepted | 14. Public Transportation | 18. Afternoon Tea |
| 3. No Children | 7. Swiming Available | 11. Off Season Rates | 15. Reservations Necessary | ★ Commissions given |
| 4. Senior Citizen Rates | 8. Skiing Available | 12. Dinner Available | 16. Private Bath | to Travel Agents |

# VERMONT

## Jeffersonville

Jurnak, Colette & Michael
Main St.
P.O. Box 288, 05464
(802) 644-2030

**Amenities:** 1,8,10,17
**Breakfast:** F.

**Dbl. Oc.:** $42.80
**Sgl. Oc.:** $26.75
**Third Person:** $16.00
**Child:** $5.35 - $10.70

**The Jefferson House Bed And Breakfast**—A fine old Victorian home in the heart of a historic Vermont village. Warm and friendly atmosphere. Attractive and comfortable rooms and a full Vermont breakfast. Near Smuggler's Notch ski area, hiking and bike trails. Pick-up for hikers on request.

## Jeffersonville

Kneeland, Craig M.
Jct. Hill Rd.
Box 5780, 05464
(800) 347-8266

**Amenities:** 1,2,5,7,8,9,10,11, 12,13,16,17
**Breakfast:** F.

**Dbl. Oc.:** $60.00
**Sgl. Oc.:** $45.00

**Sterling Ridge Inn**—Quiet and rural elegance on 85 acres of fields, woods and streams. Nearby are Mount Mansfield, Stowe, Smugglers Notch and Lamoille River area. Three- and five-day packages for cross-country and down hill skiing, canoeing, backroad and inn-to-inn cycling.

## Jericho *

Royce, Blanche
RD #2, Box 35, Underhill, 05481
(802) 899-2234

**Amenities:** 1,2,3,5,6,7,8,9,10, 11,15,16,18
**Breakfast:** F.

**Dbl. Oc.:** $60.00 - $70.00
**Sgl. Oc.:** $50.00 - $60.00
**Third Person:** $10.00

**Sinclair Towers B&B Inn**—An elegant, yet comfortable, fully restored 1890 Victorian landmark. Close to Burlington, ski areas, hiking trails, bike routes and fine restaurants. Six air-conditioned rooms, parlor, living room with fireplace, barbecue area and handicap bath.

## Killington

MacKenzie, Vickie
RR 1, Box 2848, 05751
(802) 422-3731

**Amenities:** 2,4,6,7,8,9,11,12, 13,16
**Breakfast:** F.

**Dbl. Oc.:** $140.00
**Sgl. Oc.:** $115.00
**Third Person:** $34.00
**Child:** under 12 yrs. - $25.00

**Cascades Lodge**—Set in the heart of Killington with spectacular mountain views. Large and comfortable rooms with private bath, phone and cable TV. Fireplaced lounge, sauna, whirlpool and heated indoor pool. Walk to ski slopes and golf. A great getaway area for all seasons.

---

| | | | | |
|---|---|---|---|---|
| 1. No Smoking | 5. Tennis Available | 9. Credit Cards Accepted | 13. Lunch Available | 17. Shared Bath |
| 2. No Pets | 6. Golf Available | 10. Personal Checks Accepted | 14. Public Transportation | 18. Afternoon Tea |
| 3. No Children | 7. Swiming Available | 11. Off Season Rates | 15. Reservations Necessary | ★ Commissions given |
| 4. Senior Citizen Rates | 8. Skiing Available | 12. Dinner Available | 16. Private Bath | to Travel Agents |

# VERMONT

## Killington *

McGrath, Kyram
Rt. 4, Box 267, 05751
(802) 775-7181

**Amenities:** 4,9,10,11,12, 13,16

**Breakfast:** F.

**Dbl. Oc.:** $77.70 - $392.70
**Sgl. Oc.:** $67.20 - $278.30
**Third Person: $31.50 -** $105.00
**Child:** $31.50 - $105.00

**The Inn At Long Run**—Historic country inn nest to famous Long Trail and Appalachian Trail. Cozy immaculate rooms. Fireplaced suites. Hot tub. Irish pub with live music on weekends. Weekend rates include all meals. Restaurant offers fulldelicious candlelight dinners as well as a pub menu.

## Lincoln

Conway, Beverly & Michael
RD 1, Box 560, Bristol, VT, 05443
(802) 453-3233

**Amenities:** 2,5,6,7,8,10,12,13, 17,18

**Breakfast:** F.

**Dbl. Oc.:** $70.62
**Sgl. Oc.:** $35.31
**Child:** over 10 yrs. - $35.31

**Long Run Inn**—An antique-filled country inn built in 1779 by lumberjacks in Lincoln. Wrap-around rocking chair porch overlooks a trout stream. Hiking available on one long trail. Dinner available. Meals prepared by innkeeper. Restrictive smoking. Accommodations for children over 10 years.

## Londonderry *

Gross, Irving A.
Little Pond Rd.
RR 1, Box 70, 05148
(802) 824-3933

**Amenities:** 1,2,7,8,9,10,11,13, 15,16,17,18

**Breakfast:** F.

**Dbl. Oc.:** $110.00
**Sgl. Oc.:** $65.00
**Third Person: $35.00**
**Child:** under 12 yrs. - $30.00

**The Viking Guest House**—A half mile off Route 11. An 1860's farmhouse with outdoor pool and pond. Twenty-four miles of trails on 70 acres offering cross-country skiing, inn-to-inn skiing and bike tours. Near Weston Theatre and country store. Situated in scenic Vermont's four-season area.

## Londonderry, South

Brown, Brenda & Geoff
River Rd.
Box 2012, 05155
(802) 824-3673

**Amenities:** 1,2,5,6,7,8,10, 15,17

**Breakfast:** C.(M.- F.), F.(Weekends)

**Dbl. Oc.:** $50.00
**Sgl. Oc.:** $35.00

**Six West River**—A 120-year-old farmhouse in the Green Mountains of southern Vermont. Hiking, biking, cross-country and downhill skiing. Sauna for guests. Three guest rooms with shared bath. Two cats on premises.

| | | | |
|---|---|---|---|
| 1. No Smoking | 5. Tennis Available | 9. Credit Cards Accepted | 13. Lunch Available | 17. Shared Bath |
| 2. No Pets | 6. Golf Available | 10. Personal Checks Accepted | 14. Public Transportation | 18. Afternoon Tea |
| 3. No Children | 7. Swiming Available | 11. Off Season Rates | 15. Reservations Necessary | ★ Commissions given |
| 4. Senior Citizen Rates | 8. Skiing Available | 12. Dinner Available | 16. Private Bath | to Travel Agents |

## *Ludlow*

Bentzinger, Carolyn & Rick
13 Pleasant St., 05149
(802) 228-4846

**Amenities:** 1,2,3,4,5,6,7,8,9,
10,11,12,15,16
**Breakfast:** F.
**Dbl. Oc.:** $116.00 - $135.00
**Sgl. Oc.:** $104.00 - $116.00

**The Andrie Rose Inn**—A circa 1829 country village inn nestled at the base of Okemo Mountain ski resort. Luxurious antique-filled guest rooms, down comforters, whirlpool tubs and skylights. Delectable breakfasts. Complimentary fireside hors d'oeuvres. Enjoy summer theatre, lakes, golf and tennis.

## *Ludlow*

Combes, Ruth & William
RFD #1, Box 275, 05149
(802) 228-8799

**Amenities:** 5,6,7,8,9,10,12,16,
12,16,17
**Breakfast:** F.

**Dbl. Oc.:** $95.10
**Sgl. Oc.:** $77.70
**Third Person:** $23.20
**Child:** $23.20

**The Combes Family Inn**—A family inn in a secluded setting on a country back road. Surrounded by acres of meadows. The inn was an operating dairy farm for over 100 years. It has a warm and casual ambience. Bring your family home to ours. Homey and comfortable rooms. Great food.

## *Manchester* \*

Eichorn, Patricia & Robert
Highland Ave., 05255
(802) 362-4565

**Amenities:** 1,2,5,6,7,8,9,10,
11,15,16,17,18
**Breakfast:** F.

**Dbl. Oc.:** $93.60 - $122.85
**Sgl. Oc.:** $70.20 - $87.75
**Third Person:** $20.00
**Child:** no charge - $10.00

**Manchester Highlands Inn**—Discover Manchester's best-kept secret — a Victorian inn on a hilltop above town. Great view, feather beds, down comforters, lace curtains, gourmet breakfasts and home-baked afternoon snacks. Pool, game room and pub. Walk to shops and restaurants. Minutes to skiing and golf.

## *Manchester*

Lee, Jr., James
West Rd., 05254
(802) 362-2761

**Amenities:** 1,2,7,8,9,10,12,
15,16,18
**Breakfast:** F.

**Dbl. Oc.:** $118.58
**Sgl. Oc.:** $77.44
**Third Person:** $30.25

**Birch Hill Inn**—A quiet country inn away from busy village streets with panoramic views. Swimming pool, trout pond and walking trails. Serves breakfast and dinner. Member of the *Independent Innkeepers Association*. Jim and Pat are the innkeepers.

| | | | |
|---|---|---|---|
| 1. No Smoking | 5. Tennis Available | 9. Credit Cards Accepted | 13. Lunch Available | 17. Shared Bath |
| 2. No Pets | 6. Golf Available | 10. Personal Checks Accepted | 14. Public Transportation | 18. Afternoon Tea |
| 3. No Children | 7. Swiming Available | 11. Off Season Rates | 15. Reservations Necessary | ★ Commissions given |
| 4. Senior Citizen Rates | 8. Skiing Available | 12. Dinner Available | 16. Private Bath | to Travel Agents |

## Montgomery

Kane, Maureen
Main St.
P.O. Box 344, 05471
(802) 326-4306

**Amenities:** 1,2,4,8,9,10,
16,17,18
**Breakfast:** F.

**Dbl. Oc.:** $64.20
**Sgl. Oc.:** $31.50

**Phineas Swann B&B**—A cozy, bright and beautifully decorated Victorian inn. Located in northern Vermont. Ten minutes to Jay Peak ski area. Nearby biking, hiking, canoeing and fishing. Fine restaurants. Antique and craft shops. Spectacular mountain views. Great place to unwind.

## Montgomery Center *

Tullgren, Carol & Peter
Main St.
Route 118 at 242, 05471
(802) 326-4166

**Amenities:** 1,2,5,6,7,8,9,11,15,17
**Breakfast:** F.
**Dbl. Oc.:** $64.20 - $75.00
**Sgl. Oc.:** $48.15 - $55.00
**Third Person:** $32.10 - $37.50
**Child:** $21.40 - $25.00

**Seven Bridges Inn**—A charming, warm and friendly Vermont country home. Family room with fireplace, TV, books and games. All-seasons activities including bicycling, hiking, fishing and antiquing. Nearby are Jay Peak ski area and seven covered bridges. Restaurants and shops within walking distance.

## Montpelier, East *

Potter, Charyl
Cherry Tree Hill Rd., 05651
(802) 223-0549

**Amenities:** 1,2,3,7,8,9,16.17
**Breakfast:** F.

**Dbl. Oc.:** $64.20 - $80.25
**Sgl. Oc.:** $48.15
**Third Person:** $21.40

**Cherry Tree Hill Bed & Breakfast**—A meticulously restored Dutch-roof farmhouse offering breathtaking panoramic mountain views. Just three miles from the state capitol. Luxurious accommodations amid 55 acres of fields and meadows. Heated pool, jacuzzi, fieldstone fireplace, breakfast solarium and gallery.

## North Hero

Apgar, John
P.O. Box 106, Route 2
Champlain Islands, 05474

(802) 372-8237

**Amenities:** 2,5,6,7,10,11,12,
13,15,16,18
**Breakfast:** F.

**Dbl. Oc.:** $50.00 - $95.00
**Third Person:** $15.00
**Child:** under 3 yrs. -
no charge

**North Hero House**—An intimate island inn long-famous for its fine food, gracious accommodations and old-fashioned hospitality. We invite you to visit us this season.

| | | | |
|---|---|---|---|
| 1. No Smoking | 5. Tennis Available | 9. Credit Cards Accepted | 13. Lunch Available | 17. Shared Bath |
| 2. No Pets | 6. Golf Available | 10. Personal Checks Accepted | 14. Public Transportation | 18. Afternoon Tea |
| 3. No Children | 7. Swiming Available | 11. Off Season Rates | 15. Reservations Necessary | ★ Commissions given |
| 4. Senior Citizen Rates | 8. Skiing Available | 12. Dinner Available | 16. Private Bath | to Travel Agents |

# VERMONT

## Orleans *

Boldac, David
4 Memorial Square, 05860
(802) 754-6665

**Amenities:** 2,4,6,7,8,9,10,11,12,13,16,18
**Breakfast:** F.
**Dbl. Oc.:** $37.50 - $64.00
**Sgl. Oc.:** $28.00 - $37.50
**Third Person:** $8.50
**Child:** under 5 yrs. - no charge

**Valley House Inn**—Fine lodging and dining in an 1800's country inn. Located in the center of the northeast kingdom's lakes region. Top 18-hole golf course is one mile away. Skiing at Jay Peak and Burke Mountains is just 30 minutes away. One-quarter mile from Exit 26 off I-91.

## Orwell *

Korda, Joan & Murray
Route 22A, 05760
(802) 948-2727

**Amenities:** 1,2,4,8,10,12,13,
16,17,18
**Breakfast:** F.
**Dbl. Oc.:** $100.00 - $180.00
**Sgl. Oc.:** $60.00 - $90.00
**Third Person:** $40.00
**Child:** $18.00 - $30.00

**Historic Brookside Farms**—An 1843 Greek Revival mansion that adjoins a 1789 farmhouse on 300 scenic acres. Hike and cross-country ski through our forest. Canoe and fish in our lake. Cozy up to crackling fireplaces. Savor candlelit dining. Period antiques and country rarities in our shop.

## Peru *

Okun, Nancy & Gary
Route 11, Bromley Mountain, 05152
(802) 824-5533

**Amenities:** 5,7,8,9,10,12,15,
16
**Breakfast:** F.

**Dbl. Oc.:** $64.00 - $234.00
**Child:** $7.00 - $48.00

**Johnny Seesaw's**—The essential Vermont experience. A unique log lodge featuring cozy rooms. Charming cottages with fireplaces. Game room. Casual and candlelit country dining. All amidst the beautiful Green Mountains. "The best Yankee cuisine in New England." - *Ski Magazine*.

## Pittsfield *

Morris, Barbara
Route 100, Box 675, 05762
(802) 746-8943

**Amenities:** 2,6,8,9,10,12,16
**Breakfast:** F.

**Dbl. Oc.:** $80.00
**Sgl. Oc.:** $70.00
**Third Person:** $40.00
**Child:** $40.00

**The Inn At Pittsfield**—A classic inn overlooking the village green in a tiny valley hamlet. Our central location puts you minutes away from all that Vermont has to offer. Nine rooms individually decorated and accented with handmade quilts, tie-back curtains and antiques.

| | | | | |
|---|---|---|---|---|
| 1. No Smoking | 5. Tennis Available | 9. Credit Cards Accepted | 13. Lunch Available | 17. Shared Bath |
| 2. No Pets | 6. Golf Available | 10. Personal Checks Accepted | 14. Public Transportation | 18. Afternoon Tea |
| 3. No Children | 7. Swiming Available | 11. Off Season Rates | 15. Reservations Necessary | ★ Commissions given |
| 4. Senior Citizen Rates | 8. Skiing Available | 12. Dinner Available | 16. Private Bath | to Travel Agents |

## *Plainfield*

Yankee, Joani & Glenn
RD #2, Box 1000, 05667
(802) 454-7191

**Amenities:** 1,5,6,7,8,10,11,12,
13,15,17,18
**Breakfast:** F.

**Dbl. Oc.:** $40.00 - $55.00
**Sgl. Oc.:** $30.00 - $40.00
**Third Person:** $10.00
**Child:** under 6 yrs. -
no charge

**Yankees' Northview Bed & Breakfast**—Off quiet country road in historic Calais. Antiques, heirloom quilts, bouquets and sitting room with fireplace. Breakfast on garden patio with mountain views. Nearby museums, antiques and quaking bog. Year-round recreation. Nine miles to the capitol and quarries.

## *Proctorsville* *

Allen, Eleanor
Depot St., Box 78, 05153
(802) 226-7970

**Amenities:** 1,2,3,4,6,7,8,9,
10,11,16,17,18
**Breakfast:** F.
**Dbl. Oc.:** $70.00 - $90.00
**Third Person:** $20.00

**Allens' Inn Of Proctorsville**—Immaculate and attractive accommodations with a friendly home-away-from-home atmosphere. The inn was completely renovated during the last three years and is decorated with charming country antiques. Four miles from Okemo Mountain. Nearby fine restaurants and shops.

## *Putney*

Miller, Jeffrey
RD 2, Box 510, 05346

**Amenities:** 1,2,3,7,8,9,10,
16,17
**Breakfast:** F.

**Dbl. Oc.:** $52.00 - $73.00
**Sgl. Oc.:** $42.00 - $63.00
**Third Person:** $15.00

**Mapleton Farm Bed & Breakfast**—An 1803 Vermont farmhouse is a step back in time. Decorated with antiques and old country furnishings, situated on 25 beautiful acres. It's the perfect place to unwind. Convenient to Brattleboro and Putney's fine shops and restaurants.

## *Reading* *

Taylor, Joan & Bill
Route 106, 05062
(802) 484-9192

**Amenities:** 6,8,10,15,18
**Breakfast:** C.

**Dbl. Oc.:** $60.00
**Sgl. Oc.:** $40.00
**Third Person:** $15.00

**1797 House**—A charming 18th-century home set on 25 acres. Nearby skiing, antiquing and all sports. Beautiful fall foliage.

| | | | | |
|---|---|---|---|---|
| 1. No Smoking | 5. Tennis Available | 9. Credit Cards Accepted | 13. Lunch Available | 17. Shared Bath |
| 2. No Pets | 6. Golf Available | 10. Personal Checks Accepted | 14. Public Transportation | 18. Afternoon Tea |
| 3. No Children | 7. Swiming Available | 11. Off Season Rates | 15. Reservations Necessary | ★ Commissions given |
| 4. Senior Citizen Rates | 8. Skiing Available | 12. Dinner Available | 16. Private Bath | to Travel Agents |

## Roxbury

Rogler, Debra & Jim
Carrie Howe Rd., 0569
(802) 485-8961

**Amenities:** 1,6,7,8,10,17,18
**Breakfast:** C.

**Dbl. Oc.:** $53.50
**Sgl. Oc.:** $37.45
**Third Person:** $26.75
**Child:** under 3 yrs. -
no charge

**Inn At Johnnycake Flats**—Our small inn is located in a valley known to the locals as Johnnycake Flats. A restored 1800's stagecoach stop. Guest rooms are thoughtfully decorated with family antiques. Enjoy cross-country skiing, trout fishing or a quiet walk down country lanes. Informal atmosphere.

## Royalton

Curley, Jean & Gary
Route 14, RR 1
Box 108F, 05068
(802) 763-8437

**Amenities:** 2,9,10,12,15,17
**Breakfast:** F.

**Dbl. Oc.:** $53.00
**Sgl. Oc.:** $37.10
**Third Person:** $10.60

**Fox Stand Inn**—A brick building built in 1818 on the bank of the White River. Located one mile off Interstate 89 (Exit 3). Restaurant and tavern are open to the public. Five guest rooms are available. River swimming, tubing and fishing on premises. Nearby skiing.

## Rutland, West *

Bliss, Pamela
Route 133
RFD 1, Box 1222, 05777
(802) 438-5555

**Amenities:** 2,4,5,6,7,8,9, 10,11,12,16
**Breakfast:** F.
**Dbl. Oc.:** $104.40
**Sgl. Oc.:** $69.60
**Third Person:** $17.40
**Child:** $17.40

**The Silver Fox Inn**—A special place surrounded by green pastures, sugar-maple forests and mountains. Hike to a waterfall or explore old logging trails. Seven guest rooms, antiques, wide-board floors and wonderful gourmet dining. A great place!

## Shrewsbury

Husselman, Grace & Samuel
Lincoln Hill Rd., 05738
(802) 492-3485

**Amenities:** 1,2,4,5,6,7,8,10, 15,16,17,18
**Breakfast:** C. and F.

**Dbl. Oc.:** $53.00 - $63.60
**Sgl. Oc.:** $42.40
**Third Person:** $21.20
**Child:** under 12 yrs. -
$15.90

**Buckmaster Inn (Bed & Breakfast)**—A circa 1801 inn standing on a knoll overlooking a picturesque red barn and valley scene. Its center hall, grand staircase, wide-pine floors and antiques grace the home. Spacious rooms and porches. Beautifully landscaped. Fireplaces and library/lounge area. Rural mountains.

| | | | | |
|---|---|---|---|---|
| 1. No Smoking | 5. Tennis Available | 9. Credit Cards Accepted | 13. Lunch Available | 17. Shared Bath |
| 2. No Pets | 6. Golf Available | 10. Personal Checks Accepted | 14. Public Transportation | 18. Afternoon Tea |
| 3. No Children | 7. Swiming Available | 11. Off Season Rates | 15. Reservations Necessary | ★ Commissions given |
| 4. Senior Citizen Rates | 8. Skiing Available | 12. Dinner Available | 16. Private Bath | to Travel Agents |

## *Starksboro*

Mashburn, Kathy & Gene
Route 116, 05487
(802) 453-3911

**Amenities:** 1,2,3,9,12
**Breakfast:** F.
**Dbl. Oc.:** $55.00
**Sgl. Oc.:** $40.00

**North Country Bed & Breakfast**—Centrally located between Burlington and Middlebury. We are a B&B of European tradition. Two queen-size and one twin-bedded rooms. Full breakfast served family style. Reservations preferred.

## *Starksboro*

Messer, Patricia
P.O. Box 22, 05487
(802) 453-2008

**Amenities:** 1,2,6,7,8,10,15,16, 17,18
**Breakfast:** C.
**Dbl. Oc.:** $64.20 - $74.90
**Sgl. Oc.:** $32.10 - $37.45

**Millhouse Bed And Breakfast**—An elegant and historic Vermont country home. Within 25 miles of ski resorts, golf courses and Lake Champlain. Apres ski room with fireplace. Homemade and regional specialties. Fine dining in Bristol, Middlebury, Waitsfield and Burlington. Much more!

## *Stockbridge*

Hughes, Jan
Route 100N, 05772
(802) 746-8165

**Amenities:** 2,6,7,8,9,10,11,12, 15,17
**Breakfast:** F.
**Dbl. Oc.:** $74.20
**Sgl. Oc.:** $63.60
**Third Person:** $10.60
**Child:** $10.60

**The Stockbridge Inn Bed & Breakfast**—Nestled near the banks of the White River, close to ski areas and golf. This large Victorian home is a historic landmark. Guest and public rooms are furnished with an old-world atmosphere to insure your comfort. Relax and enjoy. Our home is your home.

## *Stowe* \*

Aldrich, Mindy, Andy & Dustin
Route 100N,
RR 2, Box 2610, 05672
(802) 253-2229

**Amenities:** 1,2,5,6,7,8,9,10, 11,12,13
**Breakfast:** F.
**Dbl. Oc.:** $80.00 & up
**Sgl. Oc.:** $70.00 & up
**Third Person:** $25.00
**Child:** $25.00

**The Inn At The Brass Lantern**—A traditional B&B country inn, within an award-winning restoration of an 1800 farmhouse. Features antiques, handmade quilts, fireplaces and air conditioning. Mountain views and patio. Many activity packages available.

---

| | | | | |
|---|---|---|---|---|
| 1. No Smoking | 5. Tennis Available | 9. Credit Cards Accepted | 13. Lunch Available | 17. Shared Bath |
| 2. No Pets | 6. Golf Available | 10. Personal Checks Accepted | 14. Public Transportation | 18. Afternoon Tea |
| 3. No Children | 7. Swiming Available | 11. Off Season Rates | 15. Reservations Necessary | \* Commissions given |
| 4. Senior Citizen Rates | 8. Skiing Available | 12. Dinner Available | 16. Private Bath | to Travel Agents |

# VERMONT

## Stowe

Baas, Jr., M/M John C.
Edson Hill, RR 1,
Box 2280, 05672
(802) 253-8376

**Amenities:** 2,5,6,7,8,10,11,14,
15,16,17
**Breakfast:** C.

**Dbl. Oc.:** $45.00 - $55.00
**Sgl. Oc.:** $35.00 - $40.00
**Third Person:** $8.00 -
$10.00
**Child:** under 3 yrs. - $5.00

**Baas' Gastehaus**—Member of American Bed & Breakfast. A "B&B" in the traditional sense. Private retirement estate on three acres. Pastoral setting in prestigious area. Early American. Antiques. Twin and double beds. Minutes to Mt. Mansfield, recreation path and best cross-country areas.

## Stowe

Francis, Linda & Christopher
Mountain Rd., 05672
(802) 253-7558

**Amenities:** 1,5,6,7,8,9,10,11,
12,13,15,16,18
**Breakfast:** F.
**Dbl. Oc.:** $95.00 & up
**Sgl. Oc.:** $95.00 & up
**Third Person:** $20.00

**Ye Olde England Inne**—Classic English luxury. Laura Ashley rooms and cottages, four-poster beds, fireplaces and jacuzzis. Elegant and romantic gourmet dining by candlelight in Copperfields. Mr. Pickwick's Polo Pub internationally acclaimed for traditional English fare - 120 beers and ales. Cheers!

## Stowe *

Heiss, Gertrude & Dietmar
RD #1, Box 1450, 05672
(802) 253-7336

**Amenities:** 4,5,6,7,8,9,10,
11,12,15,16,17
**Breakfast:** C. and F.
**Dbl. Oc.:** $82.08
**Sgl. Oc.:** $50.52
**Third Person:** $10.00
**Child:** under 12 yrs. - $6.00

**Andersen Lodge - An Austrian Inn**—A warm and friendly atmosphere awaits you at the Andersen Lodge. You'll find spacious bedrooms, private baths, TV, game room, heated pool, tennis court and more. Nearby recreation path for walking and biking.

---

| | | | | |
|---|---|---|---|---|
| 1. No Smoking | 5. Tennis Available | 9. Credit Cards Accepted | 13. Lunch Available | 17. Shared Bath |
| 2. No Pets | 6. Golf Available | 10. Personal Checks Accepted | 14. Public Transportation | 18. Afternoon Tea |
| 3. No Children | 7. Swiming Available | 11. Off Season Rates | 15. Reservations Necessary | ★ Commissions given |
| 4. Senior Citizen Rates | 8. Skiing Available | 12. Dinner Available | 16. Private Bath | to Travel Agents |

# VERMONT

## Stowe *

Heyer, M/M Larry
Route #108, 05672
(802) 253-4050

**Amenities:** 5,6,7,8,10,11,

**Breakfast:** C.

**Dbl. Oc.:** $60.00 - $75.00
**Sgl. Oc.:** $30.00 - $45.00
**Third Person:** $35.00

**Ski Inn**—A Vermont country inn noted for good food and conversation. The warmth and informality of an old-fashioned ski lodge where guests enjoy themselves and each other. Dinner is available to guests during the ski season.

## Stowe *

Hildebrand, Kay
Cottage Club Rd.
RR 1, Box 810, 05672
(802) 253-7603, (800) 753-7603

**Amenities:** 2,5,6,7,8,9,10,11,
                16,18

**Breakfast:** F.

**Dbl. Oc.:** $70.00
**Sgl. Oc.:** $41.00
**Third Person:** $15.00
**Child:** $15.00

**Timberholm Inn**—A delightful country inn in a quiet wooded setting. We have 10 individually decorated rooms with antiques and private baths. Spacious common room with large fieldstone fireplace. Game room with cable TV and shuffleboard. Deck overlooks mountains.

## Stowe *

Horman, Christel
Mountain Rd., 05672
(802) 253-4846

**Amenities:** 2,5,6,7,8,9,10,11,
                15,16

**Breakfast:** F.

**Dbl. Oc.:** $64.20 & up
**Sgl. Oc.:** $45.00 & up
**Third Person:** $20.00 & up

**Guest House Christel Horman**—A European B&B with eight large, comfortable double rooms and private baths. Guest living room on first floor. TV and VCR can be watched while sitting by the hearthstone fireplace. 1-1/2 miles to cross-country and downhill skiing. Swimming pool, trout brook and barbecue.

## Stowe *

Matulionis, Rose Marie
School St.
P.O. Box 276, 05672
(802) 253-7351, (800) 248-1860

**Amenities:** 1,5,6,7,8,9,10,11,16
**Breakfast:** F.
**Dbl. Oc.:** $90.10 - $121.90
**Sgl. Oc.:** $68.90 - $121.90
**Third Person:** $21.20
**Child:** under 2 yrs. - no charge

**The 1860 House**—A *Register of Historic Places* inn with exceptional center village accommodations. King/queen beds with private baths. Enjoy classical music and friendly conversation. Jacuzzi, health club and a pool included. Ask about our "rent-the-inn" option for your small group.

| | | | |
|---|---|---|---|
| 1. No Smoking | 5. Tennis Available | 9. Credit Cards Accepted | 13. Lunch Available | 17. Shared Bath |
| 2. No Pets | 6. Golf Available | 10. Personal Checks Accepted | 14. Public Transportation | 18. Afternoon Tea |
| 3. No Children | 7. Swiming Available | 11. Off Season Rates | 15. Reservations Necessary | ★ Commissions given |
| 4. Senior Citizen Rates | 8. Skiing Available | 12. Dinner Available | 16. Private Bath | to Travel Agents |

# VERMONT

## Stowe

Shelter, Leonard
RR #1, Box 2290, 05672
(800) 426-6697,
(802) 253-7354

**Amenities:** 2,5,6,7,8,9,10,11, 15,16,17
**Breakfast:** F.

**Dbl. Oc.:** $75.00 - $85.00
**Sgl. Oc.:** $45.00 - $55.00
**Third Person:** $15.00
**Child:** under 12 yrs. - $10.00

**Logwood Inn & Chalets**—Enjoy a private setting on five acres with white birches and spacious lawns. Large swimming pool, clay tennis court and a babbling brook on the premises. Start your day with Len's hearty country breakfast in a relaxed atmosphere. Play golf at nearby Stowe Country Club.

## Stowe *

Wimberly, Deborah & Jim
Mountain Rd.,
RR #1, Box 950, 05672
(802) 253-4277, (800) 3-BUTTER

**Amenities:** 1,2,3,5,6,7,8,9, 16,18
**Breakfast:** F.

**Dbl. Oc.:** $101.65 - $128.75

**Butternut Inn At Stowe**—An award-winning, non-smoking country inn for adults. Antiques, pool and landscaped grounds. Written up as one of the better B&B inns of the Northeast. Near sleigh rides. Hospitable country inn atmosphere at its finest.

## Strafford, South *

Alden, Anna & Lincoln
Route 132, 05070
(802) 765-4314, (800) 562-5110

**Amenities:** 1,2,7,9,10,11,17
**Breakfast:** F.

**Dbl. Oc.:** $60.00
**Sgl. Oc.:** $40.00
**Third Person:** $10.00
**Child:** under 5 yrs.- no charge

**Watercourse Way Bed & Breakfast**—An authentic 1850 B&B overlooking Ompompanoosuc River in central Vermont countryside. Hiking, fishing and skiing. Fireside breakfast, gardens, goats, homemade delights and gourmet coffee. Near Hanover, NH and Woodstock, VT. Simple satisfaction away from the crowds.

## Townsend, West

Montenieri, Jan & Jim
Route 30, P.O. Box 111, 05359
(802) 874-4853

**Amenities:** 1,2,6,7,8,10,12,13, 15,16
**Breakfast:** F.

**Dbl. Oc.:** $59.55 - $64.20
**Sgl. Oc.:** $48.15 - $53.50
**Third Person:** $10.70 (cot)
**Child:** $10.70 (cot)

**The General Fletcher Homestead Bed And Breakfast**—The warmth and charm of a historic (circa 1773) farmhouse near the Green Mountains. Three comfortable bedrooms. Nearby scenery, swimming, hiking, fishing, antiquing, shopping, flea markets and skiing. Enjoy our farm animals and relax by our pond. Gracious Vermont hospitality.

---

| | | | | |
|---|---|---|---|---|
| 1. No Smoking | 5. Tennis Available | 9. Credit Cards Accepted | 13. Lunch Available | 17. Shared Bath |
| 2. No Pets | 6. Golf Available | 10. Personal Checks Accepted | 14. Public Transportation | 18. Afternoon Tea |
| 3. No Children | 7. Swiming Available | 11. Off Season Rates | 15. Reservations Necessary | ★ Commissions given |
| 4. Senior Citizen Rates | 8. Skiing Available | 12. Dinner Available | 16. Private Bath | to Travel Agents |

## *Vergennes*

Emerson, Patricia
82 Main St., 05491
(802) 877-3293

**Amenities:** 1,2,5,6,7,10, 14,17
**Breakfast:** F.

**Dbl. Oc.:** $42.40
**Sgl. Oc.:** $31.80
**Third Person:** $10.60
**Child:** $10.60

**Emersons' Guest House - Bed & Breakfast**—Enjoy a comfortable stay in a beautifully decorated old (circa 1850) Victorian home. Four double rooms and 1-1/2 shared baths. A full breakfast includes delicious homemade bread, muffins and jams served in a warm and friendly kitchen.

## *Waitsfield*

Day, Ann
Bragg Hill Rd., 05673
(802) 496-3939

**Amenities:** 1,2,4,5,6,7,8,10, 12,14,15,17,18
**Breakfast:** F.
**Dbl. Oc.:** $74.20
**Sgl. Oc.:** $42.40
**Third Person:** $26.50

**Knoll Farm Country Inn**—A unique, old-fashioned farm/inn high in the mountains on 150 acres. Large lawn, pond, barn and pastures for highland cattle and horses. Delicious farm breakfasts and dinners. Downhill and cross-country skiing at Sugarbush and Mad River Glen. Long trail for hiking. Many shops.

## *Waitsfield* \*

Gorman, Thomas
RD, Box 62, 05673
(802) 496-2405

**Amenities:** 1,2,6,8,9,10,11,12, 16,17
**Breakfast:** F.

**Dbl. Oc.:** $80.00- $108.00
**Sgl. Oc.:** $60.00 - $78.00
**Third Person:** $42.00

**Millbrook Inn**—A classic Cape-style farmhouse decorated with antiques, handmade quilts and hand stenciling. Reputation for fine dining. Homemade soups, breads, desserts and pasta made with fresh local ingredients. Candlelit atmosphere with fireside dining.

## *Waitsfield* \*

Newton, Joyce & Nicholas
Route 100, Box 159, 05673
(802) 496-7555

**Amenities:** 1,2,5,6,7,8,9,10,11,14,16,18
**Breakfast:** F.
**Dbl. Oc.:** $101.65
**Sgl. Oc.:** $90.95
**Third Person:** $20.00
**Child:** $20.00

**Newtons' 1824 House Inn**—Enjoy relaxed elegance in a perfect country setting. Six guest rooms. Classical music, Oriental rugs, fireplaces and sun porch. Souffles and fresh-squeezed orange juice. 52 acres on the Mad River. Private swimming hole. World's best B&B, say our guests.

| | | | |
|---|---|---|---|
| 1. No Smoking | 5. Tennis Available | 9. Credit Cards Accepted | 13. Lunch Available | 17. Shared Bath |
| 2. No Pets | 6. Golf Available | 10. Personal Checks Accepted | 14. Public Transportation | 18. Afternoon Tea |
| 3. No Children | 7. Swiming Available | 11. Off Season Rates | 15. Reservations Necessary | ★ Commissions given |
| 4. Senior Citizen Rates | 8. Skiing Available | 12. Dinner Available | 16. Private Bath | to Travel Agents |

# VERMONT

## Waitsfield *

Pratt, Betsy
Route 17, Box 88, 05073
(802) 496-3310

**Amenities:** 4,5,6,7,8,9,10,11, 12,16,18
**Breakfast:** F.

**Dbl. Oc.:** $55.00 - $75.00
**Sgl. Oc.:** $55.00
**Third Person:** $10.00
**Child:** under 10 yrs. - no charge

**Mad River Barn**—A friendly and informal lodge with 15 rooms, private baths, outdoor pool, gardens and stone walls. Wake up to the quiet of the mountains.

## Waitsfield *

Spencer, Fred
RFD, Route 17,Box 69, 05673
(802) 496-2426

**Amenities:** 1,2,8,9,10,12,16
**Breakfast:** F.

**Dbl. Oc.:** $106.00
**Sgl. Oc.:** $58.30
**Child:** under 12 yrs. - $26.50

**Mountain View Inn**—An old colonial farmhouse with wide pine-board floors, braided rugs and quilts. Meals served around a large harvest table with beautiful mountain views. Good fellowship around a woodstove and piano in living room. Near downhill and cross-country skiing.

## Waitsfield

The Stinson, Family
Route 100,
RR 1, Box 8, 05673
(802) 496-3450, (800) 638-8466

**Amenities:** 1,2,5,6,7,8,9,10,11,12,16
**Breakfast:** F.
**Dbl. Oc.:** $75.00
**Sgl. Oc.:** $54.00
**Third Person:** $30.00
**Child:** under 6 yrs. - no charge

**Valley Inn**—A fine example of an Austrian-style inn offering extraordinary appeal and gracious family hospitality. All freshly decorated private rooms with bath. Sauna, gamerooms and licensed lounge. Nearby activities, skiing and antiques. Winter and off-season rates available.

## Wallingford

Lombardo, Kathleen & Joseph
9 N. Main St., 05773
(802) 446-2849

**Amenities:** 2,5,6,7,8,9,10,12, 14,16,17
**Breakfast:** F.

**Dbl. Oc.:** $74.90
**Sgl. Oc.:** $53.50
**Third Person:** $20.00
**Child:** under 1 yr. - no charge

**Wallingford Inn**—A charming 1876 Victorian country inn. Rooms furnished in period decor. Interior features include oak woodwork, elegant chandeliers and polished wood floors. Candlelit dining. Full-service bar. Near skiing, hiking, fishing, antiquing and shopping. Open year round.

| | | | | |
|---|---|---|---|---|
| 1. No Smoking | 5. Tennis Available | 9. Credit Cards Accepted | 13. Lunch Available | 17. Shared Bath |
| 2. No Pets | 6. Golf Available | 10. Personal Checks Accepted | 14. Public Transportation | 18. Afternoon Tea |
| 3. No Children | 7. Swiming Available | 11. Off Season Rates | 15. Reservations Necessary | ★ Commissions given |
| 4. Senior Citizen Rates | 8. Skiing Available | 12. Dinner Available | 16. Private Bath | to Travel Agents |

## Warren

Chapman, Howard
RR, Box 38, 05674
(802) 583-3211

**Amenities:** 2,3,4,5,6,7,8
,9,10,11,16
**Breakfast:** F.
**Dbl. Oc.:** $90.0
**Sgl. Oc.:** $60.00
**Third Person:** $20.00

**Sugartree Country Inn**—An intimate mountainside country inn featuring handmade quilts atop canopy and brass four-poster beds. Antiques, oil lamps, stained glass and original art. Cool mountain evenings and warm hospitality.

## Waterbury *

Gajdos, Anita & George
RR 1, Box 715, 05677
(802) 244-7490,
(800) 366-5592

**Amenities:** 1,2,3,4,5,6,7,8,9,
10,11,15,16,18
**Breakfast:** F.

**Dbl. Oc.:** $75.00 - $95.00
**Sgl. Oc.:** $60.00 - $70.00
**Third Person:** $20.00

**The Black Locust Inn**—An 1832 restored farmhouse with large living room. Books, music, 45-inch TV and videos. Game area, wood-burning stove, antiques and Oriental rugs. Near all winter and summer outdoor activities. Many wonderful restaurants, shops, museums and theatre! Beautiful and comfortable inn.

## Waterbury

Gosselin, Pamela
Blush Hill Rd.,
Box 1266,, 05676
(802) 244-7529, (800) 736-7522

**Amenities:** 2,4,5,6,7,8,9,10,11,16,17,18
**Breakfast:** F.
**Dbl. Oc.:** $68.00 - $106.00
**Sgl. Oc.:** $60.00 - $95.00
**Third Person:** $15.00
**Child:** $15.00

**Inn At Blush Hill**—A circa 1790 Cape Cod with fabulous mountain views on five acres of lawns and gardens. A quiet area with nearby fine restaurants. Atmosphere is warm and cozy. Lots of antiques and four fireplaces. Adjacent to Ben and Jerry's Ice Cream Factory. Minutes to Stowe and Sugarbush for skiing.

---

| | | | |
|---|---|---|---|
| 1. No Smoking | 5. Tennis Available | 9. Credit Cards Accepted | 13. Lunch Available | 17. Shared Bath |
| 2. No Pets | 6. Golf Available | 10. Personal Checks Accepted | 14. Public Transportation | 18. Afternoon Tea |
| 3. No Children | 7. Swiming Available | 11. Off Season Rates | 15. Reservations Necessary | ★ Commissions given |
| 4. Senior Citizen Rates | 8. Skiing Available | 12. Dinner Available | 16. Private Bath | to Travel Agents |

# VERMONT

## Waterbury

Sellers, Christopher
RR 2, Box 1595, 05676
(802) 244-7726

**Amenities:** 1,2,4,5,6,7,8,9,10,11,12,
13,14,17,18
**Breakfast:** F.
**Dbl. Oc.:** $64.00
**Sgl. Oc.:** $43.00
**Third Person:** $16.00
**Child:** $16.00

**Grunberg Haus Bed & Breakfast**—A hand-built Tyrolean chalet on 10 wooded acres. Huge fireplace, library, pub, sauna, grand piano, balconies, chickens, trails and breakfast specialties. Situated in the mountains. Nearby Stowe, Sugarbush, covered bridges, 14 cross-country ski centers, shops, antiques and galleries.

## Waterbury

Varty, Kelly
Route 100N, RR #2, Box 62, 05676
(802) 244-5911

**Amenities:** 1,2,4,5,6,7,8,9,10,11,12,16
**Breakfast:** C. Plus
**Dbl. Oc.:** $80.25
**Sgl. Oc.:** $64.20
**Third Person:** $20.00
**Child:** under 5 yrs. - no charge

**Thatcher Brook Inn**—A cozy Vermont country inn centrally located with a variety of things to do and see. Visit Ben & Jerry's Ice Cream Factory or watch apple cider being made at Cold Hollow Cider Mill. Our inn features gourmet dining nightly in our small, but cozy, dining room "for couples only."

## Weathersfield *

Thorburn, Mary Louise
Route 106, P.O. Box 165, 05151
(802) 263-9217

**Amenities:** 2,3,5,6,7,8,9,10,
11,12,15,16,18
**Breakfast:** F.
**Dbl. Oc.:** $193.60
**Sgl. Oc.:** $127.05
**Third Person:** $78.65
**Child:** over 8 yrs.- $78.65

**The Inn At Weathersfield**—English 'High Tea,' internationally acclaimed, five-course nouvelle cuisine dinners with piano entertainment and four-course breakfasts are served at this 1795 owner-operated colonial inn. 12 fireplaces and an extensive wine cellar. Rates include meals and high tea.

| | | | |
|---|---|---|---|
| 1. No Smoking | 5. Tennis Available | 9. Credit Cards Accepted | 13. Lunch Available | 17. Shared Bath |
| 2. No Pets | 6. Golf Available | 10. Personal Checks Accepted | 14. Public Transportation | 18. Afternoon Tea |
| 3. No Children | 7. Swiming Available | 11. Off Season Rates | 15. Reservations Necessary | ★ Commissions given |
| 4. Senior Citizen Rates | 8. Skiing Available | 12. Dinner Available | 16. Private Bath | to Travel Agents |

# VERMONT

## West Dover

Chabot, Ernest
57 Dorr Fitch Rd., 05356
(802) 464-5426

**Amenities:** 5,6,7,8,10,15,16, 17,18
**Breakfast:** F.

**Dbl. Oc.:** $70.75 - $107.35
**Sgl. Oc.:** $42.75 - $65.80
**Third Person:** $29.00 - $44.00
**Child:** under 5 yrs. - no charge

**Weathervane Lodge B&B**—Four miles from Mt. Snow and Haystack. This Tyrolean-style lodge is decorated with authentic antiques and colonial charm. The lounge and recreation room have fireplaces and a B.Y.O.B. bar. Marked trails for cross-country skiing. Swimming, boating, tennis, golf and riding in summer.

## West Dover *

Sweeney, Robbie
Route 100, Box 859, 05356
(800) 332-RELAX, (802) 464-5281

**Amenities:** 1,2,3,5,6,7,8,9,10, 11,12,16,17
**Breakfast:** F.
**Dbl. Oc.:** $75.00 - $125.00
**Sgl. Oc.:** $75.00 - $125.00
**Third Person:** $25.00 - $35.00

The Austin Hill Inn

**Austin Hill Inn**—Escape to "timeless relaxation." Secluded from the mainroad. This completely renovated inn has walls of barnboard, Victorian wallpapers, fireplaces, family heirlooms, pool, wine list, afternoon tea and fine dining. Minutes to Mount Snow skiing and championship golf courses.

## Weston

Granger, David
Route E #100, Box 104, 05161
(802) 824-6789

**Amenities:** 1,2,3,5,6,7,8,9,10, 16,17,18
**Breakfast:** F.

**Dbl. Oc.:** $60.00 - $80.00
**Sgl. Oc.:** $55.00 - $75.00

**1830 Inn On The Green**—A graciously restored dwelling overlooking the village green. Within walking distance to shopping, playhouse and dining. Nearby is the Weston Priory. A full breakfast, afternoon tea and bedtime sweets are served. Open all year.

---

| | | | |
|---|---|---|---|
| 1. No Smoking | 5. Tennis Available | 9. Credit Cards Accepted | 13. Lunch Available | 17. Shared Bath |
| 2. No Pets | 6. Golf Available | 10. Personal Checks Accepted | 14. Public Transportation | 18. Afternoon Tea |
| 3. No Children | 7. Swiming Available | 11. Off Season Rates | 15. Reservations Necessary | ★ Commissions given |
| 4. Senior Citizen Rates | 8. Skiing Available | 12. Dinner Available | 16. Private Bath | to Travel Agents |

## *Weston*

Varner, Roy
Lawrence Hill Rd.
Box 106D, 05161
(802) 824-8172

**Amenities:** 1,2,6,8,9,10,
11,15,16,17,18
**Breakfast:** F.
**Dbl. Oc.:** $90.95
**Sgl. Oc.:** $85.60
**Third Person:** $26.75
**Child:** 6-10 yrs. - $16.05

**The Wilder Homestead Inn**—This 1827 brick home is just a step across the bridge from the village green, shops, museums and summer theatre. Nearby fine restaurants. Four miles to Weston Priory. Common rooms with fireplaces. Antiques, original 1830 stenciling and canopy beds - all in a country atmosphere.

## *Williston*

Bryant, Sally & Roger
102 Partridge Hill
P.O. Box 52, 05495
(802) 878-4741

**Amenities:** 1,2,6,10,17
**Breakfast:** F.

**Dbl. Oc.:** $60.00
**Sgl. Oc.:** $35.00

**Partridge Hill Bed And Breakfast**—On a quiet, wooded hilltop overlooking a panorama of the Green Mountains. 5.8 miles from Burlington Airport. Private entrance to guests' level and common room. King, queen or twin beds. Fireplace in common room. Fourth double bedroom available for families. Open all year.

## *Woodstock* *

Deignan, LIza
61 River St., Route 4, 05091
(802) 457-3896

**Amenities:** 1,2,5,6,7,8,9,10,
11,13,14,16,18
**Breakfast:** F.

**Dbl. Oc.:** $65.00 - $110.00
**Sgl. Oc.:** $60.00 - $105.00
**Third Person:** $20.00
**Child:** under 11 yrs. -
$10.00

**The Woodstocker Bed & Breakfast**—Located in historic Woodstock Village. Within walking distance to dining, shops and theatre. Enjoy our nine lovely rooms, spacious suites and relaxing whirlpool. The living room provides a library, games and cable TV. Buffet breakfast will start off your special Vermont getaway.

| | | | |
|---|---|---|---|
| 1. No Smoking | 5. Tennis Available | 9. Credit Cards Accepted | 13. Lunch Available | 17. Shared Bath |
| 2. No Pets | 6. Golf Available | 10. Personal Checks Accepted | 14. Public Transportation | 18. Afternoon Tea |
| 3. No Children | 7. Swiming Available | 11. Off Season Rates | 15. Reservations Necessary | ★ Commissions given |
| 4. Senior Citizen Rates | 8. Skiing Available | 12. Dinner Available | 16. Private Bath | to Travel Agents |

## *Woodstock*

McGinty, Rosemary & Brian
HCR 68, Box 443
Route 4, 05091
(802) 672-3713

**Amenities:** 1,2,5,6,7,8,9, 10,16
**Breakfast:** F.

**Dbl. Oc.:** $69.55 - $90.95
**Sgl. Oc.:** $53.50 - $64.20
**Third Person:** $10.70
**Child:** under 10 yrs. - no charge

**Deer Brook Inn**—A restored 1820 farmhouse with wide-pine floors, handmade quilts and open fireplace. Summer and winter sports activities abound. Nearby shopping and fine dining. Four spacious guest rooms with private baths. 4.5 miles west on Route 4 from the village green.

---

## *Woodstock*

Staab, Eunice & John
Box 13. Barnard, VT, 05031
(802) 234-9957

**Amenities:** 1,2,3,5,6,7,10,15, 17,18
**Breakfast:** F.

**Dbl. Oc.:** $50.00 - $60.00

**The Silver Lake House**—Nine miles north of Woodstock. North Road off Route 12. A circa 1820 gingerbread-trimmed, seven-gabled house overlooking picturesque Silver Lake. Tea served on granny porch. Nearby are all activities. VISA and personal checks accepted.

| | | | | |
|---|---|---|---|---|
| 1. No Smoking | 5. Tennis Available | 9. Credit Cards Accepted | 13. Lunch Available | 17. Shared Bath |
| 2. No Pets | 6. Golf Available | 10. Personal Checks Accepted | 14. Public Transportation | 18. Afternoon Tea |
| 3. No Children | 7. Swiming Available | 11. Off Season Rates | 15. Reservations Necessary | ★ Commissions given |
| 4. Senior Citizen Rates | 8. Skiing Available | 12. Dinner Available | 16. Private Bath | to Travel Agents |

# VIRGINIA

## The Mother Of Presidents

Capitol:  Richmond
Statehood:  June 25, 1788; the 10th state
State Motto:  Thus Always To Tyrants
State Song:  "Carry Me Back To Old Virginia"
State Bird:  Cardinal
State Flower:  Flowering Dogwood
State Tree:  Sugar Maple

Virginia is perhaps one of the most beautiful and historic states in the union. The climate is never too hot or too cold, an ideal vacation area. There is so much to see in this state, from the beautiful sandy beaches on the east coast to the rolling horse farms in the interior to the natural beauty of the Shenandoah Mountains and the breathtaking Skyline Drive.

The battlefield scars of two wars are here, along with their surrender points, Yorktown and Appomattox Court House. Historians come here to visit historic Jamestown, Colonial Williamsburg, Thomas Jefferson's home, Monticello, and his University of Virginia, as well as Mount Vernon, our first president's home.

Eight presidents of the United States were born here: George Washington, Thomas Jefferson, James Madison, James Monroe, William Harrison, Zackary Taylor, James Tyler and Woodrow Wilson.

## *Arlington* *

McGrath, Marlys & John
6404 No. Washington Blvd., 22205
(703) 534-4607

**Amenities:** 1,2,3,5,7,10,14,15,16,17
**Breakfast:** C.
**Dbl. Oc.:** $73.15
**Sgl. Oc.:** $67.93
**Child:** over 12 yrs. - $10.00

**Memory House**—An ornate 1899 Victorian lovingly decorated with antiques and collectibles. Convenient base for exploring the nation's capitol. One block from subway. Two blocks off I-66. Air-conditioned guest rooms. A notable house filled with comfort, hospitality and charm. Ten minutes to D.C.

## *Blacksburg*

Good, Vera
Route 1, Box 348, 24060
(703) 951-1808

**Amenities:** 1,2,4,5,6,10, 15,16
**Breakfast:** F.

**Dbl. Oc.:** $65.00
**Sgl. Oc.:** $65.00
**Third Person:** $10.00

**L'Arche Farm Bed And Breakfast**—A cozy 1790 southwest Virginia farmhouse on five rural acres. Convenient to Virginia Tech, Radford University and the scenic and recreational attractions of the New River Valley. Two miles down on Mt. Tabor Road. Good food and gracious hospitality on a country farm.

## *Boyce* *

Niemann, Cornelia S.
Route 2, Box 135, 22620
(703) 837-1476

**Amenities:** 4,6,7,9,10,15,16
**Breakfast:** F.

**Dbl. Oc.:** $78.38 - $99.28
**Sgl. Oc.:** $78.38 - $99.28
**Third Person:** $10.45
**Child:** $10.45

**The River House**—Convenient to historic, scenic and recreational areas, this rural 1780 getaway is near the Shenandoah River. Relaxing book-filled bed/sitting rooms offer fireplaces, air conditioning and private baths. House parties, small workshops and family reunions invited.

## *Burke*

Bayly, Luisa
6011 Liberty Bell Ct., 22015
(703) 451-1661

**Amenities:** 10,11,12,14,15,17
**Breakfast:** F.

**Dbl. Oc.:** $60.00
**Sgl. Oc.:** $48.00

**Heritage House**—Tastefully decorated with antiques. Twenty minutes to Mt. Vernon, Old Town in Alexandria and Washington, D.C. Weekend rates available.

---

| | | | | |
|---|---|---|---|---|
| 1. No Smoking | 5. Tennis Available | 9. Credit Cards Accepted | 13. Lunch Available | 17. Shared Bath |
| 2. No Pets | 6. Golf Available | 10. Personal Checks Accepted | 14. Public Transportation | 18. Afternoon Tea |
| 3. No Children | 7. Swiming Available | 11. Off Season Rates | 15. Reservations Necessary | ★ Commissions given |
| 4. Senior Citizen Rates | 8. Skiing Available | 12. Dinner Available | 16. Private Bath | to Travel Agents |

# VIRGINIA

## Cape Charles

Goffigon, Sara
Box 97AA, 23310
(804) 331-2212

**Amenities:** 1,5,6,7,10,16,17,18
**Breakfast:** F.
**Dbl. Oc.:** $75.00 - $85.00
**Sgl. Oc.:** $60.00
**Third Person:** $25.00

**Pickett's Harbor**—Seventeen acres of private beach on Chesapeake Bay. A rural retreat on Virginia's eastern shore. Natural flora and fauna. Colonial home with antiques. All rooms overlook the Bay. Breakfast served in your room. Nearby fish and wildlife reserve and nature conservancy.

## Cape Charles *

Wells, James
9 Tazewell Ave., 23310
(804) 331-2206

**Amenities:** 1,2,6,7,10,
16,17,18
**Breakfast:** F.

**Dbl. Oc.:** $65.10 - $75.95
**Sgl. Oc.:** $65.10 - $75.95
**Third Person:** $15.00
**Child:** $10.00

**Sea-Gate**—Located on Virginia's eastern shore. Sea-Gate invites the traveler to rest, relax and recharge. Enjoy our porches and beach. Sunsets are awing! Our home is your home. A full breakfast and afternoon tea completes a perfect getaway in the land of gentle living.

## Charles City

Copland, Mrs. Ridgely
Route 1, Box 13A, 23030
(804) 829-5176

**Amenities:** 2,7,10,11,15,
16,17
**Breakfast:** F.

**Dbl. Oc.:** $80.00 - $90.00
**Sgl. Oc.:** $70.00 - $80.00
**Third Person:** $20.00

**North Bend Plantation**—Built in 1819 and rich in Civil War history. Antique dolls, rare books, heirlooms and antiques fill this historic Virginia landmark that is still actively farmed. 25 miles west of Williamsburg and 30 miles east of Richmond. Located in James River Plantation country.

## Charlottesville *

Putalik, Sue
Box 412, Route 9, 22314
(804) 971-1800

**Amenities:** 1,4,5,6,7,8,9,10,
11,15,16
**Breakfast:** F.

**Dbl. Oc.:** $175.00
**Sgl. Oc.:** $175.00
**Third Person:** $20.00
**Child:** under 10 yrs. -
$10.00

**Clifton - The Country Inn**—An elegant 18th-century Virginia estate. Seven suites, all with fireplaces and luxurious baths. Lovely common rooms with antique furnishings. 40 acres of woods, lake, croquet and an elegant garden. Four miles east of Charlottesville. Near the University of Virginia, Monticello and vineyards.

| | | | | |
|---|---|---|---|---|
| 1. No Smoking | 5. Tennis Available | 9. Credit Cards Accepted | 13. Lunch Available | 17. Shared Bath |
| 2. No Pets | 6. Golf Available | 10. Personal Checks Accepted | 14. Public Transportation | 18. Afternoon Tea |
| 3. No Children | 7. Swiming Available | 11. Off Season Rates | 15. Reservations Necessary | ★ Commissions given |
| 4. Senior Citizen Rates | 8. Skiing Available | 12. Dinner Available | 16. Private Bath | to Travel Agents |

## Chincoteague

Bond, Carlton
600 S. Main St., 23336
(804) 336-3221

Amenities: 2,5,6,7,9,10,
11,16
Breakfast: C.

Dbl. Oc.: $85.20
Sgl. Oc.: $63.90
Third Person: $10.00

**Year Of The Horse Inn**—All rooms on the water. Pier for crabbing or fishing. Ten minutes to wildlife refuge and ocean beach. Home of famous wild ponies. The inn is tastefully decorated and we pride ourselves on the homey atmosphere.

## Chincoteague *

Olian, Victoria
Route 710, New Church, VA 22415
(804) 824-0672

Amenities: 1,2,5,6,7,9,10,11,
12,15,16,18
Breakfast: C. Plus

Dbl. Oc.: $101.17
Sgl. Oc.: $101.17
Third Person: $15.00
Child: $15.00

**The Garden And The Sea Inn**—A historic and romantic inn featuring elegant lodging and French-style gourmet dining in the European tradition. Large rooms, large private baths, antiques and Victorian detail. Nearby beautiful beach and Assateague Wildlife Refuge. Historic side trips. Tours arranged.

## Chincoteague

Stam, James
113 No. Main St., 23336
(804) 336-6686

Amenities: 1,2,5,7,10,11,
15,16,17,18
Breakfast: F.
Dbl. Oc.: $65.00 - $105.00
Sgl. Oc.: $55.00 - $85.00
Third Person: $20.00

**Miss Molly's Inn**—A charming Victorian B&B (circa 1886) with five porches, gazebo, sun deck and picket fences. Loaded with pink and red roses. Lobster boats tied up behind the house. All rooms are air-conditioned and furnished with period antiques. Marguerite Henry wrote "Misty" here.

| | | | |
|---|---|---|---|
| 1. No Smoking | 5. Tennis Available | 9. Credit Cards Accepted | 13. Lunch Available | 17. Shared Bath |
| 2. No Pets | 6. Golf Available | 10. Personal Checks Accepted | 14. Public Transportation | 18. Afternoon Tea |
| 3. No Children | 7. Swiming Available | 11. Off Season Rates | 15. Reservations Necessary | ★ Commissions given |
| 4. Senior Citizen Rates | 8. Skiing Available | 12. Dinner Available | 16. Private Bath | to Travel Agents |

# *VIRGINIA*

## *Christiansburg* *

Ray, Margaret & Tom
311 E. Main, 24073
(703) 381-1500, (800) 336-OAKS

**Amenities:** 1,2,3,4,5,6,7,
8,10,15,16,18
**Breakfast:** F.
**Dbl. Oc.:** $70.50 - $103.00
**Sgl. Oc.:** $70.50 - $103.00
**Third Person:** $10.00

**The Oaks Bed & Breakfast Inn**—A classic 1889 Queen Anne Victorian. Relaxed, tranquil, lavish breakfasts, fine antiques, fireplaces and enchanting porches. A garden gazebo with spa and sauna. Located in Virginia's beautiful Blue Ridge Mountains. Near I-81, 77 and the Blue Ridge Parkway.

## *Columbia* *

Kaz-Jepsen, Ivona
6452 River Rd. W. ,
(Route 6), 23038
(804) 842-2240

**Amenities:** 1,2,3,7,10,15,17
**Breakfast:** F.

**Dbl. Oc.:** $70.00
**Sgl. Oc.:** $65.00

**Upper Byrd Farm Bed & Breakfast**—A turn-of-the-century farmhouse nestled in the Virginia countryside on 26 acres. Overlooks the James River in the town of Columbia. Visit Ashlawn and Monticello. See the state's capitol or simply relax by the fire surrounded by antiques and original art.

## *Culpeper* *

Walker, Kathi & Steve
609 S. East St., 22701
(800) 476-2944

**Amenities:** 1,2,5,6,7,8,9,10,
12,13,14,16,18
**Breakfast:** C. plus
**Dbl. Oc.:** $71.00
**Sgl. Oc.:** $60.00
**Third Person:** $11.00
**Child:** $11.00

**Fountain Hall B&B**—Built in 1859, this grand B&B is furnished with antiques and warmly welcomes business and leisure travelers. Area activities and attractions include wineries, historic battlefields, antique shops, tennis, swimming, golf, Skyline Drive and more.

---

| | | | | |
|---|---|---|---|---|
| 1. No Smoking | 5. Tennis Available | 9. Credit Cards Accepted | 13. Lunch Available | 17. Shared Bath |
| 2. No Pets | 6. Golf Available | 10. Personal Checks Accepted | 14. Public Transportation | 18. Afternoon Tea |
| 3. No Children | 7. Swiming Available | 11. Off Season Rates | 15. Reservations Necessary | ★ Commissions given |
| 4. Senior Citizen Rates | 8. Skiing Available | 12. Dinner Available | 16. Private Bath | to Travel Agents |

## *Fairfax*

Smith, Anne & Ray
4023 Chain Bridge Rd., 22030
(703) 691-2266

**Amenities:** 1,2,9,10,14,15,16,18
**Breakfast:** F.
**Dbl. Oc.:** $101.17 - $186.37
**Sgl. Oc.:** $101.17 - $186.37

**The Bailiwick Inn**—Located in the historic city of Fairfax, only 15 miles from the nation's capitol. Rooms with fireplaces, jacuzzis, feather beds and private baths. Bridal suite available. Afternoon tea and gourmet breakfast. Colonial furnishings create an ambience of famous Virginians' homes.

---

## *Flint Hill* *

Irwin, Phil
Route 1, Box 2080, 22627
(703) 675-3693

**Amenities:** 1,2,3,5,6,7,8,9,10, **Dbl. Oc.:** $73.15 - $104.50
12,13,16,17,18 **Third Person:** $31.35
**Breakfast:** F.

**Caledonia Farm Bed & Breakfast**—A working cattle farm adjacent to Shenandoah National Park. Elegant 1812 stone home with fireplaces, air conditioning, mountain scenery, outstanding comfort, hospitality and recreation for overnight, vacation or conference. Washington, VA - 4 miles away; Washington, DC - 68 miles.

---

## *Flint Hill*

Tokash, Megan & Ronald
P.O. Box 31, 22627
(703) 675-3030

**Amenities:** 2,5,6,9,10,
11,12,13,16
**Breakfast:** F.
**Dbl. Oc.:** $131.00
**Sgl. Oc.:** $131.00
**Third Person:** $25.00
**Child:** under 10 yrs. - $10.00

**The School House Restaurant And Inn**—Set on five acres in the beautiful Blue Ridge Mountains. Dine in original classrooms with a country flair. We have two suites decorated with country antiques and fresh-cut flowers. Flint Hill's friendliest Southern inn! Visit us!

---

| | | | | |
|---|---|---|---|---|
| 1. No Smoking | 5. Tennis Available | 9. Credit Cards Accepted | 13. Lunch Available | 17. Shared Bath |
| 2. No Pets | 6. Golf Available | 10. Personal Checks Accepted | 14. Public Transportation | 18. Afternoon Tea |
| 3. No Children | 7. Swiming Available | 11. Off Season Rates | 15. Reservations Necessary | ★ Commissions given |
| 4. Senior Citizen Rates | 8. Skiing Available | 12. Dinner Available | 16. Private Bath | to Travel Agents |

# VIRGINIA

## Fredericksburg *

Bannan, Alice & Ed
1200 Princess Anne St., 22401
(703) 371-7622

**Amenities:** 2,3,4,5,6,9,
10,12,13,16,18
**Breakfast:** C.
**Dbl. Oc.:** $85.44 - $108.23
**Sgl. Oc.:** $70.53 - $97.38
**Third Person:** $10.00

**Kenmore Inn**—An elegant, circa 1800, colonial with 13 guest rooms, all with private bath and some with fireplaces. Beautiful gardens for dining or relaxing. Gourmet dining on premise featuring Virginia wines. On historical walking tour. Nearby all shops and river.

## Fredericksburg

Gowin, Dennis
711 Caroline St., 22402
(703) 899-7606

**Amenities:** 1,2,4,9,10,15,
16,17
**Breakfast:** C.

**Dbl. Oc.:** $60.00 - $131.00
**Sgl. Oc.:** $60.00 - $131.00
**Third Person:** $60.00 -
$131.00
**Child:** $60.00 - $131.00

**Richard Johnston Inn**—A romantic country inn restored with period antiques. Continental breakfast included. An ideal setting for weekend getaways, weddings and conferences.

## Fredericksburg *

Schiesser, Michele
4420 Guinea Station Rd., 22401
(703) 898-8444

**Amenities:** 2,9,10,15,16
**Breakfast:** F.

**Dbl. Oc.:** $74.55
**Sgl. Oc.:** $58.58
**Third Person:** $10.65
**Child:** no charge - $5.33

**La Vista Plantation**—An 1838 classic revival country home on 10 acres surrounded by woods, pastures, farm fields and stocked pond. Six fireplaces, radio, TV, refrigerator, phone, bicycle and nearby historic attractions. Fresh eggs and homemade jams. Air-conditioned.

## Front Royal *

Wilson, Ann & Bill
43 Chester St., 22630
(703) 635-3937, (800) 621-0441

**Amenities:** 2,3,5,6,7,8,9,10,16,17
**Breakfast:** C.
**Dbl. Oc.:** $60.00 - $110.00

**Chester House**—A Georgian mansion in the historic district. An elegant and relaxed atmosphere. Two acres. Elaborate gardens. Shenandoah Valley, River-Skyline Drive, caverns and Blue Ridge Mountains. Near antiques, gift shops, wineries, sports, recreational activities and excellent restaurants.

| | | | | |
|---|---|---|---|---|
| 1. No Smoking | 5. Tennis Available | 9. Credit Cards Accepted | 13. Lunch Available | 17. Shared Bath |
| 2. No Pets | 6. Golf Available | 10. Personal Checks Accepted | 14. Public Transportation | 18. Afternoon Tea |
| 3. No Children | 7. Swiming Available | 11. Off Season Rates | 15. Reservations Necessary | ★ Commissions give |
| 4. Senior Citizen Rates | 8. Skiing Available | 12. Dinner Available | 16. Private Bath | to Travel Agents |

## *Gordonsville* *

Allison, Beverly
Route 3, Box 43, 22942
(703) 832-5555

**Amenities:** 5,6,7,9,10,16,18
**Breakfast:** F.
**Dbl. Oc.:** $59.00 - $91.00
**Sgl. Oc.:** $43.00 - $60.00
**Third Person:** $15.00
**Child:** under 5 yrs. - no charge

**Sleepy Hollow Farm**—Located on historic Route 231, between Somerset and Gordonsville. Lovely countryside. Restored farmhouse with cottage and pond. Near Montpelier, horse trails, historic sites and fine dining. Dinner and lunch by arrangement.

---

## *Irvington* *

Stephen, Ford
King Carter Dr., 22480
(804) 438-6053

**Amenities:** 1,5,6,7,10, 15,16,17
**Breakfast:** F.

**Dbl. Oc.:**$85.00
**Sgl. Oc.:** $75.00
**Third Person:** no charge
**Child:** no charge

**Irvington House**—Luxurious suite with private loggia entry. Living room, kitchen with stocked breakfast larder. Two large doubel bedrooms with a bath between. On golf course. Near five star restaurants, Williamsburg, Jamestown, Yorktown, Chesapeake Bay. Boats available.

---

## *Irvington*

Taylor, Marilyn
King Carter Dr., 22480
(804) 438-6053

**Amenities:** 5,6,7,10,15,16,17
**Breakfast:** F.

**Dbl. Oc.:** $62.70 - $67.92
**Sgl. Oc.:** $52.25 - $57.47
**Third Person:** no charge
**Child:** no charge

**King Carter Inn**—A Victorian inn in a picturesque waterfront community. Eight rooms — four guest rooms with private baths and four guest rooms sharing two baths. Private, fully furnished cottage. Free bicycles for use of guests. Antique furnishings. Cottage available - $78.37-$104.50

---

## *Lexington*

Roberts, Ellen & John
603 So. Main St., 24450
(703) 463-3235

**Amenities:** 2,3,4,5,6,7,9,10, 11,16
**Breakfast:** F.

**Dbl. Oc.:** $69.88
**Sgl. Oc.:** $53.75
**Third Person:** $10.00

**Llewellyn Lodge At Lexington**—Lexington's oldest B&B is a short walk from the historic district. A warm, friendly atmosphere. Offers country charm with a touch of class. Home of the Lee Chapel and Stonewall Jackson. A must for Civil War buffs. Many repeat visits just for our breakfast!

---

| | | | |
|---|---|---|---|
| 1. No Smoking | 5. Tennis Available | 9. Credit Cards Accepted | 13. Lunch Available | 17. Shared Bath |
| 2. No Pets | 6. Golf Available | 10. Personal Checks Accepted | 14. Public Transportation | 18. Afternoon Tea |
| 3. No Children | 7. Swiming Available | 11. Off Season Rates | 15. Reservations Necessary | ★ Commissions given |
| 4. Senior Citizen Rates | 8. Skiing Available | 12. Dinner Available | 16. Private Bath | to Travel Agents |

## *Luray* *

Merrigan, Ann
Route 4, Box 620, 22835
(703) 743-7855

**Amenities:** 5,6,7,8,9,10,16,1
16,17
**Breakfast:** F.

**Dbl. Oc.:** $91.37 - $134.37

**The Ruffner House Inn**—A 251-year-old manor house. A romantic getawy on an 18-acre horse farm. Elegant antique-filled rooms, private baths, fireplaces, swimming pool and gourmet foods. Located in beautiful Shenandoah Valley.

---

## *Lynchburg*

Pfister, LoisAnn & Ed
Route 1, Box 362,
Madison Heights, 24572
(804) 384-7220

**Amenities:** 1,2,5,6,7,8,10,
15,17
**Breakfast:** F.

**Dbl. Oc.:** $52.19 - $62.84
**Sgl. Oc.:** $52.19 - $62.84
**Child:** under 12 yrs. -
$10.00

**Winridge Bed & Breakfast**—A grand Southern colonial home on a 14-acre country estate with a view of the mountains. Close to Blue Ridge Parkway. Queen- and twin-bedded rooms. Southern hospitality at its finest. A warm and casual atmosphere. Library, parlor, two large porches, swings and shade trees.

---

## *Maurertown*

Rohrbaugh, Fran
Route 1, Box 435, 22644
(703) 459-2985

**Amenities:** 1,2,3,10,15,16,17
**Breakfast:** F.

**Dbl. Oc.:** $48.00 - $80.00
**Sgl. Oc.:** $38.00
**Third Person:** $15.00

**Good Intent**—A restored 1890 farmhouse on 20 rolling acres in the Shenandoah Valley, two hours from Washington, D.C. A quiet and pastoral setting with lovely mountain views. Two guest rooms in main house and charming, rustic guest cottage with fireplace and sitting room.

---

## *Morattico*

Graham, Mary Chilton
P.O. Box 64, 22523
(804) 462-7759

**Amenities:** 7,10,15,16,17
**Breakfast:** C.

**Dbl. Oc.:** $35.00
**Sgl. Oc.:** $30.00
**Third Person:** $10.00
**Child:** $10.00

**"Holly Point"**—Your hostess at this country home claims to be related to George Washington and will be happy to direct you to the local historic sites. You will enjoy the 120 acres of pine forest and views of the scenic Rappahannock River. Land and water sports. Open May 1 to November 1.

---

| | | | |
|---|---|---|---|
| 1. No Smoking | 5. Tennis Available | 9. Credit Cards Accepted | 13. Lunch Available | 17. Shared Bath |
| 2. No Pets | 6. Golf Available | 10. Personal Checks Accepted | 14. Public Transportation | 18. Afternoon Tea |
| 3. No Children | 7. Swiming Available | 11. Off Season Rates | 15. Reservations Necessary | ★ Commissions given |
| 4. Senior Citizen Rates | 8. Skiing Available | 12. Dinner Available | 16. Private Bath | to Travel Agents |

## *New Market* *

Kasow, Dawn
9329 Congress St., 22844
(703) 740-8030

Amenities: 2,5,6,7,8,9,10,16
Breakfast: F.

Dbl. Oc.: $63.90 - $69.32
Sgl. Oc.: $53.35 - $58.68
Third Person: $10.00
Child: over 12 yrs. - $10.00

**A Touch Of Country**—Come and relax at our 1870's restored home on Main Street in historic New Market. Enjoy the porch swings or visit the antique shops, gift shops, restaurants and nearby attractions. Rest comfortably in one of six bedrooms decorated with antiques and collectibles.

## *Orange* *

Ramsey, Shirley & Stephen
U.S. Route 15, Box 707, 22960
(703) 672-5597

Amenities: 1,2,3,9,10,11,
            12,15,16,18
Breakfast: F.
Dbl. Oc.: $95.00 - $250.00
Sgl. Oc.: $50.00 (mid-week only)
Third Person: $20.00

**Mayhurst Inn**—A four-story Italianate villa on 36 acres of old oaks, cedars and magnolias. Seven rooms or suites with period antique furnishings. Civil War history. Near homes of Jefferson, Madison and Monroe. Fishing pond, walking paths and antique shop on premises.

## *Palmyra* *

Palmer, Gregory
Route 2, Box 1390, 22963
(804) 589-1300

Amenities: 7,9,10,11,
            12,13,15,16
Breakfast: F.
Dbl. Oc.: $125.00
Sgl. Oc.: $95.00
Third Person: $25.00
Child: under 10 yrs. - $10.00

**Palmer Country Manor**—Situated on 180 wooded acres. Private cottages with a large living area, fireplace, color TV and deck. Swimming pool, fishing, ballooning, hiking, historic sightseeing, wine tasting and white-water rafting. Call or write for brochure.

## *Raphine*

Tichenor, Pat & Jim
Route 1, Box 356, 24472
(703) 377-2398

Amenities: 1,2,3,5,6,7,8,9,10,
            15,16
Breakfast: C. Plus

Dbl. Oc.: $58.58 - $69.23
Sgl. Oc.: $47.93 - $58.58
Third Person: $15.00

**Oak Spring Farm & Vineyard**—An 1826 plantation house with modern comforts on a 40-acre working farm and vineyard. Filled with antiques, family and military memorabilia. Amenities, warm hospitality, peace and quiet are our trademarks. Nearby good restaurants. Lots to see and do. Child over 14 only.

| | | | |
|---|---|---|---|
| 1. No Smoking | 5. Tennis Available | 9. Credit Cards Accepted | 13. Lunch Available | 17. Shared Bath |
| 2. No Pets | 6. Golf Available | 10. Personal Checks Accepted | 14. Public Transportation | 18. Afternoon Tea |
| 3. No Children | 7. Swiming Available | 11. Off Season Rates | 15. Reservations Necessary | ★ Commissions given |
| 4. Senior Citizen Rates | 8. Skiing Available | 12. Dinner Available | 16. Private Bath | to Travel Agents |

## *Richmond* *

Benson, Lyn
2036 Monument Ave., 23220
(804) 353-6900

**Amenities:** 1,2,4,9,10,16
**Breakfast:** F.

**Dbl. Oc.:** $97.50 - $125.50
**Sgl. Oc.:** $97.50 - $125.50
**Third Person:** $20.00
**Child:** 10 - 15 yrs. - $15.00

**The Emmanuel Hutzler House**—Elegant, yet unpretenious, describes this large, renovated historic Italian Renaissance home. Guests can use the living room with mahogany paneling, marble fireplace and leaded glass. Four guest rooms with private baths (one with jacuzzi and two with fireplaces).

## *Richmond*

Fleming, Barbara & Bill
P.O. Box 4503, 23220
(804) 355-5855,
Fax: (804) 353-4656

**Amenities:** 1,2,3,9,10,14,15,
16,17,18
**Breakfast:** F.

**Dbl. Oc.:** $75.00 - $95.00
**Sgl. Oc.:** $55.00 - $75.00
**Third Person:** $20.00

**Abbie Hill Bed & Breakfast**—Comfort and elegance in an urban historic district. Convenient to museums, good eateries, tours, shopping and historic sites. Tastefully decorated, antiques and porch for rocking. Full Virginia breakfast. Rail, air and bus pick-up available. Complimentary tea on arrival.

## *Richmond*

West, Billie Rees
1107 Grove Ave., 23220
(804) 358-6174

**Amenities:** 2,10,14,15,16,18   **Dbl. Oc.:** $65.00 - $75.00
**Breakfast:** F.

**West-Bocock House**—An elegant historic house located in the heart of Richmond, specializing in Southern hospitality. French linens, fresh flowers, antiques and an eclectic art collection. Nearby museums, restaurants and shopping.

## *Smith Mountain Lake* *

Tucker, Mary Lynn & Lee
Route 1, Box 533, 24184
(703) 721-3951

**Amenities:** 1,2,5,6,7,8,9,10,
15,16,17,18
**Breakfast:** F.
**Dbl. Oc.:** $63.90 - $90.00

**The Manor At Taylor's Store**—Warm hospitality, idyllic setting and many luxurious amenities make this historic estate a very special place. On 120 acres with six private lakes to fish, swim and canoe. Hot tub, air conditioning and elaborate breakfast. Near Blue Ridge Parkway and Roanoke, VA.

| | | | | |
|---|---|---|---|---|
| 1. No Smoking | 5. Tennis Available | 9. Credit Cards Accepted | 13. Lunch Available | 17. Shared Bath |
| 2. No Pets | 6. Golf Available | 10. Personal Checks Accepted | 14. Public Transportation | 18. Afternoon Tea |
| 3. No Children | 7. Swiming Available | 11. Off Season Rates | 15. Reservations Necessary | ★ Commissions given |
| 4. Senior Citizen Rates | 8. Skiing Available | 12. Dinner Available | 16. Private Bath | to Travel Agents |

## Smithfield

Hart, Robert
1607 S. Church St., 23430
(804) 357-3176

**Amenities:** 2,4,5,6,9,10,16
**Breakfast:** F.

**Dbl. Oc.:** $62.84
**Sgl. Oc.:** $52.19
**Third Person:** $10.65
**Child:** under 3 yrs. -
no charge

**Isle Of Wight Inn**—A luxurious inn located in a delightful and historic riverport town. Suites with fireplaces and jacuzzi. Some 60 old homes dating from 1750. Thirty minutes to Williamsburg and Jamestown. Near Norfolk, Hampton and Virginia Beach. Antique and gift shop.

## Stanardsville *

Schwartz, Eleanor & Norman
Route 2, Box 303, 22973
(804) 985-3782

**Amenities:** 1,2,10,12,15,16
**Breakfast:** F.
**Dbl. Oc.:** $70.00
**Sgl. Oc.:** $60.00
**Third Person:** $10.00

**Edgewood Farm Bed And Breakfast**—A circa 1790 restored farmhouse on 130 acres in the Blue Ridge foothills. Off the beaten track, yet within 30 miles of Skyline, Monticello, Montpelier, vineyards, antique and craft shops and fine restaurants. For the gardener visit our herb and perennial nursery.

## Stanley *

Beers, Marley
Route 2, Box 375, 22851
(703) 778-2285

**Amenities:** 1,2,3,5,6,7,8,9,10,
12,13,15,16
**Breakfast:** C. and F.

**Dbl. Oc.:** $75.00 - $125.00
**Sgl. Oc.:** $65.00 - $95.00
**Third Person:** $10.00

**Jordan Hollow Farm Inn**—A restored colonial horse-farm inn. Beautiful mountain views. Twenty-two rooms, one with whirlpool and fireplace. Full-service restaurant and pub. Riding stable with trail rides on premises. Near Skyline Drive, Luray Caverns and much more.

## Staunton *

Harman, Joe
18 E. Frederick St., 24401
(703) 885-4220,
(800) 334-5575 (outside VA)
**Amenities:** 1,2,4,5,6,7,8,9,10,
11,12,13,14,16,18
**Breakfast:** C.
**Dbl. Oc.:** $69.23
**Sgl. Oc.:** $42.60
**Third Person:** $15.98
**Child:** under 2 yrs. - $5.33

**Frederick House**—A small historic inn in the European tradition. The Gallery Cafe at Frederick House serves breakfast, lunch and dinner. Guest rooms in the inn have private baths, TVs, phones and are air conditioned. Private parking.

| | | | |
|---|---|---|---|
| 1. No Smoking | 5. Tennis Available | 9. Credit Cards Accepted | 13. Lunch Available | 17. Shared Bath |
| 2. No Pets | 6. Golf Available | 10. Personal Checks Accepted | 14. Public Transportation | 18. Afternoon Tea |
| 3. No Children | 7. Swiming Available | 11. Off Season Rates | 15. Reservations Necessary | ★ Commissions given |
| 4. Senior Citizen Rates | 8. Skiing Available | 12. Dinner Available | 16. Private Bath | to Travel Agents |

## *Swoope* *

Fannon, Elizabeth & Daniel
Route 1, Box 63, 24479
(703) 337-6929

**Amenities:** 1,2,10,17
**Breakfast:** F.

**Dbl. Oc.:** $36.58
**Sgl. Oc.:** $31.35

**Lambsgate Bed And Breakfast**—In the historic Shenandoah Valley, six miles west of Staunton on Route 254. A restored 1816 farmhouse in a pastoral setting facing the Allegheny Mountains. This working sheep farm offers pleasant, comfortable lodging near antiquing, hiking and scenic attractions.

## *Virginia Beach*

Yates, Barbara
302 24th St., 23451
(804) 428-4690

**Amenities:** 1,5,6,7,11,14,16,17
**Breakfast:** C. Plus
**Dbl. Oc.:** $47.96 - $65.40
**Sgl. Oc.:** $34.88 - $52.32
**Third Person:** $10.00
**Child:** under 10 yrs. - $6.00

**Angie's Guest Cottage**—A cute, clean and cozy beach house in the heart of the resort area, one block from the beach. International atmosphere with casual and comfortable surroundings. Sun deck and cookout facilities available.

## *White Post*

Borel, Celeste & Alain
P.O. Box 119, 22663
(703) 837-1375

**Amenities:** 2,3,4,5,6,7,8,9,10,
12,15,16
**Breakfast:** F.

**Dbl. Oc.:** $115.00 - $175.00
**Sgl. Oc.:** $100.00 - $160.00
**Third Person:** $20.00
**Child:** under 10 yrs. -
$15.00

**L'Auberge Provencale**—Luxurious overnight accommodations. Elegant and romantic dining. The perfect getaway. Weddings and rehearsaldinners. Country charm with city sophistication. Superb French "cuisine moderne." "Mt. Airy" re-created as an inn of southern France.

## *Williamsburg*

Cottle, June
8691 Barhamsville Rd.,
Toano, VA, 23168
(804) 566-0177

**Amenities:** 10,12,16,18
**Breakfast:** F.

**Dbl. Oc.:** $48.00 - $58.00
**Sgl. Oc.:** $48.00 - $58.00
**Third Person:** $15.00
**Child:** under 6 yrs. - $10.00

**Blue Bird Haven B&B**—June welcomes you to her ranch-style home located 20 minutes from colonial Williamsburg. Guest rooms are in a private wing and feature handmade quilts and rugs. Breakfast includes homemade granola, country ham and blueberry pancakes. Complimentary evening desserts.

| | | | | |
|---|---|---|---|---|
| 1. No Smoking | 5. Tennis Available | 9. Credit Cards Accepted | 13. Lunch Available | 17. Shared Bath |
| 2. No Pets | 6. Golf Available | 10. Personal Checks Accepted | 14. Public Transportation | 18. Afternoon Tea |
| 3. No Children | 7. Swiming Available | 11. Off Season Rates | 15. Reservations Necessary | ★ Commissions given |
| 4. Senior Citizen Rates | 8. Skiing Available | 12. Dinner Available | 16. Private Bath | to Travel Agents |

## *Williamsburg*

| | | |
|---|---|---|
| Hirz, Sandra & Brad | **Amenities:** 1,2,9,10,15,16 | **Dbl. Oc.:** $85.20 - $133.10 |
| 1022 Jamestown Rd., 23185 | **Breakfast:** F. | **Third Person:** $37.27 |
| (804) 253-1260 | | |

**Liberty Rose**—A most romantic and charming restoration. Antiques, canopy beds, wallpapers and lace. Beautiful private baths. Parlor with fireplaces. Scrumptious home-cooked full breakfast. Perfectly located in a wooded setting. Suites available. Queen-size beds. Unexpected delights.

## *Williamsburg*

| | | |
|---|---|---|
| Hite, Faye | **Amenities:** 2,10,17 | **Dbl. Oc.:** $55.00 - $60.00 |
| 704 Monumental Ave., 23185 | **Breakfast:** C. | **Sgl. Oc.:** $55.00 - $60.00 |
| (804) 229-4814 | | **Third Person:** $10.00 |
| | | **Child:** under 10 yrs. - no charge |

Attractive Cape Cod within walking distance to Colonial Williamsburg and the visitor's center. Large rooms with antiques. One room has a sitting area. Each room has aTV, radio, phone and coffee maker. Breakfast in your room.Three miles to Bush Gardens.

## *Williamsburg*

Lucas, Mary Ann & Ed
930 Jamestown Rd., 23185
(804) 220-0524, (800) WMBGS-BB

**Amenities:** 1,2,3,9,10,11,15,16
**Breakfast:** F.
**Dbl. Oc.:** $79.00 - $130.00
**Sgl. Oc.:** $79.00 - $130.00
**Third Person:** $25.00

**The Legacy Of Williamsburg Tavern Bed & Breakfast**—Williamsburg's finest 18th-century ambience and the furnishings make you feel like you just stepped back in time. We have suites and rooms, all private baths, fireplaces and canopy beds. Within walking distance to everything. Homemade muffins, breads and waffles.

## *Williamsburg*

| | | |
|---|---|---|
| Orendorff, Pat & Robert | **Amenities:** 2,4,5,6,9,10,11,14, | **Dbl. Oc.:** $48.00 - $59.00 |
| 701 Monumental Ave., 23185 | 15,16,17 | **Sgl. Oc.:** $43.00 - $54.00 |
| (804) 229-6914 | **Breakfast:** C. | **Child:** $10.00 |

**Fox Grape Bed & Breakfast**—Warm hospitality awaits you within a 10-minute walk north of Virginia's restored colonial capitol. Furnishings include antiques, counted cross-stitch, stained glass, stenciled walls, duck decoys and a cup and plate collection.

| | | | |
|---|---|---|---|
| 1. No Smoking | 5. Tennis Available | 9. Credit Cards Accepted | 13. Lunch Available | 17. Shared Bath |
| 2. No Pets | 6. Golf Available | 10. Personal Checks Accepted | 14. Public Transportation | 18. Afternoon Tea |
| 3. No Children | 7. Swiming Available | 11. Off Season Rates | 15. Reservations Necessary | ★ Commissions given |
| 4. Senior Citizen Rates | 8. Skiing Available | 12. Dinner Available | 16. Private Bath | to Travel Agents |

# VIRGINIA

## Williamsburg *

Strout, Fred
605 Richmond Rd., 23185
(804) 229-0205,
  (800) 899-APLE

**Amenities:** 1,2,5,6,9,10,11,14,
  15,16,18
**Breakfast:** C. Plus

**Dbl. Oc.:** $65.00 - $95.00
**Sgl. Oc.:** $65.00 - $95.00
**Third Person:** $15.00
**Child:** $10.00

**Applewood Colonial Bed & Breakfast**—The owner's unique apple collection is evidenced throughout this colonial home. Four elegant rooms with private baths. Located four blocks from Colonial Williamsburg. Close to William & Mary College. Antiques compliment the romantic atmosphere. Fireplaces.

## Wintergreen *

Dinwiddie, M/M Edward
P.O. Box 280, Nellysford, VA, 22958
(804) 325-9126,
  (800) 325-9126 (reservations)

**Amenities:** 2,5,6,7,8,9,10,12,
  15,16
**Breakfast:** F.

**Dbl. Oc.:** $83.60 - $94.05
**Sgl. Oc.:** $67.93 - $73.15
**Third Person:** $36.58

**Trillium House**—Located within a 10,000-acre resort of Wintergreen. One mile from Blue Ridge Parkway. Featured in *Country Inns And Back Roads*, AAA - 4 diamond, *Mobile Guide* - 3 stars and *Great Inns of America*. Dinner - Friday and Saturday, 7:30p.m. By reservation only, $20.00 - $24.00.

## Woodstock

Hallgren, Bette
402 No. Main St., 22664
(703) 459-4828

**Amenities:** 1,2,10,15,16,17
**Breakfast:** C.

**Dbl. Oc.:** $58.60
**Sgl. Oc.:** $37.30
**Third Person:** $10.00
**Child:** under 12 yrs. -
  $10.00

**The Country Fare**—A small and cozy country inn where old-fashion hospitality has not gone out of style. Relax and unwind in one of the three hand-stenciled bedrooms furnished with a comfortable blend of country and collectibles. A continental breakfast of home-baked breads is served.

## Woodstock

McDonald, Margaret & Price
551 So. Main St., 22664
(703) 459-3500

**Amenities:** 1,2,8,10,15,16,17
**Breakfast:** F.

**Dbl. Oc.:** $57.48
**Sgl. Oc.:** $57.48
**Child:** under 10 yrs. -
  $15.68

**Azalea House**—A 100-year-old Victorian home complete with antiques and charming decor. Located in the Shenandoah Valley. Near fine restaurants, shops, vineyards, Civil War sites, fishing, hiking, caverns and mountainous sightseeing. Breakfast is special.

| | | | | |
|---|---|---|---|---|
| 1. No Smoking | 5. Tennis Available | 9. Credit Cards Accepted | 13. Lunch Available | 17. Shared Bath |
| 2. No Pets | 6. Golf Available | 10. Personal Checks Accepted | 14. Public Transportation | 18. Afternoon Tea |
| 3. No Children | 7. Swiming Available | 11. Off Season Rates | 15. Reservations Necessary | ★ Commissions given |
| 4. Senior Citizen Rates | 8. Skiing Available | 12. Dinner Available | 16. Private Bath | to Travel Agents |

# *WASHINGTON*

## *The Evergreen State*

Capitol: Olympia
Statehood: November 11, 1889; the 42nd state
State Motto: Alki (Bye & Bye)
State Song: "Washington, My Home"
State Bird: Willow Goldfinch
State Flower: Coast Rhododendron
State Tree: Western Hemlock

The state of Washington receives an abundance of rain. Because of this, it has great forests and lumber is its major industry. It also is known as a great land for hunting and fishing.

Olympia, the capitol, and other cities on Puget Sound are sheltered from most of the heavy rain and are able to maintain a busy harbor to send supplies north to Alaska and receive in return oil to be refined.

There are also farmlands here irrigated by means of the harnessing of the water by dams. The chief dam being the Coulee Dam, is considered to be one of the greatest pieces of engineering ever completed.

The state of Washington is also well known for her delicious Washington state apples.

## Anacortes *

Hasty, Melinda
1312 8th St., 98221
(206) 293-5773

**Amenities:** 1,2,5,6,7,9,10, **Dbl. Oc.:** $59.25 - $80.25
16,17          **Sgl. Oc.:** $59.25 - $80.25
**Breakfast:** F.        **Third Person:** $15.00
**Child:** $15.00

**Hasty Pudding House**—Exquisitely romantic! Enjoy authentic Victorian decor in this delightful 1913 home. Light and charming guest rooms invite quiet slumber. Walk to historic downtown. Near restaurants, marinas and quaint shops.

## Anacortes *

Harker, Hal
100 Sunset Beach, 98221
(206) 293-5428

**Amenities:** 1,2,9,10,11,15,16, **Dbl. Oc.:** $79.00
17,18          **Sgl. Oc.:** $68.00
**Breakfast:** C. Plus     **Third Person:** $25.00
**Child:** under 5 yrs. - $10.00

**Sunset Beach Bed And Breakfast**—On exciting Rosario Straits. Come and relax. Enjoy the views of the San Juan Islands, wild deer, sea lions and unusual water birds. Take a stroll on the beach and relax on our decks. Private bath, entry, TV and queen beds. Close to ferry, restaurants and marina.

## Anacortes *

Jones, Sarah
917 36th, 98221
(206) 293-4910

**Amenities:** 1,2,9,10,17    **Dbl. Oc.:** $59.13
**Breakfast:** F.           **Sgl. Oc.:** $48.38
**Third Person:** $10.00
**Child:** under 2 yrs. -
no charge

**Campbell House**—A conveniently located turn-of-the-century home. Large rooms comfortably furnished with antiques and queen-size beds. Delicious breakfasts. Views of Fidalgo Bay and Mt. Baker. Families welcome. A very comfortable place.

## Anacortes *

McIntyre, Pat & Dennis
2902 Oakes Ave., 98221
(206) 293-9382

**Amenities:** 1,2,9,10,11,16,17 **Dbl. Oc.:** $69.88 - $91.37
**Breakfast:** F.           **Sgl. Oc.:** $59.13 - $80.63
**Third Person:** $10.00

**Channell House**—A classic 1902 island home located within minutes of the ferry dock. We offer comfortable rooms (two with fireplaces), private and shared baths and views. Guests enjoy use of our living room, library and hot tub.

---

| | | | |
|---|---|---|---|
| 1. No Smoking | 5. Tennis Available | 9. Credit Cards Accepted | 13. Lunch Available | 17. Shared Bath |
| 2. No Pets | 6. Golf Available | 10. Personal Checks Accepted | 14. Public Transportation | 18. Afternoon Tea |
| 3. No Children | 7. Swiming Available | 11. Off Season Rates | 15. Reservations Necessary | ★ Commissions given |
| 4. Senior Citizen Rates | 8. Skiing Available | 12. Dinner Available | 16. Private Bath | to Travel Agents |

## Anacortes *

Short, Marilyn & Cecil
5708 Kingsway W., 98221
(206) 293-0677

**Amenities:** 6,7,9,10,11,15,16
**Breakfast:** F.
**Dbl. Oc.:** $72.00
**Sgl. Oc.:** $72.00
**Third Person:** $20.00
**Child:** under 2 yrs. - no charge

**Albatross Bed & Breakfast**—A charming Cape Cod-style home with a large viewing deck across the street from the Skyline Marina, charter boats and restaurant. Near Washington Park and ferry to San Jaun Islands and Victoria, B.C. Airport/ferry pick-up. Four rooms with king and queen beds. AAA.

## Anderson Island

Burg, Annie & Ken
8808 Villa Beach Rd., 98303
(206) 884-9185

**Amenities:** 1,2,5,6,7,9,12,13, 15,16,17
**Breakfast:** F.

**Dbl. Oc.:** $55.00 - $76.00
**Sgl. Oc.:** $55.00 - $76.00
**Third Person:** $15.00
**Child:** under 16 yrs. - $10.00

**The Inn At Burg's Landing**—Take a relaxing 30-minute ferry ride from Steilacoom. Enjoy a spectacular view of Puget Sound, Mt. Rainier and the Cascade Mountains from our rustic log home. Two rooms, private bath and hydro tub for two. Nearby golf, tennis and fishing. Bicycling.

## Ashford *

Darrah, John Chad
28912 S.R. 7065, 98304
(206) 569-2788

**Amenities:** 1,3,7,8,9,10, 11,16
**Breakfast:** F.

**Dbl. Oc.:** $82.13
**Sgl. Oc.:** $71.18
**Third Person:** $15.00

**Mountain Meadows Inn Bed & Breakfast**—Built in 1910 on 14 acres. Antiques, model trains, nature trails, trout pond, campfire and S'mores in the evenings. Six miles from Mt. Rainier National Park. Player piano. Cab rides on Mt. Rainier's scenic railroad. Your home-away-from-home. Hospitality at its finest.

## Ashford *

Jenny, Susan
37311 SR 706, 98304
(206) 569-2339

**Amenities:** 1,2,8,9,10,16,17
**Breakfast:** F.

**Dbl. Oc.:** $70.00 - $90.00
**Sgl. Oc.:** $60.00 - $85.00
**Third Person:** $16.50

**Growly Bear Bed And Breakfast**—Experience a bit of history. Enjoy your mountain stay at a rustic 1890 homestead house. Hike in nearby Mt. Ranier National Park. Dine at unique restaurants. Listen to Goat Creek just outside your window. Indulge in a basket of warm pastries from The Growly Bear Bakery.

| | | | | |
|---|---|---|---|---|
| 1. No Smoking | 5. Tennis Available | 9. Credit Cards Accepted | 13. Lunch Available | 17. Shared Bath |
| 2. No Pets | 6. Golf Available | 10. Personal Checks Accepted | 14. Public Transportation | 18. Afternoon Tea |
| 3. No Children | 7. Swiming Available | 11. Off Season Rates | 15. Reservations Necessary | ★ Commissions given |
| 4. Senior Citizen Rates | 8. Skiing Available | 12. Dinner Available | 16. Private Bath | to Travel Agents |

## *Bellevue* *

Garnett, Carol & Cy
830-100 Ave. S.E., 98004
(206) 453-1048

**Amenities:** 1,2,3,6,7,8,9
11,12,13,14,15,16
**Breakfast:** F.

**Dbl. Oc.:** $55.00
**Sgl. Oc.:** $50.00

**Bellevue Bed & Breakfast**—Mountain and city views. Private suite or single rooms with private baths and entrance. Central location. Full breakfast. Gourmet coffee. In Seattle's Best Places. Reasonable rates.

## *Bellingham* *

DeFreytas, Barbara & Frank
1014 N. Garden, 98225
(206) 671-7828,
(800) 922-6414

**Amenities:** 1,2,3,9,10,15,
16,17
**Breakfast:** F.

**Dbl. Oc.:** $58.22 - $62.60
**Sgl. Oc.:** $52.82 - $58.22
**Third Person:** $10.00

**North Garden Inn**—A Queen Anne Victorian in the *Register of Historic Pla*ce. Views of Bellingham Bay. Ten elegant guest rooms. Near university, shopping and dining.

## *Bellingham*

McAllister, Donna
4421 Lakeway Dr., 98226
(206) 733-0055

**Amenities:** 1,5,7,9,10,15,16
**Breakfast:** F.

**Dbl. Oc.:** $92.00 - $130.00
**Third Person:** $20.00
**Child:** $10.00

**Schnauzer Crossing Bed & Breakfast**—A luxury bed and breakfast on Lake Whatcom. King-size suite with fireplace, TV and jacuzzi tub. Queen room with lake view and private modern bath. Beautiful gardens with blueberries, raspberries and birds everywhere! Northwest hospitality at its finest!

## *Camano Island*

Harmon, Esther
1462 Larkspur Lane, 98292
(206) 629-4746

**Amenities:** 1,2,10,15,16,17
**Breakfast:** F.

**Dbl. Oc.:** $59.13 - $64.50
**Sgl. Oc.:** $43.00
**Third Person:** $16.13
**Child:** under 10 yrs. -
$16.13

**Willcox House Bed & Breakfast**—A country-style inn only one mile from the small town of Stanwood, on an island. Pleasantly serene. Furnished with antiques. Wonderful view of Cascades and Mt. Baker. A great place to relax, yet only one hour from Seattle and 30 minutes to historic Snohomish or LaConner.

## *Carnation*

Baer, Trivia
4548 Tolt River Rd., 98014
(206) 333-4262

**Amenities:** 1,2,3,6,7,9,10,
16,17
**Breakfast:** F.

**Dbl. Oc.:** $81.08 - $160.00
**Sgl. Oc.:** $70.50
**Third Person:** $27.03

**Idyl Inn On The River**—An exquisite villa country retreat with solar power. Indoor pool, sauna and steam room. Panoramic river setting. Large facilites. Privacy. Groups. Solo health stays. Rejuvenating. Romantic. Holistic. Hiking. Gardens. Near Snoqualmie Falls. Best in the Northwest. Antiques.

| | | | | |
|---|---|---|---|---|
| 1. No Smoking | 5. Tennis Available | 9. Credit Cards Accepted | 13. Lunch Available | 17. Shared Bath |
| 2. No Pets | 6. Golf Available | 10. Personal Checks Accepted | 14. Public Transportation | 18. Afternoon Tea |
| 3. No Children | 7. Swiming Available | 11. Off Season Rates | 15. Reservations Necessary | ★ Commissions given |
| 4. Senior Citizen Rates | 8. Skiing Available | 12. Dinner Available | 16. Private Bath | to Travel Agents |

## Coupeville

Cinney, Barbara & Jim
702 N. Main
P.O. Box 85, 98239
(206) 678-8000

**Amenities:** 1,2,3,4,5,6,7,9
,10,11,14,15,16
**Breakfast:** F.
**Dbl. Oc.:** $80.85 - $134.75
**Sgl. Oc.:** $75.85 - $129.75
**Third Person:** $15.00
**Child:** $15.00

**The Inn At Penn Cove**—Luxurious and historic. Two 100-year-old restored Victorians with all the comforts of today. Soak in claw-foot tubs or spas. Located in historic the seaport village of Coupeville on beautiful Whidbey Island, WA. Handicapped/ executive retreats/meetings.

## Coupeville *

Fresh, Dolores
602 N. Main
P.O. Box 761, 98239
(206) 678-5305

**Amenities:** 1,2,9,10,11,14,15,
16,18
**Breakfast:** F.

**Dbl. Oc.:** $80.85
**Third Person:** $10.00
**Child:** $10.00

**The Victorian Bed And Breakfast**—A graceful Italianate Victorian in the heart of a historic reserve. Two rooms in the house feature queen beds and private baths. The charming cottage is a private hideaway with queen bedroom, sitting room and bath - $102.41. Gourmet breakfast.

## Eatonville *

Gallagher, Catharine
116 Oak St. E., 98328
(206) 832-6506

**Amenities:** 1,4,7,8,9,10,16,17
**Breakfast:** F.
**Dbl. Oc.:** $60.00 - $80.00
**Sgl. Oc.:** $54.00 - $76.00
**Third Person:** $15.00
**Child:** under 10 yrs. - $5.00

**Old Mill House B&B**—Your password to the '20s! Built at a time of economic optimism, this lumber baron's home possesses spacious rooms, a shower in the master suite with seven heads and a Prohibition bar off the library. Put a wrinkle in time. Just say, "Joe sent me!"

| | | | | |
|---|---|---|---|---|
| 1. No Smoking | 5. Tennis Available | 9. Credit Cards Accepted | 13. Lunch Available | 17. Shared Bath |
| 2. No Pets | 6. Golf Available | 10. Personal Checks Accepted | 14. Public Transportation | 18. Afternoon Tea |
| 3. No Children | 7. Swiming Available | 11. Off Season Rates | 15. Reservations Necessary | ★ Commissions given |
| 4. Senior Citizen Rates | 8. Skiing Available | 12. Dinner Available | 16. Private Bath | to Travel Agents |

## *Edmonds*

Pinkham, Lynda & Tom
202 - 3rd Ave. So., 98020
(206) 774-3406

**Amenities:** 1,2,9,10,14,15,
16,18
**Breakfast:** F.

**Dbl. Oc.:** $60.00 - $93.00
**Sgl. Oc.:** $52.00 - $85.00
**Third Person:** $8.00
**Child:** $8.00

**Pinkham's Pillow Bed & Breakfast**—Our charming guest house offers turn-of-the-century decor and modern-day comfort in beautiful and historic Edmonds.

## *Ferndale* *

Anderson, Kelly & Dave
2140 Main St.
Box 1547, 98248
(206)384-3450

**Amenities:** 1,2,5,6,8,9,
10,14,15,16,17
**Breakfast:** F.
**Dbl. Oc.:** $48.84 - $80.85
**Sgl. Oc.:** $48.84 - $80.85
**Third Person:** $10.00
**Child:** $12.00

Anderson House

Bed & Breakfast Inn

**Anderson House Bed & Breakfast**—Perhaps the most famous of Whatcom country inns. Built in 1897. Dave and Kelly Anderson have restored the old landmark to its former charm. If this is your first B&B, it's a perfect choice. The guest book tells the entire story. This is where authors of B&B books stay!

## *Ferndale* *

Matz, Doris
5832 Church Rd., 98248
(206) 384-3619

**Amenities:** 1,4,6,9,10,14,
16,17
**Breakfast:** F.

**Dbl. Oc.:** $44.00 - $54.00
**Sgl. Oc.:** $39.00 - $44.00
**Third Person:** $10.00
**Child:** under 2 yrs. -
no charge

**Hill Top B&B**—"A quilt-lover's delight!" Large and comfortable rooms, one with a fireplace. Beds and walls warmed with an array of quilts made by your hostess. Private entry and patio. Spectacular mountain view. Children OK. Deposit required.

## *Friday Harbor* *

Robinson, Richard
365 Carter Ave., 98250
(206) 378-4730

**Amenities:** 1,2,3,5,6,7,9,10,
15,16,17,18
**Breakfast:** F.

**Dbl. Oc.:** $80.62 - $102.13
**Sgl. Oc.:** $75.25 - $96.75
**Third Person:** $26.88

**Hillside House**—A contemporary home on wooded acre. Panoramic views of harbor. Less than a mile from town. Six guest rooms; two with private bath and four sharing two baths. All with window seats. Country breakfast, coffee, tea, juices and ice always available. Perfect for reunions and groups.

| | | | | |
|---|---|---|---|---|
| 1. No Smoking | 5. Tennis Available | 9. Credit Cards Accepted | 13. Lunch Available | 17. Shared Bath |
| 2. No Pets | 6. Golf Available | 10. Personal Checks Accepted | 14. Public Transportation | 18. Afternoon Tea |
| 3. No Children | 7. Swiming Available | 11. Off Season Rates | 15. Reservations Necessary | ★ Commissions given |
| 4. Senior Citizen Rates | 8. Skiing Available | 12. Dinner Available | 16. Private Bath | to Travel Agents |

## *La Conner* *

Goldfarb, Peter
1388 Moore Rd.,
Mt. Vernon, 98273
(206) 445-6805

**Amenities:** 1,9,10,15,16,17
**Breakfast:** C.

**Dbl. Oc.:** $69.88 - $107.50
**Sgl. Oc.:** $64.50
**Third Person:** $25.00

**The White Swan Guest House**—A storybook Victorian farmhouse. Six miles to LaConner. Three guest rooms sharing two baths. Romantic garden cottage. English gardens, chocolate-chip cookies and country charm. One hour north of Seattle. Nearby are wonderful shops, galleries and restaurants. Birding,

## *Langley*

Metcalf, Senator Jack & Mrs. Norma
3273 E. Saratoga Rd., 98260
(206) 321-5483

**Amenities:** 1,2,3,9,10,14,16
**Breakfast:** F.
**Dbl. Oc.:** $65.00 - $97.00
**Sgl. Oc.:** $60.00 - $92.00
**Third Person:** $13.50

**Log Castle**—Escape to a log lodge on a secluded beach located on Whidbey Island. Big stone fireplace and turret bedrooms. Panoramic views of Puget Sound and Cascade Mountains. Norma's breakfasts are legendary. Watch for bald eagles and orca whales from the widow's walk.

## *Leavenworth* *

Turner, Karen & Monty
9308 E. Leavenworth Rd., 98826
(509) 548-7171

**Amenities:** 1,2,3,4,5,6,8,9,
      10,15,16,17,18
**Breakfast:** F.
**Dbl. Oc.:** $74.00 - $106.00
**Sgl. Oc.:** $64.00 - $96.00

**Run Of The River Bed & Breakfast**—Imagine the quintessential N.W. log bed and breakfast inn. Hand-hewn log beds, hand-stitched quilts and high pine cathedral ceilings. Spectacular Cascade views surrounded by bird refuge. Bountiful breakfasts. Smoke-free tranquility.

| | | |
|---|---|---|
| 1. No Smoking | 5. Tennis Available | 9. Credit Cards Accepted |
| 2. No Pets | 6. Golf Available | 10. Personal Checks Accepted |
| 3. No Children | 7. Swiming Available | 11. Off Season Rates |
| 4. Senior Citizen Rates | 8. Skiing Available | 12. Dinner Available |

| | | |
|---|---|---|
| 13. Lunch Available | 17. Shared Bath |
| 14. Public Transportation | 18. Afternoon Tea |
| 15. Reservations Necessary | ★ Commissions given |
| 16. Private Bath | to Travel Agents |

## *Mount Vernon* *

Benson, Linda & Vic
1957 Kanako Lane, 98273
(206) 428-1990

**Amenities:** 1,7,10,12,16
**Breakfast:** F.

**Dbl. Oc.:** $70.00 - $80.00
**Sgl. Oc.:** $60.00 - $70.00
**Third Person:** $10.00
**Child:** under 12 yrs. - $5.00

**Whispering Firs Bed And Breakfast**—One mile east of I-5 between the two LaConner exits. Set on our own 200 acres, high on a hill overlooking Skagit Valley and San Jaun Islands. Nearby hiking, private fishing, shops and dining. Large rooms, astounding views, 1 private baths, hot tub, huge deck and waterwheel.

## *Olympia* *

Williams-Young, Penny & Bob
1304 7th Ave. W., 98502
(206) 357-5520

**Amenities:** 1,10,11,14,15,16
**Breakfast:** F.

**Dbl. Oc.:** $55.40
**Sgl. Oc.:** $49.86
**Third Person:** $11.08
**Child:** under 6 yrs. -
no charge

**The Cinnamon Rabbit Bed & Breakfast**—A comfortable, older home in a quiet neighborhood. Close to downtown, Capital Mall and bus line. Relax in the hot tub, play the piano or borrow a cat for the evening. Check-in after 4:00 p.m. unless prearranged. No dogs, please.

## *Port Angeles*

Glass, Jane
1108 So. Oak, 98362
(206) 452-3138

**Amenities:** 1,2,5,6,7,8,9,10,
11,14,16,17,18
**Breakfast:** F.
**Dbl. Oc.:** $59.50 - $91.63

**Tudor Inn**—An award-winning bed and breakfast built in 1910. A historic home with European decor, antiques and English gardens. Five bedrooms with queen and king beds, one with private bath and four share two baths. Two downstairs fireplaces. Water or mountain views. Delicious breakfast.

## *Port Angeles*

Kennedy, Ann & Robert
214 Whidbey, 98362
(206) 457-6177

**Amenities:** 1,2,3,8,9,10,
11,17
**Breakfast:** F.

**Dbl. Oc.:** $53.90
**Sgl. Oc.:** $53.90

**Anniken's Bed And Breakfast**—A Scandinavian-type home with Northwestern hospitality. Wonderful views of the Olympic Mountains, Port Angeles harbor and Victoria, B.C. Five minutes to Olympic National Park and Victoria ferries. Comfortable.

| | | | | |
|---|---|---|---|---|
| 1. No Smoking | 5. Tennis Available | 9. Credit Cards Accepted | 13. Lunch Available | 17. Shared Bath |
| 2. No Pets | 6. Golf Available | 10. Personal Checks Accepted | 14. Public Transportation | 18. Afternoon Tea |
| 3. No Children | 7. Swiming Available | 11. Off Season Rates | 15. Reservations Necessary | ★ Commissions given |
| 4. Senior Citizen Rates | 8. Skiing Available | 12. Dinner Available | 16. Private Bath | to Travel Agents |

## Port Orchard

Ogle, Louise
1307 Dogwood Hill, SW., 98366
(206) 876-9170

Amenities:1,2,3,9,10,15,17

Breakfast: F.

Dbl. Oc.: $48.50
Sgl. Oc.: $37.75

**Ogle's Bed And Breakfast**—A single-story hillside home overlooking Puget Sound, Sinclair Inlet and moored Navy ships. Enjoy a full private breakfast in front of windows with beautiful views. Nearby marinas, antique shops, restaurants and outdoor farmers market. Ferry to Seattle.

## Port Townsend *

Deering, Joan & David
1208 Franklin St., 98368
(206) 385-6239

Amenities: 1,2,5,6,10,11,14, 16,17,18

Breakfast: F.

Dbl. Oc.: $64.50 - $97.00
Sgl. Oc.: $59.00 - $92.00

**The Apartment/Inn Deering**—Built in 1876 and renovated in 1986. Located in the heart of the national historic district. We know you will delight in the scrumptiously self-contained guest house and/or three comfortable rooms in the main house. Sparkling views of the mountains and Puget Bay.

## Port Townsend

Kelly, Michael
2037 Haines, 98368
(206) 385-6059

Amenities: 1,2,5,6,7,9,10,14, 15,16,17,18

Breakfast: F.

Dbl. Oc.: $60.00 - $100.00
Sgl. Oc.: $60.00 - $100.00
Third Person: $10.00

**Trenholm House Bed & Breakfast**—An 1890 Victorian farmhouse inn. Original woodwork. Five guest rooms and cottage furnished in country antiques. Gourmet breakfast. Beautiful lagoon and bay views. Make every stay memorable.

## Port Townsend

Sokol, Edel & Bob
744 Clay St., 98368
(206) 385-3205

Amenities: 1,2,3,5,6,7,8,9,10, 11,14,15,16,17

Breakfast: F.

Dbl. Oc.: $75.00 - $130.00
Third Person: $20.00

**Ann Starrett Mansion B&B**—The most photographed house in the Northwest. Features a one-of-a-kind spiral staircase, frescoed ceilings and solar calendar. Magnificent water and mountain views. The scrumptious breakfast will make you want to stay forever. A national historic landmark.

## Puyallup

Hart, Donna & Ray
7406 80th St. E.,, 98371
(206) 848-4594

Amenities: 1,2,3,4,5,8,10,15, 16,17

Breakfast: F.

Dbl. Oc.: $40.00 - $60.00
Third Person: $10.00

**Hart's Tayberry House**—A Victorian house with claw-foot tubs, tin-ceilinged kitchen and open stairway. Set amidst rolling country hills. Near Tacoma, Puget Sound and an hour from ski areas. Antiques, collectibles and vintage photographs reflect the warm hospitality of the hosts.

| | | | | |
|---|---|---|---|---|
| 1. No Smoking | 5. Tennis Available | 9. Credit Cards Accepted | 13. Lunch Available | 17. Shared Bath |
| 2. No Pets | 6. Golf Available | 10. Personal Checks Accepted | 14. Public Transportation | 18. Afternoon Tea |
| 3. No Children | 7. Swiming Available | 11. Off Season Rates | 15. Reservations Necessary | ★ Commissions given |
| 4. Senior Citizen Rates | 8. Skiing Available | 12. Dinner Available | 16. Private Bath | to Travel Agents |

## Republic *

| | | |
|---|---|---|
| Klemp, Jay | **Amenities:** 1,5,6,7,8,9,10, | **Dbl. Oc.:** $32.25 |
| P.O. Box 31, 99166 | 15,17 | **Sgl. Oc.:** $26.88 |
| (509) 775-3933 | **Breakfast:** C. Plus | **Third Person:** $5.38 |

**Triangle J. Ranch B&B**—Rest and relax on our 75-acre ranch. Enjoy a dip in the pool (summer) or a soak in the hot tub. Enjoy our many lakes, hiking/biking trails and Stonerose fossil dig. Winter activities in the area include skiing and fishing. We are also an American youth hostel.

## Seattle

| | | |
|---|---|---|
| Brown, Jerry | **Amenities:** 1,2,7,9,10,12,13, | **Dbl. Oc.:** $65.00 - $118.00 |
| 809 Fairview Pl. N., 98109 | 14,15,16,17 | **Sgl. Oc.:** $50.00 - $118.00 |
| (206) 340-1201 | **Breakfast:** F. | |

**Tugboat Challenger**—A fully functional tugboat with granite fireplace, laundry and hot-water heat. Downtown Seattle. TV, VCR, rental boats and views. Restaurants, shopping, Seattle Center and Seattle Convention Center are all within six blocks. Recognized in major publications (McCalls).

## Seattle *

Hagemeyer, Bunny & Bill
5005-22nd Ave. NE., 98105
(206) 522-2536

**Amenities:** 1,2,5,6,7,8,9,10,
1,14,15,16,17,18
**Breakfast:** F.
**Dbl. Oc.:** $89.00
**Sgl. Oc.:** $79.00
**Third Person:** $15.00
**Child:** under 12 yrs. - $10.00

**Chambered Nautilus Bed & Breakfast Inn**—Seattle's finest! A magnificent Georgian colonial set high on a hill in a convenient university district. Ten minutes from downtown. Carved ceilings, fireplaces, fully stocked bookcases and Persian rugs. English and American antiques. A gracious family welcome!

## Seattle *

| | | |
|---|---|---|
| Jones, Marylou & Dick | **Amenities:** 1,2,3,5,7,9,10,11, | **Dbl. Oc.:** $75.00 - $91.00 |
| 4915 Linden Ave. N., 98103 | 14,15,16,18 | **Third Person:** $11.00 |
| (206) 547-6077 | **Breakfast:** F. | |

**Chelsea Station Bed And Breakfast Inn**—Nestled amidst the city's activities and amenities in a peaceful, wooded setting. Near Greenlake and Seattle Zoo. Keep the comforts of home. Private baths, hot tub, full breakfast and bottomless cookie jar!

| | | | | |
|---|---|---|---|---|
| 1. No Smoking | 5. Tennis Available | 9. Credit Cards Accepted | 13. Lunch Available | 17. Shared Bath |
| 2. No Pets | 6. Golf Available | 10. Personal Checks Accepted | 14. Public Transportation | 18. Afternoon Tea |
| 3. No Children | 7. Swiming Available | 11. Off Season Rates | 15. Reservations Necessary | ★ Commissions given |
| 4. Senior Citizen Rates | 8. Skiing Available | 12. Dinner Available | 16. Private Bath | to Travel Agents |

## *Seattle*

Muia, Charlotte
2657 37th SW., 98126
(206) 938-1020

**Amenities:** 1,2,3,9,10,14,1
15,16
**Breakfast:** F.

**Dbl. Oc.:** $81.09 - $91.89
**Sgl. Oc.:** $75.67 - $86.48

**Hainsworth House**—West Seattle's historic mansion. Spectacular city and mountain views. Stroll along nearby Alki Beach. Ten minutes to downtown and 15 minutes from the airport. From the airport take I-5N to exit 163 West Seattle Freeway. Take Admiral Way exit to top of the hill and take 1st left.

## *Seattle*

Nichols, Nancy & Lindsey
1923 First Ave. #300, 98101
(206) 441-7125

**Amenities:** 9,10,11,14,17
**Breakfast:** C.

**Dbl. Oc.:** $65.00 - $85.00
**Sgl. Oc.:** $45.00 - $65.00
**Third Person:** $10.00 -
$15.00

**Pensione Nichols**—Seattle's only downtown bed and breakfast. Located in the Pike Place Market. European style, with a spectacular view of Puget Sound and the Market. Walk to Seattle's best sightseeing, shopping and restaurants. Relaxed and comfortable atmosphere.

## *Seattle*

Sarver, Mildred J.
1202-15th Ave. E., 98112
(206) 325-6072

**Amenities:** 1,2,5,6,9,10,14,
15,17,18
**Breakfast:** F.
**Dbl. Oc.:** $60.00
**Sgl. Oc.:** $50.00
**Third Person:** $15.00
**Child:** under 4 yrs. - no charge

**Mildred's Bed & Breakfast**—Step back in time at this 1890 Victorian home. Old-fashioned hospitality. Three guest rooms and private suite for two to four persons. A park and art museum across the street. City bus at the door. Minutes to freeway.

## *Silverdale* *

Fulton, Dennis
16609 Olympic View Rd. NW, 98383
(206) 692-4648

**Amenities:** 4,6,7,9,10,11,15,
16
**Breakfast:** C.

**Dbl. Oc.:** $149.00
**Sgl. Oc.:** $129.00
**Third Person:** $15.00
**Child:** under 3 yrs. -
no charge

**Seabreeze Beach Cottage**—Challenged by lapping waves at high tide, this private retreat will awaken your five senses with the smell of salty air and a taste of fresh oysters and clams. Views of the Olympic Mountains and the exhilaration of sun, surf and sand. Free brochure.

| | | | | |
|---|---|---|---|---|
| 1. No Smoking | 5. Tennis Available | 9. Credit Cards Accepted | 13. Lunch Available | 17. Shared Bath |
| 2. No Pets | 6. Golf Available | 10. Personal Checks Accepted | 14. Public Transportation | 18. Afternoon Tea |
| 3. No Children | 7. Swiming Available | 11. Off Season Rates | 15. Reservations Necessary | ★ Commissions given |
| 4. Senior Citizen Rates | 8. Skiing Available | 12. Dinner Available | 16. Private Bath | to Travel Agents |

## *So. Cle Elum* *

Moore, Monty
526 Marie St.
Box 2861, 98943
(509) 674-5939

**Amenities:** 1,2,5,6,7,8,9,10, 12,13,15,16,17
**Breakfast:** F.

**Dbl. Oc.:** $41.00 - $95.00
**Sgl. Oc.:** $30.00 - $95.00
**Third Person:** $10.00
**Child:** $10.00

**The Moore House Bed & Breakfast Country Inn**—Come and play with the seasons at our 11-room historic railway inn. Bring your family and stay in a caboose. Bring your loved one and enjoy the intimacy of the bridal suite. Stroll along adjacent Iron Horse State Park. Awake to the smell of fresh coffee and a country breakfast.

## *Spokane*

Bender, Jo Ann
E. 1729 18th St., 99203
(509) 534-1426 (day),
(509) 535-1893 (night)

**Amenities:** 1,2,9,14,15,17
**Breakfast:** C. and F.

**Dbl. Oc.:** $51.74
**Sgl. Oc.:** $46.35
**Third Person:** $10.00
**Child:** $10.00

**Hillside House B&B**—A house on a hillside overlooking the city and mountains. Hospitable hosts cater to traveling reps, as well as tourists. Quick or gourmet breakfasts. Adaptable to guests' needs. Nearby parks. Three miles to town. Airport pick-up. A member of the *Spokane B&B Association*.

## *Stevenson* *

Newmann, Neil
P.O. Box 377, 98648
(509) 427-4773

**Amenities:** 1,4,9,10,11,1, 16,17
**Breakfast:** F.

**Dbl. Oc.:** $59.18 - $134.50
**Sgl. Oc.:** $48.42 - 64.56
**Third Person:** $10.00

**Home Valley Bed & Breakfast**—A large cedar tri-level home on five grassy and wooded acres. Air conditioned. Furnished with antiques and items from around the world. Magnificent view high above the Columbia and Wind Rivers. Two spacious lounges with fireplaces, picture windows and large decks.

## *Sunnyside*

Vlieger, Karen & Donavon
800 E. Edison
P.O. Box 441, 98944
(509) 839-5557

**Amenities:** 1,5,6,9,12,13,16
**Breakfast:** F.

**Dbl. Oc.:** $45.00 - $65.00
**Third Person:** $15.00
**Child:** $15.00

**Sunnyside Inn Bed & Breakfast**—Eight luxurious rooms, all with private baths and seven with in-room jacuzzi tubs. Located in the heart of Washington wine country. Visit our 20 wineries and sample the abundance of the Yakima Valley. Come and stay at our house!

---

| | | | |
|---|---|---|---|
| 1. No Smoking | 5. Tennis Available | 9. Credit Cards Accepted | 13. Lunch Available | 17. Shared Bath |
| 2. No Pets | 6. Golf Available | 10. Personal Checks Accepted | 14. Public Transportation | 18. Afternoon Tea |
| 3. No Children | 7. Swiming Available | 11. Off Season Rates | 15. Reservations Necessary | ★ Commissions given |
| 4. Senior Citizen Rates | 8. Skiing Available | 12. Dinner Available | 16. Private Bath | to Travel Agents |

## *Vashon Island ★*

Kassik, Jacqueline
16529 - 91st Ave. SW, 98070
206) 463-2583

**Amenities:** 1,2,3,6,10,14,16
**Breakfast:** C.

**Dbl. Oc.:** $65.00
**Sgl. Oc.:** $65.00

**Artist's Studio Loft**—A lovely, private and spacious studio. Oak parquet floors, cathedral ceiling, skylights, stained glass and sun deck. Five acres. Features queen-size bed, TV, stereo, Mr. Coffee, refrigerator, microwave and bathroom with shower. Also, a wonderfully relaxing hot tub, deck and gazebo.

## *Winthrop*

Arquette, Joan
Hwy. 20
P.O. Box 371, 98862
(509) 996-2616

**Amenities:** 1,2,6,8,10,11, 15,17
**Breakfast:** C.

**Dbl. Oc.:** $59.50 - $70.00
**Sgl. Oc.:** $49.50 - $60.00
**Third Person:** $10.00
**Child:** under 12 yrs. - $5.00

**Piney Woods Inn**—Situated on 10 acres of pines, the inn has six rooms in two houses. Close to 150 Km. of cross-country track. Two miles from Winthrop, with many miles of hiking and biking. Hot tubs and kitchens. Great access to the Methow Valley and the North Cascades.

## *Winthrop ★*

Herman, Joan
Rader Rd., 98862
(509) 996-2173

**Amenities:** 1,6,7,8,10,12, 13,17
**Breakfast:** F.

**Dbl. Oc.:** $51.60
**Sgl. Oc.:** $46.23
**Third Person:** $5.00
**Child:** under 12 yrs. - $3.00

**Rader Road Inn**—Situated on 1-1/2 wooded acres in the beautiful Methow Valley. Within walking distance to historic downtown, Winthrop shops and restaurants. Enclosed pool and hot tub. Fifty yards from Methow River.

| | | | | |
|---|---|---|---|---|
| 1. No Smoking | 5. Tennis Available | 9. Credit Cards Accepted | 13. Lunch Available | 17. Shared Bath |
| 2. No Pets | 6. Golf Available | 10. Personal Checks Accepted | 14. Public Transportation | 18. Afternoon Tea |
| 3. No Children | 7. Swiming Available | 11. Off Season Rates | 15. Reservations Necessary | ★ Commissions given |
| 4. Senior Citizen Rates | 8. Skiing Available | 12. Dinner Available | 16. Private Bath | to Travel Agents |

# WEST VIRGINIA

## *The Mountain State*

Capitol:  Charleston
Statehood:  June 20, 1863, the 35th state
State Motto:  Mountaineers Are Always Free
State Song:  "The West Virginia Hills" and
                    "West Virginia, My Home Sweet Home"
State Bird:  Cardinal
State Flower:  Rhododendron
State Tree:  Sugar Maple


The state of West Virginia is an outgrowth of the Civil War. Unable to reconcile themselves to the southern philosophy, these western Virginians separated from Virginia at the height of the War and became allied with the union states, and subsequently called this area West Virginia.

West Virginia has some of the same beautiful scenery that Virginia has, along with mineral springs and plenty of hunting and fishing that brings delight to the many fishermen and hunters who come here every year.

The land is very mountainous and rugged, and has extensive bituminous coal beds. The major industry here has been and is coal mining.

Its pleasant climate, hunting, fishing and mineral springs has made it a most attractive state for tourists.

## Berkeley

Rudden, Jane
501 Johnson Mill Rd., 25411
(304) 258-4079

**Amenities:** 1,2,5,6,7,9,10,15, 16,17
**Breakfast:** F.

**Dbl. Oc.:** $65.00 - $87.00
**Sgl. Oc.:** $60.00 - $82.00
**Child:** under 5 yrs. - no charge

**Janesway Bed & Breakfast**—A century country home in the mountains with wrap-around porch and spectacular view of Warm Springs Ridge. Four guest rooms comfortably furnished for a getaway or romantic interlude. Come and enjoy a time you won't soon forget.

## Charles Town

Heiler, Jean
P.O. Box 1104, 25414
(304) 725-0637

**Amenities:** 2,3,6,9,10,15, **16,18**
**Breakfast:** F.

**Dbl. Oc.:** $85.00 - $130.00
**Sgl. Oc.:** $50.00 (weekdays)
**Third Person:** $20.00

**Gilbert House**—A beautiful, historic stone house (circa 1760) near Harpers Ferry and Antietam Battlefield. Close to I-81. Tasteful antiques, spacious rooms and bridal suite. Fireplace and private beaches. Nearby stream and gazebo. Located in a quaint village with its own ghost!

## Charles Town *

Simpson, Eleanor
Kabletown Rd. & Mill Lane
RR 2, Box 61-S, 25414
(304) 725-3371

**Amenities:** 2,5,6,9,10, 15,16,18
**Breakfast:** F.

**Dbl. Oc.:** $81.75 - $92.65
**Sgl. Oc.:** $70.85
**Third Person:** $10.00
**Child:** over 5 yrs. - $10.00

**Cottonwood Inn**—A beautifully restored Georgian farmhouse with six secluded acres on Bullskin Run. Seven guest rooms have private baths, TV, A/C, queen-size beds and sitting areas. Afternoon tea and sumptuous breakfasts are included. Children welcome.

## Elkins

Beardslee, Anne & Paul
Route 1, Box 59-1, 26241
(304) 636-1684

**Amenities:** 2,4,5,6,8,10,16
**Breakfast:** C.

**Dbl. Oc.:** $60.00
**Sgl. Oc.:** $60.00
**Third Person:** $15.00

**Tunnel Mountain Bed & Breakfast**—A charming three-story fieldstone B&B nestled on fivewooded acres surrounded by mountains. Year-round attractions include skiing, hiking, rafting, canoeing, antiquing, fishing, spelunking, fall leaves, festivals and more. Next to National Forest and Stuart recreation area.

| | | | | |
|---|---|---|---|---|
| 1. No Smoking | 5. Tennis Available | 9. Credit Cards Accepted | 13. Lunch Available | 17. Shared Bath |
| 2. No Pets | 6. Golf Available | 10. Personal Checks Accepted | 14. Public Transportation | 18. Afternoon Tea |
| 3. No Children | 7. Swiming Available | 11. Off Season Rates | 15. Reservations Necessary | ★ Commissions given |
| 4. Senior Citizen Rates | 8. Skiing Available | 12. Dinner Available | 16. Private Bath | to Travel Agents |

# WEST VIRGINIA

## Huttonsville

Murray, Loretta
General Delivery, 26273
(304) 335-6701

**Amenities:** 1,2,4,6,8,9,10,11, 12,13,16,17
**Breakfast:** F.

**Dbl. Oc.:** $49.05
**Sgl. Oc.:** $44.69
**Third Person:** $10.00
**Child:** under 10 yrs. - $5.00

**The Hutton House**—Visit our historically registered Queen Anne Victorian that is ideally located near many attractions. Gaze at the mountains as you sit on our wrap-around porch, while being served refreshments at your leisure.

## Martinsburg

Dunn, Dianna & Prince
Route 3, Box 33J, 25401
(304) 263-8646

**Amenities:** 1,2,3,9,10,15, 16,17
**Breakfast:** F.

**Dbl. Oc.:** $81.75 - $109.00
**Sgl. Oc.:** $76.30 - $103.55

**Dunn Country Inn**—Surrounded by acres of rolling pastures and woodlands providing a tranquil setting. Stone manor house built in 1805/1873 offers diversity in design and decor. Scrumptious breakfast specialties. Near Harpers Ferry National Historical Park and 60-store outlet mall.

## Martinsburg

Hotch, Ripley
601 S. Queen St., 25401
(304) 263-1448

**Amenities:** 1,2,3,6,7,8,9,10, 15,16,18
**Breakfast:** F.

**Dbl. Oc.:** $109.00 - $125.35
**Third Person:** $20.00

**Bodyville, The Inn At Martinsburg**—An 1812 plantation manor house in its own 14-acre park. Beautiful woodwork, huge rooms, spacious guest sitting areas and antiques. Books and magazines everywhere. Recommended by *Travel & Leisure magazine* and many others. Most important private historic house in the state.

## White Sulphur Springs

Griffith, Cheryl & Joe
208 E. Main St., 24986
(304) 536-9444

**Amenities:** 1,2,9,10,15,16
**Breakfast:** F.

**Dbl. Oc.:** $55.00
**Sgl. Oc.:** $50.00
**Third Person:** $10.00
**Child:** under 10 yrs. - $10.00

**The James Wylie House**—Located near the five-star resort (The Greenbier) in White Sulphur Springs. It is listed in the the *Register of Historic Places*. Less than a mile from I-64. Nearby fine resturants, shops, theatre and state parks. Nearby ski resorts. Hospitality! Two-bedroom suite available.

---

| | | | | |
|---|---|---|---|---|
| 1. No Smoking | 5. Tennis Available | 9. Credit Cards Accepted | 13. Lunch Available | 17. Shared Bath |
| 2. No Pets | 6. Golf Available | 10. Personal Checks Accepted | 14. Public Transportation | 18. Afternoon Tea |
| 3. No Children | 7. Swiming Available | 11. Off Season Rates | 15. Reservations Necessary | ★ Commissions given |
| 4. Senior Citizen Rates | 8. Skiing Available | 12. Dinner Available | 16. Private Bath | to Travel Agents |

# WISCONSIN

## *The Badger State*

Capitol:  Madison
Statehood:  May 29, 1848; the 30th state
State Motto:  Forward
State Song:  "On Wisconsin"
State Bird:  Robin
State Flower:  Wood Violet
State Tree:  Sugar Maple

Wisconsin means gathering of the waters. Water is everywhere in this state and water means fun. There is much boating and swimming and general all-around recreational activities. The cold and snow of winter brings downhill and cross-country skiing, with great ice-skating on the many ponds and lakes.

Dairy products and farming are the major industries here. Wisconsin is famous for its cheese. The early settlers from Switzerland and Germany brought their knowledge of how to make cheese with them, and it has been something Wisconsin has been famous for since those early times. The farms here also produce wonderful apples and berries.

The people of Wisconsin are proud of their state and are most hospitable and eager that you come and enjoy all their state has to offer.

## *Algoma*

Warren, Janice
N. 7136 Hwy. 42, 54201
(414) 487-3471 (summer),
(602) 968-2850 (winter)

**Amenities:** 6,7,9,10,16
**Breakfast:** F.

**Dbl. Oc.:** $57.75 - $78.75
**Sgl. Oc.:** $47.25
**Third Person:** $5.00
**Child:** $5.00

**Amberwood Inn**—A country inn on the shore of Lake Michigan. All rooms have decks and double French doors that face the lake. Multi-room suites with wet bar available. Sleep to the soothing sound of the waves. Awaken to spectacular sun rise over the water. Experience country hospitality and charm.

## *Cedarburg*

Brown, Elizabeth & Brook
W61, N520 Washington, 53012
(414) 375-0208

**Amenities:** 1,2,3,5,6,8,9,10, 11,15,16
**Breakfast:** C. Plus

**Dbl. Oc.:** $57.75 - $89.25
**Sgl. Oc.:** $47.25 - $89.25
**Third Person:** $10.00

**Stagecoach Inn Bed & Breakfast**—A historic and restored 1853 Greek Revival stone building. Twelve cozy and comfortable rooms offer the charm of stenciled walls, Laura Ashley comforters and modern conveniences. Breakfast includes hot croissants, cereal, coffee, juice and delicious homemade jams and jellies.

## *Cedarburg* *

Porterfield, Wendy
W62 N573 Washington Ave., 53012
(800) 369-4088,
(414) 375-3550

**Amenities:** 2,4,6,9,10,11,12, 13,15,16
**Breakfast:** C. (buffet)

**Dbl. Oc.:** $61.95 - $145.95
**Third Person:** $10.00
**Child:** $10.00

**Washington House Inn**—Located 25 minutes north of Milwaukee, in historic Cedarburg. Twenty-nine rooms, all with private baths, most with whirlpools and some with fireplaces. Features country and Victorian rooms with antiques and down quilts. Meeting room and sauna available.

## *Eagle*

Herriges, Riene & Dean
W370 S9590, Hwy .67, 53119
(414) 594-3304

**Amenities:** 1,2,6,7,8,10,16
**Breakfast:** C. and F.

**Dbl. Oc.:** $72.45 - $103.95
**Third Person:** $15.75

**Eagle Centre House Bed & Breakfast**—A replicated 1850's Greek Revival stagecoach inn decorated in antiques. Four rooms with private baths, two with whirlpools. In Southern Kettle Moraine Forest, near Old World, Wisconsin. Outdoor Living Historic Museum. Ninety miles from Chicago and 30 miles from Milwaukee.

| | | | |
|---|---|---|---|
| 1. No Smoking | 5. Tennis Available | 9. Credit Cards Accepted | 13. Lunch Available | 17. Shared Bath |
| 2. No Pets | 6. Golf Available | 10. Personal Checks Accepted | 14. Public Transportation | 18. Afternoon Tea |
| 3. No Children | 7. Swiming Available | 11. Off Season Rates | 15. Reservations Necessary | ★ Commissions given |
| 4. Senior Citizen Rates | 8. Skiing Available | 12. Dinner Available | 16. Private Bath | to Travel Agents |

## Eagle River *

Kalous, Darlene
1429 Silver Lake Rd., 54521
(715) 479-2215

**Amenities:** 2,3,5,6,7,8,10, 15,16
**Breakfast:** F.

**Dbl. Oc.:** $88.00
**Sgl. Oc.:** $88.00

**Cranberry Inn**—A converted coach house in a north woods setting. Clean and comfortable rooms. Situated on eight acres on Yellow Birch Lake, a chain of 28 lakes. Fishing and boating. Adjacent to authentic Finnish sauna. One mile to town; 3-20 miles to Nicolet and Ottowa National Forests.

## East Troy *

Leibner, Ruth
770 Adam's Church Rd., 53120
(414) 495-8485

**Amenities:** 2,9,10,15,17
**Breakfast:** F.

**Dbl. Oc.:** $58.00
**Sgl. Oc.:** $42.20
**Third Person:** $10.55
**Child:** under 12 yrs. - $5.28

**Greystone Farms Bed & Breakfast**—Tucked away on a hill above a quiet back road in the Southern Kettle Moraine sits this 1880's farmhome. Clean, comfortable lodging with great food. Old-fashioned charm and hospitality. Only 40 minutes southwest of Milwaukee and two hours northwest of Chicago. Hike, bike and rest.

## Ephraim

Fisher, Walt
3052 Spruce Lane
Box 129, 54211
(414) 854-4001

**Amenities:** 1,2,3,5,6,7,8,10,11,16,17
**Breakfast:** C.
**Dbl. Oc.:** $47.50 - $72.00
**Sgl. Oc.:** $42.50 - $67.00

**The French Country Inn Of Ephraim**—Seven guest rooms (four in winter) and a two-bedroom cottage. Peaceful garden setting. 100 yards from the water. Large stone fireplace, French doors, casement windows, lace curtains, ceiling fans and spacious common rooms. Gift certificates. Door County. Free brochure.

---

| | | | |
|---|---|---|---|
| 1. No Smoking | 5. Tennis Available | 9. Credit Cards Accepted | 13. Lunch Available | 17. Shared Bath |
| 2. No Pets | 6. Golf Available | 10. Personal Checks Accepted | 14. Public Transportation | 18. Afternoon Tea |
| 3. No Children | 7. Swiming Available | 11. Off Season Rates | 15. Reservations Necessary | ★ Commissions given |
| 4. Senior Citizen Rates | 8. Skiing Available | 12. Dinner Available | 16. Private Bath | to Travel Agents |

## Fish Creek

Falck-Pedersen, Christine & Sverre
4135 Bluff Rd.
P.O. Box 490, 54212
(414) 868-2444

**Amenities:** 1,2,3,5,6,7,8,10,11,17
**Breakfast:** C.
**Dbl. Oc.:** $55.92 - $69.63
**Sgl. Oc.:** $50.64 - $64.36

**Thorp House Inn**—Located just 1-1/2 blocks from the water's edge in the tiny village of Fish Creek (center of Door County). History and romance. Four antique-filled guest rooms, parlor with fireplace and cozy library. Also, "country antique" cottages, some with fireplaces.

## Hudson

Miller, Sharon
1109 3rd St., 54016
(715) 386-7111

**Amenities:** 1,2,3,6,7,8,10,15, 16,18
**Breakfast:** C.(weekday), F.(weekend)

**Dbl. Oc.:** $70.73 - $146.48
**Sgl. Oc.:** $59.68
**Third Person:** $20.00
**Child:** 9-18 yrs. - $10.00

**Jefferson-Day House**—This 1857 antique-filled Italianate home on a historic tree-lined street is two blocks from the St. Croix River and 20 minutes from St. Paul and Minneapolis. All rooms have private baths and air-conditioning. Two are suites with double whirlpools. Three-course fireside breakfasts.

## La Farge

Boyett, Rosanne
Route 2, Box 121, 54639
(608) 625-4492

**Amenities:** 2,5,6,7,8,10, 11,1516
**Breakfast:** F.

**Dbl. Oc.:** $63.00
**Sgl. Oc.:** $45.00
**Third Person:** $15.00
**Child:** under 13 yrs. -
no charge

**Trillium Country Cottage**—A cozy and private cottage. Fully furnished. Large porch, hammock, grill, picnic table, full kitchen and complete bath. Near state parks, three rivers, historic sites, Amish farms, lakes, House on the Rock and Circus World.

## Madison

Elder, Polly
424 N. Pinckney St., 53703
(608) 255-3999

**Amenities:** 2,3,9,10,11,12,15, 16,18
**Breakfast:** C.

**Dbl. Oc.:** $112.00 - $280.00
**Sgl. Oc.:** $90.00 - $260.00
**Third Person:** $20.00

**Mansion Hill Inn**—Victorian elegance abounds in our 11 exquisite suites. Bask in the luxury of whirlpool baths, fireplaces and 24-hour valet service. Located downtown, near the capitol and university. We await your pleasure.

| | | | |
|---|---|---|---|
| 1. No Smoking | 5. Tennis Available | 9. Credit Cards Accepted | 13. Lunch Available | 17. Shared Bath |
| 2. No Pets | 6. Golf Available | 10. Personal Checks Accepted | 14. Public Transportation | 18. Afternoon Tea |
| 3. No Children | 7. Swiming Available | 11. Off Season Rates | 15. Reservations Necessary | ★ Commissions given |
| 4. Senior Citizen Rates | 8. Skiing Available | 12. Dinner Available | 16. Private Bath | to Travel Agents |

# WISCONSIN

## Merrill

Ullmer, Kris & Randy
108 S. Cleveland St., 54452
(715) 536-3230

**Amenities:** 1,2,3,5,6,7,8,9,10, 14,17
**Breakfast:** F.

**Dbl. Oc.:** $45.00 - $50.00
**Sgl. Oc.:** $40.00 - $45.00

**The Brick House Bed & Breakfast**—Beveled glass doors lead to a crackling fireplace in this 1915 prairie-style home. The Daly Room features antique furnishings. A ceiling fan stirs a breeze in the pastel veranda room. Nearby cross-country ski trails, canoeing, parks and golfing.

## Merrill *

Zimmerman, Loretta & Dan
700 W. Main St., 54452
(715) 536-7744

**Amenities:** 1,2,3,5,6,7,8,9,10,16
**Breakfast:** F.
**Dbl. Oc.:** $55.00 - $90.00
**Third Person:** $10.00

**Candlewick Inn**—Experience the beauty of the past at this elegantly restored 1883 mansion. All guest rooms are appointed with antiques, complementing this former lumber baron's home. Fireplaces, gift shop and spacious screened porch. Hiking, biking and state parks.

## Newton *

Stuntz, Judie & Pete
8825 Willever Lane, 53063
(414) 726-4388

**Amenities:** 7,8,10,15,16,17
**Breakfast:** F.

**Dbl. Oc.:** $42.00
**Sgl. Oc.:** $31.50
**Third Person:** $10.50
**Child:** under 18 yrs. - $10.50

**Rambling Hills Tree Farm**—A modern country home on 50 acres with scenic views of a lake and pond. Nestled among rolling hills with hiking trails. Popular lakeshore area, 71 miles north of Milwaukee and three miles off I-43. Near Maritime Museum, Kohler Design and Road America.

## Port Washington *

Merg, Richard
832 W. Grand Ave. (Hwy. 33), 53074
(414) 284-6719

**Amenities:** 1,2,3,4,5,6,9,10, 15,16
**Breakfast:** C. and F.

**Dbl. Oc.:** $63.00 - $99.75
**Sgl. Oc.:** $63.00 - $99.75

**The Grand Inn**—Looking for a hideaway? Our turn-of-the-century Victorian is two miles from I-43, in a small New England-like community. Our home is elegantly furnished with antiques and period furniture. Queen-size beds and private bath with two-person whirlpools. Friday and Saturday - $150.00.

| | | | |
|---|---|---|---|
| 1. No Smoking | 5. Tennis Available | 9. Credit Cards Accepted | 13. Lunch Available | 17. Shared Bath |
| 2. No Pets | 6. Golf Available | 10. Personal Checks Accepted | 14. Public Transportation | 18. Afternoon Tea |
| 3. No Children | 7. Swiming Available | 11. Off Season Rates | 15. Reservations Necessary | ★ Commissions given |
| 4. Senior Citizen Rates | 8. Skiing Available | 12. Dinner Available | 16. Private Bath | to Travel Agents |

# WISCONSIN

## Sparta *

Justin, Donna & Don
Route 1, Box 274, 54656
(608) 269-4522

**Amenities:** 1,2,4,8,9,10,
15,1617
**Breakfast:** F.

**Dbl. Oc.:** $58.00 - $100.22
**Sgl. Oc.:** $52.75 - $89.67
**Child:** no charge

**Just-N-Trails B&B Farm Vacation**—New plush and granary heart-shaped whirlpool. Fireplace, air-conditioning and queen bed. A 1988 "Little House on the Prairie" log cabin. Perfect for children. Loft, bath, four rooms in farmhouse, two private baths, Laura Ashley linens, active dairy farm, zoo and acres to roam. Miles of trails.

## Sturgeon Bay

Pichette, James
132 N. 2nd Ave., 54235
(414) 743-4854

**Amenities:** 2,9,10,11,15,16
**Breakfast:** C.

**Dbl. Oc.:** $89.68 - $126.60
**Sgl. Oc.:** $71.74 - $101.28

**The Barbican**—Elegant lodging in beautiful Door County. Two turn-of-the-century homes furnished with quality antiques. Suites include double whirlpool, queen-size bed, fireplace, refrigerator, TV, stereo and room-service breakfast. Minutes from all Door County activities.

| | | | |
|---|---|---|---|
| 1. No Smoking | 5. Tennis Available | 9. Credit Cards Accepted | 13. Lunch Available | 17. Shared Bath |
| 2. No Pets | 6. Golf Available | 10. Personal Checks Accepted | 14. Public Transportation | 18. Afternoon Tea |
| 3. No Children | 7. Swiming Available | 11. Off Season Rates | 15. Reservations Necessary | ★ Commissions given |
| 4. Senior Citizen Rates | 8. Skiing Available | 12. Dinner Available | 16. Private Bath | to Travel Agents |

# WYOMING

## *The Equality State*

Capitol: Cheyenne
Statehood: July 10, 1890; the 44th state
State Motto: Equal Rights
State Song: "Wyoming"
State Bird: Meadow Lark
State Flower: Indian Paintbrush
State Tree: Cottonwood

This is a very beautiful and scenic state. Its climate is dry and sunny with cold and snowy winters and warm summers. The majestic Rocky Mountain peaks tower over much of this land. The oldest national park, Yellowstone, was founded here by John Colter in 1807. The first national monument, Devil's Tower, was dedicated by President Teddy Roosevelt. The beautiful Teton Park and Fort Laramie, established in 1840 to protect the white man from Indians as he crossed this state in covered wagons, contribute to the fascination of this state for tourists.

Women won the right to vote here in 1869 and in 1870, Esther Morris became the first Justice of the Peace in the U.S. In 1925, Nellie Tayloe Ross became the first woman to become Governor.

# WYOMING

## Casper *

McInroy, Opal L.
6905 Speas Rd., 5120 Alcova Route
P.O. Box 40, 82604
(307) 265-6819

**Amenities:** 1,2,5,6,7,8,10,12, 13,17,18
**Breakfast:** F.

**Dbl. Oc.:** $42.50
**Sgl. Oc.:** $32.00
**Third Person:** $11.00
**Child:** $11.00

**Bessemer Bend Bed And Breakfast**—A large home in a scenic area 10 miles southwest of Casper, on North Platte River. Two miles from fish hatchery. Historic area with wildlife. Tours arranged. Fishing, recreation room and hiking.

---

## Douglas

Middleton, Pauline
1200 Poison Lake Rd., 82633
(307) 358-2033

**Amenities:** 1,9,10,12,13, 15,16,18
**Breakfast:** F.

**Dbl. Oc.:** $74.20
**Sgl. Oc.:** $37.10
**Third Person:** $37.10
**Child:** under 16 yrs. - $15.90

**Deer Forks Ranch**—A working cattle and sheep ranch. 19,000 acres available for outdoor recreation, including riding, hiking, fishing and hunting. Guest houses are fully furnished for housekeeping. Guests can bring their own food at reduced rates. Open June through October.

---

## Encampment

Platt, Mayvon
Star Route 49, 82325
(307) 327-5539

**Amenities:** 1,8,10,15,17
**Breakfast:** F.

**Dbl. Oc.:** $72.80
**Sgl. Oc.:** $36.40
**Child:** under 6 yrs. - $10.70

**Platt's Rustic Mountain Lodge**—Peaceful mountain view and wholesome country atmosphere with lots of Western hospitality. Hayrides, horseback riding, fishing, hiking and rock hounding. Guided tours to scenic mountain areas. Enjoy the flora and fauna, historic trails, mining camps, snowmobiling and cross-country skiing.

---

## Guernsey

Dombeck, Annette
239 S. Dakota, 82214
(307) 836-2148

**Amenities:** 5,6,7,10,17
**Breakfast:** C. and F.

**Dbl. Oc.:** $30.00
**Sgl. Oc.:** $25.00
**Third Person:** $5.00
**Child:** under 5 yrs. - $5.00

**Annette's White House**—Located in an area where there are many historical sites. Beautiful Lake Guernsey State Park, golfing, swimming and fishing. Platte River runs along the city. Nearby are three restaurants. On the way to Yellowstone and wonderful Wyoming. Three bedrooms.

---

| | | | |
|---|---|---|---|
| 1. No Smoking | 5. Tennis Available | 9. Credit Cards Accepted | 13. Lunch Available | 17. Shared Bath |
| 2. No Pets | 6. Golf Available | 10. Personal Checks Accepted | 14. Public Transportation | 18. Afternoon Tea |
| 3. No Children | 7. Swiming Available | 11. Off Season Rates | 15. Reservations Necessary | ★ Commissions given |
| 4. Senior Citizen Rates | 8. Skiing Available | 12. Dinner Available | 16. Private Bath | to Travel Agents |

## Jackson

Jern, Sherrie & Ken
3725 Teton Village Rd., 83001
(307) 733-4710

**Amenities:** 1,2,5,6,7,8,9,10, 15,16
**Breakfast:** F.

**Dbl. Oc.:** $120.00
**Third Person:** $15.00
**Child:** under 12 yrs. - no charge

**The Wildflower Inn**—A lovely log home on three acres within 10 minutes of skiing, town and national parks. We have five guest rooms, a large jacuzzi and wonderful mountain views. A full breakfast is served overlooking our pond.

## Lander

Ratigan, Rose & Dan
548 No. Fork Rd., 82520
(307) 332-6442

**Amenities:** 1,2,4,9,10,15, 16,17
**Breakfast:** F.

**Dbl. Oc.:** $60.00
**Sgl. Oc.:** $55.00
**Third Person:** $15.00
**Child:** no charge - $15.00

**Black Mountain Ranch**—Discover our treasures and country comfort. Nestled along the Popo Agie River in the foothills of the Wind River Mountains. On the way to Yellowstone. Nearby trout fishing, hiking, horseback riding and Wind River Indian Reservation. Open May 1 - October 1.

## Laramie *

Harm, Duane
2091 State Hwy. 130, 82070
(307) 745-7036

**Amenities:** 6,8,9,10,11,12, 13,14,15,16
**Breakfast:** F.
**Dbl. Oc.:** $78.98
**Sgl. Oc.:** $69.45
**Third Person:** $9.53
**Child:** under 12 yrs. - $10.50

**Vee Bar Guest Ranch**—A beautiful and historic 100-year-old lodge located 21 miles west of Laramie. Lovely antique furniture throughout. Private bath in each room. Fishing, horseback riding and meals available.

## Laramie *

Kopulos, Diana
819 University, 82070
(307) 721-4177

**Amenities:** 1,2,9,10,15,17
**Breakfast:** C.

**Dbl. Oc.:** $48.15 - $58.85
**Sgl. Oc.:** $37.45 - $48.15
**Third Person:** $10.00
**Child:** under 1 yr. - no charge

**Annie Moore's Guest House**—A cheerfully decorated Queen Anne-style home. Six guest rooms with sunny common areas. Across the street from the University of Wyoming. Close to downtown shops and restaurants. Thirty minutes from spectacular and uncrowded wilderness. Skiing, hiking and fishing.

| | | | | |
|---|---|---|---|---|
| 1. No Smoking | 5. Tennis Available | 9. Credit Cards Accepted | 13. Lunch Available | 17. Shared Bath |
| 2. No Pets | 6. Golf Available | 10. Personal Checks Accepted | 14. Public Transportation | 18. Afternoon Tea |
| 3. No Children | 7. Swiming Available | 11. Off Season Rates | 15. Reservations Necessary | ★ Commissions given |
| 4. Senior Citizen Rates | 8. Skiing Available | 12. Dinner Available | 16. Private Bath | to Travel Agents |

## *Wilson*

Becker, Chris & Denny
Box 550, 83014
(307) 733-3233

**Amenities:** 1,2,9,10,11,15,16
**Breakfast:** F.

**Dbl. Oc.:** $90.95 - $112.35
**Sgl. Oc.:** $85.60 - $107.00
**Third Person:** $17.00
**Child:** $17.00

**Teton Tree House**—Our mountain house is a rustic open-beam home with a large living and dining room where our guests are welcome. The five bedrooms have large windows and decks with special views. Featured in Sunday travel section of the *New York Times* - May 21, 1989.

## *Wilson* *

Neil, Jane
2136 Coyote Loop, 83014
(307) 733-7954

**Amenities:** 1,5,6,7,8,9,10,11,
15,16,17
**Breakfast:** C.

**Dbl. Oc.:** $64.20 - $85.60
**Sgl. Oc.:** $58.85 - $80.25
**Third Person:** $10.70
**Child:** under 2 yrs. -
no charge

**Teton View Bed And Breakfast**—Cozy country-decor rooms with spectacular ski-resort views. Large deck and backyard for relaxation and games. Private entrance. Wonderful homemade pastries and coffee. Laundry and refrigerator available. Ten miles from Grand Teton National Park and one hour from Yellowstone.

---

| | | | |
|---|---|---|---|
| 1. No Smoking | 5. Tennis Available | 9. Credit Cards Accepted | 13. Lunch Available | 17. Shared Bath |
| 2. No Pets | 6. Golf Available | 10. Personal Checks Accepted | 14. Public Transportation | 18. Afternoon Tea |
| 3. No Children | 7. Swiming Available | 11. Off Season Rates | 15. Reservations Necessary | ★ Commissions given |
| 4. Senior Citizen Rates | 8. Skiing Available | 12. Dinner Available | 16. Private Bath | to Travel Agents |

# BED & BREAKFAST HOMES & INNS IN THE PROVINCES OF CANADA AND THE CARIBBEAN

# ALBERTA

## *The Westernmost Prairie Province of Canada*

Capitol: Edmonton
Entered The Dominion: September 1, 1905; the
8th province
The Floral Emblem: Wild Rose

Alberta is the largest of the prairie provinces. Because of the oil boom in 1947, it is one of the wealthiest provinces as well.

Some of the most attractive scenery to be found is in this area are the majestic snow-capped Canadian Rockies, and Banff and Jasper National Parks. Tourists can ride horseback through these areas, as well as enjoy boating, golfing and swimming.

## Calgary

Turgeon, Eileen
4903 Viceroy Dr., N.W., T3A 0V2
(403) 288-0494

**Amenities:** 1,2,3,12,14,15,17
**Breakfast:** F.
**Dbl. Oc.:** $45.00(CN)
**Sgl. Oc.:** $30.00(CN)

**Turgeons Bed & Breakfast**—Warm and friendly Western hospitality. Home is located in a quiet northwest residential area. Park at end of street, close to two shopping centers, University of Calgary, Canada Olympic Park and many other attractions. There is a dog and cat on the premises.

## Canmore *

Doucette, Mrs. Patricia
P.O. Box 1162, T0L 0M0
(403) 678-4751

**Amenities:** 1,2,3,5,6,7,8, 13,17
**Breakfast:** F.

**Dbl. Oc.:** $50.00(CN)
**Sgl. Oc.:** $35.00(CN)
**Third Person:** $10.00(CN)
**Child:** under 18 yrs. - $5.00(CN)

**Cougar Creek Inn**—A quiet, rustic cedar chalet with mountain views in each direction. Grounds border Cougar Creek. Walk along creek into mountains where wildlife is often seen. Area offers skiing, hiking, mountain biking, backpacking, tennis and golf. Relax by the fire or picnic in the backyard.

## Claresholm *

Laing, Anola & Gordon
Box 340, T0L 0T0
(403) 625-4389

**Amenities:** 1,2,17,18
**Breakfast:** F.

**Dbl. Oc.:** $45.00 - $95.00(CN)
**Sgl. Oc.:** $35.00(CN)

**Anola's Bed & Breakfast**—A three-room cozy country cottage. Ideal for honeymooners. Decorated in early 1900's. Or stay in our farmhouse. Private two-bedroom suite. Hot tub. Browse through Grandad's museum. 3,800-acre grain farm located on Highway 520. Nine miles north of Lethbridge.

---

| | | | |
|---|---|---|---|
| 1. No Smoking | 5. Tennis Available | 9. Credit Cards Accepted | 13. Lunch Available | 17. Shared Bath |
| 2. No Pets | 6. Golf Available | 10. Personal Checks Accepted | 14. Public Transportation | 18. Afternoon Tea |
| 3. No Children | 7. Swiming Available | 11. Off Season Rates | 15. Reservations Necessary | ★ Commissions given |
| 4. Senior Citizen Rates | 8. Skiing Available | 12. Dinner Available | 16. Private Bath | to Travel Agents |

# BRITISH COLUMBIA

## Canada's Third Largest Province

Capitol: Victoria
Entered The Dominion: July 20, 1871; the 6th province
Motto: Unfailing Splendor
The Floral Emblem: Flowering Dogwood

British Columbia is the westernmost province of Canada. It is a powerful province with great potential. It possesses great lands that can be used to grow crops, large mineral deposits, and enormous tracts of forest.

Victoria is the capitol of this province and has an excellent harbor. Visitors come from all over to purchase imported goods that come into this harbor as well as Vancouver's harbor on this southwestern coast.

The temperature is pleasant. Because of the mild winds from the Pacific Ocean, British Columbia's coast in the winter is fairly warm and cool in the summer. This king of moderate climate makes for a wide range of recreational advantages.

# BRITISH COLUMBIA

## Ganges *

DeWest, Mrs. Maureen
930 Sunset Dr., RR 1, V0S 1E0
(604) 537-2879,
Fax: (604) 537-4747

**Amenities:** 1,2,3,5,6,7,9,10,
15,16
**Breakfast:** F.

**Dbl. Oc.:** $150.00 (CN)
**Sgl. Oc.:** $150.00 (CN)
**Third Person:** $25.00(CN)

**Beach House B&B**—At the water's edge on 400 feet of beach. Two cottages, suites with ocean views, balcony and private entrances. Charter salmon fishing or island day tours by boat. Complimentary sherry, fresh fruit and flowers.

---

## Greater Vancouve *

McCurrach, Norma
4390 Frances St., Burnaby,
V5C 2R3
(604) 298-8815, (Fax) (604) 298-5917

**Amenities:** 4,9,11,14,15,16,17
**Breakfast:** F.

**Dbl. Oc.:** $60.00(CN)
**Sgl. Oc.:** $45.00(CN)
**Third Person:** $45.00(CN)
**Child:** under 11 yrs. -
$10.00(CN)

**An English Garden Bed & Breakfast, Ltd.**—Offers a king bed and private bath, plus an adjoining loft room with twin beds suitable for second couple or friends traveling together. Fifteen minutes to major tourist attractions and excellent restaurants.

---

## Mill Bay *

Clarke, Clifford
3191 Mutter Rd., V0R 2P0
(604) 743-4083

**Amenities:** 1,2,6,7,9,10,15,16
**Breakfast:** F.
**Dbl. Oc.:** $75.00 - $85.00(CN)
**Sgl. Oc.:** $50.00 - $60.00(CN)
**Third Person:** $15.00(CN)
**Child:** under 5 yrs. - $10.00(CN)

**Pine Lodge Farm Bed & Breakfast**—Situated on a 30-acre farm overlooking the sea and islands. Magnificent arbutus trees, farm animals and walking trails add to the Paradise-like setting. Each room, furnished with antiques, looks over a magnificent lounge and floor-to-ceiling fireplace.

---

## Nanoose Bay

Chapman, Leone
3161 Dolphin Dr. (location)
Box 26, Blueback Dr. RR2, V0R 2R0 (mail)
(604) 468-9241

**Amenities:** 1,2,7,15,16,17,1
**Breakfast:** C. and F.

**Dbl. Oc.:** $55.00 - $85.00(CN)
**Sgl. Oc.:** $55.00 - $75.00(CN)
**Third Person:** $20.00(CN)
**Child:** under 12 yrs.-
$15.00(CN)

**Oceanside Bed And Breakfast And Vacation Suite**—On Vancouver Island secluded among tall evergreens with spectacular ocean view. Relax on the deck or sandy beach and watch eagles, herons, otters and seals. Swim in the ocean or go salmon fishing with your hosts. Nearby golfing, hiking, trail riding and dining.

---

| | | | |
|---|---|---|---|
| 1. No Smoking | 5. Tennis Available | 9. Credit Cards Accepted | 13. Lunch Available | 17. Shared Bath |
| 2. No Pets | 6. Golf Available | 10. Personal Checks Accepted | 14. Public Transportation | 18. Afternoon Tea |
| 3. No Children | 7. Swiming Available | 11. Off Season Rates | 15. Reservations Necessary | ★ Commissions given |
| 4. Senior Citizen Rates | 8. Skiing Available | 12. Dinner Available | 16. Private Bath | to Travel Agents |

## Nanoose Bay

Wilkie, Marjorie
3381 Dolphin Dr., RR 2, V0R 2R0
(604) 468-9796

**Amenities:** 1,2,3,5,6,7,8,10, 10,11,15,16,17
**Breakfast:** F.

**Dbl. Oc.:** $50.00 - $70.00 (CN)
**Sgl. Oc.:** $40.00(CN)
**Third Person:** $15.00(CN)

**"The Lookout"**—Mid-way from Victoria to Tofino. Spectacular view of Georgia Strait. Relax on wrap-around deck and enjoy boats, cruise ships, eagles and majestic mountains. Fair winds golf four minutes away. Marina and resort two minutes away. What you want, when you want it.

## Saanichton

Black, Johanna
8243 Alec Rd., RR 2, V0S 1M0
(604) 652-9183

**Amenities:** 1,2,4,5,6,7,9,10, 11,12,13,15,16,18
**Breakfast:** F.

**Dbl. Oc.:** $80.00 - $130.00 (CN)
**Sgl. Oc.:** $60.00 - $100.00 (CN)
**Third Person:** $30.00(CN)
**Child:** under 10 yrs.- $10.00(CN)

**Arbutus Acres**—Where trees, mountains, water and sky fill the view from this 4,000-square-foot home set on 13 wooded acres. Vast skylights, 60 feet of deck, five bedrooms (one that sleeps six), jacuzzi, music and VCR await you. Come soon! Johanna welcomes you.

## Saanichton *

Laschuk, Tairroyn
629 Senanus Dr., V0S 1M0
(604) 652-4434

**Amenities:** 2,3,5,6,7,10,15, 16,17,18
**Breakfast:** F.

**Dbl. Oc.:** $95.00 - $125.00(CN)
**Sgl. Oc.:** $75.00(CN)
**Third Person:** $25.00(CN)

**Tiffany Bay Oceanfront Bed And Breakfast**—For those special moments, join us on the water's edge amid sights and sounds of seals and sea lions. Experience moonlit swims form private cove or oceanside pool. Nestled on two acres of woodland, discover tranquility when you breakfast at Tiffany's.

## Snoke

Pettinger, C. June
1965 Glenidle Rd., V0S 1N0
(604) 642-6168

**Amenities:** 2,3,6,9,15
**Breakfast:** F.

**Dbl. Oc.:** $45.00(CN)
**Sgl. Oc.:** $35.00(CN)

**Lavender Lane Bed & Breakfast**—Enjoy the west coast of Vancouver Island from our delightful two story home. A lovely rural setting provides easy access to shops, restaurants, salmon fishing, golfing, bird watching, coastal beaches and hiking trails. At days end, we are a nice place to come home to.

## Vernon

Dyde, Rosemary & Jeremy
5672 Learmouth Rd.
S 19A, C2, RR1, V1T 6L4
(604) 549-2804

**Amenities:** 1,2,4,11,15,16, 17,18
**Breakfast:** F.

**Dbl. Oc.:** $42.40(CN)
**Sgl. Oc.:** $35.50(CN)
**Third Person:** negotiable
**Child:** negotiable

**The Windmill House**—A beautiful replica windmill 15 km. east of Vernon. Lakes, beaches, orchards, skiing, hot springs, winery, lumber mill tours, gold panning and trail riding. Great for walking, hiking, jogging and cycling. Ideal Vancouver/Calgary half-way house. Great food!

| | | | |
|---|---|---|---|
| 1. No Smoking | 5. Tennis Available | 9. Credit Cards Accepted | 13. Lunch Available | 17. Shared Bath |
| 2. No Pets | 6. Golf Available | 10. Personal Checks Accepted | 14. Public Transportation | 18. Afternoon Tea |
| 3. No Children | 7. Swiming Available | 11. Off Season Rates | 15. Reservations Necessary | ★ Commissions given |
| 4. Senior Citizen Rates | 8. Skiing Available | 12. Dinner Available | 16. Private Bath | to Travel Agents |

# BRITISH COLUMBIA

## *Victoria* *

Barr, Rene
3844 Hobbs St., V8N 4C4
(604) 477-6558

**Amenities:** 1,2,5,6,7,10,
14,15,16,17,18
**Breakfast:** F.

**Dbl. Oc.:** $50.00 - $60.00(CN)
**Sgl. Oc.:** $35.00(CN)
**Child:** under 16 yrs. -
$10.00(CN)

**Cadboro Bay Bed & Breakfast**—Very comfortable accommodations. Also has separate cottage. A generous gourmet breakfast that changes daily. A short walk to the university, beach, parks (windsurfing and tennis), restaurants and village pub. Only 15 minutes to downtown Victoria and all local attractions.

## *Victoria*

Decter, Donna
1121 Faithful St., V8V 2R5
(604) 388-4889

**Amenities:** 1,2,3,5,6,9,11,
14,16,17
**Breakfast:** F.

**Dbl. Oc.:** $45.00 - $65.00(CN)
**Sgl. Oc.:** $40.00 - $60.00(CN)
**Third Person:** $20.00(CN)

**D&D's Bed & Breakfast**—Treat yourself to a relaxing, warm and friendly retreat within walking distance to downtown Victoria. Stroll along scenic ocean beaches or through 187 acres of gardens and parkland, both just one block from our beautifully restored character home.

## *Victoria* *

Flavelle, Sharon & Bill
10858 Madrona Dr. RR #1, V8L 3R9
(604) 656-9549

**Amenities:** 2,5,6,7,9,10,11,15,16,17
**Breakfast:** F.
**Dbl. Oc.:** $85.00 - $150.00(CN)
**Sgl. Oc.:** $85.00 - $150.00(CN)
**Third Person:** $50.00(CN)

**"Great-Snoring-On-Sea"**—Let us pamper you at our very British villa situated among rhododendrons, high on a cliff overlooking the sea. Artifacts, antiques and concert piano. Wander our flower gardens or ocean shore to see eagles and whales. Butchart Gardens and Empress Hotel tea nearby.

## *Victoria*

Gray, Sandra
3808 Heritage Lane, V8Z 7A7
(604) 479-0892

**Amenities:** 1,2,3,9,14,15,
17,18
**Breakfast:** F.

**Dbl. Oc.:** $85.00(CN)
**Sgl. Oc.:** $60.00(CN)
**Third Person:** $25.00(CN)

**Heritage House Bed And Breakfast**—Designated heritage home on 3/4 acre. Quiet private road. Lounging veranda, large rooms, guest parlor with fireplace and library/den. Private parking. Convenient to ferries, downtown and all highways

| | | | | |
|---|---|---|---|---|
| 1. No Smoking | 5. Tennis Available | 9. Credit Cards Accepted | 13. Lunch Available | 17. Shared Bath |
| 2. No Pets | 6. Golf Available | 10. Personal Checks Accepted | 14. Public Transportation | 18. Afternoon Tea |
| 3. No Children | 7. Swiming Available | 11. Off Season Rates | 15. Reservations Necessary | ★ Commissions given |
| 4. Senior Citizen Rates | 8. Skiing Available | 12. Dinner Available | 16. Private Bath | to Travel Agents |

# BRITISH COLUMBIA

## Victoria *

Lydon, Mrs. Aideen      **Amenities:** 1,2,5,6,7,10,17
747 Helvetia Crescent, V8Y 1M1
(604) 658-5519      **Breakfast:** F.

**Dbl. Oc.:** $50.00(CN)
**Sgl. Oc.:** $35.00(CN)
**Child:** under 5yrs. - no charge

**Hibernia Bed & Breakfast**—Large country home on cul-de-sac. Lawns, trees, vines, antique furnishings, TV and music room with grand piano. Comfortable beds, full Irish breakfast served on vine-covered patio. Fifteen minutes from airport, ferries, Butchart Gardens, beaches, restaurants and sports.

## Victoria *

McKechnie, William
998 Humboldt St., V8V 2Z6
(604) 384-8422
**Amenities:** 1,2,9
**Breakfast:** F.

**Dbl. Oc.:** $87.00 - $171.00(CN)
**Third Person:** $22.50(CN)
**Child:** under 10 yrs. - no charge

**The Beaconsfield**—An award-winning restored English mansion. A few blocks from downtown Victoria. Enter into a world of rich textures: velvets, leather, warm woods and goose down quilts. Antiques throughout. Delicious breakfast and service to pamper you.

## Victoria

McQuade, Marie      **Amenities:** 1,2,3,7,9,11,
5259 Patricia Bay Hwy., V8Y 1S8      15,16,17
(604) 658-8879      **Breakfast:** F.

**Dbl. Oc.:** $64.80 - $81.00(CN)
**Sgl. Oc.:** $51.84(CN)
**Third Person:** $21.60(CN)

**Elklake Lodge**—The living room (once a chapel for the monks who lived here) is octagon shaped. Clerestory windows and peaceful aura still remain today. Beautiful surroundings with an outdoor hot tub. Unique rooms with private baths. Full gourmet breakfast. Close to ferry.

## Victoria

Ranzinger, Sue & Inge      **Amenities:** 1,2,5,6,7,9,14,15,
66 Wellington Ave., V8V 4H5      16,18
(604) 383-5976      **Breakfast:** F.

**Dbl. Oc.:** $55.00 & up
**Sgl. Oc.:** $40.00 & up
**Third Person:** $10.00

**Wellington Bed & Breakfast**—A designer's delight! Large, beautifully furnished rooms with queen or king beds, walk-in closets and private baths. Close to downtown, 1/2 block from bus and beaches. Enjoy great hospitality, superb breakfasts and a good sleep! Relax in the living room, on sun deck or on the sunporch.

---

| | | | | |
|---|---|---|---|---|
| 1. No Smoking | 5. Tennis Available | 9. Credit Cards Accepted | 13. Lunch Available | 17. Shared Bath |
| 2. No Pets | 6. Golf Available | 10. Personal Checks Accepted | 14. Public Transportation | 18. Afternoon Tea |
| 3. No Children | 7. Swiming Available | 11. Off Season Rates | 15. Reservations Necessary | ★ Commissions given |
| 4. Senior Citizen Rates | 8. Skiing Available | 12. Dinner Available | 16. Private Bath | to Travel Agents |

## Victoria *

| | | |
|---|---|---|
| Wensley, M. Doreen | **Amenities:** 1,2,9,14,15,17 | **Dbl. Oc.:** $55.00(CN) |
| 660 Jones Terrace, V8Z 2L7 | **Breakfast:** F. | **Sgl. Oc.:** $40.00(CN) |
| (604) 479-9999 | | **Third Person:** $20.00(CN) |
| | | **Child:** under 12 yrs - $10.00(CN) |

**Garden City B&B.**—Surrounded by flowers. Fifteen minutes from city centre. A charming small ranch able to accommodate child or extra person. Peaceful and quiet neighborhood. Excellent breakfast. Relaxing atmosphere.

## Whistler

| | | |
|---|---|---|
| Morel, Ursula | **Amenities:** 1,2,4,5,6,7,8,9,10, | **Dbl.Oc.:** $69.03- $115.83(CN) |
| 7162 Nancy Greene Dr., V0N 1B0 | 11,12,13,14,15,16, | **Sgl. Oc.:** $57.33 - $104.13(CN) |
| (604) 932-3641 | 18 | **Third Person:** $23.40(CN) |
| | **Breakfast:** F. | **Child:** under 6 yrs. - $11.70(CN) |

**Edelweiss Pension**—Traditional European hospitality. Rooms with a view, balconies, down comforters, private bathroom, sauna and fireside guest lounge. Rate includes full breakfast. Easy walk to lifts, village and park. Non-smoking establishment.

## Whistler

| | | |
|---|---|---|
| Zinsli, Luise & Eric | **Amenities:** 1,2,4,5,6,7,8,9,11, | **Dbl. Oc.:** $122.00(CN) |
| 7461 Ambassador Crescent | 15,16 | **Sgl. Oc.:** $104.00(CN) |
| P.O. Box 352, V0N 1B0 | **Breakfast:** F. | **Third Person:** $23.00(CN) |
| (604) 932-4187: | | **Child:** under 10 yrs.- $12.00(CN) |
| Fax (604) 938-1531 | | |

**Chalet Luise Pension B&B Inn**—Swiss-style hospitality. Rooms with a view, balconies, down quilts, ensuite bathrooms, whirlpool, sauna, fireside guest lounge and garden/patio. Non-smoking establishment. An easy walk to lifts, village, lost lake park and trails. Home-baked bread

| | | | | |
|---|---|---|---|---|
| 1. No Smoking | 5. Tennis Available | 9. Credit Cards Accepted | 13. Lunch Available | 17. Shared Bath |
| 2. No Pets | 6. Golf Available | 10. Personal Checks Accepted | 14. Public Transportation | 18. Afternoon Tea |
| 3. No Children | 7. Swiming Available | 11. Off Season Rates | 15. Reservations Necessary | ★ Commissions given |
| 4. Senior Citizen Rates | 8. Skiing Available | 12. Dinner Available | 16. Private Bath | to Travel Agents |

# NEW BRUNSWICK

## *One of Canada's Four Atlantic Provinces*

Capitol: Fredericton
Entered The Dominion: July 1, 1867
Provincial Motto: Hope Restored
Floral Emblem: Purple Violet

New Brunswick is one of the original provinces of Canada. It has great natural beauty. Forest covers about 90% of the land yet in the St. John River Valley area there is rich farmland where potatoes are grown in great abundance.

More than one half of the people of this province live in the cities and towns. St. John is the largest city and chief industrial and shipping center. Most of the people are French descent, some are decendents from the United Empire Loyalists who left the U.S. after the Revolutionary War. This event of 1783 is still celebrated every year on May 18th in St. John.

New Brunswick has one of the best fishing grounds in North America. Thousands of visitors come here yearly to enjoy fishing, boating and swimming off the Banks of the Bay of Fundy and the Gulf of St. Lawrence.

## Grand Manan

Bowden, Cecilia
North Head, E0G 2M0
(416) 662-8570

**Amenities:** 5,6,7,9,10,12,13, 17,18
**Breakfast:** F.

**Dbl. Oc.:** $55.72(CN)
**Sgl. Oc.:** $42.18(CN)
**Third Person:** $6.66(CN)
**Child:** under 2 yrs. - no charge

**The Compass Rose**—Consists of two charming old houses by the sea, close to the ferry wharf. The rooms are furnished with pine antiques. The menu comes from our own ovens, our own garden, wild fruits, berries, lobster, scallops and a variety of local fish.

## Sackville

Hanrahan, Georgette & Richard
82 West Main St., E0A 3C0
(506) 536-1291

**Amenities:** 5,6,7,9,16
**Breakfast:** C.

**Dbl. Oc.:** $50.00(CN)
**Sgl. Oc.:** $39.00(CN)
**Third Person:** $9.00(CN)

**The Different Drummer**—A spacious Victorian home furnished with antiques. Eigh bedrooms with private baths. Close to restaurants,waterfowl park, university and shops. Fifteen minutes to the Nova Scotia border and 45 minutes to Prince Edward Ferry.

## St. Andrews

Lazare, Kathleen & Michael
59 Carleton St.
P.O. Box 349, E0G 2X0
(506) 529-3834

**Amenities:** 1,5,6,7,9,10,12,13, 15,17,18
**Breakfast:** F.

**Dbl. Oc.:** $90.00(CN)
**Sgl. Oc.:** $80.00(CN)
**Third Person:** $20.00(CN)
**Child:** $20.00(CN)

**Pansy Patch**—Located in the resort town of St. Andrews. It has a well-deserved reputation for its beautifully furnished rooms, superb water view and the warmth and charm of its atmosphere. The house itself is the most photographed building in New Brunswick.

## Sussex

Stark, Elizabeth & Peter
Walker Settlement Rd.
RR#4, E0E 1P0
(506) 433-3764

**Amenities:** 1,6,8,10,12,13,16,17,18
**Breakfast:** F.
**Dbl. Oc.:** $50.00(CN)
**Sgl. Oc.:** $40.00(CN)
**Third Person:** $10.00(CN)
**Child:** under 10 yrs. - $5.00(CN)

**Stark's Hillside Bed And Breakfast**—Relax on the veranda with panoramic view of a beautiful valley. Four golf courses within an hour's drive. Country roads to bike and hike. Poley Mountain and Ski Hill nearby. 17 covered bridges in our county. Short or long stays welcome. Bridge-playing hosts. Open all year.

| | | | |
|---|---|---|---|
| 1. No Smoking | 5. Tennis Available | 9. Credit Cards Accepted | 13. Lunch Available | 17. Shared Bath |
| 2. No Pets | 6. Golf Available | 10. Personal Checks Accepted | 14. Public Transportation | 18. Afternoon Tea |
| 3. No Children | 7. Swiming Available | 11. Off Season Rates | 15. Reservations Necessary | ★ Commissions given |
| 4. Senior Citizen Rates | 8. Skiing Available | 12. Dinner Available | 16. Private Bath | to Travel Agents |

# NOVA SCOTIA

## *One Of The Four Atlantic Provinces Of Canada*

Capitol:  Halifax
Entered The Dominion:  July 1, 1867;
                             one of the four original provinces
Provincial Motto:  One Offends and The Other Conquers
The Floral Emblem:  Trailing Arbutus

Halifax is the capitol of Nova Scotia and was founded in 1749 by an English Governor named Cornwallis. He made this city the capitol, and to this day it has remained very pro English and proud of its British connection.

Halifax is an extremely busy and large shipping port, perhaps one of the busiest in the world.

The beaches and resorts of Nova Scotia are beautiful, and visitors travel from all over to see and enjoy them. There is great hunting and fishing in this area as well. The climate is conducive to many sports; it never gets too hot nor too cold.

One can read more about Nova Scotia and its early times in Henry Wadsworth Longfellow's poem, Evangeline.

## *Annapolis Royal*

Williams, Iris
124 Victoria St.
Box 277, B0S 1A0
(902) 532-7936

**Amenities:** 1,2,15,16,17
**Breakfast:** C.

**Dbl. Oc.:** $38.50 - $52.80(CN)
**Sgl. Oc.:** $36.30 - $49.50(CN)
**Third Person:** $8.00(CN)
**Child:** under 2 yrs.-$2.00(CN)

**The Poplars Bed & Breakfast**—A restored Victorian home in the heart of Canada's oldest permanent European settlement. Registered heritage home on a large treed lot with huge 300-year-old poplars. Color cable TV in family room, evening coffee and conversation. Two blocks from amenities.

| | | | |
|---|---|---|---|
| 1. No Smoking | 5. Tennis Available | 9. Credit Cards Accepted | 13. Lunch Available | 17. Shared Bath |
| 2. No Pets | 6. Golf Available | 10. Personal Checks Accepted | 14. Public Transportation | 18. Afternoon Tea |
| 3. No Children | 7. Swiming Available | 11. Off Season Rates | 15. Reservations Necessary | ★ Commissions given |
| 4. Senior Citizen Rates | 8. Skiing Available | 12. Dinner Available | 16. Private Bath | to Travel Agents |

# ONTARIO

## Canada's Second Largest Province

Capitol: Toronto
Entered The Dominion: July 1, 1867;
                    one of the four original provinces
Motto: Loyal She Began, Loyal She Remains
The Floral Emblem: White Trillium

Ontario is most properous in agriculture and industry. There are still large farms in this province, even though more than half of its population is urbanized.

Ottawa, the capitol of Canada, is situated in this province, and here most of the population is employed by the government. Toronto, the capitol of Ontario, is large and modern, and gradually becoming the metropolis and center for all English Canada.

The history of this province is interesting. It was first settled by British loyalists who left the American colonies after the Revolutionary War ended in defeat for the English. As a result, they set the pattern for social behavior, architecture and style of living, which gives it a stong American bond.

There are many lakes which offer a variety of vacation attractions in Ontario. The southern areas along Lake Erie and Ontario are sunny and make for enjoyable vacationing.

The Dionne quintuplets were born here in Callander in 1934, and insulin was discovered here by Frederick Banting and Charles Best in 1921.

# ONTARIO

## Aton *

Hough, Jennifer & Rodney
1498 Cataract St.
RR #2,, L0N 1A0
(519) 927-3033: Fax (519) 927-5779

**Amenities:** 2,5,6,8,9,12,13,15,17
**Breakfast:** C.
**Dbl. Oc.:** $81.00(CN)
**Sgl. Oc.:** $59.40(CN)
**Third Person:** $37.80(CN)

**Cataract Inn**—Antiques and cotton prints suited to the 130-year-old inn. Terry cloth gowns hang behind the door, cover-ups as you make the short walk down the hall to the spacious bathroom. Imagine waking from a sound sleep with the sun pouring in your window and the birds singing.

## Ancaster

Morin, George
1034 Highway 53 W., L9G 3KG
(416) 648-5225

**Amenities:** 2,6,8,9,10,12, 15,16
**Breakfast:** F.

**Dbl. Oc.:** $90.00(CN)
**Sgl. Oc.:** $85.00 (CN)

**Philip Shaver House Country Inn**—This Georgian house, situated in a country setting, was built in 1835 by an Empire Loyalist family who came to Ontario from New Jersey in 1789. Diners are invited to ponder an extensive menu selection of French, Italian and continental cuisine.

## Bracebridge

Rickard, Jan
17 Dominion St., P0B 1C0
(705) 645-2245

**Amenities:** 2,5,6,7,8,9,11, 12,13,15,16,18
**Breakfast:** F.
**Dbl. Oc.:** $100.00(CN)
**Sgl. Oc.:** $80.00(CN)
**Third Person:** $12.00(CN)
**Child:** under 12 yrs. - no charge

**Inn At The Falls**—Located in a wooded, small-town setting overlooking Breacebridge Falls. This fine old Victorian inn exudes traditional old-fashioned hospitality and charm. Superb dining. Authentic English pub. Beautiful outdoor patio. Fireplaces. Voted most scenic location.

| | | | | |
|---|---|---|---|---|
| 1. No Smoking | 5. Tennis Available | 9. Credit Cards Accepted | 13. Lunch Available | 17. Shared Bath |
| 2. No Pets | 6. Golf Available | 10. Personal Checks Accepted | 14. Public Transportation | 18. Afternoon Tea |
| 3. No Children | 7. Swiming Available | 11. Off Season Rates | 15. Reservations Necessary | ★ Commissions given |
| 4. Senior Citizen Rates | 8. Skiing Available | 12. Dinner Available | 16. Private Bath | to Travel Agents |

# ONTARIO

## Braeside

McGregor, Noreen & Steve
R.R. #1, K0A 1G0
(613) 432-6248

**Amenities:** 1,2,12,15,17
**Breakfast:** F.

**Dbl. Oc.:** $35.00(CN)
**Sgl. Oc.:** $25.00(CN)
**Third Person:** $10.00(CN)
**Child:** under 6 yrs. -
$5.00(CN)

**Glenroy Farm**—Our heritage stone home was built over 100 years ago by host's grandfather. Family antiques help to furnish our home and make interesting conversation pieces. Pleasant and practical facilities on our working family farm. Enjoy Ottawa Valley hospitality and scenery.

---

## Dunrobin

Zeyl, Carole
3028 Barlow Crescent,
K0A 1T0
(613) 832-1612

**Amenities:** 1,5,6,7,8,9,15
**Breakfast:** C.

**Dbl. Oc.:** $50.00(CN)
**Sgl. Oc.:** $40.00(CN)
**Third Person:** $20.00(CN)
**Child:** under 13 yrs.-
$15.00(CN)

**Ottawa River Bed & Breakfast**—A waterfront home overlooking picturesque site of Gatineau Mountains. Close to Pinhey historical site, marina, hiking, horseback riding, flea market and restaurants. Half- hour drive to downtown Ottawa, where you can visit museums, Parliament buildings and much more.

---

## Hensall

Etherington, Karen & Rick
R.R. #1, N0M 1X0
(519) 235-1628

**Amenities:** 2,6,7,12,13,16
**Breakfast:** F.

**Dbl. Oc.:** $45.00(CN)
**Sgl. Oc.:** $30.00(CN)
**Third Person:** family rate -
$65.00(CN)
**Child:** under 12 yrs. -
$15.00(CN)

**D&D Stock Farm**—An attractive operating sheep and hog farm. Derek (11) and Robyn (8) would enjoy your company! Close to Lake Huron resorts, live theatre at Great Bend and Stratford. You'll always receive a warm welcome in southwestern Ontario.

---

## Hunta

Landis, Judy & Larry
P0L 1P0
(705) 272-6302

**Amenities:** 6,7,8,12,13,15,16
**Breakfast:** C.

**Dbl. Oc.:** $50.00 (CN)
**Sgl. Oc.:** $40.00 (CN)
**Third Person:** $15.00(CN)
**Child:** under 5 yrs. -
$10.00(CN)

**Long Lake Farm**—In northern Ontario, amid many lakes and rivers. Our log house has three bedrooms for guests. Breakfast is served in the great room or solarium. A log cottage with fireplace, three bedrooms, 1-1/2 baths, overlooking a river is available for $500.00 (CN) per week. Come and relax!

---

| | | | | |
|---|---|---|---|---|
| 1. No Smoking | 5. Tennis Available | 9. Credit Cards Accepted | 13. Lunch Available | 17. Shared Bath |
| 2. No Pets | 6. Golf Available | 10. Personal Checks Accepted | 14. Public Transportation | 18. Afternoon Tea |
| 3. No Children | 7. Swiming Available | 11. Off Season Rates | 15. Reservations Necessary | ★ Commissions given |
| 4. Senior Citizen Rates | 8. Skiing Available | 12. Dinner Available | 16. Private Bath | to Travel Agents |

## *Hunta* *

Moyer, Nancy & Tom
P0L 1P0
(705) 272-6802

**Amenities:** 4,7,8,11,12,13,
17,18
**Breakfast:** F.

**Dbl. Oc.:** $45.00
**Sgl. Oc.:** $35.00
**Third Person:** $10.00
**Child:** under 5 yrs. -
no charge

**Country Haven B&B**—Truly a country haven. Twelve miles from Cochrane, home of the Polar Bear Express. Clean, comfortable rooms and lots of hospitality. Experience nature at its finest on our 150 acre farm. A great place to get away, relax and unwind.

## *Lakefield* *

Wilkins, Joan & Wally
Slwyn, RR 3, K0L 2H0
(705) 652-6290,
Fax: (705) 652-6949

**Amenities:** 1,2,6,7,8,15,16,17
**Breakfast:** F.

**Dbl. Oc.:**$42.00-$48.00(CN)
**Sgl. Oc.:** $34.00 (CN)
**Third Person:** $12.00 (CN)
**Child:** $12.00 (CN)

**Windmere Farm Bed & Breakfast**—Our spacious century stone home is an oasis of country comfort in the heart of the Kawartha Lakes. Local attractions include art galleries, the Trent Canal System,with the world's highest lift lock. Fishing and swimming available.

## *Lansdown*

Hart, Ms. Nensi
Hart Country Estate
RR # 4, K0E 1L0
(613) 659-2873

**Amenities:** 1,5,7,12,13,15,
17,18
**Breakfast:** C. and F

**Dbl. Oc.:** $45.00 (CN)
**Sgl. Oc.:** $32.00 (CN)
**Child:** under 10 yrs.-
$10.00(CN)

**Hart Country Estate**—In the 1,000 islands. Large red brick 1890 farmhouse on 75 acres. Menagerie of farm animals. Quiet spot for a getaway. Close to beaches and U.S. border. Children are especially welcome. Enjoy a home-grown dinner on arrival. Write for brochure.

## *Millbank*

Henderson, Mrs. E. Alveretta
RR #1, N0K 1L0
(519) 595-4604

**Amenities:** 1,2,3,10,12,13,15,16,17,18
**Breakfast:** F.
**Dbl. Oc.:** $45.00 (CN)
**Sgl. Oc.:** $30.00 (CN)
**Third Person:** $15.00 (CN)

**Honeybrook Farm**—A beautiful restored 1866 stone house in the country, 20 minutes from the Stratford Festival, Waterloo Markets and St. Jacobs Mennonite culture. Large bedrooms and guest bathrooms. Menu breakfast. Meals and transportation available. Open all year.

---

| | | | | |
|---|---|---|---|---|
| 1. No Smoking | 5. Tennis Available | 9. Credit Cards Accepted | 13. Lunch Available | 17. Shared Bath |
| 2. No Pets | 6. Golf Available | 10. Personal Checks Accepted | 14. Public Transportation | 18. Afternoon Tea |
| 3. No Children | 7. Swiming Available | 11. Off Season Rates | 15. Reservations Necessary | ★ Commissions given |
| 4. Senior Citizen Rates | 8. Skiing Available | 12. Dinner Available | 16. Private Bath | to Travel Agents |

## *Niagara Falls*

| | | |
|---|---|---|
| Sieiliano, Luciana Bertoechi | **Amenities:** 9,11,14,16,17 | **Dbl. Oc.:** $75.00 (CN) |
| 4917 River Rd., L2E 3G5 | **Breakfast:** F. | **Sgl. Oc.:** $70.00 (CN) |
| (416) 357-1124 | | **Third Person:** $15.00 (CN) |
| | | **Child:** under 10 yrs.- $10.00 (CN) |

**Butterfly Manor**—Overlooking the Niagara River, within easy walking distance to the falls. Short drive from Niagara-on-the-Lake and a five-minute walk from the train or bus station. Our homeis a delightful blend of old and new. Warm kitchen with a friendly fireplace and the smell of freshly baked muffins.

## *Niagara On The Lake*

| | | |
|---|---|---|
| Hernder, Pat | **Amenities:** 1,2,5,6,7,10, | **Dbl. Oc.:** $55.00 (CN) |
| 753 Line 3, RR 2, L0S 1J0 | 16,17 | **Sgl. Oc.:** $50.00 (CN) |
| (416) 468-3192 | **Breakfast:** F. | **Third Person:** $15.00 (CN) |

**Hernder's Country Home**—Located on the wine route in the heart of Niagara's fruitland, our modern and spacious air-conditioned home offers the best of both worlds. A quiet country setting with queen-size beds. Five minutes to Shaw Festival Theatre and shops. Ten minutes to Niagara Falls.

## *Niagara-On-The-Lake*

| | | |
|---|---|---|
| Hiebert, Marlene & Otto | **Amenities:** 1,2,5,6,7,8,10,11, | **Dbl. Oc.:** $60.00 (CN) |
| 275 John St., W. | 15,17 | **Sgl. Oc.:** $55.00 (CN) |
| Box 1371, L0S 1J0 | **Breakfast:** F. | **Third Person:** $15.00(CN) |
| (416) 468-3687 | | **Child:** under 13 yrs.- $10.00(CN) |

**Hiebert's Guest House**—We are located in a historic town 13 miles north of Niagara Falls. Take time to attend the Shaw Festival Theatre and browse through the many shops. We offer firm queen and twin beds. Full homemade breakfasts. Non-smoking home. Air conditioned. Reservations recommended.

## *Norland*

| | | |
|---|---|---|
| Lowry, Rosemary & Derek | **Amenities:** 2,6,7,8,9,11,12,14, | **Dbl. Oc.:** $98.00 (CN) |
| RR 1, Highway 35, K0M 2L0 | 16,18 | **Sgl. Oc.:** $73.00 (CN) |
| (705) 454-1753 | **Breakfast:** F. | |

**Moore Lake Inn**—Two hours from Toronto in Haliburton. A turn-of-the-century farmhouse/ tavern offering comfort, civility and cuisine. Six double rooms, all with private baths. Our restaurant is considered the best for miles. Close to riding, marinas, winter sports and antiques.

## *Omemee*

| | | |
|---|---|---|
| Jones, Ella & Milburn | **Amenities:** 1,2,8,12,13,15,17 | **Dbl. Oc.:** $35.00 (CN) |
| RR #2, K0L 2W0 | **Breakfast:** F. | **Sgl. Oc.:** $25.00 (CN) |
| (705) 799-5149 | | **Child:** under 10 yrs.- $10.00(CN) |

**Lebanon Farm**—Welcome to our renovated farmhouse in the heart of theKawarthas. Picturesque home on 99 acres, 20 minutes from Peterborough, with its live theatre, lift locks and other attractions. Skiing at Devil's Elbow and Sunega is 10 minutes away. Open year round.

| | | | |
|---|---|---|---|
| 1. No Smoking | 5. Tennis Available | 9. Credit Cards Accepted | 13. Lunch Available | 17. Shared Bath |
| 2. No Pets | 6. Golf Available | 10. Personal Checks Accepted | 14. Public Transportation | 18. Afternoon Tea |
| 3. No Children | 7. Swiming Available | 11. Off Season Rates | 15. Reservations Necessary | ★ Commissions given |
| 4. Senior Citizen Rates | 8. Skiing Available | 12. Dinner Available | 16. Private Bath | to Travel Agents |

# ONTARIO

## Ottawa *

Bradley, Donna
172 O'Connor St., K2P 1T5
(613) 236-4221,
Fax: (613) 236-4232

**Amenities:** 2,5,9,10,11,
14,17,18
**Breakfast:** F.

**Dbl. Oc.:** $48.00 - $51.00 (US)
**Sgl. Oc.:** $39.00 - $47.00 (US)
**Third Person:** $3.00 -
$17.00(US)
**Child:** under 12 yrs. -
no charge

**O'Connor House Bed & Breakfast**—The most central B&B in Ottawa, with a short walk to Parliament buildings, Rideau Canal, National Gallery and shopping. Friendly, comfortable accommodations, air conditioned and parking. Free use of bicycles or ice skates. Half an hour to beaches, lakes and ski resorts.

## Ottawa

Delroy, Cathy & John
478 Albert St., K1R 5B5
(613) 236-4479,
(800) 267-1982 (Canada only)

**Amenities:** 2,3,9,11,14,
16,18
**Breakfast:** F.

**Dbl. Oc.:** $65.00 - $85.00 (CN)
**Sgl Oc.:** $55.00 -$75.00 (CN)
**Third Person:** $10.00 (CN)

**Albert House**—Our large Victorian home, built in 1875, in the heart ofdowntown Ottawa. All guest rooms are individually decorated and have en-suite facilities. Famous Albert House breakfast. We have two large, but very, friendly dogs.

## Ottawa

Waters, Carol
35 Marlborough Ave.,
K1N 8E6
(613) 235-8461

**Amenities:** 2,11,16,17,18
**Breakfast:** F

**Dbl. Oc.:** $42.00 - $58.00(CN)
**Sgl. Oc.:** 35.00(CN)
**Third Person:** $10.00(CN)

**Australis Guest House**—Award-winning, oldest-established B&B in Ottawa. Classic residence with leaded windows and fireplaces. Close to downtown and all amenities in an area of parks, embassies and Rideau River. Hosts have Australian and English backgrounds. Off-street parking. Great breakfasts.

## Port Carling

Heineck, John K.
P.O. Box 400, P0B 1C0
(705) 765-3131

**Amenities:** 2,5,6,7,8,9,11,12,
13,15,16,18
**Breakfast:** F.

**Dbl. Oc.:** $288.00 (CN)
**Sgl. Oc.:** $216.00 (CN)
**Third Person:** $94.00 (CN)
**Child:** under 6yrs. -
$58.00 (CN)

**Sherwood Inn, Limited**—In Muskoka on beautiful Lake Joseph. Charming main inn rooms or beach-side cottages. Private baths and superb dining. Nearby billiards, tennis, swimming, boating, skiing, golf, sightseeing, theatre and shopping. Very private, intimate and very special. Rates include dinner.

---

| | | | | |
|---|---|---|---|---|
| 1. No Smoking | 5. Tennis Available | 9. Credit Cards Accepted | 13. Lunch Available | 17. Shared Bath |
| 2. No Pets | 6. Golf Available | 10. Personal Checks Accepted | 14. Public Transportation | 18. Afternoon Tea |
| 3. No Children | 7. Swiming Available | 11. Off Season Rates | 15. Reservations Necessary | ★ Commissions given |
| 4. Senior Citizen Rates | 8. Skiing Available | 12. Dinner Available | 16. Private Bath | to Travel Agents |

# ONTARIO

## Rockport *

Bergen, Pieter
Box C-10, K0E 1V0
(613) 659-3513
**Amenities:** 1,2,5,6,7,10,11,12,14,16
**Breakfast:** F.
**Dbl. Oc.:** $80.00 (CN)
**Sgl. Oc.:** $60.00 (CN)
**Third Person:** $30.00 (CN)
**Child:** under 12yrs. - $25.00(CN)

**Houseboat "Amaryllis" B&B Inn**—A 100-foot double-deck houseboat located on its own island of 7.5 acres in the center of the '1000 Islands,' St.Lawrence River. Veranda deck, living room and fireplaces on water and forested shores. 1920 vintage island tours available in classic wooden boats.

---

## Toronto *

Bosher, Kenneth     **Amenities:** 1,2,9,14,15,17     **Dbl. Oc.:** $63.00 - $68.25(CN)
322 Palmerston Blvd., M6G 2N6                    **Sgl. Oc.:** $52.50 - $57.75(CN)
(416) 920-7842     **Breakfast:** C     **Third Person:** $30.00(CN)

**Burken Guest House**—Splendidly situated on a charming residential boulevard adjacent to downtown. Eight tastefully appointed rooms. Limited parking nearby with public transportation. Friendly, capable service and excellent reputation.

## Toronto *

Ketchen, Donna & Ken     **Amenities:** 1,2,3,14,16,17     **Dbl. Oc.:** $55.00(CN)
92 Orchard View Blvd., M4R 1C2                    **Sgl. Oc.:** $45.00(CN)
(416) 488-6826     **Breakfast:** F.

**Orchard View**—Our spacious renovated home is located at the hub of metropolitan Toronto and vicinity. Quick and easy access to a short transit ride takes you to all major attractions. We offer two rooms. A double with private ensuite or a twin which includes a sunroom and shared bath.

## Toronto *

Riciuto, William     **Amenities:** 1,2,9,15,16,17     **Dbl. Oc.:** $55.00 - $65.00(CN)
235 Beverley St., M5T 1Z4     **Breakfast:** F.     **Sgl. Oc.:** $40.00 - $45.00(CN)
(416) 977-0077                                  **Third Person:** $20.00(CN)
                                                     **Child:** under 1 yr. -
                                                           no charge

**Beverly Place**—An 1887 Victorian house lovingly restored to its original beauty, complete with exquisite antique furnishings. Grand piano for the music lover. Stroll to all attractions: CityHall, historic Queen's Park, Royal Ontario Museum, art gallery, University of Toronto, Convention Centre and more.

---

| | | | |
|---|---|---|---|
| 1. No Smoking | 5. Tennis Available | 9. Credit Cards Accepted | 13. Lunch Available | 17. Shared Bath |
| 2. No Pets | 6. Golf Available | 10. Personal Checks Accepted | 14. Public Transportation | 18. Afternoon Tea |
| 3. No Children | 7. Swiming Available | 11. Off Season Rates | 15. Reservations Necessary | ★ Commissions given |
| 4. Senior Citizen Rates | 8. Skiing Available | 12. Dinner Available | 16. Private Bath | to Travel Agents |

# PRINCE EDWARD ISLAND

Capitol:  Charlottetown
Entered The Dominion:  July 1, 1873; the 7th province
Provincial Motto:  The Small Under The Protection
                   Of The Great
The Floral Emblem:  Lady's Slipper


P.E.I., as it is often referred to, is the smallest yet the most densely populated province of the Canadian provinces. It is the only one of the provinces that is separated from the main land of North America.

The people of this island depend greatly upon its green meadows and rich red soil for the agriculture which brings them their yearly income.

Tourism helps the economy, too. Over 600,000 vacationers visit Prince Edward Island each year. The climate is mild during the summer, and the beaches are beautiful.

The biggest event of the year takes place in August in the capitol of Charlottetown. It is called Old Home Week. People come from all over to enjoy this happy event.

# PRINCE EDWARD ISLAND

## Augustine Cove

Cutcliffe, Mrs. Roy
Borden R.R. #1, C0B 1X0
(902) 855-2871

**Amenities:** 1,2,3,4,7,
15,16,17
**Breakfast:** C.

**Dbl. Oc.:** $34.00(CN)
**Sgl. Oc.:** $30.00(CN)
**Third Person:** $5.00(CN)

**Shore Farm Bed & Breakfast**—Welcome to our quiet 200-acre farm overlooking Northumberland Strait, on Route 10, eight km. east of the Borden Ferry. Mixed farming operation, growing potatoes and barley. 600 yards to the beach and patio. Three large guest rooms with private entrance. Open May - October 31.

---

## Montague

Partridge, Gertrude
RR 2, C0A 1R0
(902) 838-4687

**Amenities:** 1,4,7,8,9,10,
11,16
**Breakfast:** F.

**Dbl. Oc.:** $55.00(CN)
**Sgl. Oc.:** $44.00(CN)
**Third Person:** $10.00(CN)
**Child:** under 6 yrs. -
no charge

**Partridge Bed And Breakfast**—Four rooms with private bath, two rooms with shared bath. Cots and cribs available. White sandy beaches, kitchen and laundry. Wheelchair facilities in one room with private bath. Bicycles, rowboat and canoe. Babysitting. Open year round.

| | | | | |
|---|---|---|---|---|
| 1. No Smoking | 5. Tennis Available | 9. Credit Cards Accepted | 13. Lunch Available | 17. Shared Bath |
| 2. No Pets | 6. Golf Available | 10. Personal Checks Accepted | 14. Public Transportation | 18. Afternoon Tea |
| 3. No Children | 7. Swiming Available | 11. Off Season Rates | 15. Reservations Necessary | ★ Commissions given |
| 4. Senior Citizen Rates | 8. Skiing Available | 12. Dinner Available | 16. Private Bath | to Travel Agents |

# QUEBEC

## *The Largest Province Of Canada*

Capital: Quebec
Entered The Dominion: July 1, 1867
Provincial Motto: I Remember
The Floral Emblem: White Garden Lily
Provincial Tree: Sugar Maple

The province of Quebec is quite different from all the other provinces. Most of its people speak French and adhere to French customs. Old Quebec is a site of much history, and visitors come here and enjoy the charm of this city and its 300-year-old winding and cobblestone streets.

Montreal is the largest city in this province and it is a beautiful city. It has lovely parks and shops and a large community of business from around the world. It has a metropolitan air about it.

In Montreal, the University of McGill is located. This particular university is English speaking.

Quebec is known for its great religious faith. There are many Catholic and Protestant churches available for the people. Tourists love Quebec, and return here by the thousands every day.

# QUEBEC

## Aylmer

Berube, Jacqueline
56 Hemlock St., J9H 3T9
(819) 684-8250

**Amenities:** 1,5,6,7,8,14,15,16, 17
**Breakfast:** C. and F.

**Dbl. Oc.:** $50.00(CN)
**Sgl. Oc.:** $40.00(CN)
**Third Person:** $20.00(CN)
**Child:** under 12 yrs.- $15.00(CN)

**Jacki & Norm Bed & Breakfast**—Aylmer is 15 minutes to downtown Ottawa: Art Gallery of Canada, museums, Parliament, Bulgs exciting marketplace, Rideau shopping center and much more. Our B&B is within walking distance to shops, restaurants, golf, marina, bicycle path and public transportation.

## Baie St. Paul *

Arsenault, Robert
39 St. Jean Baptiste, G0A 1B0
(418) 435-6839

**Amenities:** 5,6,8,9,10,11,14, 15,16,17
**Breakfast:** C.

**Dbl. Oc.:** $55.00(CN)
**Sgl. Oc.:** $40.00(CN)
**Third Person:** $15.00(CN)
**Child:** under 12 yrs.-

$10.00(CN)

**La Muse**—Å uniquely restored 1881 Victorian house in the heart of the village. Quiet, comfortable, elegant and tastefully decorated historic home. Homemade breads with breakfast. Walk to restaurants, art galleries and shops. Nature-lovers paradise: hike, fish and whale watch.

## Beauport

Tremblay, Gisele
2515 Ave. Royale, G1C 1S2
(418) 666-4755

**Amenities:** 2,5,6,7,8,14,15
**Breakfast:** F.

**Dbl. Oc.:** $45.00-$50.00(CN)
**Sgl. Oc.:** $30.00-$35.00(CN)
**Third Person:** $20.00(CN)
**Child:** under 12 yrs.- $10.00(CN)

**En Haut De La Chute**—Family run B&B home with five rooms with both shared and private baths. Full family style breakfast is served. 10 minutes from Quebec City and 30 minutes to great skiing areas. Public bus stop right outside the front door.

## Bishopton *

Van Brimbergen, Jany & Jean
35 Gosford, J0B 1G0
(819) 884-2237

**Amenities:** 4,6,7,8,9,12,13,14, 15,167,18
**Breakfast:** C. and F.

**Dbl. Oc.:** $45.00(CN)
**Sgl. Oc.:** $32.00(CN)
**Third Person:** $10.00(CN)
**Child:** under 5 yrs. - $5.00(CN)

**Au Relais Des Mesanges**—We invite you to our little mountain farm by the lake. Your breakfast is served to you on the terrace. Located near Sherbrooke, junction of Route 11 and 2 exit 255. Bird watching, waterbikes, boats, cross country skiing, ice fishing and skating on the property. Welcome.

---

| | | | |
|---|---|---|---|
| 1. No Smoking | 5. Tennis Available | 9. Credit Cards Accepted | 13. Lunch Available | 17. Shared Bath |
| 2. No Pets | 6. Golf Available | 10. Personal Checks Accepted | 14. Public Transportation | 18. Afternoon Tea |
| 3. No Children | 7. Swiming Available | 11. Off Season Rates | 15. Reservations Necessary | ★ Commissions given |
| 4. Senior Citizen Rates | 8. Skiing Available | 12. Dinner Available | 16. Private Bath | to Travel Agents |

## Cap A L'Aigle

Potvin, Pierrette
21 Fleurie, G0T 1B0
(418) 665-6393

**Amenities:** 1,5,6,7,8,15,17
**Breakfast:** F.

**Dbl. Oc.:** $40.00(CN)
**Sgl. Oc.:** $30.00(CN)
**Child:** under 12 yrs.-
$10.00(CN)

**Les Chanterelles**—Warm, typical French Canadian century home facing the St. Lawrence River, where the heart of Quebec beats between mountains and river. Cachet, cultural, artistic and friendly atmosphere. Restricted smoking. Nearby activities: whales, canyon, golf, museum and concerts.

## Chambord *

Fortin-Bouchard, Martine & Serge
824 Route 169, G0W 1G0
(418) 342-8446, (418) 275-5054

**Amenities:** 6,7,8,15
**Breakfast:** F.
**Dbl. Oc.:** $40.00(CN)
**Sgl. Oc.:** $30.00(CN)
**Third Person:** $15.00(CN)
**Child:** under 12 yrs.-$10.00(CN)

**Chez Martine Et Serge**—Come and see wonderful Lac St-Jean. Lie down on a quiet, private beach and smell the odor of the freshly cut hay. Listen to the soft whispering of the nearby Val-Jalbert's Falls and try, in the night, to listen to the ghost's story. Fishermen are also welcome.

## Chateau Richer *

Cloutier, Gaston
8790 Rue Royale, G0A 1N0
(418) 824-4478

**Amenities:** 2,6,8,9,10,11,12,13,14,15,16,17
**Breakfast:** F.
**Dbl. Oc.:** $45.00 - $80.00(CN)
**Sgl. Oc.:** $40.00 - $75.00(CN)
**Third Person:** $15.00(CN)
**Child:** under 6 yrs. - no charge

**Logis Du Restaurant Baker**—For a real taste of Quebec, come and stay above the famous Baker's Restaurant. Located in a beautifully restored 150-year-old country home. Each room (six) is unique and charmingly decorated with personal antiques. Ten minutes from Mt. Ste. Anne's ski slopes.

| | | | |
|---|---|---|---|
| 1. No Smoking | 5. Tennis Available | 9. Credit Cards Accepted | 13. Lunch Available | 17. Shared Bath |
| 2. No Pets | 6. Golf Available | 10. Personal Checks Accepted | 14. Public Transportation | 18. Afternoon Tea |
| 3. No Children | 7. Swiming Available | 11. Off Season Rates | 15. Reservations Necessary | |
| 4. Senior Citizen Rates | 8. Skiing Available | 12. Dinner Available | 16. Private Bath | ★ Commissions given to Travel Agents |

## *Chateau Richer* *

Langevin, Michel
394 Ve. Pichette, G0A 1N0
(418) 824-3654

**Amenities:** 2,6,8,9,10,11,12,14,15,16,17
**Breakfast:** F.
**Dbl. Oc.:** $45.00-$80.00(CN)
**Sgl. Oc.:** $35.00-$70.00(CN)
**Third Person:** $15.00(CN)
**Child:** under 6 yrs. - no charge

**Le Petite Sejour**—Only 15 minutes from old Quebec City. Nearby are the Mont Ste. Anne's slopes. Discover a spacious Victorian house (1868). Cozy living room, fireplaces and stone walls. Enjoy breakfast overlooking the St. Lawrence River. Romantic atmosphere in which to unwind.

## *Desbiens*

Deschenes, Monique & Samuel
362-13 S. Ave., G0W 1N0
(418) 346-5274

**Amenities:** 2,6,7,8,11,15, 17,18
**Breakfast:** F.

**Dbl. Oc.:** $38.00(CN)
**Sgl. Oc.:** $28.00(CN)
**Third Person:** $15.00(CN)
**Child:** $15.00(CN)

Located 10 minutes from beautiful Lake St. James. Best place for fishing and the most beautiful sandy beaches. Center of al tourist attractions. We look forward to your visit. Picnic table, swing and swimming pool. Rest in our garden. Just like home.

## *Dunham* *

Charbonneau, Rachel
Route Des Vins (Road 202), J0E 1M0
(514) 295-2667,
(514) 295-3511

**Amenities:** 2,6,7,8
**Breakfast:** F.

**Dbl. Oc.:** $50.00(CN)
**Sgl. Oc.:** $35.00(CN)
**Third Person:** $15.00(CN)
**Child:** under 12 yrs.- $10.00(CN)

**Domaine Paradis Des Fruits**—Welcome to a stone house built by Loyalist pioneers. Pick your own fresh fruits and taste our natural honey. From the hilltop, a wonderful panoramic view of flourishing orchards, in the neighborhood of the famous vineyards ofDunham. Swimming pool and private entrance.

## *Havelock*

Schulman, Anne & John
164 Route 202, J0S 1E0
(514) 826-0196

**Amenities:** 1,2,6,7,8,10,12,15, 17,18
**Breakfast:** F.

**Dbl. Oc.:** $55.00(CN)
**Sgl. Oc.:** $27.50(CN)
**Third Person:** $15.00(CN)
**Child:** under 2 yrs.- $10.00(CN)

**Stoneboro Farm**—Picturesque 140-year-old stone house on 100-acre hillside farm. Cozy home, antiques and flower gardens. Thirty-five miles south of Montreal. A tranquil place to rekindle worn spirits. Maple syrup and apple region. Golf and skiing. Park Safari African 15 miles away. Two miles to New York.

| | | | |
|---|---|---|---|
| 1. No Smoking | 5. Tennis Available | 9. Credit Cards Accepted | 13. Lunch Available | 17. Shared Bath |
| 2. No Pets | 6. Golf Available | 10. Personal Checks Accepted | 14. Public Transportation | 18. Afternoon Tea |
| 3. No Children | 7. Swiming Available | 11. Off Season Rates | 15. Reservations Necessary | ★ Commissions given |
| 4. Senior Citizen Rates | 8. Skiing Available | 12. Dinner Available | 16. Private Bath | to Travel Agents |

# QUEBEC

## Longueuil

Girouard, Andre
725 Victoria, J4H 2K2
(514) 651-8167

**Amenities:** 1,2,14,16
**Breakfast:** F.

**Dbl. Oc.:** $45.00(CN)
**Sgl. Oc.:** $35.00(CN)
**Third Person:** $20.00(CN)
**Child:** under 12 yrs.-
    $10.00(CN)

**Le Gite Du Passant**—Near subway to downtown Montreal, just a few minutes away.  Close to highways from U.S.A.  A quiet residential area.We speak fluent English.  Enjoy the French environment.  Exit 8 on Highway 132, take St. Charles Street, two blocks after shopping center, "Place Longueuil."

## Magog

Fear, Marion
RR #7, 990 Ch. Colline Bunker,
J1X 3W2
(819) 843-1742

**Amenities:** 1,2,6,7,15,16,17
**Breakfast:** F.

**Dbl. Oc.:** $46.00 - $60.00(CN)
**Sgl. Oc.:** $40.00 - $45.00(CN)
**Third Person:** $22.00 -
    $30.00 (CN)
**Child:** under 12 yrs.-
    $14.00(CN)

**Ferme L'Ere Nouvell**—Plan a restover on our organic vegetable farm, 10 miles from Magog, five minutes from #55 (I-91) to Quebec City or Montreal.  Vegetarian breakfasts, large studio (sleeps five), attractive bedroom (sleeps four) and superb mountain view.  Sports, theatre, crafts and scenic area.

## Matane

Lavoie, Jacqueline
2112 Matane Sur Mer, G4W 3M6
(418) 562-2019

**Amenities:** 3,5,6,7,8,11,16,17
**Breakfast:** C.
**Dbl. Oc.:** $45.00 - $50.00(CN)
**Sgl. Oc.:** $30.00 - $35.00(CN)
**Third Person:** $15.00(CN)
**Child:** no charge - $10.00(CN)

**Maison Sur Le Fleuve**—A warm, hospitable home on the St. Lawrence River.  A nice place to relax, to walk on the beach and look at the sunset.  Two miles to the ferry, Matine-Baie Comeau. Good food and nice restaurants available.

## Mont Tremblant

Riddell, Judy & Alex
616 Montee Ryan, J0T 1Z0
(819) 425-7275
(819) 843-1742

**Amenities:** 2,5,6,7,8,10,11,
    16,17
**Breakfast:** F.

**Dbl. Oc.:** $52.00(CN)
**Sgl. Oc.:** $26.00(CN)
**Third Person:** $26.00(CN)
**Child:** under 12 yrs.-
    $13.00(CN)

**Chateau Beauvallen**—An intimate country inn on private beach and wooded property. The inn possesses a collection of antique Quebecois needlepoint tapestries on display in the pine-paneled lounge and guest rooms.  All summer and winter activities available.

| | | | | |
|---|---|---|---|---|
| 1. No Smoking | 5. Tennis Available | 9. Credit Cards Accepted | 13. Lunch Available | 17. Shared Bath |
| 2. No Pets | 6. Golf Available | 10. Personal Checks Accepted | 14. Public Transportation | 18. Afternoon Tea |
| 3. No Children | 7. Swiming Available | 11. Off Season Rates | 15. Reservations Necessary | ★ Commissions given |
| 4. Senior Citizen Rates | 8. Skiing Available | 12. Dinner Available | 16. Private Bath | to Travel Agents |

# QUEBEC

## *Montreal* *

Blondel, Lena
3000 Chemin De Breslax, H3Y 2G7
(514) 935-2312

**Amenities:** 1,9,14,17

**Breakfast:** F.

**Dbl. Oc.:** 60.00 - $65.00(CN)
**Sgl. Oc.:** $50.00 - $60.00(CN)
**Third Person:** $15.00(CN)
**Child:** under 12 yrs.-
$10.00(CN)

**Montreal Oasis Bed And Breakfast**—A spacious home in downtown Montreal. Located in a lovely neighborhood with pretty gardens. Nearby restaurants, museums and shopping. Swedish hostess is world travelled, loves all kinds of music and African art. Friendly Siamese Cat. Gourmet breakfast.

## *Montreal*

Chang, Liling Tokes
3497 Girouard Ave., H4A 3C5
(514) 487-4242

**Amenities:** 2,4,11,15,17

**Breakfast:** F.

**Dbl. Oc.:** $55.00(CN)
**Sgl. Oc.:** $45.00(CN)
**Third Person:** $20.00(CN)
**Child:** under 12 yrs.-
$10.00(CN)

**Bed & Breakfast Overseas**—There is no better way to be in Montreal than a private home offering you comfort and friendly service at the right price. Five minutes from downtown.

## *Montreal*

Fournier, Diane & Alexis
3445 St. Andre, H2L 3V4
(514) 598-0898

**Amenities:** 5,7,14,15,17

**Breakfast:** C.

**Dbl. Oc.:** $60.00 - $70.00(CN)
**Sgl. Oc.:** $40.00 - $45.00(CN)
**Third Person:** $30.00(CN)
**Child:** under 12 yrs.-
$15.00(CN)

**Chez Alexis**—A tall, elegant Victorian residence on a quiet street awaits discerning visitors seeking the distinguished charm of European hospitality. We are located in the very hear of all that makes Montreal one of the cultural, gastronomical and recreational capitals of the world.

## *Montreal*

Jouhannet, Claude
3422 Stanely St., M3A 1R8
(514) 288-6922,
 Fax: (514) 288-5757

**Amenities:** 9,11,14,15,16,17

**Breakfast:** C.

**Dbl. Oc.:** $64.25(CN)
**Sgl. Oc.:** $53.50(CN)
**Third Person:** $10.00(CN)
**Child:** under 12 yrs.-
no charge

**Manoir Ambrose**—Situated on the quiet and restful slope of beautiful MountRoyal, within walking distance of Montreal's restaurants, theatres, shopping districts and metro system. Comfortably furnished rooms in a Victorian setting with phone and cable TV. Your personal host is Lucie.

---

| | | | |
|---|---|---|---|
| 1. No Smoking | 5. Tennis Available | 9. Credit Cards Accepted | 13. Lunch Available | 17. Shared Bath |
| 2. No Pets | 6. Golf Available | 10. Personal Checks Accepted | 14. Public Transportation | 18. Afternoon Tea |
| 3. No Children | 7. Swiming Available | 11. Off Season Rates | 15. Reservations Necessary | ★ Commissions given |
| 4. Senior Citizen Rates | 8. Skiing Available | 12. Dinner Available | 16. Private Bath | to Travel Agents |

# QUEBEC

## Montreal

Lauzon, Jean-Paul
4660 de Grand-Pre, H2T 2H7
514) 843-6458

**Amenities:** 11,14,15,17,18
**Breakfast:** F.
**Dbl. Oc.:** $55.00 - $70.00(CN)
**Sgl. Oc.:** $40.00(CN)
**Child:** under 2 yrs. - no charge

**La Maison De Grand Pre**—A cozy and quiet 19th-century house with warm hospitality. Near the famous St.-Denis Street, with its restaurants, boutiques and open-door cafes. Two minutes from subway and 15 minutes from the business district. Breakfast has four different menus, fruits and hot bread.

---

## Montreal *

Morvaw, Annick
151 Sherbrooke Est, H2X 1C7
(514) 285-0895

**Amenities:** 2,4,9,14,15, 16,17
**Breakfast:** C.

**Dbl. Oc.:** $48.00 - $58.00(CN)
**Sgl. Oc.:** $42.00 - $54.00(CN)
**Third Person:** $6.00(CN)
**Child:** under 12 yrs. - no charge

**Armor Inn**—A small inn with typical European character. Situated in the heart of Montreal. Ideally located, close to the Metro and Prince Arthur Street. Near the Notre Dame Cathedral and old Montreal. Excellent underground shopping.

---

## New Carlisle West

Sawyer, Helen
337 Route 132, G0C 1Z0
(418) 752-2725, 752-6718

**Amenities:** 2,5,6,7,8,12,13,14, 17,18
**Breakfast:** F.

**Dbl. Oc.:** $35.00(CN)
**Sgl. Oc.:** $25.00(CN)
**Third Person:** $10.00(CN)
**Child:** under 12 yrs. - $5.00(CN)

**Bay View Farm B&B**—Five cozy guest rooms. Seaside home. Extra meals available with farm-fresh produce, homemade jams and home-baked food. Folk music and dances. Quilts, and crafts on display and for sale. Hiking and bird watching. Quiet and restful. Cottage available. Folk Festival second week in August.

---

## North Hatley *

Bardati, Sonya & Robert
RR 1, J0B 2C0
(819) 842-4213

**Amenities:** 1,2,4,8,9,15, 16,18
**Breakfast:** F.

**Dbl. Oc.:** $55.00(CN)
**Sgl. Oc.:** $40.00(CN)
**Third Person:** $25.00(CN)
**Child:** under 12 yrs.- $15.00(CN)

**La Casa Del Sol**—Peace and tranquility — a place to get away. This is where you will want to stay. A smiling welcome to our mini-farm with clean air and superb views add to the charm. A quiet, restful, comfortable sleep at night and good food to start your day off right. Biennvenue — Benvenuto!

---

| | | | | |
|---|---|---|---|---|
| 1. No Smoking | 5. Tennis Available | 9. Credit Cards Accepted | 13. Lunch Available | 17. Shared Bath |
| 2. No Pets | 6. Golf Available | 10. Personal Checks Accepted | 14. Public Transportation | 18. Afternoon Tea |
| 3. No Children | 7. Swiming Available | 11. Off Season Rates | 15. Reservations Necessary | ★ Commissions given |
| 4. Senior Citizen Rates | 8. Skiing Available | 12. Dinner Available | 16. Private Bath | to Travel Agents |

# QUEBEC

## Nouvelle, Gaspesie

Gauthier, Marguerite
628 Route 132 E., G0C 2 E0
(418) 794-2767

**Amenities:** 2,5,6,7,15,17
**Breakfast:** F.

**Dbl. Oc.:** $45.00(CN)
**Sgl. Oc.:** $30.00(CN)
**Third Person:** $15.00 - $20.00(CN)
**Child:** under 12 yrs - $10.00(CN)

**Maison Gauthier**—Our house is located near Carleton, where the mountains meet the sea at the "Baie Des Chaleurs." The fossil museumat "Miguasha" is interesting to visit. Quiet area. Open June-October.

## Quebec City

Dumais, Dolores
820 Eymard Ave., G1S 4A1
(418) 681-6804

**Amenities:** 6,8,14,15
**Breakfast:** F.

**Dbl. Oc.:** $45.00(CN)
**Sgl. Oc.:** $35.00(CN)
**Third Person:** $15.00(CN)

**The Battlefield Bed And Breakfast**—Between Laval Campus and Walled City. Quebec is a place of history, culture, gastronomy, heritage, nature and distinctiveness. Starting point to Ile-D'Orleans, Ste.-Anne De Beaupre Shrine, Jacques Carteir, Saguenay and St.-Lawrence Vallies and restaurants.

## Riviere du Loup *

Levesque, Louiselle
280 Anse Au Persil, RR 132, G5R 3Y5
(418) 862-9494

**Amenities:** 2,3,4,5,6,7,8,11, 14,15,16,17
**Breakfast:** F.

**Dbl. Oc.:** $48.00 - $55.00(CN)
**Sgl. Oc.:** $32.00(CN)
**Third Person:** $15.00(CN)
**Child:** under 12 yrs.- $12.00(CN)

**Le Nouveau Jardin**—Warm hospitality. Retired hosts of French culture. Typical Quebecois home. Riverfront with view. Quiet, safe and beautiful. Natural food and delicious water. Close to town, gourmet restaurants, whale watching, cruises and health center. Come, enjoy the difference — Francaise.

## Sacre-Coeur

Deschenis, Adeline
65 Rue Morin Est, G0T 1Y0
(418) 236-4307
**Amenities:** 1,9,12,13
**Breakfast:** F.
**Dbl. Oc.:** $40.00(CN)
**Sgl. Oc.:** $38.00(CN)
**Third Person:** $10.00(CN)
**Child:** $28.00(CN)

**"Les Marguerites"**—Hospitable and restful. Fifteen minutes to Ta Doussac.Within an agricultural and forested village. Come and sample household bread and fresh garden produces. Tourist attractions, whale cruises, salmon fishing and lakes.Welcome everyone!

| | | | | |
|---|---|---|---|---|
| 1. No Smoking | 5. Tennis Available | 9. Credit Cards Accepted | 13. Lunch Available | 17. Shared Bath |
| 2. No Pets | 6. Golf Available | 10. Personal Checks Accepted | 14. Public Transportation | 18. Afternoon Tea |
| 3. No Children | 7. Swiming Available | 11. Off Season Rates | 15. Reservations Necessary | ★ Commissions given |
| 4. Senior Citizen Rates | 8. Skiing Available | 12. Dinner Available | 16. Private Bath | to Travel Agents |

# QUEBEC

## Sillery

Butler-Coutts, Joyce
2156 Rue Dickson, G1T 1C9
(418) 683-3847

**Amenities:** 5,6,7,8,14,
17,18
**Breakfast:** F.

**Dbl. Oc.:** $55.00 - $75.00(CN)
**Sgl. Oc.:** $55.00 - $75.00(CN)
**Third Person:** $15.00(CN)
**Child:** under 18 yrs.-
$15.00(CN)

"Fernlea"—A beautiful home with a lovely garden. Quiet residential neighborhood where one can jog, cycle or just stroll. Ten minutes to large shopping malls. One minute to bus for Old Quebec. Easy access to hundreds of fine restaurants. Superb skiing in mid-December. Pick-up tours at door.

## Sillery *

Clibbon, Beth & Peter
1355 Pasteur Ave., G1T 2B8
(418) 683-9755

**Amenities:** 1,2,7,14,15,17,18
**Breakfast:** F.

**Dbl. Oc.:** $55.00(CN)
**Sgl. Oc.:** $45.00(CN)
**Child:** under 5 yrs.-
$10.00(CN)

Beth's Bed And Breakfast—Sillery is an inner suburb of Quebec, 10 minutes from the heart of the city by car and 20 minutes by bus. Attractive home in large private grounds on quiet street with heated in-ground pool. Excellent restaurants two streets away. Open May 1 to October 31.

## St.-Armand

Fontaine, Luce
295 Ch des erables, J0J 1T0
(514) 248-3575

**Amenities:** 2,5,7,8,15,17
**Breakfast:** F.

**Dbl. Oc.:** $55.00(CN)
**Sgl. Oc.:** $40.00(CN)
**Third Person:** $20.00(CN)
**Child:** under 12 yrs.-
$10.00(CN)

Domaine Fonberg—A quiet country setting situated on an 11-acre Christmas tree plantation. Tennis court, swimming pool and cross-country skiing. Private living room with fireplace. Near the Dunham's wine region. Come and enjoy a peaceful existence.

## St. Bruno De Montarville *

Richard, Dominique
1959 Montarville, J3V 3V8
(514) 653-2149

**Amenities:** 5,6,7,12,14,17,18
**Breakfast:** F.

**Dbl. Oc.:** $50.00(CN)
**Sgl. Oc.:** $35.00(CN)
**Third Person:** $15.00(CN)
**Child:** under 1 yr. -
no charge

Gite St. Bruno B&B—Offers quick and easy access to Montreal or airports. Quebec City or Ottawa are 2-1/2 hours away via Highway 20. Acre of land, fruit trees, vegetable and flower garden. Barbeque and picnic area. Screen house for guests. French, Dutch and English spoken. Open April-November.

---

| | | | |
|---|---|---|---|
| 1. No Smoking | 5. Tennis Available | 9. Credit Cards Accepted | 13. Lunch Available | 17. Shared Bath |
| 2. No Pets | 6. Golf Available | 10. Personal Checks Accepted | 14. Public Transportation | 18. Afternoon Tea |
| 3. No Children | 7. Swiming Available | 11. Off Season Rates | 15. Reservations Necessary | ★ Commissions given |
| 4. Senior Citizen Rates | 8. Skiing Available | 12. Dinner Available | 16. Private Bath | to Travel Agents |

## St. Jean, Ile d'Orleans

Godolphin, Lorraine & John  **Amenities:** 1,6,7,10,16  **Dbl. Oc.:** $60.00 - $75.00(CN)
170 Chemin Marie-Carreau,  **Breakfast:** F.  **Sgl. Oc.:** $50.00(CN)
G0A 3W0
(418) 829-2613, (418) 829-2871

**La Vigie Du Pilote (The Pilot's Lookout)**—Come and stay at the river pilot's home. Our tranquil cliff-top setting on four acres of land gives our luxurious home magnificent views of the St. Lawrence River and shipping channel. Only 30 minutes from Quebec City. Fluent English and French spoken.

## St.-Marc *

Handfield, Conrad
555 Richelieu, J0L 2E0
(514) 584-2226

**Amenities:** 2,5,6,7,8,9,12,13,15,16,18
**Breakfast:** F.
**Dbl. Oc.:** $50.00(CN)
**Sgl. Oc.:** $43.00(CN)
**Third Person:** $8.00(CN)
**Child:** under 10 yrs. - no charge

**Handfield Inn**—Quintessentially French is this inn on the Richelieu River. The rustic decor of this 160-year-old home is complemented with antiques and locally crafted furnishings. Outstanding cuisine, a marina and other facilities make this a unique holiday spot.

## St. Ulric

Dube, Rene & Nicole  **Amenities:** 14,15,17  **Dbl. Oc.:** $35.00(CN)
3371 Route 132, G0J 3H0  **Sgl. Oc.:** $25.00(CN)
(418) 737-4896  **Breakfast:** F.  **Third Person:** $45.00(CN)
**Child:** 6 - 12 yrs. -
$8.00(CN)

**After having** watched the fishermen at work loading shrimp and after visiting the salmon migrating fishway come home and breathe the fresh air of the St. Laurence River. See the marvelous sunsets and enjoy the savour of our homemade jam. Welcome.

## Ste. Agathe *

Fleurent, Claude  **Amenities:** 5,6,7,8,9,11,  **Dbl. Oc.:** $40.00 - $60.00(CN)
230 St. Venant, J8C 3A3  12,1516,18  **Sgl. Oc.:** $35.00 - $55.00(CN)
(819) 326-7016  **Breakfast:** F.  **Third Person:** $15.00(CN)
**Child:** under 16 yrs.-
no charge

**Auberge Du Lac Des Sables**—Two inns with 20 rooms each on the lake. TV, jacuzzi, air-conditioning, fireplace, piano, veranda, playroom, meeting room and outdoor whirlpool on the terrace. Watch beautiful sunsets on the lake. Country inn one mile from the city, 60 miles north of Montreal. Skiing nearby.

| | | | | |
|---|---|---|---|---|
| 1. No Smoking | 5. Tennis Available | 9. Credit Cards Accepted | 13. Lunch Available | 17. Shared Bath |
| 2. No Pets | 6. Golf Available | 10. Personal Checks Accepted | 14. Public Transportation | 18. Afternoon Tea |
| 3. No Children | 7. Swiming Available | 11. Off Season Rates | 15. Reservations Necessary | ★ Commissions given |
| 4. Senior Citizen Rates | 8. Skiing Available | 12. Dinner Available | 16. Private Bath | to Travel Agents |

## Ste. Agnes Charlevoix *

Maltais, Huguet
102 PrincIpale, G0T 1R0
(418) 439-4017

**Amenities:** 4,5,6,7,8,10,11,12,13,
14,15,16,17,18
**Breakfast:** F.
**Dbl. Oc.:** $50.00 - $60.00(CN)
**Sgl. Oc.:** $40.00 - $50.00(CN)
**Third Person:** $10.00(CN)
**Child:** $10.00(CN)

**La Louviere**—A warm, hospitable and charmingly restored house, circa1 830. A great place to relax and unwind. Situated eight miles from theatres, museum, cross-country and downhill skiing. Snowmobiling at the door. Fondu, fireplace, homemade breads and jams and regional cuisine.

## Ste Foy

Bastien, Jules
825 De Mons Ave., G1X 2R6
(418) 653-5884

**Amenities:** 2,3,4,5,9,10,11,12, 13,14,15,16,18
**Breakfast:** F.

**Dbl. Oc.:** $55.00(CN)
**Sgl. Oc.:** $35.00(CN)

**Best Value Lodging**—You'll like the real hospitality. You'll feel at home away from home. A privileged and warm place to stay. A quiet atmosphere for a perfect rest. Private bathroom, leisure room and color TV.

## Ste. Foy *

Godbout, Ghislaine
891 Chanoine Martin, G1V 3P8
(418) 651-8521

**Amenities:** 2,6,8,14
**Breakfast:** F.

**Dbl. Oc.:** $50.00(CN)
**Sgl. Oc.:** $30.00(CN)
**Third Person:** $10.00(CN)

**Bienvenue Chez-Nous**—Feel the warm French hospitality of Quebec in a private and quiet home within walking distance of shopping centers and fine restaurants. Just 20 minutes from the walls of Old Quebec.

## Ste.-Jeanne D'Arc

Harvey, Denyse
230 RG 7 D'Almas, G0W 1E0
(418) 276-2810

**Amenities:** 4,11,17
**Breakfast:** F.

**Dbl. Oc.:** $35.00(CN)
**Sgl. Oc.:** $25.00(CN)
**Third Person:** $15.00(CN)
**Child:** $15.00(CN)

**Co-Lac St. Jean**—Older home on a small farm with modern facilities. Breakfast includes home-made jellies and jams. Picnic area with table. Church 3 Km away in the town of Ste. Jean D'arc.

| | | | |
|---|---|---|---|
| 1. No Smoking | 5. Tennis Available | 9. Credit Cards Accepted | 13. Lunch Available | 17. Shared Bath |
| 2. No Pets | 6. Golf Available | 10. Personal Checks Accepted | 14. Public Transportation | 18. Afternoon Tea |
| 3. No Children | 7. Swiming Available | 11. Off Season Rates | 15. Reservations Necessary | ★ Commissions given |
| 4. Senior Citizen Rates | 8. Skiing Available | 12. Dinner Available | 16. Private Bath | to Travel Agents |

## Tadoussac

Hovington, Lise & Paulin
285 Des Pionniers, G0T 2A0
(514) 671-4656 (winter),
(418) 235-4466 (summer)
**Amenities:** 5,6,7,9,11,15,16,17
**Breakfast:** C.
**Dbl. Oc.:** $50.00 - $60.00(CN)
**Sgl. Oc.:** $40.00(CN)
**Third Person:** $15.00(CN)
**Child:** under 5 yrs. - $10.00(CN)

**Maison Hovington**—An old ancestral house with view of St. Lawrence and Saguenay Rivers. Whale watching country. Pedestrian paths. The Hovingtons are happy to welcome you into their family home.

## Val-David

Bourque, Camille & Lise
1267 Ch. de la Sapiniere, J0T 2N0
(819) 322-6379

**Amenities:** 1,2,3,4,8,15,17

**Breakfast:** C.

**Dbl. Oc.:** $50.00(CN)
**Sgl. Oc.:** $30.00(CN)
**Third Person:** $20.00(CN)
**Child:** under 12 yrs.-
$15.00(CN)

**La Chaumiere Aux Marguerites**—One hour north of Montreal. Enjoy a healthy breakfast and relaxing music by the fireplace in this large house. In winter there is a downhill and cross-country skiing area.In summer there are pedestrian walks and mountain climbing. Fine restaurants and genuine arts and crafts shops.

| | | | | |
|---|---|---|---|---|
| 1. No Smoking | 5. Tennis Available | 9. Credit Cards Accepted | 13. Lunch Available | 17. Shared Bath |
| 2. No Pets | 6. Golf Available | 10. Personal Checks Accepted | 14. Public Transportation | 18. Afternoon Tea |
| 3. No Children | 7. Swiming Available | 11. Off Season Rates | 15. Reservations Necessary | ★ Commissions given |
| 4. Senior Citizen Rates | 8. Skiing Available | 12. Dinner Available | 16. Private Bath | to Travel Agents |

# SASKATCHEWAN

## Ile-a-la Crosse

Cornett, Ken
Box 238, S0M 1C0
(306) 833-2590

**Amenities:** 1,2,4,6,7,8,9,10,
12,13,17,18
**Breakfast:** F.

**Dbl. Oc.:** $60.00(CN)
**Sgl. Oc.:** $44.00(CN)
**Third Person:** $10.00(CN)
**Child:** under 6 yrs. -
no charge

**Rainbow Ridge Bed & Breakfast**—Become one of the family in one of our six luxurious rooms located on a beautiful 14-acre peninsula. To our guests we provide complimentary boats, canoes, Ski-Doo and mini-golf. A very quiet, peaceful and scenic location.

# YUKON

## Dawson City

Magnusson, Inday & Jon
451 Craig St.
Box 954, Y0B 1G0
(403) 993-5649:
Fax (403) 993-5648

**Amenities:** 1,2,7,8,9,10,11,12,
13,15,16,17,18
**Breakfast:** C.(summer)
F.(winter)

**Dbl. Oc.:** $63.00(CN)
**Sgl. Oc.:** $53.00(CN)
**Third Person:** $19.00(CN)
**Child:** under 3 yrs. -
no charge

**Dawson City Bed & Breakfast**—Located at junction of Klondike and Yukon Rivers. Within walking distance to downtown attractions. Oriental lunches and dinner available upon request. Airport, bus and waterfront transportation provided. Northern and Oriental hospitality and decor. VISA and Diners cards accepted.

| | | | |
|---|---|---|---|
| 1. No Smoking | 5. Tennis Available | 9. Credit Cards Accepted | 13. Lunch Available | 17. Shared Bath |
| 2. No Pets | 6. Golf Available | 10. Personal Checks Accepted | 14. Public Transportation | 18. Afternoon Tea |
| 3. No Children | 7. Swiming Available | 11. Off Season Rates | 15. Reservations Necessary | ★ Commissions given |
| 4. Senior Citizen Rates | 8. Skiing Available | 12. Dinner Available | 16. Private Bath | to Travel Agents |

# COSTA RICA

Watkins, John A
3018 San Isidro de Heredia
Box 308, Greenfield, MO 65661 (U.S. address)
(506) 39-8096
(417) 637-2066 (U.S.)

**Amenities:** 9,12,14,15,16
**Breakfast:** F.

**Dbl. Oc.:** $45.20
**Sgl. Oc.:** $39.55
**Third Person:** $11.30

**La Posada De La Montana**—Great headquarters for birding trips. Less than three hours to either the Pacific or the Atlantic. Best climate with clean air at 4,500 feet elevation. 5 1/2 acres. Terrific mountain views. Twenty minutes to San Jose. We grow our own coffee, fruit, melons. American owned.

# PUERTO RICO

## Ceiba

Treat, Nicki
P.O. Box 1067, 00635
CARR 977 Km. 1.2
(809) 885-0471

**Amenities:** 2,9,15,16

**Breakfast:** C.

**Dbl. Oc.:** $55.00
**Sgl. Oc.:** $45.00
**Third Person:** $10.00

**Ceiba Country Inn**—A nine room tropical inn located in the hills above town. A magnificent view of the ocean and the Isle of Culebra. A cozy cocktail lounge for your eveining libation. Three miles to Rooosevelt Roads Navy Base. 35 miles to the night life of San Jaun.

## Patillas

Geller, Esther
HC 764, BZ 8490, 00723
(809) 839-6339

**Amenities:** 1,2,3,7,9,11,12,
13,15,16,18
**Breakfast:** C.

**Dbl. Oc.:** $77.70
**Sgl. Oc.:** $77.70
**Third Person:** $12.00

**Hotel Caribe Playa, Inc.**—Our extraordinary combination of sea and mountains in a tropical environment provides Puerto Rico's best year-round climate for enjoyable vacationing. Caribe Playa attracts friendly, adventurous guests from all walks of life for relaxation and fun..

| | | | |
|---|---|---|---|
| 1. No Smoking | 5. Tennis Available | 9. Credit Cards Accepted | 13. Lunch Available | 17. Shared Bath |
| 2. No Pets | 6. Golf Available | 10. Personal Checks Accepted | 14. Public Transportation | 18. Afternoon Tea |
| 3. No Children | 7. Swiming Available | 11. Off Season Rates | 15. Reservations Necessary | ★ Commissions given |
| 4. Senior Citizen Rates | 8. Skiing Available | 12. Dinner Available | 16. Private Bath | to Travel Agents |

# UNITED STATES VIRGIN ISLANDS

## St. John

Straubinger, Eric
P.O. Box 350, 00831
(809) 776-6378

**Amenities:** 2,5,9,11,12,14,
          16,17
**Breakfast:** C.

**Dbl. Oc.:** $53.00 & up
**Sgl. Oc.:** $38.00 & up
**Third Person:** $15.00

**The Inn At Tamarind Court**—The inn's 20 rooms offer guests a complimentary continental breakfast. Secure, intimate, yet only two blocks from the ferry dock. A most convenient retreat while you explore St. John's National Park and unspoiled beaches.

## St. Thomas

Cooper, Barbara
P.O. Box 1903, 00803
(809) 774-4270

**Amenities:** 2,3,7,9,11,15
**Breakfast:** C.

**Dbl. Oc.:** $92.00
**Sgl. Oc.:** $86.00
**Third Person:** $18.00

**Island View Guest House**—Fifteen rooms, 545 feet in elevation, overlooking the harbor and town. Five minutes to town, airport and beach. King, queen and twin accommodations, most with private bath and balcony. Telephones in rooms. Kitchens and air-conditioning available. Freshwater pool.

## St. Thomas

Hepworth, Jack
Blackbeard's Hill, 00802
(800) 343-4085, (809) 774-5511

**Amenities:** 2,7,9,11,12,14,15,16
**Breakfast:** C.
**Dbl. Oc.:** $92.00 - $210.00
**Sgl. Oc.:** $92.00 - $210.00
**Third Person:** $25.00
**Child:** under 3 yrs. - no charge

**The Mark St. Thomas Inn & Restaurant**—A top a majestic hillside overlooking St. Thomas Harbor. Offers eight intimate guest rooms, housed in a historic home. On the site are terraced gardens, outdoor pool and nightly dinner at the Mark's highly acclaimed restaurant.

| | | | |
|---|---|---|---|
| 1. No Smoking | 5. Tennis Available | 9. Credit Cards Accepted | 13. Lunch Available | 17. Shared Bath |
| 2. No Pets | 6. Golf Available | 10. Personal Checks Accepted | 14. Public Transportation | 18. Afternoon Tea |
| 3. No Children | 7. Swiming Available | 11. Off Season Rates | 15. Reservations Necessary | ★ Commissions given |
| 4. Senior Citizen Rates | 8. Skiing Available | 12. Dinner Available | 16. Private Bath | to Travel Agents |

# *Reservation Services*

# Alabama

## Leeds

Rice, Kay
Route 2, Box 275, 35094
(205) 699-9841

**Amenities:** 4,6

**Dbl. Oc.:** $40.00 - $75.00
**Sgl. Oc.:** $30.00 - 70.00

**Bed & Breakfast Birmingham**—Southern hospitality assured from north Alabama to the Gulf Coast. Homes in a variety of settings and state-wide locations. Descriptive directory available for $2.00.
**Areas Covered:**Tennessee into Florida.

# Alaska

## Anchorage

Dennis, Mercy
4631 Caravelle Dr., 99502
(907) 248-2292

**Amenities:** 3,4,5,6

**Dbl. Oc.:** $45.00 - $95.00
**Sgl. Oc.:** $45.00 - $60.00

**Alaska Private Lodgings**—Carefully selected Alaskan homes offer rooms or suites with private or shared baths. We have homes with wonderful views, lakeside cabins and locations close to downtown. Write for brochure.
**Areas Covered:** Anchorage, Seward, Homer, Wasilla, Healy, Fairbanks, Glennallen, Valdez, Girdwood.

# Arizona

## Prescott

Thomson, George
P.O. Box 3999, 86302-3999
(602) 776-1102

**Amenities:** 4,6

**Dbl. Oc.:** $45.00 - $130.00
**Sgl. Oc.:** $40.00 - $130.00

**B&B Scottsdale And The West**—Enjoy the desert sunning by your private pool. Hike among the unique cacti and flora, or soar aloft on a hot-air balloon! Experience the fresh pine air and the scenery of the forested high country. Explore ancient Indian ruins and tour old historic mining towns.
**Areas Covered:** State of Arizona (We network with services in other western states).

## Scottsdale

Thomas, Thomas
P.O. Box 8628, 85252
(602) 995-2831, (800) 266-7829

**Amenities:** 1,3,4,5,6

**Dbl. Oc.:** $35.00 - $125.00
**Sgl. Oc.:** $30.00 - $100.00

**Bed & Breakfast In Arizona**—Homes, inns and ranches state-wide. All are inspected and have warm, friendly hosts who know about local things to do and see. An intimate and personalized, yet private, experience. From Bisbee to Page and from Lake Havasu to Lakeside, we represent the best in Arizona.
**Areas Covered:** Arizona statewide.

1. American Express
2. Senior Citizen Rate
3. VISA
4. Personal Check
5. Master Card
6. Brochure Available
7. Discover Card
8. Diner's Club

# RESERVATION SERVICES

## *Tempe*

Young, Ruth                    **Amenities: 6**        **Dbl. Oc.: $35.00 - $125.00**
P.O. Box 950 NB, 85281                                 **Sgl. Oc.: $25.00 - $90.00**
(602) 990-0682

**Mi Casa Su Casa**—Modest and luxurious homestays, cottages and ranches. Most are near golf, tennis, pools, national and state parks, canyons, mountains, lakes, birds, Indians, art and sports. **Areas Covered:** Phoenix, Scottsdale, Tempe, Mesa, Tucson, Sedona, Flagstaff, Paradise Valley, Prescott, Yuma, Wickenburg, Ajo, Bisbee etc.

## *Tucson*

Kiekebusch, Rena               **Amenities: 6**        **Dbl. Oc.: $35.00 - $104.55**
P.O. Box 13603, 85732                                  **Sgl. Oc.: $25.00 - $93.65**
(602) 790-2399

**Old Pueblo Homestays**—A wide variety of homes in Tucson proper, the foothills and surrounding areas. All are inspected and hosts carefully chosen. Truly friendly people who enjoy offering that personal touch. For free brochure, send self-addressed, stamped envelope. **Areas Covered:** Tucson, Green Valley, Bisbee, Oracle, Ajo and Oro Valley.

# California

## *Altadena*

Judkins, Ruth                  **Amenities: 3,5**      **Dbl. Oc.: $35.00 - $150.00**
P.O. Box 694, 91003                                    **Sgl. Oc.: $30.00 - $125.00**
(213) 684-4428, (818) 797-2055

**Eye Openers Bed & Breakfast Reservations**—A reservation service that strives to match travelers'requests with a wide range of B&B homes and inns throughout California. **Areas Covered:** State of California.

## *Fullerton*

Garrison, Joyce                **Amenities: 1,4,5,6**  **Dbl. Oc.: $50.00 - $200.00**
1943 Sunny Crest Dr., Ste. 304, 92635                  **Sgl. Oc.: $50.00 - $200.00**
(714) 738-8361

**Bed And Breakfast Of Southern California**—We make reservations for bed and breakfast homes and inns throughout the world. We have our network of homes in southern California. **Areas Covered:** All of southern California.

## *Pt.Reyes Station*

Fields, Sandy                  **Amenities: 4,6**      **Dbl. Oc.: $81.00 - $135.00**
P.O. Box 1162, 94956
(415) 663-1351

**Coastal Lodging Of West Marin**—Bed and breakfast availability an hour north of San Francisco and minutes from Pt. Reyes National Seashore. Inns, cottages and guest homes offer country hospitality, privacy, beaches, views, gardens, hot tubs, fireplaces, kitchens and quiet relaxation. **Areas Covered:** Pt. Reyes Station, Inverness and Bolinas.

| 1. American Express | 2. Senior Citizen Rate | 3. VISA | 4. Personal Check |
| 5. Master Card | 6. Brochure Available | 7. Discover Card | 8. Diner's Club |

# RESERVATION SERVICES

## San Francisco

Kreibich, Susan  
P.O. Box 349, 94101  
(415) 931-3083

**Amenities:** 1,3,4,5,6  
**Breakfast:** F.

**Dbl. Oc.:** $55.00 - $200.00  
**Sgl. Oc.:** $45.00 - $200.00

**Bed And Breakfast San Francisco**—Bed and breakfast in small inns, mansions, homes and yachts in San Francisco, Monterey, Carmel, the wine country and the Pacific Coast. Enjoy the real hospitality of San Franciscans. A full breakfast is served.  
**Areas Covered:** San Francisco, wine country, Monterey, Carmel and Pacific coast.

## San Francisco

Walsh, Sharon  
1181-B Solano Ave., Albany 94706  
(415) 525-4569

**Amenities:** 1,3,4,5,6,8

**Dbl. Oc.:** $55.00 - $125.00  
**Sgl. Oc.:** $45.00 - $125.00

**Bed & Breakfast International**—Offers over 300 private homes and professional inns throughout California with a focus on San Francisco, the wine country, Carmel and popular destinations in southern California. Try our houseboats in Sausalito for a uniqueway to stay at a B&B.  
**Areas Covered:** San Francisco, Berkeley, Palo Alto, Santa Cruz, Monterey, Lake Tahoe, Yosemite, Cambria, Santa Barbara, Los Angeles, San Diego and Las Vegas.

## Ventura

Hutton, Clara  
10890 Galvin, 93004  
(805) 647-0651

**Amenities:** 6

**Dbl. Oc.:** $50.00 - $85.00  
**Sgl. Oc.:** $45.00 - $85.00

**Bed And Breakfast Approved Hosts**—Seaside city, historic Sapnis-Chumash Museum; National Park Musuem.  
**Areas Covered:** Ventura county, California.

## Whittier

Davis, Coleen  
11715 S. Circle Dr., 90601  
(213) 699-8427

**Amenities:** 2,4,6

**Dbl. Oc.:** $40.00 - $85.00  
**Sgl. Oc.:** $35.00 - $70.00

**CoHost, America's Bed And Breakfast**—CoHosts enjoy guests, full breakfast, clean bath, good bed, help with planning, baby sitting, dinner, lunch, tour guides, wine & cheese, swimming, golf, skiing in some areas. Homes available near Disneyland, Knotts Berry Farm, Queen Mary, Spruce Goose and Universal Studios.  
**Areas Covered:** All of California, Lake Tahoe, as well as selected small towns and establishments throughout the U.S

| 1. American Express | 2. Senior Citizen Rate | 3. VISA | 4. Personal Check |
| 5. Master Card | 6. Brochure Available | 7. Discover Card | 8. Diner's Club |

# Colorado

## *Colorado Springs*

Field, Betty Ann
P.O. Box 804, 80901
(719) 630-3433

**Amenities:** 3,4,5,6

**Dbl. Oc.:** $40.00 - $175.00
**Sgl. Oc.:** $30.00 - $125.00

**Bed And Breakfast Rocky Mountains**—A reservation service for 100 B&Bs in Colorado, New Mexico and Utah. Budget to luxury rates. Descriptive directory available for $4.50. For general information call (800)825-0225. For reservations call (719) 630-3433.
**Areas Covered:** Colorado, Utah and New Mexico.

# Connecticut

## *New Haven*

Argenio, Jack
P.O. Box 216, 06513
(203) 469-3260

**Amenities:** 4,6

**Dbl. Oc.:** $50.00 - $75.00
**Sgl. Oc.:** $40.00 - $60.00

**Bed & Breakfast, Ltd.**—Offers 125 listings of gracious and affordable accommodations in Connecticut, from elegantly simple to simply elegant. B&B Ltd. takes pride in the variety and quality of its host homes and in the personalized service we provide to our guests.
**Areas Covered:** Connecticut, Massachusettes and Rhode Island.

## *Norfolk*

Trembley, Diane
Maple Ave.
Box 447, 06058
(203) 542-5944

**Amenities:** 1,3,4,5,6

**Dbl. Oc.:** $55.00 - $160.00
**Sgl. Oc.:** $50.00 - $150.00

**Covered Bridge**—Let us help you plan an ideal getaway. Idyllic B&B catering to the discriminating traveler. Charming farmhouses, Victorian estates or beautifully restored colonials. Guest rooms, several with fireplaces and decorated with antiques, offer a romantic retreat.
**Areas Covered:** Connecticut, Berkshires of Massachusettes, Hudson Valley of New York, shoreline of Rhode Island and southern Vermont.

# Delaware

## *Wilmington*

Alford, Millie
Box 177, 3650 Silverside Rd., 19810
(302) 479-9500, (800) 233-4689

**Amenities:** 3,4,5,6

**Dbl. Oc.:** $60.00 - $95.00
**Sgl. Oc.:** $35.00 - $55.00

**Bed & Breakfast Of Delaware**—Whatever your reason for visiting greater Delaware — beach or musuem, parkland, or boardroom, outdoor sports or indoor leisure - count on our reservation service for accommodations most appropriate to your full satisfaction. Reasonable monthly/weekly rates available.
**Areas Covered:** Delaware—Wilmington, Newark, New Castle, Odessa, Middletown, Dover, Bridgeville, Laurel, Lewes, Milford, Milton and Selbyville. Maryland—Fairhill, Elkton, Chesapeake City and Ocean City. Pennsylvania—Landenberg, Chadds Ford and West Chester.

| | | | |
|---|---|---|---|
| 1. American Express | 2. Senior Citizen Rate | 3. VISA | 4. Personal Check |
| 5. Master Card | 6. Brochure Available | 7. Discover Card | 8. Diner's Club |

# District of Columbia

## *Washington*

| | | |
|---|---|---|
| Groobey, Millie<br>P.O. Box 9490, 20016<br>(202) 363-7767 | Amenities: 1,3,4,5,6 | Dbl. Oc.: $51.45 - $119.55<br>Sgl. Oc.: $40.35 - $106.95 |

**Bed And Breakfast League/Sweet Dreams And Toast**—Represents accommodations in privately owned homes and apartments in the best and most convenient sections of the city. Many homes are in the historic sections. All offer easy access to public transportation and many offer parking. All B&Bs are carefully screened by us.
**Areas Covered:** Washington, D.C.; Arlington and Alexandria, Virginia; Bethesda and Rockville, Maryland.

## *Washington*

| | | |
|---|---|---|
| Simeone, Karen<br>P.O. Box 12011, 20009<br>(202) 328-3510 | Amenities: 1,3,5,8 | Dbl. Oc.: $52.25 - $196.00<br>Sgl. Oc.: $41.80 - $168.00 |

**Bed 'N' Breakfast Ltd. Of Washington, D.C.**—Reservation service for Washington, Maryland and Virginia. Convenient to public transportation. Some large, historic homes filled with antiques. We also have apartments for family groups or longer stays. Friendly, helpful, interesting hosts. Budget to luxury accommodations.
**Areas Covered:** Washington, D.C., Maryland and Virginia.

# Georgia

## *Thomasville*

| | | |
|---|---|---|
| Watt, Mercer<br>1104 Old Monticello Rd., 31792<br>(912) 226-7218, (912) 226-6882 | Amenities: 4,6 | Dbl. Oc.: $40.00 - $75.00<br>Sgl. Oc.: $30.00 - $50.00 |

**Quail Country Bed & Breakfast, Ltd.**—A professional service arranges lodging in carefully selected homes and private guest houses in historic Thomasville. Activities of interest include plantation tours, historic restoraitions and nearby hunting preserves.
**Areas Covered:** Thomasville.

# Hawaii

## *Hilo*

| | | |
|---|---|---|
| Diamond, Fred<br>P.O. Box 11418, 96721<br>(800) 662-8483, (808) 935-4178 | Amenities: 2,4,6 | Dbl. Oc.: $54.50<br>Sgl. Oc.: $49.05 |

**Go Native..Hawaii**—A celebratiion of Aloha! Go Native. Hawaii offers a rainbow of choices from a restored ambassador's mansion in Hilo, to a romantic cliff-top gazebo on Maui. From modest to luxury, our island B&Bs are special. A native's view of Paradise. Call or write for details.
**Areas Covered:** Each major island of the state of Hawaii.

| | | | |
|---|---|---|---|
| 1. American Express | 2. Senior Citizen Rate | 3. VISA | 4. Personal Check |
| 5. Master Card | 6. Brochure Available | 7. Discover Card | 8. Diner's Club |

# RESERVATION SERVICES

## Honolulu

Bridges, Gene          **Amenities:** 3,4,5,6      **Dbl. Oc.:** $38.50 - $176.00
3242 Kaohinani Dr., 96817                           **Sgl. Oc.:** $27.50 - $165.00
(808) 595-7533, (800) 288-4666, Fax:(808) 595-2030

**Bed & Breakfast Honolulu & Statewide**—Over 300 personally inspected homestays and studios on all islands. Free brochure. Toll-free reservations. Our homestays are like having friends in the islands!
**Areas Covered:** All the islands in the state of Hawaii.

---

## Kailua

Carlin, Ann           **Amenities:** 3,4,5       **Dbl. Oc.:** $49.00 - $275.00
823 Kainui Dr., 96734                             **Sgl. Oc.:** $38.00 & up
(800) 263-2342

**All Islands Bed And Breakfast**—Over 300 unique private homes, cottages and studios. Luxurious to modest. Inspected. On the ocean, in the mountains, in a city or on a flower farm. Low rates on rental cars and inter-island air fares. Call toll-free,( 800) 263-2342 for information and reservations.
**Areas Covered:** All the islands in the state of Hawaii.

---

## Kailua

Carlin, Ann           **Amenities:** 3,4,5       **Dbl. Oc.:** $49.00 - $275.00
823 Kainui Dr., 96734                             **Sgl. Oc.:** $38.00 & up
(800) 263-2342

**All Islands Bed And Breakfast**—Over 300 unique private homes, cottages and studios. Luxurious to modest. Inspected. On the ocean, in the mountains, in a city or on a flower farm. Low rates on rental cars and inter-island air fares. Call toll-free,( 800) 263-2342 for information and reservations.
**Areas Covered:** All the islands in the state of Hawaii.

---

## Kapaa (Kauai)

Epp, Doris           **Amenities:**           **Dbl. Oc.:** $45.00 and up
218-A, 970 No. Kalaheo, 96734
(808) 262-6026 (808) 254-5030
Fax: (808) 261-6573

**Pacific Hawaii Bed and Breakfast**—Beach front retreats, white sand beach. Ideal swimming or just walking the two mile stretch of beach. Executive-type homes. Non-tourist environment, yet only 15 minute drive to downtown Honlulu or 30 minute drive to Wakiki.
**Areas Covered:** Kailua, Oahu, Hawaii.

| | | | |
|---|---|---|---|
| 1. American Express | 2. Senior Citizen Rate | 3. VISA | 4. Personal Check |
| 5. Master Card | 6. Brochure Available | 7. Discover Card | 8. Diner's Club |

# Illinois

## *Chicago*

Shaw, Mary
P.O. Box 14088, 60614-0088
(312) 9510-0085

**Amenities:** 1,3,4,5,6

**Dbl. Oc.:** $50.00 - $80.00
**Sgl. Oc.:** $40.00 - $70.00

**Bed & Breakfast/Chicago, Inc.**—As a distinctive alternative to hotels and motels, we provide pleasant, reasonably priced lodging in either private homes or furnished self-contained apartments. Your" home-away-from-home" may be a room in a historic area, a high-rise condo with a panoramic view or a coach house.
**Areas Covered:** Downtown Chicago ( near north side), Hyde Park/Kenwood and the north shore suburbs.

## *Hoffman Estates*

McDonald-Swan, Martha
P.O. Box 95503, 60195-0503
(708) 310-9010

**Amenities:** 3,4,5,6,7

**Dbl. Oc.:** $50.00 - $170.00
**Sgl. Oc.:** $45.00 - $90.00

**B&B Northwest Suburban — Chicago**—A vast array of homes in northern Illinois range from a country farmhouse to an elegant Italianate villa with fireplace and jacuzzi  Some suburban conveniences while others offer the perfect getaway,  Most non-smoking.  Call early for reservations that are ideal for you.
**Areas Covered:** North and west suburbs of Chicago, west to Galena, Illinois (covering the northern sector of Illinois except Chicago proper).

# Louisiana

## *Metairie*

Brown, Sarah Margaret
671 Rosa St., 70005
(504) 838-0071, (504) 838-0072, (504) 838-0073

**Amenities:** 1,3,4,5,6

**Dbl. Oc.:** $40.00 - $275.00
**Sgl. Oc.:** $35.00 - $275.00

**New Orleans Bed And Breakfast And Accommodations**—French Quarter hideaways, old New Orleans homes and apartments for one or a bunch. All have been inspected for your comfort. Rates are based on type of home, location and private or shared bath. Free listing. Budget, moderate and deluxe rates.
**Areas Covered:** New Orleans, Metairie and Kenner, Louisiana.

| | | | |
|---|---|---|---|
| 1. American Express | 2. Senior Citizen Rate | 3. VISA | 4. Personal Check |
| 5. Master Card | 6. Brochure Available | 7. Discover Card | 8. Diner's Club |

# RESERVATION SERVICES

## *New Orleans*

Brown, Sarah Margaret
P.O. Box 8128, 70182
(504) 838-0071, 838-0072

**Amenities:** 1,3,5,6,7

**Dbl. Oc.:** $45.00 - $150.00
**Sgl. Oc.:** $45.00 - $150.00

**New Orleans Bed And Breakfast**—Many lovely homes offering Southern hospitality to visitors are available at budget, moderate or deluxe rates. We can arrange and we can offer our assistance for almost anything a visitor might want.
**Areas Covered:** Greater New Orleans area.

# Maine

## *Falmouth*

Tierney, Peg
32 Colonial Village, 04105
(207) 781-4528

Amenities: 3,5

Dbl.Oc.: $49.00 - $140.00
Sgl.Oc.: $38.00 - $90.00

**Bed & Breakfast of Maine**—A one stop booking service for B&B homes in the most popular parts of the state. Accommodation list is available for $1.00. Plan your trip and we handle reservations. Enjoy coastal or inland areas. We are open to phone calls evenings or weekends.
**Areas Covered:** State of Maine.

# Maryland

## *Baltimore*

Grater, Betsy
1428 Park Ave., 21217
(301) 225-0001

**Amenities:** 1,3,4,5,6

**Dbl. Oc.:** $45.00 & up
**Sgl. Oc.:** $40.00 & up

**Amanda's Bed & Breakfast Reservation Service**—Amanda's offers a fine selection of private homes, small inns and yachts. Historic locations on the water. Pools, fireplaces and private beaches. Urban and rural. Near public transportation, cultural events, antiques and shops.
**Areas Covered:** Maryland, Virginia, Pennsylvania, Delaware, West Virginia, New Jersey and District of Columbia.

| | | | |
|---|---|---|---|
| 1. American Express | 2. Senior Citizen Rate | 3. VISA | 4. Personal Check |
| 5. Master Card | 6. Brochure Available | 7. Discover Card | 8. Diner's Club |

# Massachusetts

## *Bedford*

Phillips, Phyllis
48 Spring Rd., 01730
(617) 275-9025

**Amenities:** 4,6

Dbl. Oc.: $50.00 - $70.00
Sgl. Oc.: $40.00 - $60.00

**Bed & Breakfast Folks**—A B&B reservation service offering a warm, homey alternative to hotels and motels. Located in 14 towns north and west of Boston.
**Areas Covered:** North and west of Boston, Bedford, Lexington, Concord, Chelmsford, Lowell, Westford, Groton, Reading, Tyngsboro, Dunstable, Boxford, Boxboro, Brookline and Nashua, New Hampshire.

## *Boston*

Handler, Steven
248 Newbury St., 02116
(617) 266-7142

**Amenities:** 3,4,5,6

Dbl. Oc.: $76.38
Sgl. Oc.: $60.36

**Beacon Inns & Guesthouses**—Located in historic Back Bay offering guest rooms with private bath, kitchenette and air-conditioning. On the Green Line MBTA (public transit system) and Cambridge bus line. Welcome to Boston!
**Areas Covered:** Boston.

## *Boston*

Mintz, Ferne
47 Commercial Wharf, 02110
(800) 248-9262, (617) 720-3540

**Amenities:** 1,3,4,5,6

Dbl. Oc.: $70.00 - $100.00
Sgl. Oc.: $55.00 - $80.00

**A Bed & Breakfast Agency Of Boston**—Downtown Boston's largest selection of historic, private homes, 1840 waterfront lofts and Victorian townhouses. Exclusive locations include waterfront, Fanueil Hall, Quincy Market, Freedom Trail, Back Bay, Beacon Hill and Copley Square. Furnished apartments also available.
**Areas Covered:** Boston.

## *Boston*

Mitchell, Marilyn
P.O. Box 57166, Babson Park, 02157-0166
(617) 449-5302, Fax: (617) 449-5958

**Amenities:** 1,3,4,5,6

Dbl. Oc.: $60.00 - $100.00
Sgl. Oc.: $50.00 - $90.00

**Bed & Breakfast Associates Bay Colony, Ltd.**—Boston's largest selection of fine, fully inspected host homes are offered by our experienced reservation staff. Call us weekdays from 10:00-5:00 and let us show you the very best of B&Bs throughout eastern Massachusetts.
**Areas Covered:** Boston, Cambridge, Brookline, surrounding suburbs, north and south shores and Cape Cod.

| | | | |
|---|---|---|---|
| 1. American Express | 2. Senior Citizen Rate | 3. VISA | 4. Personal Check |
| 5. Master Card | 6. Brochure Available | 7. Discover Card | 8. Diner's Club |

# RESERVATION SERVICES

## Boston

Whittington, Marcia  **Amenities:** 1,3,4,5  **Dbl. Oc.:** $54.00 - $99.00
P.O. Box 117, Waban Branch, 02168  **Sgl. Oc.:** $45.00 - $85.00
(617) 244-1308

**Host Homes Of Boston**—Since 1982, Marcia has culled the best B&B homes close to historic, cultural and business sites. Cordial hosts at exclusive addresses include Beacon Hill, Back Bay, Faneuil Hall and nearby suburbs on the "T." Two-night minimum. Call Monday-Friday, 9:00-4:30. Free directory.
**Areas Covered:** Boston, Brookline, Newton, Cambridge, Needham, Lexington, Concord, Wellesley, Dover, Westwood, Weymouth, Marblehead and Cape Cod.

## Cambridge

Carruthers, Pamela  **Amenities:** 1,2,3,4,5,6  **Dbl. Oc.:** $60.00 - $95.00
P.O. Box 665, 02140  **Sgl. Oc.:** $45.00 - $80.00
(617) 576-1492, 576-2112

**Bed & Breakfast Cambridge & Greater Boston B&B**—In Minuteman country. Charming, regularly inspected host homes in safe areas. Near colleges and historic sites. Good public transportation; therefore, you may not need a car. Call 9:00-6:00, Monday - Friday and 10:00-3:00, Saturday. We look forward to serving you. Come home to us!
**Areas Coverd:** Boston, Cambridge, Lexington and surrounding towns.

## Cambridge

Goldberg, Charlotte  **Amenities:** 1,3,5,6  **Dbl. Oc.:** $60.00 - $95.00
335 Pearl St., 02139  **Sgl. Oc.:** $60.00 - $90.00
(617) 491-0274

**ABC: Accommodations Of Boston & Cambridge**—Our family of host homes is ready to great you warmly and offer you home, hearth and a healthy breakfast, together with hospitality, comfort and good conversation. Call 24 hours a day, or write to the above address.
**Areas Covered:** Boston, Cambridge, Brookline, Newton, Weston and surrounding towns.

## Hyannis, West

Diehl, Clark  **Amenities:** 1,3,4,5,6  **Dbl. Oc.:** $48.00 - $175.00
Box 341, 02672  **Sgl. Oc.:** $40.00 - $60.00
(508) 775-2772

**Bed & Breakfast Cape Cod**—Select from 80 romantic, historic inns or host homes. Beaches, whale watches, seafood and hospitality at its best. Deluxe or modest accommodations. Write or call for information.
**Areas Covered:** Cape Cod, Nantucket, Martha's Vineyard, north and south of Boston.

| | | | |
|---|---|---|---|
| 1. American Express | 2. Senior Citizen Rate | 3. VISA | 4. Personal Check |
| 5. Master Card | 6. Brochure Available | 7. Discover Card | 8. Diner's Club |

## New Bedford

Mulford, Judy
P.O. Box F 821, 02742
(508) 990-1696

**Amenities:** 1,3,4,5,6

**Dbl. Oc.:** $43.00 - $145.00
**Sgl. Oc.:** $35.00 - $65.00

**Pineapple Hospitality New England-Wide**—Offers tips on fun itinerary for your travels in New England. Knowledgable tour operators will place you in pre-inspected bed and breakfasts. Hours: weekdays 9 a.m. - 6 p.m.
**Areas Covered:** Connecticut, Rhode Island, Vermont, New Hampshire, Maine and Massachusettes.

## Orleans

Griffin, Richard
Box 1881, 02653
(800) 666-HOST

**Amenities:** 1,2,3,4,5,6

**Dbl. Oc.:** $48.00 - $187.00
**Sgl. Oc.:** $35.00 - $150.00

**House Guests Cape Cod And The Islands**—B&B lodgings in expertly restored sea and whaling captains' homes dating from 1712. Many are in lovely, wooded settings; others are ocean-front or water view. A selection of cottages and apartments is also available. Send $3.95 for 68-page illustrated directory.
**Areas Covered:** Cape Cod, Martha's Vineyard and Nantucket.

## Plymouth

Gillis, Diane
P.O. Box 1333, 02360
(617) 837-9867

**Amenities:** 1,3,4,5,6

**Dbl. Oc.:** $50.00 - $110.00
**Sgl. Oc.:** $38.00 - $65.00

**Be Our Guest Bed & Breakfast, Ltd.**—Homes range from historic to traditional New England. Hosted by people dedicated to making your stay a memorable experience. Visit Plymouth Rock, The Mayflower, Boston and Cape Cod. Enjoy the ocean, fine restaurants and antiquing. Easy commuting to all points of interest. Brochure: $1.00.
**Area Covered:** Boston, Cohasset, Duxbury, Falmouth, Hanover, Kingston, Marshfield, Plymouth, Sandwich, Scituate and Cape Cod.

# Michigan

## Dearborn

Shields, Diane M.
23522 Lawrence, 48128
(313) 561-6041

**Amenities:** 3,4,5,6

**Dbl. Oc.:** $45.00 - $125.00
**Sgl. Oc.:** $40.00 - $100.00

**Bed and Breakfast Michigan**—Modest or magnificent, rustic or romantic, city or country, Michigan's B&Bs share one thing in common — a genuine concern for you, the guest. Let us arrange accommodations for you in Michigan's finest B&Bs. All personally inspected and guaranteed.
**Areas Covered:** Michigan.

| 1. American Express | 2. Senior Citizen Rate | 3. VISA | 4. Personal Check |
|---|---|---|---|
| 5. Master Card | 6. Brochure Available | 7. Discover Card | 8. Diner's Club |

# Mississippi

## *Meridian*

Hall, Barbara Lincoln
2303 23rd Ave.
P.O. Box 3497, 39303
(601) 482-5483

**Amenities:** 3,4,5,6

**Dbl. Oc.:** $45.00 - $150.00
**Sgl. Oc.:** $45.00 - $85.00

**Lincoln Ltd., Bed & Breakfast**—Gracious Southern hospitality in Mississippi's loveliest historic inns and private homes. Your personal preferences are carefully considered when placing you with one of our charming hosts.
**Areas Covered:** Mississippi, SW Tennessee, NW Florida, SW Alabama and New Orleans.

## *Natchez*

Ater, Phyllis
Canal at State St.
P.O. Box 347, 39120
(800) 647-6742, (601) 446-6631

**Amenities:** 1,3,4,5,6

**Dbl. Oc.:** $75.00 - $165.00
**Sgl. Oc.:** $70.00 - $160.00

**Natchez Pilgrimage Tours**—Experience true Southern hospitality in one of our magnificent antebellums. Accommodations in main houses, servants' quarters and guest cottages. Furnished in period antiques. Private baths. Full Southern breakfast included at most locations.
**Areas Covered:** Natchez.

## *Natchez*

Dunn, Roger
Canal St. Depot, 39120
(800) 824-0355

**Amenities:** 1,3,4,5,6

**Dbl. Oc.:** $65.00 - $130.00
**Sgl. Oc.:** $55.00 & up

**Creative Travel B&B Center**—We represent B&Bs historically significant, dating from 1785 to the 1850's, city and country, and all are special. Each is inspected by us and each maintains excellent ratings. A stay in Natchez is more rewarding when living in an old mansion or plantation.
**Areas Covered:** Natchez and Woodville.

# Missouri

## *Branson*

Cameron, Kay
P.O. Box 295, 65616
(417) 334-4720

**Amenities:** 1,2,3,4,5,6

**Dbl. Oc.:** $35.00 - $90.00
**Sgl. Oc.:** $30.00 - $80.00

**Ozark Mountain Country Bed & Breakfast Service**—All homes, guest cottages and inns are carefully selected to provide the quality B&B guests expect! Singles, couples and families can get away from it all and still be close to attractions. Most include gourmet breakfasts. A few have pools, spas and fireplaces.
**Areas Covered:** SW Missouri and NW Arkansas.

| | | | |
|---|---|---|---|
| 1. American Express | 3. Senior Citizen Rate | 3. VISA | 4. Personal Check |
| 5. Master Card | 6. Brochure Available | 7. Discover Card | 8. Diner's Club |

## Lenexa, Kansas

Monroe, Edwina T.
P.O. Box 14781, 66215
(913) 888-3636

**Amenities:** 4,6

**Dbl. Oc.:** $35.00 - $100.00
**Sgl. Oc.:** $30.00 - $100.00

**Bed & Breakfast—Kansas City**—Forty Victorian, turn-of-the-century homes and two inns. All serve full breakfasts and have private baths. Two B&Bs have hot tubs and three B&Bs have pools. Country and city getaways.
**Areas Covered:** Kansas City, MO. and nearby towns.

## St. Louis

Tessaro, Janell
P.O. Box 30069, 63119
(800) 666-5656 (out of state), (314) 961-2252 (Mo)

**Amenities:** 4,6

**Dbl. Oc.:** $40.00 - $95.00
**Sgl. Oc.:** $35.0 0- $85.00

**Bed & Breakfast Greater Saint Louis Reservation Service** - Select listing of the exclusive and private St.Louis B&B homes and small inns. All offer full, often gourmet, breakfasts. Lovley furnishings, personalized amenities and prime locations. Advance reservations of one month or more enhance availability.
**Areas Covered:** St. Louis, MO - city, county and outlying towns.

# Montana

## Billings

Deigert, Paula
806 Poly Dr.
P.O. Box 20972, 59104
(406) 259-7993

**Amenities:** 3,4,5,6
**Breakfast:** C. and F.

**Dbl. Oc.:** $28.00 - $175.00
**Sgl. Oc.:** $25.00 - $100.00

**Bed & Breakfast Western Adventure**—Glacier and Yellowstone Parks, blue-ribbon trout streams, roving ranches, Western history and mountain beauty are everywhere. All B&Bs are inspected. Hosts of ranches, homes, cabins and guest houses offer warm Western hospitality. Directory available for $5.00.
**Areas Covered:** Montana, Wyoming and Eastern Idaho.

# New Hampshire

## Meredith

Taddei, Ernie
Red Gate Lane
RFD 4, Box 88, 03253
(603) 279-8348

**Amenities:** 4,6

**Dbl. Oc.:** $45.00 - $115.00
**Sgl. Oc.:** $40.00 - $90.00

**New Hampshire Bed & Breakfast**—Over 60 locations close to breath taking scenery, four-season recreation, tax-free shopping and exciting attractions. Experience 18th-century colonial inns, lake-front homes, private mountainside residences. All with gracious owner hospitality and wonderful breakfasts.
**Areas Covered:** State of New Hampshire.

| | | | |
|---|---|---|---|
| 1. American Express | 2. Senior Citizen Rate | 3. VISA | 4. Personal Check |
| 5. Master Card | 6. Brochure Available | 7. Discover Card | 8. Diner's Club |

# RESERVATION SERVICES

# New Jersey

## *Denville*

Bergins, Alex      Amenities: 4,6      Dbl.Oc.: $80.00
11 Sunset Trail, 07834      Sgl.Oc.: $35.00
(201) 625-5129

Northern New Jersey Bed & Breakfast—We welcome B&B travelers for several day stays, as well as corporate transferees for stays of one week or one year. We offer temporary lodgings and a network of furnished lodgings. We cater to transferees and consultants. Rates allow for efficient management of relocation allotments.
**Areas Covered:** Northern and central New Jersey.

## *Midland Park*

Mould, Aster      **Amenities:** 1,2,3,4,5,6,7      **Dbl. Oc.:** $55.00 - $160.00
Suite 132, 103 Godwin Ave., 07432      **Sgl. Oc.:** $50.00 - $95.00
(201) 444-7409

**Bed & Breakfast Adventure**—Indulge in a lavish high-rise condo overlooking a metropolitan skyline. Stay in a restored mansion, on a yacht or enjoy the view from a cozy mountain cottage. Interesting and affordable Gold Medallion accommodations. Optional $25.00 membership fee.
**Areas Covered:** New Jersey, NE Pennsylvania, Poconos, southern New York state, New York City, SW Connecticut and southern Florida.

## *Princeton*

Hurley, John      **Amenities:**      **Dbl. Oc.:** $50.00 - $65.00
P.O. Box 571, 08540      **Sgl. Oc.:** $40.00 - $55.00
(609) 924-3189

**Bed And Breakfast Of Princeton**—Provides a pleasant alternative to local hotel lodging. Private homes that are either a few miles drive or within walking distance of the town center and universities.
**Areas Covered:** Princeton.

# New York

## *Buffalo*

Brannan, Georgia A.      **Amenities:** 3,4,5,6      **Dbl. Oc.:** $55.00 - $65.00
466 Amherst St., 14207      **Sgl. Oc.:** $35.00 - $45.00
(716) 874-8797

**Rainbow Hospitality, Inc.**—Rainbows are "bright, multi-colored arrangements or displays." We provide a multi-faceted display of bed and breakfast accommodations, from the rushing roar of Niagara Falls to Chinaman's Lighthouse welcoming you to Buffalo. Experience a memorable stay and an unforgettable adventure.
**Areas Covered:** Western New York, Niagara Falls, Buffalo and southern Ontario, Canada.

| | | | |
|---|---|---|---|
| 1. American Express | 2. Senior Citizen Rate | 3. VISA | 4. Personal Check |
| 5. Master Card | 6. Brochure Available | 7. Discover Card | 8. Diner's Club |

# RESERVATION SERVICES

## Elbridge

Samuels, Elaine
4987 Kingston Rd., 13060
(315) 689-2082

**Amenities:** 4,6

**Dbl. Oc.:** $45.00 & up
**Sgl. Oc.:** $35.00 & up

**Elaine's Bed & Brekfast And Inn Reservation Serv.**—A delightful contemporary high on a hill with views for 30 miles. A 200-year-old, 22-room inn in the Berkshires. Cabins and B&B inns in Vermont. Nearby lakes, arts and crafts, university, boutiques, malls, state fair and antiques. Convenience, clean air, peace and quiet.
**Area Covered:** Central New York, Syracuse and suburbs, Finger Lakes, Vernon, Cazenovia, the Berkshires in western Massachusettes and Vermont.

---

## Groton

Camin, Susan E.
384 Pleasant Valley Rd., 13073
(800) 221-2215, (607) 898-3814

**Amenities:** 1,7

**Dbl. Oc.:** $48.50 - $175.00
**Sgl. Oc.:** $37.50 - $77.00

**Blue Heron B&B Reservation Service**—Specializing in up-state New York, endless mountains of Pennsylvania and worldwide. Pre-inspected and quality-controlled B&Bs. Corporate and metaphysical retreats, seminars and workshops.
**Areas Covered:** Upstate New York, Endless Mtns., Pennsylvania and world-wide.

---

## New York

Goldberg, Leslie
134 W. 32nd, Suite 602, 10001
(212) 645-8134

**Amenities:** 6

**Dbl. Oc.:** $70.00 - $90.00
**Sgl. Oc.:** $50.00 - $60.00

**Bed & Breakfast Network Of New York**—Accommodations ranging from the funky to the fabulous. Mostly in Manhattan. Hosted and unhosted. We do our best to find the most suitable situation for every guest and to offer a friendly, inexpensive alternative to hotels.
**Areas Covered:** New York City.

---

## New York

Goldberg, Judith
35 W. 92nd St., 10025
(212) 865-8740

**Amenities:** 1,4,6

**Dbl. Oc.:** $70.00 - $90.00
**Sgl. Oc.:** $60.00 - $75.00

**Bed & Breakfast**—Accommodations are conveniently located in residential and commercial areas near transportation and within walking distance of many cultural and tourist attractions. Unhosted apartments are $90.00-$160.00 for two-four people. Call Monday-Friday, 9:30 a.m. - 5:00 p.m.
**Areas Covered:** Manhattan, New York.

---

| | | | |
|---|---|---|---|
| 1. American Express | 2. Senior Citizen Rate | 3. VISA | 4. Personal Check |
| 5. Master Card | 6. Brochure Available | 7. Discover Card | 8. Diner's Club |

# RESERVATION SERVICES

## New York

Leifer, Shelli                    **Amenities:** 1,4,6              **Dbl. Oc.:** $60.00 - $95.00
P.O. Box 20022, 10028                                              **Sgl. Oc.:** $50.00 - $80.00
(212) 472-2000

**Abode Bed & Breakfast, Ltd.**—Have your heart set on staying in a delightful old brownstone or in a contemporary, luxury apartment in the heart of Manhattan? All homes personally inspected. Abode aims to find just the right "home away from home" to suite guest's needs. Unhosted apartments: $85.00-$275.00.
**Areas Covered:** Manhattan and Brooklyn Heights.

---

## New York

Nielsen, Dee Staff                **Amenities:** 1,3,4,5            **Dbl. Oc.:** $60.00 - $95.00
P.O. Box 20355, Cherokee Station, 10028                           **Sgl. Oc.:** $40.00 - $75.00
(212) 737-7049, Fax: (212) 535-2755

**City Lights Bed & Breakfast, Ltd., R.S.O.**—All accommodations are readily accessible to any area of Manhattan via a short bus, taxi or subway ride. Hosts are screened and rooms/apartments inspected and approved by means of a personal visit by a reservation service associate. All provide privacy and comfort.
**Areas Covered:** New York City (Manhattan and outer boroughs) and Europe.

---

## New York

Salisbury, William                **Amenities:** 1,6               **Dbl. Oc.:** $80.00
P.O. Box 200, 10108                                               **Sgl. Oc.:** $60.00
(212) 246-4000

**Aaah Bed & Breakfast**—Used frequently by savvy business travelers since its inception. Aaah B&B has offered accommodations for 50 percent less than hotels. All Manhattan locations. Hosted and unhosted. Personal and friendly service. Call for free borchure.
**Areas Covered:** New York City, London and Paris.

---

## Rochester

Kinsman, Betty                    **Amenities:** 4,6               **Dbl. Oc.:** $50.00 - $135.00
P.O. Box 444, Fairport, NY (mail), 14450                          **Sgl. Oc.:** $45.00 - $55.00
(716) 223-8877

**Bed & Breakfast Rochester**—Wonderful and carefully selected homes in city, suburban and lakeside locations. All have easy access to Rochester's many attractions — museums, art galleries, parks and colleges. Full breakfasts. Advance reservations advised. Hosts help with maps and area information.
**Areas Covered:** Rochester, Pittsford, Greece, Webster, Ontario, Lima, Victor, Fairport, Penn Yan (Fingerlakes area).

---

| 1. American Express | 2. Senior Citizen Rate | 3. VISA | 4. Personal Check |
| 5. Master Card | 6. Brochure Available | 7. Discover Card | 8. Diner's Club |

# RESERVATION SERVICES

## Vernon

Degni, Rose
Seneca Turnpike E.
RD 1, Box 325, 13476
(315) 829-4888

**Amenities:** 1,2,3,4,5,6

**Dbl. Oc.:** $45.00 - $125.00
**Sgl. Oc.:** $40.00 - $75.00

**Bed & Breakfast Connection Reservation Service**—Central New York - Clean, hospitable, safe, personally inspected; from Victorian elegance to country charm. Skiing, snowmobiling, horse racing, riding and stabling, ballooning, hiking, biking, water sports, craft shows, shops and historic sites. One phone call does it all!
**Area Covered:** Syracuse, Utica, Mohawk Valley, Southern Tier Adirondaks, Cooperstown, Catskills - Leatherstocking region.

# Ohio

## Cleveland

Phillips, Elaine
P.O. Box 18590, 44118
(216) 321-3213

**Amenities:**

**Dbl. Oc.:** $45.00 - $75.00
**Sgl. Oc.:** $35.00 - $50.00

**Private Lodgings, Inc.**—Accommodations include houses and apartments near universities, hospitals and musuems. B&B homes have private bathrooms. Hours 9:00 a.m. - 12:00 p.m. and 3:00p.m. - 5:00 p.m., Monday, Tuesday, Thursday and Friday. Extended stays available.
**Areas Covered:** Cleveland suburbs.

## Columbus

Burns, Howard W.
763 So. Third St., German Village, 43206
(614) 444-8888, (614) 443-3680

**Amenities:** 4,6

**Dbl. Oc.:** $55.00
**Sgl. Oc.:** $45.00

**Columbus Bed & Breakfast**—All homes located in German Village - a registered national historic area. Close to downtown Columbus in measurement- a century away in character. Nearby are some of the city's best restaurants and all connecting lines of the thruway.
**Areas Covered:** Columbus.

# Pennsylvania

## Devon (Philadelphia)

Gregg, Peggy
P.O. Box 21, 19333
(215) 687-3565, (800) 448-3619

**Amenities:** 1,3,4,5,6

**Dbl. Oc.:** $35.00 - $125.00
**Sgl. Oc.:** $25.0 - $125.00

**Bed and Breakfast Connections**—Gracious hosts welcome you to pre-Revolutionary colonials, quaint 1800's townhouses & farmhouses, turn-of-the-century mansions and contemporary homes. All personally inspected and Gold Medallion certified. Reservations: Monday -Saturday, 9 a.m. - 9 p.m., Sunday, 1 p.m. - 9 p.m.
**Areas Covered:** Philadelphia, suburbs, Valley Forge, Brandywine Valley, Pennsylvania Dutch Country and Redding.

| | | | |
|---|---|---|---|
| 1. American Express | 2. Senior Citizen Rate | 3. VISA | 4. Personal Check |
| 5. Master Card | 6. Brochure Available | 7. Discover Card | 8. Diner's Club |

# RESERVATION SERVICES

## Gradyville

Ralston, Joan R.
P.O. Box 252, 19039
(800) 733-4747, (215) 358-4747

**Amenities:** 1,3,4,5,6

**Dbl. Oc.:** $35.00 - $125.00
**Sgl. Oc.:** $25.00 - $85.00

**Bed & Breakfast Philadelphia**—Pennsylvania's original bed and breakfast service. Center of city townhouses, suburban manors, country inns and farms. Historic areas, Valley Forge, New Hope, Brandywine Valley and Amish country. Short- and long-term stays. Monday - Friday 9 a.m. - 7 p.m.; Saturday 10 a.m. - 4 p.m.
**Areas Covered:** Philadelphia, Bucks county, Chester county and Lancaster county.

## Hershey

Deutel, Renee
P.O. Box 208, 17033
(717) 533-2928

**Amenities:** 3,4,5,6

**Dbl. Oc.:** $48.00 - $75.00
**Sgl. Oc.:** $43.00 - $65.00

**Hershey Bed & Breakfast Service**—Experience country living in a warm and friendly atmosphere with easy access to many recreational facilities. Be it a private home, farm or country inn, our hosts are pleased to extend their hospitality.
**Areas Covered:** Hershey, Middletown, Harrisburg, Lebanon, Elizabethtown, Annville, New Cumberland, Gettysburg (southereastern Pennsylvania) and Lancaster county.

## Mountville

Reno, Patricia
P.O. Box 19, 17554
(717) 285-5956

**Amenities:** 2,3,5,6

**Dbl. Oc.:** $58.30 - $106.00
**Sgl. Oc.:** $47.70 - $68.90

**Bed & Breakfast Of Lancaster County**—Sample a slice of unique Lancaster country lifestyle from within. Enjoy the flavor of true country living and old-fashioned hospitality by planning your next vacation through us. Gracious homes, hospitable farms and quaint inns provide warm hospitality to you and your family.
**Areas Covered:** Lancaster county (Pennsylvania Dutch country), Hershey, Gettysburg, York, Reading, Harrisburg and surrounding areas.

## Valley Forge

Williams, Carolyn
P.O. Box 562, 19481
(215) 783-7838

**Amenities:** 1,3,4,5,6,8

**Dbl. Oc.:** $31.80 - $159.00
**Sgl. Oc.:** $21.20 - $68.90

**All About Town B&B**—Reserve by phone or mail. Town, country, historic and ski locations. Garden townhouses, suites, apartments, historic homes, guest cottages, carriage houses, farms and country inns. Kitchens, cribs, family plans. One B&B has a resident ghost. Gift certificates. Weekly rates.
**Areas Covered:** Philadelphia, Valley Forge, Brandywine Valley, Bucks county and Lancaster county.

| 1. American Express | 2. Senior Citizen Rate | 3. VISA | 4. Personal Check |
| 5. Master Card | 6. Brochure Available | 7. Discover Card | 8. Diner's Club |

# RESERVATION SERVICES

## West Chester

Archbold, Janice K.
Box 2137, 19380
(800) 950-9130

**Amenities:** 1,3,4,5,6

**Dbl. Oc.:** $50.00 - $200.00 & up
**Sgl. Oc.:** $40.00 - $200.00 & up

**Guesthouse, Inc.**—Specializing in historic private and public landmarks and *National Register* sites. "Brandywine Breakaway" package -three days, two nights, admissions, dinner - $320.00 per couple. Includes taxes and gratuities. Call Monday-Friday,12 p.m. - 4 p.m. to make reservations.
**Areas Covered:** Pennsylvania, Delaware, Maryland, New Jersey, District of Columbia and the Chesapeake Bay.

---

# Rhode Island

## Newport

Farmer, Joan
P.O. Box 981, 02840
(401) 846-ROOM

**Amenities:** 1,3,4,5,6

**Dbl. Oc.:** $55.00 - $200.00
**Sgl. Oc.:** $45.00 - $130.00

**Newport Historic Inns**—An association of fine inns decorated with period antiques in historic properties. The list includes four18th-century colonials, a Georgian "summer cottage" and seven elegant Victorians. Most offer private baths, some are air conditioned, and all offer the ambience of Newport.
**Areas Covered:** Newport.

---

## Newport

Meiser, Joy
38 Bellevue Ave., 02840
(401) 849-1298(reservations), (800) 628-INNS(info)

**Amenities:** 1,3,4,5

**Dbl. Oc.:** $50.00 - $115.00
**Sgl. Oc.:** $45.00 - $85.00

**Bed & Breakfast Of Rhode Island**—We have selected B&Bs that will add to your comfort during your visit to Rhode Island. Personally inspected. All our B&Bs meet our high standards of cleanliness, comfort and represent a wide range of styles and prices.
**Areas Covered:** Rhode Island and southern Massachusettes.

---

# South Carolina

## Charleston

Fairy, Charlotte
43 Legare St., 29401
(803) 722-6606

**Amenities:** 1,3,4,5,6,7,8

**Dbl. Oc.:** $65.00 - $125.00
**Sgl. Oc.:** $65.00 - $125.00

**Historic Charleston And South Carolina Bed &**—Breakfast - A reservation service for the state of South Carolina with the largest number of homes in Charleston's historic district. Many historic homes, two plantationsand several inns are included in our listings. Near beaches, lakes, museums and many cultural activities.
Areas Covered: South Carolina.

---

| 1. American Express | 2. Senior Citizen Rate | 3. VISA | 4. Personal Check |
|---|---|---|---|
| 5. Master Card | 6. Brochure Available | 7. Discover Card | 8. Diner's Club |

# RESERVATION SERVICES

## *Charleston*

Rogers, Eleanor        **Amenities: 4**        **Dbl. Oc.:** $90.00 - $150.00
84 Murray Blvd., 29401                              **Sgl. Oc.:** $75.00
(803) 723-4948

**Charleston Society Bed And Breakfast**—Accommodations in private homes and carriage houses. All are located in the historic district and include pre-Revolutionary, post-Revolutionary and antebellum homes.
**Areas Covered:** Charleston historic district.

# Tennessee

## *Nashville*

Odom, Fredda        **Amenities:** 1,3,5,6,7        **Dbl. Oc.:** $50.00 - $150.00
P.O. Box 110227, 37222                            **Sgl. Oc.:** $40.00.- $125.00
(615) 331-5244, (800) 458-2421, Fax:(615) 833-7701

**Bed & Breakfast Hospitality International**—Use our service to save toll calls for domestic and international reservations in over 700 inns and homestays all over the world. A small processing fee will be accessed and a credit-card number is required.
**Areas Covered:** Tennessee, U.S.A. and world-wide.

# Virginia

## *Berryville*

Duncan, Rita        Amenities:        Dbl.Oc.: $45.00 - $150.00
Rocks & Rills Farm, Route 2,                   Sgl.Oc.: $35.00 - $100.00
Box 3895, 22611
(703) 955-1246

**Blue Ridge Bed & Breakfast**—Historic farms, gracious homes, quaint inns with romantic rooms. Fishing, canoeing, skiing, hiking, hunting, antique shopping, swimming, horse racing and mountain foliage. Shenandoah Valley, Applachian Trail and Harper's Ferry.
**Areas Covered:** Virginia, West Virginia, Maryland and Pennsylvania.

## *Charlottesville*

Capertown, Mary Hill        **Amenities:** 1,3,4,5,6        **Dbl. Oc.:** $56.42 - $162.75
P.O. Box 5737, 22903                           **Sgl. Oc.:** $52.08 - $141.05
(804) 979-7264

**Guesthouses**—Accommodations in distinctive private homes, suites and guest cottages. Country and town locations near Jefferson's Monticello, the University of Virginia and the Blue Ridge Mountains. Call or send for descriptive brochure - $1.00.
**Areas Covered:** Charlottesville and Albemarle country area.

| | | | |
|---|---|---|---|
| 1. American Express | 2. Senior Citizen Rate | 3. VISA | 4. Personal Check |
| 5. Master Card | 6. Brochure Available | 7. Discover Card | 8. Diner's Club |

# RESERVATION SERVICES

## Norfolk

Hubbard, Susan
P.O. Box 3343, 23507
(804) 627-1983, (804) 627-9409

Amenities: 4,6

Dbl. Oc.: $35.00 - $75.00
Sgl. Oc.: $30.00 - $50.00

**Bed And Breakfast Of Tidewater Virginia**—Coastal Virginia: Selected homes in Norfolk's colorful and historic Ghent, in Virginia Beach, beautiful resort area on the Atlantic Ocean and on the picturesque Eastern Shore overlooking the Chesapeake Bay.
**Area Covered:** Eastern Virginia (coastal), Norfolk, Virginia Beach, the Eastern Shore, Northern Neck and Mathews County.

## Richmond

Benson, Lyn
2036 Monumnet Ave., 23220
(804) 353-6900

Amenities: 2,3,4,5,6

Dbl. Oc.: $65.00 - $140.00
Sgl. Oc.: $60.00 - $135.00

**Bensonhouse Reservation Service Of Virginia**—Representing 40 carefully selected small inns and private homes in Fredericksburg, Richmond, Williamsburg, the Blue Ridge Mountains and eastern shore. Most are of architectural interest and in historic areas. Most have private baths and some have fireplaces and jacuzzis.
**Areas Covered:** Fredericksburg, Petersburg, Orange, Richmond, Williamsburg, the Blue Ridge Mountains and the eastern shore of Virginia.

## Williamsburg

Zubkoff, Sheila R.
P.O. Box 838, 23187
(804) 253-1571

Amenities: 4,6

Dbl. Oc.: $52.40 - $101.18
Sgl. Oc.: $42.08 - $90.53

**The Travel Tree Reservation Service**—Williamsburg's B&B reservation service offers the finest accommodations: quaint dormered rooms, elegant suites, a cozy cottage and more! Choose gracious private homes or small inns, some within walking distance to historic area, others within 1-4 miles. Mon. - Fri., 6 p.m. - 9 p.m.
**Areas Covered:** Williamsburg.

# Wisconsin

## Mequon

Zabrinsky, Suzanne
1916 W. Donges Bay Rd., 53092
(414) 242-9680

Amenities: 1,2,3,4,5,6

Dbl. Oc.: $42.00 - $105.00
Sgl. Oc.: $36.75 - $94.50

**Bed & Breakfast Of Milwaukee, Inc.**—A free reservation service. We'll match your needs to accommodations. A variety of homes and amenities. Any occasion or corporate stay. Caring *hosts.* All homes inspected. Reserve across the U.S., Canada and abroad. Member of B&B Worldwide (trade association).
**Areas Covered:** Eastern Wisconsin to South Centreal Wisconsin.

| | | | |
|---|---|---|---|
| 1. American Express | 2. Senior Citizen Rate | 3. VISA | 4. Personal Check |
| 5. Master Card | 6. Brochure Available | 7. Discover Card | 8. Diner's Club |

# Canada

## *Greater Vancouver, BritishColumbia*

McCurrach, Norma     **Amenities:** 1,2,3,5,6     **Dbl. Oc.:** $60.00 - $105.00(CN)
4390 Frances St., V5C 2R3                     **Sgl. Oc.:** $40.00 - $55.00(CN)
(604) 263-5595, Fax: (604) 298-5917

**AB&C Bed & Breakfast Of Vancouver**—We list from cabins to mansions, also suites and special accommodations. Norma was founder and presently director of the *BC/Bed & Breakfast Association.*
**Areas Covered:** Greater Vancouver, Victoria, Whistler and all surrounding cities of the Provinceof British Columbia.

---

## *North Vancouver, British Columbia*

Massey, Ellison     **Amenities:** 1,3,4,5,6     **Dbl. Oc.:** $60.00 - $85.00(CN)
P.O. Box 86607, V7L 4L2                     **Sgl. Oc.:** $40.00 - $60.00(CN)
(604) 929-1424

**Canada-West Accommodations B&B Registry**—Efficient reservation system that places guests into quality private homes in British Columbia. Private and shared baths. Full breakfast. Inquiries by phone rather than by mail suggested.
**Areas Covered:** Vancouver, Victoria, Whistler and Okanagan Valley(Kelowna).

---

## *North Vancouver,British Columbia*

Tyndall, Vicki     **Amenities:** 3,4,5,6     **Dbl. Oc.:** $55.00 - $120.00(CN)
P.O. Box 86818, V7L 4L3                     **Sgl. Oc.:** $40.00 - $70.00(CN)
(604) 986-5069

**Old English Bed & Breakfast Registry**—A professional reservation service for quality B&B accommodations throughout greater Vancouver. Our gues thomes provide a friendly, hospitable environment and valuable knowledge about the area you'll be visiting.
**Areas Covered:** Vancouver, north Vancouver and west Vancouver.

---

## *Vancouver, British Columbia*

Burich, Helen     **Amenities:**     **Dbl. Oc.:** $65.00 - $150.00(CN)
P.O. Box 46544, V6R 4G8                     **Sgl. Oc.:** $45.00 - $65.00(CN)
(604) 731-5942

**Town & Country Bed & Breakfast In B.C., Canada**—Modest to luxurious with rates accordingly. Guide also available for $12.00 (U.S.). Personal checks accepted for deposit only.
**Areas Covered:** Vancouver and Victoria.

| | | | |
|---|---|---|---|
| 1. American Express | 2. Senior Citizen Rate | 3. VISA | 4. Personal Check |
| 5. Master Card | 6. Brochure Available | 7. Discover Card | 8. Diner's Club |

# RESERVATION SERVICES

## Victoria, British Columbia

Doreen, Wensley M.  **Amenities:** 1,3,5
660 Jones Terrace, V8Z 2L7
(604) 479-9999

**Dbl. Oc.:** $45.00 - $150.00(CN)
**Sgl. Oc.:** $30.00 - $65.00(CN)

**Garden City Bed & Breakfast Reservation Service**—No fee for service. Owner-operator provides personal attention to details. Itinerary assistance. Cater to travelers, honeymooners. Hospitality plus king, queen, double, twin and single rooms. Majestic heritage to demure cozy cottage in top-rated area. Business began in 1985.
**Areas Covered:** Victoria, Vanouver Island, Vancouver and Gulf Islands.

## Victoria, British Columbia

Von Epp, Kate & David  **Amenities:** 3,5,6
P.O. Box 5511 NA Station 'B', V8R 6S4
(604) 595-2337

**Dbl. Oc.:** $50.00 - $150.00(CN)
**Sgl. Oc.:** $40.00 - $75.00(CN)

**All Seasons Bed & Breakfast Agency, Inc.**—Fifty heritage, garden or sea view homes in Victoria, on Vancouver Island or the Gulf Islands. Each one personally vetted with emphasis on luxury, privacy and affordability. Posh holiday , eh? What?
Areas Covered: Victoria, Vancouver Island and Gulf Islands.

## Alma, Ontario

Grose, Sharon  **Amenities:** 2,4,6
R.R.#2,, N0B 1A0
(519) 846-9788

**Dbl. Oc.:** $35.00 - $65.00(CN)
**Sgl. Oc.:** $25.00 - $35.00(CN)

**Ontario Vacation Farm Association**—Enjoy country hospitality. A quiet rest from the hustle and bustle of your busy life. Each season the Ontario Vacation Farm Association farm offers a unique holiday experience. Enjoy horseback riding, hiking, swimming and biking down country lanes. 100 farms.
**Areas Covered:** Province of Ontario.

## Leamington, Ontario

Tressen, Agatha  **Amenities:** 6
115 Erie St. S., N8H 3B5
(519) 326-7169

**Dbl. Oc.:** $45.00 - $55.00(CN)
**Sgl. Oc.:** $37.00 - $45.00(CN)

**Point Pelee Bed & Breakfast Association**—A bed and breakfast service in Canada's most southern point. Famous for bird watching. Enjoy warm hospitality in our unique area of homes. Breakfast at your convenience. Tourist area - July and August. Fine beaches. Trip to Pelee Island. Air-conditioned.
**Areas Covered:** Point Pelee.

| | | | |
|---|---|---|---|
| 1. American Express | 2. Senior Citizen Rate | 3. VISA | 4. Personal Check |
| 5. Master Card | 6. Brochure Available | 7. Discover Card | 8. Diner's Club |

# RESERVATION SERVICES

## Montreal, Quebec

Finkelstein, Bob       **Amenities:** 1,3,5,6      **Dbl. Oc.:** $40.00 - $55.00(CN)
3458 Laval Ave. at Sherbrooke St., H2X 3C8      **Sgl. Oc.:** $30.00(CN) & up
(514) 289-9749

**A Bed & Breakfast - A Downtown Network**—A network of fine private homes offering comfortable accommodations, including a complete breakfast, at prices you can well afford. Downtown old Montreal, Latin Quarterour specialty. One of Canada's oldest bed and breakfast networks.
**Areas Covered:** Montreal (particularly downtown), Old Montreal and the Latin Quarter.

## Niagara Falls, Ontario

Siciliano/Bertoechi, Luciene    **Amenities:** 1,3,5      **Dbl.Oc.:**$55.00 - $85.00(CN)
4917 River Rd., L2E 3G5                     **Sgl.Oc.:**$50.00 - $80.00(CN)
(416) 358-8988

**NR. & N.O.T.L. B&B Service.**
**Aeas Covered:** Niagara on the Lake, Niagara Falls.

## Ottawa, Ontario

Rivoire, Robert         **Amenities:** 6       **Dbl. Oc.:** $50.00 - $64.00
488 Cooper St., K1R 5H9                     **Sgl. Oc.:** $40.00(CN)
(613) 563-0161

**Ottawa Area Bed & Breakfast**—Welcome to friendly and affordable accommodations in Canada's capital. Your hosts are residents of Ottawa who are anxious to meet you and show you their homes and provide you with much advice about our city.
**Areas Covered:** Ottawa and Ontario.

## Peterborough, Ontario

Wilkins, Joan & Wally     **Amenities:** 6       **Dbl. Oc.:** $38.00 - $55.00(CN)
P.O. Box 2264, K9J 7Y8                     **Sgl. Oc.:** $32.00 - $45.00(CN)
(705) 652-6290, Fax: (705) 652-6949

**Bed & Breakfast Registry of Peterborough & Area**—Choose your style of accommodations - a period home in the country, a modern lakeside bungalow, or a restful house on a quiet street in a village or town. All homes are inspected for cleanliness and comfort and are owned by friendly, informed hosts. Call Wally Wilkins.
**Areas Covered:** Peterborough and surrounding area.

| 1. American Express | 2. Senior Citizen Rate | 3. VISA | 4. Personal Check |
|---|---|---|---|
| 5. Master Card | 6. Brochure Available | 7. Discover Card | 8. Diner's Club |

# RESERVATION SERVICES

## St. Catherines, Ontario

Worth, M. & A.　　　　　**Amenities:** 1,3,4,6　　　　**Dbl. Oc.:** $40.00 - $50.00(CN)
489 Carlton St., L2M 4W9　　　　　　　　　　　　　**Sgl. Oc.:** $30.00(CN)

(416) 937-2422

**St. Catherines Bed And Breakfast Association**—Offers a variety of homes in the Niagara region. St. Catherines is in the heart of the wine country, located 15 minutes from Niagara Falls and Niagara-on-the-Lake. All lodgings are quality assured.
**Areas Covered:** Niagara region.

---

## Toronto, Ontario

Oppenheim, Susan　　　　　**Amenities:** 3,4,6　　　　**Dbl. Oc.:** $55.00 - $75.00(CN)
P.O. Box 190, Station B., M5T 2B6　　　　　　　　　**Sgl. Oc.:** $45.00 - $65.00(CN)
(416) 977-6841, (416) 598-4562

**Downtown Tour Association of B&B Guesthouses**—In our 10th year with the largest selection of downtown properties. All non-smoking. Parking. Apartments, suites, private homes and ensuites, some air-conditioned. Six languages spoken. All hosts are active in the arts and hospitality industry. Tell us your needs.
**Areas Covered:** Downtown Toronto.

---

## Toronto, Ontario

Page, Larry　　　　　**Amenities:** 3,5,6,8　　　　**Dbl. Oc.:** $50.00 - $75.00(CN)
P.O. Box 269, 253 College St., M6G 3A7　　　　　　**Sgl. Oc.:** $40.00 - $65.00(CN)
(416) 588-8800

**Toronto Bed & Breakfast**—Toronto's oldest professional bed and breakfast reservation service. A quality registry, now in its 13th year. 25 selected hosts help you discover Toronto with a variety of homes throughout the metropolitan area. A free brochure is available upon request.
**Areas Covered:** Toronto.

---

## Quebec, Quebec

Blanchet, Denise　　　　　**Amenities:** 4,6　　　　**Dbl. Oc.:** $45.00 - $95.00(CN)
3765 Rd. Monaco, G1P 3J3　　　　　　　　　　　　**Sgl. Oc.:** $35.00 - $45.00(CN)
(418) 527-1465

**Bed & Breakfast Bonjour Quebec**—For reservations: write or phone to the above. Denise and Raymond Blanchet will forward, by mail, information as well as a city map with directions. The first R.S.O. of Quebecre presents 11 homes selected to make your visit a genuine French experience.
**Areas Covered:** Quebec City.

| 1. American Express | 2. Senior Citizen Rate | 3. VISA | 4. Personal Check |
|---|---|---|---|
| 5. Master Card | 6. Brochure Available | 7. Discover Card | 8. Diner's Club |

# United States Virgin Islands

## *St. John*

Zalis, Annellen
P.O. Box 191, 00830
(809) 779-4094, (809) 776-7836

Amenities: 6

Dbl.Oc.: $75.00 - $115.00
Sgl.Oc.: $60.00 - $105.00

**V.I. B&B Homestays**—Stay in a hillside home with breathtaking ocean views or in a luxurious waterfront setting. V.I. B&B will reserve your host home. Let us arrange for you jeep rentals, island tours, day sails, dive trips and space on the most beautiful beaches in the world!
**Areas Covered:** St. John, St. Thomas and St. Croix.

| | | | |
|---|---|---|---|
| 1. American Express | 2. Senior Citizen Rate | 3. VISA | 4. Personal Check |
| 5. Master Card | 6. Brochure Available | 7. Discover Card | 8. Diner's Club |

# Restaurant Guide Section

# RESTAURANTS

# Arkansas

## *Eureka Springs*

**Cafe Armagost**
 52 Kingshighway, 72632
(501) 253-8075

**Amenities:** 1,2,3,4,7,11

**Breakfast:** $4.75 - $8.00,
        (Sun. Brunch)

Dine in a romantic atmosphere with linen tablecloths, candlelight and fresh flowers. All food is made fresh on the premises. Famous Sunday brunch. Children's menu available.

---

# California

## *Healdsburg*

**Restaurant At Madrona Manor**
1001 Westside Rd., 95448
(707) 433-4231

**Amenities:** 1,4,5,6,7,8,11,12
**Breakfast:** $14.95
       (Sunday Brunch)

**Appetizer:** $5,75 - $8.00
**Lunch:** not open
**Dinner:** $18.00 - $22.00
**Desserts:** $3.75

Pat Ricia Unterman of the *San Francisco Chronicle,* May 13, 1990, proclaimed "Todd Muir has developed the Madrona Manor dining room to the point where it is the equal of any in the city." Come for the food stay for the lodging.

**Hours:** Dinner—6p.m.- p.m. (7 nights a week).
       Sunday Brunch - 11a.m.-2 p.m.

---

## *Moss Beach*

**Moss Beach Distillery**
Beach & Ocean, 940398
(415) 728-5595

**Amenities:** 1,3,4,5,7,8,9,11

**Lunch:** $3.95 - $13.95
**Dinner:** $11.95 - $24.95
**Dessert:** $1.50 - $3.75

Built in 1928, this historic restaurant offers an ocean view from every seat in the house. Fresh fish, seafood specialties, prime rib and meats from our own smoker. Outdoor deck overlooks the Pacific Ocean. Jazz in our lounge on Sundays. A classic coastal dining experience.

**Hours:** Dining Room—5p.m. (Mon.-Fri.), 4p.m. (Sun.).
       Lounge—5p.m. (Mon.-Sat.), 4p.m. (Sun.).

---

| 1.American Express | 4. VISA | 7. Public Parking | 10. Senior Citizen Rates |
| 2. Discover Card | 5. Diners Club | 8. Beer & Wine Served | 11. Handicap Accessibliity |
| 3. Mastercard | 6. Valet Parking | 9. Full Bar | 12. Function Room(s) |

# RESTAURANTS

## Colorado

### Colorado Springs

**The Mason Jar**
2925 W. Colorado Ave., 80904
(719) 531-6186

**Amenities:** 2,3,4,7,9,11,12

**Breakfast:** not open

**Appetizer:** $2.39 - $2.99
**Lunch:** $3.95 - $5.49
**Dinner:** $4.29 - $11.99
**Dessert:** $1.99 - $2.29

Selections from the farm and the sea, home-made desserts and cocktails. Old-fashioned hospitality and exceptional service. Non-smoking section. Children's menu. Affordable family dining.

**Hours:** 11a.m.-10p.m. (daily in summer), 11:30a.m. 9p.m. (Sun-Thurs in winter) 11:30a.m.-9:3 p.m. (Fri. & Sat. in winter).

---

### Colorado Springs

**The Mason Jar**
6716 No. Academy Blvd., 8
(719) 531-6186

**Amenities:** 2,3,4,7,9,11

**Breakfast:** not open

**Appetizer:** $2.39 - $2.99
**Lunch:** $3.59 - $5.49
**Dinner:** $4.29 - $11.99
**Dessert:** $1.99 - $2.29

Selections from the farm and the sea, home-made desserts and cocktails. Old-fashioned hospitality and exceptional service. Non smoking section. Children's menu. Affordable family dining.

**Hours:** 11a.m.-10p.m. (daily in summer), 11:30a.m.-9p.m. (Sun. - Thurs. in winter), 11:30a.m.-9:30p.m. (Fri. & Sat. in winter).

---

### Denver

**Buckhorn Exchange**
1000 Osage St., 80204
(303) 534-9505

**Amenities:** 1,2,3,4,5,7,8,9, 11,12

**Breakfast:** not open

**Appetizer:** $4.25 - $6.50
**Lunch:** $4.95 - $9.50
**Dinner:** $14.00 - $24.00
**Dessert:** $2.25 - $3.50

Established in 1893. This is Colorado's oldest and most historic eating and drinking emporium. Marvelously heartyfare including prime dry-aged beef steaks, buffalo, ribs and game specialties. Lunch features five enormous burgers and a pot-roast sandwich.

**Hours:** Lunch: 11 a.m. - 3 p.m. (Mon.-Fri.), Dinner: 5 p.m. - 10:30 p.m. (Mon.-Fri.).

---

| | | | |
|---|---|---|---|
| 1.American Express | 4. VISA | 7. Public Parking | 10. Senior Citizen Rates |
| 2. Discover Card | 5. Diners Club | 8. Beer & Wine Served | 11. Handicap Accessbiliity |
| 3. Mastercard | 6. Valet Parking | 9. Full Bar | 12. Function Room(s) |

# RESTAURANTS

# Connecticut

## *Norwalk, East*

**Skippers, Restaurant**
Beach Rd., 06855
(203) 838-2211

**Amenities:** 1,3,4,5,7,8,9,11, 12

**Breakfast:** $14.95
(Sunday brunch)

**Appetizer:** $3.50 - $7.25
**Lunch:** $4.50 - $8.95
**Dinner:** $11.00 - $23.75
**Dessert:** $2.00 - $3.50

Located on the harbor, enjoy your meal while watching the beautiful boats just outside your table window. Skippers is well known for its food, atmosphere and service. Lobster, prime rib, steaks, chops and homemade desserts. Banquet rooms available. Dancing on Fridays and Saturdays.

**Hours:** Lunch: 11:30a.m.-3:30p.m.,
Dinner: 4p.m.-10:30p.m. (weekdays), 4p.m.-10:30p.m. (Fri, & Sat.).
Sunday Brunch: 11:30a.m.-2:30p.m.

## *Old Mystic*

**J.P. Daniels**
Route 184, 06372
(203) 572-9564

**Amenities:** 1,3,4,7,9,11,12

**Breakfast:** $11.95
(Sunday brunch)

**Appetizer:** $3.25 - $9.95
**Lunch:** not open
**Dinner:** $14.95 - $19.95
**Dessert:** $2.50 - $4.25

A historic old-barn setting resplendent with candlelight, fresh flowers and crisp white linen. Our award-winning atmosphere is complimented by our superb cuisine and attentive service. Our international cuisine includes fresh seafood, duck, veal, beef and chicken.

**Hours:** Dinner: 5p.m.-9:30p.m. (7 days a week).

# Delaware

## *New Castle*

**Cellar Gourmet**
Route 184, 06372
(203) 572-9564

**Amenities:** 7

**Breakfast:** $2.00 - $5.95
**Lunch:** $2.75 - $5.95

Cozy restaurant in historic New Castle with an original Gilpin well in the dining area. Specializes in homemade soups, quiche, hearty sandwiches, salads, vegetarian options, desserts, muffins, ice cream and frozen yogurt. Picnic lunches available.

**Hours:** April-Oct.:Breakfast: 8a.m. - 11a.m. (Mon. - Sat.), Sunday Buffet: 9a.m.-12a.m.,
Lunch: 8a.m. - 6p.m. (Mon. - Fri.),8a.m. - 8p.m. (Sat. & Sun.).
Nov.-March:Breakfast: 8a.m.-11a.m. (Mon.-Sun.),
Lunch: 8a.m.-4p.m. (Mon.-Sun.).

| | | | |
|---|---|---|---|
| 1.American Express | 4. VISA | 7. Public Parking | 10. Senior Citizen Rates |
| 2. Discover Card | 5. Diners Club | 8. Beer & Wine Served | 11. Handicap Accessiblity |
| 3. Mastercard | 6. Valet Parking | 9. Full Bar | 12. Function Room(s) |

# RESTAURANTS

## Florida

### Cedar Key

**Historic Restaurant Island Hotel**
Main St.
P.O. Box 460, 32625
(904) 543-5111

**Amenities:**2,3,4,7,
8,11,12
**Breakfast:** $8.00 - $10.00

**Appetizer** $3.95 - $6.50
**Lunch:** $8.00 - $10.00
**Dinner:** $9.95 - $18.95
**Dessert:** $3.95

Gourmet-natural foods. Specializing in Florida seafood and vegetarian dishes. Unique original recipes such as poppyseed bread, fish in paper, masterpiece soup, bouillabaisse, soft-shell crabs finished with sherry and dessert delicacies. Internationally reviewed. Filtered water.

**Hours:** Dinner: 6p.m.-10p.m., Breakfast served on weekends only.

---

### Daytona Beach

**Live Oak Inn**
448 So. Beach, 32114
(904) 252-INNS

**Amenities:** 1,3,4,7,9,11,12

**Breakfast:** B&B guests only.

**Appetizer:** $2.00 - $6.00
**Lunch:** - $6.00
(Afternoon tea)
**Dinner:** $12.00 - $16.00
**Dessert:** $2.00 - $6.00

Dine in historic 1881 home. Gracious and relaxed with attentive service, river views, verandas and garden dining. Specialties: fresh fish, bouillibaisse, range chicken and healthful meals. Berries A la Brugges, souffles, tarts, fresh fruit and cheese desserts.

**Hours—:**Afternoon Tea: 3p.m.-4:30p.m., Cocktail Hour: 4p.m.-5:30p.m.,
Dinner: 5p.m.-9:30p.m. (Tues.-Sun.)

---

### St. Augustine

**Le Pavillon**
45 San Marco Ave., 32084
(904) 824-6202

**Amenities:** 1,2,3,4,5,7,8,
9,12
**Breakfast:** not served

**Appetizer:** $2.50 - $7.75
**Lunch:** $4.95 - $5.95
**Dinner:** $6.95 - $16.95
**Dessert:** $2.75 - $2.95

House specials include rack of lamb, bouillabaisse, veal dishes and fresh seafood. An intimate and elegant dining experience. Food prepared by our award-winning Swiss chef and served in the European manner inside a gracious old home.

**Hours:** Lunch: 11:30a.m.-2:30p.m., Dinner: 5:00p.m.-10.00p.m.

| | | | |
|---|---|---|---|
| 1.American Express | 4. VISA | 7. Public Parking | 10. Senior Citizen Rates |
| 2. Discover Card | 5. Diners Club | 8. Beer & Wine Served | 11. Handicap Accessiblity |
| 3. Mastercard | 6. Valet Parking | 9. Full Bar | 12. Function Room(s) |

# RESTAURANTS

# Georgia

## *Savannah*

**Palmers Seafood House**      **Amenities:** 1,3,4,5,7,8,9,11,     **Appetizer:** $1.75 - $2.95
80 Wilmington Island Rd., 31410     12     **Lunch:** $5.50
(912) 897-2611     **Breakfast:** not open     (average price)
    **Dinner:** $9.50
    (average price)
    **Dessert:** $1.25 - $2.95

We are located on the beautiful Wilmington River only ten minutes from downtown historic Savannah. We are nationally famous for our broiled, steamed and fried seafood. Casual dress. Family prices.

**Hours:** 12p.m.-10p.m. (Tues.-Sat.), 12p.m.-9p.m. (Sun.), 5p.m.-10p.m. (Mon.).

---

# Illinois

## *Galena*

**Stillman Country Inn**     **Amenities:** 1,2,3,4,7,9,12     **Appetizer:** $1.50 - $6.25
513 Bouthillier, 61036     **Lunch.:** not open
(815) 777-0557     **Breakfast:** not open     **Dinner:** $9.75 - $27.95
    **Dessert:** $1.50 - $3.25

Stillman's is an 1858 Victorian mansion featuring fine dining in three lovely dining rooms. Dinner offers steaks, chicken, ribs and seafood. Weekend entertainment is available in the adjacent nightclub.

**Hours:** Dinner: 5p.m.-9p.m. (Mon.-Sun.),
Lounge: 8p.m.-1a.m. (Fri. & Sat.)

| | | | |
|---|---|---|---|
| 1.American Express | 4. VISA | 7. Public Parking | 10. Senior Citizen Rates |
| 2. Discover Card | 5. Diners Club | 8. Beer & Wine Served | 11. Handicap Accessibliity |
| 3. Mastercard | 6. Valet Parking | 9. Full Bar | 12. Function Room(s) |

# RESTAURANTS

# Indiana

## *Indianapolis*

**Peter's Restaurant**
936 Virginia Ave., 46203
(317) 637-9333

**Amenities:** 3,4,5,7,8,9,11,12
**Breakfast:** not open
**Appetizer:** $3.50 - $9.50
**Lunch.:** not open
**Dinner:** $4.00 - $7.00
**Dessert:** $11.50 - $21.50

Peter's offers an ever-changing menu of Midwest regional fare. Indiana duckling and veal, Angus beef and fresh waterfish. Every creation is prepared in-house, from hickory smoked game to persimmon ice cream. Accessible from I-65 or I-70. Reservations appreciated.

**Hours:** 5:30p.m.-9:30p.m. (Mon.-Thurs.), 5:30p.m.-10p.m. (Fri. & Sat.).

## *Jasper*

**Schnitzelbank Restaurant**   **Amenities:** 2,3,4,7,8,9,10,
393 Third Ave., Hwy. 162, So., 47546       11,12       **Lunch:** $4.00 - $6.00
(812) 482-2640       **Breakfast:** not open       **Dinner:** $6.95 - $18.95

The Schnitzelbank has served generations of diners for over 85 years. This popular restaurant features the finest in German foods, in addition to an outstanding varied menu. The Schnitzelbank is one of the finest eating establishments in the Midwest.

**Hours:** Lunch 10a.m.-3p.m., Dinner: 4p.m.-10p.m. (Closed Sundays).

# Massachusetts

## *S. Dartmouth Padanaram Village*

**Bridge Street Cafe**
10A Bridge St., 02748
(508) 994-7200
**Amenities:** 3,4,9

Located in the seaside village of Padanaram. Casual, unpretentious restaurant that features native seafood, pasta, saute dishes and Angus beef. The canopied outdoor patio is a great spot to relax and enjoy lunch, dinner and Sunday brunch.
**Hours:** May-October—Lunch: 11:30a.m.-2:30p.m., Dinner: 5:30p.m.-10:00p.m. Open 7 days.
Nov.-April—Lunch: 11:30a.m.-2:30p.m.,
Dinner: 5:30p.m.-9p.m. (open til 9:30 p.m. on Fri. & Sat., closed Mondays. )

| 1.American Express | 4. VISA | 7. Public Parking | 10. Senior Citizen Rates |
|---|---|---|---|
| 2. Discover Card | 5. Diners Club | 8. Beer & Wine Served | 11. Handicap Accessibliity |
| 3. Mastercard | 6. Valet Parking | 9. Full Bar | 12. Function Room(s) |

# RESTAURANTS

## *Salem*

**Lyceum Bar & Grill**
43 Church St., 01945
(508) 745-7665

**Amenities:** 1,3,4,7,8,9,11,12

**Breakfast:** not open

**Appetizer:** $3.50 - $6.00
**Lunch:** $4.50 - $7.95
**Dinner:** $10.90 - $14.90
**Dessert:** $3.50

Located in the heart of historic Salem in a beautifully restored landmark. The Lyceum Bar & Grill is one of the north shore's best. Serving contemporary American cuisine seven days a week in a casual, affordable but stylish setting. Piano entertainment.

**Hours:** Open 7 days a week.

# Missouri

## *Kansas City*

**Cafe Nile**
8433 Wornall Rd., 64114
(816) 361-9097

**Amenities:** 3,4,7,9

Award-winning Mediterranean cuisine. Menu favorites are:Sole with spinach sauce, rack of lamb with garlic sauce,veal scallopini, Beef Oscar and seafood in puffed pastry. Escargot and shrimp garlic are our appetizer leaders along with Hummus and Dolmas.

# Nebraska

## *Grand Island*

**Nonna's Palazzo Restaurant**
820 W. Second St., 68801
(308) 384-3029

**Amenities:** 3,4,8
**Breakfast:** not open
**Lunch:** $3.95 - $5.95
**Dinner:** $5.95 - $12.95
**Dessert:** $1.25 - $2.50

Fine Italian cuisine served in the national historic landmark, the Hamilton Donald Mansion. Newly redecorated in the European style. All foods — pastas, sauces and breads are homemade from traditional family recipes of the proprietor's own heritage.

**Hours:** Lunch 11a.m.-2p.m. (Tues.-Fri.), Dinner 5p.m.-9p.m. (Fri.-Sat.).

| 1.American Express | 4. VISA | 7. Public Parking | 10. Senior Citizen Rates |
|---|---|---|---|
| 2. Discover Card | 5. Diners Club | 8. Beer & Wine Served | 11. Handicap Accessibliity |
| 3. Mastercard | 6. Valet Parking | 9. Full Bar | 12. Function Room(s) |

# RESTAURANTS

## New Jersey

### Cape May

**Peaches Cafe**
322 Carpenter's Lane
P.O. Box 155, 08204
(609) 884-0202

**Amenities:** 3,4,11
**Breakfast:**

**Dinner:** $13.95 - $23.95
Appetizers: $3.00 - $6.95
Dessert: $4.25

A cozy cafe with indoor and outdoor seating. Features exotic international dishes, local seafood and scrumptious desserts. Personal and friendly service in an intimate atmosphere with fresh flowers and good music. A true adventure in dining. Please bring your own beer or wine.

**Hours:** Dinner: 5:30p.m.-9:30p.m. (Every night June-Sept.)
Closed Tuesday and Wednesdays in April, May, October and November.

## New Mexico

### Albuquerque

**66 Diner**
1405 Central Ave., NE, 87106
(505) 247-1421

**Amenities:** 1,3,4,7,8,11

**Breakfast:** $1.50 - $4.9

**Appetizer:** $1.50
(average price)
**Lunch.:** $2.00 - $5.56
**Dinner:** $2.00 - $5.56
**Dessert:** $2.25

Located on historic Route 66. This roadside diner is home to Albuquerque's best milkshake. Try the famous green chili cheeseburger, chicken fried steak or the day's blue plate special. Homemade desserts. Complete soda fountain. Beer and wine served with your meal.

**Hours:** Breakfast: 8a.m.-1p.m. (Sat. & Sun.)
Lunch/Dinner: 10:30a.m.-10p.m. (Mon.-Thurs.), 10:30a.m.-11p.m. (Fri. & Sat.),
10:30a.m.-9p.m. (Sun.)

### Albuquerque

**Cafe Oceana**
1414 Central Ave., SE, 87106
(506) 247-2233

**Amenities:** 1,3,4,5,7,9,11,12

**Appetizer:**$4.95 - $6.95
**Lunch.:** $4.95 - $8.95
**Dessert:** $2.50

Selected Albuquerque's "Best Seafood," this unique shrimp and oyster bar and fresh seafood cafe features daily fresh fish selections plus an extensive menu including lobster and crab. Enjoy cocktails or fine wines in the patio lounge. Shrimp and oyster hour daily.

**Hours:** Lunch: 11a.m. - 3p.m. (Mon.-Fri.),
Dinner: 3p.m.-111p.m. (Mon.-Thurs.), 3p.m.-11:30p.m. (Fri.&Sat.)
Oyster Hour: 3p.m-6:30p.m. (Mon.-Fri.), 5p.m.-7p.m.(Sat.).

| 1.American Express | 4. VISA | 7. Public Parking | 10. Senior Citizen Rates |
| 2. Discover Card | 5. Diners Club | 8. Beer & Wine Served | 11. Handicap Accessibliity |
| 3. Mastercard | 6. Valet Parking | 9. Full Bar | 12. Function Room(s) |

# RESTAURANTS

## *Bernalillo*

**Prairie Star**
P.O. Box 1509, 87004
(505) 867-3327

**Amenities:** 1,3,4,7,9,11,12

Extraordinary cuisine in the comfort of a rambling adobe with a stunning view of the Sandias. Entres include Truchas Pinon, Santa Ana Tenderlion, and Shrimp Margarita. Exceptional wine list. A short drive north of Albuquerque. Reservations recommended.

**Hours:** Dinner: 5p.m.-10p.m. (Mon.-Thurs.), 5p.m.-11p.m. (Fri. & Sat.).
Lounge opens 4p.m. daily.

---

# New Hampshire

## *Portsmouth*

**Oar House**
23 Page Ave., 28803
(704) 252-3685

**Amenities:** 3,4,6,8,9,11,12

Traditional foods, uniquely prepared, describes the cuisine at the Oar House. Located on Portsmouth's historic waterfront in an old grain warehouse dating back to the early 1800's. Reservations suggested.

---

# New York

## *L:ittle Falls*

**Canal Side Inn**
395 S. Ann, 13365
(315) 823-1170

**Amenities:** 3,4,5,7,8,9,11

Located in a recently restored section of town. Owned and operated by the chef. The menu and daily specials offer the finest in French and American cuisine. Included are duckling, rack of lamb, veal and a variety of fresh fish.

## *Lake Placid*

**Lindsays & The Woodshed**
237 Main St., 12946
(518) 523-3824

**Amenities:** 1,2,3,4,5,7,
8,9,11,12

Two great restaurants, one convenient location. Woodshed is casual dining with an Italian American menu. Lindsays is elegant dining with a continental menu. Children's menu available. Bar room lunch with Italian specialties. Open for dinner.

**Hours:** Dinner: 5p.m.-10p.

| 1. American Express | 4. VISA | 7. Public Parking | 10. Senior Citizen Rates |
|---|---|---|---|
| 2. Discover Card | 5. Diners Club | 8. Beer & Wine Served | 11. Handicap Accessiblity |
| 3. Mastercard | 6. Valet Parking | 9. Full Bar | 12. Function Room(s) |

# RESTAURANTS

## *Lake Placid*

**Epicuran Cafe**
Baron Steuben Place,
Market St., 14830
(607) 962-6553

**Amenities:**1,5,7,10,11

"The whole world in a single bite." Continental breakfast, superb lunches, lite dinner, pastries, desserts, specialty cakes and box lunches. The one restaurant to include while in Corning. Casual. First floor. Quality. Reasonable.

**Hours:** 8a.m.-6p.m. (Mon.-Sat.)

---

# North Carolina

## *Asheville*

**23Page**
23 Page Ave., 28803
(704) 252-3685

**Amenities:** 1,3,4,5,7,8,9,10, 11,12

**Breakfast:** not open

**Appetizer:** $5.50 - $7.95
**Lunch:** $5.50 - $6.50
(box lunch)
**Dinner:** $12.50 - $18.50
**Dessert:** $3.50 - $6.50

Fine American cuisine and attentive service in a relaxed setting. Serving dinner only and lunch for take-out. Full service catering and private parties accepted. Exceptional wine list. Conveniently located in downtown Asheville around the corner from the Civic Center.

**Hours:** 5:30 p.m. (Mon.-Sat.)

---

## *Asheville*
**The Greenery Restaurant**
148 Tunnel Rd.,,, 28805
(704) 253-2809

**Amenities:** 1,3,4,7,9,11

**Breakfast:** not open

**Appetizer:** $4.25 - $7.50
**Lunch:** $4.95 - $8.95
**Dinner:** $9.95 - $18.95
**Dessert:** $2.25 - $4.50

Original and classic cuisine served in a warm, inviting setting of antique table sets and soft candlelight. Exceptional selection of fine wines. Located near downtown and the mall. Reservations suggested.

**Hours:** Lunch: 11:30a.m.-2:00p.m.,  Dinner: 5:30p.m. (nightly)

---

| | | | |
|---|---|---|---|
| 1.American Express | 4. VISA | 7. Public Parking | 10. Senior Citizen Rates |
| 2. Discover Card | 5. Diners Club | 8. Beer & Wine Served | 11. Handicap Accessibliity |
| 3. Mastercard | 6. Valet Parking | 9. Full Bar | 12. Function Room(s) |

# RESTAURANTS

## New Bern

**Henderson House Restaurant**
216 Pollock St., 28560
(919) 637-4784

**Amenities:** 1,3,4,7,8, 9,12

**Appetizer:** $3.95 - $7.95
**Lunch:** $7.00 - $13.00

**Dessert:** $2.00 - $4.50

Chef-owned award-winning dining since 1973. *AAA, Mobil, Fodor, Master Chefs of America* and *Who's Who in America's Restuarants*. Continental and regional specialties. No children's facilities. Located in a red brick Federal house listed in the *National Register of Historic Places*.

**Hours:** Lunch: 11:30a.m.-2:00p.m., Dinner: 6p.m.-9p.m. (Wed., Thurs., Fri. and Sat.). Open other days by prior arrangement.

## Weaverville

**Weaverville Milling Co.**
26 Reems Cr. Rd.,
P.O. Box 26, 28787
(704) 645-4700

**Amenities:** 3,4,7,8,11,12

**Appetizer:** $1.00 - $5.50
**Dinner:** $6.95 - $13.95
**Dessert:** $2.25 - $2.75

Friendly hospitality and good food await you at historic Weaverville Milling Co. We serve delicious prime rib steaks, veal and chicken. Fresh mountain trout is our speciality. Our homemade desserts with homemade ice cream are spectacular.

**Hours:** 5p.m. (closed Wednesdays).

## Wilmington

**Cafe Atlantique**
10 Market St., 28401
(919) 763-8100

**Amenities:** 3,4,7,8,9

**Breakfast:** not open

**Appetizer** $4.75 - $8.50
**Lunch:** not open
**Dinner:** $17.50 - $21.50
**Dessert:** $4.50 - $6.50

A classic French bistro in the heart of historic downtown Wilmington. Famous for it's crusty homemade baguettes, local seafood, Barbarie duck and black angus beef. Award-winning wine list. Menu changes weekly. Reservations are required.

**Hours:** 6p.m.-10p.m. (Mon.-Sat.).

| | | | |
|---|---|---|---|
| 1.American Express | 4. VISA | 7. Public Parking | 10. Senior Citizen Rates |
| 2. Discover Card | 5. Diners Club | 8. Beer & Wine Served | 11. Handicap Accessibliity |
| 3. Mastercard | 6. Valet Parking | 9. Full Bar | 12. Function Room(s) |

# RESTAURANTS

## Ohio

### Ashtabula

**Hulberts**
1033 Bridge St., 44004
(216) 964-2594

**Amenities:**3,4,7,8,11,12

Casual family dining in a charming Victorian atmosphere. Specializing in roast beef, steaks, quiche, salads. The areas largest selection of homemade desserts. Located in the heart of a Victorian shopping district that is listed on the *National Register of Historic Places.*

**Hours:** Breakfast: 8a.m.-11:30a.m. (Sat. & Sun.)
Lunch/Dinner: 11a.m.-8p.m. (Tues.-Thurs.), 11a.m.-9p.m. (Fri.),
8a.m.-9p.m. (Sat.), 8a.m.-7p.m. (Sun.)

### Millersburg

**Millersburg, Emperor's Cove/ Hotel**
9 W. Jackson,, 44654
(216) 674-1457

**Amenities:**3,4,7,9,12

**Breakfast:** not open

**Appetizer:**$1.25 -$3.00
**Lunch:** $2.95 - $5.25
**Dinner:** $7.95 - $13.95
**Dessert:** $1.25 - $3.75

Menu changes daily. Dinner includes a homemade muffin, salad, potato or rice and vegetable. Featured in *Ohio Magazine Country Restaurant Worth The Drive.* Lunch features soup, delicious sandwiches, salads, quiches and much more. Complete bar featuring Ohio wines.

**Hours:** Lunch: 11a.m.-2p.m. (Mon.-Sat.),
Dinner: 5p.m.-9p.m. (Mon.-Thurs.), 5p.m.-10-p.m. (Fri.-Sat.)

## Pennsylvania

### Benton

**Jamison City Hotel**
Broad St.
RD #2, Box 243A, 17814
(717) 925-6978

**Amenities:** 7,8,9,11,12

**Breakfast:** not open

**Lunch:** $1.95-$4.95
(Mon.-Thurs.)
**Dinner** $1.95-$4.95
(Mon.-Thurs.)

Enjoy our prime rib and seafood buffet on Friday, Saturday and Sunday for $7.95 - $12.95 with salad bar, homemade breads and desserts. Lounge with music and dancing. Unwind and relax! Excellent area for hunting, fishing and cross-country skiing.

**Hours:** 12p.m.-10p.m. (Fri., Sat. and Sun.)
12p.m.-9p.m. (Mon.-Thurs.)

| | | | |
|---|---|---|---|
| 1.American Express | 4. VISA | 7. Public Parking | 10. Senior Citizen Rates |
| 2. Discover Card | 5. Diners Club | 8. Beer & Wine Served | 11. Handicap Accessibliity |
| 3. Mastercard | 6. Valet Parking | 9. Full Bar | 12. Function Room(s) |

# RESTAURANTS

## Ephrata

The Restaurant At Doneckers
333 N. State St., 17522
(717) 738-2421

**Amenities:** 1,2,3,4,5,7,8,9,11, 12
**Breakfast.:** not open

**Appetizer:** $3.95 - $9.25
**Lunch:** $6.75 - $12.75
**Dinner:** $16.95 - $22.95
**Dessert:** $2.25 - $4.25

Classic French cuisine with an innovative American flair. Attentive service and gracious surroundings. Heart-healthy dining options on all menus. Banquet facilities for groups from 12 to 200. Near Doneckers fashion stores and art galleries. An elegant country inn. Supper menu available.

**Hours:** 11a.m.-10p.m. (Mon.-Sat.), 11:30a.m.-3p.m. (Sun.). Closed Wednesdays.

## Lancaster

Market Fare Restaurant
25 W. King St., 17603
(717) 299-7090

**Amenities:** 1,3,4,5,7,9,11,12

Serving classic American cuisine. Extensive wine list. Menu features fresh seafood, pasta, chicken and grilled steaks. Don't forget to try our poppyseed bread and chocolate decadance.

## Philadelphia

Dickens Inn
421 South 2nd St., 19147
(215) 928-9307
(215) 928-0232 (Fax)

**Amenities:** 1,2,3,4,5,7, 9,11,12

**Appetizer:** $3.50-$7.50
**Lunch:** $6.95-$12.00
**Dinner:** $16.25-$24.75
**Dessert:** $3.75

Country cuisine served in a restored 18th century coaching inn with unique Dickensian prints. Fillet of Beef Wellington and Prime Rib with Yorkshire Pudding are offered along with lighter dishes. Desserts prepared in the inn's bakery. Private rooms available. Our 11th year.

**Hours:** Sunday Brunch: 11:30a.m.-3:30p.m.
Lunch: 11:30a.m.-3:00p.m. (Mon.-Sun.)
Dinner: 5:30p.m.-10:00p.m. (Mon.-Sat.), Tavern: 11:30a.m.-2p.m. (Mon.-Sun.).

## Pomeroy

Stottsville Inn
Strasburg & Valley Rds., 19367
(215) 857-1133

**Amenities:** 1,3,4,5,6,7,8, 9,10,11,12

**Appetizer:** $3.95 - $5.95
**Lunch:** $3.95 - $8.95
**Dinner:** $13.95 - $19.95
**Dessert:** $4.00

Fine country gourmet dining in an elegant Victorian inn. Our exquisite fare is prepared with only the freshest ingredients from the surrounding Amish farms. Our country pub relaxes you with our famous ice cream drinks and casual pub menu. Our service is legendary.

**Hours:** Lunch: 11:30a.m.-2:30p.m. (Tues.-Sat.).
Dinner: 5:30p.m.-9:30p.m.(Tues.-Sat.). Pub: 11:30a.m.-12p.m. (Tues.-Sat.).

| | | |
|---|---|---|
| 1.American Express | 4. VISA | 7. Public Parking | 10. Senior Citizen Rates |
| 2. Discover Card | 5. Diners Club | 8. Beer & Wine Served | 11. Handicap Accessibliity |
| 3. Mastercard | 6. Valet Parking | 9. Full Bar | 12. Function Room(s) |

# RESTAURANTS

## Tennessee

### Sewanee

**4 Seasons**
Midway Rd.
Route 1, Box 585, 37375
(615) 598-5544

Amenities: 7,11

Appetizer: $1.75
Lunch: $1.80 - $5.99
Dinner: $1.80 - $5.99
Dessert: $1.50 - $2.00

All-U-Can-Eat Catfish, chicken, shrimp, vegetable and salad. Pizza, burgers and homemade pies. We raise our own fish and vegetables and prepare our food from scratch. Satisfaction guaranteed!

**Hours:** Lunch: 11a.m.-3p.m. (Sunday only).
Dinner: 4p.m.-9p.m. (Thurs.-Sun.).

## Texas

### Galveston Island

**Dinner On The Diner**
123 Rosenberg (25th) & Strand
P.O. Box 637, 77553 (mail)
(409) 763-4759, (800) 683-2053

Amenities: 1,3,4,5,7,8,11,12

Board the "Silver Hours" club car (circa 1940). Your dinner begins with a menu from the past and foods of today, expertly prepared. Crisp white linen, sparkling china and glassware. Come for an evening of good food, drink and entertainment.

**Hours:** Lunch: 11:00a.m.-2:00p.m. (Mon. - Sat.)
Dinner: From 5:00p.m.
Sunday Brunch: 11:00a.m.-3:00p.m.

## Virginia

### Charlottesville

**Le Snail Restaurant**
320 W. Main St., 22901
(804) 295-4456

Amenities: 1,2,3,4,5,8,9,
11,12

Appetizer: $4.75 - $6.95
Lunch: not open
Dinner: $15.50 - $22.50
Dessert: $2.95 - $4.95

Outstanding French cuisine served in intimate, elegant surroundings. Viennese chef/owner. Prix-fixe menu Monday to Thursday - $16.95. A la carte daily, Monday to Saturday. Reservations recommended. Jacket required. Tradition of excellence since 1979. Full bar & wine list.

**Hours:** 6p.m.-10p.m. (Mon.-Sat.).

| | | | |
|---|---|---|---|
| 1.American Express | 4. VISA | 7. Public Parking | 10. Senior Citizen Rates |
| 2. Discover Card | 5. Diners Club | 8. Beer & Wine Served | 11. Handicap Accessibliity |
| 3. Mastercard | 6. Valet Parking | 9. Full Bar | 12. Function Room(s) |

# RESTAURANTS

## Richmond

**The Tobacco, Restaurant Compamy**
1201 E. Cary St., 23219
(804) 782-9431

**Amenities:** 1,3,4,5,7,8,9,11
**Appetizer:** $2.95 - $7.95
**Lunch.:** $3.95 - $9.95
**Dinner:** $11.95 - $24.95
**Dessert:** $4.95(buffet)

A landmark in Richmond's historic Shockoe Slip The Tobacco Company Restaurant combines old south gentility and east coast sophistication. Within a four-floor renovated 1870's tobacco warehouse. Nightly entertainment on first floor and dancing in the club Tuesday to Saturday.

**Hours:** Lunch: 11:30a.m.-2:30p.m. (Mon.-Sat.).
Dinner: 5:30p.m.- 10:30p.m. (Mon.-Frid.), 5:30p.m.-12a.m. (Sat.)
5:30p.m.-10p.m. (Sun.)
Brunch: 10:30a.m.-2p.m. (Sunday)

# West Virginia

## Charles Town

**Charles, Washington Inn**
210 W. Liberty St., 25414
(304) 725-1030

**Amenities:** 1,2,3,4,
5,7,8,9
**Breakfast:** $3.95 - $8.95

**Appetizer:** $4.95 - $6.95
**Lunch:** $3.95 - $7.95
**Dinner:** $10.95 - $28.00
**Dessert:** $2.50 - $3.95

Open seven days per week. Full lunch and dinner menu. Extended pub hours.

**Hours:** 11a.m.-10p.m..

## Elkins

**Cheat River Inn**
Route 33, E., 26241
(304) 636-6265

**Amenities:** 3,4,7,8,9

**Lunch:** $3.75 - $12.95
**Dinner:** $7.95 - $16.95

Fine riverside dining. Seafood and steaks.

**Hours:** Lunch: 11a.m.-3p.m. (Tues.-Sun.).
Dinner: 4p.m.-10p.m. (Tues.-Sun.), Lounge: 4p.m.-11p.m.

| | | | |
|---|---|---|---|
| 1.American Express | 4. VISA | 7. Public Parking | 10. Senior Citizen Rates |
| 2. Discover Card | 5. Diners Club | 8. Beer & Wine Served | 11. Handicap Accessibliity |
| 3. Mastercard | 6. Valet Parking | 9. Full Bar | 12. Function Room(s) |

## MEMBERSHIP CARD

Please send me at the address below, an application for membership in The National Bed & Breakfast Assoc. which will entitle me to a listing in your Bed & Breakfast Guide for the U.S. & Canada.

_____

_____

_____

_____
                                          Zip Code


                    Thank you,
                    Phyllis Featherston, President
                    Barbara F. Ostler, Vice President


## MEMBERSHIP CARD

Please send me at the address below, an application for membership in The National Bed & Breakfast Assoc. which will entitle me to a listing in your Bed & Breakfast Guide for the U.S. & Canada.

_____

_____

_____

_____
                                          Zip Code


                    Thank you,
                    Phyllis Featherston, President
                    Barbara F. Ostler, Vice President

**NATIONAL B. & B. ASSOCIATION**
**P.O. Box 332**
**Norwalk, CT 06852**

**NATIONAL B. & B. ASSOCIATION**
**P.O. Box 332**
**Norwalk, CT 06852**

# THE NATIONAL BED & BREAKFAST GUIDE • (Comments)

Help us serve you better!
Aidez-nous à vous mieux servir!
¡Ayúdennos servirles mejor!

Name of B. & B. _____

Address_____

_____

| I found this B. & B. to be | Excellent | _____ | Good | _____ | Poor | _____ |
|---|---|---|---|---|---|---|
| J'ai trouvé cette pension | Excellente | _____ | Bonne | _____ | Mauvaise | _____ |
| Encontré esta pensión | Excelente | _____ | Bueno | _____ | Malo | _____ |

Signature _____

Address_____

_____

Comments _____

Remarques _____

Comentos_____


# THE NATIONAL BED & BREAKFAST GUIDE • (Comments)

Help us serve you better!
Aidez-nous à vous mieux servir!
¡Ayúdennos servirles mejor!

Name of B. & B. _____

Address_____

_____

| I found this B. & B. to be | Excellent | _____ | Good | _____ | Poor | _____ |
|---|---|---|---|---|---|---|
| J'ai trouvé cette pension | Excellente | _____ | Bonne | _____ | Mauvaise | _____ |
| Encontré esta pensión | Excelente | _____ | Bueno | _____ | Malo | _____ |

Signature _____

Address_____

_____

Comments _____

Remarques _____

Comentos_____

**NATIONAL B. & B. ASSOCIATION**
**P.O. Box 332**
**Norwalk, CT 06852**

**NATIONAL B. & B. ASSOCIATION**
**P.O. Box 332**
**Norwalk, CT 06852**

# TRAVELERS NOTES

# TRAVELERS NOTES

# TRAVELERS NOTES

# TRAVELERS NOTES

# TRAVELERS NOTES

# TRAVELERS NOTES

# TRAVELERS NOTES

# TRAVELERS NOTES

# TRAVELERS NOTES

# *TRAVELERS NOTES*